Commercial Knowledge Module: Preparatory Study Manual

Twomey/Jennings/Fox

CENGAGE
Learning™

Australia • Brazil • Japan • Korea • Mexico • Singapore • Spain • United Kingdom • United States

CENGAGE
Learning™

Commercial Knowledge Module:
Preparatory Study Manual

Twomey/Jennings/Fox

Executive Editors:
Michele Baird

Maureen Staudt

Michael Stranz

Project Development Manager:
Linda deStefano

Senior Marketing Coordinators:
Sara Mercurio

Lindsay Shapiro

Production/Manufacturing Manager:
Donna M. Brown

PreMedia Services Supervisor:
Rebecca A. Walker

Rights & Permissions Specialist:
Kalina Hintz

Cover Image:
Getty Images*

ISBN-13: 978-0-324-21308-9

ISBN-10: 0-324-21308-5

Cengage Learning
5191 Natorp Boulevard
Mason, Ohio 45040
USA

Cengage Learning is a leading provider of customized learning solutions with office locations around the globe, including Singapore, the United Kingdom, Australia, Mexico, Brazil, and Japan. Locate your local office at:
international.cengage.com/region

Cengage Learning products are represented in Canada by Nelson Education, Ltd.

For your lifelong learning solutions, visit **custom.cengage.com**

Visit our corporate website at **cengage.com**

Custom Contents

About the National Contract Management Association

More than 22,000 professionals enhance their knowledge and leverage opportunities in purchasing, procurement, project management, and contract management with the National Contract Management Association. Comprised of individual volunteer members and other professional groups from nonprofit, industry, and government, NCMA continues to provide unique resources for the contracting community. For over 40 years, members have taken advantage of NCMA membership benefits to advance their careers. Practical, proven survival techniques and industry news help members stay informed about current contract management events. NCMA continues to provide vital information about the field through the association's prestigious publications, educational materials, and professional resources.

NCMA is committed to the following values:

- An open exchange of ideas in neutral forums
- Our members' independence of purpose, freedom of action, and responsibilities to their employers
- Responsible behavior as defined by NCMA's Code of Ethics
- A culturally and professionally diverse membership
- Excellence of service to our members and the contract management community
- Effective, vibrant local chapters
- Continuous professional development
- Education and training
- Demonstration of professional status through certification
- Research and study
- Quality volunteer leadership
- Generation of leading edge ideas

NCMA Vision

NCMA's vision is to be the preeminent source of professional development for contract managers. Contract management is a strategic management discipline employed by both buyers and sellers whose objectives are to manage customer and supplier expectations and relationships, control risk and cost, and contribute to organizational profitability/ success.

Foreword

NCMA has served the contract management profession for almost half a century. During that time, NCMA has provided education, information, and certification. While the certification program has been continually updated, today's program has been reconfigured to take advantage of more modern means of delivery and administration.

As industry and governments continue to acquire goods and services, the men and women charged with awarding and administering contracts for these goods and services must attain certain core competencies, a particular defined level of knowledge. The contract manager needs to know core areas of business management. The most adept contract managers will possess knowledge in the areas of contract principles, acquisition strategy, contract administration and all the steps involved in contracting from initiation to archival.

NCMA's certifications are valuable and valid evidence of this professional knowledge. NCMA recently developed a new certification program with a modular structure (more details can be found on our web site at www.ncmahq.org). There are three modules consisting of three multiple-choice examinations; a General Business Knowledge exam, a Federal Knowledge exam and a Commercial Knowledge exam.

The material you find in the Commercial Knowledge Module Preparatory Study Manual is intended to help you prepare to take the Commercial Knowledge examination module. The material is organized around the Contract Management Body of Knowledge and contains those pieces that are especially relevant to anyone wishing to learn the scope of general business topics in contract management. NCMA does not guarantee that if you read this book, you will pass the examination: it is intended to help you prepare for the examination. You are the only person who can accurately gauge the depth of your knowledge on any one topic. You are encouraged to use this book as a tool to help you find information where you need it.

Different people use different ways of preparing to take examinations. You might use study guides, such as this one, or you might join a local study group, such as those given by NCMA Chapters, or you could register for and take an on-line study course on General Business Knowledge for contract managers. These courses might be available through NCMA, or they may be available through NCMA affiliates or other providers who have specifically designed courses for NCMA certification examinations.

In any case, the essential point is that you have decided to seek certification and join the ranks of professional contract managers. NCMA salutes your intent and wishes you every success in your professional career.

Business Ethics, Social Forces, and the Law

Learning Objectives

After studying this chapter, you should be able to

1. Describe the role of ethics in business and law
2. List the methods for recognizing ethical dilemmas
3. Explain the questions to address in resolving ethical dilemmas

Each day businesspeople work together on contracts and projects. Their completion of the work is partially the result of the laws that protect contract rights. Much of what business people do, however, is simply a matter of their word. Executives arrive at a 9:00 A.M. meeting because they promised they would be there. An employee meets a deadline for an ad display board because she said she would. Business transactions are completed through a combination of the values of the parties and the laws that reflect those values and the importance of one's word in business. Over time, the rules that govern business, from written laws to unwritten expressions of value, have evolved to provide a framework of operation that ensures good faith in our dealings with each other.

This chapter takes you behind the rules of law to examine the objectives in establishing rules for business conduct. Both social forces and business needs contribute to the standards that govern businesses and their operations.

A. WHAT IS BUSINESS ETHICS?

Some people have said that the term *business ethics* is an oxymoron, that the word *business* and the word *ethics* contradict each other. **Ethics** is a branch of philosophy dealing with values that relate to the nature of human conduct and values associated with that conduct. Conduct and values within the context of business operations become more complex because individuals are working together to maximize profit. Balancing the goal of profits with the values of individuals and society is the focus of **business ethics.** Some economists make the point that insider trading on the stock market is an efficient way to run that market. To an economist, inside information allows those with the best information to make the most money. This quantitative view ignores the issues of fairness: What about those who trade stock who do not have access to that information? Is the philosophy fair to them? What will happen to the stock market if investors perceive there is not a level playing field? In the U.S. Supreme Court decision *United States v O'Hagan*[1] on insider trad-

[1] 521 US 657 (1997).

ing, Justice Ruth Ginsburg noted, "Investors wouldn't invest in a market where trading based on misappropriated nonpublic information is unchecked." The field of business ethics seeks to balance the values of society with the need for businesses to remain profitable.

1. The Law as the Standard for Business Ethics

Moral standards come from different sources, and philosophers debate the origin of moral standards and which ones are appropriate for application. One set of moral standards is simply what codified or **positive law** requires. The application of the test of whether an act is legal as a moral standard is common in business. Codified law is used as the standard for ethical behavior. Absent illegality, all behavior is ethical under this simple standard. For example, the phrase "AS IS" when written conspicuously on a contract (see Chapter 26 for further discussion) means, by law, that there are no warranties for the goods being sold. If a buyer purchases a used car and the phrase "AS IS" is in the contract, the seller has no legal obligation, in most states, if the transmission falls apart the day after the buyer's purchase. Following a positive law standard, the seller who refuses to repair the transmission has acted ethically. However, the issue of fairness still arises. We know there was no legal obligation to fix the transmission, but was it fair to have the car fall apart the day after it was purchased?

2. The Notion of Universal Standards for Business Ethics

Another view of ethics holds that standards exist universally and cannot be changed or modified by law. In many cases, individuals feel the universal standards stem from religious beliefs. In some countries today, the standards for business are still determined by religious tenets. Proponents of this **natural law** theory maintain that higher standards of behavior than those required by law must be followed even if those higher standards run contrary to the law. In the early nineteenth century when slavery was legally permissible in the United States, a positive law standard would sanction such ownership as legal. However, such deprivation of a person's rights violated the natural law principle of individual freedom and would be unethical.

Accordingly, **civil disobedience** occurs when natural law proponents violate positive law.

Supreme Court Justice Sandra Day O'Connor, who was second in her class at Stanford Law School (Chief Justice William Rehnquist was first), was unable to secure employment as an attorney. She found a job as a receptionist for a law firm instead. At that time, no law prohibited discrimination against women, so the law firms' hiring practices, using only a positive law standard, were ethical. However, if the natural law standard of equality is applied, the refusal to hire Sandra O'Connor as a lawyer, a position for which she was qualified, was discriminatory conduct and unethical.

3. The Standard of Situational Business Ethics or Moral Relativism

Situational ethics or **moral relativism** is a flexible standard of ethics that permits an examination of circumstances and motivation before attaching the label of right or wrong to conduct. The classic example of moral relativism: Would it be unethical to steal a loaf of bread to feed a starving child? More recently, a question a Florida court faced was whether to go forward with the prosecution for arson of a man who set fire to an abandoned property in his neighborhood that was used as a crack-cocaine house. In both cases, the law has been broken. The first crime is theft, and the second crime is arson. Neither person denied committing the crime. The issue in both cases is not whether the crime was committed but whether the motivation and circumstances excuse the actions and eliminate the punishment. An employee embezzles money from his employer because he is a single parent trying to make ends meet. Was his conduct unethical? The conduct is illegal, but moral relativism would consider the employee's personal circumstances in determining whether it is ethical. Businesses use moral relativism standards frequently in their international operations. Bribery is illegal in the United States, but, as many businesses argue, it is an accepted method of doing business in other countries.[2]

[2] The United States, Mexico, Korea, and most of the countries in the European Union have joined together and signed a resolution denouncing bribery and specifically noted that its practice is neither legally nor culturally accepted in their nations.

The standard of moral relativism is used to allow behavior in international business transactions that would be a violation of the law in the United States.

4. The Business Stakeholder Standard of Behavior

Businesses have different constituencies, referred to as **stakeholders,** often with conflicting goals for the business. Shareholders, for example, may share economists' view that earnings, and hence dividends, should be maximized. Members of the community where a business is located are also stakeholders in the business and have an interest in preserving jobs. The employees of the business itself are stakeholders and certainly wish to retain their jobs. A **downsizing,** or reduction in workforce, would offer the shareholders of the company a boost in earnings and share price. But that same reduction will impact the local economy and community in a negative way. Balancing the interests of these various stakeholders is a standard used in resolving ethical dilemmas in business. Figure 3.1 lists the areas of concern that should be examined as businesses analyze an ethical dilemma.

As Figure 3.1 indicates, **stakeholder analysis** requires the decision maker to view a problem from different perspectives in the light of day. Stakeholder analysis requires measurement of the impact of a decision on various groups but also

FIGURE 3.1 *Guidelines for Analyzing a Contemplated Action*

1. Define the problem from the decision maker's point of view.
2. Identify who could be injured by the contemplated action.
3. Define the problem from the opposing point of view.
4. Would you (as the decision maker) be willing to tell your family, your supervisor, your CEO, and the board of directors about the planned action?
5. Would you be willing to go before a community meeting, a congressional hearing, or a public forum to describe the action?
6. With full consideration of the facts and alternatives, reach a decision about whether the contemplated action should be taken.

requires that public disclosure of that decision be defensible. The questions help the employee who is about to leave the office for half a day without taking vacation time: Could I tell my family or my supervisor that I have done this? These questions also help a company faced with the temptation of price fixing: Could I describe before a congressional committee what I am about to do?

In other situations, a business is not facing questions of dishonesty or unfair competition. In many ethical dilemmas, a business faces the question of taking voluntary action or simply complying with the law. Some experts maintain that the shareholders' interest is paramount in resolving these conflicts among stakeholders. Others maintain that a business must assume some responsibility for social issues and their resolution. Economist Milton Friedman expresses his views on resolving the conflicts among stakeholders as follows:

A corporate executive's responsibility is to make as much money for the shareholders as possible, as long as he operates within the rules of the game. When an executive decides to take action for reasons of social responsibility, he is taking money from someone else—from the stockholders, in the form of lower dividends; from the employees, in the form of lower wages; or from the consumer, in the form of higher prices. The responsibility of the corporate executive is to fulfill the terms of his contract. If he can't do that in good conscience, then he should quit his job and find another way to do good. He has the right to promote what he regards as desirable moral objectives only with his own money.[3]

In direct opposition to the Friedman view is the social responsibility views of Anita Roddick, the CEO of the Body Shop International. She has stated that she does not care about earning money because the sole reason for a business to exist is to solve social problems. In between these two views are compromise positions in which businesses exist primarily to benefit the shareholders but do take opportunities to solve social problems. Many businesses today have created flextime, job sharing, and telecommuting as work options for their employees to accommodate family needs. These options are a response to larger societal issues sur-rounding children and their care but may also serve as a way to retain a quality workforce that is more productive without the worry of poor child-care arrangements. The law currently does not require businesses to furnish such options, but the businesses offer the programs voluntarily as a means of addressing a social issue.

In between the Friedman and Roddick views on business ethics and social responsibility are businesses with varying views on the role of business in society. Among these businesses are very profitable firms that are also involved in their communities through employees' volunteer work and companies' charitable donations. For example, Bill Gates, the CEO of Microsoft and ranked as the richest man in the United States, pledged, in 1999, $1 billion from his charitable foundation for minority scholarships. One different view on the social responsibility of business comes from Warren Buffett, the second-richest man in the United States according to the *Forbes* ranking, and the CEO of Berkshire Hathaway, a company with shares selling for more than $60,000 each. Mr. Buffett asks his shareholders whether they would like to donate to any charitable organization and then asks them to specify their charity of choice. Mr. Buffett's view is that the shareholders, not he, should make decisions about corporate profits and their use. In 1998, the average amount for corporate charitable giving was 2 percent of pre-tax income.

---

[3] From "Interview: Milton Friedman," *Playboy,* February 1973 © 1973 *Playboy.*

ETHICS AND THE LAW

Ethics and Social Responsibility

Ben & Jerry's Homemade, Inc., is a Vermont-based ice-cream company founded by Ben Cohen and Jerry Greenfield, who began the company with the goal of social contribution. A portion of all proceeds from the sale of their ice cream is donated to charity. The company issues strong position statements on social issues.

Following some slowing in market growth and reduction in profits, Cohen and Greenfield retired as officers of the company (although they remain majority shareholders and therefore in control of the board) and hired Robert Holland as CEO. After Holland had been CEO for a year, a Japanese supplier approached him and offered to distribute Ben & Jerry's ice cream in Japan. Holland turned down the offer because the Japanese company had no history of involvement in social issues, explaining, "The only clear reason to take the opportunity was to make money."

Do you agree with Holland's decision? What approach do Ben & Jerry's and Holland take with respect to their stakeholders? Is it troublesome that the company had not turned around financially when the offer was declined? Holland added that the only growth opportunities are in international markets. Is Ben & Jerry's passing up business? Is this a good or bad practice for a company? Holland left the company shortly after the decision on the Japanese opportunity had been made. How do you view Holland's position on business ethics and social responsibility? Is it best to find a company with values consistent with your own? How would you be able to tell the values of a company?

B. WHY IS BUSINESS ETHICS IMPORTANT?

Regardless of a firm's views on social responsibility issues, the notions of compliance with the law and fairness in business transactions and operations are universal concerns. Values are an important part of business success. Business ethics is important for more than the simple justification that "it's the right thing to do." This section covers the significance of ethics in business success.

5. The Importance of Trust

Capitalism succeeds because of trust. Investors provide capital for a business because they believe the business will use it and return it with earnings. Customers are willing to purchase products and services from businesses because they believe the businesses will honor their commitments to deliver quality and then stand behind their product or service. Businesses are willing to purchase equipment and hire employees on the assumption that investors will continue to honor their commitment to furnish the necessary funds and will not withdraw their promises or funds. Busi-

ness investment, growth, and sales are a circle of trust. While courts provide remedies for breaches of agreements, no economy could grow if it were based solely on positive law and court-mandated performance. It is the reliance on promises, not the reliance on litigation, that produces good business relationships. In economics, the concept of rational expectations of investors and consumers plays a role in economic growth and performance. The assumption every investor makes is that his or her initial investment will earn a return. An assumption that employees make is, absent problems with their performance, their employment will continue. Those assumptions encourage investment by investors and spending by employees. Their assumptions demonstrate trust in the relationship and in the underlying economic system.

E T H I C S   A N D   T H E   L A W

Ethics in Government Employees

The state of Arizona mandates emission testing for cars prior to obtaining updated registrations. The emissions tests are conducted by a contractor hired by the state to operate the various emissions testing facilities around the state. In October 1999, the Arizona attorney general announced the arrest of 13 workers at one of the emissions testing facilities for allegedly taking between $50 and $200 from car owners to pass their cars on the emissions tests when those cars fell below emissions standards and would not have been registered. Nearly half of the staff at the emissions facility were arrested.

Why is it a crime for someone working in a government-sponsored facility to accept a payment for a desired outcome? Is anyone really harmed by the payoffs to the workers?

As economists have had the opportunity to watch nations with new forms of government enter the international markets, they have documented distinctions in growth rates. In those countries where government officials control market access through individual payments to them, the business climate is stalled and growth lags behind free-market nations.

ETHICS AND THE LAW

Michael Irvin, a professional football player with the Dallas Cowboys, was hired as a spokesman for the Dallas area Toyota dealers. Irvin was given a $50,000 Toyota Landcruiser and fees for promotional activities as part of his contract. Shortly after entering into the contract, he entered a no contest plea to drug possession charges, was given a deferred prosecution, and was sentenced to 800 hours of community service. The Toyota dealers brought suit against Irvin seeking the return of the Landcruiser and damages of $1.4 million for the loss of sales and cost of the abandoned campaign. The dealers said that they assumed their contract was with a "moral" person.* The dealers explained that Irvin's activities made him a questionable spokesperson and that they had assumed his personal life did not involve illegal or immoral activities.

Did the dealers have trust in Irvin? Do you think that moral behavior is a condition for acting as a product's spokesperson?

*Lane, Randall. "Nice Guys Finish First." *Forbes* 16 Dec. 1996, 236–242.

---

6. Business Ethics and Financial Performance

Studies centering around a business's commitment to values and its financial performance suggest that those with the strongest value systems survive and do so successfully. In the book *Built to Last,* by James C. Collins and Jerry I. Porras, an in-depth look at companies with long-term growth and profits produced a common thread. That common thread was the companies' commitment to values. All the firms studied had focused on high standards for product quality, employee welfare, and customer service.

A study of companies that had paid dividends for 100 years without interruption revealed the same pattern of values.[4] Companies that had survived two world wars and a depression without missing a dividend remained committed to their customers and employees with standards of fairness and honesty.

An examination of companies involved in an ethical breach demonstrates the impact of poor

value choices on financial performance. A study of the impact of breaches of the law by companies shows that for five years after their regulatory or legal misstep, these companies are still struggling to recover the financial performances they had achieved prior to their legal difficulties.[5]

After Salomon Brothers illegally controlled the bond market, its Wall Street rank in terms of earnings and asset base slipped dramatically. Salomon's earnings dropped $29 million in one quarter. The firm paid $122 million in fines and was required to establish a $100 million fund to compensate the victims of its bond market activity. After the scandal at Kidder, Peabody in which falsification of trades and income were uncovered, the firm had to be sold at a $600 million loss. Kidder, Peabody was eventually liquidated. Columbia Health Care has seen its share price drop and experienced a 53 percent drop in earnings as a result of government charges that it overbilled for Medicare reimbursements. The nation's largest hospital chain has had to spin off 100 hospitals and has paid record fines to settle the charges.[6]

Asbestos liability bankrupted Johns-Manville because documentation showed that, despite knowledge of the company's executives about the lethal effect of asbestos on the lungs, no action was taken to warn buyers and users of the product. Bausch & Lomb, Leslie Fay, Phar-Mor, Cendant, and Sunbeam are all financial victims of accounting improprieties carried out by company officers assisted by many employees. Bankruptcy and/or free falls in the worth of shares are the fates that await firms that make poor ethical choices.

7. The Importance of a Good Reputation

Richard Teerlink, the CEO of Harley-Davidson, once said, "A reputation, good or bad, is tough to shake."[7] A breach of ethics is costly to a firm not

---

[4] Louis Grossman and Marianne Jennings, IN IT FOR THE MONEY (forthcoming)

[5] Melinda S. Baucus and David A. Baucus, "Paying the Piper: An Empirical Examination of Longer-Term Financial Consequences of Illegal Corporate Behavior," *40 Academy of Management Journal* 129 (1997).

[6] Gilpin, Kenneth N. "Salomon Profit Drops 93% in Quarter," *New York Times*, 23 Oct. 1992. Cl; Siconolfi, Michael. "How Kidder, a Tiger in April, Found Itself the Prey by December," *Wall Street Journal*, 29 December 1994, A1, A4; Lagnado, Lucette, "Columbia/HCA Warns of Profit Decline." *Wall Street Journal*, 10 September 1987, A3.

[7] David K. Wright, *The Harley-Davidson Motor Co.: An Official Ninety-Year History* (Motorbook Int'l 1993).

FIGURE 3.2 *The Endless Cycle of Societal Interaction*

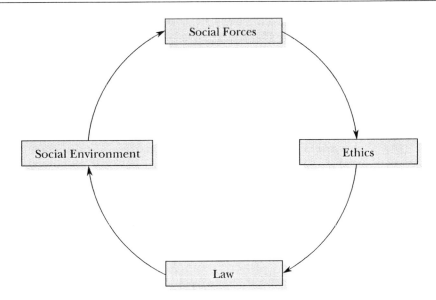

only in the financial sense of drops in earnings and possible fines. A breach of ethics often carries with it a lasting memory that impacts the business and its sales for years to come. Following Sears, Roebuck's settlement with the California Consumer Affairs Department of fraud charges involving the operation of its auto centers, Montgomery Ward Auto Centers enjoyed an increase in business.[8] Customers were concerned about taking their cars to Sears because of the scandal surrounding the nationally reported charges of unnecessary repairs. Because business declined, Sears was forced to close some of its auto centers.

When an ethical breach occurs, businesses lose that component of trust important to customers' decisions to buy and invest. Beech-Nut, the baby food company, has an outstanding product line and offers quality at a good price. Yet, it has not regained its former market share as a result of the federal charges it faced in 1986.[9] Its apple juice tasted good, but it was a chemical concoction containing no apple juice despite advertising claims to the contrary. Even though no one was harmed, the customers' view of Beech-Nut changed. Trust disappeared and so did a good portion of the company's market share. A decade later, the company continues to struggle to overcome that one-time breach in ethics.

8. Business Ethics and Business Regulation: Public Policy, Law, and Ethics

When business behavior results in complaints from employees, investors, or customers, laws or regulations are often used to change the behavior. ◆ For example, the bankruptcy of Orange County and the large losses experienced by Procter & Gamble and Gibson Greetings resulting from their heavy investments in high-risk financial instruments[10] motivated the Securities and Exchange Commission (SEC) (see Chapter 47) to promulgate regulations about disclosures in financial statements on high-risk investments, known as derivatives. The Federal Reserve stepped in to regulate virtually all aspects of credit transactions, focusing on the disclosure of the actual costs of credit to ensure full information for borrowers. ◆ Confusion among consumers about car leasing and its true costs and the fees applicable at the

---

[8] "Sears Fires Head of Its Auto Unit." *Wall Street Journal,* 21 December 1992, B6.

[9] Chris Welles, "What Led Beech-Nut Down the Road to Disgrace." *Business Week,* 22 February 1988: 128.

[10] Antilla, Susan. "P & G Sees Charge on Derivatives." *New York Times,* 13 April 1994, C1, C16; Murray, Matt, and Paulette Thomas. "After the Fall: Fingers Point and Heads Roll." *Wall Street Journal,* 23 December 1994, B1, B4; and Jones, Del. "County Seeks Bankruptcy Protection." *USA Today,* 7 December 1994, 1C, 2C.

end of the lease terms caused the Federal Reserve to expand its regulation of credit to car leases. Figure 3.2 depicts the relationships among ethics, the social forces of customers and investors, and the laws that are passed to remedy the problems raised as part of the social forces movement.

From the nutrition facts that appear on food packages to the type of pump at the gas station, government regulation of business activity is evident. Congress begins its legislative role and administrative agencies begin their process of regulation (see Chapter 6) when congressional hearings and studies reveal abuses and problems within an industry or throughout business. Legislation and regulation are responses to activities of businesses that are perfectly legal but raise questions of fairness that cause customer and investor protests.

Antidiscrimination laws were passed when evidence established that many companies had policies that required, for example, pregnant employees to stop working. Hotels at one time had policies that permitted minorities to work in kitchens and perform housekeeping tasks but did not permit them to hold "guest-contact" positions. These policies did not violate any laws at the time. However, employees justifiably raised concerns about the fairness or the ethics of such policies. Because, in large part, of the unwillingness of business to change its practices, legislation was passed to remedy employees' concerns. Businesses that act voluntarily on the basis of value choices often avoid the costs and sometimes arbitrariness of legislation and regulation. Voluntary change by businesses is less costly and considered less intrusive. Regulation costs are substantial, and regulation is extensive. The ethical issues of cost and compliance are covered in the following problem.

ETHICS AND THE LAW

Ethics and Government Regulation

Rowena Fullinwider is the founder of Rowena's, Inc., which makes Rowena Fullinwider's Wonderful Almond Pound Cake and other products, such as lemon curd and carrot jam. The specialty gourmet food manufacturer specializes in high-calorie and, often, high-fat treats. When the Nutrition Labeling and Education Act requiring disclosure of food products' nutrients and contents went into effect in 1995, compliance with the new federal mandates for Rowena's 30 products cost $100,000 for the redesign of labels, the testing of the products for verification of ingredients, and printing and production.

Rowena's, like many other specialty food manufacturers, has very narrow profit margins ranging from 0.5 percent to 5 percent. It employs 16 people and has $1 million in annual sales. At the top end of its profit margin, Rowena's has a net profit of $50,000.

Fullinwider expresses her concerns with the labeling act as follows:

"I am not going to put new products out. In the gourmet industry, we are always improving our recipes. I want to make improvements, but I can't afford to if I'm all bound up by regulations."

Why do you believe the federal food labeling act was necessary? Do you think Rowena's was guilty of deception in the sale of its products? Should food manufacturers have disclosed voluntarily the content of their products? Why would they resist? Is it possible that the label requirements will put some companies out of business? Is it desirable to have regulations that eliminate businesses?

Businesses that respond to social forces and the movements of the cycle of societal interaction gain a competitive advantage. Businesses that act irresponsibly and disregard society's views and desire for change will speed the transition from value choice to enforceable law. Businesses should watch the cycle of social forces and follow trends there to understand the values attached to certain activities and responses. These values motivate change, either in the form of voluntary business activity or legislation. All values that precipitate change have one of several basic underlying goals. These underlying goals offer signals about the pattern of social change.

(a) **Protection of the State.** A number of laws exist today because of the underlying goal or value of protection of the state. Laws that condemn treason are examples of laws passed to preserve the government of the state. Other less dramatic laws that offer protection to the state are the tax codes, which provide authority for collecting taxes for the operation of government facilities and enforcement agencies. The armed forces and draft registration are also examples of government programs and regulations created with protection and security of the state as the goals.

(b) Protection of the Person. A second social force is protection of the person. From the earliest times, laws were developed to protect the individual from being injured or killed. Criminal laws are devoted to protection of individuals and their properties. In addition, civil suits permit private remedies for wrongful acts toward people and their property. Over time, the protection of personal rights has expanded to include the rights of privacy and the protection of individuals from defamation. Contract rights are protected from interference by others. Laws continue to evolve to protect the reputations, privacy, and mental and physical well-being of individuals.

Individual rights have been the values at the core of legislation and regulation relating to governmental assistance programs, public schools, service on a jury, and access to public facilities. The antidiscrimination laws that affect nearly all businesses are grounded in the value of protection of the individual. Labor laws and regulations exist to protect the individual rights of workers.

(c) Protection of Public Health, Safety, and Morals. The food-labeling regulations discussed earlier were an example of laws grounded in the value of protecting the safety and health of individuals. Food and restaurant inspections, mandatory inoculation, speed limits on roadways, mandatory smoke detectors and sprinkler systems in hotels, and prohibitions on the sale of alcohol to minors are all examples of laws based on the value of safety for the public. Zoning laws that prohibit the operation of adult bookstores and movie theaters near schools and churches are examples of laws based on moral values.

(d) Protection of Property: Its Use and Title. Someone who steals another's automobile is a thief and is punished by law with fines and/or imprisonment. A zoning law that prohibits the operation of a steel mill in a residential area also provides protection for property. A civil suit

brought to recover royalties lost because of another's infringement of one's copyrighted materials is based on federal laws that afford protection for property rights in nontangible or intellectual property (see Chapter 10). Laws afford protection of title for all forms of property. The deed that is recorded in the land record is the legal mechanism for protecting the owner's title. The copyright on a software program or a song protects the creator's rights in that intellectual property. The title documents issued by a department of motor vehicles afford protection of title for the owner of a car.

Those who have title to property are free to use the property in any manner they see fit. However, even ownership has restrictions imposed by law. A landowner cannot engage in activities on his property that damage another's land or interfere with another's use of land. A business may operate a factory on its real property, but if the factory creates a great deal of noise, adjoining landowners may successfully establish it a nuisance (see Chapter 50) that interferes with their use and enjoyment of their land. The law affords remedies for such a nuisance that might be an injunction, or court order, limiting the hours of the factory's operation so that neighbors have the opportunity to sleep.

If that factory releases chemicals into the river flowing nearby, others' rights and use of their land are affected. Environmental laws (see Chapter 51) have been passed that regulate the use of property. Those environmental laws evolved through social activism after landowners and residents located near factories and other operations with harmful emissions became concerned about the impact on the value of their properties as well as the impact on their health and safety. Environmental laws thus emerged as regulation of land use in response to concerns about legal, but harmful, emissions by companies.

(e) Protection of Personal Rights. The desire for individual freedom to practice religion and freedom from political domination gave rise to the colonization of the United States and, eventually, the American Revolution. The desire for freedom from economic domination resulted in the free enterprise philosophy that exists in the United States today. Individual freedoms and personal rights continue as a focus of values discussions followed by legislation if those individual rights are violated.

Economic freedoms and the free enterprise system were in jeopardy at the end of the nineteenth century as large conglomerates began to dominate certain markets and inhibit the ability of individuals to compete. Repressive activities in the marketplace by some companies led to federal regulation in the form of antitrust laws. These laws were passed in response to social concerns about economic freedom and individual opportunities within the economy.

(f) Enforcement of Individual Intent. When someone has voluntarily entered into a transaction, there is a responsibility to carry forward the promises made. Principles of honesty and honoring commitments are the ethical values at the heart of the parties' conduct in carrying out contracts. If, however, the parties do not keep their promises, the law does enforce transactions through sets of rules governing requirements for them. ◆ For example, if a person provides by will for the distribution of property at death, the law will generally allow the property to pass to the persons intended by the deceased owner. ◆ The law will also carry out the intentions of the parties to a business transaction. Laws exist to honor the intent of parties because not all commitments are fulfilled voluntarily. The law may impose requirements that a transaction or agreement be in writing to ensure that the intent of the parties is documented adequately and fulfilled (see Chapter 16). The law may also place restrictions on honoring intentions. A contract to commit a murder may be evidenced by intent and fully documented in writing. However, the intent of parties will not be honored because of the social values manifested in the protection of individuals and individuals' rights and safety.

(g) Protection from Exploitation, Fraud, and Oppression. Many laws have evolved because businesses took advantage of another group. Some groups or individuals have been given protection by the law because of excesses by businesses in dealing with them. **Minors,** or persons under legal age (see Chapter 13), are given special protections under contract laws that permit them to disaffirm their contracts so they are not disadvantaged by excessive commitments without the benefit of the wisdom of age and with the oppressive presence of an adult party. The federal laws on disclosure with respect to the sales of securities and shareholder relations (see Chapters 46 and 49) were developed following the 1929 stock market crash when many investors lost all they had because of the lack of candor and information by the businesses in which they were investing.

Food manufacturers have exclusive control over the canning and processing of their products. The opportunity for taking advantage of customers who do not generally have access to the factories and plants is great. The contents of canned products are not visible to consumers before they make their purchases. Because of excesses and exploitations by food processors, there are both federal and state regulations of food processing and food labeling. Adulteration or poisoning of food products carries criminal penalties. Misrepresenting the contents in food packages may constitute a federal felony.

(h) Furtherance of Trade. Some laws are the result of social forces seeking to simplify business and trade. Installment sales and credit transactions, and their accompanying laws and regulations, have made additional capital available for businesses and provided consumers with alternatives to cash purchases. The laws on checks, drafts, and notes have created instruments used to facilitate trade. The Federal Reserve System's Board of Governors and its oversight of federal banks and interest rates have mitigated the harmful effects of alternating economic periods of depression and inflation.

(i) Protection of Creditors and Rehabilitation of Debtors. Society seeks to protect the rights of creditors and to protect them from dishonest or fraudulent acts of debtors. Initially, creditors are protected by the laws that make contracts binding and enforceable. Creditors are also protected by statutes that make it a fraud for a debtor to conceal property from a creditor. To meet the social demands for facilitation of trade, credit transactions were authorized. But with that authorization came the demand for the creditor's assurance of repayment by the debtor. Mortgages, security interests, and surety relationships (see Chapters 34, 35, and 50) are mechanisms created by law to provide creditors with legal mechanisms for collecting their obligations.

When collection techniques became excessive and exploitative, new laws on debtors' rights were enacted. Debtors' prisons were abolished. Disclosure requirements for credit contracts were mandated by Congress. Collection techniques were limited through the Fair Debt Collections Practices Act (see Chapter 29). The remedy of bankruptcy was afforded debtors under federal law to provide them with an opportunity to begin a new economic life when their existing debts reached an excessive level and could no longer be paid in a timely fashion (see Chapter 36).

(j) **Stability and Flexibility.** Stability is particularly important in business transactions. When you buy a house, for example, you not only want to know the exact meaning of the transaction under today's law, but you also want the transaction to have the same meaning in the future.

Because of the desire for stability, courts will ordinarily follow former decisions unless there is a strong reason to depart from them. Similarly, when no former case bears on the point involved, a court will try to reach a decision that is a logical extension of some former decision or that follows a former decision by analogy rather than strike out on a new path to reach a decision unrelated to the past.

If stability were always required, the cause of justice would often be defeated. The reason that originally existed for a rule of law may have ceased to exist. Also, a rule may later appear unjust because it reflects a concept of justice that is outmoded or obsolete. The policies surrounding adoption of children and the rights of natural versus adopted parents have continued to evolve because of changing attitudes about the relationships of the parties and new technology that permits laboratory creation and insemination.

The typical modern statute, particularly in the area of business regulation, often contains an escape clause by which a person can "escape" from the operation of the statute under certain circumstances. For example, a rent control law may impose a rent ceiling, that is, a maximum rent a landlord can charge a tenant. The same law may also authorize a greater charge when special circumstances make it just to allow such an exception. For example, the landlord may have made expensive repairs to the property or taxes on the property may have increased substantially.

Protection of the person is frequently the controlling factor in determining whether a court should adhere to the common law, thereby furthering stability; or whether it should change the law, thereby furthering flexibility.

In the following case, the court grapples with issues of ethics, law, technology, contract rights, stability, and the new methods of doing business under e-commerce.

Mortenson Co., Inc. v Timberline Software Corp.
970 P.2d 803 (Wash. 1999)

The One Click Warranty Waiver

Mortenson Company, Inc., a contractor, upgraded its version of Timberline Software's Bid Analysis Software. Bid Analysis Software is used by contractors in preparation of construction bids.

Mortenson negotiated a price and issued a purchase order for eight copies. Employees of both firms initialed the purchase order.

When the software arrived at Mortenson, employees unpacked and activated it. Mortenson employees did not notice that a license agreement is printed on the outside of each sealed envelope containing the diskettes. The license agreement instructs the buyer to read the terms ". . .before using the programs. Use of the programs indicates your acknowledgement that you have read this license, understand it, and agree to be bound by its terms and conditions." The terms also provided "If you do not agree to these terms and conditions, promptly return the programs and user manuals to the place of purchase and your purchase price will be refunded."

The terms limited Timberline's liability for any errors caused by the software programs to a reimbursement for the license fee. Buyers could not recover either compensatory or consequential damages.

After using the Timberline software and submitting a bid, Mortenson discovered a $2 million error and sought to recover damages from Timberline for being forced to perform on the contract for which it had accidentally submitted the incorrect bid that was $2 million low. Timberline defended on the grounds of its warranty limitation placed in the packaging of its software. The trial court granted summary judgment for Timberline and Mortenson appealed.

WEBSTER, Justice "Transactions in which the exchange of money precedes the communication of detailed terms are common." *ProCD, Inc.* v. *Zeidenberg,* 86 F.3d 1447, 1451 (7th Cir.1996). In *ProCD* the Seventh Circuit held that shrinkwrap licenses accompanying off-the-shelf computer software are enforceable unless their terms are objectionable under general contract law. See 86 F.3d at 1449. The defendant purchased ProCD software at a retail outlet and made the database information therein available on the World Wide Web at a cost less than what ProCD charged consumers. See id. at 1450. The district court refused to enforce the license agreement that came with the software because the purchaser did not agree to "hidden terms"—those inside the box—even though a printed notice on the outside of the box referred to the license terms inside. See id. The Seventh Circuit reversed. See id. at 1449. The court stated: "Notice on the outside, terms on the inside, and a right to return the software for a refund if the terms are unacceptable (a right that the license expressly extends), may be a means of doing business valuable to buyers and sellers alike." Id. at 1451 (citing E. Allan Farnsworth, 1 FARNSWORTH ON CONTRACTS § 4.26 (1990) and RESTATEMENT (SECOND) OF CONTRACTS § 211 cmt. a (1981). The court discussed several examples of "money now, terms later" transactions. See id. at 1451 (the purchase of insurance, airline tickets, electronic goods containing warranties inside the box, and drugs with inserts describing interactions and contraindications). Turning to the software industry, the court noted that software is often ordered over the phone and the Internet and that increasingly the delivery is also over the Internet. The court

rejected the defendant's theory that would make these sales "unfettered by terms—so the seller has made a broad warranty and must pay consequential damages for any shortfalls in performance, two 'promises' that if taken seriously would drive prices through the ceiling or return transactions to the horse-and-buggy age."

The Seventh Circuit again upheld license terms in a pay-now- terms-later transaction with an accept-or-return provision in *Hill v. Gateway 2000, Inc.,* 105 F.3d 1147, 1150 (7th Cir.), cert. denied, — U.S. ——, 118 S.Ct. 47, 139 L.Ed.2d 13 (1997). In *Hill,* the customer ordered a computer over the phone, paying with a credit card, and received the computer in the mail accompanied by a list of terms to govern if the customer did not return the computer within 30 days. The court posed this question: "Are these terms effective as the parties' contract, or is the contract term-free because the order-taker did not read any terms over the phone and elicit the customer's assent?" Relying in part on *ProCD,* the court held that the terms were effective, stating: "Practical considerations support allowing vendors to enclose the full legal terms with their products."

ProCD and *Hill* allow a vendor to propose that a sale contract be formed, not when the product is requested or the money is paid, but after the customer has inspected the item and the terms. We find the Seventh Circuit's reasoning persuasive and see similarities between these cases and the present appeal. Timberline's license agreement, included with the software, is fairly standard and contains an accept-or-return provision. Mortenson argues that the negotiations between it and Timberline distinguishes this case from *ProCD* and

Hill, cases involving off-the-shelf purchases where no negotiations took place between the buyer and seller. But although the software provided by Timberline is specialized to a specific market, no evidence suggests that the software was customized for Mortenson, and we find that it is analogous to an off-the-shelf package.

Mortenson makes much of the fact that Reich never mentioned the license agreement or any of its terms during the negotiations. But the negotiations between the parties involved only the number of copies and the price. Reich's failure to bring up the license terms during price-quantity discussions is hardly surprising. Reich knew that Mortenson had a license to a prior version of the software and that it licensed other software. Consider negotiation of a law firm's Westlaw license —a Westlaw representative may negotiate an hourly rate versus a flat rate and the cost of training and customer support, but is unlikely to bring up a choice of law provision or limitations of remedies clause if those terms are not negotiable. Does failure in such a case to elicit the customer's express assent to the license terms before a purchase order is issued make a contract "unfettered by terms—so the seller has made a broad warranty and must pay consequential damages for any shortfalls in performance?" We conclude that it does not and hold that the terms of the present license agreement are part of the contract as formed between the parties. We find that Mortenson's installation and use of the software manifested its assent to the terms of the license and that it is bound by all terms of that license that are not found to be illegal or unconscionable.

Considering all the circumstances surrounding the transaction in this case, the limitations clause is not procedurally unconscionable. Although Mortenson and Timberline did not specifically negotiate the limitations of remedies clause, this one factor is not conclusive. The introductory screen warned that use of the program was subject to a license. This warning placed Mortenson on notice that use of the software was governed by a license. Mortenson had reasonable opportunity to learn and understand the terms of the agreement. The limitations provision was not hidden in a maze of fine print, but appeared in all capital letters. Finally, such limitations provisions are widely used in the computer software industry.

Mortenson argues that the fact that Timberline knew about the bug before it sold the software to Mortenson and did not inform Mortenson of the defect or send a new version to Mortenson contributes to the unconscionability of the license terms. However, the evidence regarding Timberline's knowledge of the bug indicates that it considered it to be an "obscure" bug, "not a major problem." There is no evidence showing that Timberline was aware that the bug would lead to an inaccurate bid. Considering the totality of the circumstances, we conclude that the limitations of remedies provision is not procedurally unconscionable.

Turning to substantive unconscionability, RCW 62A.2-719(3) provides in part that "[l]imitation of . . . consequential damages is valid unless it is established that the limitation is unconscionable." Limitations on consequential damages in commercial transactions are prima facie conscionable. See American Nursery Prods., 115 Wash.2d at 222, 797 P.2d 477. Such clauses are standard in the software industry and do not shock the conscience. Indeed, they are useful in making software affordable. If software developers were prohibited from limiting consequential damages, the significant costs to the industry would be passed on to the consumer. We conclude that the limitations of remedies provision is not substantively unconscionable. Thus, the limitations of remedies clause bars Mortenson's claim for consequential damages, and we affirm the trial court's order granting summary judgment.

Questions

1. How do E-commerce and the methods for doing business change the nature of contract laws?
2. What would happen if software manufacturers could not limit their liability?
3. Do you think a click and use of software is enough to bind a party to the contract terms?

FIGURE 3.3 *Categories of Ethical Behavior*

1. Integrity and truthfulness
2. Promise keeping
3. Loyalty—avoiding conflicts of interest
4. Fairness
5. Doing no harm
6. Maintaining confidentiality

C. HOW TO RECOGNIZE AND RESOLVE ETHICAL DILEMMAS

Business managers find themselves in circumstances in which they are unclear about right and wrong, and confused about how to resolve the dilemmas they face. A recent survey showed that 98 percent of all Fortune 500 companies have codes of ethics designed to help their employees recognize and resolve ethical dilemmas. Nearly 65 percent of those firms provide their employees with some form of training in ethics.[11] These codes of ethics provide for employees categories of behavior that constitute ethical breaches. Regardless of the industry, the type of business, or the size of the company, certain universal categories can help managers recognize ethical dilemmas. Figure 3.3 provides a list of those categories.

9. Categories of Ethical Behavior

(a) Integrity and Truthfulness. Mark Twain once wrote, "Always tell the truth. That way you don't have to remember anything." As discussed earlier, trust is a key component of business relationships and of the free enterprise system. Trust begins with the belief that honesty is at the heart of relationships. Many contract remedies in law are based on the failure of the parties to be truthful with each other. If you purchase a home that has been certified as termite-free and you then discover termites in the home shortly after you move in, someone has not been truthful. If you then discover there were two termite inspections conducted and the first one, which revealed there were termites, was concealed from you, then your trust in sellers and exterminators is diminished.

An assurance that a seller has the expertise to handle your project is important in building that

[11] Survey of the Society for Human Resource Management and Ethics Resource Center.

relationship. If you discover later that the seller lacks the expertise, you are harmed by the delay and possible poor work that has been done. When the prospectus for a stock offering fails to provide full information about the company's obsolete inventory, investors are not given the full truth and are harmed when they invest without complete disclosure. Investors become skeptical when offerings do not carry with them a very basic level of honesty in their disclosures. Honesty is necessary for the wheels of commerce to turn.

Integrity is the adherence to one's values and principles despite the costs and consequences. An executive contracted with a variety of companies to sell his hard-to-find computer components. When he was approached by one of his largest customers to break a contract with a small customer, the executive refused. The customer assured the executive it would be his last order with the company if he did not get more components. Despite facing the threat of losing a multimillion-dollar customer, the executive fulfilled his promises to the small purchasers. The executive kept his word on all of his contracts and demonstrated integrity.

ETHICS AND THE LAW

Ethics and Lying to Get Ahead

A study by an executive search firm revealed that 20 percent of all the résumés they review contain inaccurate information about the individual's educational background or past employment. The types of inaccuracies include listing attendance at a university as a degree and misrepresenting responsibilities at previous jobs (sales manager refers to himself as "director of marketing" on his résumé).*

Another study by Rutgers University concluded, based on surveys conducted of students, that 75 percent of all students in masters of business administration (MBA) programs lied or cheated to get into their graduate programs. Examples of their listed misconduct included cheating in undergraduate school, falsifying letters of reference, and having someone else take the (GMAT) for them.**

Why do people lie about their backgrounds and qualifications? Is anyone really hurt by this individual misconduct? Why is it important that the information on résumés and applications for graduate school be accurate?

* Barry, Dan. "Cheating Hearts and Lying Resumes." *New York Times*, 14 December 1997, WK1, WK4.
** Carol Innerst, "Colleges Are Stepping Up the War Against Cheaters," *Washington Times*, Nov. 6–12, 1995, p. 25.

(b) Promise Keeping. If we examine the types of things we do in a day, most are based on promises. We promise to deliver goods either with or without a contract. We promise to pay the dentist for our dental work. We promise to provide someone with a ride. Keeping those promises, regardless of whether there is a legal obligation, is a key component of an ethical person and an ethical business. Keeping promises is also evidence of integrity. The issue of employee downsizing is debated with the underlying question of whether the "downsized" employees had a promise from their company of continued employment. As stakeholder analysis is reviewed, the ethical issue surrounding the question is whether there are promises to others who are at risk. Weren't shareholders promised a return on their investment? Weren't suppliers promised payment? In many circumstances, the question is not *whether* a promise is kept but rather *which* promise will be kept. The strategic issue is whether businesses should make commitments and promises in circumstances that create a very thin margin of profit and perhaps even thinner margin for error. Over the long term, the importance of keeping its promises to all stakeholders translates into the reputation of the business.

ETHICS AND THE LAW

Ethics and Downsizing

Aaron Feuerstein is the owner of Malden Mills, a textile plant in Methuen, Massachusetts. The company was founded by Feuerstein's grandfather in 1906 as a swimsuit and sweater manufacturer. Feuerstein changed the direction of traditional garment manufacturing when he switched the factory to Polartec® production. Polartec is a revolutionary fabric made from recycled plastic bottles and used in skiing and hiking clothing because of its unique qualities of being very warm, very lightweight, and easy to dry and dye. L.L. Bean, Patagonia, and Eddie Bauer are all on Malden Mills' customer list, which has generated $425 million in sales each year.

On December 11, 1995, the Malden Mills factory was nearly completely destroyed by a fire started by a boiler that exploded. Feuerstein held a meeting with his employees several days later and guaranteed their pay for 30 days and their health benefits for 90 days. Malden Mills has 3,000 employees and an annual payroll of $65 million.

Feuerstein gave all of his employees three months of pay and had all but 20 percent working full-time again by March 1996. By midsummer 1996, Malden Mills was back at full production. One employee said, "Another person would have taken the insurance money and walked away. I might have done that."

Feuerstein describes his role as follows:

"The fundamental difference is that I consider our workers an asset, not an expense. I have a responsibility to the worker, both blue-collar and white-collar. I have an equal responsibility to the community. It would have been unconscionable to put 3,000 people on the streets and deliver a death blow to the cities of Lawrence and Methuen. Maybe on paper our company is worth less to Wall Street, but I can tell you it's worth more. We're doing fine."

Was it right for Feuerstein to keep his promise to employees? Did he really have a promise to keep? Does it matter that Malden Mills is not a publicly held company?

* Steve Wulf, "The Glow From a Fire," *Time*, January 8, 1996, p. 49.

(c) Loyalty–Avoiding Conflicts of Interest. An employee who works for a company owes his or her allegiance to that company. Conduct that compromises that loyalty is a **conflict of interest.** For example, suppose that your sister operates her own catering business. Your company is seeking a caterer for its monthly management meetings. You are responsible for these meetings and could hire your sister to handle the lunches furnished at the meetings. Your sister would have a substantial contract, and your problems with meal logistics would be solved. Nearly all companies have a provision in their codes of ethics covering this situation. An employee cannot hire a relative, friend, or even his own company without special permission because it is a conflict of interest. Your loyalty to your sister conflicts with the loyalty to your employer, which requires you to make the best decision at the best price.

A conflict of interest arises when a purchasing agent accepts gifts from suppliers, vendors, or manufacturers' representatives. The purchasing agent has introduced into the buy/sell relationship an element of *quid pro quo* or the supplier's expectation that the gift will enjoy a return from the agent in the form of a contract. Some companies have a "zero" tolerance for conflicts with a complete prohibition on any gifts from suppliers and manufacturers. ◆ For example, Wal-Mart buyers are not permitted to accept even a cup of coffee from potential merchandise suppliers, and Amgen's buyers can go out to dinner with a supplier only if Amgen pays. ◆

ETHICS AND THE LAW

Ethics and Conflicts of Interest

ABC news correspondent and *20/20* anchorwoman Barbara Walters did a profile piece for *20/20* on composer Andrew Lloyd Webber. After the flattering piece ran on network television, the *New York Daily News* revealed that Ms. Walters had invested $100,000 in Webber's new production of *Sunset Boulevard,* which was mentioned in the *20/20* piece. Further, ABC's parent company, Disney, produced Webber's *Evita* and has an interest in a number of Webber's other musicals. Disney's relationship with Webber was disclosed in the *20/20* profile, but Walter's investment was not.

Should the information about Walter's investment have been disclosed? Should Ms. Walters have done the story on Webber? How could the conflict have been avoided?

(d) Fairness. In business transactions in which the buyer was not told about the crack in the engine block or the dry well on the property, a typical response is, "That's not fair. I wouldn't have bought it if I'd known." A question often

posed to the buyer in response is, "Wouldn't you have done the same thing?" It feels different when we are the victims of unfairness than when we hold the superior knowledge in the transaction. The ethical standard of fairness requires both sides to ask the questions, "How would I want to be treated? Would this information make a difference to me?" Imposing our own standards and expectations on our own behavior in business transactions produces fairness in business.

ETHICS AND THE LAW

Ethics and Fairness

Dateline NBC, a television newsmagazine program that airs several nights a week, presented a segment on General Motors (GM) and the safety of GM's trucks with sidesaddle gas tanks. *Dateline* producers staged and taped an accident with a GM truck that showed a gas tank explosion and subsequent fire that engulfed the pickup truck. The tape was shown on *Dateline.* Through disclosures of several crew members, it was later revealed that explosive devices had been used to create the scene for the cameras. The use of those devices was not disclosed during the *Dateline* piece.*

Was it fair to use the explosive devices? Was it fair to use the explosive devices and not disclose that to the audience? Was it fair to GM?

Note: Dateline later read an on-air apology for the tape.

* Jensen, Elizabeth. "Some Journalists Join GM in Criticizing NBC's Treatment of Truck-Crash Story." *Wall Street Journal,* 10 February 1993, B1, B8.

(e) Doing No Harm. Imagine selling a product that your company's internal research shows presents significant health dangers to its users. Selling the product without disclosure of the information is unfair. But there is the additional ethical breach of physical harm to your customers and users. Ford designed and sold its Pinto with a fundamental flaw in the placement of the car's gas tank. Rear-end collisions in which a Pinto was involved resulted, even at very low speeds, in fires that engulfed the car so quickly that occupants could not always escape from it. An internal memo from engineers at Ford revealed that an analysis about the risk of the tanks versus the cost of redesign was considered but never done. Peter Drucker's advice on ethics for businesses is *primum non nocere,* or above all do no harm.

(f) **Maintain Confidentiality.** Often the success of a business depends on information or technology that it holds. If the competitive edge that comes from the business's peculiar niche or knowledge is lost through disclosure, so also are profits. Employees not only owe a duty of loyalty to their employers, they owe an obligation of confidentiality. Information that employees obtain through their employer's work or research should not be used by the employee either personally or through a competitor. Providing customer lists or leads is a breach of that confidentiality.

In addition, managers have responsibilities regarding their employees' privacy. Performance evaluations of individual employees are private and should never be disclosed or revealed, even in one-on-one conversations outside the lines of authority and the workplace.

ETHICS AND THE LAW

Ethics and Competition

In a long-running case that involves international competition, General Motors and Volkswagen AG have battled in courts and in newspapers over the departure of several GM employees for Volkswagen and their alleged taking of proprietary information regarding GM's supply chain management system in Europe.* The case resulted in the passage of the Economic Espionage Act (EEA) in the United States, which makes it a crime to download or in any way electronically or otherwise take proprietary information from one company to give or sell to another company.

Why is it an ethical issue to take from an employee's mind information about his or her former employer? What risks do you see in hiring someone who offers to bring to you proprietary information? What precautions could companies take to prevent employees from taking proprietary information to competitors?

* "Judge sets Michigan Venue for GM Suit Against VW." *Wall Street Journal,* 18 October 1996, B5.

---

10. Resolving Ethical Dilemmas

Recognizing an ethical dilemma is perhaps the easiest part of business ethics. Resolution of that dilemma is more difficult. The earlier section on stakeholders offers one model for resolution of ethical dilemmas (see Figure 3-1). Other models have been developed to provide managers with methods of analysis for resolving dilemmas in a timely fashion.

(a) **Blanchard and Peale Three-Part Test.** Dr. Kenneth Blanchard, author of books on the one-minute manager, and the late Dr. Norman Vincent Peale developed a model for evaluating ethical breaches that is widely used among Fortune 500 companies.[12] The following three questions should be asked: Is it legal? Is it balanced? How does it make me feel?

In answering the questions on legality, a manager should look to positive law both within and outside the company. If the proposed conduct would be a violation of antitrust laws, then the manager's analysis can stop there. If the proposed conduct would violate company policy, then the manager's analysis can stop. In the field of business ethics, there is little room for civil disobedience. Compliance with the law is a critical component of a successful ethics policy in any company.

The question on balance forces the manager to examine the ethical value of fairness. Perhaps the decision to downsize must be made, but couldn't the company offer the employees a severance package and outplacement assistance to ease the transition?

The final question of the Blanchard/Peale model is conscience based. While some managers may employ any tactics to maximize profits, this final question forces a manager to examine the physical impact of a decision: Does it cause sleeplessness or appetite changes? Personalizing business choices often helps managers to see the potential harm that comes from poor ethical choices.

---

[12] Kenneth Blanchard and Norman Vincent Peale, *The Power of Ethical Management* (1986).

Bribery and Ethics

Salt Lake City, Utah, had been a contender as a potential site for the Winter Olympics for 30 years. Each time, the city, famous for its extensive ski resorts and powder snow, lost to other cities around the world. When city and state officials and representatives from business made their bid for the 2002 Winter Olympics, they were determined to win. During the course of the International Olympic Committee's decision-making process, some members of the Salt Lake City Olympic Committee gave benefits to members of the International Committee. Those benefits included everything from entertainment to medical care and college educations for the family members of Olympic Committee members.

When all of the perks were revealed, members of the International Olympic Committee as well as the Salt Lake City Olympic Committee resigned. Some Olympic sponsors withdrew.*

How could the Blanchard/Peale test have helped those involved in courting the Olympic Committee? Does it matter that those kinds of benefits and perks are expected in the cultures of some of the International Olympic Committee members?

* Ira Berkow, "Greed Knows Few Bounds in Olympics," *New York Times*, Feb. 10, 1999, C23.

Ethics and the Glare of Public Disclosure

Edwin Garrity, the assistant fire chief, retired from the Phoenix Fire Department after an internal audit revealed he had issued holiday pay for employees who had actually never worked. The audit also revealed that Garrity and his family owned a company that sold T-shirts and other fire department souvenirs.*

What categories of ethical breaches occurred here? Could any of the ethical models have helped Garrity avoid the pitfalls that forced his retirement?

* Fiscus, Chris. "Key Official Forced to Retire." *Arizona Republic,* 18 Oct. 1996, A1, A12.

(b) The Front-Page-of-the-Newspaper Test. This simple but effective model for ethical evaluation helps a manager to visualize the public disclosure of proposed conduct. When he took over Salomon Brothers after its bond-trading controversy, Warren Buffett described the newspaper test as follows:

Contemplating any business act, an employee should ask himself whether he would be willing to see it immediately described by an informed and critical reporter on the front page of his local paper, there to be read by his spouse, children, and friends. At Salomon, we simply want no part of any activities that pass legal tests but that we, as citizens, would find offensive.[13]

[13] Janet Lowe, *Warren Buffett Speaks: Wit and Wisdom from the World's Greatest Investor* (Wiley 1997).

(c) Laura Nash Model. In her work, business ethicist Laura Nash has developed a series of questions to help business people reach the right decision in ethical dilemmas. Her questions are: Have you defined the problem accurately? How would you define the problem if you stood on the other side of the fence? How did this situation occur in the first place? What is your intention in making this decision? How does the intention compare with the probable results? Whom could your decision or action injure? Can you discuss your decision with the affected parties? Are you confident that your position will be as valid over a long period of time as it seems now? Could you discuss your decision with your supervisor, co-workers, officers, board, friends, and family? The Nash model requires an examination of the dilemma from all perspectives. Defining the problem and how the problem arose provides the business with assistance in avoiding the dilemma again. For example, suppose that a supervisor is asked to provide a reference for a friend who works for her. The supervisor is hesitant because the friend has not been a very good employee. The ethical dilemma the manager believes she faces is whether to lie or tell the truth about the employee. The real ethical dilemma is why the supervisor never provided evaluation or feedback indicating the friend's poor performance. Avoiding the problem in the future is possible through candid evaluations. Resolving the problem requires that the supervisor talk to her friend now about the issue of performance and the problem with serving as a reference.

One final note about the Nash model that business people find helpful is a question that asks for a perspective on an issue from family and friends. The problem of groupthink in business situations is very real. As business people sit together in a room and discuss an ethical dilemma, they can persuade each other to think the same way. The power of consensus overwhelms each person's concerns and values. There is a certain fear in bringing up a different point of view in a business meeting. Proper perspective is often lost as the discussion centers around numbers, but bringing in views of an outsider is often helpful. For example, when McNeil, the manufacturer of Tylenol, was faced with the cyanide poisonings in the Chicago area, the decision about existing inventory had to be made. It was clear to both insiders and outsiders that the poisonings had not occurred at McNeil, but rather after delivery to the stores. Despite the huge numbers involved in the recall and destruction of inventory, the McNeil managers made the decision easily because they viewed the risk to their own families, that is, "from the outside." From this standpoint, it became a question of life and not a question of numbers.[14]

ETHICS AND THE LAW
Ethics When No One Knows
While making a sales call using a company car, you hit another vehicle in a customer's parking lot. You are positive no one has seen you. You cannot locate the owner of the vehicle.

Would you leave a note with full information and ask the owner to contact you? Use all of the models discussed to reach a decision.

(d) *Wall Street Journal* Model. The *Wall Street Journal* presented a simple, three-prong test for resolving ethical dilemmas known as the three-C model: (1) Will this *conduct* be in compliance with the law? (2) What *contribution* does this decision make to the shareholders? To the community? To the employees? And (3) What are the *consequences* of this decision? This model requires an examination of the impact of a choice, which then produces a look from a different perspective on a course of conduct. ◆ For example, Sears recently paid $475 million in fines and penalties for its unauthorized collection of debts from debtors who were in bankruptcy or had debts discharged in bankruptcy. Such collection beyond what the law allows was not in compliance with the law.[15] The contribution to the company was more collections and hence more cash, but the consequences were the large fine and the damage to Sears' reputation for putting its interests above the law and above other creditors who conducted themselves within the limits of the bankruptcy law. While Sears may resent the fact that debtors have not paid, it is not justified in taking the law into its own hands or profiting at the expense of other creditors. ◆

SUMMARY

Business ethics is the application of values and standards to business conduct and decisions. These values originate in various sources, from positive (codified) law to natural law to stakeholder values. Business ethics is important because trust is a critical component of good business relationships and free enterprise. A business with values will enjoy the additional competitive advantage of a good reputation and, over the long term, better earnings. When businesses make decisions that violate basic ethical standards, social forces are set into motion and the area of abuse is regulated with resulting additional costs and restrictions for business. Voluntary value choices by businesses position them for a competitive advantage.

---

[14] Brief History of Johnson: Johnson (1992) (Company Pamphlet)

[15] Leslie Kaufman. "Sears Settles Suit on Raising of Its Credit Card Rates," *New York Times,* March 11, 1999, C2.

The categories of ethical values in business are truthfulness and integrity, promise keeping, loyalty and avoiding conflicts of interest, fairness, doing no harm, and maintaining confidentiality.

Resolution of ethical dilemmas is possible through the use of various models that require a businessperson to examine the impact of a decision before it is made. The models include stakeholder analysis, Blanchard/Peale, the front-page-of-the-newspaper test, the Laura Nash model, and the *Wall Street Journal* model.

WEBSITE REFERENCES

Visit Inc. Online's Ethics Corner, a site that addresses ethical dilemmas faced by entrepreneurs:

www.inc.com/extra/columns/ethics

Visit also the website for the Markula Ethics Center of Santa Clara University:

www.scu.edu/Ethics/
Note: the E must be uppercase.

QUESTIONS AND CASE PROBLEMS

1. What is the relationship between ethics and law? How does one affect the other? How do social forces connect the two?

2. Ann Elkin, who works for Brill Co., has been sent out to conduct two customer evaluations, which have gone much more quickly than Ann anticipated. Her supervisor does not expect Ann back until after lunch. It is now 10:30 A.M., and Ann would like to run some personal errands and then go to lunch before returning to work at 1:00 P.M. Should Ann take the time? Would you? Why or why not? Be sure to consider the categories of ethical values and apply one or two models before reaching your conclusion.

3. Fred Sanguine is a New York City produce broker. Ned Santini is a 19-year-old college student who works for Sanguine from 4:00 A.M. until 7:00 A.M. each weekday before he attends classes at Pace University. Fred has instructed Ned on the proper packing of produce as follows: "Look, put the bad and small cherries at the bottom. Do the same with the strawberries and blueberries. Put the best fruit on top and hide the bad stuff at the bottom. This way I get top dollar on all that I sell." Ned is uncomfortable about the instructions, but, as he explains to his roommate, "It's not me doing it. I'm just following orders. Besides, I need the job." Should Ned just follow instructions? Is the manner in which the fruit is packed unethical? Would you do it? Why or why not? Is anyone really harmed by the practice?

4. Alan Gellen is the facilities manager for the city of Milwaukee and makes all final decisions on purchasing items such as chairs and lights as well as other supplies and materials. Alan also makes the final decisions for the award of contracts to food vendors at event sites. Grand Beef Franks has submitted a bid to be one of the city's vendors. Alan went to school with Grand Beef's owner, Steve Grand, who phones Alan and explains that Grand Beef owns a condominium in Maui that Alan could use. "All it would cost you for a vacation is your airfare. The condo is fully stocked with food. Just let me know," was Steve's offer to Alan. Should Alan take the offer? Would you? Be sure to determine which category of ethical values this situation involves, and apply several models as you resolve the question of whether Alan should accept the invitation.

5. CNBC and other television networks have been working to develop policies for their business correspondents and guests on their business shows because of a practice known as "pump and dump." Pump and dump is the practice of a Wall Street professional or network business correspondent appearing on television to tout a particular stock as being a good buy. Often unbeknownst to the viewing audience, the guest or correspondent promoting the stock has a large holding in that stock and, after the television show runs and the stock price creeps up, sells his or her interest at a higher price than before the show and

their raves about the stock. What category of ethical issue exists here? If you were a network executive, what would you do to remedy the problem? Could the government regulate such practices? What kind of regulation could it impose?

6. Adam Smith wrote the following in *The Theory of Moral Sentiments:*

   In the practice of the other virtues, our conduct should rather be directed by a certain idea of propriety, by a certain taste for a particular tenor of conduct, than by any regard to a precise maxim or rule; and we should consider the end and foundation of the rule, more than the rule itself.[16]

   Do you think Adam Smith adhered to positive law as his ethical standard? Is he a moral relativist? Does his quote match stakeholder analysis? What would the ethical posture be on violating the law?

7. If you were asked by your new employer to reveal your salary at your previous job, would you include your bonus as part of your salary and not reveal the bonus? Why or why not?

8. Marv Albert, the longtime NBC sportscaster famous for his "Yes!" commentary, was charged with violations of several Virginia statutes, including criminal assault, battery, and sodomy, for his alleged conduct with a woman in a hotel room. Initially, Mr. Albert went to trial on the case and denied that the charges were true. During the trial, another woman testified that Mr. Albert had engaged in similar behavior with her. Following plea negotiations, Mr. Albert entered a guilty plea the next day. He was then fired by NBC under a provision in his contract that prohibited employees from making false statements. Mr. Albert had assured his superiors at NBC that the charges were baseless. Do you agree with NBC's decision to fire Mr. Albert? Is his personal behavior relevant for his job performance? Do you agree that lying to your employer should result in automatic termination? How do you compare Michael Irvin's conduct with Mr. Albert's? Mr. Albert is back as a network commentator. Does his reinstatement mean that moral issues and private conduct the irrelevant in business decisions?

9. In 1997, the Federal Trade Commission (FTC) issued a "cease and desist" order against Toys 'R' Us. The order requires Toys 'R' Us to stop what the FTC calls its "blacklisting" practices. The FTC ruled that Toys 'R' Us had forced the large toy manufacturers, such as Mattel and Hasbro, to withhold their products from the discount warehouse stores such as Sam's Club and Costco. Toys 'R' Us allegedly threatened not to carry these companies' products if they were also sold at the discount warehouse chains. Mattel's Barbie doll is one example of a toy Toys 'R' Us carried that the discount warehouses were not permitted to carry. Costco's CEO, James Sinegal, said, "You could fill Madison Square Garden with the people who don't want to sell to us." Are these types of sales agreements ethical? Is it fair for Toys 'R' Us to insist on these arrangements? What do you think these arrangements do to price?

10. The president and athletic director at UCLA fired the school's basketball coach because an expense form he had submitted for reimbursement had the names of two students he said had joined him for a recruiting dinner. The students had not been to the dinner. The coach was stunned because he had been there eight years and had established a winning program. He said, "And to throw it all away on a meal?" Do you agree with the coach's assessment? Was it too harsh to fire him for one inaccurate expense form? Did the coach commit an ethical breach?

[16] Adam Smith, *The Theory of Moral Sentiments* (Arlington House, 1969; originally published in 1769).

Nature and Classes of Contracts

Learning Objectives

After studying this chapter, you should be able to

1. List the essential elements of a contract
2. Describe the way in which a contract arises
3. State how contracts are classified
4. Differentiate contracts from agreements that are not contracts
5. Differentiate formal contracts from simple contracts
6. Differentiate express contracts from implied contracts
7. Differentiate contractual liability from quasi-contractual liability

Practically every business transaction affecting anyone involves a contract.

A. NATURE OF CONTRACTS

This introductory chapter will familiarize you with the terminology needed to work with contract law. In addition, the chapter introduces quasi contracts, which are not true contracts but rather obligations imposed by law.

1. Definition of a Contract

A **contract** is a legally binding agreement.[1] By one definition, "a contract is a promise or a set of promises for the breach of which the law gives a remedy, or the performance of which the law in some way recognizes as a duty."[2] Contracts arise out of agreements, so a contract may be defined as an agreement creating an obligation.

The substance of the definition of a contract is that by mutual agreement or assent the parties create enforceable duties or obligations. That is, each party is legally bound to do or to refrain from doing certain acts.

2. Elements of a Contract

The elements of a contract are (1) an agreement (2) between competent parties (3) based on the genuine assent of the parties that is (4) supported by consideration, (5) made for a lawful objective, and (6) in the form required by law, if any. These elements will be considered in the chapters that follow.

3. Subject Matter of Contracts

The subject matter of a contract may relate to the performance of personal services, such as contracts of employment to work developing computer software or to play professional football. A contract may provide for the transfer of ownership of property, such as a house (real property) or an automobile (personal property), from one person to another.

4. Parties to a Contract

The person who makes a promise is the **promisor,** and the person to whom the promise is made is the **promisee.** If the promise is binding, it imposes on the promisor a duty or obligation, and the promisor may be called the **obligor.** The promisee who can claim the benefit of the obligation is called the **obligee.** The parties to a contract are said to stand in **privity** with each other, and the relationship between them is termed **privity of contract.** ◆ For example, when the state of North Carolina and the architectural firm of O'Brien/ Atkins Associates executed a contract for the construction of a new building at the University of North Carolina, Chapel Hill, these parties were in privity of contract. However, a building contractor, RPR & Associates, who worked on the project did not have standing to sue on the contract between the architect and the state, because the contractor was not in privity of contract.[3] ◆

In written contracts, parties may be referred to by name. More often, however, they are given special names that serve to better identify each party. For example, consider a contract by which one person agrees that another may occupy a house upon the payment of money. The parties to this contract are called *landlord* and *tenant,* or *lessor* and *lessee,* and the contract between them is known as a *lease.* Parties to other types of contracts also have distinctive names, such as *vendor* and *vendee* for the parties to a sales contract, *shipper* and *carrier* for the parties to a transportation contract, and *insurer* and *insured* for the parties to an insurance policy.

A party to a contract may be an individual, a partnership, a corporation, or a government. One or more persons may be on each side of a contract. Some contracts are three-sided, as in a credit card transaction, which involves the company issuing the card, the holder of the card, and the business furnishing goods and services on the basis of the credit card.

---

[1] The Uniform Commercial Code defines *contract* as "the total legal obligation which results from the parties' agreement as affected by [the UCC] and any other applicable rules of law." UCC § 1–201 (11).

[2] Restatement (Second) of Contracts § 1.

[3] *RPR & Associates v O'Brien/Atkins Associates, P. A.,* 24 FSupp 2d 515 (MDNC 1998).

If a contract is written, the persons who are the parties and who are bound by it will ordinarily be determined by reading what the paper says and seeing how it is signed. A contract binds only the parties to the contract. It cannot impose a duty on a person who is not a party to it.[4] Ordinarily, only a party to a contract has any rights against another party to the contract.[5] In some cases, third persons have rights on a contract as third-party beneficiaries or assignees. But a person cannot be bound by the terms of a contract to which that person is not a party.[6]

5. How a Contract Arises

A contract is based on an agreement. An agreement arises when one person, the **offeror,** makes an offer and the person to whom the offer is made, the **offeree,** accepts. There must be both an offer and an acceptance. If either is lacking, there is no contract.[7]

6. Intent to Make a Binding Agreement

Because a contract is based on the consent of the parties and is a legally binding agreement, it follows that the parties must have an intent to enter into an agreement that is binding. Sometimes the parties are in agreement, but their agreement does not produce a contract. Sometimes there is merely a preliminary agreement, but the parties never actually make a contract, or there is merely an agreement as to future plans or intentions without any contractual obligation to carry out those plans or intentions.

7. Freedom of Contract

In the absence of some ground for declaring a contract void or voidable, parties may make such contracts as they choose. The law does not require parties to be fair, or kind, or reasonable, or to share gains or losses equitably.

B. CLASSES OF CONTRACTS

Contracts are classified according to their form, the way in which they were created, their binding character, and the extent to which they have been performed.

8. Formal and Informal Contracts

Contracts can be classified as formal or informal.

(a) Formal Contracts. Formal contracts are enforced because the formality with which they are executed is considered sufficient to signify that the parties intend to be bound by their terms. Formal contracts include (1) contracts under seal, (2) contracts of record, and (3) negotiable instruments.

(1) Contracts under Seal. A **contract under seal** is executed by affixing a seal or making an impression on the paper or on some adhering substance, such as wax, attached to the document. Although at common law an impression was necessary, the courts now treat various signs or marks to be the equivalent of a seal. Most states hold that there is a seal if a person's signature or a corporation's name is followed by a scroll or scrawl, the word *seal,* or the letters *L.S.*[8] In some jurisdictions, the body of the contract must recite that the parties are sealing the contract in addition to their making a seal following their signatures.[9]

A contract under seal was binding at common law solely because of its formality. In many states, this has been changed by statute. The Uniform Commercial Code makes the law of seals inapplicable to the sale of goods. In some states, the law of seals has been abolished generally without regard to the nature of the transaction involved.

(2) Contracts of Record. A contract of record is an agreement or obligation that has been recorded by a court. One form of contract of record arises when one acknowledges before a proper court the obligation to pay a certain sum unless a speci-

[4] *Continental Casualty Co. v Campbell Design Group, Inc.,* 914 SW2d 43 (Mo App 1996).

[5] *Hooper v Yakima County,* 904 P2d 1193 (Wash App 1995).

[6] *Walsh v Telesector Resources Group, Inc.,* 662 NE2d 1043 (Mass App 1996).

[7] *Orcutt v S&L Paint Contractors, Ltd.,* 791 P2d 71 (NM App 1990).

[8] Some authorities explain *L.S.* as an abbreviation for *Locus Sigilium* (place for the seal).

[9] *Dunes South Homeowners Ass'n, Inc. v First Flight Builders, Inc.,* 451 SE2d 636 (NC App 1994) (corporate seal).

FIGURE 11.1 *Contractual Liability*

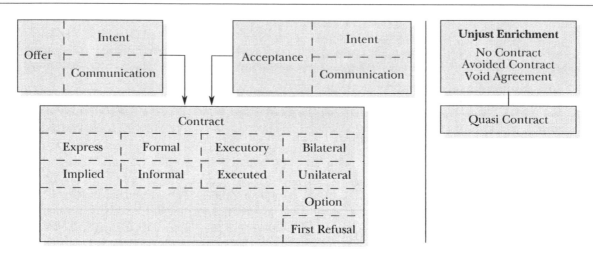

fied condition is met. ◆ For example, a party who has been arrested may be released on a promise to appear in court and may agree to pay a certain sum on failing to do so. An obligation of this kind is known as a **recognizance.** ◆

(b) Informal Contracts. All contracts other than formal contracts are called **informal** (or simple) **contracts** without regard to whether they are oral or written. These contracts are enforceable, not because of the form of the transaction, but because they represent agreement of the parties.

9. Express and Implied Contracts

Simple contracts may be classified as express contracts or implied contracts according to the way they are created.

(a) Express Contracts. An **express contract** is one in which the agreement of the parties is manifested by their words, whether spoken or written.

(b) Implied Contracts. An **implied contract** (or, as sometimes stated, a contract implied in fact) is one in which the agreement is shown not by words, written or spoken, but by the acts and conduct of the parties. ◆ For example, such a contract arises when one person renders services under circumstances indicating that payment for them is expected and the other person, knowing such cir-

cumstances, accepts the benefit of those services.[10] Similarly, when a building owner requests a professional roofer to make repairs to the roof of a building, an obligation arises to pay the reasonable value of such services, although no agreement has been made about compensation. ◆

An implied contract cannot arise when there is an existing express contract on the same subject. However, the existence of a written contract does not bar recovery on an implied contract for extra work that was not covered by the contract.[11]

No contract is implied when the relationship of the parties is such that, by a reasonable interpretation, the performance of services or the supplying of goods was intended as a gift. The fact that the services are rendered by a neighbor does not show that the services were rendered as a gift.[12]

10. Valid and Voidable Contracts and Void Agreements

Contracts may be classified in terms of enforceability or validity.

[10] *Vortt Exploration Co. v Chevron U.S.A., Inc.,* 787 SW2d 942 (Tex 1990).

[11] *Jensen Construction Co. v Dallas County,* 920 SW2d 761 (Tex App 1996).

[12] *Estate of Holtmeyer v Piontek,* 913 SW2d 352 (Mo App 1996).

FIGURE 11.2 *Contract*

Note that this contract includes the following important items of information: (1) the name and address of each party, (2) the promise or consideration of the seller, (3) the promise or consideration of the buyer, (4) the signature of the two parties, and (5) the date.

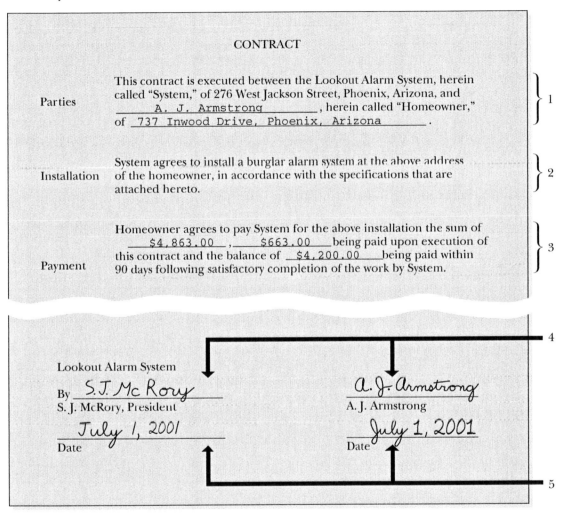

(a) **Valid Contracts.** A **valid contract** is an agreement that is binding and enforceable.

(b) **Voidable Contracts.** A **voidable contract** is an agreement that is otherwise binding and enforceable, but, because of the circumstances surrounding its execution or the lack of capacity of one of the parties, it may be rejected at the option of one of the parties. ◆ For example, a person who has been forced to sign an agreement that that person would not have voluntarily signed may, in some instances, avoid the contract. ◆

(c) **Void Agreements.** A **void agreement** is without legal effect. An agreement that contemplates the performance of an act prohibited by law is usually incapable of enforcement; hence it is void. Likewise, it cannot be made binding by later approval or ratification.

11. Executed and Executory Contracts

Contracts may be classified as executed contracts and executory contracts according to the extent to which they have been performed.

(a) Executed Contracts. An **executed contract** is one that has been completely performed. In other words, an executed contract is one under which nothing remains to be done by either party.[13] A contract may be executed at once, as in the case of a cash sale, or it may be executed or performed in the future.

(b) Executory Contracts. In an **executory contract,** something remains to be done by one or both parties. ♦ For example, on July 10, Mark agreed to sell to Chris his Pearl drum set for $600, the terms being $200 upon delivery on July 14, with $200 to be paid on July 21, and the final $200 being due July 28. Prior to the July 14 delivery of the drums to Chris, the contract was entirely executory. After the delivery by Mark, the contract was executed as to Mark and executory as to Chris, until the final payment was received on July 28. ♦

12. Bilateral and Unilateral Contracts

In making an offer, the offeror is in effect extending a promise to do something, such as pay a sum of money, if the offeree will do what the offeror requests. Contracts are classified as bilateral or unilateral. Some bilateral contracts look ahead to the making of a later contract. Depending on their terms, these are called option contracts or first-refusal contracts.

(a) Bilateral Contract. If the offeror extends a promise and asks for a promise in return and if the offeree accepts the offer by making the promise, the contract is called a **bilateral contract.** One promise is given in exchange for another, and each party is bound by the obligation. ♦ For example, when the house painter offers to paint the owner's house for $3,700 and the owner promises to pay $3,700 for the job, there is an exchange of promises, and the agreement gives rise to a bilateral contract. ♦

(b) Unilateral Contract. In contrast with a bilateral contract, the offeror may offer to do something only when something is done by the offeree. Because only one party is obligated to perform

after the contract has been made, this kind of contract is called a **unilateral contract.**[14] This is illustrated by the case of the reward for the return of lost property. The offeror does not wish to have promises by members of the public that they will try to find and return the property. The offeror wants the property and promises to pay anyone who returns the property. The offer of a unilateral contract calls for an act.

(c) Option and First-Refusal Contracts. The parties may make a contract that gives a right to one of them to enter into a second contract at a later date. If one party has an absolute right to enter into the later contract, the initial contract is called an **option contract.** Thus, a bilateral contract may be made today giving one of the parties the right to buy the other party's house for a specified amount. This is an option contract because the party with the privilege has the freedom of choice, or option, to buy or not buy. If the option is exercised, the other party to the contract must follow the terms of the option and enter into the second contract. If the option is never exercised, no second contract ever arises, and the offer protected by the option contract merely expires.

In contrast with an option contract, a contract may merely give a **right of first refusal.** This imposes only the duty to make the first offer to the party having the right of first refusal.

13. Quasi Contracts

In some cases, a court will impose an obligation even though there is no contract. Such an obligation is called a **quasi contract,** which is an obligation imposed by law.[15]

(a) Prevention of Unjust Enrichment. A *quasi contract* is not a true contract, reflecting all of the elements of a contract set forth previously in this chapter. The court is not seeking to enforce the intentions of the parties contained in an agreement. Rather, where a person or enterprise receives a benefit from another, even in the absence of a promise to pay for the benefit, a court

---

[13] *Marsh v Rheinecker,* 641 NE2d 1256 (Ill App 1994).

[14] *Anderson v Douglas & Lomason Co.,* 540 NW2d 277 (Iowa 1995).

[15] *Dana Larson, Roubal, and Associates v Board of Commissioners of Canyon County,* 864 P2d 632 (Idaho App 1993).

may impose an obligation to pay for the reasonable value of that benefit, to avoid *unjust enrichment*.

Sometimes a contract may be unenforceable due to a failure to set forth the contract in writing in compliance with the statute of frauds. In other circumstances there is no enforceable contract because of a lack of definite and certain terms. Yet, in both situations one party may have performed services for the benefit of the other party; and the court will require payment of the reasonable value of services to avoid the unjust enrichment of the party receiving the services without paying for them. These damages are sometimes referred to as *restitution damages*. Some courts refer to this situation as an action or recovery in *quantum meruit* (as much as he or she deserved).

A situation may arise as to the mistaken conference of a benefit. ♦ For example, Nantucket Island has a few approved colors for houses in its historic district. Using the approved gray color, Martin Kane and his crew began painting Sheldon Adams's house in the historic district due to a mistaken address. Adams observed the initiation of the work from his office across the street but did nothing to stop the painters. At the end of the day when the work was done, Adams refused to pay for the work, saying, "I signed no contract, and never approved this work." The law deems it inequitable that Adams should have received the benefit of this work, having observed the benefit being conferred and knowing that the painters expected payment. Adams would be unjustly enriched if he were allowed to retain the benefit without payment for the reasonable value of the work. If Adams did not have knowledge that the work was being done and thus that payment was expected, quasi-contractual liability would not be imposed. ♦

ETHICS AND THE LAW

Professor Arthur Bernstein was asked by the Association of Oil and Gas Executives (AOGE) to conduct a session on business ethics at the group's annual meeting in Houston, Texas. Professor Bernstein, a member of the faculty at UCLA, agreed to conduct the session for an honorarium of $1,200 plus travel expenses. The agreement between Professor Bernstein and AOGE was an oral one completed over the phone.

The professor took an early morning flight from Los Angeles to Houston to conduct his 3:30 P.M. session for AOGE. Because Houston was experiencing severe thunderstorms and the Dallas airport was under fog, Professor Bernstein's flight could not land in either Houston or Dallas until 8 P.M. Professor Bernstein called the AOGE offices and left word about the difficulties. The plane was low on fuel and was routed to San Antonio for refueling.

At 3:30 P.M. (Houston time), the pilot offered anyone on board the opportunity to deplane and catch flights out of San Antonio. Professor Bernstein deplaned and caught a 4:30 flight back to Los Angeles because he would not be able to get to Houston on time.

When he returned, Professor Bernstein submitted a bill to AOGE for his airfare of $598. AOGE refused to pay and wrote in a letter, "Frankly, we're a bit surprised that you would submit a bill. We received absolutely no benefit from you. We were left without a presentation."

Professor Bernstein responded, "Frankly, I'm surprised that you can't compromise on the airfare. I put in a great deal of time preparing for my presentation, and I spent an entire day on an airplane trying to get there. I certainly had no benefit. And we had an understanding on travel expenses."

After you review the legal standing of these parties, consider the ethical issues. Is the weather anyone's fault? Did Professor Bernstein act in good faith? Is there unjust enrichment on the part of AOGE? Is AOGE's refusal to pay the airfare an ethical position? What would you do?

(b) When Quasi-Contractual Liability Does Not Exist. While the objective of the quasi contract is to do justice, one must not conclude that a quasi contract arises every time there is an injustice.

(1) Unexpected Cost. The fact that performance of a contract proves more difficult or more expensive than had been expected does not entitle a party to extra compensation.

(2) Existing Contract. A plaintiff cannot sue for restitution damages or for reasonable value of services rendered when there is an express contract fixing the amount due.[16]

(3) Gift Benefit There can be no recovery for unjust enrichment when the circumstances are such that it is reasonable to conclude that goods or services were furnished to the benefited party with the intent to make a gift and not in the expectation of being compensated. ◆ **For example,** personal care services provided between family members are generally considered gratuitous, unless they exceed those customarily rendered by reason of the family relationship. ◆

(c) Extent of Recovery When recovery is allowed in quasi contract, the plaintiff recovers the reasonable value of the benefit conferred on the defendant.[17] The fact that the plaintiff may have sustained greater damages or have been put to greater expense is ignored. Thus, the plaintiff cannot recover lost profits or other kinds of damages that would be recovered in a suit for breach of a contract.

◆ **For example,** Peabody New England, Inc., is in the business of constructing waste system facilities for cities and towns. A facility that Peabody contracted to build for the town of Marshfield was not completed on time. The project's completion date was delayed in part by the contractor's mismanagement. The town also contributed to the delays. The court refused to allow Peabody to recover under the terms of the contract because Peabody did not live up to the contract's terms. However, the court did allow limited damages to Peabody for the reasonable value of the services rendered, which amount was less than the contract price and did not include lost profits and "overhead" expenses.[18] ◆

SUMMARY

A contract is a binding agreement between two or more parties. A contract arises when an offer is accepted with contractual intent (the intent to make a binding agreement).

Contracts may be classified in a number of ways according to form, the way in which they were created, validity, and obligations. With respect to form, a contract may be either informal or formal, such as those under seal or those appearing on the records of courts. Contracts may be classified by the way they were created as those that are expressed by words—written or oral—and those that are implied or deduced from conduct. The question of validity requires distinguishing between contracts that are valid, those that are voidable, and those that are not contracts at all but are merely void agreements. Contracts can be distinguished on the basis of the obligations created as executed contracts, in which everything has been performed, and executory contracts, in which something remains to be done. The bilateral contract is formed by exchanging a promise for a promise, so each party has the obligation of thereafter rendering the promised performance. In the unilateral contract, which is the doing of an act in exchange for a promise, no further performance is required of the offeree who performed the act.

In certain situations, the law regards it as unjust for a person to receive a benefit and not pay for it. In such a case, the law of quasi contracts allows the performing person to recover the reasonable value of the benefit conferred on the benefited person even though no contract between them requires any payment. Unjust enrichment, which a quasi contract is designed to prevent, sometimes arises when there was never any contract between the persons involved or when there was a contract, but for some reason it was avoided or held to be merely a void agreement.

---

[16] *Threadgill v Farmers Ins. Exchange,* 912 SW2d 264 (Tex App 1995).

[17] *Ramsey v Ellis,* 484 NW2d 331 (Wis 1992).

[18] *Peabody New England, Inc. v Town of Marshfield,* 689 NE2d 774 (Mass 198).

WEBSITE REFERENCES

For a look at ancient contracts from Mesopotamia visit:

http://www.fordham.edu/halsall/ancient/mesopotamia-contracts.html

For an international perspective on contract law, survey several cases from Australia dealing with contract formation by visiting the following site:

http://www.anu.edu.au/law/pub/edinst/anu/contract/OverviewB.html#Overview - B4

For a brief overview on the nature of contracts and their importance in society visit:

http://www.st-hawaii.com/com-con.html

QUESTIONS AND CASE PROBLEMS

1. What social forces that shape the law (from the list in Chapter 3, Section 8) are illustrated by the following quotation: "A person shall not be allowed to enrich himself unjustly at the expense of another." *Note:* As you study the various rules of law in this chapter and the chapters that follow, consider each rule in relationship to its social, economic, and ethical background. Try to determine the particular objective(s) of each important rule. To the extent that you are able to analyze law as the product of society's striving for justice, you will have greater insight into the law itself, the world in which you live, the field of business, and the human mind.

2. What is a contract?

3. Karl sent letters to names randomly selected from the phone book. Each letter stated: "It is agreed that we will paint your house for a price based on the cost of our labor and paint plus an additional 10 percent for profit." Maria received such a letter. Is there a contract between Karl and Maria?

4. Compare an implied contract with a quasi contract.

5. Stephen said to Hilda, "I want to buy your old Chevy." She replied, "It's yours for $495." Stephen replied, "I'll take it." Later, Stephen changed his mind and refused to take or pay for the car. When Hilda sued him for damages, he contended that he had never made a contract with her because they had never expressly stated, "We hereby make a contract for the sale of the car." Stephen claimed that, in the absence of such an express declaration showing that they intended to make a contract, there could not be a binding agreement to purchase the car. Was he correct?

6. Beck was the general manager of Chilkoot Lumber Co. Haines sold fuel to the company. To persuade Haines to sell on credit, Beck signed a paper by which he promised to pay any debt the lumber company owed Haines. He signed this paper with his name followed by "general manager." Haines later sued Beck on this promise, and Beck raised the defense that the addition of "general manager" showed that Beck was signing on behalf of Chilkoot, was not personally liable, and did not intend to be bound by the paper. Was Beck liable on the paper? [*Beck v Haines Terminal and Highway Co.*, 843 P2d 1229 (Alaska)]

7. *A* made a contract to construct a house for *B*. Subsequently, *B* sued *A* for breach of contract. *A* raised the defense that the contract was not binding because it was not sealed. Is this a valid defense? [*Cooper v G. E. Construction Co.*, 158 SE2d 305 (Ga App)]

8. While Clara Novak was sick, her daughter Janie helped her in many ways. Clara died, and Janie then claimed that she was entitled to be paid for the services she had rendered her mother. This claim was opposed by three brothers and sisters who also rendered services to the mother. They claimed that Janie was barred because of the presumption that services rendered between family members are gratuitous. Janie claimed that this presumption was not applicable because she had not lived with her mother but had her own house. Was Janie correct? [*In re Estate of Novak* 398 NW2d 653 (Minn App)]

9. Dozier and his wife, daughter, and grandson lived in the house Dozier owned. At the request of the daughter and grandson, Paschall made

some improvements to the house. Dozier did not authorize these, but he knew that the improvements were being made and did not object to them. Paschall sued Dozier for the reasonable value of the improvements, Dozier argued that he had not made any contract for such improvements. Was he obligated to pay for such improvements?

10. When Harriet went away for the summer, Landry, a house painter, painted her house. He had a contract to paint a neighbor's house but painted Harriet's house by mistake. When Harriet returned from vacation, Landry billed her for $1,200, which was what the painting was worth. She refused to pay. Landry claimed that she had a quasi-contractual liability for that amount. Was he correct?

11. Margrethe and Charles Pyeatte, a married couple, agreed that she would work so that he could go to law school and that when he finished, she would go back to school for her master's degree. After Charles was admitted to the bar and before Margrethe went back to school, the two were divorced. She sued Charles, claiming that she was entitled to quasi-contractual recovery of the money that she had paid for Charles's support and law school tuition. He denied liability. Was she entitled to recover for the money she spent for Charles's maintenance and law school tuition? (*Pyeatte v Pyeatte*, 661 P2d 196 (Ariz App)]

12. Carriage Way was a real estate development of approximately 80 houses and 132 apartments. The property owners were members of the Carriage Way Property Owners Association. Each year, the association would take care of certain open neighboring areas that were used by the property owners, including a nearby lake. The board of directors of the association would make an assessment or charge against the property owners to cover the cost of this work. The property owners paid these assessments for a number of years and then refused to pay any more. In spite of this refusal, the association continued to take care of the areas in question. The association then sued the property owners and claimed that they were liable for the benefit that had been conferred on them. Were the owners liable? [*Board of Directors of Carriage Way Property Owners Ass'n v Western National Bank*, 487 NE2d 974 (Ill App)]

13. Lombard insured his car, and when it was damaged, the insurer sent the car to General Auto Service for repairs. The insurance company went bankrupt and did not pay the repair bill. General Auto Service then sued Lombard for the bill because he had benefited from the repair work. Was he liable?

14. When a college student complained about a particular course, the vice president of the college asked the teacher to prepare a detailed report about the course. The teacher did and then demanded additional compensation for the time spent in preparing the report. He claimed that the college was liable to provide compensation on an implied contract. Was he correct? [*Zadrozny v City Colleges of Chicago*, 581 NE2d 44 (Ill App)]

15. Smith made a contract to sell automatic rifles to a foreign country. Because the sale of such weapons to that country was illegal under an act of Congress, Smith was prosecuted by the U.S. government for making the contract. He raised the defense that because the contract was illegal, it was void and there is no binding obligation when a contract is void; therefore, no contract for which he could be prosecuted existed. Was he correct?

CPA QUESTION

1. Kay, an art collector, promised Hammer, an art student, that if Hammer could obtain certain rare artifacts within two weeks, Kay would pay for Hammer's postgraduate education. At considerable effort and expense, Hammer obtained the specified artifacts within the two-week period. When Hammer requested payment, Kay refused. Kay claimed that there was no consideration for the promise. Hammer would prevail against Kay based on
   a. Unilateral contract
   b. Unjust enrichment
   c. Public policy
   d. Quasi contract

The Agreement

Learning Objectives

After studying this chapter, you should be able to

1. Decide whether a statement is an offer or an invitation to negotiate
2. Decide whether an agreement is too indefinite to be enforced
3. Describe the exceptions that the law makes to the requirement of definiteness
4. List all the ways an offer is terminated
5. Compare offers, firm offers, and option contracts
6. Define what constitutes the acceptance of an offer

A contract consists of enforceable obligations that have been voluntarily assumed. Thus, one of the essential elements of a contract is an agreement. This chapter explains how the basic agreement arises, when there is a contract, and how there can be merely unsuccessful negotiations without a resulting contract.

A. REQUIREMENTS OF AN OFFER

An **offer** expresses the willingness of the offeror to enter into a contractual agreement regarding a particular subject. It is a promise that is conditional upon an act, a forbearance (a refraining from doing something one has a legal right to do), or a return promise.

1. Contractual Intention

To make an offer, the offeror must appear to intend to create a binding obligation. Whether this intent exists is determined by objective standards.[1] This intent may be shown by conduct. ◆ For example, when one party signs a written contract and sends it to the other party, such action is an offer to enter into a contract on the terms of the writing. ◆

There is no contract when a social invitation is made or when an offer is made in jest or excitement. A reasonable person would not regard such an offer as indicating a willingness to enter into a binding agreement.

(a) Invitation to Negotiate. The first statement made by one of two persons is not necessarily an offer. In many instances, there may be a preliminary discussion or an invitation by one party to the other to negotiate or to make an offer. Thus, an inquiry by a school as to whether a teacher wished to continue the following year was merely a survey or invitation to negotiate and was not an offer that could be accepted. Therefore, the teacher's affirmative response did not create a contract.

Ordinarily, a seller sending out circulars or catalogs listing prices is not regarded as making an offer to sell at those prices. The seller is merely indicating a willingness to consider an offer made by a buyer on those terms. The reason for this rule is, in part, the practical consideration that because a seller does not have an unlimited supply of any commodity, the seller cannot possibly intend to make a contract with everyone who sees the circular. The same principle is applied to merchandise that is displayed with price tags in stores or store windows and to most advertisements. An advertisement in a newspaper is ordinarily considered an invitation to negotiate and is not an offer that can be accepted by a reader of the paper.[2] However, some court decisions have construed advertisements as offers that called for an act on the part of the customer thereby forming a unilateral contract, such as an advertisement of a reward for the return of lost property.

ETHICS AND THE LAW

PepsiCo ran an ad and promotional campaign in 1996 called the "Drink Pepsi Get Stuff" campaign. The enormously successful campaign allowed customers to claim prizes in exchange for points on PepsiCo beverage containers, and the points could be combined with cash payments to obtain the prizes. The campaign was so successful that the second round of ads and promotions was not run because the prizes were nearly exhausted.

In one television ad, PepsiCo pictured a Harrier jet as a satirical spoof on the prizes available under the campaign. The jet was offered in the ad for 7 million beverage points. Harrier jets are made only for the Marine Corps and are not sold in the open market. They cost $33.8 million each and can be produced at a rate of only one dozen at a time.

John Leonard, a 21-year-old business student, called PepsiCo and was told he would need to drink 16.8 million cans of Pepsi in order to obtain the required points. He was also told that he had the option of buying PepsiCo points for 10¢ each. Leonard developed a pool of investors (Pepsi drinkers) and delivered 15 PepsiCo points and a check for $700,008.50 for the remaining 6,999,985 points plus shipping and handling.

---

[1] *Glass Service Co. v State Farm Mutual Automobile Ins. Co.,* 530 NW2d 867 (Minn App 1995).

[2] *Ford Motor Credit Co. v Russell,* 519 NW2d 460 (Minn App 1994).

PepsiCo refused to provide Leonard with a Harrier jet because it said the ad was not an offer but a joke. Leonard filed suit on August 6, 1996, but PepsiCo had already filed a preemptive suit on July 18, asking that Leonard's suit be dismissed and declared frivolous and that PepsiCo be reimbursed for its legal expenses.

Did PepsiCo make an offer? Did Leonard accept? What is the significance of Leonard's phone call and the verification of the PepsiCo points needed? Is there a contract? If you were a PepsiCo executive, what would you do? If there is a misunderstanding about the ad, is there an ethical obligation on the part of PepsiCo? Was Leonard taken advantage of, or is he taking advantage of PepsiCo? Leonard v. PepsiCo, Inc., 39 UCC Rep Serv 2d (CBC 1999).

Quotations of prices, even when sent on request, are likewise not offers unless there have been previous dealings between the parties or unless a trade custom exists that would give the recipient of the quotation reason to believe that an offer was being made. Whether a price quotation is to be treated as an offer or merely an invitation to negotiate is a question of the intent of the party giving the quotation. Although sellers are not bound by quotations and price tags, they will, as a matter of goodwill, ordinarily make every effort to deliver the merchandise at those prices.[3]

In some cases, the fact that important terms are missing indicates that the parties are merely negotiating and that a contract has not been made. When a letter or printed promotional matter of a party leaves many significant details to be worked out later, the letter or printed matter is merely an invitation to negotiate. It is not an offer that may be accepted and a contract thereby formed.[4]

(b) Agreement to Make a Contract at a Future Date. No contract arises when the parties merely agree that at a future date they will consider making a contract or will make a contract on terms to be agreed on at that time.[5] In such a case, neither party is under any obligation until the future contract is made. No binding contract to renew a contract when it expires is created by a provision in the original contract that, when it expires, the parties intend to "negotiate in good faith to renew this agreement for an additional year upon terms and conditions to be negotiated." When the parties have prepared a draft agreement but it is clear that such agreement is not regarded by them as final, the draft is merely a step in negotiations and is not a contract.

The fact that all material terms have not been agreed on is significant in concluding that there is no contract. Thus, an agreement to construct a house was not binding when the size and shape of the house were not specified.[6]

2. Definiteness

An offer, and the resulting contract, must be definite and certain. If an offer is indefinite or vague or if an essential provision is lacking,[7] no contract arises from an attempt to accept it. The reason is that courts cannot tell what the parties are to do. Thus, an offer to conduct a business for as long as it is profitable is too vague to be a valid offer. The acceptance of such an offer does not result in a contract that can be enforced. Statements by a bank that it was "with" the debtors and would "support" them in their proposed business venture were too vague to be regarded as a promise by the bank to make necessary loans to the debtors.

The fact that minor, ministerial and nonessential terms are left for future determination does not make an agreement too vague to be a contract.[8]

In the *McCarthy* case, the court was faced with the question of whether a legally enforceable contract had been made where the parties expressed their intent to execute a subsequent purchase and sale agreement.

---

[3] Statutes prohibiting false or misleading advertising may also require adherence to advertised prices.

[4] *Lynx Exploration and Production Co. v 4-Sight Operating Co.*, 891 SW2d 785 (Tex App 1995).

[5] *Ellis v Taylor*, 49 SE2d 487 (SC 1994).

[6] *Manley v Athan*, 915 SW2d 792 (Mo App 1996).

[7] *T.O. Stanley Boot Co. v Bank of El Paso*, 847 SW2d 218 (Tex 1993).

[8] *Hsu v Vet-A-Mix, Inc.* 479 NW2d 336 (Iowa App 1991).

FIGURE 12.1 *Offer and Acceptances*

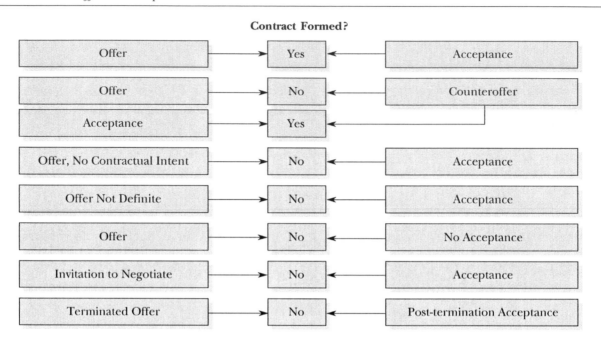

McCarthy v Tobin
706 NE2d 629 (Mass 1999)

Offer to Purchase is Controlling Legal Document

John McCarthy Jr. brought an action for specific performance against Ann Tobin claiming that the parties created a binding contract when they signed an offer to purchase (OTP) form on August 9, 1995. Robert Diminico and his wife intervened because they thereafter agreed to purchase the property in question from Ms. Tobin. The trial court granted summary judgment for Tobin and the Diminicos, which was vacated by the Appeals Court. The Supreme Judicial Court granted further appellate review.

ABRAMS, J. . . . The facts, which are undisputed, are as follows. On August 9, 1995, McCarthy executed an offer to purchase real estate on a pre-printed form generated by the Greater Boston Real Estate Board. The OTP contained, among other provisions, a description of the property, the price to be paid, deposit requirements, limited title requirements, and the time and place for closing. The OTP also included several provisions that are the basis of this dispute. The OTP required that the parties "shall, on or before 5 P.M. August 16, 1995, execute the applicable Standard Form Purchase and Sale Agreement recommended by the Greater Boston Real Estate Board . . . which, when executed, shall be the agreement between the parties hereto." . . . Finally, an unnumbered paragraph immediately above the signature line states: "NOTICE: This is a legal document that creates binding obligations. If not understood, consult an attorney." Tobin signed the OTP on August 11, 1995.

On August 16, 1995, sometime after 5 P.M., Tobin's lawyer sent a first draft of the pur-chase and sale agreement by facsimile transmission to McCarthy's lawyer. On August 21, McCarthy's lawyer sent a letter by facsimile transmission containing his comments and proposing several changes to Tobin's lawyer. The changes laid out the requirements for good title; imposed on Tobin the risk of casualty to the premises before sale; solicited indemnification, for title insurance purposes, regarding mechanics' liens, parties in possession, and hazardous materials; and sought an acknowledgment that the premises' systems were operational. The next day, the two lawyers discussed the proposed revisions. They did not discuss an extension of the deadline for signing the purchase and sale agreement, and Tobin's lawyer did not object to the fact that the deadline had already passed. On August 23, Tobin's lawyer sent a second draft of the agreement to McCarthy's lawyer. On August 25, a Friday, McCarthy's lawyer informed Tobin's lawyer that the agreement was acceptable, McCarthy would sign it, and it would be delivered the following Monday. On Saturday, August 26, McCarthy signed the purchase and sale agreement. On the same day, Tobin accepted the DiMinicos' offer to purchase the property.

On August 28, McCarthy delivered the executed agreement and a deposit to Tobin's broker. The next day, Tobin's lawyer told McCarthy's lawyer that the agreement was late and that Tobin had already accepted the DiMinicos' offer. In September, 1995, Tobin and the DiMinicos executed a purchase and sale agreement. Before the deal closed, McCarthy filed this action for specific performance and damages.

1. *Firm offer.* The primary issue is whether the OTP executed by McCarthy and Tobin was a binding contract. Tobin and the DiMinicos argue that it was not because of the provision requiring the execution of a purchase and sale agreement. McCarthy urges that he and Tobin intended to be bound by the OTP and that execution of the purchase and sale agreement was merely a formality.

McCarthy argues that the OTP adequately described the property to be sold and the price to be paid. The remaining terms covered by the purchase and sale agreement were subsidiary matters which did not preclude the formation of a binding contract. We agree.

The controlling fact is the intention of the parties. . . . Tobin argues that language contemplating the execution of a final written agreement gives rise to a strong inference that she and McCarthy have not agreed to all material aspects of a transaction and thus that they do not intend to be bound. . . .

Although the provisions of the purchase and sale agreement can be the subject of negotiation, "norms exist for their customary resolution." . . .

The interveners argue that McCarthy departed from the customary resolution of any open issues, and therefore manifested his intent not to be bound, by requesting several additions to the purchase and sale agreement. We agree with the Appeals Court, however, that McCarthy's revisions were "ministerial and nonessential terms of the bargain." . . .

The inference that the OTP was binding is bolstered by the notice printed on the form. McCarthy and Tobin were alerted to the fact that the OTP "create[d] binding obligations." The question is what those obligations were. The DiMinicos argue that the OTP merely obligated the parties to negotiate the purchase and sale agreement in good faith. We disagree. The OTP employs familiar contractual language. It states that McCarthy "hereby offer[s] to buy" the property, and Tobin's signature indicates that "[t]his Offer is hereby accepted." The OTP also details the amount to be paid and when, describes the property bought, and specifies for how long the offer was open. This was a firm offer, the acceptance of which bound Tobin to sell and McCarthy to buy the subject property. We conclude that the OTP reflects the parties' intention to be bound.

[The court found that Tobin had waived the August 16 deadline by words and conduct attributable to her, including her lawyer's failure to object to the passage of the deadline and his continued dealing with McCarthy's lawyer to craft an agreement.]

2. *Specific performance.* . . . McCarthy's right to specific performance is unaltered by Tobin's execution of a purchase and sale agreement with the DiMinicos. McCarthy filed this action prior to the execution of that agreement. The DiMinicos had actual notice of McCarthy's claim to the property and assumed the risk of a result favorable to McCarthy. . . .

The judgment is vacated. The case is remanded to the Superior Court for the entry of a judgment in favor of McCarthy's claim for specific performance.

[Judgment for McCarthy]

Questions

1. State Tobin's position before the court.
2. Were there definite and certain terms agreed to by the parties regarding the purchase to Tobin's property?
3. Evaluate Ms. Tobin's strategy, after signing the OTP, of hiring an attorney to handle the purchase and sale agreement and closing.

The law does not favor the destruction of contracts because that would go against the social force of carrying out the intent of the parties.[9] Consequently, when it is claimed that a contract is too indefinite to be enforced, a court will do its best to find the intent of the parties and thereby reach the conclusion that the contract is not too indefinite. ◆ For example, boxing promoter Don King had both a Promotional Agreement and a Bout Agreement with boxer Miguel Angel Gonzalez. The Bout Agreement for a boxing match held on March 7, 1998, with Julio Cesar Chavez gave King the option to promote the next four of Gonzalez's matches. The contract made clear that if Gonzalez won the Chavez match, he would receive at least $75,000 for the next fight, unless the parties agreed otherwise and if he lost, he would receive at least $25,000 for the subsequent fight, unless otherwise agreed. The agreement did not explicitly state the purse for the subsequent match in the event of a draw. The Chavez match ended in a draw, and Gonzalez contended that this omission rendered the contract so indefinite that it was unenforceable. The court disagreed, stating that striking down a contract as indefinite and in essence meaningless is at best a last resort. The court held that although the contract was poorly drafted the Promotional Agreement contained explicit price terms for which a minimum purse for fights following a draw may be inferred.[10] ◆ A court may not rewrite the agreement of the parties in order to make it definite.

(a) Definite by Incorporation. An offer and the resulting contract that by themselves may appear "too indefinite" may be made definite by reference to another writing ◆ For example, a lease agreement that was too vague by itself was made definite because the parties agreed that the lease should follow the standard form with which both were familiar. ◆ An agreement may also be made definite by reference to the prior dealings of the parties and to trade practices.

(b) Implied Terms. Although an offer must be definite and certain, not all of its terms need to be expressed. Some omitted terms may be implied by law. ◆ For example, an offer "to pay $400" for a certain Movado time piece does not state the terms of payment. A court, however, would not condemn this provision as too vague but would hold that it required that cash be paid and that the payment be made on delivery of the watch. ◆ Likewise, terms may be implied from conduct. As an illustration, where borrowed money was given to the borrower by a check on which the word *loan* was written, the act of the borrower in endorsing the check constituted an agreement to repay the amount of the check.

(c) Precision Not Required. The fact that a contract's term is not precise does not mean that it is not sufficiently definite. Thus, a provision that an employee would be discharged only for "good cause" is not too vague to be binding.[11]

[9] *Mears v Nationwide Mut. Ins. Co.* 91 F3d 1118 (8th Cir 1996)

[10] *Gonzalez v Don King Productions, Inc.*, 17 F Supp 2d 313 (SDNY 1998).

[11] *Scott v Pacific Gas & Electric Co.*, 46 Cal Rptr 2d 427 (Cal App 1995).

(d) Divisible Contracts. When the agreement consists of two or more parts and calls for corresponding performances of each part by the parties, the agreement is a **divisible contract.** Thus, in a promise to buy several separate articles at different prices at the same time, the agreement may be regarded as separate or divisible promises for the articles. When a contract contains a number of provisions or performances to be rendered, the question arises as to whether the parties intended merely a group of separate, divisible contracts or whether it was to be a package deal so that complete performance by each party was essential.

(e) Exceptions to Definiteness. The law has come to recognize certain situations in which the practical necessity of doing business makes it desirable to have a contract, yet the situation is such that it is either impossible or undesirable to adopt definite terms in advance. In these cases, the indefinite term is often tied to the concept of good-faith performance or to some independent factor that will be definitely ascertainable at some time in the future. For example, the indefinite term might be tied to market price, cost to complete, or production requirements. Thus, the law recognizes binding contracts in the case of a **requirements contract,** a contract to buy all requirements of the buyer from the seller. The law also recognizes as binding an **output contract,** the contract of a producer to sell the entire production or output to a given buyer. These are binding contracts even though they do not state the exact quantity of goods that are to be bought or sold.

3. Communication of Offer to Offeree

An offer must be communicated to the offeree. Otherwise, the offeree cannot accept even though knowledge of the offer has been indirectly acquired. Internal management communications of an enterprise that are not intended for outsiders or employees do not constitute offers and cannot be accepted by them. Sometimes, particularly in the case of unilateral contracts, the offeree performs the act called for by the offeror without knowing of the offer's existence. Such performance does not constitute an acceptance. Thus, without knowing that a reward is offered for information leading to the arrest of a particular criminal, a person may provide information that leads to the arrest of the criminal. In most states, if that person subsequently learns of the reward the reward cannot be recovered.[12]

Not only must the offer be communicated, but also it must be communicated by the offeror or at the offeror's direction.

B. TERMINATION OF OFFER

An offeree cannot accept a terminated offer. Offers may be terminated by revocation, counteroffer, rejection, lapse of time, death or disability of a party, or subsequent illegality.

4. Revocation of Offer by Offeror

Ordinarily, an offeror can revoke the offer before it is accepted. If this is done, the offeree cannot create a contract by accepting the revoked offer. Thus, the bidder at an auction sale may withdraw (revoke) a bid (offer) before it is accepted, and the auctioneer cannot accept that bid later.

An ordinary offer may be revoked at any time before it is accepted even though the offeror has expressly promised that the offer will be good for a stated period and that period has not yet expired. It may also be revoked even though the offeror has expressly promised to the offeree that the offer would not be revoked before a specified later date.

The fact that the offeror expressly promised to keep the offer open has no effect when no consideration was given for that promise.[13]

(a) What Constitutes a Revocation? No particular form or words are required to constitute a revocation. Any words indicating the offeror's termination of the offer are sufficient. A notice sent to the offeree that the property that is the subject of the offer has been sold to a third person is a revocation of the offer. A customer's order for goods, which is an offer to purchase at certain prices, is revoked by a notice to the seller of the

---

[12] With respect to the offeror, it should not make any difference, as a practical matter, whether the services were rendered with or without knowledge of the existence of the offer. Only a small number of states have adopted this view, however.

[13] *Prenger v Baumhoer,* 914 SW2d 413 (Mo App 1996).

cancellation of the order provided such notice is communicated before the order is accepted.

(b) Communication of Revocation. A revocation of an offer is ordinarily effective only when it is made known to the offeree. Until it is communicated to the offeree, directly or indirectly, the offeree has reason to believe that there is still an offer that may be accepted, and the offeree may rely on this belief. A letter revoking an offer made to a particular offeree is not effective until received by the offeree. It is not a revocation at the time it is written by the offeror or even when it is mailed or dispatched. A written revocation is effective, however, when it is delivered to the offeree's agent or to the offeree's residence or place of business under such circumstances that the offeree may be reasonably expected to be aware of its receipt.

It is ordinarily held that there is a sufficient communication of the revocation when the offeree learns indirectly of the offeror's revocation. This is particularly true in a land sale when the seller-offeror, after making an offer to sell the land to the offeree, sells the land to a third person and the offeree indirectly learns of such sale. The offeree necessarily realizes that the seller cannot perform the original offer and therefore must be considered to have revoked it.

If the offeree accepts an offer before it is effectively revoked, a valid contract is created.

(c) Option Contracts. An **option contract** is a binding promise to keep an offer open for a stated period of time or until a specified date. An option contract requires that the promisor receive consideration—that is, something, such as a sum of money, as the price for the promise to keep the offer open. In other words, the option is a contract to refrain from revoking an offer.

(d) Firm Offers. As another exception to the rule that an offer can be revoked at any time before acceptance, statutes in some states provide that an offeror cannot revoke an offer prior to its expiration when the offeror makes a firm offer. A **firm offer** is an offer that states that it is to be irrevocable, or irrevocable for a stated period of time. Under the Uniform Commercial Code, this doctrine of firm offers applies to a merchant's signed, written offer to buy or sell goods but

with a maximum of three months on its period of irrevocability.[14]

5. Counteroffer by Offeree

The offeree rejects the offer when he ignores the original offer and replies with a different offer.[15] If the offeree purports to accept an offer but in so doing makes any change to the terms of the offer, such action is a **counteroffer** that rejects the original offer. An "acceptance" that changes the terms of the offer or adds new terms is a rejection of the original offer and constitutes a counteroffer.[16]

Ordinarily, if *A* makes an offer, such as to sell a used automobile to *B* for $1,000, and *B* in reply makes an offer to buy at $750, the original offer is terminated. *B* is in effect indicating refusal of the original offer and in its place making a different offer. Such an offer by the offeree is known as a **counteroffer.** No contract arises unless the original offeror accepts the counteroffer.

Counteroffers are not limited to offers that directly contradict the original offers. Any departure from or addition to the original offer is a counteroffer even though the original offer was silent on the point added by the counteroffer.

6. Rejection of Offer by Offeree

If the offeree rejects the offer and communicates this rejection to the offeror, the offer is terminated. Communication of a rejection terminates an offer even though the period for which the offeror agreed to keep the offer open has not yet expired. It may be that the offeror is willing to renew the offer, but, unless this is done, there is no longer any offer for the offeree to accept.

7. Lapse of Time

When the offer states that it is open until a particular date, the offer terminates on that date if it has not yet been accepted. This is particularly so where the offeror declares that the offer shall be void after the expiration of the specified time. Such limitations are strictly construed.

---

[14] UCC § 2-205.

[15] *Bourque v FDIC,* 42 F3d 704 (1st Cir 1994)

[16] *L.B. v State Committee of Psychologists,* 912 SW2d 611 (Mo App 1995).

If the offer contains a time limitation for acceptance, an attempted acceptance after the expiration of that time has no effect and does not give rise to a contract.[17] When a specified time limitation is imposed on an option, the option cannot be exercised after the expiration of that time, regardless of whether the option was exercised within what would have been held a reasonable time if no time period had been specified.

If the offer does not specify a time, it will terminate after the lapse of a reasonable time. What constitutes a reasonable time depends on the circumstances of each case—that is, on the nature of the subject matter, the nature of the market in which it is sold, the time of year, and other factors of supply and demand. If a commodity is perishable or fluctuates greatly in value, the reasonable time will be much shorter than if the subject matter is of a stable value. An offer to sell a harvested crop of tomatoes would expire within a very short time. When a seller purports to accept an offer after it has lapsed by the expiration of time, the seller's acceptance is merely a counteroffer and does not create a contract unless that counteroffer is accepted by the buyer.

8. Death or Disability of Either Party

If either the offeror or the offeree dies or becomes insane before the offer is accepted, the offer is automatically terminated. ◆ **For example,** Johann offers to sell his ranch to Interport, Inc. Five days later, Johann dies in a plane crash. Interport writes to his son, Mateo, that his father's offer is accepted. This cannot be done, as the offer made by Johann died with him. ◆

9. Subsequent Illegality

If the performance of the contract becomes illegal after the offer is made, the offer is terminated. ◆ **For example,** if an offer is made to sell six semi-automatic handguns to a commercial firing range for $550 per weapon, but a new law prohibiting such sales is enacted before the offer is accepted, the offer is terminated. ◆

C. ACCEPTANCE OF OFFER

An **acceptance** is the assent of the offeree to the terms of the offer. Whether there has been an agreement of the parties is determined by objective standards.

10. What Constitutes an Acceptance?

No particular form of words or mode of expression is required, but there must be a clear expression that the offeree agrees to be bound by the terms of the offer.

If the offeree reserves the right to reject the offer, such action is not an acceptance.[18]

11. Privilege of Offeree

Ordinarily, the offeree may refuse to accept an offer. If there is no acceptance, by definition there is no contract. The fact that there had been a series of contracts between the parties and that one party's offer had always been accepted before by the other does not create any legal obligation to continue to accept subsequent offers.

12. Effect of Acceptance

When an offer has been accepted, a binding agreement or contract is created,[19] assuming that all of the other elements of a contract are present. Neither party can subsequently withdraw from or cancel the contract without the consent of the other party.

13. Nature of Acceptance

An acceptance is the offeree's manifestation of intent to enter into a binding agreement on the terms stated in the offer. Whether there is an acceptance depends on whether the offeree has manifested an intent to accept. It is the objective or outward appearance that is controlling rather than the subjective or unexpressed intent of the offeree.[20]

In the absence of a contrary requirement in the offer, an acceptance may be indicated by an

---

[17] *Century 21 Pinetree Properties, Inc. v Cason,* 469 SE2d 458 (Ga App 1996).

[18] *Pantano v McGowan,* 530 NW2d 912 (*Neb* 1995).

[19] *Ochoa v Ford,* 641 NE2d 1042 (Ind App 1994).

[20] *Cowan v Mervin Mewes, Inc.,* 546 NW2d 104 (SD 1996).

informal "okay," by a mere affirmative nod of the head, or, in the case of an offer of a unilateral contract, by performance of the act called for.

The acceptance must be absolute and unconditional. It must accept just what is offered. If the offeree changes any terms of the offer or adds any new term, there is no acceptance because the offeree does not agree to what was offered.

Where the offeree does not accept the offer exactly as made, the addition of any qualification converts the "acceptance" into a counteroffer, and no contract arises unless such a counteroffer is accepted by the original offeror.[21]

14. Who May Accept?

An offer may be accepted only by the person to whom it is directed. If anyone else attempts to accept it, no agreement or contract with that person arises.

If the offer is directed to a particular class rather than a specified individual, it may be accepted by anyone within that class. If the offer is made to the public at large, it may be accepted by any member of the public at large having knowledge of the existence of the offer.

When a person to whom an offer was not made attempts to accept it, the attempted acceptance has the effect of an offer. If the original offeror is willing to accept this offer, a binding contract arises. If the original offeror does not accept the new offer, there is no contract.

E-COMMERCE AND CYBERLAW

Contract Formation on the Internet

It is not possible for an on-line service provider or seller to individually bargain with each person who visits its website. The website owner, therefore, as offeror places its proposed terms on its website and requires visitors to assent to these terms in order to access the site, or download software, or purchase a product or service.

In a written contract the parties sign a paper document indicating their intention to be bound by the terms of the contract. On-line however, an agreement may be accomplished by the visitor-offeree simply typing the words "I Accept" in an on-screen box and then clicking a "send" or similar key which indicates acceptance. Or, the individual clicks an "I Agree" or "I Accept" icon. Access to the site is commonly denied those who do not agree to the terms. The agreements have come to be called *clickon* or *clickwrap* agreements. The agreements contain fee schedules and other financial terms, and may contain terms such as a notice of the proprietary nature of the material contained on the site, limitations on the use of the site, and the downloading of software. Moreover, the clickon agreements can contain limitations on liability, including losses associated with the use of downloaded software or products or services purchased from the site.

The use of clickon or clickwrap agreements have become standard practice for the sale of certain products and services on-line and the distribution of software. And, although case law is scarce, where the agreements are not contrary to the basic principles of contract law, the contracts are legally enforceable.*

In *Caspi v Microsoft Network***the Superior Court of New Jersey Appellate Division upheld the enforcement of certain terms of Microsoft Network's (MSN) clickon membership agreement and dismissed a suit brought by subscribers on the basis of a forum selection clause

* As will be seen in Chapter 24, Article Two of the Uniform Commercial Code deals with the sale of goods. It was adopted by most states in the 1960s, well before the contemplation and existence of the Internet and electronic contracting issues. The Uniform Computer Information Transactions Act (UCITA), a new uniform law promulgated in July of 1999 by the National Conference of Commissioners on Uniform State Laws if adopted by individual states will govern all contracts involving the sale, licensing, maintenance and support of computer software. As of April 12, 2000, the UCITA has been adopted by one state, Virginia, effective July 1, 2001. (See **www. Ucitaonline.com/whathap.html** for and update on adoption of this act.) The UCITA is clear that clickon agreements that allow a user to convey consent through an on screen click are legally enforceable so long as there was an opportunity to review the terms before assenting. See UCITA§112, Reporter Notes No. 5, Illustration 1. The UCITA is not applicable to an electronically conducted transaction for the sale of goods that contain no embedded software.

** 732 A.2d 528 (N.J. Super 1999).

---

[21] *Logan Ranch, Karg Partnership v Farm Credit Bank of Omaha,* 472 NW2d 704 (Neb 1991).

contained in the membership agreement. The plaintiff-subscribers had argued in part that the forum selection clause did not apply to them because they did not receive adequate notice of the clause. The agreement formation process was explained by the trial court as follows:

Before becoming an MSN member, a prospective subscriber is prompted by MSN software to view multiple computer screens of information, including a membership agreement which contains the above clause. MSN's membership agreement appears on the computer screen in a scrollable window next to blocks providing the choices "I Agree" and "I Don't Agree." Prospective members assent to the terms of the agreement by clicking on "I Agree" using a computer mouse.

The court stated that the plaintiffs were free to scroll through the various computer screens that presented the terms of their contracts before clicking their agreement. The court found that in any sense that matters, there is no significant distinction between the electronic form of this contract and a contract in printed form. Accordingly, the plaintiffs were forced to comply with the forum selection clause and bring their lawsuit challenging MSN's billing practices in the state of Washington rather than New Jersey.

15. Manner of Acceptance

The offeror may specify the manner for accepting the offer. When the offeror specifies that there must be a written acceptance, no contract arises when the offeree makes an oral acceptance. If the offeror calls for acceptance by a specified date, a late acceptance has no effect. When an acceptance is required by return mail, it is usually held that the letter of acceptance must be mailed the same day that the offer was received by the offeree. If the offer specifies that the acceptance be made by the performance of an act by the offeree, the latter cannot accept by making a promise to do the act but must actually perform it.

When the offer calls for the performance of an act or of certain conduct, the performance thereof is an acceptance of the offer and creates a unilateral contract.

When a person accepts services offered by another and it reasonably appears that compensation was expected, the acceptance of the services without any protest constitutes an acceptance of the offer. As a result, a contract exists for payment for the services.

When the offeror has specified a particular manner of acceptance, the offeree cannot accept in any other way.[22] However, acceptance in some other way is effective (1) if the manner of acceptance specified was merely a suggested alternative and was not clearly the exclusive method of acceptance, or (2) if the offeror has proceeded on the basis that there had been an effective acceptance.

(a) Silence as Acceptance. In most cases, the offeree's silence and failure to act cannot be regarded as an acceptance. Ordinarily, the offeror is not permitted to frame an offer in such a way as to make the silence and inaction of the offeree operate as an acceptance. Nor can a party to an existing contract effect a modification of that agreement without actual acceptance or approval from the other party. ◆ For example, H. H. Taylor made a contract with Andy Stricker, a civil engineer, to design a small hotel. The parties agreed on an hourly rate with "total price not to exceed $7,200," and required that additional charges would be presented to Taylor prior to proceeding with any changes. Andy was required to dedicate more hours to the project than anticipated, but could not present the additional charges to Taylor, because Taylor would not return his phone calls. He billed Taylor $9,035 for his services. Taylor's failure to act in not returning phone calls is not a substitute for the assent needed to modify a contract. Stricker is thus only entitled to $7,200.[23] ◆

(b) Unordered Goods and Tickets. Sometimes a seller writes to a person with whom the seller has not had any prior dealings, stating that, unless notified to the contrary, the seller will send specified merchandise and the recipient is obligated to pay for it at stated prices. There is no acceptance if the recipient of the letter ignores the offer and does nothing. The silence of the person receiving the letter is not an acceptance, and the sender, as a reasonable person, should recognize that none was intended.

This rule applies to all kinds of goods, books, magazines, and tickets sent through the mail when

---

[22] *Hreha v Nemecek,* 849 P2d 1131 (Or App 1993).

[23] *Stricker v Taylor,* 975 Pad 930 (Or App 1999).

they have not been ordered. The fact that the items are not returned does not mean that they have been accepted; that is, the offeree is required neither to pay for nor to return the items. If desired, the recipient of the unordered goods may write "Return to Sender" on the unopened package and put the package back into the mail without any additional postage. The Postal Reorganization Act provides that the person who receives unordered mailed merchandise from a commercial sender has the right "to retain, use, discard, or dispose of it in any manner the recipient sees fit without any obligation whatsoever to the sender."[24] It provides further that any unordered merchandise that is mailed must have attached to it a clear and conspicuous statement of the recipient's right to treat the goods in this manner.

16. Communication of Acceptance: Unilateral Contracts

If the offeror makes an offer of a unilateral contract, communication of acceptance is ordinarily not necessary. In such a case, the offeror calls for a completed or accomplished act. If that act is performed by the offeree with knowledge of the offer, the offer is accepted without any further action by way of notifying the offeror. As a practical matter, there will eventually be some notice to the offeror because the offeree who has performed the act will ask the offeror to pay for the performance that has been rendered.

When the offer of a unilateral contract calls for a performance that requires some time to complete, there is authority that there is an acceptance when the offeree commences the performance.[25]

17. Communication of Acceptance: Bilateral Contracts

Acceptance by the offeree is the last step in the formation of a bilateral contract. Intuitively, the receipt of the acceptance by the offeror should be the point in time when the contract is formed and its terms apply. Where the parties are involved in face-to-face negotiations, a contract is formed upon receipt of the acceptance by the offeror.

When the offeror hears the offeree's words of acceptance, the parties may at that point in time shake hands, signifying their understanding that the contract has been formed.

(a) The Mailbox Rule. When the parties are negotiating at a distance from each other, special rules have developed as to when the acceptance takes effect based on the commercial expediency of creating a contract at the earliest period of time and the protection of the offeree. Under the so-called *mailbox rule,* a properly addressed, postage paid mailed acceptance takes effect when the acceptance is placed into the control of the U.S. Postal Service[26] or, by judicial extension, placed in the control of a private third-party carrier such as Federal Express or United Parcel Service. That is, the acceptance is effective upon dispatch even before it is received by the offeror. The offeror may avoid the application of this rule by stating in the offer that acceptance shall take effect upon receipt by the offeror.

(b) Determining the Applicable Means of Communication. The modern rule on the selection of the appropriate medium of communication of acceptance is that unless otherwise unambiguously indicated in the offer, it shall be construed as inviting acceptance in any manner and by any medium reasonable under the circumstances.[27] A medium of communication is normally reasonable if it is one used by the offeror or if it is customary in similar transactions at the time and place the offer is received. Thus, if the offeror uses the mails to extend an offer, the offeree may accept by using the mails. Indeed, acceptance by mail is ordinarily reasonable when the parties are negotiating at a distance even if the offer is not made by mail.

The *Cantu* case raises the question whether a hand-delivered offer can be accepted by mail. In negotiations with respect to property with rapidly fluctuating value, such as corporate securities, an acceptance by mail may be too slow. It may be the custom of the parties to the negotiations to accept by telephone, E-mail, or fax.

[24] Federal Postal Reorganization Act § 3009.

[25] *Strata Production Co. v Mercury Exploration Co.,* 916 P2d 822 (NM 1996).

[26] See *Adams v Lindsell,* 106 Eng Rep 250 (KB 1818). Common law jurisdictions have unanimously adopted the mailbox rule as has the Restatement (Second) of Contracts § 63, and the UCC (see UCC § 1-201 (26),(38).

[27] Rest 2d §30; UCC§ 2-206 (1)(a).

Cantu v Central Education Agency
884 SW2d 563 (Tex App 1994)

Acceptance By Mail Must Be Reasonable

Cantu had a teaching contract with the San Benito Consolidated Independent School District. She hand-delivered to her supervisor a written offer to resign. Three days later, the superintendent of schools mailed her a letter accepting the offer of resignation. Cantu then changed her mind and the next day hand-delivered a letter withdrawing her resignation. The superintendent refused to recognize the attempted rescission of the resignation. Cantu appealed to the state district court. It decided against her, and she again appealed.

SMITH, J. . . . On Saturday, August 18, 1990, shortly before the start of the school year, Cantu hand-delivered to her supervisor a letter of resignation, effective August 17, 1990. In this letter, Cantu requested that her final paycheck be forwarded to an address in McAllen, Texas, some fifty miles from the San Benito office where she tendered the resignation. The San Benito superintendent of schools, the only official authorized to accept resignations on behalf of the school district, received Cantu's resignation on Monday, August 20. The superintendent wrote a letter accepting Cantu's resignation the same day and deposited the letter, properly stamped and addressed, in the mail at approximately 5:15 P.M. that afternoon. At about 8:00 A.M. the next morning, August 21, Cantu hand-delivered to the superintendent's office a letter withdrawing her resignation. . . .

The aphorism "the offeror is the master of his offer" reflects the power of the offeror to impose conditions on acceptance of an offer, specify the manner of acceptance, or withdraw the offer before the offeree has effectively exercised the power of acceptance. However, more often than not, an offeror does not expressly authorize a particular mode, medium, or manner of acceptance. Consequently, particularly with parties communicating at a distance, a rule of law is needed to establish the point of contract formation and allocate the risk of loss and inconvenience that inevitably falls to one of the parties between the time that the offeree

exercises, and the offeror receives, the acceptance. See 1 Arthur L. Corbin, *Contracts* § 78 (1963).

As Professor Corbin notes, courts could adopt a rule that no acceptance is effective until received, absent express authorization by the offeror; however, the mailbox rule, which makes acceptance effective on dispatch, closes the deal and enables performance more promptly, and places the risk of inconvenience on the party who originally has power to control the manner of acceptance. . . . "Even though the offer was not made by mail and there was no [express] authorization, the existing circumstances may be such as to make it reasonable for the offeree to accept by mail and to give the offeror reason to know that the acceptance will be so made." . . . In short, acceptance by mail is impliedly authorized if reasonable under the circumstances. . . .

We hold that it is proper to consider whether acceptance by mail is reasonably implied under the circumstances, whether or not the offer was delivered by mail.

. . . It was reasonable for the superintendent to accept Cantu's offer of resignation by mail. Cantu tendered her resignation shortly before the start of the school year—at a time when both parties could not fail to appreciate the need for immediate action by the district to locate a replacement. In fact, she delivered the letter on a Saturday, when the Superintendent could neither receive nor respond to her offer, further delaying matters by two days. Finally, Cantu's request that her final paycheck be forwarded to an address some fifty miles away indicated that she could no longer be reached in San Benito and that she did not intend to return to the school premises or school-district offices. The Commissioner of Education and district court properly considered that it was reasonable for the school district to accept Cantu's offer by mail. . . .

[Judgment affirmed]

Questions

1. At what point in time did the agreement to rescind Cantu's employment contract take effect?
2. Why did the court refer to the fact that Cantu's forwarding address was 50 miles away from the place where she delivered her offer to resign?
3. The *Cantu* case holds that a hand-delivered offer may always be accepted by a mailed acceptance. Appraise this statement.

(c) Telephone and Electronic Communication of Acceptance. Although telephonic communication is very similar to face-to-face communication, most U.S. courts have nevertheless applied the mailbox rule, holding that telephoned acceptances are effective where and when dispatched.

The courts have yet to address the applicability of the mailbox rule to E-mail. However, where the offeree's server is under the control of an independent entity such as an on-line service provider and the offeree cannot withdraw the message, it is anticipated that the courts will apply the mailbox rule and acceptance will take effect on proper dispatch. In the case of companies that operate their own servers, the acceptance will take effect when the message is passed onto the Internet.

Facsimile transmissions are substantially instantaneous and could be treated as face-to-face communications. However, it is anticipated that U.S. courts, when called upon to deal with this issue, will apply the mailbox acceptance-upon-dispatch rule as it does with telephoned acceptances.

(d) Effects of the Mailbox Rule. If an offer requires that acceptance be communicated by a specific date and the acceptance is properly dispatched by the offeree on the final date, the acceptance is timely and the contract is formed, even though the acceptance is actually received by the offeror well after the specified date has passed.

A situation may occur when a revocation and acceptance cross in the mail. As set forth previously, a revocation is effective only on receipt by the offeree. If an offeree dispatches an acceptance after the offeror has dispatched a revocation but before the revocation arrives, a contract is formed.

18. Auction Sales

At an auction sale, the statements made by the auctioneer to draw forth bids are merely invitations to negotiate. Each bid is an offer, which is not accepted until the auctioneer indicates that a particular offer or bid is accepted. Usually this is done by the fall of the auctioneer's hammer, indicating that the highest bid made has been accepted.[28] Since a bid is merely an offer, the bidder may withdraw the bid at any time before it is accepted by the auctioneer.

Ordinarily, the auctioneer may withdraw any article or all of the property from the sale if not satisfied with the amounts of the bids that are being made. Once a bid is accepted, however, the auctioneer cannot cancel the sale. In addition, if it had been announced that the sale was to be made "without reserve," the property must be sold to the person making the highest bid regardless of how low that bid may be.

In an auction "with reserve," bids are taken by the auctioneer as agent for the seller with the understanding that no contract is formed until the seller accepts the transaction.[29]

---

[28] *Dry Creek Cattle Co. v Harriet Bros. Limited Partnership*, 908 P2d 399 (Wyo 1995).

[29] *Marten v Staab*, 543 NW2d 436 (Neb 1996).

SUMMARY

Because a contract arises when an offer is accepted, it is necessary to find that there was an offer and that it was accepted. If either element is missing, there is no contract.

An offer does not exist unless the offeror has contractual intent. This intent is lacking if the statement of the person is merely an invitation to negotiate, a statement of intention, or an agreement to agree at a later date. Newspaper ads, price quotations, and catalog prices are ordinarily merely invitations to negotiate and cannot be accepted.

An offer must be definite. If an offer is indefinite, its acceptance will not create a contract because it will be held that the resulting agreement is too vague to enforce. In some cases, an offer that is by itself too indefinite is made definite because some writing or standard is incorporated by reference and made part of the offer. In some cases, the offer is made definite by implying terms that were not stated. In other cases, the indefinite part of the offer is ignored when that part can be divided or separated from the balance of the offer. In other cases, the requirement of definiteness is ignored either because the matter that is not definite is unimportant or because there is an exception to the rule requiring definiteness.

Assuming that there is in fact an offer that is made with contractual intent and that it is sufficiently definite, it still does not have the legal effect of an offer unless it is communicated to the offeree by or at the direction of the offeror.

In some cases, no contract arises because there is no offer that satisfies the requirements just stated. In other cases, there was an offer, but it was terminated before it was accepted. By definition, an attempted acceptance made after the offer has been terminated has no effect. The ordinary offer may be revoked at any time by the offeror. All that is required is the showing of intent to revoke and the communication of that intent to the offeree.

The offeror's power to revoke is barred by the existence of an option contract under common law or a firm offer under the Uniform Commercial Code or local non-Code statute and by the application of the doctrine of detrimental reliance by the offeree. An offer is also terminated by the express rejection of the offer or by the making of a counteroffer, by the lapse of the time stated in the offer or of a reasonable time when none is stated, by the death or disability of either party, or by a change of law that makes illegal a contract based on the particular offer.

When the offer is accepted, a contract arises. Only the offeree can accept an offer, and the acceptance must be of the offer exactly as made without any qualification or change. Ordinarily, the offeree may accept or reject as the offeree chooses. Limitations on this freedom of action have been imposed by antidiscrimination and consumer protection laws.

The acceptance is any manifestation of intent to agree to the terms of the offer. Ordinarily, silence or failure to act does not constitute acceptance. The recipient of unordered goods and tickets may dispose of the goods or use the goods without such action constituting an acceptance. An acceptance does not exist until the words or conduct demonstrating assent to the offer is communicated to the offeror. Acceptance by mail takes effect at the time and place when and where the letter is mailed or the fax is transmitted. A telephoned acceptance is effective when and where dispatched.

In an auction sale, the auctioneer asking for bids makes an invitation to negotiate. A person making a bid is making an offer, and the acceptance of the highest bid by the auctioneer is an acceptance of that offer and gives rise to a contract. When the auction sale is without reserve, the auctioneer must accept the highest bid. If the auction is not expressly without reserve, the auctioneer may refuse to accept any of the bids.

WEBSITE REFERENCES

For more discussion and case analyses on the law of offer and acceptance visit:

http://uniserve.edu.au/law/pub/edinst/ anu/contract/MCONTRACTFORMATION OFFER ANDACCEP.html

To explore option contracts from a multinational financial management perspective, watch an internet slide show at:

http://cyberprof.bradley.edu/Rubash/ FIN_323/LECT/323ch8/sld001.htm

For more discussion on the legality of good faith in contract law visit:

http://www.mayerbrown.com/legal/deitrick. htm

QUESTIONS AND CASE PROBLEMS

1. Bernie and Phil's Great American Surplus store placed an ad in the *Sunday Times* stating, "Next Saturday at 8:00 A.M. sharp 3 brand new mink coats worth $5,000 each will be sold for $500 each! First come, First served." Marsha Lufklin was first in line when the store opened and went directly to the coat department, but the coats identified in the ad were not available for sale. She identified herself to the manager and pointed out that she was first in line in conformity to the store's advertised offer and that she was ready to pay the $500 price set forth in the store's offer. The manager responded that a newspaper ad is just an invitation to negotiate and that the store decided to withdraw "the mink coat promotion." Review the text on unilateral contracts in Section 12(b) of the Chapter 11. Decide.

2. Brown made an offer to purchase Overman's house on a standard printed form. Underneath Brown's signature was the statement: "ACCEPTANCE ON REVERSE SIDE." Overman did not sign the offer on the back but sent Brown a letter accepting the offer. Later, Brown refused to perform the contract, and Overman sued him for breach of contract. Brown claimed there was no contract because the offer had not been accepted in the manner specified by the offer. Decide. [*Overman v Brown,* 372 NW2d 102 (Neb)]

3. Katherine mailed Paul an offer stating that it was good for 10 days. Two days later, she mailed Paul another letter stating that the original offer was revoked. That evening Paul phoned Katherine to say he accepted the offer. She said that he could not because she had mailed him a letter of revocation that he would undoubtedly receive in the next morning's mail. Was the offer revoked by Katherine?

4. Nelson wanted to sell his home. Baker sent him a written offer to purchase the home. Nelson made some changes to Baker's offer and wrote him that he, Nelson, was accepting the offer as amended. Baker notified Nelson that he was dropping out of the transaction. Nelson sued Baker for breach of contract. Decide. What social forces and ethical values are involved? [*Nelson v Baker,* 776 SW2d 52 (Mo App)]

5. Lessack Auctioneers advertised an auction sale that was open to the public and was to be conducted with reserve. Gordon attended the auction and bid $100 for a work of art that was worth much more. No higher bid, however, was made. Lessack refused to sell the item for $100 and withdrew the item from the sale. Gordon claimed that because he was the highest bidder, Lessack was required to sell the item to him. Was he correct?

6. Willis Music Co. advertised a television set at $22.50 in the Sunday newspaper. Ehrlich ordered a set, but the company refused to deliver it on the ground that the price in the newspaper ad was a mistake. Ehrlich sued the company. Was it liable? Why or why not? [*Ehrlich v Willis Music Co.,* 113 NE2d 252 (Ohio App)]

7. When a movement was organized to build Charles City College, Hauser and others signed pledges to contribute to the college. At the time of signing, Hauser inquired what would happen if he should die or be unable to pay. The representative of the college stated that the pledge would then not be binding and that it was merely a statement of intent. The college failed financially, and Pappas was appointed receiver to collect and liquidate the assets of the college corporation. He sued Hauser for the amount due on his pledge. Hauser raised the defense that the pledge was

not a binding contract. Decide. What ethical values are involved? [*Pappas v Hauser,* 197 NW2d 607 (Iowa)]

8. *A* signed a contract agreeing to sell land he owned but reserved the right to take the hay from the land until the following October. He gave the contract form to *B*, a broker. *C*, a prospective buyer, agreed to buy the land and signed the contract but crossed out the provision regarding the hay crop. Was there a binding contract between *A* and *C*?

9. A. H. Zehmer discussed selling a farm to Lucy. After a 40-minute discussion of the first draft of a contract, Zehmer and his wife, Ida, signed a second draft stating: "We hereby agree to sell to W. O. Lucy the Ferguson farm complete for $50,000 title satisfactory to buyer." Lucy agreed to purchase the farm on these terms. Thereafter, the Zehmers refused to transfer title to Lucy and claimed they had made the contract for sale as a joke. Lucy brought an action to compel performance of the contract. The Zehmers claimed there was no contract. Were they correct? [*Lucy v Zehmer,* 84 SE2d 516 (Va App)]

10. Wheeler operated an automobile service station, which he leased from W. C. Cornitius, Inc. The lease ran for three years. Although the lease did not contain any provision for renewal, it was in fact renewed six times for successive three-year terms. The landlord refused to renew the lease for a seventh time. Wheeler brought suit to compel the landlord to accept his offer to renew the lease. Decide. [*William C. Cornitius, Inc. v Wheeler,* 556 P2d 666 (Or)]

11. Buster Cogdill, a real estate developer, made an offer to the Bank of Bellevue to have the bank provide construction financing for the development of an outlet mall, with funds to be provided at prime rate plus two percentage points. The bank's president Julio Plunkett thanked Buster for the proposal and said, "I will start the paper work." Did Cogdill have a contract with the Bank of Bellevue?

[*Bank of Benton v Cogdill,* 454 NE 2d 1120 (Ill App)]

12. Jake Fries had an option to purchase at $223 an acre a 160-acre farm owned by Mary Fries. He transferred this option to his seven children and died from cancer a few months later. Six of the seven children then claimed six-sevenths of the land by virtue of the option, but one, Mary, refused to recognize a fractional exercise of the option. Could she do this? [*Fries v Fries,* 470 NW2d 232 (ND)]

13. An agreement was made between *C* Corporation and *S*, a shareholder of *C*, that *S* would sell his stock to *C*. The agreement did not specify any price but stated that the price should be determined by Lenox, a certified public accountant. The agreement also specified that the computations would be made on the basis of the value of corporate assets as shown by the corporate books. Lenox determined the value of the stock on that basis. *S* then refused to carry out the terms of the agreement. He claimed (1) there was no contract because the agreement failed for lack of definiteness by not stating the price to be paid, and (2) he was not bound by the price determined by Lenox because inflation and other factors made the corporate assets worth much more than appeared from the corporate books. *S* also claimed that the formula specified in the agreement was not in accord with good accounting practices. Was *S* required to sell his stock to *C* at the price determined by Lenox?

14. Sanchis owned a building. He agreed to rent it to Rosell for commercial purposes for three years at $50,000 a year. The agreement provided that at the end of that time Rosell had the option to extend the lease for another three years at a rent to be determined then. The first three years expired, and the parties could not agree to the rent to be paid for the next three years. Rosell insisted that Sanchis was required to lease the building for another three years at the same rent as for the first three years. Was he correct?

CPA QUESTIONS

1. Able Sofa, Inc., sent Noll a letter offering to sell Noll a custom-made sofa for $5,000. Noll immediately sent a telegram to Able purporting to accept the offer. However, the telegraph company erroneously delivered the telegram to Abel Soda, Inc. Three days later, Able mailed a letter of revocation to Noll, which was received by Noll. Able refused to sell Noll the sofa. Noll sued Able for breach of contract. Able

    a. Would have been liable under the deposited acceptance rule only if Noll had accepted by mail
    b. Will avoid liability since it revoked its offer prior to receiving Noll's acceptance
    c. Will be liable for breach of contract
    d. Will avoid liability due to the telegraph company's error

    (Law, #2, 9911)

2. On September 27, Summers sent Fox a letter offering to sell Fox a vacation home for $150,000. On October 2, Fox replied by mail agreeing to buy the home for $145,000. Summers did not reply to Fox. Do Fox and Summers have a binding contract?

    a. No, because Fox failed to sign and return Summers' letter.
    b. No, because Fox's letter was a counteroffer.
    c. Yes, because Summers' offer was validly accepted.
    d. Yes, because Summers' silence is an implied acceptance of Fox's letter.

    (Law, #2, 0462)

3. On June 15, Peters orally offered to sell a used lawn mower to Mason for $125. Peters specified that Mason had until June 20 to accept the offer. On June 16, Peters received an offer to purchase the lawn mower for $150 from Bronson, Mason's neighbor. Peters accepted Bronson's offer. On June 17, Mason saw Bronson using the lawn mower and was told the mower had been sold to Bronson. Mason immediately wrote to Peters to accept the June 15 offer. Which of the following statements is correct?

    a. Mason's acceptance would be effective when received by Peters.
    b. Mason's acceptance would be effective when mailed.
    c. Peters' offer had been revoked and Mason's acceptance was ineffective.
    d. Peters was obligated to keep the June 15 offer open until June 20.

    (Law, #13, 3095)

Capacity and Genuine Assent

Learning Objectives

After studying this chapter, you should be able to

1. Define contractual capacity
2. State the extent and effect of avoidance of a contract by a minor
3. Classify unilateral and bilateral mistakes
4. Distinguish between innocent misrepresentation, fraud, and nondisclosure
5. List those classes of persons who lack contractual capacity
6. Distinguish between undue influence and duress

A contract is a binding agreement. This agreement must be made between parties who have the capacity to do so. They must also truly agree so that all parties have really consented to the contract. This chapter explores the elements of contractual capacity of the parties and the genuineness of their assent.

A. CONTRACTUAL CAPACITY

Some persons lack contractual capacity, a lack that embraces both those who have a status incapacity, such as minors, and those who have a factual incapacity, such as insane persons.

1. Contractual Capacity Defined

Contractual capacity is the ability to understand that a contract is being made and to understand its general meaning. However, the fact that a person does not understand the full legal meaning of a contract does not mean that contractual capacity is lacking. Everyone is presumed to have capacity unless it is proven that capacity is lacking, or unless there is status incapacity.[1] ◆ For example, Jacqueline, aged 22, entered into a contract with Sunrise Storage Co. but later claimed it was not binding because she did not understand several clauses in the printed contract. The contract was binding. No evidence supported her claim that she lacked capacity to contract or to understand its subject. Contractual capacity can exist even though a party does not understand every provision of the contract. ◆

(a) Status Incapacity. Over the centuries, the law has declared that some classes of persons lack contractual capacity. The purpose is to protect these classes by giving them the power to get out of unwise contracts. Of these classes, the most important today is the class identified as minors.

Until recent times, some other classes were held to lack contractual capacity in order to discriminate against them. Examples are married women and aliens. Still other classes, such as persons convicted of and sentenced for a felony, were held to lack contractual capacity in order to punish them. Today, these discriminatory and puni-

tive incapacities have largely disappeared. Married women have the same contractual capacity as unmarried persons.[2]

By virtue of international treaties, the discrimination against aliens has been removed.

(b) Factual Incapacity. A factual incapacity contrasts with incapacity imposed because of the class or group to which a person belongs. A factual incapacity may exist when, because of mental or physical condition caused by medication, drugs, alcohol, illness, or age, a person does not understand that a contract is being made or understand its general nature. If the factual incapacity later disappears, the party affected can ordinarily avoid the contract. In some extreme cases, the contract made while the incapacity existed is void.

2. Minors

Minors may make contracts.[3] To protect them, however, the law has always treated minors as a class lacking contractual capacity.

(a) Who Is a Minor? At common law, any person, male or female, under 21 years of age was a minor. At common law, minority ended the day before the 21st birthday. The "day before the birthday" rule is still followed, but the age of majority has been reduced from 21 years to 18 years.

(b) Minor's Power to Avoid Contracts. With exceptions that will be noted later, a contract made by a minor is voidable at the election of the minor. The minor may affirm or ratify the contract on attaining majority by performing the contract, by expressly approving the contract, or by allowing a reasonable time to lapse without avoiding the contract.

(1) What Constitutes Avoidance? A minor may avoid or *disaffirm* a contract by any expression of an intention to repudiate the contract. Any act inconsistent with the continuing validity of the contract is also an avoidance.

---

[1] *Re* Adoption of Smith, 578 So 2d 988 (La App 1991).

[2] A few states have a limitation that a married woman cannot make a binding contract to pay the debt of her husband if he fails to.

[3] *Buffington v State Automobile Mutual Ins. Co.,* 384 SE2d 873 (Ga App 1989).

(2) Time for Avoidance. A minor can disaffirm a contract only during minority and for a reasonable time after attaining majority. After the lapse of a reasonable time, the contract is deemed ratified and cannot be avoided by the minor.

(3) Minor's Misrepresentation of Age. Generally, the fact that the minor has misrepresented his or her age does not affect the minor's power to disaffirm the contract. Some states hold that such fraud of a minor bars contract avoidance. Some states permit the minor to disaffirm the contract in such a case but require the minor to pay for any damage to the property received under the contract.

In any case, the other party to the contract may disaffirm it because of the minor's fraud.

(c) Restitution by Minor after Avoidance. When a minor disaffirms a contract, the question arises as to what must be returned by the minor to the other contracting party.

(1) Original Consideration Intact. When a minor still has what was received from the other party, the minor, on avoiding the contract, must return it to the other party or offer to do so. That is, the minor must put things back to the original position or, as it is called, restore the **status quo ante.**

(2) Original Consideration Damaged or Destroyed. What happens if the minor cannot return what has been received because it has been spent, used, damaged, or destroyed? The minor's right to disaffirm the contract is not affected. The minor can still disaffirm the contract and is required to return only what remains. The fact that nothing remains or that what remains is damaged does not bar the right to disaffirm the contract. In states that follow the common law rule, minors can thus refuse to pay for what has been received under a contract or can get back what had been paid or given even though they do not have anything to return or return property in a damaged condition. There is, however, a trend to limit this rule.

(d) Recovery of Property by Minor on Avoidance. When a minor disaffirms contract, the other contracting party must return the money received. Any property received from the minor must also be returned. If the property has been sold to a third person who did not know of the original seller's minority, the minor cannot get the property back. In such cases, however, the minor is entitled to recover the property's monetary value or the money received by the other contracting party.

(e) Contracts for Necessaries. A minor can disaffirm a contract for necessaries but must pay the reasonable value for furnished necessaries. This duty of the minor is a quasi-contractual liability. It is a duty that the law imposes on the minor rather than a duty created by contract.

(1) What Constitutes Necessaries? Originally, **necessaries** were limited to those things absolutely necessary for the sustenance and shelter of the minor. Thus limited, the term would extend only to food, clothing, and lodging. In the course of time, the rule was relaxed to extend generally to things relating to the health, education, and comfort of the minor. Thus, the rental of a house used by a married minor is a necessary. Services reasonably necessary to obtaining employment by a minor have been held to be necessaries.

(2) Contract with Parent or Guardian. When a third person supplies the parents or guardian of a minor with goods or services that the minor needs, the minor is not liable for these necessaries because the third person's contract is with the parent or guardian, not with the minor.

(f) Ratification of Former Minor's Voidable Contract. A former minor cannot disaffirm a contract that has been ratified after reaching majority.[4]

(1) What Constitutes Ratification? Ratification consists of any words or conduct of the former minor manifesting an intent to be bound by the terms of a contract made while a minor.

(2) Form of Ratification. Generally, no special form is required for ratification of a minor's voidable contract, although in some states a written ratification or declaration of intention is required.

(3) Time for Ratification. A person can disaffirm a contract any time during minority and for a rea-

---

[4] *Fletcher v Marshall,* 632 NE2d 1105 (Ill App 1994).

sonable time after that but, of necessity, can ratify a contract only after attaining majority. The minor must have attained majority, or the ratification would itself be regarded as voidable.

(g) Contracts That Minors Cannot Avoid. Statutes in many states deprive a minor of the right to avoid an educational loan;[5] a contract for medical care; a contract made while running a business; a contract approved by a court; a contract made in performance of a legal duty; or a contract relating to bank accounts, insurance policies, or corporate stock.

(h) Liability of Third Person for a Minor's Contract. The question arises whether parents are bound by the contract of their minor child. The question also arises whether a person cosigning a minor's contract is bound if the contract is avoided.

(1) Liability of Parent. Ordinarily, a parent is not liable on a contract made by a minor child. The parent may be liable, however, if the child is acting as the agent of the parent in making the contract. Also, the parent is liable to a seller for the reasonable value of necessaries supplied by the seller to the child if the parent had deserted the child.

(2) Liability of Cosigner. When the minor makes a contract, another person, such as a parent or a friend, may sign along with the minor to make the contract more acceptable to the third person.

With respect to the other contracting party, the cosigner is bound independently of the minor. Consequently, if the minor disaffirms the contract, the cosigner remains bound by it. When the debt to the creditor is actually paid, the obligation of the cosigner is discharged.

If the minor disaffirms a sales contract but does not return the goods, the cosigner remains liable for the purchase price.

---

[5] A Model Student Capacity to Borrow Act makes educational loans binding on minors in Arizona, Mississippi, New Mexico, North Dakota, Oklahoma, and Washington. This act was reclassified from a uniform act to a model act by the Commissioners on Uniform State Law, indicating that uniformity was viewed as unimportant and that the matter was primarily local in character.

3. Mentally Incompetent Persons

A person with a mental disorder may be so disabled as to lack capacity to make a contract. If the person is so mentally incompetent as to be unable to understand that a contract is being made or the general nature of the contract, the person lacks contractual capacity.

(a) Effect of Incompetency. An incompetent person may ordinarily avoid a contract in the same manner as a minor. Upon the removal of the disability (that is, upon becoming competent), the formerly incompetent person can either ratify or disaffirm the contract. A mentally incompetent person or his or her estate is liable for the reasonable value of all necessaries furnished that individual.

(b) Appointment of Guardian. If a court appoints a guardian for the incompetent person, a contract made by that person before the appointment may be ratified or, in some cases, disaffirmed by the guardian. If the incompetent person makes a contract after a guardian has been appointed, the contract is void and not merely voidable.

4. Intoxicated Persons

The capacity of a party to contract and the validity of the contract are not affected by the party's being impaired by alcohol at the time of making the contract so long as the party knew that a contract was being made.

If the degree of intoxication is such that a person does not know that a contract is being made, the contract is voidable by that person. The situation is the same as though the person were insane at the time and did not know what was being done. On becoming sober, the person may avoid or rescind the contract. However, an unreasonable delay in taking steps to set aside a known contract entered into while intoxicated may bar the intoxicated person from asserting this right.[6] ◆ For example, Edward made a contract while intoxicated. When he sobered up, he immediately disaffirmed the contract for lack of capacity as the result of his intoxication. The other contracting party claimed that voluntary intoxication cannot

---

[6] *Diedrich v Diedrich*, 424 NW2d 580 (Minn App 1988).

FIGURE 13.1 *Avoidance of Contract*

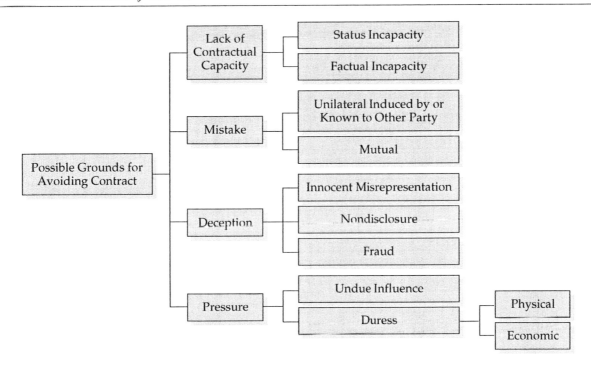

void a contract, but Edward could disaffirm the contract because he lacked the legal capacity to enter a contract. ◆

The courts treat impairment caused by the use of drugs the same as impairment caused by the excessive use of alcohol.

ETHICS AND THE LAW

Globe Life Insurance Co. has undertaken a new sales program that targets neighborhoods in Los Angeles where drive-by shootings are a nightly occurrence. Over the past two months, two such shootings occurred in which children were killed as they sat in their living rooms. Another child was paralyzed by a bullet from a drive-by shooting three months ago.

Globe salespeople are instructed to "hit" the houses surrounding those where children were victims. They are also told to contact the parents of those children to sell policies for their other children.

Tom Raskin, an experienced Globe salesman, read of a drive-by shooting last night at Nancy Leonard's home, in which Leonard's five-year-old son was killed. The *Los Angeles Times* reported that Leonard was a single parent with four other children.

Raskin traveled to Leonard's home and described the benefits of a Globe policy for her other children. He offered her the $10,000 term life policy for each of the children for a total cost of $21 per month. Leonard was in the process of making funeral arrangements for her son, and Raskin noted, "See how much it costs for a funeral."

Leonard had been given several tranquilizers the night before by a physician at the hospital's emergency room. The physician had also given her 15 more tranquilizers to help her through the following week. She had taken one additional tranquilizer an hour before Raskin arrived, using a Coors Lite beer to take the pill.

Leonard signed the contract for the policy. After her son's funeral, she received the first month's bill for it and exclaimed, "I didn't buy any life insurance! Where did this come from?"

After you discuss Leonard's legal standing, discuss the ethical issues involved in Globe's sales program. Discuss the legal issues involved in Raskin's decision to target Leonard the day after her son's death.

B. MISTAKE

The validity of a contract may be affected by the fact that one or both of the parties made a mistake. In some cases, the mistake may be caused by the misconduct of one of the parties.

5. Unilateral Mistake

A unilateral mistake—that is, a mistake by only one of the parties—as to a fact does not affect the contract when the mistake is unknown to the other contracting party.[7] When a contract is made on the basis of a quoted price, the validity of the contract is not affected by the fact that the party furnishing the quotation had made a mathematical mistake in computing the price if there was no reason for the other party to recognize that there was a mistake.[8] The party making the mistake may avoid the contract if the mistake is known, or should be known or recognized, by the other contracting party. ◆ For example, Office Supply Outlet, Inc., a single store office equipment and supply retailer, ordered 100 model RVX-414 computers from Compuserve, Inc. A clerical error had been made on the order form by a new staff member, and the quantity ordered was far in excess of what it could sell in a year. Office Supply realized their mistake when the delivery trucks arrived at its warehouse. Office Supply's manager called Compuserve and explained that it intended to order just 10 computers. Compuserve declined to accept the return of the machines. Because Office Supply's mistake was unilateral, the contract for the 100 machines is enforceable. If, however, a regular Compuserve salesperson called on Office Supply and knew of Office Supply's policy not to stock more than 10 model RVX-414 machines at any one period of time and the order for 100 machines was placed through this regular salesperson, Office Supply could avoid the contract for the additional 90 machines because Compuserve knew or should have known a mistake had been made. ◆

(a) Mistake as to Nature of Document. When a party makes a negligent mistake as to the nature of a document, the party is bound according to its terms. For example, when the printed form for a corporation's loan application contained a guarantee of the corporate debt by the president of the corporation, the president signing the application without reading it was bound by this guarantee. This is true even though the president did not know that it was in the application and the application was headed merely "Application for Credit."

(b) Mistake as to Terms of Document. A person who has the ability and the opportunity to read a document before signing is bound by its terms even though the person signed without reading it.[9] Such a signer cannot avoid liability on the ground there had not been any explanation given of the terms of the writing.

6. Mutual Mistake

When both parties enter into a contract under a mutually mistaken understanding concerning a basic assumption of fact or law on which the contract is made, the contract is voidable by the adversely affected party if the mistake has a material effect on the agreed exchange.[10] In the *Mattson* case both parties to the contract were mistaken in their belief that a lifetime agricultural leaseback was legal and a proper device to utilize in structuring their land contract, and the mistake had a material effect on the agreed exchange.

[7] *Oh v Wilson,* 210 P2d 276 (Nev 1996).
[8] *Procan Construction Co. v Oceanside Development Corp.,* 539 NYS2d 437 (App Div2d 1989).
[9] *Huber v Hovey,* 501 NW2d 53 (Iowa 1993).
[10] See *Browning v Howerton,* 966 P2d 367 (Wash App 1998).

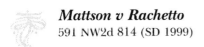

Mattson v Rachetto
591 NW2d 814 (SD 1999)

Ignorance of the Law Is an Excuse in This Case

Jon and Barbara Mattson brought an action against Jerry and Joan Rachetto for rescission of a land contract after the contract's agricultural leaseback provision was found to be illegal. From a judgment for the Mattsons, the Rachettos appealed.

GILBERTSON, J. . . . Jon and Barbara Mattson are husband and wife. Jerry and Joan Rachetto are husband and wife. Jerry Rachetto and Barbara Mattson are brother and sister. Additionally, Jon Mattson and Jerry Rachetto are both attorneys who shared a law office in Deadwood. . . .

In 1974 when Jerry Rachetto returned to Deadwood from law school, he went to work for Jon Mattson. He later expressed a desire to build a house on Tract A of the Mattson Ranch. The Mattsons deeded Tract A to Jerry and Joan Rachetto. Tract A consisted of 1.837 acres. No money was paid for this land. The Mattsons also gave the Rachettos an easement through their ranch property so the Rachettos could access their house from the highway. The easement passed through Tract C and the Ray Placer Sub-division.

In 1984, the Rachettos approached the Mattsons about buying Tract C so they could have a buffer zone between Rachettos' property and the Ray Placer Sub-division to ensure no future development adjacent to the Rachetto home. Tract C was composed of approximately eighteen (18) acres. The Mattsons were willing to sell Tract C but not without a specific lease-back provision that allowed them to cultivate hay and graze livestock on the tract for their lifetime. The Mattsons sold Tract C to the Rachettos for the consideration of $26,959.50 and the agricultural leaseback. The Mattsons also agreed to reimburse the Rachettos for the real property tax levied against the property for the term of the agricultural lease. The price charged was far less than the value of other lots on the ranch.

After several drafts of the agreement, the parties agreed to the terms for the sale. Neither party knew or realized the agricultural lease was void under SDCL 43–32–2.* In 1996, Jerry Rachetto came across the decision of *Commercial Trust & Sav. Bank v. Christensen,* 535 N.W.2d 853 (S.D. 1995), in which we interpreted part of SDCL 43–32–2. The Rachettos, without informing the Mattsons of this discovery, erected an electric fence around Tract C. The Mattsons did not discover the mistake until the Rachettos put up the electric fence. Jerry Rachetto, when confronted, brought the *Christensen* case to the Mattsons' attention.

When the Mattsons learned the agricultural lease was invalid as a matter of law, they attempted to negotiate some type of compromise. All offers were rejected by the Rachettos, as they wanted to use the land for their own purposes.** The Mattsons attempted to tender rescission offering the purchase price plus interest. The Rachettos refused.

The Mattsons then filed a complaint for rescission of the land contract. . . .

The Rachettos claim the trial court erred or abused its discretion in allowing summary judgment on the Mattsons' count for rescission of the 1984 land sale. They claim the Mattsons do not need the land for agricultural use but instead want it back because of its significant increase in value and their desire to sub-divide the land.

* SDCL 43–32–2 states:

   No lease or grant of agricultural land for a longer period than twenty years . . . shall be valid.

** Jerry Rachetto has built a golf course green and tee box on the property.

The Mattsons . . . claim rescission is permissible due to a mistake of law. The Mattsons contend both parties made a mutual mistake of law—the lifetime agricultural leaseback in the contract. . . .

Mistake of Law.

The Mattsons claim that both parties made a mistake of law as defined in SDCL 53–4–10. This provision states:

A mistake of law in relation to consent to contract constitutes a mistake resulting in voidable consent only when it arises from:

(1) A misapprehension of the law by all parties, all supposing that they knew and understood it and all making substantially the same mistake as to the law[.]

"The equitable relief of rescission, being extraordinary, should never be granted, except where the evidence is clear and convincing." In an equity case, we are required to read all the evidence produced and give consideration to the facts and circumstances in the record.

The Mattsons had worked very hard over the years to build up their family ranch. They only acquired title to Tract C after a long struggle with the federal government. Tract C was the best hay and watering ground they had for their livestock. They sold Tract C to their relatives, the Rachettos, only because the Rachettos were close relatives, expressed their concerns over the encroaching sub-division and because they assured the Mattsons via the agricultural leaseback provision they could continue to graze cattle. It is quite clear that the Mattsons would not have sold Tract C at this price if they were not assured the use of the land via the agricultural leaseback. Tract C was the Mattsons' best grazing and hay land which is exhibited by the fact that after they were denied access to Tract C, the Mattsons were forced to purchase hay to feed their cattle.

Although there clearly was a mistake of law neither side took advantage of the other. Both parties admitted they did not know the agricultural leaseback was illegal. Mattson and Rachetto were licensed attorneys working in the same office who negotiated the terms of the agreement in good faith which went through several drafts before becoming acceptable to all parties.

The mere fact the statute is a public record is not the controlling factor in this case. It is a statutorily recognized exception to the old axiom "ignorance of the law is no excuse." Freedom from negligence is not a requirement to invoke the mistake of law claim provided by SDLC 53–4–10. . . .

The trial court restored the parties to where they were before they made their contractual mistake. The trial court did not abuse its discretion in righting a wrong caused by a mutual mistake of law. As there is no genuine issue of material fact, we affirm. . . .

Following rescission of the contract the trial court ordered the Mattsons to repay Rachettos the purchase price of Tract C, $26,950.50 and pay an additional $24,212.69 in interest. . . .

[Judgment Affirmed]

Questions

1. Is the ignorance of the applicable law a defense to a lawsuit based on mutual mistake of law?
2. Explain how the mutual mistake concerning a basic assumption of law on which the contract was made had a material effect on the agreed exchange between Mattson and Rachetto.

A contract based on a *mutual mistake in judgment* is not voidable by the adversely affected party. ◆ For example, if both parties believe that a colt is not fast enough to develop into a competitive race horse and effect a sale accordingly, when the animal later develops into the winner of the Preakness as a three-year-old, the seller cannot rescind the contract based on mutual mistake, because the mutual mistake was a mistake in judgment. ◆ In contrast, where two parties to a contract believe a cow to be barren at the time they contract for its sale, but, before delivery of the animal to the buyer, it is discovered that the assumption was mistaken, such is a mutual mistake of fact making the contract void.[11]

7. Mistake in the Transcription or Printing of the Contract

In some instances, the parties make an oral agreement and, in the process of committing it to writing, or in the process of printing the agreement from a manuscript, a phrase, term or segment is inadvertently left out of the final, signed document. The aggrieved party may petition the court to *reform* the contract to reflect the actual agreement of the parties. However, the burden of proof required is that of clear and convincing evidence that such a mistake was made. ◆ For example, the Printers International Union reached agreement for a new three-year contract with a large regional printing company. As was their practice, the union negotiators then met with Sullivan Brothers Printers, Inc., a small specialty shop employing 10 union printers, and Sullivan Brothers and the union agreed to follow the contractual pattern set by the union and the large printer. That is, Sullivan Brothers agreed to give its workers all of the benefits negotiated for the employees of the large printing company. In typing up the contract, a new benefit of 75 percent employer-paid coverage for a dental plan was inadvertently not typed into the final contract that the parties signed. The mistake was not discovered until later, and Sullivan Brothers, Inc., is now reluctant to assume the additional expense. Based on the clear and convincing evidence of a practice of following the contractual pattern set by the large printer and Sullivan's assent to again follow the pattern, a court or arbitrator will reform the contract. ◆

C. DECEPTION

One of the parties may have been misled by a fraudulent statement or a failure to disclose information when there was a duty to do so. In such situations, there is no true or genuine assent to the contract, and it is therefore voidable at the innocent parties' option.

8. Intentional Misrepresentation

Fraud is a generic term embracing all multifarious means that human ingenuity can devise and that are resorted to by one individual to get advantage over another. It is classified in the law as a tort. However, where a party is induced into making a contract by a material misrepresentation of fact, this form of fraudulent activity adversely affects the genuineness of the assent of the innocent party, and it is this type of fraud that is the focus of our discussion in the chapters on contracts.

9. Fraud

Fraud is the making of a material misrepresentation (or false statement) of fact with (1) knowledge of its falsity or reckless indifference to its truth, (2) the intent that the listener rely on it, (3) the result that the listener does so rely, and (4) the consequence that the listener is harmed.[12]

The *Tschira* case deals with the tort of fraudulent misrepresentation and is a clear example of how fraud impacts on the genuineness of the contractual assent of the affected party. Note that the Tschiras did not seek to *rescind* (cancel) the two contracts they entered as a result of the fraudulent misrepresentations, which ordinarily is the first remedy sought in fraud cases, because they canceled the management agreement upon discovery of the fraud, and they later sold at a loss the property that was the subject of the second contract. The remedies they sought were the actual damages they suffered as a result of the fraud and punitive damages to punish and make an example of the perpetrators of the wrongdoings.

---

[11] See *Sherwood v Walker,* 66 Mich 568 (1887).

[12] *Maack v Resource Design & Construction, Inc.,* 875 P2d 570 (Utah 1994); *Bortz v Noon,* 729 A2d 555 (Pa 1999).

Tschira v Willingham
135 F3rd 1077 (6th Cir 1998)

Watch Out! Some People Have a Lot of Nerve

German citizens Klaus and Gerda Tschira brought suit against Corim, Inc., a U.S. real estate investment firm and its president Ben Willingham Jr. for fraudulent misrepresentation during a real estate transaction between the Tschiras and Corim. From a judgment for the Tschiras, Corim and Willingham appealed.

GIBSON, J. . . . In 1988, Klaus Tschira benefitted financially when the company he helped to create, SAP AG ("SAP"), went public in Germany. In search of investment opportunities, Klaus learned through a German real estate broker, Claus Schenk, that Appellants were soliciting investors for commercial property in the southeastern United States. Intrigued by this information, Klaus, who was joined by other SAP founders, attended a meeting in Walldorf, Germany at which Willingham, who speaks fluent German, made a presentation. According to trial testimony, Willingham explained that Corim proposed to obtain buildings for purchase by investors at a "fair market price"; Corim then intended to enter into management contracts with the new owners. By the terms of the management contracts, Corim and Willingham would lease the buildings from the investors and, in return, would then pay the investors a contractually established rent amounting to approximately eight percent annually of the purchase price of the building. Klaus testified that he inquired as to how Willingham and Corim would earn a profit, and Willingham responded that Corim would receive revenue via the difference between the rents Corim would charge for its subleases and the rent Corim itself paid the investors.

The Tschiras found the investment attractive and initially agreed to buy four buildings in various southern cities and lease those properties back to Corim. The Tschiras did not procure independent American counsel for these transactions, as they claim to have regarded Willingham as their trusted agent. . . .

In late 1990, Schenk brought Klaus a Corim brochure about One Church Street, a Nashville, Tennessee property. The brochure advertised One Church Street as a five story commercial building erected in 1872, available for $1,985,000. The pamphlet described the property as having "a special architectural character" and said the building had been "recently renovated with substantial effort and expense." J.A. at 358. Corim guaranteed rent payments of $158,000 the first two years of the lease back, $165,000 the third and fourth years, and $171,000 the fifth year. The Tschiras expressed interest, and soon thereafter they received the Letter from Willingham. The document guaranteed that the building would be "insured sufficiently, so that it can be restored from the proceeds of the insurance in the event of destruction or damage." J.A. at 182. The final paragraph of the letter states that "[t]he powers of attorney given to us will only be used according to the forthcoming agreement." *Id.* Willingham had signed the copy of the Letter he mailed to the Tschiras. After reviewing the available materials, the Tschiras decided to invest in the property. They did not, however, secure independent counsel for the deal, visit One Church Street prior to the purchase, or obtain an appraisal from any source other than Corim.

The Tschiras and Corim subsequently entered into a Purchase Agreement for the Nashville property. They simultaneously executed a Management Agreement for the building. . . .

Several years later, the Tschiras discovered other details surrounding the sale of the Nashville building. Namely, they learned that two closings occurred on December 14, 1990. In the first, One Church Street, Inc., shell corporation owned by Corim and Willingham, purchased the property from its owner, First Atlanta Services Corporation. The selling price in this deal was $774,000. In the second transaction, One Church Street, Inc. sold the building to the Tschiras for $1,985,000. Schenk, the German national who referred the Tschiras to Corim, received a $79,400 commission from Corim for his part in the sale. Willingham admitted at trial that the Tschiras were never advised that the shell company purchased the property and then resold it for an instant profit of $1,211,000. When the Tschiras became aware of these facts in the Spring of 1992, they canceled the Management Agreement with Corim and brought the instant lawsuit. In 1995, the Tschiras sold One Church Street for $665,000.

In their Complaint, the Tschiras claimed that Corim and Willingham . . . committed the tort of intentional misrepresentation. Two key pieces of evidence at trial were the title and liability insurance policies issued for One Church Street. The title insurance policy Willingham forwarded to the Tschiras indicated that the Ticor Title Insurance Company had provided protection up to $1,985,000. In actuality, Lisa Wilson, the local branch manager of Ticor, testified that the policy the company extended for the property was for only $774,000. Evidence also suggested that the liability insurance policy the Tschiras received, which purported to originate from Palmer Cay/Carswell and indicated coverage in the amount of $1,985,000, only provided protection up to $774,000. . . .

The jury awarded $1,420,000 in compensatory damages against Corim and Willingham, as well as $1,000,000 in punitive damages against Corim and $750,000 in punitive damages against Willingham. . . .

To establish a cause of action for fraudulent misrepresentation, a plaintiff must prove: (1) an intentional misrepresentation, (2) knowledge of the representation's falsity, (3) the plaintiff reasonably relied on the misrepresentation and suffered damages, and (4) the misrepresentation relates to an existing or past fact. *See Hill v. John Banks Buick, Inc.*, 875 S.W.2d 667, 670 (Tenn.Ct.App.1993). The evidence presented at trial was sufficient to uphold the jury's finding of fraudulent misrepresentation. Willingham promised the Tschiras a fair market price for the property they were buying, as well as adequate title and property insurance to cover any losses. The evidence was sufficient to establish that, at the time Willingham promised this to the Tschiras, he knew the property's value was closer to $774,000, which is the price Corim paid for the property. The jury could have reasonably found that Willingham had knowledge of the false title and property insurance policies which only covered the property up to $774,000, while the Tschiras believed the property was covered up to $1,985,000—the price they paid for the property.

Appellants argue that the representations were not material because they provided a "guaranteed" return on the Tschiras' investment through the rental income. However, the jury could have reasonably found otherwise. The Tschiras believed they were paying "fair market price" for the purchase of the property, *in addition to* receiving a guaranteed return on their investment. The Tschiras believed, and the jury could have reasonably concluded, that the Tschiras actually paid $1,211,000 over the fair market price of the property and therefore lost that amount on their investment at the time of purchase. Finally, we conclude that the evidence was sufficient to support the jury's determination that the Tschiras reasonably relied on the representations and suffered damages as a result of that reliance. The Tschiras believed, based on the letter of November 26, 1990, that Willingham was their trusted agent and would not sell them property for above the "fair market value." As a result of that belief, the Tschiras paid well over the "fair market price" for the property, thereby losing a great deal of money on the "investment." . . .

For the reasons set forth in this opinion. we affirm the district court's judgment in all respects.

[Judgment Affirmed]

Questions

1. Identify the material misrepresentations of fact evident in this case.
2. What was the measure of damages received by the Tschiras?
3. Assess Corim, Inc., and Willingham's argument on appeal that the representations made were not material because they provided a "guaranteed" return on the Tschiras' investment through rental income.

In order to prove fraud, there must be a material misrepresentation of fact. Such a misrepresentation is one that is likely to induce a reasonable person to assent to a contract. ◆ **For example,** when a used car salesman says "this Buick had but one owner, a retired teacher who kept it in mint condition," when in fact the auto had several owners, the last of which was an auto salvage company that rebuilt the car after a serious accident, such is a material misrepresentation of fact. ◆

(a) Statement of Opinion or Value. Ordinarily, matters of opinion or value are not regarded as fraudulent. Thus, statements that a building was "very good," it "required only normal maintenance," and the "deal was excellent" were merely matters of opinion. Therefore, a court considered the sophistication and expertise of the parties and the commercial setting of the transaction and enforced the contract "as is." The theory is that the person hearing the statement recognizes or should recognize that it is merely the speaker's personal view and not a statement of fact. A statement that is mere sales talk cannot be the basis of fraud liability.

If the defendant made a statement about future expectations and had knowledge that showed such expectations could not be realized, the statement can be held fraudulent. A statement of opinion may be fraudulent when the speaker knows of past or present facts that make the opinion false. ◆ **For example,** Biff Williams, the sales manager of Abrasives International (AI) sold an exclusive dealership selling AI products to Fred Farkas for $100,000 down and a 3 percent royalty on all gross proceeds. Williams told Farkas, "You have the potential to earn $300,000 to $400,000 a year in this territory." He later added, "We have four dealerships making that kind of money today." Farkas was thus persuaded by the business potential of the territory and executed the purchase contract. He later found out AI had a total of just four distributorships at that time and the actual earnings of the highest producer was $43,000. Assertions of opinions about the future profit potential alone may not amount to fraud, but the assertion of present fact that four dealerships were presently earning $300,000 to $400,000 a year was a material misstatement of fact, which made the forecast sales potential for Farkas' territory a material misstatement of fact as well. Since there was reliance and damages, Farkas can rescind the contract based on fraud and recover all damages resulting from the fraud.[13] ◆

(b) Reliance on Statement. A fraudulent statement made by one party has no importance unless the other party relies on the statement's truth. Consequently, fraud is not present when the victim has the same knowledge of the true facts as the alleged wrongdoer or should have known these facts. When false statements are made after a contract has been signed, it is obvious that the making of the contract was not induced by the statements and that the other party to the contract had not relied on them. ◆ **For example,** after making thorough tests of the Nagel Co.'s pump, Allstate Services Co. ordered 100 pumps. It later sued Nagel on the ground that advertising statements made about the pumps were false. Allstate Services cannot impose fraud liability on Nagel for the advertisements, even if they were false, because it had not relied on them in making the purchase but had acted on the basis of its own tests. ◆

[13] The Federal Trade Commission and state agencies have franchise disclosure rules that will penalize the franchisor in this case. See Chapter 43.

If the alleged victim of the fraud knew that the statements were false, because the truth was commonly known, the victim cannot rely on the false statements. When the statements of a seller are so "indefinite and extravagant" that reasonable persons would not rely thereon, the statements cannot be the basis of a claim of fraud.[14]

(c) Proof of harm. For an individual to recover damages for fraud, proof of harm to that individual is required. The injured party may recover the actual losses suffered as a result of the fraud, as well as punitive damages where the fraud is gross or oppressive. The injured party has the right to have the court order the rescission or cancellation of the contract that has been induced by fraud.

10. Nondisclosure

Under certain circumstances, nondisclosure will serve to make a contract voidable, especially when the nondisclosure consists of active concealment.

(a) General Rule of Nonliability. Ordinarily, a party to a contract has no duty to volunteer information to the other party. ◆ For example, if Fox does not ask Tehan any questions, Tehan is not under any duty to make a full statement of material facts. ◆ Consequently, the nondisclosure of information that is not asked for does not impose fraud liability or impair the validity of a contract.

(b) Exceptions. The following exceptions exist to the general rule of nonliability for nondisclosure.

(1) Unknown Defect or Condition. A duty is developing in the law for one party who knows of a defect or condition to disclose that information to the other party where the defect or condition is obviously unknown to the other person and is of such a nature that it is unlikely that the other person would discover the truth or inquire about it. However, a defendant who had no knowledge of the defect cannot be held liable for failure to disclose it.[15]

(2) Confidential Relationship. If parties stand in a **confidential relationship,** failure to disclose information may be regarded as fraudulent. For example, in an attorney-client relationship,[16] the attorney has a duty to reveal anything that is material to the client's interest when dealing with the client. The attorney's silence has the same legal consequence as a knowingly made false statement that there was no material fact to be told the client.

(3) Active Concealment. Nondisclosure may be more than the passive failure to volunteer information. It may consist of a positive act of hiding information from the other party by physical concealment, or it may consist of knowingly or recklessly furnishing the wrong information. Such conduct constitutes fraud. ◆ For example, when Nigel wanted to sell his house, he covered the wooden cellar beams with plywood to hide extensive termite damage. He sold the house to Kuehne, who sued Nigel for damages on later discovering the termite damage. Nigel claimed he had no duty to volunteer information about the termites, but by covering the damage with plywood, he committed active fraud as if he had made a false statement that there were no termites. ◆

D. PRESSURE

What appears to be an agreement may not in fact be voluntary because one of the parties entered into it as the result of undue influence or physical or economic duress.

11. Undue Influence

An aged parent may entrust all business affairs to a trusted child; a disabled person may rely on a nurse; a client may follow implicitly whatever an attorney recommends. The relationship may be

---

[14] *Eckert v Flair Agency, Inc.,* 909 P2d 1201 (Okla App 1995) (seller's statement that house would never be flooded again).

[15] *Nesbitt v Dunn,* 672 So2d 226 (La App 1996).

[16] *Re Boss Trust,* 487 NW2d 256 (Minn App 1992).

such that for practical purposes one person is helpless in the hands of the other. When such a confidential relationship exists, it is apparent that the parent, the disabled person, or the client is not exercising free will in making a contract suggested by the child, nurse, or attorney but is merely following the will of the other person. Because of the great possibility of unfair advantage, the law presumes that the dominating person exerts **undue influence** on the other person whenever the dominating person obtains any benefit from a contract made with the dominated person. The contract is then voidable. It may be set aside by the dominated person unless the dominating person can prove that, at the time the contract was made, no unfair advantage had been taken.

The class of confidential relationships is not well defined. It ordinarily includes the relationships of parent and child, guardian and ward, physician and patient, and attorney and client and any other relationship of trust and confidence in which one party exercises a control or influence over another.

Whether undue influence exists is a difficult question for courts (ordinarily juries) to determine. The law does not regard every influence as undue.

An essential element of undue influence is that the person making the contract does not exercise free will. In the absence of a recognized type of confidential relationship, such as that between parent and child, courts are likely to take the attitude that the person who claims to have been dominated was merely persuaded and there was therefore no undue influence.

12. Duress

A party may enter into a contract to avoid a threatened danger. The danger threatened may be a physical harm to person or property, called **physical duress,** or it may be a threat of financial loss, called **economic duress.**

(a) Physical Duress A person makes a contract under **duress** when there is such violence or threat of violence that the person is deprived of free will and makes the contract to avoid harm. The threatened harm may be directed either at a near relative of the contracting party or against the contracting party. If a contract is made under duress, the resulting agreement is voidable at the victim's election.

Agreements made to bring an end to mass disorder or violence are ordinarily not binding contracts because they were obtained by duress.

One may not void a contract on grounds of duress merely because it was entered into with great reluctance and proves to be very disadvantageous to that individual.[17]

(b) Economic Duress. Economic duress is a condition where one is induced by a wrongful act or threat of another to make a contract under circumstances that deprive one of the exercise of their own free will.[18] ◆ **For example,** Richard Case, an importer of parts used in the manufacture of high quality mountain bicycles had a contractual duty to supply Katahdin Manufacturing Co.'s needs for specifically manufactured stainless steel brakes for the 2001 season. Katahdin's president, Bill Reed, was in constant contact with Case about the delay in delivery of the parts and the adverse consequences it was having on Katahdin's relationship with its retailers. Near the absolute deadline for meeting orders for the 2001 season, Case called Reed and said, "I've got the parts in but I'm not sure I'll be able to send them to you, because I'm working on next year's contracts and you haven't signed yours yet." Case's 2002 contract increased the cost of parts by 38 percent. Reed signed the contract to obtain the delivery but later found a new supplier and gave notice to Case of this action. The defense of economic duress would apply in a breach of contract suit brought by Case on the 2002 contract, because Case implicitly threatened to commit the wrongful act of not delivering parts due under the prior contract, and Katahdin Co. had no means available to obtain parts elsewhere to prevent the economic loss that would occur if it did not receive these parts. ◆

---

[17] *Miller v Calhoun Johnson Co.*, 497 SE2d 397 (Ga App 1998).
[18] *Hurd v Wildman, Harrold, Allen, and Dixon*, 707 NE2d 609 (Ill App 1999).

SUMMARY

An agreement that otherwise appears to be a contract may not be binding because one of the parties lacks contractual capacity. In such a case, the contract is ordinarily voidable at the election of that party who lacks contractual capacity. In some cases, the contract is void. Ordinarily, contractual incapacity is the inability, for mental or physical reasons, to understand that a contract is being made and to understand its general terms and nature. This is typically the case when it is claimed that incapacity exists because of insanity, intoxication, or use of drugs. The incapacity of minors arises because society is discriminating in favor of that class to protect them from unwise contracts.

The age of majority is 18. Minors can disaffirm most contracts. If a minor received anything from the other party, the minor, on avoiding the contract, must return what had been received from the other party if the minor still has it.

When a minor disaffirms a contract for a necessary, the minor must pay the reasonable value of any benefit received.

Only minors are liable for their contracts. Parents of a minor are not liable on the minor's contracts merely because they are the parents. Frequently, an adult will enter into the contract as a co-party of the minor and is then liable without regard to whether the minor has avoided the contract.

The contract of an insane person is voidable to much the same extent as the contract of a minor. An important distinction is that if a guardian has been appointed for the insane person, a contract made by the insane person is void and not merely voidable.

An intoxicated person lacks contractual capacity to make a contract if the intoxication is such that the person does not understand that a contract is being made.

The consent of a party to an agreement is not genuine or voluntary in certain cases of mistake, deception, or pressure. When this occurs, what appears to be a contract can be avoided by the victim of such circumstances or conduct.

As to mistake, it is necessary to distinguish between unilateral mistakes that are unknown to the other contracting party and those that are known. Mistakes that are unknown to the other party usually do not affect the binding character of the agreement. A unilateral mistake of which the other contracting party has knowledge or has reason to know makes the contract avoidable by the victim of the mistake.

The deception situation may be one of innocent misrepresentation, nondisclosure, or fraud. A few courts allow recovery of damages. When one party to the contract knows of a fact that has a bearing on the transaction, the failure to volunteer information about that fact to the other contracting party is called nondisclosure. The law ordinarily does not attach any significance to nondisclosure. Contrary to this rule, there is a duty to volunteer information when a confidential relationship exists between the possessor of the knowledge and the other contracting party.

When concealment goes beyond mere silence and consists of actively taking steps to hide the truth, the conduct may be classified as fraud. A statement of opinion or value cannot ordinarily be the basis for fraud liability.

The free will of a person, essential to the voluntary character of a contract, may be lacking because the agreement had been obtained by pressure. This may range from undue influence through the array of threats of extreme economic loss (called economic duress) to the threat of physical force that would cause serious personal injury or damage to property (called physical duress).

When the voluntary character of an agreement has been destroyed by mistake, deception, or pressure, the victim may avoid or rescind the contract or may obtain money damages from the wrongdoer. When the mistake consists of an error in putting an oral contract in writing, either party may ask the court to reform the writing so that it states the parties' actual agreement.

WEBSITE REFERENCES

For a brief glimpse at the law of capacity in terms of who can draft a visit:

http://www.nolo.com/encyclopedia/faqs/ep/legalwill.html

For a glimpse of the law of capacity and marriage visit:

http://www.nolo.com/encyclopedia/faqs/mlt/sp14.html

To explore the principle of assent in the context of agreement visit:

http://www.nolo.com/dictionary/dictionary_alpha.cfm?wordnumber=1040&alpha=I

QUESTIONS AND CASE PROBLEMS

1. Lester purchased a used automobile from MacKintosh Motors. He asked the seller if the car had ever been in a wreck. The MacKintosh salesperson had never seen the car before that morning and knew nothing of its history but quickly answered Lester's question by stating: "No. It has never been in a wreck." In fact, the auto had been seriously damaged in a wreck and, although repaired, was worth much less than the value it would have had if there had been no wreck. When Lester learned the truth, he sued MacKintosh Motors and the salesperson for damages for fraud. They raised the defense that the salesperson did not know the statement was false and had not intended to deceive Lester. Did the conduct of the salesperson constitute fraud?

2. Helen, aged 17, wanted to buy a motorcycle. She did not have the money to pay cash but persuaded the dealer to sell a cycle to her on credit. The dealer did so partly because Helen said that she was 22 and showed the dealer an identification card that falsely stated her age as 22. Helen drove the motorcycle away. A few days later, she damaged it and then returned it to the dealer and stated that she disaffirmed the contract because she was a minor. The dealer said that she could not because (1) she had misrepresented her age and (2) the motorcycle was damaged. Can she avoid the contract?

3. Alama and Richard make a contract for the sale of an automobile. They orally agree that the price Richard is to pay is $2,000, but when the written contract is typed, the amount is wrongly stated as $3,000. This contract is signed before anyone notices the mistake. Alama then claims that the written contract is binding and that Richard is required to pay $3,000. Richard claims that he is required to pay only the originally agreed-on amount of $2,000. Is he correct?

4. High-Tech Collieries borrowed money from Holland. High-Tech later refused to be bound by the loan contract, claiming the contract was not binding because it had been obtained by duress. The evidence showed that the offer to make the loan was made on a take-it-or-leave-it basis. Was the defense of duress valid? [*Holland v High-Tech Collieries, Inc.*, 911 F Supp 1021 (DC WA)]

5. Thomas Bell, a minor, went to work in the Pittsburgh beauty parlor of Sam Pankas and agreed that when he left the employment, he would not work in or run a beauty parlor business within a 10-mile radius of downtown Pittsburgh for a period of two years. Contrary to this provision, Bell and another employee of Pankas' opened a beauty shop three blocks from Pankas' shop and advertised themselves as Pankas' former employees. Pankas sued Bell to stop the breach of the noncompetition, or restrictive, covenant. Bell claimed that he was not bound because he was a minor when he had agreed to the covenant. Was he bound by the covenant? [*Pankas v Bell*, 198 A2d 312 (Pa)]

6. Aldrich and Co. sold goods to Donovan on credit. The amount owed grew steadily, and finally Aldrich refused to sell any more to Donovan unless Donovan signed a promissory note for the amount due. Donovan did not want to but signed the note because he had no money and needed more goods. When Aldrich brought an action to enforce the note, Donovan claimed that the note was not binding because it had been obtained by economic duress. Was he correct? [*Aldrich & Co. v Donovan*, 778 P2d 397 (Mont)]

7. Adams claimed that Boyd owed him money but was under the impression that Boyd did not have much money. On the basis of this impression, Adams made a settlement agreement with Boyd for a nominal amount.

When Adams later learned that Boyd was in fact reasonably wealthy, Adams sought to set the agreement aside. Was Adams entitled to do so?

8. An agent of Thor Food Service Corp. was seeking to sell Makofske a combination refrigerator-freezer and food purchase plan. Makofske was married and had three children. After being informed of the eating habits of Makofske and his family, the agent stated that the cost of the freezer and food would be about $95 to $100 a month. Makofske carefully examined the agent's itemized estimate and made some changes to it. Makofske then signed the contract and purchased the refrigerator-freezer. The cost proved to be greater than the estimated $95 to $100 a month, and Makofske claimed that the contract had been obtained by fraud. Decide. [*Thor Food Service Corp. v Makofske*, 28 Misc 2d 872, 218 NYS2d 93]

9. Blubaugh was a district manager of Schlumberger Well Services. Turner was an executive employee of Schlumberger. Blubaugh was told that he would be fired unless he chose to resign. He was also told that if he would resign and release the company and its employees from all claims for wrongful discharge, he would receive about $5,000 in addition to his regular severance pay of approximately $25,000 and would be given job-relocation counseling. He resigned, signed the release, and received about $40,000 and job counseling. Some time thereafter, he brought an action claiming that he had been wrongfully discharged. He claimed that the release did not protect the defendants because the release had been obtained by economic duress. Were the defendants protected by the release? [*Blubaugh v Turner* 842 P2d 1072 (Wyo)]

10. Sippy was thinking of buying Christich's house. He noticed watermarks on the ceiling, but the agent showing the house stated that the roof had been repaired and was in good condition. Sippy was not told that the roof still leaked and that the repairs had not been able to stop the leaking. Sippy bought the house. Some time later, heavy rains caused water to leak into the house, and Sippy claimed that Christich was guilty of fraud. Was he correct? [*Sippy v Christich* 609 P2d 204 (Kan App)]

11. Pileggi owed Young money. Young threatened to bring suit against Pileggi for the amount due. Pileggi feared the embarrassment of being sued and the possibility that he might be thrown into bankruptcy. To avoid being sued, Pileggi executed a promissory note to pay Young the amount due. He later asserted that the note was not binding because he had executed it under duress. Is this defense valid? [*Young v Pileggi*, 455 A2d 1228 (Pa Super)]

12. Scott was employed by Litigation Reprographics and Support Services, Inc. The contract of employment was "at will," which gave the employer the right to fire Scott at any time for any reason or for no reason. Reprographics told Scott that if he wanted to keep his job, he would have to sign a contract stating that he would not compete with Reprographics when he was no longer employed by it. He signed the contract but later claimed he was not bound by it because it had been obtained by economic duress, as he had to have the job. Decide.

13. C&J Publishing Co. told a computer salesman that it wanted a computer system that would operate its printing presses. C&J specified that it wanted only new equipment and no used equipment would be acceptable. The seller delivered a system to C&J that was a combination of new and secondhand parts because it did not have sufficient new parts to fill the order. When the buyer later learned what had happened, it sued the seller for fraud. The seller contended that no statement or warranty had been made that all parts of the system were new and that it would not therefore be liable for fraud. Decide.

14. The city of Salinas entered into a contract with Souza & McCue Construction Co. to construct a sewer. City officials knew unusual subsoil conditions (including extensive quicksand) existed that would make performance of the contract unusually difficult. This information was not disclosed when city officials advertised for bids. The advertisement for bids directed bidders to examine carefully the site of the work and declared that the submission of a bid would constitute evidence that

the bidder had made an examination. Souza & McCue was awarded the contract, but, because of the subsoil conditions, it could not complete on time and was sued by Salinas for breach of contract. Souza & McCue counter-claimed on the basis that the city had not revealed its information on the subsoil conditions and was thus liable for the loss. Was the city liable? [*City of Salinas v Souza & McCue Construction Co.*, 424 P2d 921 (Cal App 3d)]

CPA QUESTIONS

1. A building subcontractor submitted a bid for construction of a portion of a high-rise office building. The bid contained material computational errors. The general contractor accepted the bid with knowledge of the errors. Which of the following statements best represents the subcontractor's liability?
   a. Not liable, because the contractor knew of the errors
   b. Not liable, because the errors were a result of gross negligence
   c. Liable, because the errors were unilateral
   d. Liable, because the errors were material
   (5/95, Law, #17, 5351)

2. Egan, a minor, contracted with Baker to purchase Baker's used computer for $400. The computer was purchased for Egan's personal use. The agreement provided that Egan would pay $200 down on delivery and $200 thirty days later. Egan took delivery and paid the $200 down payment. Twenty days later, the computer was damaged seriously as a result of Egan's negligence. Five days after the damage occurred and one day after Egan reached the age of majority, Egan attempted to disaffirm the contract with Baker. Egan will
   a. Be able to disaffirm despite the fact that Egan was *not* a minor at the time of disaffirmance
   b. Be able to disaffirm only if Egan does so in writing
   c. Not be able to disaffirm because Egan had failed to pay the balance of the purchase price
   d. Not be able to disaffirm because the computer was damaged as a result of Egan's negligence
   (11/93, Law, #21, 4318)

5

C H A P T E R   1 2

Consideration

LEARNING OBJECTIVES
After studying this chapter, you should be able to:

1. *Define what constitutes consideration*
2. *State the effect of the absence of consideration*
3. *Identify promises that can serve as consideration*
4. *Distinguish between present consideration and past consideration*
5. *State when forbearance can be consideration*
6. *Recognize situations in which adequacy of consideration has significance*
7. *List the exceptions to the requirement of consideration*

231

Will the law enforce every promise? Generally, a promise will not be enforced unless something is given or received for the promise.

A. GENERAL PRINCIPLES

As a general rule, one of the elements needed to make an agreement binding is consideration.

1. Definition

Consideration is what a promisor demands and receives as the price for the promise.[1] Consideration is something to which the promisor is not otherwise entitled and which the promisor specifies as the price for the promise.

_____
[1] *Roark v Stallworth Oil and Gas, Inc.*, 813 SW2d 492 (Tex 1991).

It is not necessary that the promisor expressly use the word *consideration*.

Because consideration is the price paid for the promise, it is unimportant who pays that price as long as it has been agreed that it should be paid in that way. For example, consideration may be the extending of credit to a third person, such as extending credit to the corporation of which the promisor is a stockholder. Likewise, when a bank lends money to a third person, such lending is consideration for the promise of its customer to repay the loan to the bank if it will loan the money to the third person.[2]

The *Schering-Plough* case illustrates the point that a promise without consideration is not a binding contract.

_____
[2] *FDIC v Diamond C Nurseries*, 629 So 2d 157 (Fla Dist Ct App 1993).

SCHERING-PLOUGH HEALTHCARE PRODUCTS, INC. v NBD BANK

890 F Supp 651 (D Mich 1995)

Schering sold goods on credit to F&M, which paid with checks drawn on NBD Bank. The bank refused to honor the checks because the F&M account had insufficient funds. Schering claimed that an officer of the bank promised that the checks would be certified if Schering brought them into the bank.*

Author's note: A certification of a check is a guarantee by the bank that the amount of the check will be paid. The certification must be written on the check. Oral or written separate agreements are not valid.

The checks were brought to the bank but the bank refused to certify them. Schering sued the bank on the theory that it had promised to certify the checks. The bank raised the defense that there was no consideration for such a promise and therefore the promise, if made, was not binding. The bank moved for judgment in its favor.

GADOLA, J. ... The court finds that no agreement existed between NBD and Schering-Plough to certify the checks in question. Under the facts alleged in the affidavits submitted by Schering-Plough's employees, the alleged agreements merely amounted to preliminary discussions, invitations to deal, and estimates of the availability of funds rather than the firm and objective commitment that is required for contractual liability.

In the same way, the alleged agreement to certify the checks was not an agreement at all. Instead, NBD personnel merely informed a Schering-Plough employee that certification of checks could occur at a certain branch office as long as checks were presented and they were accepted. In this case, once a Schering-Plough employee appeared at the named branch office with checks in hand, the real decision of whether to certify the checks was made. The invitation to deal by traveling from Memphis to Dearborn does not amount to an agreement to certify. It amounted to an agreement to consider certification once the checks were presented. The request for certification was ultimately denied.... NBD...was under no obligation to certify the checks.... An indication that certification was available does not amount to the kind of contractual agreement that would bind NBD....

The court also finds that the alleged promises to certify the checks and to make funds available were not supported by consideration. The essence of consideration is a legal detriment that has been bargained for and exchanged for the promise sought....

In this case, Schering-Plough alleges that the consideration given in exchange for the promise to certify the checks was the trip from Memphis to Dearborn. Schering-Plough contends that NBD employee Sandra Martin stated that if the checks were brought to Dearborn from Memphis, then the checks would be certified. The point that

Schering-Plough appears to miss, however, is that a reasonable person would surely recognize that the trip from Memphis was not *bargained for in exchange for* the promise to certify; rather, the trip was merely a necessary prerequisite for NBD to even consider certification. Under these circumstances, there was no consideration to support the alleged agreement to certify the two checks at issue.

[Summary judgment entered for the bank]

Questions

1. What is the significance of Schering's bringing the checks to the bank?
2. Because the bank requested that the checks be brought to the bank, presentation of the checks was the consideration for the promise of the bank to certify the checks. Appraise this statement.
3. What practical lesson in decision making can be drawn from the *Schering* case?

(a) NATURE OF CONTRACT. In a unilateral contract, the consideration for the promise is the doing of the act called for. The doing of the act in such case is also the acceptance of the offer of the promisor.

In a bilateral contract, which is an exchange of promises, each promise is the consideration for the other promise. When a lawsuit is brought for breaking a promise, it is the consideration for the broken promise to which attention is directed.

(b) AGREED EXCHANGE. Consideration is what is agreed to in return for the promise. In most cases, this will directly benefit the promisor and will be some burden or detriment to the promisee. For example, an employer who promises to pay wages sustains detriment by promising to pay the wages in exchange for the benefit of receiving the employee's promise to work. The important thing, however, is that what is received is what was asked for as the

price of the promise. **For example, Rodney, a retailer, ordered goods from Daniel, a distributor. With his order Rodney sent a check for payment in full. In a later dispute, Rodney claimed that Daniel had promised to take back unsold goods and that the consideration of this promise was the check for the goods ordered. Rodney is wrong. Daniel had not specified that if Rodney would pay at the time he ordered, Daniel would allow him to return unsold goods. Although the payment for the goods at the time of ordering was a benefit to Daniel, it did not constitute consideration.**

As long as someone gives what was asked for by the promisor, the promisor's obligation is supported by consideration even though the economic benefit of the promise is not received by the person giving the consideration. Thus, when a third person comes to the financial aid of a debtor by making some promise to the creditor in exchange for some promise from the creditor, consideration exists. The contract is binding even though the creditor's promise benefits the debtor rather than the third person. A promise guaranteeing repayment of a loan to a corporation is binding although all the money loaned was received by the corporation and nothing was received by the promisor, even though the promisor is not a shareholder of the corporation.[3]

(c) UNSPECIFIED BENEFIT. The fact that the promisor receives a benefit does not show that there was consideration for the promise. The benefit received must have been the price demanded for the making of the promise. Consequently, the fact that a creditor does not enforce a debt is not consideration for the promise of a third person to pay the debt when there was no agreement that the guarantor would pay the debt if the creditor would not enforce it.

(d) MODIFICATION OF TERMINABLE CONTRACT. A contract may be terminated by either party. If one party proposes a modification of a contract's terms and the other party continues to perform under the contract, such continued performance is consideration for the proposed modification. Consequently, when an at-will employee continues to work after the employer announces a proposed change in employment terms, such continuation of working constitutes consideration, and the modification is binding.[4]

2. Effect of Absence of Consideration

The absence of consideration makes a promise not binding.[5] Thus, a person sued for breaking a promise will not be held liable when no consideration was received for the promise. For example, an employee may promise to refrain from competing with the employer when the employment relationship ends. If the promise is not supported by consideration, the promise is not binding and the former employee may compete with the former employer.

(a) MORAL OBLIGATION. The fact that the promisor feels morally obligated to make the promise does not make the promise binding when there is no consideration for it.[6] **For example, when Abdul learned that his younger brother Bendigo was unemployed and owed his landlord rent, Abdul promised the landlord to pay the rent Bendigo owed. Abdul later reneged and claimed that his promise was not binding because it lacked consideration. Abdul is correct. The promise was nothing more than a moral obligation to pay rent to aid members of his family in need. Moral obligations do not constitute consideration.**

(b) LEGALITY DISTINGUISHED. While the absence of consideration ordinarily prevents enforcing a promise, the absence of consideration has no greater effect; that is, the agreement is not illegal because there was no consideration. Consequently, when a person keeps the promise, the performance rendered cannot later be revoked on the ground that there was no consideration. To illustrate, a promise to make a gift cannot be enforced because there is no consideration for the promise. However, once the gift is made, the donor cannot take the gift back because there was no consideration.

3. Legality of Consideration

The law will not permit persons to make contracts that violate the law. Accordingly, a promise to do something that the law prohibits or a promise to refrain from doing something that the law requires is not valid consideration, and the contract is illegal. **For example, Sandrovar, a security guard for Apex Co., promised to obtain the secret access code to the company's computer system and deliver it to Tancred Co., a competitor of Apex, for $1 million. Sandrovar's promise is not consideration because it involves the commission of an illegal act—revealing trade secrets. An illegal act is not a valid form of consideration.**

3 *Dunkin Donuts of America, Inc. v Liberatore*, 526 NYS2d 141 (App Div 1988).
4 *Habeck v MacDonald*, 520 NW2d 808 (ND 1994).
5 *Rothell v Continental Casualty Co.*, 402 SE2d 283 (Ga Ct App 1991).

6 *Production Credit Ass'n of Mandan v Rub*, 475 NW2d 532 (ND 1991). As to the Louisiana rule of moral consideration, see *Thomas v Bryant*, 596 So 2d 1065 (La Ct App 1992).

4. Failure of Consideration

When a promise is given as consideration, the question arises whether the promisor will perform the promise.

(a) NONPERFORMANCE OF PROMISE. If the promise is not performed, the law describes the default as a failure of consideration. This is a breach of the contract because what was required by the contract has not been performed.[7]

(b) BAD BARGAIN DISTINGUISHED. When the promisor performs the promise, there is never a failure of consideration. The fact that the consideration turns out to be disappointing does not mean there has been a failure of consideration. In other words, the fact that the contract proves to be a bad bargain for the promisor does not constitute a failure of consideration, nor does it affect the binding character of the contract. Thus, the fact that a business purchased by a group of buyers proves unprofitable does not constitute a failure of consideration that releases the buyers from their obligation to the seller.[8]

B. WHAT CONSTITUTES CONSIDERATION

The sections that follow analyze certain common situations in which a lawsuit turned on whether the promisor received consideration for the promise sued upon.

5. A Promise as Consideration

In a bilateral contract, each party makes a promise to the other. The promise that one party makes is consideration for the promise made by the other.

The fact that parties appear to be in agreement does not mean that there is a promise. Thus, a statement that a proposed loan would be no problem does not constitute a promise to make a loan.

(a) BINDING CHARACTER OF PROMISE. To constitute consideration, a promise must be binding; that is, it must impose a liability or create a duty. An unenforceable promise cannot be consideration. Suppose that a coal company promises to sell to a factory at a specific price all the coal that it orders, and that the factory agrees to pay that price for any coal that it orders from the coal company. The promise of the factory is not consideration because it does not obligate the factory to buy any coal from the coal company.

A promise that in fact does not impose any obligation on the promisor is often called an **illusory promise** because, although it looks like a binding promise, it is not.

(b) CONDITIONAL PROMISE. Can a conditional promise be consideration? Assume that an agreement states that buyer promises to buy, provided buyer can obtain financing. Is such a promise consideration for the seller's promise to sell, or is the buyer's promise not consideration because it does not impose any obligation on the buyer at the time that the promise is made?

The fact that a promise is conditional does not prevent it from being consideration, even when, as a practical matter, it is unlikely that the condition would ever be satisfied.[9] Thus, the promise of a fire insurance company to pay the homeowner in case of fire is consideration for the payment of premiums by the homeowner even though it is probable that there will never be a fire.

(c) CANCELLATION PROVISION. Although a promise must impose a binding obligation, it may authorize one or either party to terminate or cancel the agreement under certain circumstances or on giving notice to the other party. The fact that the contract may be terminated in this manner does not make the contract any less binding prior to such termination. **For example, Stu obtained an automobile insurance policy from Coverall Insurance Co. stating that either party could cancel the policy on five days' notice. Later, Coverall claimed it was**

---

7   *Check Control, Inc. v Shepherd*, 462 NW2d 644 (ND 1990).
8   *Commerce Bank of Joplin v Shallenburger*, 766 SW2d 764 (Mo Ct App 1989).

9   *Charles Hester Enterprises, Inc. v Illinois Founders Ins. Co.*, 114 Ill 2d 278, 102 Ill Dec 306, 499 NE2d 1319 (1986).

not bound by the policy because Stu could cancel it. Coverall is wrong. While theoretically the ability to cancel violates the requirement that promises be binding in order to be consideration, the law accepts that a power to cancel does not destroy the obligation of the contract. Until there is a cancellation, there is a binding contract. Therefore, if a loss is sustained before the insurance company cancels the policy, the insurance company is bound to pay even though it could have canceled the policy before the loss was sustained.

6. Promise to Perform Existing Obligation

Ordinarily, doing or promising to do what one is already under a legal obligation to do is not consideration.[10] Similarly, a promise to refrain from doing what one has no legal right to do is not consideration. This preexisting duty or legal obligation can be based on statute, on general principles of law, on responsibilities of an office held by the promisor, or on a preexisting contract.

(a) COMPLETION OF CONTRACT. Suppose a contractor refuses to complete a building unless the owner promises a payment or bonus in addition to the sum specified in the original contract, and the owner promises to make that payment. The question then arises whether the owner's promise is binding. Most courts hold that the second promise of the owner is without consideration.

If the promise of the contractor is to do something that is neither expressed nor implied as part of the first contract, then the promise of the other party is binding. For example, if a bonus of $1,000 is promised in return for the promise of a contractor to complete the building at a date earlier than that specified in the original agreement, the promise to pay the bonus is binding. **For example, Exterior Painters made a contract with Sonya to paint her house by the end of the month for $2,000. Later, Sonya promised to pay an additional $500 if the work was finished by the 15th of the month. Exterior completed the painting on the 14th of the month but Sonya refused**

to pay the $500 on the ground that Exterior was already obligated to paint the house for $2,000. Sonya is wrong in ignoring the fact that the $2,000 price was tied to finishing the job by the end of the month. By getting the job done earlier, Sonya was getting something to which she was not already entitled and therefore the promise of Exterior to finish by the 15th was effective as consideration to support the promise to pay the $500 extra.

(1) Good-Faith Adjustment. A recent trend is to enforce a second promise to pay a contractor a greater amount for the performance of the original contract when there are extraordinary circumstances caused by unforeseeable difficulties and when the additional amount promised the contractor is reasonable under the circumstances.

When parties to a contract, in a good-faith effort to meet the business realities of a situation, agree to a reduction of contract terms, there is some authority that the promise of the one party to accept the lesser performance of the other is binding. These cases have held that the promise is binding even though technically the promise to render the lesser performance is not consideration because the obligor was already obligated to render the greater performance. Thus, a landlord's promise to reduce the rent was binding when the tenant could not pay the original rent and the landlord preferred to have the building occupied even though receiving a smaller rental.

(2) Contract for Sale of Goods. When the contract is for the sale of goods, any modification made in good faith by the parties to the contract is binding without regard to the existence of consideration for the modification.

(b) COMPROMISE AND RELEASE OF CLAIMS. The rule that doing or promising to do what one is bound to do is not consideration applies to a part payment made in satisfaction of an admitted debt. Thus, a promise to pay part of an amount that is admittedly owed is not consideration for a promise to discharge the balance. It will not prevent the creditor from demanding the remainder later.

If the debtor pays before the debt is due, there is consideration because on the day when

---

10 *Waide v Tractor and Equipment Co.*, 545 So 2d 1327 (Ala 1989).

the payment was made, the creditor was not entitled to demand any payment. Likewise, if the creditor accepts some article (even of slight value) in addition to the part payment, consideration exists and the agreement is held to be binding.

A debtor and creditor may have a bona fide dispute over the amount owed or whether any amount is owed. In such a case, payment by the debtor of less than the amount claimed by the creditor is consideration for the latter's agreement to release or settle the claim. It is generally regarded as sufficient if the claimant believes in the merit of the claim.[11] Conversely, if the claimant knows that the claim does not have any merit and is merely pressing the claim to force the other party to make some payment to buy peace from the annoyance of a lawsuit, the settlement agreement based on the part payment is not binding.

(c) PART-PAYMENT CHECKS. The acceptance and cashing of a check for part of a debt releases the entire debt when the check bears a notation that it is intended as final or full payment and the total amount due is disputed or unliquidated. It probably has this same effect even though the debt is not disputed or is liquidated.[12] In some jurisdictions, this principle is applied without regard to the form of payment or whether the claim is disputed. Section 1541 of the California Civil Code provides: "An obligation is extinguished by a release therefrom given to the debtor by the creditor upon a new consideration, or in writing, with or without new consideration."

(d) COMPOSITION OF CREDITORS. In a **composition of creditors**, the various creditors of one debtor mutually agree to accept a fractional part of their claims in full satisfaction of the claims. Such agreements are binding and are supported by consideration. When creditors agree to extend the due date of their debts, the promise of each creditor to forbear is likewise consideration for the promise of other creditors to forbear.

7. Present Consideration versus Past Benefits

If consideration is what the promisor states must be received in return for the promise, then consideration must be given when or after the promisor states what is demanded.

(a) PAST CONSIDERATION. Past benefits already received by the promisor cannot be consideration for a later promise.[13] **For example: Magda was so pleased with the school work of her daughter, Sharon, during the preceding year that Magda promised to buy Sharon a new car. After a family fight, Magda stated that she would not buy the car. Sharon claimed that the promise to buy the car was binding because it was supported by consideration—her high grades. Sharon is wrong. Past consideration is not binding consideration for a promise given.**

(b) COMPLEX TRANSACTIONS. In applying the rule that past benefits cannot be consideration, care must be taken to distinguish between the situation in which the consideration is in fact past and the situation in which the earlier consideration and subsequent promises were all part of one complex transaction. In such cases, the earlier consideration is not regarded as past and supports the later promises.[14]

8. Forbearance as Consideration

In most cases, consideration consists of the performance of an act or the making of a promise to act.[15] Consideration may also consist of forbearance, which is refraining from doing an act, or a promise of forbearance. In other words, the promisor may desire to buy the inaction or a promise of inaction of the other party.

The waiving or giving up of any right can be consideration for the promise of another. Thus, the relinquishment of a right in property or of a right to sue for damages will support a promise given in return for it.

C
P
A

---

[11] *F. H. Prince & Co. v Towers Financial Corp.*, 656 NE2d 142 (Ill App Ct 1995).
[12] *Hearst Corp. v Lauerer, Martin & Gibbs, Inc.*, 524 NE2d 193 (Ohio Ct App 1987).

[13] *Sager v Basham*, 401 SE2d 676 (Va 1991).
[14] Such a complex transaction is called "contemporaneous" in some states. *Soukop v Snyder*, 709 P2d 109 (Haw Ct App 1985).
[15] *Kapoor v Robins*, 573 NE2d 292 (Ill App Ct 1991).

The promise of a creditor to forbear collecting the debt is consideration for a promise by the debtor to modify the terms of the transaction. **For example, Rex was the major stockholder of Wyndham Corp., which owed a large bill to Natural Gas Co. Rex asked Natural to "go easy" and stated that he would pay the bill if necessary. Natural delayed taking any action for a month, then demanded payment from Rex. Rex is not bound by his promise to pay the Wyndham debt owed to Natural because there was no consideration for it. The voluntary forbearance of Natural was not consideration because it was not the price of Rex's promise as the promise was made without any commitment to forbear and there was nothing to show that the parties regarded the promise as the price for the forbearance.**

The right that is surrendered in return for a promise may be a right against a third person as well as against the promisor. Consequently, when a creditor has a claim against a corporation, the creditor's promise to forbear his legal right can be consideration for the guaranty of the debt by the corporation's president.[16]

As under the rule governing compromises, forbearance to assert a claim is consideration when the claim has been asserted in good faith even if it is without merit.[17] In the absence of a good-faith belief, forbearance with respect to a worthless claim is not consideration.

(a) WHAT CONSTITUTES CONSIDERATION. The consideration for forbearance is anything that constitutes consideration under the general rules discussed in this chapter. Usually, it is a payment of money to the promisor or a third person to guarantee the debt of another. The extending of the date for payment of a debt is consideration for the promise of a third person that the debt will be paid.[18]

(b) CONSIDERATION IN EMPLOYMENT CONTRACTS. In employment contracts, an employee may promise not to compete with the employer after leaving the employment. What is the consideration for this promise? When the promise is made at the time of the making of the contract of employment, the promise of the employer to employ and to pay compensation is consideration for the employee's promise to refrain from competing after leaving the employment. If the employee's promise is made after the contract of employment has been made, it is necessary to see whether the contract (1) is for an indefinite duration with no job security provision or (2) is for a definite period of time, such as five years, or contains job security provisions that prevent the employer from discharging the employee at will.

If the employment contract is for a definite period or is covered by job security provisions, the employee's promise not to compete when made after the contract of employment has been made is not binding on the employee unless the employer gives some consideration for the promise not to compete. In the case of the indefinite-duration contract that has no job security provision, the employer can ordinarily terminate the contract at will. Therefore, according to some courts, the employer's continuing to employ the person after the employee's making of the promise not to compete is consideration for that promise even though the parties did not express these thoughts in words. Other courts, however, do not make a distinction based on the type of employment contract. These courts follow the common law rule that a restrictive covenant agreed to by an employee already under a contract of employment is not binding because it is not supported by consideration.

(c) OBLIGATION TO FORBEAR DISTINGUISHED. Forbearance as consideration for a promise is distinct from an obligation to forbear. When the latter arises, it is necessary to find consideration to forbear; without consideration, the ordinary rule is followed. There is accordingly no obligation to forbear when consideration is lacking.[19]

9. Adequacy of Consideration

Ordinarily, courts do not consider the adequacy of the consideration given for a promise. The fact that the consideration supplied by one

---

[16] *Gooch v American Sling Co.*, 902 SW2d 181 (Tex App 1995).
[17] *Stueber v Picard*, 816 P2d 1111 (NM 1991).
[18] *Hope Petty Motors of Columbia, Inc. v Hyatt*, 425 SE2d 786 (SC Ct App 1992).

---

[19] *GECC Financial Corp. v Jaffarian*, 904 P2d 530 (Haw Ct App 1995).

C
P
A
C
P
A
C
P
A
C
P
A
C
P
A
C
P
A

party is slight when compared with the burden undertaken by the other party is immaterial. It is a matter for the parties to decide when they make their contract whether each is getting a fair return. In the absence of fraud or other misconduct, courts usually will not interfere to make sure that each side is getting a fair return.

Because the adequacy of consideration is ignored, it is immaterial that consideration is so slight that the transaction is in part a "gift."[20] **For example, Collier promised to buy Gustav's motor bike for $2,000. Gustav later claimed that he was not bound by the agreement because he was not getting enough money for the bike. Whether he was getting enough money is irrelevant because the law ignores the adequacy of consideration.**

E T H I C S   A N D   T H E   L A W

Alan Fulkins, who owns a construction company that specializes in single-family residences, is constructing a small subdivision with 23 homes. Tretorn Plumbing, owned by Jason Tretorn, was awarded the contract for the plumbing work on the homes at a price of $4,300 per home.

Plumbing contractors complete their residential projects in three phases. Phase one consists of digging the lines for the plumbing and installing the pipes that are placed in the foundation of the house. Phase two consists of the pipes within the walls of the home, and phase three is the surface plumbing, such as sinks and tubs. However, industry practice dictates that the plumbing contractor receive one-half of the contract amount after completion of phase one.

Tretorn completed the digs of phase one for Fulkins and received payment of $2,150. Tretorn then went to Fulkins and demanded an additional $600 per house for completion of the work. Fulkins said, "But you already have a contract for $4,300!" Tretorn responded, "I know, but the costs are killing me. I need the additional $600."

Fulkins explained the hardship of the demand, "Look, I've already paid you half. If I hire someone else, I'll have to pay them two-thirds for the work not done. It'll cost me $5,000 per house." Tretorn responded,

"Exactly. I'm a bargain because the additional $600 I want only puts you at $4,900. If you don't pay it, I'll just lien the houses and then you'll be stuck without a way to close the sales. I've got the contract all drawn up. Just sign it and everything goes smoothly."

Should Fulkins sign the agreement? Does Tretorn have the right to the additional $600? Was it ethical for Tretorn to demand the $600? Is there any legal advice you can offer Fulkins?

C. EXCEPTIONS TO THE LAW OF CONSIDERATION

The ever-changing character of law clearly appears in the area of consideration, because the rules stated earlier in this chapter are slowly eroding.

10. Exceptions to Adequacy of Consideration Rule

The insufficiency or inadequacy of the consideration may lead a court to the conclusion that a contract is not binding because it is unconscionable.[21] Inadequate consideration may also indicate that fraud was practiced on the promisor.

The inadequacy of the consideration may be evidence of the exercise of undue influence or the taking advantage of the condition of the other contracting party. Several factors may combine to challenge the validity of the contract.

For the enforcement of unconscionable contract, some courts may consider the adequacy of consideration. For example, "if the sum total of the provisions of a contract drive too hard a bargain, a court of conscience will not assist its enforcement."[22] **For example, Pasterno owned a tract of moderately good farm land that Urena Sales Co. purchased from Pasterno for about one-tenth of its fair market value. Pasterno later sued to set aside the sale to Urena because he had been induced by false**

---

20 *Pasant v Jackson Nat'l Life Ins. Co.*, 52 F3d 94 (5th Cir 1995).
21 *Mimica v Area Interstate Trucking, Inc.*, 620 NE2d 1328 (Ill App Ct 1993).
22 *Waters v Min Ltd.*, 587 NE2d 231 (Mass 1992).

Figure 12-1   Consideration and Promises

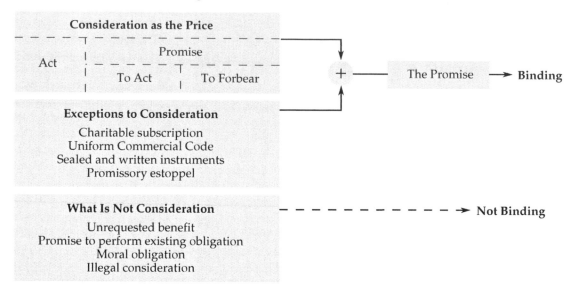

"inside information" provided by Urena. Pasterno claimed that a plant manufacturing dangerous radioactive products would be constructed on the neighboring land and Urena failed to disclose this information. In such a case, Pasterno can argue that the consideration for the farm was inadequate as a result of Urena's misrepresentations.

11. Exceptions to Requirement of Consideration

By statute or decision, consideration is no longer required in a number of situations.

(a) CHARITABLE SUBSCRIPTIONS. When charitable enterprises are financed by voluntary subscriptions of a number of persons, the promise of each is generally enforceable. For example, when a number of people make pledges or subscriptions for the construction of a church, for a charitable institution, or for a college, the subscriptions are binding. Some states require proof that the charity has relied on the subscription.[23]

The theories for sustaining such promises vary. Consideration is lacking according to the technical standards applied in ordinary contract cases. Nevertheless, the courts enforce such promises as a matter of public policy.

(b) UNIFORM COMMERCIAL CODE. In a number of situations, the Uniform Commercial Code abolishes the requirement of consideration. For example, under the Code consideration is not required for (1) a merchant's written, firm offer for goods stated to be irrevocable; (2) a written discharge of a claim for an alleged breach of a commercial contract; or (3) an agreement to modify a contract for the sale of goods.[24] **For example, Stanley wrote to Rojas Personal Computer Store asking the price of a particular computer. He received a letter signed by the manager stating that the price was $1,500 for the next 30 days. Five days later, Stanley went to Personal for the computer but was told that the price had been raised to $1,700. He claimed that he could purchase at the price stated in the letter. Personal replied that the statement in the letter was not binding because there was no consideration for a promise to keep the offer open for 30 days. The letter from its manager constituted a firm offer by a merchant. It is therefore binding according to its terms even though no consideration is present.**

---

[23] *King v Trustees of Boston University*, 647 NE2d 1196 (Mass 1995).

[24] UCC § 2-209(1).

(c) SEALED AND WRITTEN INSTRUMENTS. At common law, consideration was not necessary to support a promise under seal. In a state that gives the seal its original common law effect, the gratuitous promise or a promise to make a gift is enforceable when it is set forth in a sealed instrument.[25]

In some states, a promise under seal must be supported by consideration, just as though it did not have a seal. Other states take a middle position and hold that the presence of a seal is prima facie proof that there is consideration to support the promise. This means that if nothing more than the existence of the sealed promise is shown, it is deemed supported by consideration. The party making the promise, however, may prove that there was no consideration. In that case, the promise is not binding.

In some states a rebuttable presumption arises whenever a contract is in writing that the promises of the parties are supported by consideration.

When a sealed instrument calls also for consideration, the instrument cannot be enforced if there is a failure of consideration despite the fact that an ordinary sealed instrument would be enforced even without consideration.[26]

12. Promissory Estoppel

A promise that is not supported by consideration may still be binding if the doctrine of promissory estoppel can be applied. A person may make a promise to another under circumstances that the promisor should reasonably foresee will induce the promisee to rely on it and will cause the promisee to sustain substantial loss if the promise is not kept. Under the doctrine of **promissory estoppel**, such a promise is binding even though there is no consideration for it.[27] In applying the doctrine of promissory estoppel, courts are ignoring the requirement of consideration in order to attain a just result.

Legal difficulties often arise because parties take certain things for granted. Frequently they will be sure that they have agreed to everything and that they have a valid contract. Sometimes, however, they do not. The courts are then faced with the problem of leaving them with their broken dreams or coming to their rescue as in the *Hoffman* case.

---

[25] *Hopkins v Griffin*, 402 SE2d 11 (Va 1991).
[26] *Thomas v Webster Spring Co.*, 638 NE2d 51 (Mass App Ct 1994).

[27] *Hill v Mayers*, 802 P2d 694 (Or Ct App 1990).

HOFFMAN v RED OWL STORES, INC.
133 NW2d 267 (Wis 1965)

Red Owl was a corporation that maintained a system of chain stores. Joseph H. Hoffman wanted to acquire a franchise for a Red Owl grocery store. Red Owl's agent informed Hoffman and his wife that if they would sell their bakery in Wautoma, acquire a certain tract of land in Chilton (another city), and put up a specified amount of money, they would be given a franchise. Hoffman sold his business and acquired the land in Chilton but was never granted a franchise. He and his wife sued Red Owl, which raised the defense that there had only been an assurance that Hoffman would receive a franchise but no promise supported by consideration. Thus, there was no binding contract to give him a franchise. From a judgment in the Hoffmans' favor, Red Owl appealed.

CURRIE, C. J. ... The development of the law of promissory estoppel "is an attempt by the court to keep remedies abreast of increased moral consciousness of honesty and fair representations in all business dealings." *Peoples National Bank of Little Rock v Lineberger Constr. Co.*, 219 Ark. 11, 240 S.W.2d 12, (1951). ...

The Restatement avoids use of the term "promissory estoppel," and there has been criticism of it as an inaccurate term.... Use of the word "estoppel" to describe a doctrine upon which a party to a lawsuit may obtain affirmative relief offends the traditional concept that estoppel merely serves as a shield and cannot serve as a sword to create a cause of action....

Because we deem the doctrine of promissory estoppel, as stated in Sec 90 of Restatement, 1 Contracts, as one which supplies a needed weapon which courts may employ in a proper cause to prevent injustice, we endorse and adopt it.

The record here discloses a number of promises and assurances given to Hoffman by Lukowitz on behalf of Red Owl upon which plaintiffs relied and acted upon to their detriment. ...

Originally the doctrine of promissory estoppel was invoked as a substitute for consideration rendering a gratuitous promise enforceable as a contract.... In other words, the acts of reliance by the promisee to his detriment provided a substitute for consideration.... [Under] Sec 90 of Restatement, 1 Contracts,...the conditions imposed are:

1. *Was the promise one which the promisor should reasonably expect to induce action or forbearance of a definite and substantial character on the part of the promisee?*
2. *Did the promise induce such action or forbearance?*
3. *Can injustice be avoided only by enforcement of the promise?...*

We conclude that injustice would result here if plaintiffs were not granted some relief because of the failure of defendants to keep their promises which induced plaintiffs to act to their detriment. ...

[Judgment affirmed on this phase of the case]

Questions

1. Could the court in the *Hoffman* case have reached the same conclusion by applying the common law rule as to consideration?

2. Compare the concept of firm offer with promissory estoppel.

3. How could Hoffman have avoided the problem that arose in his case?

(a) PROMISSORY ESTOPPEL DISTINGUISHED FROM CONSIDERATION. Promissory estoppel differs from consideration in that with promissory estoppel the reliance of the promisee is not the bargained-for price or response sought by the promisor. Under promissory estoppel it is sufficient that the promisor foresees that there will be such reliance. The doctrine of promissory estoppel applies only when (1) the promisor has reason to foresee the detrimental reliance by the promisee, and (2) the promisee in fact would sustain a substantial loss because of such reliance if the promise were not performed.

Promissory estoppel cannot be applied unless the promise is sufficiently definite for the court to determine what the promisor is required to do.[28]

(b) PROMISE ESSENTIAL. The making of an express promise is essential to applying the concept of promissory estoppel. Thus the fact that one party has certain hopes or expectations is in itself not sufficient. There must be a promise by the other party to produce the hoped-for result before promissory estoppel can be applied. Vague statements are not sufficient. Thus a statement by the creditor bank that it was "with" the debtors and would "support" them in their proposed venture was too vague to constitute a promise to make loans to the debtors. Likewise, a promissory estoppel cannot be based on a statement that "good employees are taken care of."[29]

---

[28] *Black Canyon Racquetball Club, Inc. v Idaho First National Bank*, 804 P2d 900 (Idaho 1987).

[29] *Ruud v Great Plains Supply, Inc.*, 526 NW2d 369 (Minn 1995).

(c) DETRIMENTAL RELIANCE ESSENTIAL.
Promissory estoppel cannot be applied merely because the promisor has not performed the promise. In the absence of the promisee's detrimental reliance on the promise, the doctrine of promissory estoppel is not applicable. Thus a promise made to the debt or by the creditor that the creditor would collect only $20 a month on the debt of approximately $12,000 was not binding because there was no proof that the debtor relied in any manner on that promise.[30]

What constitutes detrimental reliance sufficient to satisfy the promissory estoppel rule has been diluted in recent years. In the early promissory estoppel cases, it was necessary to show that if the defendant did not perform the promise, the plaintiff would suffer a substantial loss—of a nature that could not be compensated for by the payment of money. Many courts are now willing to accept any financial loss as sufficient to show detrimental reliance. Thus, it has been held that when the plaintiff quit a job in reliance on the defendant's promise to employ the plaintiff, there was sufficient detrimental reliance to make the defendant's promise binding.[31] **For example, Thomas was working for Long Island Water Co. when San Jose Water Co. promised to give him a job.**

Nothing further was done by either San Jose or Thomas, but Thomas quit his job with Long Island, took his three small children from the local New York schools, and moved with his wife and children near San Jose. When San Jose refused to give him a job, Thomas claimed it was bound by promissory estoppel. San Jose claimed that promissory estoppel was not applicable because there was no detrimental reliance by Thomas. San Jose is wrong. The disruption in Thomas' work, his family, and his children's schooling caused by moving from the extreme East to the extreme West was substantial and satisfied the requirement of detrimental reliance for the doctrine of promissory estoppel.

---

[30] *Lawrence v Board of Education*, 503 NE2d 1201 (Ill App Ct 1987). Some courts hold the promisor liable for tort damages when the promisee has sustained harm because the promisee relied on the promise but the promise was never kept. *ITT Terryphone Corp. v Tri-State Steel Drum, Inc.*, 344 SE2d 686 (Ga Ct App 1986). The explanation for these differing views is that those courts do not believe it is just for the promisor to break a promise on which the promisee had detrimentally relied, but at the same time they do not feel that they can flatly state that consideration is not required to make the broken promise binding on the defendant.
[31] *Roberts v Geosource Drilling Services, Inc.*, 757 SW2d 48 (Tex App 1988).

SUMMARY

A promise is not binding if there is no consideration for the promise. Consideration is what the promisor requires as the price for the promise. That price may be the doing of an act, refraining from the doing of an act, or merely a promise to do or to refrain. In a bilateral contract, it is necessary to find that the promise of each party is supported by consideration. If either promise is not so supported, it is not binding and the agreement of the parties is not a contract. Consequently, the agreement cannot be enforced. When a promise is the consideration, it must be a binding promise. The binding character of a promise is not affected by the circumstance that there is a condition precedent to the performance promised. Likewise, the binding character of the promise and of the contract is not affected by a provision in the contract for its cancellation by either one or both of the parties.

A promise to do what one is already obligated to do is not consideration, although some exceptions are made. Such exceptions include when the rendering of a partial performance or a modified performance is accepted as a good-faith adjustment to a changed situation, a compromise and release of claims, a part-payment check, or a compromise of creditors. Because consideration is the price that is given to obtain the promise, past benefits conferred on the promisor cannot be consideration. In the case of a complex transaction, however, the past benefit and the subsequent transaction relating to the promise may in fact have been intended by the parties as one transaction. In such a case, the earlier benefit is not past consideration but is the consideration contemplated by the promisor as the price for the promise subsequently made.

A promise to refrain from doing an act can be consideration. A promise to refrain from suing or asserting a particular claim can be consideration. Generally, the promise to forbear must be for a specified time as distinguished from agreeing to forbear at will. When consideration is forbearance to assert a claim, it is immaterial whether the claim is valid as long as the claim has been asserted in good faith in the belief that it was valid.

When the promisor obtains the consideration specified for the promise, the law is not ordinarily concerned with the value or adequacy of that consideration. Exceptions are sometimes made in the case of fraud or unconscionability and under consumer protection statutes.

There is a current trend to abandon the requirement of consideration with promissory estoppel the most extensive repudiation of that requirement.

All transactions must be lawful; therefore, consideration for a promise must be legal. If it is not, there is no consideration and the promise is not binding.

When the promisor does not actually receive the price promised for the promise, there is a failure of consideration, which constitutes a breach of the contract.

Although consideration is required to make a promise binding, the promise that is not supported by consideration is not unlawful or illegal. If the promisor voluntarily performs the promise, the promisor cannot undo the performance and restore matters to their position prior to the making of the agreement. The parties are free to perform their agreement, but the courts will not help either of them because there is no contract.

QUESTIONS AND CASE PROBLEMS

1. What social force is advanced by each of the following rules of law? (a) An executed gift or a performance that has been rendered without consideration cannot be rescinded for lack of consideration. (b) In the absence of fraud, the adequacy of consideration is usually immaterial.

2. Sarah's house caught on fire. Through the prompt assistance of her neighbor Odessa, the fire was quickly extinguished. In gratitude, Sarah promised to pay Odessa $1,000. Can Odessa enforce this promise if Sarah does not pay the money?

3. Clifton agreed to work for Acrylics Inc. for $400 a month. He later claimed there was no contract because the consideration for the services to be rendered was inadequate. Is there a binding contract?

4. Dale Dyer, who was employed by National By-Products, Inc., was seriously injured at work as the result of a job-related accident. He agreed to give up his right to sue the employer for damages in consideration of the employer's giving him a lifetime job. The employer later claimed that this argument was not binding because Dyer's promise not to sue could not be consideration for the promise to employ on the ground that Dyer in fact had no right to sue. Dyer's only remedy was to make a claim under workers' compensation. Was the agreement binding? [*Dyer v National By-Products, Inc.*, 380 NW2d 732 (Iowa)]

5. Galloway induced Marian to sell her house to Galloway by false statements that a factory was going to be built on the vacant lot adjoining Marian's house. No factory was ever built, and Marian then sued Galloway for damages for fraud. Marian offered to prove that Galloway had paid her only a fraction of the true value of her house. Galloway claimed that this evidence of value could not be admitted because it was immaterial whether the consideration paid Marian was adequate. Is Galloway correct?

6. Koedding hired West Roofers to put a roof on her house. She later claimed that the roofing job was defective, and she threatened to sue West. Both parties discussed the matter in good faith. Finally, West guaranteed that the roof would be free from leaks for 20 years in return for the guarantee by Koedding not to sue West for damages. The roof leaked the next year, and Koedding sued West on the guarantee. West claimed that the guarantee was not binding because there was no consideration for it. According to West, Koedding's promise not to sue had no value because Koedding in fact did not have any valid claim against West; therefore, she was not entitled to sue. Was this defense valid?

7. Fedun rented a building to Gomer, who did business under the name of Mike's Cafe. Later, Gomer was about to sell out the business to Brown and requested Fedun to release him from his liability under the lease. Fedun agreed to do so. Brown sold out shortly thereafter. The balance of the rent due by Gomer under the original lease agreement was not paid, and Fedun sued Gomer on the rent claim. Could he collect after having released Gomer? [*Fedun v Mike's Cafe*, 204 A2d 776 (Pa Super Ct)]

8. Alexander Proudfoot Co. was in the business of devising efficiency systems for industry. It told Sanitary Linen Service Co. that it could provide an improved system for Sanitary Linen that would save it money. It made a contract with Sanitary Linen to provide a money-saving system. The system was put into operation, and Proudfoot was paid the amount due under the contract. The system failed to work and did not save money. Sanitary Linen sued to get the money back. Was it entitled to do so? [*Sanitary Linen Service Co. v Alexander Proudfoot Co.*, 435 F2d 292 (5th Cir)]

9. Sears, Roebuck and Co. promised to give Forrer permanent employment. Forrer sold his farm at a loss to take the job. Shortly after beginning work, he was discharged by Sears, which claimed that the contract could be terminated at will. Forrer claimed that promissory estoppel prevented Sears from terminating the contract. Was he correct? [*Forrer v Sears, Roebuck & Co.*, 153 NW2d 587 (Wis)]

10. Kemp leased a gas filling station from Baehr. Kemp, who was heavily indebted to Penn-O-Tex Oil Corp., transferred to it his right to receive payments on all claims. When Baehr complained that the rent was not paid, he was assured by the corporation that the rent would be paid to him. Baehr did not sue Kemp for the overdue rent but later sued the corporation. The defense was raised that there was no consideration for the promise of the corporation. Decide. [*Baehr v Penn-O-Tex Corp.*, 104 NW2d 661 (Minn)]

11. Bogart owed several debts to Security Bank & Trust Co. and applied to the bank for a loan to pay the debts. The bank's employee stated that he would take the application for the loan to the loan committee and "within two or three days, we ought to have something here, ready for you to go with." The loan was not made. The bank sued Bogart for his debts. He filed a counterclaim on the theory that the bank had broken its contract to make a loan to him and that promissory estoppel prevented the bank from going back on what the employee had said. Was this counterclaim valid? [*Security Bank & Trust Co. v Bogart*, 494 NE2d 965 (Ind Ct App)]

12. Kelsoe worked for International Wood Products, Inc., for a number of years. One day Hernandez, a director and major stockholder of the company, promised Kelsoe that the corporation would give her 5 percent of the company's stock. This promise was never kept and Kelsoe sued International for breach of contract. Had the company broken its contract? [*Kelsoe v International Wood Products, Inc.*, 588 So 2nd 877 (Ala)]

13. Norma Elmore was in a Wal-Mart store when she slipped and fell on an open package of mints on the floor. She asked the store representative who came to her aid if the store would pay her medical expenses. The representative assured her that the store would pay. The store failed to do so and Norma sued for medical expenses. Was the store liable?

14. On the death of their mother, the children of Jane Smith gave their interests in their mother's estate to their father in consideration of his payment of $1 to each of them and his promise to leave them the property on his death. The father died without leaving them the property. The children sued their father's second wife to obtain the property in accordance with the agreement. The second wife claimed that the agreement was not a binding contract because the amount of $1 and future gifts given for the children's interests were so trivial and uncertain. Decide.

15. Radio Station KSCS broadcast a popular music program. It announced that it would pay $25,000 to any listener who detected that it did not play three consecutive songs. Steve Jennings listened to and heard a program in which two songs were followed by a commercial program. He claimed the $25,000. The station refused to pay on the ground that there was no consideration for its promise to pay that amount. Was the station liable? [*Jennings v Radio Station KSCS*, 708 SW2d 60 (Tex App)]

Form of Contract

<table>
<tr><td valign="top">

A. STATUTE OF FRAUDS

1. Validity of Oral Contracts
2. Contracts That Must Be Evidenced by a Writing
3. Note or Memorandum
4. Effect of Noncompliance

</td><td valign="top">

B. PAROL EVIDENCE RULE

5. Exclusion of Parol Evidence
6. When the Parol Evidence Rule Does Not Apply

</td><td valign="top">

Learning Objectives

After studying this chapter, you should be able to

1. State when a contract must be evidenced by a writing
2. List the requirements of a writing that evidence a contract
3. State the effects of the absence of a sufficient writing when a contract must be evidenced by a writing
4. List the exceptions that have been made by the courts to the laws requiring written evidence of contracts
5. Compare statute of frauds requirements with the parol evidence rule
6. List exceptions to the parol evidence rule

</td></tr>
</table>

When must a contract be written? What is the effect of a written contract? These questions lead to the statute of frauds and the parol evidence rule.

A. STATUTE OF FRAUDS

A contract is a legally binding agreement. Must the agreement be evidenced by a writing?

1. Validity of Oral Contracts

In the absence of a statute requiring a writing, a contract may be oral or written. Managers and professionals should be more fully aware that their oral communications, including telephone conversations and dinner or breakfast discussions, may be deemed legally enforceable contracts. ◆ For example, suppose Mark Wahlberg, after reviewing a script tentatively entitled *The Bulger Boys,* meets with Steven Spielberg to discuss Mark's playing mobster James "Whitey" Bulger in the film. Steven states, "You *are* 'Whitey,' Marky! The nuns at Gate of Heaven Grammar School in South Boston—or maybe it was St. Augustine's—they don't send for the Boston Police when they are troubled about drug use in the neighborhood and schools; they send for you to talk to the kids. Nobody messes with you, and the kids know it. And it works! This is true stuff, and this fugitive's brother Bill comes out of Southie to be President of U Mass." Mark likes the script. Steven and Mark block out two months of time for shooting the film this fall. They agree on Mark's usual fee and a "piece of the action" based on a set percentage of the net income from the film. Thereafter, Mark's agent does not like the deal. He believes there are better scripts for Mark. Things may come out about "Whitey" that could tarnish the film. And with Hollywood accounting, a percentage of the "net" take is usually of little value. However, all of the essential terms of a contract have been agreed upon, and such an oral agreement would be legally enforceable. As set forth in the following text, no writing is required for a services contract that can be performed within one year after the date of the agreement.

Certain contracts must be evidenced by a writing to be legally enforceable. These contracts are covered by the **statute of frauds.**[1]

Since many oral contracts are legally enforceable, it is a good business practice in the preliminary stages of discussions to stipulate that no binding agreement is intended to be formed until a written contract is prepared and signed by the parties.

2. Contracts That Must Be Evidenced by a Writing

The statute of frauds requires that certain kinds of contracts be evidenced by a writing or else they cannot be enforced.[2] This means that either the contract itself must be in writing and signed by both parties or there must be a sufficient written memorandum of the oral contract signed by the person being sued for breach of contract.

(a) Agreement That Cannot Be Performed within One Year after the Contract is Made. A writing is required when the contract, by its terms or subject matter, cannot be performed within one year after the date of the agreement. An oral agreement to supply a line of credit for two years cannot be enforced because of the statute of frauds.[3] Likewise, a joint venture agreement to construct a condominium complex was subject to the one-year provision of the statute of frauds where the contract could not reasonably have been performed within one year. The plans of the parties projected a development over the course of three years.

---

[1] *Pull v City of Corinth,* 579 So 2d 534 (Miss 1991).

[2] The name is derived from the original English Statute of Frauds and Perjuries, which was adopted in 1677 and became the pattern for similar legislation in America. The seventeenth section of that statute governed the sale of goods, and its modern counterpart is § 2-201 of the UCC. The fourth section of the English statute provided the pattern for U.S. legislation with respect to contracts other than for the sale of goods described in this section of the chapter. The English statute was repealed in 1954, except as to land sale and guarantee contracts. The U.S. statutes remain in force, but the liberalization by UCC § 2-201 of the pre-Code requirements with respect to contracts for the sale of goods lessens the applicability of the writing requirement. Additional movement away from the writing requirement is seen in the 1994 Revision of Article 8, Securities, which abolishes the statute of frauds provision of the original UCC § 8-319 and goes beyond by declaring that the one-year performance provision of the statute of frauds is not applicable to contracts for securities. UCC § 8-113 [1994 Revision].

[3] *ZBS Industries, Inc. v Anthony Cocca Videoland, Inc.,* 637 NE2d 956 (Ohio App 1994).

FIGURE 16.1 *Hurdles in the Path of a Contract*

Writing Required	
Statute of Frauds	**Exceptions**
More than One Year to Perform Sale of Land Answer for Another's Debt or Default Personal Representative to Pay Debt of Decedent Promise in Consideration of Marriage Sale of Goods for $500 or More Miscellaneous	Part Performance Promisor Benefit Detrimental Reliance
Parol Evidence Rule	**Exceptions**
Every Complete, Final Written Contract	Incomplete Contract Ambiguous Terms Fraud, Accident, or Mistake To Prove Existence or Nonbinding Character of Contract Modification of Contract Illegality

The year runs from the time the oral contract is made rather than from the date when performance is to begin. In computing the year, the day on which the contract was made is excluded.

When no time for performance is specified by the oral contract and complete performance could "conceivably occur" within one year, the statute of frauds is not applicable to the oral contract.[4] The statute of frauds does not apply if it is possible under the terms of the agreement to perform the contract within one year. Thus, a writing is not required when no time for performance is specified and the performance will not necessarily take more than a year.

When a contract may be terminated at will by either party, the statute of frauds is not applicable because the contract may be terminated within a year.

(1) Oral Extension of Contract. An oral extension of a written contract must satisfy the statute of frauds if the extension cannot be performed within one year. Thus, a two-year oral extension of a written employment contract cannot be enforced because of the statute of frauds.[5]

(b) Agreement to Sell or a Sale of an Interest in Land. All contracts to sell land, buildings, or interests in land, such as mortgages, must be evidenced by a writing. Leases are also interests in land and must be in writing, except in some states where leases for one year or less do not have to be in writing. Thus, if Mrs. O'Toole orally agrees to sell her house to the Gillespies for $250,000, and thereafter her children convince her that she could obtain $280,000 for the property if she is patient, Mrs. O'Toole can raise the defense of the

[4] *El Paso Healthcare System v Piping Rock Corp.*, 939 SW2d 695 (Tex App 1997).

[5] *Chevron USA, Inc. v Schirmer*, 11 F3d 1473 (CA9 Ariz 1993).

statute of frauds should she be sued for breach of the oral agreement. Under the *part performance doctrine,* an exception exists whereby an oral contract for the sale of land will be enforced by a court of equity in a suit for specific performance if the buyer has taken possession of the land under an oral contract and has made substantial improvements, the value of which cannot easily be ascertained, or has taken possession and paid part of the purchase price.

(c) Promise to Answer for the Debt or Default of Another. If an individual *I* promises a creditor *C* to pay the debt of *D* if *D* does not do so, *I* is promising to answer for the debt of another. Such a promise is sometimes called a **suretyship** contract and it must be in writing to be enforceable. *I* the promisor is only obligated to pay if *D* does not pay. *I*'s promise is a *collateral* or *secondary* promise, and such promises must be in writing under the statute of frauds.

(1) Main Purpose of Exception. When the main purpose of the promisor's promise to pay the debt of another is to benefit the promisor, the statute of frauds is not applicable and the oral promise to pay the debt is binding. ♦ For example, an individual *I* hires a contractor *C* to repair *I*'s building, and the supplier *S* is unwilling to extend credit to *C*. In an oral promise by *I* to pay *S* what is owed for the supplies in question if *C* does not do so, *I* is promising to pay for the debt of another, *C*. However, the *main purpose* of *I*'s promise was not to aid *C*, but rather was to get his own house repaired. This promise is not within the statute of frauds. ♦

(d) Promise by the Executor or Administrator of a Decedent's Estate to Pay a Claim against the Estate from Personal Funds. The **personal representative** (**executor** or **administrator**) has the duty of handling the affairs of a deceased person, paying the debts from the proceeds of the estate, and distributing any balance remaining. The executor or administrator is not personally liable for the claims against the estate of the **decedent.** If the personal representative promises to pay the decedent's debts with his or her own money, the promise cannot be enforced unless it is evidenced by a writing.

If the personal representative makes a contract on behalf of the estate in the course of adminis-

tering the estate, a writing is not required. The representative is then contracting on behalf of the estate. Thus, if the personal representative employs an attorney to settle the estate or makes a burial contract with an undertaker, no writing is required.

(e) Promises Made in Consideration of Marriage. Promises to pay a sum of money or give property to another in consideration of marriage must be in writing under the statute of frauds.

Thus, if Mr. Bradley orally promises to provide Karl Radford $20,000 upon Karl's marriage to Mr. Bradley's daughter Michelle, and Karl and Michelle marry, the agreement is not enforceable under the statute of frauds because it was not in writing.

Prenuptial or *antenuptial* agreements are entered into by the parties before their marriage, and, after full disclosure of each party's assets and liabilities, the parties set forth the rights of each partner regarding the property and, among other things, set forth rights and obligations should the marriage end in a separation or divorce. Such a contract must be in writing. This provision of the statute of frauds is not applicable to ordinary mutual promises to marry.

(f) Sale of Goods. As will be developed in Chapter 24 on the Nature and Form of Sales and the Uniform Commercial Code, contracts for the sale of goods priced at $500 or more must ordinarily be in writing under UCC Section 2-201.

3. Note or Memorandum

The statute of frauds requires a writing to evidence those contracts that come within its scope. This writing may be a note or memorandum as distinguished from a contract.[6] The statutory requirement is, of course, satisfied if there is a complete written contract signed by both parties.

(a) Signing. The note or memorandum must be signed by the party sought to be bound by the contract.[7] ♦ For example, in the previous sce-

---

[6] *Busler v D&H Manufacturing, Inc.,* 611 NE2d 352 (Ohio App 1992).

[7] *Blackmon v Berry,* 939 SW2d 863 (Ark App 1997).

nario involving Mark Wahlberg and Steven Spielberg, suppose the parties agree to do the film according to the same terms but agree to begin shooting the film a year from next April, and Mark writes the essential terms on a napkin, dates it and has Steven sign it, "to make sure I got it right." Mark then placed the napkin in his wallet for his records. Since the contract cannot be performed within one year after the date of the agreement a writing is required. If Steven thereafter decides not to pursue the film, Mark could enforce the contract against him because the napkin-note has been signed by the party to be bound or "sought to be charged," Steven. However, if Mark later on decides not to appear in the film, the agreement to do the film could not be enforced against Mark because no writing exists signed by Mark, the party sought to be charged. ◆

Some states require that the authorization of an agent to execute a contract coming within the statute of frauds must also be in writing.[8] In the case of an auction, it is usual practice for the auctioneer to be the agent of both parties for the purpose of signing the memorandum.

The signature may be an ordinary one or any symbol that is adopted by the party as a signature. It may consist of initials, figures, or a mark. When a signature consists of a mark made by a person who is illiterate or physically incapacitated, the name of the person is commonly required to be placed on the writing by someone else, who may be required to sign the instrument as a witness. In the absence of a local statute that provides otherwise, a signature may be made by pencil, pen, typewriter, print, or stamp.

E · COMMERCE AND CYBERLAW

Electronic Signatures in the Internet Age

Over 40 states have enacted various electronic signature statutes providing, in effect, that the use of an electronic signature on an electronic record will be treated in the same manner as a handwritten signature. Under some state laws, issues exist as to proving the authenticity of electronic signatures, however. Digital signatures using cryptographic technology are treated as self-authenticating documents in states that have digital signature laws. The lack of uniformity and certainty in the application of existing state laws has hindered the conversion of paper business transactions to an electronic environment. The Uniform Electronic Transactions Act (UETA) was adopted by the National Conference of Commissioners on Uniform State Laws in July of 1999 to establish a set of uniform rules for electronic writings and signatures that may be adopted by the states.* Clicking on "I accept" to an Internet clickwrap agreement combined with an identification procedure qualifies as an electronic signature under the UETA.

Today parties to major business and personal transactions including employment contacts of executives or the purchase of a home often use the Internet for evaluative information and use E-mail to exchange drafts of proposed contracts. However, when it comes to the execution of these contracts, the parties continue to require handwritten signatures on paper documents.

* UETA may be reviewed on the Internet at **<http://www.law.upenn.edu/bll/ulc/ulc_frame.htm>**.

(b) Content. The note or memorandum must contain all the essential terms of the contract so the court can determine just what was agreed. If any essential term is missing, the writing is not sufficient. A writing evidencing a sale of land that does not describe the land or identify the buyer does not satisfy the statute of frauds. The subject matter must be identified either within the writing itself or in other writings to which it refers. A deposit check given by the buyer to the seller does not take an oral land sales contract out of the statute of frauds. This is because the check does not set forth the terms of the sale.

The note or memorandum may consist of one writing or of separate papers, such as letters, or a combination of such papers. Separate writings cannot be considered together unless they are linked. Linkage may be express reference in each writing to the other or by the fact that each writing clearly deals with the same subject matter.

[8] *Re* W. H. Shipman, Ltd., 934 P2d 1 (Haw App 1997).

4. Effect of Noncompliance

The majority of states hold that a contract that does not comply with the statute of frauds is **voidable**.[9] A small minority of states hold that such an agreement is **void**. Under either view, if an action is brought to enforce the contract, the defendant can raise the defense that the alleged contract is not evidenced by a writing, as required by the statute of frauds.

(a) Recovery of Value Conferred. In most instances, a person who is prevented from enforcing a contract because of the statute of frauds is nevertheless entitled to recover from the other party the value of any services or property furnished or money given under the oral contract. Recovery is not based on the terms of the contract but on a quasi-contractual obligation. The other party is to restore to the plaintiff what was received in order to prevent unjust enrichment at the plaintiff's expense. ◆ For example, when an oral contract for services cannot be enforced because of the statute of frauds, the person performing the work may recover the reasonable value of the services rendered. ◆

(b) Who May Raise the Defense of Noncompliance? Only a party to the oral contract may raise a defense that it is not binding because there is no writing that satisfies the statute of frauds. Third persons, such as an insurance company or the Internal Revenue Service, cannot claim that a contract is void because the statute of frauds was not satisfied.[10]

B. PAROL EVIDENCE RULE

When the contract is evidenced by a writing, may the contract terms be changed by the testimony of witnesses?

5. Exclusion of Parol Evidence

The general rule is that parol or extrinsic evidence will not be allowed into evidence to add to, modify, or contradict the terms of a written contract that is fully integrated or complete on its face. Evidence of an alleged earlier oral or written agreement, within the scope of the fully integrated written contract, or evidence of an alleged contemporaneous oral agreement, within the scope of the fully integrated written contract, is inadmissible as *parol evidence*. Parol evidence is admissible, however, to show fraud, duress, or mistake and under certain other circumstances to be discussed in the following paragraphs.

The **parol evidence rule** is based on the theory that either there never was an oral agreement, or, if there was, the parties abandoned it when they reached the stage in negotiations of executing their written contract. The social objective of the parol evidence rule is to give stability to contracts and to prevent the assertion of terms that did not exist or did not survive the bargaining of the parties so as to reach inclusion in the final written contract.

◆ For example, L (landlord), the owner of a new development containing a five-store mall, discusses leasing one of the stores to T (tenant), who is viewing the property with his sister S, a highly credible poverty worker on leave from her duties in Central America. L, in the presence of S, agrees to give T the exclusive right to sell coffee and soft drinks in the five-store mall. Soon L and T execute a detailed written lease for the store, which makes no provision for T's exclusive right to sell soft drinks and coffee in the mall. Subsequently, when two of the mall's new tenants began to sell soft drinks and coffee, T brought suit against L for the breach of the oral promise granting him exclusive rights to sell soft drinks and coffee. T calls S as his first witness to prove the existence of the oral promise. L, through his attorney, will object to the admission of any evidence of a prior oral agreement that would add to or amend the fully integrated written lease, which set forth all restrictions on the landlord and tenant as to uses of the premises. After study of the matter, the court, based on the parol evidence rule, will not hear testimony from either S or T about the oral promise L made to T. In order to preserve his exclusive right to sell

---

[9] The UCC creates several statutes of frauds of limited applicability in which it uses the phrase "not enforceable": § 1-206 (sale of intangible personal property);§ 2-201 (sale of goods); and § 8-319 (sale of securities). The Official Code Comment, point 4, to§ 2-201 describes "not enforceable" as meaning what would ordinarily be called "voidable." Note that the 1994 Revision of Article 8 abolishes the statute of frauds with respect to securities. UCC § 8-113 [1994 Revision].

[10] *O'Daniels' Estate v United States,* 6 F3d 321 (CA5 Tex 1993).

the drinks in question, *T* should have made certain that this promise was made part of the lease. His lawsuit will not be successful. ◆

6. When the Parol Evidence Rule Does Not Apply

The parol evidence rule will not apply in certain cases. The most common of these are discussed in the following paragraphs.

(a) Ambiguity. If a written contract is **ambiguous** or may have two or more different meanings, parol evidence may generally be admitted to clarify the meaning.[11]

Parol evidence may also be admitted to show that a word used in a contract has a special trade meaning or a meaning in the particular locality that differs from the common meaning of that word.

The fact that the parties disagree about the meaning of the contract does not mean that it is ambiguous.[12]

(b) Fraud, Duress, or Mistake. A contract apparently complete on its face may have omitted a provision that should have been included. Parol evidence may be admitted to show that a provision was omitted as the result of fraud, duress, or mistake and to further show what that provision stated. Parol evidence is admissible to show that a provision of the written contract was a mistake even though the written provision is unambiguous.[13] When one party claims to have been fraudulently induced by the other to enter into a contract, the parol evidence role does not bar proof that there was a fraud. ◆ For example, the parol evidence rule does not bar proof that the seller of land intentionally misrepresented that the land was zoned to permit use as an industrial park. ◆ Such evidence does not contradict the terms of the contract but shows that the agreement is unenforceable.[14]

(c) Modification of Contract. The parol evidence rule prohibits only the contradiction of a complete written contract. It does not prohibit proof that the contract was thereafter modified or terminated.

The *Bourg* case deals with an asserted oral modification of a written agreement.

Bourg v Bristol Boat Co.
705 A2d 969 (RI 1998)

All Sail and No Anchor

On April 2, 1990, Christian Bourg hired the Bristol Boat Co., Inc., and Bristol Marine Co. (defendants) to construct and deliver a yacht on July 1, 1990. However, the defendants did not live up to their promises and the contract was breached. On October 22, 1990, the defendants executed a written settlement agreement whereby Mr. Bourg agreed to pay an additional sum of $135,000 for the delivery of the yacht and to provide the defendants a loan of $80,000 to complete the construction of the vessel. Referencing the settlement agreement, the defendants at the same time executed a promissory note obliging them to repay the $80,000 loan plus interest in

---

[11] *Berg v Hudesman,* 801 P2d 222 (Wash 1990). This is also the view followed by UCC §2-202(a), which permits terms in a contract for the sale of goods to be "explained or supplemented by a course of dealing or usage of trade . . . or by course of performance." Such evidence is admissible not because there is an ambiguity but "in order that the true understanding of the parties as to the agreement may be reached." Official Code Comment to § 2-202.

[12] *Baker's Supermarkets, Inc. v Feldman,* 502 NW2d 428 (Neb 1993).

[13] *CMI Food Service, Inc. v Hatridge Leasing,* 890 SW2d 420 (Mo App 1995).

[14] *Edwards v Centrex Real Estate Corp.,* 61 Cal Rptr 518 (Cal App 1997).

annual installments due on November 1 of each year, with the final payment due on November 1, 1994. The court stated in presenting the facts, "However, like the yacht itself, the settlement agreement soon proved to be just another hole in the water into which the plaintiff threw his money." Bourg sued the defendants after they failed to make certain payments on the note, and the trial court granted a motion for summary judgment in favor of Bourg for $59,081. The defendants appealed.

The defendants asserted that the trial court was in error because "at the time of the execution of the promissory note and settlement agreement upon which Plaintiff relies, it was understood and agreed that a substantial part of the note would be paid for by services rendered by the defendants. . . ."

FLANDERS, J. . . . [T]he statement in defendants' affidavit that the alleged oral modification was agreed to "*[a]t the time of* the execution of the promissory note and settlement agreement" (emphasis added) eviscierates defendants' contention on appeal that it was in fact a subsequent oral modification. Rather, because the affidavit recites that the alleged oral side agreement was entered into *at the time of* the settlement agreement and promissory note, it would have constituted a contemporaneous modification that would merge into the integrated promissory note and settlement agreement and thus be barred from admission into evidence under the parol evidence rule. In short, this alleged contemporaneous oral modification was legally "immaterial in ascertaining the terms of the transaction" between plaintiff and defendants. *Fram Corp.*, 121 R.I. at 587–88, 401 A.2d at 1272.

Finally, although parties to an integrated written contract—that is, "one where the parties adopt a writing or writings as a final and complete expression of [their] agreement," *id.* at 587, 401 A.2d at 1272—can modify their understanding by a subsequent oral pact, to be legally effective there must be evidence of mutual assent to the essential terms of the modification and adequate consideration. Here the defendants adduced no competent evidence of either mutual assent to particular terms or of a specific consideration that would be sufficiently definite to constitute an enforceable subsequent oral modification to the parties' earlier written agreements. Thus legally this alleged oral alteration was all sail and no anchor.

[Judgment affirmed]

Questions

1. Did the parties have a fully integrated written contract concerning the loan of $80,000 and the promissory note?
2. Can a contemporaneous oral agreement that "it was understood and agreed that a substantial part of the note would be paid for by services rendered by the defendants" be given weight as evidence to contradict the 1990 written settlement agreement and note that called for annual cash payments to repay the $80,000 loan?
3. Must a subsequent oral modification to a written agreement meet the essential elements for contract formation, including an agreement, and consideration?

ETHICS AND THE LAW

Marvin Windows and Doors Company of Minnesota is the largest custom window manufacturer in the world. The president of this privately held company, Bill Marvin and his son Jake, the company's chief operating officer, met with PPG Industries Bob Ponchot on Jake's front lawn on a summer morning in 1984 and listened to Mr. Ponchot sell PPG's new wood preservative PILT. Relying on the promises made on behalf of PPG by

Mr. Ponchot, Bill Marvin made a handshake deal to use the new product. The product was used for 4 years and soon thereafter Marvin Windows started receiving complaints about premature wood rot. Marvin Windows study of the problem concluded that PILT was the problem. PPG's analysis found PILT blameless, and it refused to help Marvin cover the cost of replacing the defective windows. In 1994 Marvin Windows sued PPG, *inter alia*, for breach of contract and four years of discovery ensued. Bill Marvin states that promises were made on Jake's lawn that summer morning and he had a right to rely on them. "We never had a written a contract, and I don't think that's naïve. They reneged on a handshake deal and simply speaking, that's not right." PPG defended that there was no written agreement obliging PPG to pay for a portion of the cost of replacing the defective windows. PPG's attorney asserted that, "Marvin Windows likes to tell you about a family run business from a small town in Minnesota who does business on a handshake . . . but they are a hundred million dollar international corporation with a long history of litigation." He further asserted that, "experienced merchants ought to be smart enough to write a contract outlining who is responsible for what if the product they are buying doesn't work properly." Is Bill Marvin or PPG correct? Is it good business practice to have a written contract in effect for all company purchases, specifying the responsibilities of the parties if each product purchased does not work properly, or will this lead to a "Battles of the Forms" and increased expenses for both parties? Based on the assertions made by both Bill and Jake Marvin about the promises made by PPG is it unethical for PPG to renege on the promises? UCC§2-725 sets forth a four years time limitation period, called a statute of limitations, after which period the party seeking a remedy can no longer resort to the courts. Did Marvin wait to long to bring the law suit?

SUMMARY

An oral agreement may be a contract unless it is the intention of the parties that they should not be bound by the agreement unless a writing is executed by them. Certain contracts must be evidenced by a writing, however, or else they cannot be enforced. The statutes that declare this exception are called statutes of frauds. Statutes of frauds commonly require that a contract be evidenced by writing in the case of (1) an agreement that cannot be performed within one year after the contract is made, (2) an agreement to sell any interest in land, (3) a promise to answer for the debt or default of another, (4) a promise by the executor or administrator of a decedent's estate to pay a claim against the estate from personal funds, (5) a promise made in consideration of marriage, and (6) a contract for the sale of goods for a purchase price of $500 or more.

To evidence a contract to satisfy a statute of frauds, there must be a writing of all essential terms. This must be signed by the defendant against whom suit is brought for enforcement of the contract or damages for its breach. The signing may be made by printing, typewriting, or any other means that is intended to identify the particular party.

Two or more writings can be combined to form a writing sufficient to satisfy the statute of frauds, provided there is an express internal reference in the writings that ties them together.

If the applicable statute of frauds is not satisfied, the oral contract cannot be enforced. To avoid unjust enrichment, a plaintiff barred from enforcing an oral contract may recover from the other contracting party the reasonable value of the benefits conferred by the plaintiff on the defendant.

When there is a written contract, the question arises whether that writing is the exclusive statement of the parties' agreement. If the writing is the complete and final statement of the contract, parol evidence as to matters agreed to before or at the time of the writing was signed is not admissible to contradict the writing. This is called the parol evidence rule. In any case, the parol evidence rule does not bar parol evidence when (1) the writing is ambiguous; (2) the writing is not a true statement of the agreement of the parties because of fraud, duress, or mistake; or (3) the existence, modification, or illegality of a contract is in controversy. The fact that the parties disagree about the meaning of a contract or that a court decision is required to settle the point does not make the writing ambiguous. Parol evidence may be used to prove that there is in fact no contract because there is a mutual mistake or the writing that has been executed does not correctly set forth the terms of the contract.

WEBSITE REFERENCES

To view a slide show addressing principals of contract interpretation visit:

> **http://falcon.cc.ukans.edu/~mlevin/slide16/ sld001.htm**

To explore the European default rules for interpreting contracts visit:

> **http://www.ufsia.ac.be/~estorme/PECL2en5. html**

QUESTIONS AND CASE PROBLEMS

1. What social forces are affected by the following rule of law? "Parol evidence is not admissible for the purpose of modifying a written contract when that evidence relates to an agreement made before or at the time that the written contract was executed."

2. In a telephone conversation, Roderick agreed to buy Dexter's house. All the details of the transaction were agreed to in the conversation. The next day Dexter wrote Roderick a letter stating: "This confirms the agreement we made last night that I should sell you my home." Later, Dexter refused to go through with the transaction. Roderick sued Dexter. Will Roderick recover?

3. Kelly made a written contract to sell certain land to Brown and gave Brown a deed to the land. Thereafter, Kelly sued Brown to get back a 20-foot strip of the land. Kelly claimed that before making the written contract it was agreed that Kelly would sell all of his land to Brown to make it easier for Brown to get a building permit, but that after that was done, the 20-foot strip would be reconveyed to Kelly. Was Kelly entitled to the 20-foot strip? What ethical values are involved? [*Brown v Kelly,* 545 So 2d 518 (Fla App)]

4. Martin made an oral contract with Cresheim Garage to work as its manager for two years. Cresheim wrote Martin a letter stating that the oral contract had been made and setting forth all its terms. Cresheim later refused to recognize the contract. Martin sued Cresheim for breach of the contract and offered Cresheim's letter in evidence as proof of the contract. Cresheim claimed that the oral contract was not binding because the contract was not in writing and the letter referring to the contract was not a contract but only a letter. Was the contract binding?

5. Lawrence loaned money to Moore, who died without repaying the loan. Lawrence claimed that when he mentioned the matter to Moore's widow, she promised to pay the debt. She did not do so, and Lawrence sued her on her promise. Does she have any defense? [*Moore v Lawrence,* 480 SW2d 941 (Ark)]

6. Jackson signed an agreement to sell 79 acres of land to Devenyns. Jackson owned 80 acres and was apparently intending to keep for himself the acre on which his home was located. The written agreement also stated, "Devenyns shall have the option to buy on property _____," but nothing was stated in the blank space. Devenyns sued to enforce the agreement. Was it binding? [*Re* Jackson's Estate, 892 P2d 786 (Wyo)]

7. Boeing Airplane Co. contracted with Pittsburgh–Des Moines Steel Co. for the latter to construct a supersonic wind tunnel. R.H. Freitag Mfg. Co. sold materials to York-Gillespie Co., which subcontracted to do part of the work. To persuade Freitag to keep supplying materials on credit, Boeing and the principal contractor both assured Freitag that he would be paid. When Freitag was not paid by

the subcontractor, he sued Boeing and the contractor. They defended on the ground that the assurances given Freitag were not written. Decide. What ethical values are involved? [*R.H. Freitag Mfg. Co. v Boeing Airplane Co.*, 347 P2d 1074 (Wash)]

8. An accounting firm sold out its business to a new firm. The sales contract stated that it was the intention of the parties that the new firm should provide service for clients of the old firm. The new firm agreed to pay the old firm 15 percent of the gross billings for assignments performed by the new firm for a period of 84 months. Later, a dispute arose as to whether the 15 percent of gross billings was limited to the billings of those who were originally clients of the old firm or whether it also included billings of new clients of the new firm. In a lawsuit over this point, parol evidence was offered to show what the contract covered. Was this evidence admissible? [*Rullman v LaFrance, Walker, Jackley & Saville*, 292 NW2d 19 (Neb)]

9. With respect to the applicability of the statute of frauds, compare (a) a promise made by an aunt to her niece to pay the niece's bill owed to a department store, (b) a promise made by the aunt to the department store to pay the amount the aunt owes the store for a television set the aunt purchased as a present for her niece, and (c) a promise made by the aunt to the department store that she would pay her niece's bill if the niece did not do so.

10. Louise Pulsifer owned a farm. She desired to sell the farm and ran an ad in the local newspaper. After Russell Gillespie agreed to purchase the farm, Pulsifer wrote him a letter stating that she would not sell it. He sued her to enforce the contract, and she raised the defense of the statute of frauds. The letter signed by her did not contain any of the terms of the sale. Gillespie, however, claimed that the newspaper ad could be combined with her letter to satisfy the statute of frauds. Was he correct? [*Gillespie v Pulsifer*, 655 SW2d 123 (Mo)]

11. McLarty claimed that he and Wright made an oral contract to start a business under the name of DeKalb Textile Mill, Inc.; to incorporate the business; and to divide the stock equally. The alleged contract was not performed, and McLarty sued Wright for breach of contract. Wright raised the defense of the statute of frauds, asserting that it was not specified that the contract should be performed within one year of making. Was this defense valid? [*McLarty v Wright*, 321 So 2d 687 (Ala Civ App)]

12. In February or March, Corning Glass Works orally agreed to retain Hanan as management consultant from May 1 of that year to April 30 of the next year for a total fee of $25,000. Was this agreement binding? Is this decision ethical? [*Hanan v Corning Glass Works*, 314 NYS2d 804 (App Div)]

13. Levina made a contract with Thompson. She later claimed that she could enforce the terms of an earlier agreement that they had made a week before. Thompson claimed that proof of that agreement was barred by the parol evidence rule. Levina claimed this was not so because (1) she never intended that the written contract should wipe out the earlier oral agreement, and (2) the written contract did not state it was the entire agreement of the parties and displaced all prior agreements. Were her objections valid?

14. When Holdings and Thriftway borrowed money from the Northland Bank, Filipek and others guaranteed that the loans would be paid back. Touche Ross was appointed to liquidate the assets of the bank. The loans to Holdings and Thriftway were not repaid when due. Touche Ross sued Filipek and the other guarantors on their obligation to repay the loans. They raised the defense that they were not bound by their guarantees because they and the borrower had been induced to enter into the transactions by the bank's fraudulent statements and promises. Touche Ross claimed that the parol evidence rule barred any evidence that the parties had been induced by fraud. Could the guarantors produce parol evidence to support their claim of fraud? [*Touche Ross Ltd. v Filipek*, 778 P2d 721 (Haw App)]

15. While Celeste was in New York, the manager of Kendall Corp. of Galveston, Texas, interviewed her for the position of head of the corporate accounting department. The manager

told her to send her application to Galveston and that he believed she would be given a five-year contract for the job. Within a few days after the manager left New York, Celeste sold her New York home, quit her New York job, and went to Texas. When she arrived, she was told that the vacancy had been filled by someone else. She sued Kendall for breach of contract, and it contended there was no writing to evidence existence of the contract. Celeste raised the counterdefense of promissory estoppel. Decide.

CPA QUESTIONS

1. Which of the following statements is true with regard to the statute of frauds?
   a. All contracts involving consideration of more than $500 must be in writing.
   b. The written contract must be signed by all parties.
   c. The statute of frauds applies to contracts that can be fully performed within one year from the date they are made.
   d. The contract terms may be stated in more than one document.
2. With regard to an agreement for the sale of real estate, the statute of frauds
   a. Requires that the entire agreement be in a single writing
   b. Requires that the purchase price be fair and adequate in relation to the value of the real estate
   c. Does *not* require that the agreement be signed by all parties
   d. Does *not* apply if the value of the real estate is less than $500
3. In negotiations with Andrews for the lease of Kemp's warehouse, Kemp orally agreed to pay one-half of the cost of the utilities. The written lease, later prepared by Kemp's attorney, provided that Andrews pay all of the utilities. Andrews failed to carefully read the lease and signed it. When Kemp demanded that Andrews pay all of the utilities, Andrews refused, claiming that the lease did not accurately reflect the oral agreement. Andrews also learned that Kemp intentionally misrepresented the condition of the structure of the warehouse during the negotiations between the parties. Andrews sued to rescind the lease and intends to introduce evidence of the parties' oral agreement about sharing the utilities and the fraudulent statements made by Kemp. The parol evidence rule will prevent the admission of evidence concerning the

	Oral agreement regarding who pays the utilities	Fraudulent statements by Kemp
a.	Yes	Yes
b.	No	Yes
c.	Yes	No
d.	No	No

Interpretation of Contracts

Learning Objectives

After studying this chapter, you should be able to

1. Compare the effects of objective and subjective intent of the parties to a contract
2. Distinguish between conditions precedent and conditions subsequent
3. State the rules for interpreting ambiguous terms in a contract
4. State the effect of contradictory terms
5. Define and illustrate implied terms
6. State what controls the choice of law applicable to an interstate contract

When it has been decided that there is a contract between the parties, the next step is to determine what the contract means.

A. RULES OF CONSTRUCTION AND INTERPRETATION

In interpreting contracts, courts are aided by certain rules.

1. Intention of the Parties

When persons enter into an agreement, it is to be presumed they intend that their agreement should have some effect. A court will strive to determine the intent of the parties and to give effect to it. A contract is therefore to be enforced according to its terms. A court cannot remake or rewrite the contract of the parties under the pretense of interpreting it.[1] If there is a dispute as to the meaning of a contract, the court examines the contract to determine what the parties intended. It will then give effect to this intent, so long as it is lawful.

No particular form of words is required, and any words manifesting the intent of the parties are sufficient. In the absence of proof that a word has a peculiar meaning or that it was employed by the parties with a particular meaning, a common word is given its ordinary meaning.[2]

(a) Objective Intent. When it is stated that the law seeks to enforce the intent of the parties, this means the intent that is outwardly manifested. That is, what would a reasonable third person believe the parties intended? It is this **objective intent** that will be enforced.

(b) Meaning of Words. Ordinary words are to be interpreted according to their ordinary meaning.[3]

When a contract requires the gasoline dealer to pay the supplier for "gallons" supplied, the term *gallons* is unambiguous and does not require that an adjustment of the gallonage be made for the temperature.[4]

If there is a common meaning to a term, that meaning will be followed even though the dictionary may contain additional meanings. If technical or trade terms are used in a contract, they are to be interpreted according to the area of technical knowledge or trade from which the terms are taken.

The prior relationships of the parties may give meaning to the words used by the parties.[5]

(c) Incorporation by Reference. The contract may not cover all the agreed terms. The missing terms may be found in another document. Frequently, the parties executing the contract will state that it embraces or incorporates the other document. Thus, a contract for storage will simply state that a storage contract is entered into and that the contract applies to the goods that are listed in the schedule that is attached to and made part of the contract. Likewise, a contract for the construction of a building may involve plans and specifications on file in a named city office. The contract will simply state that the building is to be constructed according to those plans and specifications that are "incorporated herein and made part of this contract." When there is such an **incorporation by reference,** the contract consists of both the original document and the detailed statement that is incorporated in it.

E T H I C S   A N D   T H E   L A W

John J. Mellencamp, professionally known at various times as John Cougar, John Cougar Mellencamp, or John Mellencamp, is a songwriter, performer, and recording artist who has enjoyed enormous success since the early 1980s.

Through a series of agreements, Mellencamp had assigned the copyrights to his songs to Riva Music. He was not pleased with the arrangement, however, because he felt he had not been paid all the royalties he was entitled to and that Riva had not acted in good faith in promoting his songs.

During a luncheon meeting held in a New York City restaurant in March 1987, Mellencamp's accountant Sigmund Balaban, Riva owner William Gaff, and Gaff's attorney Milton Marks,

---

[1] *Paddison Builders v Turncliff,* 672 So2d 1133 (La App 1996).

[2] *Ex parte Agee,* 669 So2d 102 (Ala 1995).

[3] *Thornton v D.F.W. Christian Television, Inc.,* 925 SW2d 17 (Tex App 1995).

[4] *Hopkins v BP Oil, Inc.,* 81 F3d 1070 (11th Cir 1996).

[5] See Section 3 of this chapter.

entered into an alleged agreement to sell Mellencamp's copyrights back to him for $3 million.

Gary Baker served as Gaff's attorney for the due diligence process and drafting the oral agreement. Henry Goldstein served as Mellencamp's attorney. Goldstein sent the following letter to Baker on April 1, 1987:

I enclose a preliminary Document Request List in connection with our preparation of an agreement pursuant to which, among other things, John Mellencamp will effect the cancellation of his songwriter agreements with Riva Music et al.

Please note that the Document Request List is designed for our due diligence, investigation and evaluation and, accordingly, is intended to be illustrative rather than exhaustive. It is expected that, during the course of our review of the materials and our preparation of the agreement, we will make requests for additional information.

On April 27, Baker received a draft agreement from Mr. Goldstein accompanied by a letter that stated the following:

I enclose a draft of the proposed agreement between John J. Mellencamp and Riva Music pursuant to which, among other things, John Mellencamp will effect the cancellation of his songwriter agreements with Riva Music et al.

Under separate cover, I will shortly be sending you the various Exhibits to the proposed agreement. I would appreciate it if, while you are reviewing the proposed agreement, you prepare the Schedules to the proposed agreement and forward same to me.

As soon as you have reviewed the proposed agreement, please call me.

Please note that I am simultaneously sending a copy of the proposed agreement to our client for review; therefore, I must reserve the right to make any changes which it may require.

On April 21, 1987, Balaban sent a letter to Mellencamp that included the following:

I have been in frequent communication with Hank Goldstein regarding the proposed contract with Riva Music Ltd. and its associated entities.

In that connection Hank forwarded to me a preliminary draft dated April 16, 1987, for my comments. I suggested to Hank that he delete certain words on page 1 of the draft because they do not

appear to me to be necessary, and may result in a hostile reaction from Gaff. . . .

I have also indicated to Hank that while Gaff and his companies should release you from all obligations under the prior agreements, there does not appear to be any reason for you to release Gaff et al. from anything, except acting as your publisher. This is of course the lawyer's domain.

Gaff had not signed the agreement. Both Mellencamp and Balaban indicated their intent was to be bound, and Balaban testified as follows at the trial about the luncheon meeting:

At the conclusion of the meeting Milton Marks, William Gaff and I joined hands and Milton Marks solemnly stated the Hebrew words "Mazel Bracha," which literally means "good fortune and good blessing" and which are customarily said in some circles to evidence a firm agreement. I am also aware that in the entertainment business handshake agreements, particularly where there have been extensive negotiations prior to the agreement, are honored and binding.

Would you interpret the letters as indicating there was a binding agreement? Was the conduct at the close of the lunch meeting relevant? Was it ethical for Gaff to withhold his signature from the agreement? Is the fact that the sale fell through after an oral agreement simply just a risk of business?

Mellencamp v Riva Music, Ltd., 698 F Supp 1154 (DC NY 1988).

(d) Expectations Distinguished from Meaning. A contract means what it says. A contracting party must avoid reading into a contract something that it does not say because that is what the party expects, hopes for, or wants. ◆ For example, the word *permanent* in a contract provision for permanent employment does not mean that the employment will continue unless the employee is discharged for cause but merely indicates that the employment is not temporary or seasonal.[6] ◆

(e) Economic Realities. In searching for the intent of the parties, a court will view their contract

---

[6] *Friedman v BRW, Inc.*, 40 F3d 293 (8th Cir 1994).

in the context of the economic realities surrounding its execution. Consequently, when uncertainty exists over whether new or used goods are to be sold, or the kind of insurance that is provided, the court may properly consider what is being paid because the payment and performance specified in a contract usually are commensurate.

2. Whole Contract

The provisions of a contract must be construed as a whole in such a way that every part is given effect.

Every word of a contract is to be given effect if reasonably possible. The contract is to be construed as a whole, and if the plain language of the contract thus viewed solves the dispute, no further analysis is to be made by the court.[7]

3. Contradictory and Ambiguous Terms

One term in a contract may conflict with another term, or one term may have two different meanings. It is then necessary for the court to determine whether there is a contract and, if so, what the contract really means. When the terms of a contract are contradictory or conflict about a significant matter, this conflict precludes the existence of any contract.

In some instances, conflict between the terms of a contract is eliminated by the introduction of parol evidence or by the application of an appropriate rule of construction.

(a) **Nature of Writing.** When a contract is partly a printed form or partly typewritten and partly handwritten, and the written part conflicts with the printed or typewritten part, the written part prevails. When there is a conflict between a printed part and a typewritten part, the latter prevails. Consequently, when a clause typewritten on a printed form conflicts with what is stated by the print, the conflicting print is ignored and the typewritten clause controls. This rule is based on the belief that the parties had given greater

thought to what they typed or wrote for the particular contract as contrasted with printed words already in a form designed to cover many transactions. Thus, a typewritten provision to pay 90 cents per unit overrode a preprinted provision setting the price as 45 cents per unit.[8]

When there is a conflict between an amount or quantity expressed both in words and figures, as on a check, the amount or quantity expressed in words prevails. Words control because there is less danger that a word will be wrong than a number.

(b) **Ambiguity.** A contract is **ambiguous** when the intent of the parties is uncertain and the contract is capable of more than one reasonable interpretation.[9] Some courts refuse to look beyond the four corners to the written contract for determining if the contract contains any ambiguity. Other courts reject this **four corners rule** and look at the contract in the light of the situation in which it was made to determine if it is ambiguous.[10]

Disagreement over the legal effect of terms used by the parties does not make the contract ambiguous. This is so because the court, by applying the law to their terms, can reach a conclusion as to the intent manifested by the contract. In contrast, if the intent would still be uncertain even after rules of law were applied the contract is ambiguous.

Whether a contract is ambiguous cannot always be determined merely by looking at it. In some cases, the written contract will look perfectly clear, and the ambiguity does not become apparent until the contract is applied to the facts or the property concerned.[11]

The fact that a particular situation is not provided for by the contract does not make it ambiguous. ◆ For example, a summer camp contract is not ambiguous because it does not contain

---

[7] *Atlantic Mut. Ins. Co. v Metron Engineering and Construction Co.,* 83 F3d 897 (7th Cir 1996).

[8] *Honingsbaum's, Inc. v Stuyvesant Plaza, Inc.,* 577 NYS2d 165 (App Div 1991).

[9] *Kauffman & Stewart v Weinbrenner Shoe Co.* 589 NW2d 499 (Minn App 1999).

[10] *R.T. Hepworth Co. v Dependable Ins. Co.,* 997 F2d 315 (CA7 III 1993).

[11] *Sparrow v Tayco Construction Co.,* 846 P2d 1323 (Utah App 1993).

any provision relating to refunds if cancellation occurs. ◆

The background from which the contract and the dispute arose may help in determining the intention of the parties. Thus, when suit was brought in Minnesota on a Canadian insurance policy, the question arose whether the dollar limit of the policy referred to Canadian or U.S. dollars. The court concluded that Canadian dollars were intended. Both the insurer and the insured were Canadian corporations; the original policy, endorsements to the policy, and policy renewals were written in Canada; over the years, premiums had been paid in Canadian dollars; and a prior claim on the policy had been settled by the payment of an amount computed on the basis of Canadian dollars.

(c) Strict Construction against Drafting Party. An ambiguous contract is interpreted strictly against the party who drafted it.[12] Thus, printed forms of insurance policies that are supplied by the insurer are interpreted against the insurer and in favor of the insured when two interpretations are reasonably possible. If the contract is clear and unambiguous, it will be enforced according to its terms even though this benefits the party who drafted the contract.

4. Implied Terms

In some cases, a court will imply a term to cover a situation for which the parties failed to provide or, when needed, to give the contract a construction or meaning that is reasonable.

A term will not be implied in a contract when the court concludes that the silence of the contract on the particular point was intentional.

(a) Duration of Contract. When a contract is to continue over a period of time but no duration is specified in the contract, courts will imply that the contract is to be performed or will continue for a reasonable time. But either party may terminate the contract by giving notice to the other party.

An employment contract that does not specify any duration may be terminated by either party at any time for any reason.[13]

(b) Details of Performance. Details of performance of a contract not expressly stated in the contract will often be implied by the court. In a contract to perform work, there is an implied promise to use such skill as is necessary for the proper performance of the work. In a "cost plus" contract, it is implied that the costs will be reasonable and proper. When a contract does not specify where money is to be paid, it will be implied that the payment is to be made to the creditor at the creditor's office or place of business.

When a contract does not specify the time for performance, a reasonable time is implied. "Reasonable time for a contract's performance is not measured by hours, days, weeks, months or years, but is to be determined from the surrounding conditions and circumstances which the parties contemplated at the time the contract was executed.[14]

(c) Good Faith. In every contract, there is an implied obligation that neither party shall do anything that will have the effect of destroying or injuring the right of the other party to receive the fruits of the contract. This means that in every contract there exists an implied covenant of **good faith** and fair dealing. Thus, an owner having the right under a contract with a real estate developer to approve or reject the plans submitted by the developer was guilty of a breach of the duty to act in good faith when it was shown that the owner refused to approve the developer's plans, not because the plans were disapproved, but because the owner was trying to get more money from the developer.

The *El Paso Natural Gas Co.* case deals with the question whether the marketer of natural gas had breached its implied obligation of good faith in negotiating a release from its obligations under a gas purchase agreement.

---

[12] *Idaho Migrant Council, Inc. v Warila*, 890 P2d 39 (Wyo 1995).

[13] *Wlasiuk v Whirlpool Corp.*, 914 P2d 102 (Wash App 1996).

[14] *Miller v. Beales*, 608 NE2d 1133 (Ohio App 1992).

El Paso Natural Gas Co. v Minco Oil & Gas Co.
964 SW2d 54 (Tex App 1998)

Natural Gas or Pure Deceit?

Minco Oil & Gas Co. executed "take-or-pay" gas purchase agreements in 1979 with El Paso Natural Gas Co. Under these agreements, Minco and other producers dedicated to El Paso all the natural gas that could be produced on their properties. In turn, El Paso agreed to purchase a specified minimum quantity per day. If it failed to purchase the minimum quantity, then El Paso was required to nevertheless pay for the difference between the amount actually taken and the minimum quantity it was required to take. That is, El Paso was required to "take or pay" up to the minimum quantity. For several years, all parties performed as expected. By the mid 1980s, natural gas prices fell substantially, and El Paso realized that its contracts with Minco were not profitable. It set out to negotiate a release from its obligation to take-or-pay from Minco and other producers, and certain releases were signed. Thereafter, Minco sued El Paso for violating the take-or-pay provision in the 1979 agreement; El Paso defended based on the releases; and Minco replied that the company had breached its implied obligation of good faith in the negotiation of the releases. From a judgment for Minco, El Paso appealed.

QUINN, J. . . . In considering the entire record, we find evidence illustrating that the gas market experienced appreciable decline several years after the 1979 Agreements were executed. And, there is no question that the drop in price was caused by factors outside the control of El Paso. Given that, one could say that El Paso had a legitimate commercial reason for endeavoring to ameliorate the situation by modifying its obligations to take-or-pay at the price and quantity set forth in the 1979 Agreements.

Yet, the record contains evidence illustrating that El Paso did more than simply approach its producers, inform them of its predicament, and attempt to negotiate a modification. Rather, in 1982, the company unilaterally reduced the amount of gas it took to less than the 80% minimum specified in the 1979 Agreements. Furthermore, it did so without disclosing its intent to Minco. It further decided, unilaterally, to eschew *voluntary* payment for the gas it did not take. That is, the 1979 Agreements contained a provision specifying the date by which El Paso had to pay for the gas it did not take. However, El Paso simply decided to ignore that provision, again without notifying its producers. Instead, the company opted to remain silent until a producer made inquiry into the situation. And, once that happened, it interposed excuses for its conduct, denied any liability, and forced them into negotiations to resolve the claim.*

Furthermore, during the "denial/negotiation" process, the producers like Minco were effectively "boxed in," as another El Paso employee eventually admitted. Again, they had dedicated 100% of their product to El Paso. So, they could not sell it to others without El Paso's consent, and needless to say, El Paso was not consenting to such sales without first being released from potential liability for not performing.

---

* A memo drafted by an El Paso employee named Bernard termed this procedure as the denial/negotiation process. And, though the company objected to the admission of the Bernard memo describing the procedure, the objection was not incorporated into a point of error. Furthermore, other evidence admitted without objection revealed that El Paso's actions comported with the general guidelines espoused by Bernard. In effect, El Paso actually did many of the things described in the memo. Given this, it can be said that the memo was merely redundant of admissible evidence, and that its admission was, therefore, not error.

So, having placed Minco in a box which at least one court believed to be unfair, El Paso tendered the Amendatory Agreement to the producer. In the cover letter accompanying the agreement, the buyer represented that it was "firmly committed to solving [the problems facing it] so as to remain capable of marketing your gas." So, El Paso proposed that if Minco would agree to *retroactively* and prospectively reduce both the price to be paid for gas and quantity to be taken, then the prospects for El Paso taking gas in the future would be enhanced.

As to the change in minimum take-or-pay percentage, El Paso maintained that the agreement was "soft"; that is, the provisions of the original 1979 Agreement could still be invoked to either reduce the percentage or entirely relieve the company of its duty to take-or-pay for a particular period. However, the producer's obligation to dedicate 100% of its gas to El Paso remained. So, in effect, the previously unfair contract was further enhanced in favor of El Paso. For all practical purposes, the latter found a way to escape potential liability for its prior conduct and make it easier for it to avoid, conceivably *in toto*, its future take-or-pay duties while keeping the producers obligated to dedicate all their gas to it. And, more importantly, all this was done under the pretense of enabling itself to acquire more gas from them.

But, instead of finding that El Paso was buying more, Minco encountered the opposite. Indeed, within a short time, El Paso began to forward to its producers monthly release letters. Though their format varied from time to time, their substance did not. Each informed the producer that El Paso did not intend to or could not buy gas during that month. The reasons given for avoiding its obligations were several. For instance, at times they were told that governmental regulations or the status of the market prevented it from complying. Yet, those two reasons proved less than accurate. For instance, a company representative admitted that no regulation actually prohibited it from taking gas in any particular month. This same representative also conceded that the gas could have actually been taken and paid for.

Another reason why El Paso chose not to perform was its supposed policy barring discrimination among its producers. In other words, since the total amount of gas it was required to take from all its producers exceeded its need, it chose either to forgo taking gas from any or to take a prorated fraction from all. Yet, in applying this policy against discrimination, El Paso again proved to be less than candid. For instance, in none of its monthly release letters did the company disclose to the producers that while it was not taking from them, it was actually buying gas on the spot market (at a reduced price) from *its own affiliates*. In other words, El Paso was using its anti-discrimination policy in a way to discriminate in favor of it and its own.

And, as to the assurances made in the monthly letters regarding its dedication to helping Minco and the others to "maximize [their] production and revenues," El Paso also omitted to tell them of other adverse affects they would suffer by agreeing to the temporary releases. Admittedly, the producers would gain the option to sell their product on the spot market (at a lesser price most likely). But, they would be extending to El Paso the option to either eliminate its take-or-pay obligation for that month or offset the amount of gas sold against its cumulative take-or-pay obligation. Moreover, El Paso admitted that the option it intended to select would be that most advantageous to it and most disadvantageous to the producer. That suggests a mode of conduct contrary to the supposed desire to maximize the production and revenues of Minco.

Finally tiring of El Paso's ongoing practice, Minco asked to end the contractual relationship. In effect, El Paso was not buying Minco's gas, and Minco could not sell it elsewhere without El Paso's approval.

When viewed as a whole, the record contains sufficient evidence from which it could reasonably be inferred that El Paso acted, with regard to each release and modification secured, like what some call a "dishonest compromiser" or extortionist. 1 J. White, R. Summers *Uniform Commercial Code* § 1–6(b) (1995). It 1) decided not to voluntarily perform its contractual obligations without informing its producers of same, 2) waited until its conduct was questioned then interjected the unwary producer into the denial/negotiation process, 3) obtained modification of its duties through the use of its power to block sales to others and by dangling hollow promises and representations in front of the producer, and 4) contrived additional reasons to avoid performing its modified duties until the producer eventually capitulated by asking to end the relationship. While this evidence may not illustrate the gross oppression implicit in unconscionability, it is some evidence of El Paso posturing its producers into granting concessions through means which were less than honest in fact. And, we found no evidence of a commercial standard proven at trial which condoned the use of deceit in obtaining modifications and releases like those won here.

Of course, there is evidence indicating that El Paso believed its defenses and posturing were legally justifiable. So too is there evidence indicating that Minco may have benefitted from the modifications and releases; after all it did gain the chance to sell gas on the spot market (at a lesser price) when El Paso could have

even denied it that. Yet, this contradictory evidence is not enough to overwhelm the court's finding of bad faith. Consequently, we overrule point two as it relates to Minco. . . .

[Judgment affirmed. El Paso was ordered to pay Minco damages equal to the amount of gas that it agreed to take or pay for under the unamended 1979 agreement.]

Questions

1. Does the court tell El Paso how it should have gone about dealing with its producers when it determined that the 1979 agreements were no longer profitable?
2. Explain the "denial/negotiation process."
3. El Paso obtained modifications of its contractual duties through the use of the power reserved to El Paso under the contract to block producers' sales to other marketers and by dangling hollow promises that the modifications would allow El Paso to market more of the producers' gas. Is it not up to the parties to the contracts, including Minco and the other producers, and not the courts, to make sure that the terms of each contract modification will lead to the promised results?

When the satisfaction of a condition involves action by a party to the contract the implied duty to act in good faith requires that the party make an honest, good faith effort to bring about the satisfaction of the condition. ♦ For example, when a contract is made subject to the condition that one of the parties obtain financing, that party must make reasonable, good-faith efforts to obtain financing. The party is not permitted to do nothing and then claim that the contract is not binding because the condition has not been satisfied. Likewise, when a contract requires a party to obtain government approval, the party must use all reasonable means to obtain it.[15] ♦ When a contract may reasonably be interpreted in different ways, a court should make the interpretation that is in harmony with good faith and fair dealing.

5. Conduct and Custom

The conduct of the parties and the customs and usages of a particular trade may give meaning to the words of the parties and thus aid in the interpretation of their contract.

(a) **Conduct of the Parties.** The conduct of the parties in carrying out the terms of a contract is the best guide to determining the parties' intent. When performance has been repeatedly tendered and accepted without protest, neither party will be permitted to claim that the contract was too indefinite to be binding. ♦ For example, a travel agent made a contract with a hotel to arrange for trips to the hotel. After some 80 trips have already been arranged and paid for by the hotel at the contract price without any dispute about whether the contract obligation was satisfied, any claim by the travel agent that it could charge additional fees must be rejected. ♦

---

[15] *Kroboth v Brent* 625 NYS2d 748 (App Div 1995)

(b) Custom and Usage of Trade. The customs and **usages of trade** or commercial activity to which the contract relates may be used to interpret the terms of a contract.[16] ◆ For example, when a contract for the construction of a building calls for a "turn-key construction," industry usage is admissible to show what this means—a construction in which all the owner needs to do is "turn the key" in the lock to open the building for use and in which all construction risks are assumed by the contractor.[17] ◆

Custom and usage, however, cannot override express provisions of a contract that are inconsistent with custom and usage.

6. Avoidance of Hardship

As a general rule, a party is bound by a contract even though it proves to be a bad bargain. If possible, a court will interpret a contract to avoid hardship, particularly when the hardship will hurt the weaker of the two parties to the contract. Courts will, if possible, interpret a vague contract in a way to avoid any forfeiture. Accordingly, a court will avoid holding that a statement or a promise is a **condition precedent,** which if unsatisfied would mean that no rights would arise under the contract, or is a **condition subsequent,** which if satisfied would mean that all rights under the contract would be terminated.

When there is ambiguity about the meaning of a contract, a court will avoid the interpretation that gives one contracting party an unreasonable advantage over the other or that causes a forfeiture of a party's interest.

When hardship arises because the contract makes no provision for the situation that has occurred, the court will sometimes imply a term in order to avoid the hardship.

In the *Perkins* case, the weaker party claimed that the court should imply or read into the contract a protective term that was not there.

Perkins v Standard Oil Co.
383 P2d 107 (Or 1963)

Court Glides with Clyde

Standard Oil Co. made a jobbing, or wholesale, dealership contract with Clyde Perkins. The contract limited Perkins to selling Standard Oil's products and required him to maintain certain minimum prices. Standard Oil had the right to approve or disapprove Perkins' customers. In order to be able to perform under this contract, Perkins had to make a substantial monetary investment, and his only income was from commissions on sales of Standard Oil's products. Standard Oil made some sales directly to Perkins' customers. When Perkins protested, Standard Oil pointed out that the contract did not contain any provision making his rights exclusive. Perkins sued Standard Oil to compel it to stop dealing with his customers. From a decision in Standard Oil's favor, Perkins appealed.

ROSSMAN, J. . . . The contract authorized the plaintiff [Perkins] to sell without Standard's written consent "on a nonexclusive basis" the products which Standard consigned to him but only to service stations or consuming accounts. Standard's written consent was required before the plaintiff could sell to any other account. The plaintiff promised in the contract to use his "best efforts to promote the sale of products consigned hereunder" and to sell a specified minimum amount during each year. . . . The plaintiff was required to deliver to Standard a complete list of the names and addresses of all his distributors and submit to it

---

[16] *Affiliated FM Ins. Co. v Constitution Reinsurance Corp.,* 626 NE2d 878 (Mass 1994).

[17] *Blue v R.L. Glossen Contracting, Inc.,* 327 SE2d 582 (Ga App 1985).

the names of any new potential distributors. . . .

The plaintiff claims that the contract by its very nature contains an implied condition that Standard would not solicit business directly from his (plaintiff's) customers. Standard protests that such an implied condition would be contrary to the express terms of the contract since the latter (1) provides that the plaintiff was authorized to sell Standard's products only "on a nonexclusive basis" and (2) reserved to Standard the "right to select its own customers." Plaintiff proposes a more restricted interpretation. . . . He concedes that the contract reserved to Standard the right to sell to any new accounts which it found, and to accept or reject any new accounts which he (the plaintiff) might obtain, but he insists that it does not permit Standard to solicit accounts which it had approved as his customers. . . .

In order to be successful in his business and to comply with the terms of his contract, the plaintiff was obliged to make substantial investments in storage facilities, delivery trucks, and other equipment. He was also obliged to hire employees. He was required to use his "best efforts" to promote the sale of Standard's products. Only if he sold Standard's products exclusively could it be said that he was using his best efforts to promote their sale. It is clear, then, that the contract limited his dealership to Standard products. Plaintiff was also required to sell a minimum quantity of other designated Standard petroleum products. If he at any time failed to sell the minimum quantity, Standard was at liberty to terminate its contract with him. Plaintiff's compensation was based exclusively on the sales he made to customers, which he secured through his own efforts. No compensation was available for the plaintiff if he obtained customers for Standard who bought directly from it. Nor does the contract obligate Standard to compensate him for sales made directly by Standard to plaintiff's customers. . . .

. . . A condition must be implied that Standard would not solicit customers which had been obtained through plaintiff's efforts. The interpretation of the contract for which Standard contends would leave plaintiff and others in a position similar to his completely at the mercy of Standard. . . .

"We cannot accept [Standard's] construction of its meaning. An intention to make so one-sided an agreement is not readily to be inferred. . . .

"In every contract there is an implied covenant that neither party shall do anything that will have the effect of destroying or injuring the right of the other party to receive the fruits of the contract, which means that in every contract there exists a covenant of good faith and fair dealing." . . . 3 *Corbin* [*on Contracts* 278] 349–352 . . .

The implication of a condition finds support in many circumstances. . . . Plaintiff's only source of return on his substantial investments in the business was the sales he made to his customers. If Standard was at liberty to solicit his direct customers, as it contends. . . . plaintiff was in a state of economic servility; we do not believe that the parties intended such a result at the time the contract was signed. . . .

The contract before us is obviously a form contract prepared by Standard. It is a contract of "adhesion" in the sense that it is a take-it-or-leave-it whole. Such contracts are regarded by some authorities as anachronistic or inconsistent with real freedom of contract. At least they should be construed with an awareness of the inequality of the bargainers. . . .

[Judgment reversed]

Questions

1. What created the problem in the *Perkins* case?
2. Could the problem in the *Perkins* case have been avoided?

B. CONFLICT OF LAWS

When a lawsuit is brought on a contract, the court will seek to apply the law under which the contract was made. In other words, a California court in many cases will not apply California law to a foreign (out-of-state) contract. The principle that determines when a court applies the law of its own state—the **law of the forum**—or some foreign law is called **conflict of laws.**

Because there are 50 state court systems and a federal court system, as well as a high degree of interstate activity, conflict of laws questions arise frequently.

7. State Courts

It is important to distinguish between the state in which the parties are **domiciled** or have their permanent home; the state in which the contract is made; and the state in which the contract is to be performed. The law of the state where the contract is made determines whether it is valid in substance and satisfies requirements of form. Matters relating to the performance of the contract, excuse or liability for nonperformance, and the measure of damages for nonperformance are generally governed by the law of the state where the contract is to be performed. Similar considerations apply to the interpretation of international contracts. Thus, a California court will apply Swiss law to a contract made in Switzerland that is to be performed in that country.

When a lawsuit is brought on a contract, the law of the forum determines the procedure and the rules of evidence.

(a) Center of Gravity. It is common for contracts with interstate aspects to specify that they shall be governed by the law of a particular state. In the absence of a law-selecting provision in the contract, there is a growing acceptance of the rule that a contract should be governed by the law of the state that has the most significant contacts with the transaction. This is the state to which the contract may be said to gravitate.[18]

◆ For example, assume the buyer's place of business and the seller's plant are located in state *A*, and the buyer is purchasing to resell to customers in state *A*. Many courts will hold that this is a contract governed by the law of state *A* in all respects. The fact that it is a state *B* contract by virtue of the chance circumstance that the seller's offer was accepted by the buyer in state *B* would not change this result. ◆ In determining which state has the most significant contacts, the court is to consider the place of contracting, negotiating, and performing; the location of the subject matter of the contract; and the domicile (residence) and states of incorporation and principal place of business of the parties.

When all states have the same rule of law, it is not important which state's law is followed. If, however, the law of the states involved is not the same, the choice of the state whose law is to govern will determine how the lawsuit will end. With the increasing interstate character of big business, the question of choice of law becomes increasingly important.

8. Federal Courts

When the parties to a contract reside in different states and the amount involved is $75,000 or more, an action may be brought in a federal court because of the parties' different citizenship. The federal court must apply the same rules of conflict of laws that would be applied by the courts of the state in which the federal court is sitting. Thus, a federal court in Chicago deciding a case involving parties from different states must apply the same rule of conflict of laws as would be applied by the state courts in Illinois. The state law must be followed by the federal court in such a case, whether or not the federal court agrees with the state law.

SUMMARY

Because a contract is based on the agreement of the parties, courts must determine the intent of the parties manifested in the contract. The intent that is to be enforced is the intent as it reasonably appears to a third person. This objective intent is followed.

In interpreting a contract, ordinary words are to be given their ordinary meanings. If trade or technical terms have been used, they are interpreted according to their technical meanings. The court must consider the whole contract and not read a particular part out of context. When different writings are executed as part of the same transaction, or one writing refers to or incorporates another, all the writings are to be read together as the contract of the parties.

---

[18] *Cleveland Vending Co. v Hercules Construction Corp.*, 23 F Supp 2d 287 (EDM/1998).

When provisions of a contract are contradictory, the court will try to reconcile or eliminate the conflict. If this cannot be done, the conclusion may be that there is no contract because the conflict makes the agreement indefinite as to a material matter. In some cases, conflict is solved by considering the form of conflicting terms. Handwriting prevails over typing and a printed form, and typing prevails over a printed form. Ambiguity will be eliminated in some cases by the admission of parol evidence or by interpreting the provision strictly against the party preparing the contract, particularly when that party has significantly greater bargaining power.

In most cases, the parties are held to their contract exactly as it has been written. In other cases, the courts will imply certain terms to preserve the contract against the objection that essential terms are missing or to prevent hardship. The law will imply that performance is to be made within a reasonable time and that details of performance are reasonable when the contract fails to be specific on these points. Also, the law will imply an obligation to act in good faith.

When a contract has interstate aspects, it is necessary to determine which state's law governs it. The rules that govern that decision are called the law of conflict of laws. The parties may specify the jurisdiction whose law is to govern. In the absence of such a provision, some courts will apply the older rule that the law of the state where the contract was made prevails in most matters and the law of the state where performance is to be made prevails in matters relating to performance. The center-of-gravity view is to choose the jurisdiction that has the most significant relationship to the parties, the contract, and its performance. When an action is brought in a federal court because it involves citizens of different states (diversity of citizenship), the federal court must apply the conflict of laws principles that would be applied by the courts of the state in which the federal court is sitting.

WEBSITE REFERENCES

For an illustration and definition of a "Quasi Contract," visit:

> **http://www.gallaudet.edu/~emwick/ bus447/quasi.html**

For a discussion on the risk of creating an unintended implied contract through the use of a management guide visit:

> **http://www.omwlaw.com/pubs/sutherland/ 00012.html**

QUESTIONS AND CASE PROBLEMS

1. What social forces are affected by the rule that a secret intention has no effect?
2. Harrison Builders made a contract to build a house for Kendall on the basis of cost plus 10 percent profit. The cost of the finished house was approximately $100,000. Kendall had expected that it would be $60,000 and claimed that Harrison was careless and extravagant in incurring costs of $100,000. Harrison asserted that since Kendall did not deny that the costs were $100,000, he could not dispute that they were proper. Is Harrison correct?
3. In letters between the two, Rita Borelli contracted to sell "my car" to Viola Smith for $2,000. It was later shown that Borelli owned two cars. Borelli refused to deliver either car to Smith, and Smith sued Borelli for breach of contract. Borelli raised the defense that the contract was too indefinite to be enforced because it could not be determined from the writing which car was the subject matter of the contract. Is the contract too indefinite to be enforced?
4. Quinn of Ohio sues Norman of California in the federal district court for the southern district of New York. Quinn claims that the court should apply the conflict of laws rules of Ohio because he is from Ohio and the plaintiff should have the choice of law. Norman claims that the federal court should apply federal law rather than the law of any particular state. Who is correct?

5. Panasonic Industrial Co. (PIC) made a contract making Manchester Equipment Co., Inc. (MECI), a nonexclusive wholesale distributor of its products. The contract stated that PIC reserves the unrestricted right to solicit and make direct sales of the products to anyone, anywhere. The contract also stated that it contained the entire agreement of the parties and that any prior agreement or statement was superseded by the contract. PIC subsequently began to make direct sales to two of MECI's established customers. MECI claimed that this was a breach of the distribution contract and sued PIC for damages. Decide. What ethical values are involved? [*Manchester Equipment Co. v Panasonic Industrial Co.* 529 NYS2d 532 (App Div)]

6. McGill and his grandson, Malo, made an agreement by which McGill would live with Malo and receive support and maintenance in return for McGill's deeding his house to Malo. After a number of years, McGill left the house because of the threats and physical violence of the grandson. There was no complaint of lack of support and maintenance. Had the grandson broken the contract? [*McGill v Malo,* 184 A2d 517 (Conn Super)]

7. A contract made for the sale of a farm stated that the buyer's deposit would be returned "if for any reason the farm cannot be sold." The seller later stated that she had changed her mind and would not sell, and she offered to return the deposit. The buyer refused to take the deposit back and brought suit to enforce the contract. The seller contended that the "any reason" provision extended to anything, including the seller's changing her mind. Was the buyer entitled to recover? [*Phillips v Rogers* 200 SE2d 676 (WVa)]

8. Integrated, Inc., entered into a contract with the state of California to construct a building. It then subcontracted the electrical work to Alec Fergusson Electrical Contractors. The subcontract was a printed form with blanks filled in by typewriting. The printed payment clause required Integrated to pay Fergusson on the 15th day of the month following the submission of invoices by Fergusson. The typewritten part of the contract required Integrated to pay Fergusson "immediately following payment" (by the state) to the general contractor. When was payment required? [*Integrated, Inc. v Alec Fergusson Electrical Contractors,* 58 Cal Rptr 503 (Cal App)]

9. Norwest Bank had been lending money to Tresch to run a dairy farm. The balance due the bank after several years was $147,000. The loan agreement stated that Tresch would not buy any new equipment in excess of $500 without the express consent of the bank. Some time later, Tresch applied to the bank for a loan of $3,100 to purchase some equipment. The bank refused to make the loan because it did not believe the new equipment would correct the condition for which it would be bought and would not result in significant additional income. Tresch then sued the bank, claiming that its refusal to make the loan was a breach of the implied covenant of good faith and fair dealing. Decide. [*Tresch v Norwest Bank of Lewistown,* 778 P2d 874 (Mont)]

10. Physicians Mutual Insurance Co. issued a policy covering Brown's life. The policy declared that it did not cover any deaths resulting from "mental disorder, alcoholism, or drug addiction." Brown was killed when she fell while intoxicated. The insurance company refused to pay because of the quoted provision. Her executor, Savage, sued the insurance company. Did the insurance company have a defense? [*Physicians Mutual Ins. Co. v Savage* 296 NE2d 165 (Ind App)]

11. Tucker was employed by Ashland Oil. Tucker's contract prohibited him from working for a competitor after the termination of his employment. Tucker worked as a district manager of Ashland in Louisiana, Missouri, and Illinois. When his employment ended, he worked for a competitor in Missouri, which would be a breach of the anticompetitive covenant. Tucker claimed, however, that the covenant did not bind him because it was invalid under the law of Louisiana, where the contract of employment had originally been made. Suit was brought in Missouri to enforce the covenant, and under Missouri law the covenant was valid. Which state law should be applied? [*Ashland Oil, Inc. v Tucker,* 768 SW2d 595 (Mo App)]

12. Carol and John, a married couple, separated and signed an agreement by which John promised to pay Carol $100 a month. A year later they were divorced, and John stopped

making payments. Carol sued him for breach of the contract. John offered to testify that it was his intention that the payments would stop when the parties were divorced. Is this testimony admissible? [*Grady v Grady,* 224 SE2d 282 (NC App)]

13. The Dickinson Elks club conducted an annual Labor Day golf tournament. Charbonneau Buick-Pontiac offered to give a new car as a prize to anyone making "a hole in one on hole no. 8." The golf course of the club was only nine holes. To play 18 holes, the players would go around the course twice, although they would play from different tees or locations for the second nine holes. On the second time around, what was originally the eight hole became the seventeenth hole. Grove was a contestant in the tournament. He scored 3 on the no. 8 hole, but on approaching it for the second time as the seventeenth hole, he made a hole in one. He claimed the prize car from Charbonneau. The latter claimed that Grove had not won the prize because he did not make the hole in one on the eighth hole. Decide. [*Grove v Charbonneau Buick-Pontiac, Inc.,* 240 NW2d 8533 (ND)]

14. Beck and Co., a brewery, gave Gianelli Distributing Co. a franchise to distribute Beck's Beer. The franchise agreement specified that it would continue "unless and until terminated at any time by 30 days' written notice by either party to the other." Some time thereafter, Beck notified Gianelli that the franchise was terminated. Gianelli claimed that the franchise could be terminated only upon proof of reasonable cause. He offered evidence of trade usage to show that common practice required cause for termination and further claimed that such usage would be read into the franchise agreement with Beck. Is this evidence admissible?

15. Drews Co. contracted to renovate a building owned by Ledwith. There were many delays in performing the contract, and finally the contractor quit the job. Ledwith sued the contractor for damages for delay and for breach of the contract. The contractor claimed that it was not liable for damages for delay because the contract did not contain any date by which the work was to be completed and did not state that time was of the essence. Did the silence of the contract excuse the delay?

Discharge of Contracts

Learning Objectives

After studying this chapter, you should be able to

1. List the ways in which a contract can be discharged
2. Distinguish between the effect of a rejected tender of payment and a rejected tender of performance
3. Define when time is of the essence
4. Compare performance to the satisfaction of the other contracting parties, performance to the satisfaction of a reasonable person, and substantial performance
5. State when a consumer contract may be rescinded by the consumer
6. Compare the discharge of a contract by rescission, cancellation, substitution, and novation
7. State the effect on a contract of the death or disability of one of the contracting parties
8. Define the concept of economic frustration

In the preceding chapters, you studied how a contract is formed, what it means, and who has rights under a contract. In this chapter, attention is turned to how a contract is ended or discharged. In other words, what puts an end to the rights and duties created by the contract?

A. CONDITIONS RELATING TO PERFORMANCE

As will be developed in the body of this chapter, the ordinary method of discharging obligations under a contract is by performance. Certain promises may be less than absolute and instead come into effect only upon the happening of a specified event, or an existing obligation may be extinguished by the occurrence of an event. Such are conditional promises.

1. Classifications of Conditions

When the occurrence or nonoccurrence of an event, as expressed in a contract, affects the duty of a party to the contract to perform, the event is called a **condition.** Terms such as *if, provided that, when, after, as soon as, subject to,* and *on the condition that* indicate the creation of a condition.[1] Conditions are classified as *conditions precedent, conditions subsequent,* and *concurrent conditions.*

(a) Condition Precedent. A **condition precedent** is a condition that must occur before a party to a contract has an obligation to perform under the contract. ◆ For example, the City of San Diego promises to hire Jane Stewart as a police officer "on condition" that she finish her training at the Regional Training Center at Mirimar College and obtain a State of California peace officer certificate. If either of the conditions do not occur, namely that Jane finish her training and obtain state certification, the City has no obligation to perform under the contract and hire Jane as a police officer. ◆

(b) Condition Subsequent. The parties to a contract may agree that a party is obligated to perform such act or pay a certain sum of money, but the contract contains a provision that relieves the obligation upon the occurrence of a certain event. That is, on the happening of a **condition subsequent,** such an event extinguishes the duty to thereafter perform. ◆ For example, Chad Newly served as the weekend anchor on *Channel 5 News* for several years. The station manager Tom O'Brien, on reviewing tapes in connection with Newly's contract renewal, believed that Newly's speech on occasion was slightly slurred, and he suspected that it was due to alcohol use. In the parties' contract discussions, O'Brien expressed his concerns about an alcohol problem and offered help. Newly denied there was a problem. O'Brien agreed to a new two-year contract with Newly at $167,000 for the first year and $175,000 for the second year with other benefits subject to "the condition" that the station reserved the right to make four unannounced drug-alcohol tests during the contract term, and should Newly test positive for drugs or alcohol, under measurements set forth in the contract, then all of Channel 5's obligations to Newly under the contract would cease. When Newly subsequently failed a urinalysis test three months into the new contract, the happening of this event extinguished the station's obligation to employ and pay him under the contract. ◆

(c) Concurrent Condition. In most bilateral contracts, the performances of the parties are **concurrent conditions.** That is, their mutual duties of performance under the contract are to take place simultaneously. ◆ For example, concerning a contract for the sale and delivery of certain goods, the buyer must tender to the seller a certified check at the time of delivery as set forth in the contract, and the seller must tender the goods to the buyer at the same time. ◆

> ### ETHICS AND THE LAW
>
> In February 2000, John Hancock Financial Services Co. (JHFS) agreed to sponsor the Olympics for a four-year period through the 2004 Athens Games for $55 million, in exchange for the right to promote itself as an Olympic sponsor. JHFS insisted on the inclusion of a so called "morals clause" in the sponsorship contract that would allow JHFS to void its payment obligations and

---

[1] *Harmon Cable Communications v Scope Cable Television, Inc.,* 468 NW2d 350 (Neb 1990).

withdraw as a sponsor if the International Olympic Committee (IOC) misbehaves during the sponsorship period. Can the courts be utilized to resolve controversies over whether or not a morals clause has been violated? If so, is the occurrence of a morals clause violation a condition precedent or condition subsequent?

B. DISCHARGE BY PERFORMANCE

When it is claimed that a contract is discharged by performance, questions arise as to the nature, time, and sufficiency of the performance.

2. Normal Discharge of Contracts

A contract is usually discharged by the performance of the terms of the agreement. In most cases, the parties perform their promises and the contract ceases to exist or is thereby discharged. A contract is also discharged by the expiration of the time period specified in the contract.[2]

3. Nature of Performance

Performance may be the doing of an act or the making of payment.

(a) **Tender.** An offer to perform is known as a **tender.** If performance of the contract requires the doing of an act, the refusal of a tender will discharge the party offering to perform and be a basis for that party to bring a lawsuit.

A valid tender of payment consists of an unconditional offer of the exact amount due on the date when due. A tender of payment is not just an expression of willingness to pay; it must be an actual offer to perform by making payment of the amount owed.

(b) **Payment.** When payment is required by the contract, performance consists of the payment of money.

(1) Application of Payments. If a debtor owes more than one debt to the creditor and pays money, a question may arise as to which debt has been paid. If the debtor specifies the debt to which the payment is to be applied and the creditor accepts the money, the creditor is bound to apply the money as specified.[3] Thus, if the debtor specifies that a payment is to be made for a current purchase, the creditor may not apply the payment to an older balance.

(2) Payment by Check. Payment by commercial paper, such as a check, is ordinarily a conditional payment. A check merely suspends the debt until the check is presented for payment. If payment is then made, the debt is discharged; if not paid, the suspension terminates, and suit may be brought on either the debt or the check. Frequently, payment must be made by a specified date. It is generally held that the payment is made on time if it is mailed on or before the final date for payment.

4. Time of Performance

When the date or period of time for performance is specified in the contract, performance should be made on that date or within that time period.

(a) **No Time Specified.** When the time for performance is not specified in the contract, an obligation to perform within a reasonable time will be implied.[4] The fact that no time is specified neither impairs the contract on the ground that it is indefinite nor allows an endless time in which to perform. What constitutes a reasonable time is determined by the nature of the subject matter of the contract and the facts and circumstances surrounding the making of the contract.

(b) **When Time Is Essential.** If performance of the contract on or within the exact time specified is vital, it is said that "time is of the essence." Time is of the essence when the contract relates to property that is perishable or that is fluctuating rapidly in value. Where a contract fixes by unambiguous language a time for performance and where there is no evidence showing that the parties did not intend that time should be of the essence, failure to perform within the specified time is a breach of

[2] *Washington National Ins. Co. v Sherwood Associates,* 795 P2d 665 (Utah App 1990).

[3] *Oakes Logging, Inc. v Green Crow, Inc.,* 832 P2d 894 (Wash App 1992).

[4] *First National Bank v Clark,* 447 SE2d 558 (W Va 1994)

FIGURE 19.1 *Causes of Contract Discharge*

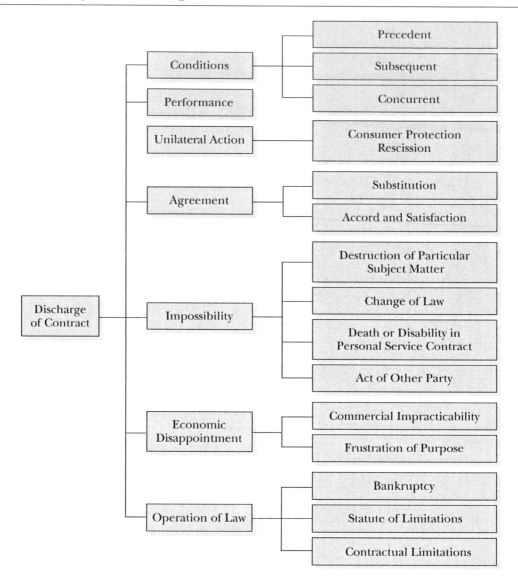

contract entitling the innocent party to damages. ◆ **For example,** Dixon and Gandhi agreed that Gandhi would close on the purchase of a motel as follows: "Closing Date. The closing shall be held . . . on the date which is within twenty (20) days after the closing of Nomura Financing." Gandhi did not close within the time period specified, and Dixon was allowed to retain $100,000 in pre-paid closing costs and fees as liquidated damages for Gandhi's breach of contract.[5] ◆

[5] *Woodhull Corp. v Saibaba Corp.* 507 SE2d 493 (Ga App 1998).

(c) When Time Is Not Essential. Unless a contract so provides, time, ordinarily, is not of the essence, and performance within a reasonable time is sufficient. In the case of the sale of property, time will not be regarded as of the essence when there has not been any appreciable change in the market value or condition of the property and when the person who delayed does not appear to have done so for the purpose of speculating on a change in market price.

(d) Waiver of Essence of Time Limitation. A provision that time is of the essence may be waived. It is waived when the specified time has expired but the party who could complain requests the delaying party to take steps necessary to perform the contract.[6]

5. Adequacy of Performance

When a party renders exactly the performance called for by the contract, no question arises as to whether the contract has been performed. In other cases, there may not have been a perfect performance, or a question arises as to whether the performance made satisfies the standard set by the contract.

(a) Substantial Performance. Perfect performance of a contract is not always possible when dealing with construction projects. A party who in good faith has provided **substantial performance** of the contract may sue to recover the payment specified in the contract. However, because the performance was not perfect, the performing party is subject to a counterclaim for the damages caused the other party. When a building contractor has substantially performed the contract to construct a building, the contractor is responsible for the cost of repairing or correcting the defects as an offset from the contract price.

The measure of damages under these circumstances is known as "cost of completion" damages. If, however, the cost of completion would be unreasonably disproportionate to the importance of the defect, the measure of damages is the diminution in value of the building due to the defective performance.

Whether there is substantial performance is a question of degree to be determined by all of the facts, including the particular type of structure involved, its intended purpose, and the nature and relative expense of repairs.

◆ **For example,** a certain building contractor (BC) and a certain owner (O) made a contract to construct a home overlooking Vineyard Sound on Martha's Vineyard according to plans and specifications that clearly called for the use of General Plumbing Blue Star piping. The contract price was $1,100,000. Upon inspecting the work before making the final $400,000 payment and accepting the building, O discovered BC had used Republic piping throughout the house. O explained to BC that his family had made its money by investing in General Plumbing and he therefore would not make the final payment until the breach of contract was remedied. BC explained that Republic pipes were of the same industrial grade and quality as the Blue Star pipes. Moreover, BC estimated that it would cost nearly $300,000 to replace all of the pipes due to the destruction of walls and fixtures necessary to accomplish such a task. BC may sue O for $400,000 for breach of contract claiming he had substantially performed the contract, and O may counterclaim for $300,000 seeking an offset for the cost of remedying the breach. The court will find in favor of the contractor and will not allow the $300,000 offset, but rather will allow a "nominal" offset of perhaps $100 to $1,000 for the amount the Republic pipes diminished the value of the building.[7] ◆

The willfullness of the departure from the specifications of the contract will not by itself preclude some recovery for the contractor on the "cost of completion" basis, but rather is a factor in consideration of whether there was substantial performance by the contractor.

The *Beeson* case raised the question of when performance is substantial.

J.M. Beeson Co. v Sartori
553 So 2d 180 (Fla Dist Ct App 1989)

When Perfection is Not Required

Beeson Co. made a contract to construct a shopping center for Sartori. Before the work was fully completed, Sartori stopped making the payments to Beeson that were required by the contract. Beeson then stopped working and sued Sartori for the balance due under the contract just as

---

[6] *Stefanelli v Vitale*, 636 NYS2d 50 (App Div 1996).

[7] *See Jacob & Youngs, Inc. v Kent*, 230 NY 239 (1921).

though it had been fully performed. Sartori's defense was that Beeson had not "substantially completed" the work as that term was defined in the contract. Beeson proved that Sartori had been able to rent most of the stores in the center. Judgment was entered in favor of Sartori, and Beeson appealed.

WARNER, J. . . . Appellant contends that the trial court erred in finding that he did not substantially complete the work. In this case the contract provided that "substantial" completion occurred when "construction is sufficiently complete in accordance with the Contract Documents, so the owner can occupy or utilize the work or designated portion thereof for the use for which it is intended." The "work" under the contract "comprises the completed construction required by the contract documents." Under the contract in this case the work consisted of "construction and completion of a Shopping Center," including all of its component parts such as landscaping and paving. . . .

We agree with appellant's contention that the contractual definition of substantial completion in this case is similar to the well established doctrine of substantial performance, and the terms are interchangeable. . . .

Substantial performance is that performance of a contract which, while not full performance, is so nearly equivalent to what was bargained for that it would be unreasonable to deny the promisee the full contract price subject to the promisor's right to recover whatever damages have been occasioned him by the promisee's failure to render full performance. See 3A *Corbin on Contracts*, Section 702 et seq.

To say that substantial performance is performance which is nearly equivalent to what was bargained for, as the case law defines the term, in essence means that the owner can use the property for the use for which it is intended. Furthermore, in defining substantial performance, one of the tests as enunciated by Corbin is the "degree of frustration of purpose":

Extremely important factors in solving the present problem [of what is substantial performance] are the character of the performance that the plaintiff promised to render, the purposes and end that it was expected to serve on behalf of the defendant, and the extent to which the nonperformance by the plaintiff has defeated those purposes and ends, or would defeat them if the errors and omissions are corrected. Corbin on Contracts, 3-A, Section 706.

Thus, substantial completion as defined in the contract is the equivalent of substantial performance under the case law and authorities hereinbefore cited.

In the instant case . . . the owner was capable of having tenants occupy the spaces and collecting rents thereon, and he was already collecting substantial rents on many of the tenant spaces. . . .

When the owner was able to occupy . . . the constructed space, the construction was substantially completed. . . . At that point, the appellant was entitled to his full contract price, less the cost to complete.

[Judgment reversed and action remanded]

Questions

1. How does the court distinguish "substantial completion" from "substantial performance"?
2. What is the characteristic of a performance that is substantial?
3. Assume that a contractor makes a contract to build a house, digs a foundation, and then quits work. Has there been a substantial performance of the contract?

(b) **Fault of Complaining Party.** A party cannot complain that a performance was defective when the performance follows the terms of the contract required by the complaining party. Thus, a homeowner who supplied the specifications for poured cement walls cannot hold a contractor liable for damages when the walls that were poured in exact compliance with those specifications proved defective.

(c) **Performance to the Satisfaction of the Contracting Party or a Third Party.** Sometimes an agreement requires performance to the satisfaction, taste, or judgment of the other party to the contract. Where the contract specifically stipulates that the performance must satisfy the contracting party, then the courts will ordinarily enforce the plain meaning of the language of the parties and the work must satisfy the contracting party, subject of course to the requirement that dissatisfaction be made in good faith and not simply to avoid payment for the work that has been done.[8] Good-faith personal satisfaction is generally required when the subject matter of the contract is personal, such as interior design work, tailoring, and the painting of a portrait.

With respect to things mechanical or routine performances, courts require that the performance be such as would satisfy a reasonable person under the circumstances.

When work is to be done subject to the approval of an architect, engineer, or another expert, most courts apply the reasonable person test of satisfaction.

C. DISCHARGE BY ACTION OF PARTIES

Contracts may be discharged by the joint action of both contracting parties or, in some cases, by the action of one party alone.

6. Discharge by Unilateral Action

Ordinarily, a contract cannot be discharged by the action of either party alone. In some cases, the contract will give one of either party the right to cancel the contract by unilateral action, such as by notice to the other party. Insurance policies covering loss commonly provide that the insurer may cancel the policy upon giving a specified number of days' notice.

(a) Consumer Protection Rescission. A basic principle of contract law is that once made, a contract between competent persons is a binding obligation. Consumer protection legislation introduces into the law a contrary concept—that of giving the consumer a chance to think things over and to rescind the contract. Thus, the federal

Consumer Credit Protection Act (CCPA) gives the debtor the right to rescind a credit transaction within three business days when the transaction would impose a lien on the debtor's home. ◆ For example, a homeowner who mortgages his or her home to obtain a loan may cancel the transaction for any reason by notifying the lender before midnight of the third full business day after the loan is made.[9] ◆

A Federal Trade Commission regulation gives the buyer three business days in which to cancel a home-solicited sale of goods or services costing more than $25.[10]

7. Discharge by Agreement

A contract may be discharged by the operation of one of its provisions or by a subsequent agreement. Thus, there may be a discharge by (1) the terms of the original contract, such as a provision that the contract should end on a specified date; (2) a mutual cancellation, in which the parties agree to end their contract; (3) a mutual **rescission,** in which the parties agree to annul the contract and return both parties to their original positions before the contract had been made;[11] (4) the **substitution** of a new contract between the same parties; (5) a **novation** or substitution of a new contract involving a new party;[12] (6) an **accord and satisfaction;** (7) a release; or (8) a **waiver.**

(a) Substitution. The parties may decide that their contract is not the one they want. They may then replace it with another contract. If they do, the original contract is discharged by **substitution.**[13]

---

[8] *Kohler v Leslie Hindman, Inc.,* 80 F3d 1181 (7th Cir 1996).

[9] If the owner is not informed of this right to cancel, the three-day period does not begin until that information is given. Consumer Credit Protection Act § 125, 15 USC § 1635 (a), (e), (f).

[10] CFR § 429.1 This displaces state laws making similar provision for rescission, such as UCCC § 2.502.

[11] *Agri Careers, Inc. v Jepsen,* 463 NW2d 93 (Iowa App 1990).

[12] *Eagle Industries, Inc. v Thompson,* 900 P2d 475 (Or 1995). In a few jurisdictions, the term *novation* is used to embrace the substitution of any new contract, whether between the original parties or not.

[13] *Shawnee Hospital Authority v Dow Construction, Inc.,* 812 P2d 1351 (Okla 1990).

(b) Accord and Satisfaction. Where the parties have differing views as to the performance required by the terms of a contract, they may agree to a different performance. Such an agreement is called an *accord.* When the accord is performed or executed, there is an **accord and satisfaction,** which discharges the original obligation. To constitute an accord and satisfaction, there must be a bona fide dispute, a proposal to settle the dispute, and performance of the agreement.[14] ◆ For example, Lymon Mitchell operated a Badcock Home Furnishing dealership, under which as dealer he was paid a commission on sales, and Badcock retained title to merchandise on display. Mitchell sold his dealership to another, and, to facilitate the sale, Badcock prepared a summary of commissions owed with certain itemized offsets it claimed that Mitchell owed Badcock. Mitchell disagreed with the calculations, but he accepted them and signed the transfer documents closing the sale on the basis of the terms set forth in the summary and was paid accordingly. Mitchell's subsequent claim asserting Badcock's offsets were improper was precluded by an accord and satisfaction; where there was a dispute over the settlement amount, Mitchell accepted the disputed calculations as the amount owed him (accord), and executed the transfer documents and received payment (the satisfaction).[15]

D. DISCHARGE BY EXTERNAL CAUSES

Circumstances beyond the control of the contracting parties may discharge the contract.

8. Discharge by Impossibility

Impossibility of performance refers to external or extrinsic conditions. This is contrasted with an individual's personal inability to perform.[16] ◆ For example, Pollard Excavating, Inc., made a contract with Comprehensive Builders, Inc., to install sewer piping from the foundation of a new home to the sewer main, but withdrew from the job asserting impossibility due to problems arising from subsurface soil conditions and the fact that the sewer main was farther underground than the builder stated. Pollard was held liable for "cost of completion" damages. The subsoil conditions and the location of the sewer main were discussed prior to making the contract and were not unanticipated events that made performance objectively impossible.[17] ◆

Shortages of materials and similar factors, even though external, ordinarily do not excuse performance under contract. However, a seller's duty may be excused by a failure of a particular source of supply that was specified by the parties to the contract. ◆ For example, if a contractor's usual gravel source cannot be used (and it is necessary to transport gravel from a more distant source, making performance more costly), such by itself does not discharge the contractor from the obligation to construct a road. If there is nothing in the contract requiring that the gravel be obtained from the unavailable source, no question of impossibility of performance exists. ◆ A contract is not discharged merely because performance proves to be more burdensome or costly than was originally contemplated.[18] However, if the parties specified the source of supply in their contract, such would constitute impossibility that would excuse performance.

(a) Destruction of Particular Subject Matter. When parties contract expressly for or with reference to a particular subject matter, the contract is discharged if the subject matter is destroyed through no fault of either party. When a contract calls for the sale of a wheat crop growing on a specific parcel of land, the contract is discharged if that crop is destroyed by blight.

On the other hand, if there is merely a contract to sell a given quantity of a specified grade of wheat, the seller is not discharged when the seller's crop is destroyed by blight. The seller had made an unqualified undertaking to deliver wheat of a specified grade. No restrictions or qualifications were imposed as to the source. If the seller does not deliver the goods called for by the

---

[14] *S&G, Inc. v Intermountain Power Agency,* 913 P2d 735 (Utah 1996).

[15] *Mitchell v W.S. Badcock Corp.,* 496 SE2d 502 (Ga App 1998).

[16] *Haessly v Safeco Title Ins. Co.,* 825 P2d 1119 (Idaho 1992).

[17] *Comprehensive Bldg. v Pollard Excavating,* 674 NYS2d 869 (App Div 1998).

[18] *Stasyszyn v Sutton East Associates,* 555 NYS2d 297 (App Div 1990).

contract, the contract is broken, and the seller is liable for damages.

The parties may, by their contract, allocate the risk of loss. Thus, a contract for the sale of a building and land may specify that any loss from damage to the building should be borne by the seller.

(b) Change of Law. A contract is discharged when its performance is made illegal by a subsequent change in the law. Thus, a contract to construct a nonfireproof building at a particular place is discharged by the adoption of a zoning law prohibiting such a building within that area. Mere inconvenience or temporary delay caused by the new law, however, does not excuse performance.

(c) Death or Disability. Where the contract obligates a party to render or receive personal services requiring peculiar skill, the death, incapacity, or illness of the party who was either to render or receive the personal services excuses both sides from a duty to perform. It is sometimes said that "the death of either party is the death of the contract."

The rule does not apply, however, where the acts called for by the contract are of such a character that (1) the acts may be as well performed by others such as the promisor's personal representatives or (2) by the contract's terms contemplate continuance of the obligations after the death of one of the parties. ◆ For example, Lynn Jones was under contract to investor Ed Jenkins to operate certain "Subway" sandwich shops and to acquire new franchises with funding provided by Jenkins. After Jenkins's death, Jones claimed he was no longer bound under the contract and was free to pursue franchise opportunities on his own. The contract between Jones and Jenkins expressed that it was binding upon the parties' "heirs and assigns" and the contract embodied property rights that passed to Jenkins's widow. The agreement's provisions thus established that the agreement survived the death of Jenkins and Jones was therefore obligated to remit profits from the franchise he acquired for himself after Jenkins's death.[19] ◆

(d) Act of Other Party. Every contract contains "an implied covenant of good faith and fair dealing." As a result of this covenant, a promisee is under an obligation to do nothing that would interfere with performance by the promisor. When the promisee prevents performance or otherwise makes performance impossible, the promisor is discharged from the contract. Thus, a subcontractor is discharged from any obligation when unable to do the work because the principal contractor refuses to deliver the material, equipment, or money required by the subcontract. When the default of the other party consists of failing to supply goods or services, the duty may rest on the party claiming a discharge of the contract to show that substitute goods or services could not be obtained elsewhere.

9. Developing Doctrines

Commercial impracticability and frustration of purpose may excuse performance.

(a) Commercial Impracticability. The doctrine of *commercial impracticability* (as opposed to *impossibility*) was developed to deal with the harsh rule that a party must perform its contracts unless it is absolutely impossible. It must be remembered that not every type of impracticability is an excuse for nonperformance. It is only available when the performance is made impractical by the subsequent occurrence of an event whose nonoccurence was a basic assumption on which the contract was made, unless the adversely affected party assumed the risk that the contingency might occur.[20] If the subsequent event is a severe shortage of raw materials or supplies that results in a marked increase in the cost of the materials or supplies and this event was foreseeable, the defense is not available.

(b) Frustration of Purpose Doctrine. Because of a change in circumstances, the purpose of the contract may have no value to the party entitled to receive performance. In such a case, performance may be excused if both parties were aware of the purpose and the event that frustrated the purpose was unforeseeable.

---

[19] *Jenkins Subway, Inc. v Jones,* 990 SW2d 713 (Tenn App 1998).

[20] Restatement (Second) of Contracts, § 261; UCC § 2-615.

♦ For example, National Southern Bank rents a home near Willowbend Country Club on the southeastern shore of North Carolina for $75,000 a week to entertain business guests at the Ryder Cup matches scheduled for the week in question. Storm damage from Hurricane David the week before the event caused the closing of the course and the transfer of the tournament to another venue in a different state. The bank's duty to pay for the house may be excused by the doctrine of *frustration of purpose*, because the transfer of the tournament fully destroyed the value of the home rental, both parties were aware of the purpose of the rental, and the cancellation of the golf tournament was unforeseeable. ♦

(c) Comparison to Common Law Rule. The traditional common law rule refuses to recognize commercial impracticability or frustration of purpose. By the common law rule, the losses and disappointments against which commercial impracticability and frustration of purpose give protection are merely the risks that one takes in entering into a contract. Moreover, the situations could have been guarded against by including an appropriate condition subsequent in the contract. A condition subsequent declares that the contract will be void if a specified event occurs. Or the contract could have provided for a readjustment of compensation if there was a basic change of circumstances. The common law approach also rejects these developing concepts because they weaken the stability of a contract.

An indication of a wider recognition of the concept that "extreme" changes of circumstances can discharge a contract is found in the Uniform Commercial Code. The UCC provides for the discharge of a contract for the sale of goods when a condition that the parties assumed existed, or would continue, ceases to exist.[21]

10. Temporary Impossibility

Ordinarily, either a temporary impossibility has no effect on the performance obligation of a party or at most it suspends the duty to perform. If the obligation to perform is suspended, it is revived on the termination of the impossibility. If, however, performance at that later date would

[21] UCC § 2-615.

impose a substantially greater burden on the party obligated to perform, some courts discharge the obligor from the contract.

(a) Weather. Acts of God, such as tornadoes, lightning, and floods, usually do not terminate a contract even though they make performance difficult. Thus, weather conditions constitute a risk that is assumed by a contracting party in the absence of a contrary agreement. Consequently, extra expense sustained by a contractor because of weather conditions is a risk that the contractor assumes in the absence of an express provision for additional compensation in such a case. ♦ For example, Danielo Contractors made a contract to construct a shopping mall for the Rubicon Center, with construction to begin November 1. Because of abnormal cold and blizzard conditions, Danielo was not able to begin work until April 1 and was five months late in completing the construction of the project. Rubicon sued Danielo for breach of contract by failing to perform on schedule. Danielo is liable. As no provision was included in the contract covering delay caused by weather, Danielo bore the risk of the delay and resulting loss. ♦

Modern contracts commonly contain a "weather clause" and reflect the parties' agreement on this matter. When the parties take the time to discuss weather issues, purchasing insurance coverage is a common resolution.

11. Discharge by Operation of Law

A contract is discharged by **operation of law** by (1) an alteration or a material change made by a party, (2) the destruction of the written contract with intent to discharge it, (3) bankruptcy, (4) the operation of a statute of limitations, or (5) a contractual limitation.

(a) Bankruptcy. As set forth in the chapter on bankruptcy, even though all creditors have not been paid in full, a discharge in **bankruptcy** eliminates ordinary contract claims against the debtor.

(b) Statute of Limitations. A **statute of limitations** provides that after a certain number of years have passed, a contract claim is barred. The time limitation provided by state statutes of limitations varies widely. The time period for bringing actions for breach of an oral contract is two to three years. The period may differ with the type of contract—ranging from a relatively short time for open accounts (ordinary customers' charge accounts) to four years for sales of goods.[22] A somewhat longer period exists for bringing actions for breach of written contracts (usually four to six years), and the maximum period for judgments of record is usually ten to twenty years.

(c) **Contractual Limitations.** Some contracts, particularly insurance contracts, contain a time limitation within which suit must be brought. This is in effect a private statute of limitations created by the agreement of the parties. A 12-month limitation in an insurance policy for the time for suit is not unconscionable even though a person obtaining the insurance has virtually no chance of successfully negotiating a change of the provision.[23]

A contract may also require that notice of any claim be given within a specified time. A party who fails to give notice within the time specified by the contract is barred from suing thereon.

A contract provision requiring that suit be brought within one year does not violate public policy, although the statute of limitations would allow two years in the absence of such a contract limitation.[24]

SUMMARY

A party's duty to perform under a contract can be affected by a condition precedent, which must occur before a party has an obligation to perform; a condition subsequent, which condition or event relieves the duty to thereafter perform; and concurrent conditions, which require mutual and often simultaneous performance.

Most contracts are discharged by performance. An offer to perform is called a tender of performance. If a tender of performance is wrongfully refused, the duty of the tenderer to perform is terminated. When the performance called for by the contract is the payment of money, it must be legal tender that is offered. In actual practice, it is common to pay and to accept payment by checks or other commercial paper.

When the debtor owes the creditor on several accounts and makes a payment, the debtor may specify which account is to be credited with the payment. If the debtor fails to specify, the creditor may choose which account to credit.

When a contract does not state when it is to be performed, it must be performed within a reasonable time. If time for performance is stated in the contract, the contract must be performed at the time specified if such time is essential (is of the essence). Performance within a reasonable time is sufficient if the specified time is not essential. Ordinarily, a contract must be performed exactly in the manner specified by the contract. A less-than-perfect performance is allowed if it is a substantial performance and if damages are allowed the other party. The other contracting party or a third person may guarantee a perfect performance. Such a guarantor is then liable if the performance is less than perfect.

A contract cannot be discharged by unilateral action unless authorized by the contract itself or by statute, as in the case of consumer protection rescission.

As a contract arises from an agreement, it may also be terminated by an agreement. A contract may also be discharged by the substitution of a new contract for the original contract; by a novation, or making a new contract with a new party; by accord and satisfaction; by release; or by waiver.

A contract is discharged when it is impossible to perform. Impossibility may result from the destruction of the subject matter of the contract, the adoption of a new law that prohibits performance, the death or disability of a party whose personal action was required for performance of the contract, or the act of the other party to the contract. Some courts will also hold that a contract is discharged when its performance is commercially impracticable or there is frustration of purpose. Temporary impossibility, such as a labor strike or bad weather, has no effect on a contract. It is common, though, to include protective

[22] UCC § 2-725(1).

[23] *Thomas v United Fire and Casualty Co.,* 426 NW2d 396 (Iowa 1988).

[24] *Keiting v Skauge,* 543 NW2d 565 (Wis App 1995).

clauses that excuse delay caused by temporary impossibility.

A contract may be discharged by operation of law. This occurs when (1) the liability arising from the contract is discharged by bankruptcy, (2) suit on the contract is barred by the applicable statute of limitations, or (3) a time limitation stated in the contract is exceeded.

WEBSITE REFERENCE

To view an actual discharge agreement visit: **http://www.asha.com/html/c-general.htm**

QUESTIONS AND CASE PROBLEMS

1. What social forces are affected by the doctrine of economic frustration?

2. McMullen Contractors made a contract with Richardson to build an apartment house for a specific price. A number of serious apartment house fires broke out in the city, and an ordinance was adopted by the city council increasing the fire precautions that had to be taken in the construction of a new building. Compliance with these new requirements would make the construction of the apartment house for Richardson more expensive than McMullen had originally contemplated. Is McMullen discharged from the contract to build the apartment house?

3. Grattan contracted to build a house and garage for Boris for $50,000. The job was completed according to the specifications in all respects except that Grattan neglected to put a tool shed next to the garage, as required by the contract specifications. Boris refused to pay Grattan, and Grattan sued Boris. Boris raised the defense that Grattan was not entitled to any money until the contract was completely performed and that the performance was incomplete because the tool shed had not been constructed. Was Boris correct?

4. American Bank loaned Koplik $50,000 to buy equipment for a restaurant about to be opened by Casual Citchen Corp. The loan was not repaid, and Fast Foods, Inc., bought out the interest of Casual Citchen. As part of the transaction, Fast Foods agreed to pay the debt owed to American Bank, and the parties agreed to a new schedule of payments to be made by Fast Foods. Fast Foods did not make the payments, and American Bank sued Koplik. He contended that his obligation to repay $50,000 had been discharged by the execution of the agreement providing for the payment of the debt by Fast Foods. Was this defense valid? [*American Bank & Trust Co. v Koplik*, 451 NYS2d 426 (App Div)]

5. Metalcrafters made a contract to design a new earth moving vehicle for Lamar Highway Construction Co. Metalcrafters was depending on the genius of Samet, the head of its research department, to design a new product. Shortly after the contract was made between Metalcrafters and Lamar, Samet was killed in an automobile accident. Metalcrafters was not able to design the product without Samet. Lamar sued Metalcrafters for damages for breach of the contract. Metalcrafters claimed that the contract was discharged by Samet's death. Is it correct?

6. The Tinchers signed a contract to sell land to Creasy. The contract specified that the sales transaction was to be completed in 90 days. At the end of the 90 days Creasy requested an extension of time. The Tinchers refused to grant an extension and stated that the contract was terminated. Creasy claimed that the 90-day clause was not binding because the contract did not state that time was of the essence. Was the contract terminated? [*Creasy v Tincher*, 173 SE2d 332 (W Va)]

7. Christopher Bloom received a medical school scholarship created by the U.S. Department of Health and Human Services to increase the number of doctors serving rural areas. In return for this assistance, Bloom agreed to practice four years in a region identified as being underserved by medical professionals. After some problem with his postgraduation assignment, Bloom requested a repayment

schedule from the agency. Although no terms were offered, Bloom tendered to the agency two checks totaling $15,500 and marked "Final Payment." Neither check was cashed, and the government sued Bloom for $480,000, the value of the assistance provided. Bloom claimed that by tendering the checks to the agency his liability had been discharged by an accord and satisfaction. Decide. [*U.S. v Bloom*, 11 F3d 200 (7th Cir)].

8. Dickson contracted to build a house for Moran. When it was approximately 25 percent to 40 percent completed, Moran would not let Dickson work any further because he was not following the building plans and specifications and there were many defects. Moran hired another contractor to correct the defects and finish the building. Dickson sued Moran for breach of contract, claiming that he had substantially performed the contract up to the point where he had been discharged. Was Dickson correct? [*Dickson v Moran*, 344 So 2d 102 (La App)]

9. A lessor leased a trailer park to a tenant. At the time, sewage was disposed of by a septic tank system that was not connected with the public sewage system. The tenant knew this, and the lease declared that the tenant had examined the premises and that the landlord made no representation or guarantee as to the condition of the premises. Some time thereafter, the septic tank system stopped working properly, and the county health department notified the tenant that he was required to connect the septic tank system with the public sewage system or else the department would close the trailer park. The tenant did not want to pay the additional cost involved in connecting with the public system. The tenant claimed that he was released from the lease and was entitled to a refund of the deposit that he had made. Was he correct? [*Glen R. Sewell Street Metal v Loverde*, 451 P2d 721 (Cal App)]

10. Oneal was a teacher employed by the Colton Consolidated School District. Because of a diabetic condition, his eyesight deteriorated so much that he offered to resign if he would be given pay for a specified number of "sick leave" days. The school district refused to do this and discharged Oneal for nonperformance of his contract. He appealed to remove the discharge from his record. Decide. What ethical values are involved? [*Oneal v Colton Consolidated School District*, 557 P2d 11 (Wash App)]

11. Northwest Construction, Inc., made a contract with the state of Washington for highway construction. Part of the work was turned over under a subcontract to Yakima Asphalt Paving Co. The contract required that any claim be asserted within 180 days. Yakima brought an action for damages after the expiration of 180 days. The defense was that the claim was too late. Yakima replied that the action was brought within the time allowed by the statute of limitations and that the contractual limitation of 180 days was therefore not binding. Was Yakima correct?

12. The Metropolitan Park District of Tacoma gave Griffith a concession to run the district's parks. The agreement gave the right to occupy the parks and use any improvements found therein. The district later wished to set this agreement aside because it was not making sufficient money from the transaction. While it was seeking to set the agreement aside, a boathouse and a gift shop in one of the parks were destroyed by fire. The district then claimed that the concession contract with Griffith was discharged by impossibility of performance. Was it correct? [*Metropolitan Park District of Tacoma v Griffith*, 723 P2d 1093 (Wash)]

13. Suburban Power Piping Corp., under contract to construct a building for LTV Steel Corp., made a subcontract with Power & Pollution Services, Inc., to do some of the work. The subcontract provided that the subcontractor would be paid when the owner (LTV) paid the contractor. LTV went into bankruptcy before making the full payment to the contractor, who then refused to pay the subcontractor on the gound that the "pay-when-paid" provision of the subcontract made payment by the owner a condition precedent to the obligation of the contractor to pay the subcontractor. Was the contractor correct? [*Power & Pollution Services, Inc. v Suburban Power Piping Corp.*, 598 NE2d 69 (Ohio App)]

14. Ellen borrowed money from Farmers' Bank. As evidence of the loan, she signed a promissory note by which she promised to pay to the bank in installments the amount of the loan together with interest and administrative costs. She was unable to make the payments on the scheduled dates. She and the bank then executed a new agreement that gave her a longer period of time for making the payments. However, after two months she was unable to pay on this new schedule. The bank then brought suit against her under the terms of the original agreement. She raised the defense that the original agreement had been discharged by the execution of the second agreement and could not be sued upon. Decide.

15. Acme Hydraulic Press Co. manufactured large presses and sold them throughout the United States. The agreement of sale contract that Acme would execute with its customers specified that they could make no claim for breach of contract unless notice of the breach had been given within 10 days after the delivery of a press in question to the buyer and that no lawsuit could thereafter be brought if notice had not been given. Was this time limitation valid?

CPA QUESTIONS

1. Parc hired Glaze to remodel and furnish an office suite. Glaze submitted plans that Parc approved. After completing all the necessary construction and painting, Glaze purchased minor accessories that Parc rejected because they did not conform to the plans. Parc refused to allow Glaze to complete the project and refused to pay Glaze any part of the contract price. Glaze sued for the value of the work performed. Which of the following statements is correct?
   a. Glaze will lose because Glaze breached the contract by *not* completing performance.
   b. Glaze will win because Glaze substantially performed and Parc prevented complete performance.
   c. Glaze will lose because Glaze materially breached the contract by buying the accessories.
   d. Glaze will win because Parc committed anticipatory breach.

2. Ordinarily, in an action for breach of a construction contract, the statute of limitations time period would be computed from the date the
   a. Contract is negotiated
   b. Contract is breached
   c. Contract is begun
   d. Contract is signed

Obligations and Performance

A. GENERAL PRINCIPLES

1. Obligation of Good Faith
2. Time Requirements of Obligations
3. Repudiation of the Contract
4. Adequate Assurance of Performance

B. DUTIES OF THE PARTIES

5. Seller's Duty to Deliver
6. Buyer's Duty upon Receipt of Goods
7. Buyer's Duty to Accept Goods
8. Buyer's Duty to Pay
9. When Duties Are Excused

Learning Objectives

After studying this chapter, you should be able to

1. Define the obligation of good faith as applied to merchants and nonmerchants
2. State what steps can be taken by a party to a sales contract who feels insecure
3. State the obligations of the seller and the buyer in a sales contract
4. Identify conduct that constitutes an acceptance

Contracts for the sale of goods impose both obligations and requirements for performance on the parties.

A. GENERAL PRINCIPLES

Each party to a sales contract is bound to perform according to the terms of the contract. Each is likewise under a duty to exercise **good faith** in the contract's performance and to do nothing that would impair the other party's expectation that the contract will be performed.

1. Obligation of Good Faith

Every contract or duty within the UCC imposes an obligation of good faith in its performance or enforcement.[1] The UCC defines good faith as "honesty in fact in the conduct or transaction concerned."[2] In the case of a merchant seller or buyer of goods, the UCC carries the concept of good faith further. The UCC imposes the additional requirement that merchants observe "reasonable commercial standards of fair dealing in the trade."[3]

2. Time Requirements of Obligations

In a cash sale that does not require the physical moving of the goods, the duties of the seller and buyer are concurrent. Each one has the right to demand that the other perform at the same time. That is, as the seller hands over the goods, the buyer theoretically must hand over the purchase money. If either party refuses to act, the other party has the right to withhold performance. In self-service stores, the performance of the parties is concurrent. The buyer pays as the items are bagged at checkout.

3. Repudiation of the Contract

If the seller or the buyer refuses to perform the contract when the time for performance arises, a **repudiation** of the contract results. Often, before the time for performance arrives, one party may inform the other that the contract will never be performed. This repudiation made in advance of the time for performance is called an **anticipatory repudiation.**[4]

4. Adequate Assurance of Performance

A party to a sales contract may become concerned that the other party will not perform the contract.[5] ♦ For example, if the seller's warehouse is destroyed by fire, the buyer could worry that the seller will not be able to make a delivery scheduled for the following month. ♦ Whenever a party to a sales contract has reasonable grounds to be concerned about the future performance of the other party, a written demand may be made for *assurance* that the contract will be performed.[6] ♦ For example, a seller who is concerned about a buyer's ability to pay for goods could demand an updated credit report, financial statement, or even additional security or payment. ♦

(a) Form of Assurance. The person on whom demand for assurance is made must give "such assurance of due performance as is adequate under the circumstances of the particular case."[7] The exact form of assurance is not specified by the UCC. If the party on whom demand is made has an established reputation, a reaffirmation of the contract obligation and a statement that it will be performed may be sufficient to assure a reasonable person that it will be performed. In contrast, if the party's reputation or economic position at the time is such that mere words and promises would not give any real assurance, it may be necessary to have a third person (or an insurance company) guarantee performance or put up property as security for performance.

[1] UCC § 1-203; *Plaza Terraces, Inc., v QSC Products, Inc.,* 868 F Supp 346 (DDC 1994).

[2] UCC § 1-201(19); *Kotis v Nowlin Jewelry, Inc.,* 844 SW2d 920 (Tex App 1992).

[3] UCC § 2-103(1)(b); *Amoco Oil Co. v Ervin,* 908 P2d 493 (Colo 1995); *El Paso Natural Gas Co. v Minco Oil & Gas Co.,* 964 SW2d 54(Tex App 1998); *General Electric Co. v Compagnie Euralair,* 945 F Supp 527 (SDNY 1996).

[4] UCC § 2-610; *Aero Consulting Corp. v Cessna Aircraft Co.,* 867 F Supp 1480 (D Kan 1994).

[5] UCC § 2-609.

[6] *S & S, Inc., v Meyer,* 478 NW2d 857 (Iowa App 1991).

[7] UCC § 2-609(4).

(b) Failure to Give Assurance. If adequate assurance is not given within 30 days from the time of demand, the demanding party may treat the contract as repudiated. The demanding party may then sue for damages for breach of contract. In addition, a demanding buyer may make a substitute contract with a third person to obtain goods covered by a broken contract.

The *Hornell Brewing Co., Inc. v Spry* case involves an issue of adequate assurances.

Hornell Brewing Co., Inc., v Spry
664 N Y S 2d 698 (Sup Ct 1997)

The Evaporating Lines of Credit for the Beverage Distributor

Hornell Brewing Company, Inc. (plaintiff or Hornell), is a supplier and marketer of alcoholic and nonalcoholic beverages, including the popular iced tea drink "Arizona." In 1992, Stephen A. Spry approached Don Vultaggio, Hornell's chairman of the board, about becoming a distributor for Hornell's beverages. In January 1993, Spry presented Vultaggio with a most ambitious plan for distributing Hornell beverages in Canada. Based on the proposed plan and Vultaggio's understanding of Spry's stellar reputation as a distributor, Hornell granted Spry the exclusive rights to distribute Arizona products in Canada. Spry formed a Canadian corporation, Arizona Iced Tea, Ltd. (defendants), for the sole purpose of distributing these products.

The initial arrangement was an oral agreement, and, in response to Spry's request for a letter he needed in order to secure financing, Hornell provided a letter that confirmed the distributorship arrangement but which contained no other details. Hornell had agreements with its other distributors, but this arrangement was unique in its lack of paperwork.

During 1993 and 1994, Hornell shipped beverages on 10-day credit terms, but between December of 1993 and February of 1994, Spry's credit balances grew from $20,000 to $100,000 and a $31,000 check from Spry was returned for insufficient funds.

In March 1994, Hornell demanded that Spry obtain a line and/or letter of credit to pay for the beverages in order to place their relationship on more secure footing. Vanguard Financial did send a letter to Spry confirming a "$1,500,000 revolving credit facility," but it never evolved into an actual line of credit. Following a meeting with Spry, during which a factor (Metro Factors, Inc.) was brought in by telephone, Vultaggio demanded that Spry pay all of his arrears and then obtain a $300,000 line of credit or the shipments of the products would not be continued. Vultaggio confirmed these terms in a letter. The deadline for the payment of arrears (April 19, 1994) passed with no payment and no response until April 25, 1994, when Spry proposed that a company named "Metro" pay the amount due of $79,316.24 by May 2, 1994.

Hornell received no payment on May 2, 1994. It did receive a wire transfer from Metro of the full amount on May 9, 1994. Upon immediate confirmation of that payment, Spry ordered 30 trailer loads of "product" from Hornell, at a total purchase price of $390,000 to $450,000. In the interim between April 25, 1994, and May 9, 1994, Hornell learned from several sources, including its regional sales manager Baumkel, that Spry's warehouse was empty, that he had no managerial, sales, or office staff, that he had no trucks, and that in effect his operation was a sham.

On May 10, 1994, Hornell wrote to Spry, acknowledging receipt of payment and confirming that they would extend up to $300, 000 of credit to him, net 14 days cash "based on your prior representation that you have secured a $1,500,000 U.S. line of credit."

Spry did not respond to this letter. Spry never even sent Hornell a copy of his agreement with Metro Factors, Inc., which Spry had signed on March 24, 1994, and which was fully executed on March 30, 1994. On May 26, 1994, Vultaggio met with Spry to discuss termination of their business relationship. Vultaggio presented Spry with a letter of agreement as to the termination, which Spry took with him but did not sign. After some months of futile negotiations by counsel, Hornell filed suit.

LOUISE GRUNER GANS, J. . . . At the outset, the court determines that an enforceable contract existed between plaintiff and defendants based on the uncontroverted facts of their conduct. Under Article 2 of the Uniform Commercial Code, parties can form a contract through their conduct rather than merely through the exchange of communications constituting an offer and acceptance.

Both parties' undisputed actions over a period of many months clearly manifested mutual recognition that a binding obligation was undertaken.

Notwithstanding the parties' conflicting contentions concerning the duration and termination of defendants' distributorship, plaintiff has demonstrated a basis for lawfully terminating its contract with defendants in accordance with section 2-609 of the Uniform Commercial Code. Section 2-609 authorizes one party upon "reasonable grounds for insecurity" to "demand adequate assurance of due performance and until he receive such assurance . . . , if commercially reasonable, suspend performance for which he has not already received the agreed return."

Whether a seller, as the plaintiff in this case, has reasonable grounds for insecurity is an issue of fact that depends upon various factors, including the buyer's exact words or actions, the course of dealing or performance between the parties, and the nature of the sales contract and the industry.

Once the seller correctly determines that it has reasonable grounds for insecurity, it must properly request assurances from the buyer. Although the Code requires that the request be made in writing, UCC § 2-609(1), courts have not strictly adhered to this formality as long as an unequivocal demand is made. After demanding assurance, the seller must determine the proper "adequate assurance." What constitutes "adequate" assurance of due performance is subject to the same test of commercial reasonableness and factual conditions.

Applying these principles to the case at bar, the overwhelming weight of the evidence establishes that at the latest by the beginning of 1994, plaintiff had reasonable grounds to be insecure about defendants' ability to perform in the future. Defendants were substantially in arrears almost from the outset of their relationship with plaintiff, had no financing in place, bounced checks, and had failed to sell even a small fraction of the product defendant Spry originally projected.

Reasonable grounds for insecurity can arise from the sole fact that a buyer has fallen behind in his account with the seller, even where the items involved have to do with separate and legally distinct contracts, because this "impairs the seller's expectation of due performance."

Here, defendants do not dispute their poor payment history, plaintiff's right to demand adequate assurances from them and that plaintiff made such demands. Rather, defendants claim that they satisfied those demands by the April 15, 1994 telephone conversation between Vultaggio and Richard Worthy of Metro Factors, Inc., followed by Vultaggio's April 18, 1994 letter to Metro, and Metro's payment of $79,316.24 to Hornell, and that thereafter plaintiff had no right to demand further assurance.

The court disagrees with both plaintiff and defendants in their insistence that only one demand for adequate assurance was made in this case to which there was and could be only a single response. Even accepting defendants' argument that payment by Metro was the sole condition Vultaggio required when he spoke and wrote to Metro, and that such condition was met by Metro's actual payment, the court is persuaded that on May 9, 1994, Hornell had further reasonable grounds for insecurity and a new basis for seeking further adequate assurances.

Here, there was a further change of circumstances. Vultaggio's reported conversation with Worthy on April 15 and his April 25 letter to Metro, both anticipate that once payment of defendants' arrears was made, Hornell would release *up to* $300,000 worth of product on the further condition that defendants met the 14 day payment terms. The arrangement, by its terms, clearly contemplated an opportunity for Hornell to test out defendants' ability to make payment within 14-day periods.

By placing a single order worth $390,000 to $450,000 immediately after receipt of Metro's payment, Spry not only demanded a shipment of product which exceeded the proposed limit, but placed Hornell in a position where it would have *no* opportunity learn whether Spry would meet the 14-day payment terms, before Spry again became indebted to Hornell for a very large sum of money.

These circumstances, coupled with information received in early May (on which it reasonably relied) that Spry had mislead Hornell about the scope of his operation, created new and more acute grounds for Hornell's insecurity and entitled Hornell to seek further adequate assurance from defendants in the form of a documented line of credit or other guarantee. Defendants' failure to respond constituted a repudiation of the distributorship agreement, which entitled plaintiff to suspend performance and terminate the agreement.

The court notes in conclusion that its evaluation of the evidence in this case was significantly influenced by Mr. Spry's regrettable lack of credibility. The court agrees with plaintiff, that to an extent far greater than was known to Hornell in May 1994, Mr. Spry was not truthful, failed to pay countless other creditors almost as a matter of course, and otherwise engaged in improper and deceptive business practices.

For the foregoing reasons, it is hereby ORDERED and ADJUDGED that plaintiff Hornell Brewing Co., Inc. have a declaratory judgment that defendants Stephen A. Spry and Arizona Tea Products, Ltd. were duly terminated and have no continuing rights with respect to plaintiff Hornell Brewing Co.'s beverage products in Canada or elsewhere.

Questions

1. What type of assurances did Hornell want?
2. Do you think Hornell was reasonable in its time demands and types of assurances?
3. Was there a breach of contracts?

B. DUTIES OF THE PARTIES

The obligations of the parties to a sales contract include (1) the seller's duty to deliver the goods, (2) the buyer's duty to accept the goods, and (3) the buyer's duty to pay for the goods.

5. Seller's Duty to Deliver

The seller has the duty to deliver the goods in accordance with the terms of the contract.

(a) Place, Time, and Manner of Delivery. The terms of the contract determine whether the seller is to send the goods or the buyer is to call for them and whether the goods are to be transported from the seller to the buyer or the transaction is to be completed by the delivery of documents without the movement of the goods. In the absence of a provision in the contract or a contrary course of performance or usage of trade, the place of delivery is the seller's place of business if the seller has one; otherwise, it is the seller's residence. (See Chapter 25 for more details on delivery and shipping terms.)[8] However, if the subject matter of the contract consists of identified goods that are known by the parties to be in some other

[8] UCC § 2-308.

place, that place is the place of delivery. If no time for shipment or delivery is stated, delivery or shipment is required within a reasonable time.

When a method of transportation called for by the contract becomes unavailable or commercially unreasonable, the seller must make delivery by means of a commercially reasonable substitute if available.

(b) Quantity Delivered. The buyer has the right to insist that all the goods be delivered at one time. If the seller delivers a smaller or larger quantity than what is stipulated in the contract, the buyer may refuse to accept the goods.[9]

6. Buyer's Duty upon Receipt of Goods

The buyer must accept goods that conform to the contract, and the refusal to do so is a breach of the contract. However, the buyer has certain rights prior to acceptance.

(a) Right to Examine Goods—The Buyer's Right of Inspection.[10] To determine whether the goods in fact conform to the contract, the buyer has the right to examine the goods when tendered by the seller. An exception to this rule occurs when goods are sent COD. In a COD shipment, the buyer has no right to examine the goods until payment is made.

The buyer's right of *inspection* includes the right to remove goods from cartons and conduct tests. ♦ For example, a buyer who is purchasing potatoes for use in making potato chips has the right to peel and test a portion of the potatoes to determine whether they are the appropriate type for "chipping." ♦

(b) Right to Refuse or Return the Goods—The Buyer's Right of Rejection.[11] If the goods the seller has tendered do not conform to the contract in any way, the buyer can *reject* the goods. ♦ For example, the buyer may reject a mobile home when it does not contain an air conditioner with the capacity specified by the contract. ♦ The buyer may reject the goods if they are not perfect. The standard for rejection does not require that

the defect in the goods or the breach be material. ♦ For example, a small pressure mark on an ottoman is not material; the ottoman will function just as well. However, the buyer still has the right to reject the ottoman because it has a defect. ♦

The buyer has the right to reject the full shipment, accept the full shipment and seek damages for the goods' diminished value (see Chapter 28) or accept any **commercial units** and reject the remainder. Commercial units are defined by trade and industry according to the customary size of cartons or containers for the goods shipped. Envelopes come in commercial units of boxes of 500. Computer disks often come in packages of 20 or 50. Rejection by a buyer in these cases would be not of individual envelopes or disks, but of boxes. ♦ For example, if Donna purchased a package of 20 disks and 4 of the 20 disks were defective, Donna would return the box of 20 disks for a new box. ♦ Rejection and acceptance in commercial units prevent the problems created when a seller has to open other units and mix and match goods in each.

After rejecting the goods, the buyer may not exercise any right of ownership over the goods. The buyer must hold the goods and await instructions from the seller. If the buyer disposes of the goods before the seller has had a reasonable time in which to give instructions, the buyer is liable for any loss.[12]

The buyer's rejection must be made within a reasonable time after the delivery or tender of the goods. The buyer must notify the seller of the rejection and, in transactions with merchants particularly, provide the seller with the reason for the rejection.[13]

(c) Cure of Defective Tender or Delivery. The reason for the notification of rejection to the seller by the buyer is that the UCC gives a right of cure to the seller if the seller tenders or delivers nonconforming goods. The buyer's rejection is not an end to the transaction. The seller is given a second chance, or a **right to cure,** to make a proper tender of conforming goods.[14]

This right of cure is restricted by whether the seller can make the second tender of the goods

---

[9] UCC § 2-307.

[10] UCC § 2-601.

[11] UCC § 2-602; *Total Foods Corp. v Wilfran Agricultural Industries, Inc.,* 945 F Supp 100 (EDPa 1996).

[12] UCC § 2-603.

[13] UCC § 2-602(1); *Loden v Drake,* 881 P2d 467 (Colo App 1994).

[14] *Allied Semi-Conductors Int'l v Pulsar Components Int'l, Inc.,* 907 F Supp 618 (EDNY 1995).

within the time remaining for performance under the contract. If the time for making delivery under the contract has not expired, the seller need only give the buyer **seasonable** (timely) notice of the intention to make a proper delivery within the time allowed by the contract. However, if the time for making the delivery has expired, the seller may be given an additional reasonable time in which to make a substitute conforming tender. Additional time is allowed if (1) the seller so notifies the buyer and (2) the seller had acted reasonably in making the original tender, believing that it would be acceptable to the buyer.

7. Buyer's Duty to Accept Goods

Assuming that the buyer has no grounds for rejection of the goods after inspection, the next step in the performance of the contract is the buyer's **acceptance** of the goods.

(a) **What Constitutes Acceptance of Goods.**[15] Acceptance of goods means that the buyer, pursuant to a contract, has, either expressly or by implication, taken the goods permanently. The buyer's statement of acceptance is an express acceptance. A buyer can accept goods by implication if there is no rejection after a reasonable opportunity to inspect them or after a reasonable time after the buyer has inspected them. Another form of acceptance by implication is conduct by the buyer that is inconsistent with rejection, as when a buyer uses or sells the delivered goods.[16]

A buyer accepts goods by making continued use of them and by not attempting to return them. A buyer, of course, accepts goods by modifying them because such action is inconsistent with a rejection or with the continued ownership of the goods by the seller.

(b) **Revocation of Acceptance.** Even after acceptance of the goods, the performance under the contract may not be finished if the buyer exercises the right to revoke acceptance of the goods.[17] The buyer may revoke acceptance of the goods when they do not conform to the contract, the defect is such that it substantially impairs the value of the

contract to the buyer, and either the defect is such that the buyer could not discover the problem or the seller has promised to correct a problem the buyer was aware of and pointed out to the seller prior to acceptance. ◆ For example, a buyer who purchased an emergency electric power generator found that the generator produced only about 65 percent of the power called for by the contract. This amount of power was insufficient for the operation of the buyer's electrical equipment. The seller's repeated attempts to improve the generator's ouput failed. The buyer, despite having used the generator for three months, could revoke his acceptance of it because its value was substantially impaired and he continued to keep it and use it only because of the seller's assurances that it would be repaired. ◆

Substantial impairment is a higher standard than the one of "fails to conform in any respect" for rejection. Substantial impairment requires proof of more than the mere fact that the goods do not conform to the contract. The buyer is not required to show that the goods are worthless, but the buyer must prove that their use to him is substantially different from what the contract promised.

A revocation of acceptance is not a cancellation of the contract with the seller. After revocation of acceptance, the buyer can choose from the remedies available for breach of contract or demand that the seller deliver conforming goods. (See Chapter 28 for more information on remedies for breach.)

(c) **Notification of Revocation of Acceptance.** To revoke acceptance properly, the buyer must take certain steps. The buyer must give the seller notice of revocation. The revocation of acceptance is effective when the buyer notifies the seller. The buyer need not actually return the goods to make the notification or the revocation effective.

The notice of revocation of acceptance must be given within a reasonable time after the buyer discovers or should have discovered the problems with the goods. The right of revocation is not lost if the buyer gives the seller a longer period of time to correct the defects in the goods. Even the lapse of a year will not cost the buyer the right of revocation of acceptance if the seller has been experimenting during that time trying to correct the problems with the goods.

The *Jackson Hole Traders, Inc v Joseph* case deals with the timeliness of revocation of acceptance.

---

[15] UCC § 2-606.

[16] *Contours, Inc., v Lee,* 874 P2d 1100 (Haw App 1994).

[17] UCC § 2-608; *Fode v Capital RV Center, Inc.,* 575 NW2d 682 (ND 1998).

Jackson Hole Traders, Inc., v Joseph
931 P 2d 244 (Wyo 1997)

Jackson Hole Traders: The Retailer Looking for a Loop hole

Catherine Joseph, who does business as Metro Classics (appellee), sold clothing to Jackson Hole Traders, Inc., a corporation owned by David and Elizabeth Speaks (appellants). Jackson Hole Traders is located in Jackson, Wyoming, and sells clothing for men and women through a retail store and mail-order catalog business. The clothing Joseph sold was specially manufactured for Jackson Hole Traders and had a total contract price of $50,000, with terms being net 30.

When the clothing items were shipped between July and September, 1994, approximately 900 items were sent. Elizabeth Speaks complained about the quality on some of the clothing items when they arrived and was given a credit of $1,096 for returned merchandise. However, Jackson Hole Traders did not pay $33,000 of the total Joseph bill despite it being well past the net-30-day period for payment. When Joseph demanded payment, Elizabeth Speaks boxed up approximately 350 items of the clothing and sent them back, demanding a credit for revocation of acceptance. Joseph filed suit for payment alleging that it was too late for revocation of acceptance. The trial court found for Joseph, and the Speakses appealed.

MACY, J. . . . Appellants claim that the trial court improperly concluded that the Uniform Commercial Code governed the parties' transaction, arguing that this transaction was principally one for labor and services. Appellee counters that the trial court appropriately applied the Uniform Commercial Code to this transaction because it was for the sale of goods.

For support of their proposition that this transaction was one for services rather than for goods, Appellants rely on *Wells v 10-X Manufacturing Company*, 609 F.2d 248 (6th Cir.1979). That case, however, differs from the case at bar because the buyer in *Wells* furnished the manufacturer with virtually everything but the labor:

In this case, 10-X agreed to "cut, make, and finish" for Wells 550 dozen hunting shirts. While 10-X was to furnish the thread, all other materials involved in the production of the shirt were to be provided by Wells. Wells was in all other respects responsible for the design and development of the shirt.

. . . The language used in the contract clearly bespeaks the intention of the parties that 10-X's obligation under the contract was essentially to provide the manpower and machine capabilities for production of the hunting shirt. That the only material supplied by 10-X in the entire production

process was thread is a factor to be considered in characterizing the contract one for services rather than goods. Wells, 609 F.2d at 255.

Although Appellants purchased and supplied the outer fabric for some of the garments produced by Appellee, Appellee supplied all the other materials which were used to manufacture the garments; i.e., buttons, linings, interfacing, special care labels, as well as the outer fabric for the remaining garments. Some garments were patterned from Appellee's own designs. Even for those styles which utilized a design provided by Appellants, Appellee and her pattern maker had to restyle them because of various changes which were requested by Appellants. Each pattern was then graded into the particular sizes to be used for that garment. Under the facts of this case, the trial court correctly applied the Uniform Commercial Code as this transaction was one for the sale of goods even though labor was involved in producing the goods.

Appellee shipped approximately 900 garments to Appellants between July 18, 1994, and the last week of September 1994 plus an additional "holiday" order during the last week of October 1994. Of the 900 garments, Appellants properly rejected ten vests and four coats, returning these garments to Appellee in early October. Appellee gave them a credit for these items. Appellants kept all the other goods until mid-December 1994 when Appellee demanded that Appellants pay the remaining $32,000 which they owed to her. In response to that demand, Appellants packed up 350 garments and shipped them back to Appellee. David Speaks gave the following testimony with regard to Appellants' response to Appellee's demand:

[APPELLEE'S ATTORNEY:] Now, I sent you a letter dated December 9 asking for thirty-two thousand dollars for [Appellee], did I not?

A. Yes, you did.

Q. And your response was to pack up 350 garments that she had manufactured at your request and ship them back in bulk to her, wasn't it?

A. That's what we did, yes.

. . . .

[Q.] Now, the goods that you shipped back to [Appellee], you instructed—either you or Ms. Speaks instructed someone working for you to take the goods off of the showroom floor and box them up and send them back. Some of the goods that were returned to [Appellee] were pulled off the showroom floor, weren't they?

A. Most likely, yes. I'm almost positive, yeah.

Q. And some of those items were pulled off the shelves where they had been stored for several months, weren't they?

A. You're talking about in the warehouse?

Q. Yes.

A. Yes, they were.

. . . .

Q. If you don't think the goods got there on time and you think that you have been put in a bad way as a result of that, you can refuse the shipment, can't you?

A. You can refuse the shipment, yes, you can. That is one option.

Q. And you could have done that, couldn't you?

A. That's an option, yes.

Q. But you didn't refuse the shipment, did you?

A. No, we did not.

Q. And you put the goods in your warehouse, didn't you?

A. Yes, they were in the warehouse.

Q. And put them on your showroom floor, didn't you?

A. Yes, we did.

Q. And you sold them through your catalog; is that right?

A. Yes, we did.

Q. And you sold many of them in your store, didn't you?

A. Yes, we did.

. . . .

[Q.] When I sent you the letter on December 9th asking for payment of the thirty-two thousand plus dollars owed to [Appellee], your response within 72 hours was to take everything and ship it back to [Appellee]; is that correct?

A. Yes, it was.

Appellants breached the contract when they failed to pay for the garments which had been sent to them and which they had accepted for resale. The trial court properly awarded damages in an amount which would place Appellee in the same position that she would have occupied had the contract been performed.

[Affirmed]

Questions

1. How long had the goods been with the buyer?
2. Where were the goods when they were packaged to be sent back?
3. Will the seller get her money?

(d) Buyer's Responsibilities upon Revocation of Acceptance. After a revocation of acceptance, the buyer must hold the goods and await instructions from the seller. If the buyer revokes acceptance after having paid the seller in advance, the buyer may retain possession of the goods as security for the refund of the money that has been paid.

At Saks Fifth Avenue, they call it the "return season." Return season occurs within the week following a major fund-raising formal dance. Women who have purchased formal evening wear return the dresses after the dance. The dresses have been worn, and the tags have been cut, but the women return the dresses with requests for a full refund. Neiman Marcus also experiences the same phenomenon of returns.

Some stores have implemented a policy that formal evening wear may not be returned if the tags are cut from it. Others require a return within a limited period of seven days. Others offer an exchange only after five days.

Are the women covered by a right of rejection under Article 2? What do you think of the conduct of the women? Is it simply revocation of acceptance? Is there good faith on the part of the women?

8. Buyer's Duty to Pay

The buyer must pay the amount stated in the sales contract for accepted goods.

(a) **Time of Payment.** The sales contract may require payment in advance or may give the buyer credit by postponing the time for payment.[18]

(b) **Form of Payment.** Unless otherwise agreed, payment by the buyer requires payment in cash.

The seller may accept a check or a promissory note from the buyer. If the check is not paid by the bank, the purchase price remains unpaid. A promissory note payable at a future date gives the buyer credit by postponing the time for payment.

The seller can refuse to accept a check or a promissory note as payment for goods but must give the buyer reasonable time in which to obtain legal tender with which to make payment.

9. When Duties Are Excused

Under Article 2, the doctrine of **commercial impracticability** is available as a defense to performance of a contract. The doctrine of commercial impracticability is the modern commercial law version of the common law doctrine of impossibility. If a party to a contract can establish that there has been an occurrence or a contingency not anticipated by the parties and not a basic assumption in their entering into a contract, the party can be excused from performance.

The standard for commercial impracticability is objective, not subjective. ♦ For example, if a farmer has contracted to sell two tons of peanuts to an airline and his crop fails, he is not excused on the grounds of commercial impracticability. So long as there are peanuts available for the farmer to buy and then sell to the buyer to satisfy their contract terms, the farmer is not excused. Commercial impracticability refers to those circumstances in which peanuts are not available anywhere because the entire peanut harvest was destroyed rather than just the individual farmer's crop. ♦

The *Alamance County Board of Education v Bobby Murray Chevrolet* case involves an issue of commercial impracticability.

Alamance County Board of Education v Bobby Murray Chevrolet, Inc.
28 UCC Rep Serv 2d 1220 (NC App 1996)

The 1,200 School Buses That Were Never Delivered

Bobby Murray Chevrolet, Inc., submitted a bid to the Alamance County Board of Education to supply 1,200 school bus chassis to the district. Bobby Murray was awarded the contract and contracted with General Motors (GM) to purchase the chassis for the school board.

---

[18] UCC § 2-310.

In between the time of Bobby Murray's contract with GM and the delivery date, the Environmental Protection Agency (EPA) enacted new emission standards for diesel vehicles, such as school buses. Under the new law, the buses Bobby Murray ordered from GM would be out of compliance, as would the buses Bobby Murray specified in its bid to the school board.

GM asked for several extensions in order to manufacture the buses within the new EPA guidelines. The school board was patient and gave several extensions, but then, due to its needs for buses, purchased them from another supplier after notifying Bobby Murray of its intent to do so. The school board had to pay an additional $150,152.94 for the buses from its alternative source and sued Bobby Murray for that amount. Bobby Murray claimed it was excused from performance on the grounds of commercial impracticability. The lower court found for the board, and Bobby Murray appealed.

JOHN, J. . . . .Bobby Murray admits the bus chassis ordered by plaintiff school boards were never delivered. However, Bobby Murray contends its lack of performance should be excused pursuant to N.C.G.S. § 25-2-615.

Bobby Murray contends the failure of GM to supply the bus chassis was "a contingency the nonoccurrence of which" was a basic assumption of the underlying contracts between Bobby Murray and plaintiffs. Second, Bobby Murray claims governmental regulation prohibiting the installation of the 8.2N engine after 1 January 1991 was an intervening factor which should operate as an excuse.

U.C.C. § 2-615 has its roots in the relatively recent common law doctrines of impossibility of performance and frustration of purpose, which evolved from the original common law rule that parties to a contract were to be held absolutely to its terms. The official comments to § 2-615 indicate that both doctrines were intended to be embraced within a U.C.C. concept denominated "commercial impracticability."

Commentators have asserted that the drafters of the U.C.C. intended "commercial impracticability" to allow a more liberal standard in releasing promisors from contracts than the common law had afforded, but have also noted that courts generally have declined to heed such alleged intent.

In order to be excused under § 2-615, a seller of goods must establish the following elements:

"(1) performance has become 'impracticable';

"(2) the impracticability was due to the occurrence of some contingency which the parties expressly or impliedly agreed would discharge the promisor's duty to perform;

"(3) the promisor did not assume the risk that the contingency would occur;

"(4) the promisor seasonably notified the promisee of the delay in delivery or that delivery would not occur at all[.]"

Utilizing the foregoing criteria as well as the official commentary to § 2-615 and case law from other jurisdictions, we now consider Bobby Murray's arguments on appeal.

Initially, Bobby Murray contends an implied condition of its contract with plaintiffs was the ability of GM to manufacture and supply the ordered bus chassis. We agree that when an exclusive source of supply is specified in a contract or may be implied by circumstances to have been contemplated by the parties, failure of that source may excuse the promisor from performance. However, neither contingency is reflected in the record herein.

Bobby Murray insists in its brief that "[a]ppellant disclosed in the bid that the chassis would be manufactured by Chevrolet and Plaintiff-Appellees had knowledge that Appellant's sole source of supply was General Motors." However, Bobby Murray points to no record evidence of such knowledge on the part of plaintiffs, and appears to rely solely upon its status as a GM franchisee to support its assertion.

By contrast, we note that the "General Contract Terms and Conditions" on Form TC-1, incorporated into the bid document, contain the following section entitled "MANUFACTURER'S NAMES":

"Any manufacturers' names, trade names, brand names, information and/or catalog numbers used herein are for purpose(s) of description and establishing general quality levels. Such references are not intended to be restrictive and products of any manufacturer may be offered."

Further, no clause in the contract between plaintiffs and Bobby Murray conditioned the latter's performance on its ability to obtain bus chassis from its manufacturer.

Moreover, assuming arguendo GM was contemplated by the parties as Bobby Murray's exclusive source, the record reflects that Bobby Murray assumed the risk of its failure to supply the vehicles, as it was foreseeable that GM might not supply the bus chassis. Failure to make express provision for a foreseeable contingency in a sales contract implicitly places the burden of loss on the seller when the contingency comes to fruition.

Foreseeability under § 2-615 is an objective standard; it matters not whether the seller thought a certain event would or would not occur, but what contingencies were reasonably foreseeable at the time the contract was made. Henning & Wallach, supra, at ¶ 5.10[2], 5-36 (1992). Examination of the record reveals that cancellation of chassis orders by GM was a risk reasonably foreseeable to Bobby Murray.

For example, the "Dealer Sales and Service Agreement" between Bobby Murray and GM provides as follows:

"Dealer's order for . . . Motor Vehicles are not binding on . . . [GM] until accepted by [GM]. . . . Orders are accepted by [GM] when Released to Production."

Vehicle orders thus bind GM only upon "Release to Production" of the subject vehicles. The bus chassis at issue herein were never "released to production."

The same document also suggests numerous factors which might affect the availability of vehicles, including "component availability" and "governmental regulations," and indicates that GM reserved the discretion to distribute vehicles based upon its own judgment.

Similarly, the record herein contains no evidence of a contract between Bobby Murray and GM to ensure delivery of the ordered chassis. Robin J. Fleming, fleet sales manager of Bobby Murray, in deposition simply claimed GM had never before failed to produce vehicles for which it had taken orders while he had been with Bobby Murray, notwithstanding provisions in the "Dealer Sales and Service Agreement" to the effect that orders did not bind GM until the vehicles were "Released to Production" and that certain specified factors might affect production.

Moreover, during the time orders were accepted from plaintiffs, Bobby Murray also received a DCS message revealing that GM was experiencing shortages of Allison automatic transmissions. Bobby Murray therefore also had actual notice its source of supply might fail.

We next examine Bobby Murray's contention its performance should be excused in consequence of intervening governmental regulations. Generally, governmental regulations do not excuse performance under a contract where a party has assumed the risk of such regulation. The contract between the parties sub judice, in its "General Contract Terms and Conditions", Form TC-1, provided as follows:

"GOVERNMENTAL RESTRICTIONS: In the event any Governmental restrictions may be imposed which would necessitate alteration of the material, quality, workmanship or performance of the items offered on this proposal prior to their delivery, it shall be the responsibility of the successful bidder to notify this Division at once, indicating in his letter the specific regulation which required such alterations. The State reserves the right to accept any such alterations, including any price adjustments occasioned thereby, or to cancel the contract."

Bobby Murray, by terms of the parties' agreement, accepted responsibility for keeping abreast of governmental regulations bearing upon the contract.

In addition, Bobby Murray was on notice 26 July 1990 that new emissions standards would preclude, effective 1 January 1991, production of bus chassis using the 8.2N engine specified in its bid. Nothing in the record indicates that this information was conveyed to plaintiffs. Bobby Murray was further notified 10 August 1990 that production dates could be pushed beyond December 1990. The record contains no evidence that Bobby Murray explored with plaintiffs, or otherwise, alternative methods of meeting its contractual obligations. Under these circumstances, equity dictates that excuse by governmental regulation be unavailable to Bobby Murray. "The absence of fault is . . . an important part of a Section 2-615 defense." In sum, governmental regulations do not supervene in this case.

[Affirmed]

Questions

1. Why could the buses not be delivered?
2. What defense to performance is raised?
3. Is Bobby Murray excused?

SUMMARY

Every sales contract imposes an obligation of good faith in its performance. Good faith means honesty in fact in the conduct or transaction concerned. For merchants, the UCC imposes the additional requirement of observing "reasonable commercial standards of fair dealing in the trade."

In the case of a cash sale where no transportation of the goods is required, both the buyer and the seller may demand concurrent performance.

A buyer's or a seller's refusal to perform a contract is called a repudiation. A repudiation made in advance of the time for performance is called an anticipatory repudiation and is a breach of the contract. If either party to a contract feels insecure about the performance of the other, that party may demand in writing adequate assurance of performance. If that assurance is not given, the demanding party may treat the contract as repudiated.

The seller has a duty to deliver the goods in accordance with the terms of the contract. This duty does not require physical transportation; it requires that the seller permit the transfer of possession of the goods to the buyer.

With the exception of COD contracts, the buyer has the right to inspect the goods upon tender or delivery. Inspection includes the right to open cartons and conduct tests.

If the inspection by the buyer reveals that the seller has tendered nonconforming goods, the buyer may reject them. Subject to certain limitations, the seller may then offer to replace the goods or cure the problems the buyer has noted.

The buyer has a duty to accept goods that conform to the contract, and refusal to do so is a breach of contract. The buyer is deemed to have accepted goods either expressly or by implication through conduct inconsistent with rejection or by lapse of time. The buyer must pay for accepted goods in accordance with the terms of the contract. The buyer can reject goods in commercial units, accept the goods and collect damages for their problems, or reject the full contract shipment. The buyer must give notice of rejection to the seller and cannot do anything with the goods that would be inconsistent with the seller's ownership rights. The buyer should await instructions from the seller on what to do with the goods.

Even following acceptance, the buyer may revoke that acceptance if the problems with the goods substantially impair their value and the problems were either not easily discoverable or the buyer kept the goods based on the seller's promises to repair them and make them whole. Upon revocation of acceptance, the buyer should await instructions from the seller on what steps to take.

Performance can be excused on the grounds of commercial impracticability, but the seller must show objective difficulties that create more than cost increases.

WEBSITE REFERENCES

For a look at consumer's rights and goods, visit

www.consumersunion.org

The electronic UCC Bulletin is available by sending an email to

listproc@assocdir.wuacc.edu

QUESTIONS AND CASE PROBLEMS

1. In 1992, Donna Smith telephoned Clark, the manager of Penbridge Farms, in response to an advertisement Clark had placed in the July issue of the Emu Finder about the availability for sale of proven breeder pairs. Clark told Smith he had a breeder pair available for purchase. Clark sold the pair to Smith for $16,500. Some months later, after Smith had had a chance to inspect the pair, she discovered that Clark had sold her two male emus. Smith immediately notified Clark and revoked her acceptance of the animals. Clark said the revocation was too late. Is it? [*Smith v Penbridge Associates, Inc.,* 655 A2d 1015 (Pa Super)]

2. On January 3, 1991, Central District Alarm (CDA) and Hal-Tuc entered into a written sales agreement providing that CDA would sell and install new security equipment described on an equipment list attached to the contract. This list included a Javelin VCR. When the system was installed, CDA installed a used JVC VCR instead of a new Javelin VCR. Hal-Tuc called CDA the day after the installation and complained that the equipment was not the Javelin brand and that the VCR was a used JVC VCR. CDA told Hal-Tuc that the equipment was not used and that a JVC VCR was better than a Javelin. Hal-Tuc telephoned CDA personnel over a two-week period during which they denied that the equipment was used. After two weeks of calls, CDA's installation manager went to the store to see the equipment and admitted that it was used. No one from CDA advised Hal-Tuc in advance that they were installing used equipment temporarily until the right equipment arrived.

   CDA offered to replace it with a new Javelin VCR as soon as one arrived, which would take one or two months. Hal-Tuc asked CDA to return its deposit and take the equipment back. but CDA refused. Hal-Tuc put all the equipment in boxes and stored it. CDA filed a petition against Hal-Tuc for damages for breach of contract. Hal-Tuc filed a counterclaim, alleging fraud. CDA asserted it had the right to cure by tendering conforming goods after Hal-Tuc rejected the nonconforming goods. Is CDA correct? [*Central District Alarm, Inc., v Hal-Tuc, Inc.,* 866 SW2d 210 (Mo App)]

3. Custom Built Homes purchased unassembled prefabricated houses from Page-Hill in Minnesota to be delivered by the seller "FOB building site Kansas." The seller brings the houses to the building site by tractor-trailer, where he unhitches the trailer and unloads the shipment. What rights of inspection and rejection does Custom Built have? Explain some defects that might permit revocation of acceptance. [*Custom Built Homes Co. v Kansas State Commission of Revenue,* 334 P2d 808 (Kan)]

4. Washington ordered a computer by mail from Grant Co. in Seattle. It was sent to her COD. To be sure that there has been no mistake, Washington has asked to examine the computer before she pays the carrier. Can she do so?

5. Lafer Enterprises sold Christmas decorations to B.P. Development & Management Corp., the owners and operators of the Osceola Square Mall. The package of decorations was delivered to Osceola Square Mall prior to Thanksgiving 1986 for a total cost of $48,775, which B.P. would pay in three installments. Cathy Trivigno, a manager at B.P. who supervised the installation of the decorations, indicated that she and the Osceola Square Mall merchants were not satisfied with the quality of the decorations but that they needed to be in place for the day after Thanksgiving (the

start of the holiday shopping season). B.P. complained to Lafer about the quality of the decorations but had the decorations installed. B.P. paid the first installment to Lafer but then stopped payment on the last two checks. B.P. claimed it had rejected the decorations. Lafer claimed breach for nonpayment because B.P. used the decorations. Did B.P. accept the decorations? [*B.P. Dev. & Management Corp. v Lafer Enterprises, Inc.*, 538 So 2d 1379 (Fla App)]

6. International Minerals and Metals Corp. contracted to sell Weinstein scrap metal that was to be delivered within 30 days. Later the seller informed the buyer that it could not make delivery within that time. The buyer agreed to an extension of time, but no limiting date was set. Within what time must the seller perform? [*International Minerals and Metals Corp. v Weinstein*, 73 SE2d 472 (NC)]

7. Carlson ordered equipment from Ventresca Foundry in St. Louis, Missouri, to be sent "FOB Chicago, Illinois." The equipment was placed on a motor freight truck under a proper shipment contract. The truck was wrecked before it reached Chicago. Ventresca demands payment of the purchase price from Carlson. Carlson says he has inspected the goods and they are defective. Must he take them?

8. Spaulding & Kimball Co. ordered from Aetna Chemical Co. 75 cartons of window washers. The buyer received them and sold about a third to its customers but later refused to pay for them, claiming that the quality was poor. The seller sued for the price. Decide. [*Aetna Chemical Co. v Spaulding & Kimball Co.*, 126 A 582 (Vt)]

9. A computer manufacturer promoted the sale of a digital computer as a "revolutionary breakthrough." The manufacturer made a contract to deliver one of these computers to a buyer. The seller failed to deliver the computer and explained that its failure was caused by unanticipated technological difficulties. Was this an excuse for nonperformance by the seller? [*United States v Wegematic Corp.*, 360 F2d 674 (2d Cir)]

10. Economy Farms Corp. sold concrete-forming equipment to Kandy. After using the equipment for over six months, Kandy notified Economy that the equipment was inadequate. Economy Farms alleged that Kandy had accepted the goods. Kandy denied liability. Was there an acceptance? Why or why not? [*Economy Forms Corp. v Kandy, Inc.*, 391 F Supp 944 (ND Ga)]

11. Teeman made a contract to purchase lumber from Oakhill Mill. The contract called for payment to be made on delivery to Teeman. When the truck from the mill arrived to deliver the lumber, Teeman gave the driver a check for the purchase price. The driver refused to take the check or leave the lumber. The driver returned to the mill, and the mill then notified Teeman that the contract was canceled. Was the mill entitled to cancel the contract?

12. Lury has a sales contract with Burns, with whom he has not previously dealt, to make four quarterly deliveries of a product on 30 days' credit. Two months after the first delivery under the contract Burns has not yet paid. Can Lury demand adequate assurance of performance?

13. Matsuda was in the process of furnishing her apartment. She purchased a leather sofa and three leather chairs from Davenport Furniture, Inc., to be delivered in 20 days. She paid part of the purchase price upon executing the order and agreed to pay the balance on delivery. Davenport delivered the sofa and the chairs a week later, but the leather chairs did not match the sofa. Matsuda thereupon rejected the sofa and the chairs. She also demanded the return of her money. What rights, if any, does Davenport have?

14. Harry Ulmas made a contract to buy a new car from Acey Oldsmobile. He was allowed to keep his old car until the new car was delivered. The sales contract gave him a trade-in value of $650 on the old car but specified that the car would be reappraised when it was actually brought to the dealer. When Ulmas brought the trade-in to the dealer, an Acey employee took it for a test drive and said that the car was worth between $300 and $400. Acey offered Ulmas only $50 for his trade-in. Ulmas refused to buy from Acey and purchased from another dealer, who appraised the trade-in at $400. Ulmas sued for breach of

contract on the grounds of violation of good faith. Is he right? [*Ulmas v Acey Oldsmobile, Inc.,* 310 NYS 2d 147 (NY Civ)]

15. Cornelia and Ed Kornfeld contracted to sell a signed Picasso print to David Tunick, Inc. The print, entitled *Le Minotauromachie,* was to be signed "Pablo Picasso." The signature on the print was discovered to be a forgery, and the Kornfelds offered Tunick a substitute Picasso print. Tunick refused the Kornfelds' substituted performance and demanded a return of the contract price. The Kornfelds refused on the grounds that their cure had been refused. Was the substitute print an adequate cure? [*David Tunick, Inc., v Kornfeld,* 838 F Supp 848 (SDNY)]

CPA QUESTIONS

1. Under the sales article of the UCC, which of the following statements is correct?
   a. The obligations of the parties to the contract must be performed in good faith.
   b. Merchants and nonmerchants are treated alike.
   c. The contract must involve the sale of goods for a price of more than $500.
   d. None of the provisions of the UCC may be disclaimed by agreement.

2. Rowe Corp. purchased goods from Stair Co. that were shipped COD. Under the sales article of the UCC, which of the following rights does Rowe have?
   a. The right to inspect the goods before paying
   b. The right to possession of the goods before paying
   c. The right to reject nonconforming goods
   d. The right to delay payment for a reasonable period of time

3. Bibbeon Manufacturing shipped 300 designer navy blue blazers to Custom Clothing Emporium. The blazers arrived on Friday, earlier than Custom had anticipated and on an exceptionally busy day for its receiving department. They were perfunctorily examined and sent to a nearby warehouse for storage until needed. On Monday of the following week, upon closer examination, it was discovered that the quality of the blazer linings was inferior to that specified in the sales contract. Which of the following is correct insofar as Custom's rights are concerned?
   a. Custom can reject the blazers upon subsequent discovery of the defects.
   b. Custom must retain the blazers since it accepted them and had an opportunity to inspect them upon delivery.
   c. Custom's only course of action is rescission.
   d. Custom had no rights if the linings were merchantable quality.

4. Parker ordered 50 cartons of soap from Riddle Wholesale Company. Each carton contains 12 packages of soap. The terms were: Eight dollars per carton 2/10, net/30, FOB buyer's delivery platform, delivery June 1. During transit approximately one half the packages were damaged by the carrier. The delivery was made on May 28. Answer the following with "Yes" or "No."
   a. Riddle had the risk of loss during transit.
   b. If Parker elects to accept the undamaged part of the shipment, he will be deemed to have accepted the entire shipment.
   c. To validly reject the goods, Parker must give timely notice of rejection to Riddle within a reasonable time after delivery.
   d. If Riddle were notified of the rejection on May 28, Riddle could cure the defect by promptly notifying Parker of intention to do so and making a second delivery to Parker of conforming goods by June 1.
   e. The statute of frauds is inapplicable to the transaction in the facts given.

Breach of Contract and Remedies

Learning Objectives

After studying this chapter, you should be able to

1. List and define the kinds of damages that may be recovered when a contract is broken
2. Describe the requirement of mitigation of damages
3. State when liquidated damages clauses are valid
4. State when liability-limiting clauses are valid
5. State when a breach of contract is waived
6. List the steps that may be used to prevent a waiver of breach of contract

What can be done when a contract is broken?

A. WHAT CONSTITUTES A BREACH OF CONTRACT?

The question of remedies does not become important until it is first determined that the contract has been violated or breached.

1. Definition of Breach

A **breach** is the failure to act or perform in the manner called for by the contract. When the contract calls for performance, such as painting an owner's home, the failure to paint or to paint properly is a *breach of contract*. If the contract calls for a creditor's forbearance, the action of the creditor in bringing a lawsuit is a breach of the contract.

2. Anticipatory Breach

When the contract calls for performance, a party may make it clear before the time for performance arrives that the contract will not be performed. This is referred to as an **anticipatory breach.**

(a) Anticipatory Repudiation. When a party expressly declares that performance will not be made when required, this declaration is called an **anticipatory repudiation** of the contract. To constitute such a repudiation, there must be a clear, absolute, unequivocal refusal to perform the contract according to its terms.

The *Tips* case deals with the issue of anticipatory repudiation and damages.

Tips v Hartland Developers, Inc.
961 SW2d 618 (Tex App 1998)

Splitting Tips—Contract Price Less Cost of Completion

In 1985, Hartland Developers, Inc., agreed to build an airplane hangar for Robert Tips of San Antonio for $300,000, payable in three installments of $100,000, with the final payment due upon the completion of the building and the issuance of a certificate of completion by the engineer representing Tips. The evidence shows that Tips's representative Mr. Lavelle instructed Hartland to cease work on the building because Tips could no longer afford to make payments. Hartland ceased work as instructed before the final completion of the building, having been paid $200,000 at that time. He sued Tips for breach of contract. On May 6, 1996, the trial court allowed Hartland the amount owing on the contract, $100,000, less the cost of completing the building according to the contract, $65,000, plus attorneys' fees and prejudgment and postjudgment interest. Tips appealed.

HARDBERGER, C. J. . . .

Substantial Performance

Tips claims that the evidence is legally or factually insufficient to support the trial court's finding that Hartland had substantially performed under the agreement. . . .

We agree with Tips that Hartland had not substantially performed under the contract. However, we find this point irrelevant to the resolution of this case. Substantial performance is a doctrine that allows *breaching* parties who have substantially completed their obligations to recover on a contract. WHITE & SUMMERS, CONTRACTS § 11–18(b) (3rd ed 1987). Hartland was not a breaching party. A contractor can recover on a contract when the failure to substantially perform is the fault of the other party. A party injured by the anticipatory breach of another may elect to sue for damages under the contract, . . . (if owner repudiates construction contract, contractor may sue in damages or for restitution); *Taylor Pub. Co. v. Systems Marketing Inc.,* 686 S.W.2d 213, 217 (when party obligated to make fixed payment absolutely repudiates the agreement, the obligee is entitled to recover [in an] action for damages and receive the present value of the payments payable under the agreement).

The trial judge based his damage assessment on anticipatory repudiation of contract. The evidence that Tips's representative, Lavelle, instructed Hartland to cease work on the project because Tips no longer could afford to make payments was sufficient to support this finding. *See Tennessee Gas Pipeline Co. v. Lenape Resources Corp.*, 870 S.W.2d 286, 302 (Tex.App.—San Antonio 1993) (anticipatory repudiation occurs when a party repudiates a contract before time for performance), *aff'd in part, rev'd in part,* 925 S.W.2d 565 (Tex. 1996).

Offset Damages

Tips claims that the trial judge erred in not offsetting Hartland's award for its failure to provide electrical connections to the hangar. Tips also claims he should be compensated $11,000 for a temporary access ramp he was forced to construct in anticipation of a permanent ramp being installed. . . . [W]e find that the $65,000 offset for the construction of a permanent ramp is sufficient compensation for that deficiency. However, we agree with Tips that the damages award must be offset by the cost of providing electrical outlets to the hangar.

Tips is entitled to an offset for electrical connections under a breach of contract theory. Damages for breach of contract are the contract price, less the cost of completion. *Sage Street Assoc. v. Northdale Const. Co.,* 937 S.W.2d 425, 426 (Tex.1996). The trial judge did not address in his findings of fact and conclusions of law whether the electrical connections were contemplated by the contract, but there was testimony at trial that they were, and electrical wiring is listed among Hartland's duties in the contract. A witness for Hartland admitted under cross examination that the work was part of the agreement and that it had not been completed. Tips testified that he had spent $23,000 to install connections. Hartland's damages should be further offset by this amount.

[Judgment affirmed as modified]

Questions

1. What facts did Hartland rely on to assert the anticipatory repudiation of the contract?
2. What is the measure of damages for a breach of a construction contract? Calculate what is owed Hartland excluding attorneys' fees and interest.
3. Why is prejudgment and postjudgment interest appropriate in a breach of contract lawsuit?

A refusal to perform a contract that is made before performance is required unless the other party to the contract does an act or makes a concession that is not required by the contract, is an anticipatory repudiation of the contract.[1]

A party making an anticipatory repudiation may *retract* or take back the repudiation if the other party has not changed position in reliance on the repudiation. However, if the other party has changed position, the party making the anticipatory repudiation cannot retract it. ◆ For example, if a buyer makes another purchase when the seller declares that the seller will not perform the contract, the buyer has acted in reliance on the seller's repudiation. The seller will therefore not be allowed to retract the repudiation. ◆

(b) **Anticipatory Repudiation by Conduct.** The anticipatory repudiation may be expressed by conduct that makes it impossible for the repudiating party to perform subsequently. To illustrate, there is a repudiation by conduct if a farmer makes a contract to sell an identified quantity of potatoes and then sells and delivers them to another buyer before the date specified for the delivery to the first buyer.

---

[1] *Chamberlain v Puckett Construction,* 921 P2d 1237 (Mont 1996).

NBC, for the 1994–1995 and 1995–1996 television seasons, had its show *Friends* place consistently among the top 10 television programs (as measured by the Nielsen ratings). The show has an ensemble cast of six "Generation X" friends who live in New York City.

In addition to the revenues from advertising on the popular show, NBC had significant profits from brisk sales of *Friends* merchandise including hats, T-shirts, and mugs.

Just prior to the August 12, 1996, start of production for the show for the 1996–1997 season, the six cast members demanded raises from their contract salaries of $40,000 per episode to $100,000. The stars of the show also demanded a percentage of profits from the show and any affiliated sales and contracts. The six actors indicated that they would not report for the start of filming if their demands for a raise were not met. None of the six had expired contracts. Their $40,000-per-episode salary was to continue at least through 1997.

NBC had just signed an agreement to sell the *Friends* episodes into syndication beginning in 1998. This syndication deal required NBC to turn over four seasons of episodes, and it was reported NBC received $40 million for the sale of the syndication rights.

When production began for the 1996–1997 season, all the members of the *Friends* cast did report for work. The network issued a statement indicating that no agreement had been reached but negotiations were ongoing.

Was it fair for the stars to threaten to strike unless their demands for higher compensation were met? Suppose that NBC signed new contracts with the six actors agreeing to all their demands. Would the contracts be enforceable? What defenses could be raised? Do you believe contracts negotiated for the higher salaries with the cast members are supported by consideration? Why or why not?

If the actors had failed to report for filming on August 12, 1996, would their conduct constitute a breach of contract? What damages would NBC experience if the stars failed to report for filming? What damages could NBC recover in the event the actors failed to complete their existing contracts?

When Jay Leno was asked about the tactics of the *Friends* stars, he responded, "You have to get what you can while you can in this business." Is Mr. Leno right? Is such an attitude ethical?

B. WAIVER OF BREACH

The breach of a contract may have no importance because the other party to the contract waives the breach.

3. Cure of Breach by Waiver

The fact that one party has broken a contract does not necessarily mean that there will be a lawsuit or a forfeiture of the contract. For practical business reasons, one party may be willing to ignore or waive the breach. When it is established that there has been a **waiver** of a breach, the party waiving the breach cannot take any action on the theory that the contract was broken. The waiver, in effect, erases the past breach. The contract continues as though the breach had not existed.

The waiver may be express or it may be implied from the continued recognition of the existence of the contract by the aggrieved party. When the conduct of a party shows an intent to give up a right, that right is waived. Once a right is waived, it cannot be revived.

4. Existence and Scope of Waiver

It is a question of fact whether there has been a waiver.

(a) Existence of Waiver. A party may express or declare that the breach of a contract is waived. A waiver of breach is more often the result of an express forgiving of a breach. Thus, a party allowing the other party to continue performance without objecting that the performance is not satisfactory waives the right to raise that objection when sued for payment by the performing party.

♦ For example, a contract promising to sell back a parcel of commercial property to Jackson

FIGURE 20.1 *What Follows the Breach?*

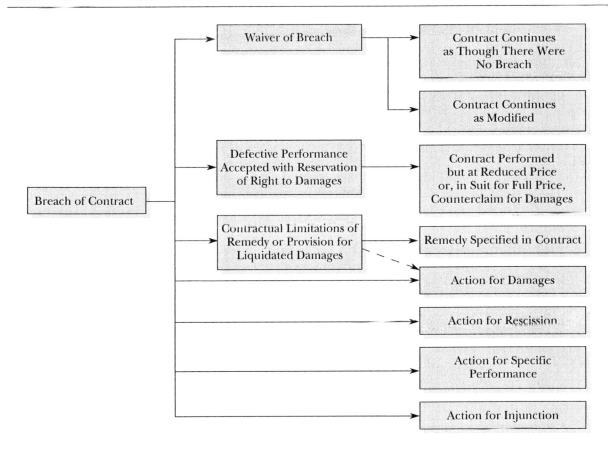

required Jackson to make a $500 payment to Massey's attorney on the first of the month for five months, December through April. It was clearly understood that the payments would be "on time without fail." Jackson made the December payment on time. New Year's Day, a holiday, fell on a Friday, and Jackson made the second payment on January 4. He made $500 payments on February 1, March 1, and March 31, respectively, and the payments were accepted and a receipt issued on each occasion. However, Massey refused to convey title back to Jackson because "the January 4 payment was untimely and the parties' agreement had been breached." The court held that the doctrine of *waiver* applied due to Massey's acceptance of the late payment and the three subsequent payments without objection, and the court declared that Jackson was entitled to possession of the land.[2] ◆

(b) **Scope of Waiver.** The waiver of a breach of contract extends only to the matter waived. It does not show any intent to ignore other provisions of the contract.

(c) **Antimodification Clause.** Modern contracts commonly specify that the terms of a contract shall not be deemed modified by waiver as to any breaches. This means that the original contract remains as agreed to. Either party may therefore return to and insist on compliance with the original contract.

In the example involving Jackson and Massey's contract, the trial court reviewed the contract to see if the court was restricted by the contract from applying the waiver. It concluded, "In this case, the parties' contract did not contain any terms that could prevent the application of the doctrine of waiver to the acceptance of late payments. . . ."[3]

[2] *Massey v Jackson,* 726 So2d 656 (Ala Civ App 1998).

[3] *Id.,* 659.

5. Reservation of Rights

It may be that a party is willing to accept a defective performance but does not wish to surrender any claim for damages for the breach. ◆ For example, Midwest Utilities, Inc., accepted 20 carloads of Powder River Basin coal (sometimes called "Western" coal) from its supplier, Maney Enterprises, because its power plants were in short supply of coal. Midwest's requirements contract with Maney called for Appalachian coal, a low sulfur, highly efficient fuel, which is sold at a premium price per ton. Midwest, in accepting the tendered performance with a **reservation of rights,** gave notice to Maney that it reserved all rights to pursue damages for the tender of a nonconforming shipment. ◆

C. REMEDIES FOR BREACH OF CONTRACT

One or more **remedies** may be available to the innocent party in the case of a breach of contract. There is also the possibility that arbitration or a streamlined out-of-court alternative dispute resolution procedure is available or required for determining the rights of the parties.

6. Remedies upon Anticipatory Repudiation

When an anticipatory repudiation of a contract occurs, the aggrieved person has several options.[4] He or she may (1) do nothing beyond stating that the performance at the proper time will be required; (2) regard the contract as having been definitively broken and bring a lawsuit against the repudiating party, without waiting to see if there will be a proper performance when the performance date arrives; or (3) regard the repudiation as an offer to cancel the contract. This offer can be accepted or rejected. If accepted, there is a discharge of the original contract by the subsequent cancellation agreement of the parties.

7. Remedies in General and the Measure of Damages

Courts provide a *quasi-contractual* or *restitution* remedy where a contract is unenforceable because it

lacked definite and certain terms or was not in compliance with the statute of frauds yet one of the parties performed services for the other. The measure of damages in these and other quasi-contract cases is the reasonable value of the services performed—and not an amount derived from the defective contract.

Where there is a breach of contract, the regular remedy is an award of *monetary damages*. In unusual circumstances, where monetary damages are inadequate, the injured party may obtain **specific performance,** whereby the court will order that the contract terms be carried out.

The measure of monetary damages where there has been a breach of contract is the sum of money that will place the injured party in the same position that would have been attained if the contract had been performed.[5] That is, the injured party will be given the *benefit of the bargain* by the court. As seen in the *Tips v Hartland Developers* case, the nonbreaching party, Hartland, was awarded the contract price less the cost of completion of the project, which had the effect of giving the builder the benefit of the bargain.

8. Monetary Damages

Monetary damages are commonly classified as compensatory damages, nominal damages, and punitive damages. **Compensatory damages** "compensate" the injured party for the damages incurred as a result of the breach of contract. Compensatory damages have two branches, *direct damages* and *consequential* (or *special*) *damages*.

An injured party who does not sustain an actual loss because of the breach of contract is entitled to a judgment of a small sum of money such as $1, and this kind of damages is called **nominal damages.**

Damages in excess of actual loss, imposed for the purpose of punishing or making an example of the defendant, are known as **punitive damages** or **exemplary damages.** In contract actions, punitive damages are not ordinarily awarded.[6]

(a) Direct and Consequential Damages. **Direct damages** (sometimes called **general damages**) are

---

[4] *Jitner v Gersch Development Co.,* 780 P2d 704 (Or App 1990).

[5] *Leingang v City of Mandan Weed Board,* 468 NW2d 397 (ND 1991).

[6] *Art's Flower Shop, Inc. v Chesapeake and Potomac Telephone Co.,* 413 SE2d 670 (W Va 1991).

those that naturally flow from the given type of breach of contract involved and include *incidental damages*, which are extra expenditures made by the injured party to rectify the breach or mitigate damages. **Consequential damages** (sometimes called **special damages**) are those that do not necessarily flow from the type of breach of contract involved but happen to do so in a particular case due to the injured party's particular circumstances. Consequential damages may only be recovered if it was reasonably foreseeable to the defendant that the kind of loss in question could be sustained by the nonbreaching party if the contract were broken.

To illustrate, in early August, Spencer Adams ordered a four-wheel-drive GMC truck with a rear-end hydraulic lift for use on his Aroostook County, Maine, potato farm. The contract price was $58,500. He told Brad Jones, the owner of the dealership, that he had to have the truck by Labor Day so he could use it to bring in his crop from the fields before the first frost, and Brad nodded that he understood. The truck did not arrive by Labor Day as promised in the written contract. After a two-week period of gradually escalating recriminations with the dealership, Adams obtained the same model GMC truck at a dealership 40 minutes away in Houlton, but at the cost of $60,500. He was also able to rent a similar truck from the Houlton dealer for $250 for the day while the new truck was being prepared. Farmhands had used other means of harvesting, but due to the lack of the truck their work was set back by five days. As a result of the delays, 30 percent of the crop was still in the fields when the first frost came, causing damages expertly estimated at $320,000. The *direct damages* for the breach of contract in this case would be the difference between the contract price for the truck of $58,500 at the market price of $60,500, or $2,000. These direct damages naturally flow from the breach of contract for the purchase of a truck. Also, the *incidental damages* of $250 for the truck rental are recoverable direct damages. The $320,000 loss of the potato crop was a consequence of not having the truck, and this sum is arguably recoverable by Spencer Adams as *consequential* or *special damages*. Adams notified Brad Jones of the reason he needed to have the truck by Labor Day, and it should have been reasonably foreseeable to Jones that loss of a portion of the crop could occur if the truck contract was breached. However, due to Spencer Adams's obligation to mitigate damages (as will be discussed below), it is unlikely that Adams will recover the full consequential damages. Truck rental availability or lack thereof within the rural area, alternative tractor usage, and the actual harvesting methods used by Adams will all relate to the mitigation issue to be resolved by the jury.

(b) **Mitigation of Damages.** The injured party is under the duty to mitigate damages if reasonably possible.[7] In other words, damages must not be permitted to increase if an increase can be prevented by reasonable efforts. This means that the injured party must generally stop any performance under the contract to avoid running up a larger bill. It may require an injured party to buy or rent elsewhere the goods that the wrongdoer was obligated to deliver under the contract. In the case of breach of an employment contract by the employer, the employee is required to seek other similar employment. The wages earned from other employment must be deducted from the damages claimed. The discharged employee, however, is not required to take employment of less-than-comparable work.

(1) Effect of Failure to Mitigate Damages. The effect of the requirement of mitigating damages is to limit recovery by the nonbreaching party to the damages that would have been sustained had this party mitigated the damages where it was possible to do so. ♦ For example, self-described "sports nut" Gary Baker signed up for a three-year club-seat "package" that entitled him and a companion to tickets for 41 Boston Bruin hockey games and 41 Boston Celtic basketball games at the New Boston Garden Corporation's Fleet Center for approximately $18,000 per year. After one year, Baker stopped paying for the tickets, thinking that he would simply lose his $5,000 security deposit. Baker, a CPA, tried to work out a compromise settlement to no avail. New Boston sued Baker for breach of contract, seeking the balance due on the tickets of $34,866. At trial, Baker argued to the jury that although he had breached his contract, New Boston had an obligation to mitigate dam-

---

[7] *West Pinal Family Health Center, Inc. v McBride,* 785 P2d 66 (Ariz 1989).

ages, for example, by treating his empty seats and those of others in the same situation as "rush seats" shortly before game time and selling them at a discount. New Boston argued that just as a used luxury car cannot be returned for a refund, a season ticket cannot be canceled without consequences. The jury accepted Baker's position on mitigation and reduced the amount owed New Boston by $21,176 to $13,690.[8] ◆

9. Rescission

When one party commits a material breach of the contract, the other party may rescind the contract; if the party in default objects, the aggrieved party may bring an action for rescission. A breach is *material* when it is so substantial that it defeats the object of the parties in making the contract.[9]

An injured party who rescinds a contract after having performed services may recover the reasonable value of the performance rendered under restitutionary or quasi-contractual damages. Money paid by the injured party may also be recovered. The purpose is to restore the injured party to the position occupied before the contract was made. However, the party seeking restitutionary damages must also return what this party has received from the party in default.

◆ **For example,** Pedro Morena purchased real estate from Jason Alexander after Alexander had assured him that the property did not have a flooding problem. In fact, the property regularly flooded after ordinary rainstorms. Morena was entitled to the return of the purchase price and payment for the reasonable value of the improvements he made to the property. Alexander is entitled to a setoff for the reasonable rental value of the property during the time Morena was in possession of this property. ◆

10. Action for Specific Performance

Under special circumstances, an injured party may obtain the equitable remedy of specific performance, which compels the other party to carry out the terms of a contract. Specific performance is ordinarily granted only if the subject matter of the contract is "unique," thereby making an award of money damages an inadequate remedy. Contracts for the purchase of land will be specifically enforced.[10]

Specific performance of a contract to sell personal property can be obtained only if the article is of unusual age, beauty, unique history, or other distinction. ◆ **For example,** Maurice owned a rare Revolutionary War musket that he agreed to sell to Herb. Maurice then changed his mind because of the uniqueness of the musket. Herb can sue and win, requesting the remedy of specific performance of the contract because of the unique nature of the goods. ◆

When the damages sustained by the plaintiff can be measured in monetary terms, specific performance will be refused. Consequently, a contract to sell a television station will not be specifically enforced when the buyer had made a contract to resell the station to a third person; the damages caused by the breach of the first contract would be the loss sustained by being unable to make the resale, and such damages would be adequate compensation to the original buyer.[11]

Ordinarily, contracts for the performance of personal services will not be specifically ordered. This is because of the difficulty of supervision by the court and the restriction of the U.S. Constitution's Thirteenth Amendment prohibiting involuntary servitude except as criminal punishment.

11. Action for an Injunction

When a breach of contract consists of doing an act prohibited by the contract, a possible remedy is an **injunction** against doing the act. ◆ For example, when the obligation in an employee's contract is to refrain from competing after resigning from the company and the obligation is broken by competing, a court may order or enjoin the former employee to stop competing. Similarly, when a vocalist breaks a contract to record exclusively for a particular label, he or she may be enjoined from recording for any other company. This may have the indirect effect of compelling the vocalist to record for the plaintiff. ◆

---

[8] Sacha Pfeiffer, "Disenchanted Fan Scores Win in Ticket Fight," *The Boston Globe*, B-4, Aug. 28, 1999.

[9] *Frank Felix Associates v Austin Drugs, Inc.,* 111 F3d 284 (CA2 NY 1997).

[10] *English v Muller,* 514 SE2d 195 (Ga 1999).

[11] *Miller v LeSea Broadcasting, Inc.,* 87 F3d 224 (7th Cir 1996).

D. CONTRACT PROVISIONS AFFECTING REMEDIES AND DAMAGES

The contract of the parties may contain provisions that affect the remedies available or the recovery of damages.

12. Limitation of Remedies

The contract of the parties may limit the remedies of the aggrieved parties. ◆ For example, the contract may give one party the right to repair or replace a defective item sold or to refund the contract price. The contract may require both parties to submit any dispute to arbitration or another streamlined out-of-court dispute resolution procedure. ◆

13. Liquidated Damages

The parties may stipulate in their contract that a certain amount should be paid in case of a breach. This amount is known as **liquidated damages** and may be variously measured by the parties. When delay is possible, liquidated damages may be a fixed sum, such as $1,000 for each day of delay. When there is a total default, damages may be a percentage of the contract price or may be the amount of the down payment.

(a) Validity. To be **valid,** a **liquidated damages clause** must satisfy two requirements: (1) The situation must be one in which it is difficult or impossible to determine the actual damages, and (2) the amount specified must not be excessive when compared with the probable damages that would be sustained.[12] The validity of a liquidated damages clause is determined on the basis of the facts existing when the clause was agreed to.

(b) Effect. When a liquidated damages clause is held valid, the injured party cannot collect more than the amount specified by the clause. The defaulting party is bound to pay such damages once the fact is established that there has been a default. The injured party is not required to make

any proof as to damages sustained, and the defendant is not permitted to show that the damages were not as great as the liquidated sum.

(c) Invalid Clauses. If the liquidated damages clause calls for the payment of a sum that is clearly unreasonably large and unrelated to the possible actual damages that might be sustained, the clause will be held to be void as a penalty. Thus, a contract term was void as a penalty by providing that a village would be entitled to $100,000 if a cable television franchisee failed to complete installation by a specified date.

When a liquidated damages clause is held invalid, the effect is merely to erase the clause from the contract and the injured party may proceed to recover damages for its breach. Instead of recovering the liquidated damages amount, the injured party will recover whatever actual damages he or she can prove.

14. Limitation of Liability Clauses

A contract may contain a provision stating that one of the parties shall not be liable for damages in case of breach. Such a provision is called an **exculpatory clause** or a **limitation-of-liability clause.** ◆ For example, a construction contract may state that the contractor shall not be liable for damages from delay caused by third persons.[13] ◆

(a) Content and Construction. An exculpatory clause, as in the case of any other contract provision, is to be given the meaning intended by the parties. An exculpatory clause must be clear and unambiguous.[14] Moreover, such a clause is strictly construed. ◆ For example, a limitation of liability for negligence does not bar liability for violation of a consumer protection statute. ◆

(b) Validity. When the public interest is not involved, the parties are free to allocate liability for negligence as they choose. If the public interest is involved, it is contrary to public policy to exempt one party from liability for that party's

---

[12] *Southeast Alaska Construction Co. v Alaska,* 791 P2d 339 (Alaska 1990).

[13] *City of Beaumont v Excavators and Constructors, Inc.,* 870 SW2d 123 (Tex App 1993).

[14] *Greater Orlando Aviation v Bulldog Airlines,* 705 SO2d 120 (Fla App 1998).

negligence.[15] Release forms signed by participants in athletic and sporting events declaring that the sponsor, proprietor, or operator of the event shall not be liable for injuries sustained by participants because of its negligence are binding. Such forms are invalid, though, when the harm was caused by "willful or wanton conduct or by gross negligence."[16]

SUMMARY

When a party fails to perform a contract or performs improperly, the other contracting party may sue for damages caused by the breach. What may be recovered by the aggrieved person is stated in terms of being direct or consequential damages. Direct damages are those that ordinarily will result from the breach. Direct damages may be recovered on proof of causation and amount. Consequential damages can be recovered only if, in addition to proving causation and amount, it is shown that they were reasonably within the contemplation of the contracting parties as a probable result of a breach of the contract. The right to recover consequential damages is lost if the aggrieved party could reasonably have taken steps to avoid such damages. In other words, the aggrieved person has a duty to mitigate or reduce damages by reasonable means.

In any case, the damages recoverable for breach of contract may be limited to a specific amount by a liquidated damages clause. Damages may be canceled out completely by a limitation-of-liability clause.

In a limited number of situations, an aggrieved party may bring an action for specific performance to compel the other contracting party to perform the acts called for by the contract. Specific performance by the seller is always obtainable for the breach of a contract to sell land or real estate on the theory that such property has a unique value. With respect to other contracts, specific performance will not be ordered unless it is shown that there was some unique element present so that the aggrieved person would suffer a damage that could not be compensated for by the payment of money damages.

The aggrieved person also has the option of rescinding the contract if (1) the breach has been made concerning a material term and (2) the aggrieved party returns everything to the way it was before the contract was made.

Although there has been a breach of the contract, the effect of this breach is nullified if the aggrieved person by word or conduct waives the right to object to the breach. Conversely, an aggrieved party may accept a defective performance without thereby waiving a claim for breach if the party makes a reservation of rights. A reservation of rights can be made by stating that the defective performance is accepted "without prejudice," "under protest," or "with reservation of rights."

WEBSITE REFERENCES

To view a slide show on breach of contract and applicable remedies visit

http://www.bevans.co.uk/letters/breachcon. htm

For a real-world perspective on the issue of defining breach of contract visit

http://www.legaltools.com/_genleg/ 00000091.htm

To view a short notice of breach visit

http://www.bevans.co.uk/letters/breachcon. htm

---

[15] *Olsen v Breeze, Inc.*, 55 Cal Rptr 2d 818 (Cal App 1996).

[16] *New Light Co. v Wells Fargo Alarm Services*, 525 NW2d 25 (Neb 1994).

QUESTIONS AND CASE PROBLEMS

1. What social forces are affected by the rule governing the mitigation of damages?

2. Anthony makes a contract to sell a rare painting to Laura for $100,000. The written contract specifies that if Anthony should fail to perform the contract, he will pay Laura $5,000 as liquidated damages. Anthony fails to deliver the painting and is sued by Laura for $5,000. Can she recover this amount?

3. Rogers made a contract with Salisbury Brick Corp. that allowed it to remove earth and sand from land he owned. The contract ran for four years, with provision to renew it for additional four-year terms up to a total of 96 years. The contract provided for compensation to Rogers based on the amount of earth and sand removed. By an unintentional mistake, Salisbury underpaid Rogers the amount of $863 for the months of November and December 1986. Salisbury offered this amount to Rogers, but he refused to accept it and claimed that he had been underpaid in other months. Rogers claimed that he was entitled to rescind the contract. Was he correct? [*Rogers v Salisbury Brick Corp.*, 882 SE2d 915 (SC)]

4. A contractor departed at a number of points from the specifications in a contract to build a house. The cost to put the house in the condition called for by the contract was approximately $1,000. The contractor was sued for $5,000 for breach of contract and emotional disturbance caused by the breach. Decide.

5. Protein Blenders, Inc., made a contract with Gingerich to buy from him the shares of stock of a small corporation. When the buyer refused to take and pay for the stock, Gingerich sued for specific performance of the contract on the ground that the value of the stock was unknown and could not be readily ascertained because it was not sold on the general market. Was he entitled to specific performance? [*Gingerich v Protein Blenders, Inc.*, 95 NW2d 522 (Iowa)]

6. The buyer of real estate made a down payment. The contract stated that the buyer would be liable for damages in an amount equal to the down payment if the buyer broke the contract. The buyer refused to go through with the contract and demanded his down payment back. The seller refused to return it and claimed that he was entitled to additional damages from the buyer because the damages that he had suffered were greater than the amount of the down payment. Decide. [*Waters v Key Colony East, Inc.*, 345 So 2d 367 (Fla App)]

7. Kuznicki made a contract for the installation of a fire detection system by Security Safety Corp. for $498. The contract was made one night and canceled at 9:00 the next morning. Security then claimed one-third of the purchase price from Kuznicki by virtue of a provision in the contract that "in the event of cancellation of this agreement . . . the owner agrees to pay 33⅓ percent of the contract price, as liquidated damages." Was Security Safety entitled to recover the amount claimed? [*Security Safety Corp. v Kuznicki*, 213 NE2d 866 (Mass)]

8. Over the telephone, Wagner agreed to sell a farm he owned to Van for $1 million. Wagner later repudiated the agreement, and Van sued him for specific performance of the agreement. Decide.

9. Melodee Lane Lingerie Co. was a tenant in a building that was protected against fire by a sprinkler and alarm system maintained by the American District Telegraph Co. (ADT). Because of the latter's fault, the controls on the system were defective and allowed the discharge of water into the building, which damaged Melodee's property. When Melodee sued ADT, its defense was that its service contract limited its liability to 10 percent of the annual service charge made to the customer. Was this limitation valid? [*Melodee Lane Lingerie Co. v American District Telegraph Co.*, NY 218 NE2d 661 (NY)]

10. In May, a homeowner made a contract with a roofer to make repairs to her house by July 1. The roofer never came to repair the roof, and heavy rains in the fall damaged the interior of the house. The homeowner sued the roofer for breach of contract and claimed damages for the harm done to the interior of the

house. Is the homeowner entitled to recover such damages?

11. Ken Sulejmanagic, aged 19, signed up for a course in scuba diving taught by Madison at the YMCA. Before the instruction began, Ken was required to sign a form releasing Madison and the YMCA from liability for any harm that might occur. At the end of the course, Madison, Ken, and another student went into deep water. After Ken made the final dive required by the course program, Madison left him alone in the water while he took the other student for a dive. When Madison returned, Ken could not be found, and it was later determined that he had drowned. Ken's parents sued Madison and the YMCA for negligence in the performance of the teaching contract. The defendants raised the defense that the release Ken signed shielded them from liability. The plaintiffs claimed that the release was invalid. Who was correct? [*Madison v Superior Court*, 250 Cal Rptr 299 (Cal App)]

12. Wassenaar worked for Panos under a three-year contract stating that if the contract were terminated wrongfully by Panos before the end of the three years, he would pay as damages the salary for the remaining time that the contract had to run. After three months, Panos terminated the contract, and Wassenaar sued him for pay for the balance of the contract term. Panos claimed that this amount could not be recovered because the contract provision for the payment was a void penalty. Was this provision valid? [*Wassenaar v Panos*, 331 NW2d 357 (Wis)]

13. Soden, a contractor, made a contract to build a house for Clevert. The sales contract stated that "if either party defaults in the performance of this contract," that party would be liable to the other for attorney fees incurred in suing the defaulter. Soden was 61 days late

in completing the contract, and some of the work was defective. In a suit by the buyer against the contractor, the contractor claimed that he was not liable for the buyer's attorney fees because he had made only a defective performance and because "default" in the phrase quoted meant "nonperformance of the contract." Was the contractor liable for the attorney fees? [*Clevert v Soden*, 400 SE2d 181 (Va)]

14. Protection Alarm Co. made a contract to provide burglar alarm security for Fretwell's home. The contract stated that the maximum liability of the alarm company was the actual loss sustained or $50, whichever was the lesser, and that this provision was agreed to "as liquidated damages and not as a penalty." When Fretwell's home was burglarized, he sued for the loss of approximately $12,000, claiming that the alarm company had been negligent. The alarm company asserted that its maximum liability was $50. Fretwell claimed that this was invalid because it bore no relationship to the loss that could have been foreseen when the contract was made or that in fact "had been sustained." Decide.

15. Shepherd-Will made a contract to sell Emma Cousar "15 acres of land adjoining property owned by the purchaser and this being formerly land of Shepherd-Will, Inc., located on north side of Highway 223. This 5 acres to be surveyed at earliest time possible at which time plat will be attached and serve as further description on property." Shepherd-Will owned only one 100-acre tract of land that adjoined Emma's property. This tract had a common boundary with her property of 1,140 feet. Shepherd-Will failed to perform this contract. Emma sued for specific performance of the contract. Decide. [*Cousar v Shepherd-Will, Inc.*, 387 SE2d 723 (SC App)]

CPA QUESTIONS

1. Master Mfg., Inc., contracted with Accur Computer Repair Corp. to maintain Master's computer system. Master's manufacturing process depends on its computer system operating properly at all times. A liquidated

damages clause in the contract provided that Accur pay $1,000 to Master for each day that Accur was late responding to a service request. On January 12, Accur was notified that Master's computer system failed. Accur did not respond to Master's service request until January 15. If Master sues Accur under the liquidated damage provision of the contract, Master will

a. Win, unless the liquidated damage provision is determined to be a penalty
b. Win, because under all circumstances liquidated damage provisions are enforceable
c. Lose, because Accur's breach was *not* material
d. Lose, because liquidated damage provisions violate public policy

(5/93, Law, #25)

2. Jones, CPA, entered into a signed contract with Foster Corp. to perform accounting and review services. If Jones repudiates the contract prior to the date performance is due to begin, which of the following is *not* correct?

a. Foster could successfully maintain an action for breach of contract after the date performance was due to begin.
b. Foster can obtain a judgment ordering Hones to perform.
c. Foster could successfully maintain an action for breach of contract prior to the date performance is due to begin.
d. Foster can obtain a judgment for the monetary damages it incurred as a result of the repudiation.

(5/89, Law, #35)

Price Determination

eBay Customers Name Their Own Price

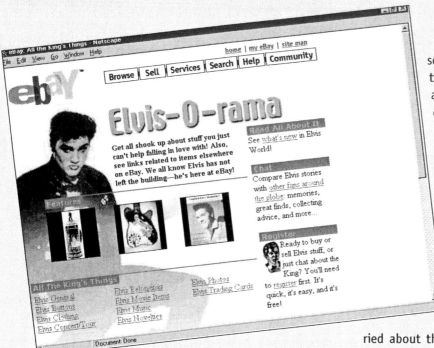

In one of the zaniest startup stories of the decade, Pierre Omidyar goes online to find Pez candy dispensers for his fiancée's collection and ends up an owner of a hot new online auction company—eBay. That was in 1995. Today, the Internet star has watched sales figures soar from just under $6 billion to nearly $50 billion in one recent year, and industry analysts predict this is only the beginning.

The number of online auctioneers is growing and now includes names such as Onsale, Buy.com, UBid, CitiAuction, icollector, and even the world's largest online bookseller, Amazon.com. However, eBay has remained the top auctioneer by building a community of buyers and sellers who have built common-interest relationships online. Says CEO Meg Whitman, "Our competitors are in anywhere between 10 and 50 other businesses. This is the only business we're in, and it's a full-time, 24-by-seven job to make person-to-person trading on the Internet fun, fast, entertaining, and easy to use."

eBay has been dubbed by some "the world's biggest flea market." It neither owns the merchandise nor sells it—eBay simply brings together ordinary people who share many of the same interests. An estimated 147 million online bidders are predicted to generate over $6.5 billion in sales of collectibles by 2003. Antiques, sports memorabilia, toys, coins, books, and artwork are some of the items that go up on eBay's virtual auction block. Despite the number of competing online auction sites, eBay is so dominant that 100 of its competitors recently agreed to share their auction listings, making an item on one site available for bidding on all the other sites. Included in this agreement are Microsoft Corp.'s MSN, Excite@Home Corp., and Lycos Inc.'s *The New York Times*. Another major new competitor is Amazon.com, which teamed up with the prestigious fine-art auction house, Sotheby's, to add name recognition and expertise to its new online auction site.

Since it now owns Butterfield & Butterfield of San Francisco, one of the largest and oldest auction houses in the world, eBay is not worried about the recent competition. Bidders on eBay can now compete for everything from Ren and Stempy toys to Rembrandt etchings. Whitman also points out that Amazon's 8 million book browsers cannot compare to eBay's 2 million dedicated buyers and sellers. After all, eBay has well over 2 million items for sale in over 1,500 categories. Amazon's approach, she explains, "is more retail. It has large dealers for the most part, selling new items. That's quite different from our community of individual and very small dealers who are selling unique items."

The family of buyers and sellers on eBay are entirely in charge of setting prices for their goods and services. The Internet auctioneer generates revenues by charging fees for its services. These fees are relatively low and structured on three levels. The first fee covers the cost of listing an item on the site. Feature fees allow an item to be placed in high-visibility areas on the site. Finally, value fees depend on the actual price paid. eBay doesn't take physical possession or title to inventory, so its operating costs are small. Starting with a very high gross margin gives eBay the flexibility to spend money where and when it is needed—mainly on advertising and promotion designed to expand its customer base of buyers and sellers even more. As one industry expert points out, "It benefits both the buyer and seller to be in the most active market." And eBay customers are in the most liquid market in the world today.

So how much is Liberace's seventh limousine worth? To a recent eBay bidder, $17,000.[1]

CHAPTER OVERVIEW

One of the first questions shoppers ask is, "How much does it cost?" Marketers understand the critical role the price of a good or service plays in the consumer's decision-making process. From lipstick and perfume to automobiles and gasoline to donuts and coffee, marketers must develop strategies that price products to achieve their firms' objectives.

As a starting point for examining pricing strategies, consider the meaning of the term *price*. A **price** is the exchange value of a good or service—in other words, what it can be exchanged for in the marketplace. Price does not necessarily involve money. In earlier times, the price of an acre of land might have been 20 bushels of wheat, three head of cattle, or one boat. This barter process still applies in some areas of the world. However, in a modern monetary system, *price* refers to the amount of funds required to purchase a product.

As eBay buyers and sellers recognize, the method of setting prices is a major component of a successful listing on the online auction site. Prices are both difficult to set and dynamic; they shift in response to a number of variables. A higher-than-average price can convey an image of prestige, while a lower-than-average price may connote good value. Price can also powerfully affect a company's overall profitability and market share.

This chapter discusses the process of determining a profitable but justifiable (fair) price. The chapter focuses on management of the pricing function and discusses pricing strategies, price-quality relationships, and pricing in both the industrial and public sectors. It also looks at the effects of various conditions on price determination, including legal constraints, competitive pressures, and changes in global and online markets. ▨

LEGAL CONSTRAINTS ON PRICING

tline the legal constraints
pricing.

Pricing decisions must be made with a variety of legal constraints imposed by both federal and state governments. The next time you pull up to a gas station, consider where each dollar goes: Almost 50 percent goes to federal, state, local, and excise taxes. Tariffs—taxes levied on the sale of imported goods and services—often permit firms to set prices on domestically produced goods well above world market levels. Restrictions on importing Mexican-grown Hass avocados mean that San Diego supermarket shoppers may pay $1.79 for the California-grown variety, while Vancouver purchasers can buy Mexican-grown produce for $.79 each. Similar restrictions result in higher prices for bananas in Europe than what Americans generally pay.[2]

If you are looking for an industry where the legal environment has had a major impact on prices, consider the handgun marketplace. Following a rash of public shootings and mass murders—often on school grounds and just as often at the hands of teenage gunmen—antigun activists pressured Congress to pass additional restrictions regulating ownership and sales. At the same time, survivors, families of victims, and even cities began filing lawsuits against handgun manufacturers. Proponents of civilian gun ownership, such as the National Rifle Association, countered that government could accomplish more by enforcing existing laws rather than simply passing additional legislation. The growing legal assault prompted handgun marketers to raise prices almost 10 percent. The industry justified the price increases citing additional legal expenses, but critics say another reason exists for the price hikes. Demand is soaring and manufacturers, wholesalers, and retailers are taking advantage of the market.[3]

Pricing is also regulated by the general constraints of U.S. antitrust legislation, as outlined in Chapter 2. The next few pages contain a discussion on some of the most important pricing laws for contemporary marketers.

Robinson-Patman Act

The **Robinson-Patman Act** (1936) typifies Depression-era legislation. Known in some circles as the *Anti-A&P Act*, it was inspired by price competition from the developing grocery store chains—in fact, the original draft was prepared by the United States Wholesale Grocers Association. Legislators saw the country in the midst of the Great Depression, and they intended the law primarily to save jobs. They perceived the developing chain stores as threats to traditional retailing and employment and established the act to reverse the trend.

The Robinson-Patman Act, which technically was an amendment to the Clayton Act, prohibits price discrimination in sales to wholesalers, retailers, and other producers; basically, differences in price must reflect cost differentials. The act also disallows selling at unreasonably low prices in order to drive competitors out of business. The Clayton Act had applied only to price discrimination between geographic areas, which injured local sellers. Supporters justified the Robinson-Patman legislation by arguing that the chain stores might secure volume discounts from suppliers, while small, independent stores would continue to pay regular prices.

The practice of price discrimination, where some customers pay more than others, goes back 3,000 years to the beginning of trade and commerce. Today, however, technology has added to the frequency and complexity of price discrimination. Many companies get around the law by inviting certain customers to become "preferred customers," entitling them to average discounts of 10 percent. As long as companies can justify their price discounts and promotional allowances without restricting competition, they will escape restrictions of the Robinson-Patman Act. Direct-mail marketers frequently send out catalogs of identical goods but with differing prices. Zip-code areas that traditionally consist of high spenders get the high-price catalogs, while price-sensitive zip-code customers get a low-price catalog. Victoria's Secret, Staples, and Simon & Schuster are among the hundreds of companies that employ legal price discrimination strategies.[4]

Firms accused of price discrimination often argue that they set price differentials to meet competitors' prices and that cost differences justify variations in prices. When a firm asserts that it maintains price differentials as good-faith methods of competing with rivals, a logical question arises: What constitutes good-faith pricing behavior? The answer depends on the particular situation.

A defense based on cost differentials works only if the price differences do not exceed the cost differences resulting from selling to various classes of buyers. Marketers must then justify the cost differences; indeed many authorities consider this provision one of the most confusing areas in the Robinson-Patman Act. The varying interpretations of the act certainly qualify it as one of the vaguest laws that affects marketing. Courts handle most charges brought under the act as individual cases. Therefore, domestic marketers must continually evaluate their pricing actions to avoid potential Robinson-Patman violations.

The Robinson-Patman Act does not cover export markets, though. U.S. law does not prohibit a domestic firm from selling a product to a foreign customer at a price significantly lower than the domestic wholesale price.

Unfair-Trade Laws

States supplement federal legislation with their own **unfair-trade laws**, which require sellers to maintain minimum prices for comparable merchandise. Enacted in the 1930s, these laws were intended to protect small specialty shops, such as dairy stores, from the *loss-leader pricing* tactics, in which chain stores might sell certain products below cost to attract customers. Typical state laws set retail price floors at cost plus some modest markup.

Although most unfair-trade laws have remained on the books for the past 70 years, marketers had all but forgotten them until recent years. Then in 1993, Wal-Mart, the nation's largest retailer, was found guilty of violating Arkansas' unfair-trade law for selling drugs and health-and-beauty aids below cost. The lawsuit filed by three independent drugstore owners accused the mass merchandiser of attempting to drive them out of business through predatory pricing practices. Wal-Mart appealed the decision and the decision was overturned, but similar lawsuits have been filed in several other states, all seeking to end the chain's low-price marketing strategy.

Fair-Trade Laws

The concept of fair trade has affected pricing decisions for decades. **Fair-trade laws** allow manufacturers to stipulate minimum retail prices for their products and to require dealers to sign contracts agreeing to abide by these prices.

FIGURE 18.1

Protecting Brand Image by Avoiding Price Discounting

The basic argument behind this legislation asserts that a product's image, determined in part by its price, is a property right of the manufacturer. Therefore, the producer should have the authority to protect its asset by requiring retailers to maintain a minimum price. The Fabergé name—internationally respected for its exquisite gold and jewel-encrusted eggs and jewelry designs—exudes images of royalty, nobility, and wealth. The name is also a registered trademark and used under license by companies such as Mozaffarian jewelers, an exclusive distributor for Fabergé fine writing instruments, such as the one shown in Figure 18.1. Enhanced with the Fabergé name, each limited-edition Shapur fountain pen retails for about $2,000. By severely restricting the number of retail stores that carry their writing instruments, Fabergé marketers can coordinate the prices charged by their retail partners and discourage price discounting, which might adversely affect the company's image.

The origins of fair-trade legislation trace back to lobbying efforts by organizations of independent retailers fearful of chain store growth. The economic mania of the Depression years was clearly reflected in these statutes. In 1931, California became the first state to enact fair-trade legislation. Most other states soon followed; only Missouri, the District of Columbia, Vermont, and Texas failed to adopt such laws.

A U.S. Supreme Court decision invalidated fair-trade contracts in interstate commerce, and Congress responded by passing the *Miller Tydings Resale Price Maintenance Act* (1937). This law exempted interstate fair-trade contracts from compliance with antitrust requirements, thus freeing states to keep these laws on their books if they so desired.

Over the years, fair-trade laws declined in importance as discounters emerged and price competition gained strength in marketing strategy. These laws became invalid with the passage of the *Consumer Goods Pricing Act* (1975), which halted all interstate enforcement of resale price maintenance provisions, an objective long sought by consumer groups.

THE ROLE OF PRICE IN THE MARKETING MIX

Ancient philosophers recognized the importance of price in an economic system. Some early written accounts refer to attempts to determine fair or just prices. Price continues to serve as a means of regulating economic activity. Employment of any or all of the four factors of production—natural resources, capital, human resources, and entrepreneurship—depends on the prices that those factors receive. An individual firm's prices and the resulting purchases by its customers determine how much revenue the company receives. Prices, therefore, influence a firm's profits as well as its employment of the factors of production.

PRICING OBJECTIVES

Just as price is a component of the total marketing mix, pricing objectives also represent components of the organization's overall objectives. As Chapter 6 explained, marketing objectives state the outcomes that executives hope to attain. They derive from and support the overall objectives of the organization. The objectives of the firm and its marketing organization guide development of pricing objectives, which in turn lead to development and implementation of more specific pricing policies and procedures.

A firm might set a major overall objective of becoming the dominant producer in its domestic market. It might then develop a marketing objective of achieving maximum sales penetration in each region, followed by a related pricing objective of setting prices at levels that maximize sales. These objectives might lead to the adoption of a low-price policy implemented by offering substantial price discounts to channel members.

Price affects and is affected by the other elements of the marketing mix. Product decisions, promotional plans, and distribution choices all impact the price of a good or service. For example, products distributed through complex channels involving several intermediaries must be priced high enough to cover the markups needed to compensate wholesalers and retailers for services they provide. Basic so-called "fighting brands" are intended to capture market share from higher-priced, options-laden competitors by offering relatively low prices to entice customers to give up some options in return for a cost savings.

While pricing objectives vary from firm to firm, they can be classified into four major groups: (1) profitability objectives, (2) volume objectives, (3) meeting competition objectives, and (4) prestige objectives. Profitability objectives include profit maximization and target-return goals. Volume objectives seek to either maximize sales or increase market share. Not-for-profit companies must also consider similar objectives in their pricing strategies. Table 18.1 outlines the pricing objectives marketers rely on to meet their organization's overall goals.

Profitability Objectives

Marketers at for-profit firms must set prices with profits in mind. Even not-for-profit organizations realize the importance of setting prices high enough to cover expenses and provide a financial cushion to cover unforeseen needs and expenses. But both groups of price setters are well aware of the Russian proverb, "There are two fools in every market: One asks too little, one asks too much." For consumers to pay these prices, they must be convinced they are receiving fair value for their money.

Classical economic theory is based on two major assumptions. First, it presumes that firms will behave rationally and, second, that this rational behavior will result in an effort to maximize

Lillian Vernon Strikes Out

BACKGROUND All over the nation, people receiving the new Lillian Vernon catalog knew something was amiss. Accustomed to receiving several catalogs a year—each overflowing with value-priced household goods for convenient in-home shopping—customers could not remember a catalog this small with so few items and with such high prices.

THE MARKETING PROBLEM When paper prices and postage costs rose during the mid-1990s, the $250 million specialty online and catalog retailer sharply reduced the number of pages in its catalogs and discontinued the distribution of one sale catalog entirely. Also, the product mix was redesigned to include more expensive items to counter the rising overhead costs.

continued on next page

2

Identify the major categories of pricing objectives.

MARKETING | **DICTIONARY**

unfair-trade laws State laws requiring sellers to maintain minimum prices for comparable merchandise.

fair-trade laws Statutes enacted in most states that permitted manufacturers to stipulate a minimum retail price for their product.

TABLE 18.1	Pricing Objectives	
OBJECTIVE	**PURPOSE**	**EXAMPLE**
Profitability objectives	• Profit maximization • Target return	Low introductory interest rates on credit cards with high standard rates after 6 months
Volume objectives	• Sales maximization • Market share	Compaq's low-priced PCs increase market share and sales of services
Meeting competition objectives	• Value pricing	Price wars among major airlines
Prestige objectives	• Lifestyle • Image	High-priced luxury autos such as Ferrari and watches by Rolex
Not-for-profit objectives	• Profit maximization • Cost recovery • Market incentives • Market suppression	High prices for tobacco and alcohol to reduce consumption

gains and minimize losses. Some marketers use elaborate calculations based on predicted future sales; others estimate profits by looking at historical sales data. It has been said that setting prices is an art, not a science. The talent lies in a marketer's ability to strike a balance between desired profits and the customer's perception of a product's value.

Marketers should evaluate and adjust prices continually to accommodate changes in the environment. The technological environment, for example, forces Internet marketers to respond quickly to competitors' pricing strategies. New search capabilities performed by *bots*, (described in Chapter 4) allow customers to compare prices locally, nationally, and globally in a matter of seconds.

Marketers at Huckleberry Mountain Co., a Jackson Hole, Wyoming–based specialty manu-facturer of candies and preserves, determine wholesale prices by multiplying ingredient costs by two then adding 20 percent. The doubling of ingredient costs covers labor and overhead, while the 20 percent addition covers distribution and sales commissions. But consumer demand can-not be ignored, and Huckleberry regularly compares their prices against those of leading com-petitors. Says Judy Johnson, co-owner with her husband, "We have to balance our ideal with what the market will pay. We attend about 40 trade shows a year and see what customers are pay-ing. If we're 40 percent higher than the competition, then we'd better have something really spe-cial or drop our prices."[5]

Profits are a function of revenue and expenses:

$$\text{Profits} = \text{Revenue} - \text{Expenses.}$$

Revenue is determined by the product's selling price and number of units sold:

$$\text{Total Revenue} = \text{Price} \times \text{Quantity Sold.}$$

Therefore, a profit maximizing price rises to the point at which further increases will cause dis-proportionate decreases in the number of units sold. A 10 percent price increase that results in only an 8 percent cut in volume will add to the firm's revenue. However, a 10 percent price hike that results in an 11 percent sales decline will reduce revenue.

Economists refer to this approach as *marginal analysis*. They identify **profit maximization** as the point at which the addition to total revenue is just balanced by the increase in total cost. Mar-keters must resolve a basic problem of how to achieve this delicate balance when they set prices. Relatively few firms actually hit this elusive target. A significantly larger number prefer to direct their effort toward more achievable goals.

Consequently, marketers commonly set **target-return objectives**—short-run or long-run goals usually stated as percentages of sales or investment. The practice has become particularly popular among large firms in which other pressures interfere with profit-maximization objectives. Target-return objectives offer several benefits for marketers in addition to resolving pricing questions. For example, these objectives serve as tools for evaluating performance. They also satisfy desires to generate "fair" profits as judged by management, stockholders, and the public.

Volume Objectives

Many business executives argue that pricing behavior actually seeks to maximize *sales* within a given profit constraint. In other words, they set a minimum acceptable profit level and then seek to maximize sales (subject to this profit constraint) in the belief that the increased sales are more important than immediate high profits to the long-run competitive picture. Such a company continues to expand sales as long as its total profits do not drop below the minimum return acceptable to management.

Hawaiian hotel and resort marketers stay in heated competition to attract business travelers and vacationers. Price is a popular and effective tool in maximizing sales in this booming travel industry. To encourage guests to prolong their stay at one of Westin's Hawaiian resorts, such as the one shown in Figure 18.2, marketers created a "splash package." In addition to golf privileges, gourmet dining, and beachfront rooms, guests receive a $100 daily resort credit—stay 3 nights and get $300 in credit.

Sales maximization can also result from non-price factors such as service and quality. For example, marketers increased sales for Dr. Scholl's new shoe insert, Dynastep, by heavily advertising in magazines. The ads explained how the Dynastep insert would help relieve leg and back pain. Priced around $14 per insert—twice as much as comparable offerings—the Dynastep ran over its competitors to become number one in its category.

Another volume-related pricing objective is the *market-share objective*—the goal set for controlling a portion of the market for a firm's good or service. Dr. Scholl's was able to increase its market share to 29 percent by focusing on the benefits of Dynastep. The company's specific goal may be to maintain its present share of a particular market, or to increase its share, for instance, from 10 percent to 20 percent. Volume-related objectives such as sales maximization and market share play an important role in most firms' pricing decisions.

The PIMS Studies

Market-share objectives may prove critical to the achievement of other organizational objectives. High sales, for example, often mean more profits. The extensive **Profit Impact of Market Strategies (PIMS) project**, conducted by the Marketing Science Institute, analyzed more than 2,000 firms and revealed that two of the most important factors influencing profitability were product quality and market share. Advertisements like the one in Figure 18.3 help to enhance profitability for the Clorox Co. As the industry leader in bleach sales, Clorox marketers do not focus on low price but rather on product benefits such as the pleasing fragrance and high-quality performance of its bleach compared to lesser-known brands that attempt to compete with a lower price. Numerous studies confirm the link between market share and profitability.

drscholls.com

MARKETING DICTIONARY

profit maximization Point at which the additional revenue gained by increasing the price of product equals the increase in total costs.

target return objective Short-run or long-run pricing objectives of achieving a specified return on either sales or investment.

Profit Impact of Market Strategies (PIMS) project Research that discovered a strong positive relationship between a firm's market share and its return on investment.

Clorox: Increasing Profitability through Product Quality and Market Share

Rain Clean Clorox Bleach smells fresh as a spring rain.

No bargain bleach has a fragrance like it.

And no bargain bleach beats that unbeatable Clorox Bleach white.
Don't be fooled by bargain bleaches. Get Rain Clean Clorox Bleach.

RAIN CLEAN

©1998 The Clorox Company

The relationship of market share and profitability is evident in PIMS data that reveal an average 32 percent return on investment (ROI) for firms with market shares over 40 percent. In contrast, average ROI decreases to 24 percent for firms whose market shares are between 20 and 40 percent. Firms with a minor market share (less than 10 percent) generate average pretax investment returns of approximately 13 percent.[6]

The relationship also applies to a firm's individual brands. The PIMS researchers compared the top four brands in each market segment they studied. Their data revealed that the leading brand typically generates after-tax ROI of 18 percent, considerably higher than the second-ranked brand. Weaker brands, on average, fail to earn adequate returns.

Marketers have developed an underlying explanation of the positive relationship between profitability and market share. Firms with large shares accumulate greater operating experience and lower overall costs relative to competitors with smaller market shares. Accordingly, segmentation strategies might focus on obtaining larger shares of smaller markets and on avoiding smaller shares of larger ones. A firm might achieve higher financial returns by becoming a major competitor in several smaller market segments than by remaining a relatively minor competitor in a larger market.

Meeting Competition Objectives

A third set of pricing objectives seeks simply to meet competitor's prices. In many lines of business, firms set their own prices to match those of established industry price leaders.

In 1999, Worldcom shook up the long-distance telephone market by advertising 5-cents-per-minute pricing for nights and weekends. AT&T countered with a 7-cents-per-minute rate all the time. Since both telecommunication firms offer a service most customers consider interchangeable, neither of these multinational giants could continue operations unless they came close to matching each other's prices. Also, any price reductions below the 5-cent level are likely to lead to flat-rate monthly service offers due to the cost of preparing and mailing itemized bills.[7]

Pricing objectives tied directly to meeting prices charged by major competitors de-emphasize the price element of the marketing mix and focus more strongly on non-price variables. Pricing is a highly visible component of a firm's marketing mix and an easy and effective tool for obtaining a differential advantage over competitors; still, other firms can easily duplicate a price reduction themselves. The airline price competition of recent years exemplifies the actions and reactions of competitors in this marketplace. Rather than emphasizing the lowest fares of any carrier, most airlines choose to compete by offering convenient arrival and departure times, an attractive frequent-flyer program, and customer-focused alliances with automobile rental, lodging, and other partners. Because price changes directly affect overall profitability in an industry, many firms attempt to promote stable prices by meeting competitors' prices and competing for market share by focusing on product strategies, promotional decisions, and distribution—the non-price elements of the marketing mix.

Ford Escort marketers focus on such non-price elements as the company's award-winning reputation for quality and the economy sedan's low price in the ad shown in Figure 18.4. In competition with Chrysler's Neon, the Kia Sephia, and Geo's Metro, the low price helps Ford to reach targeted young adults and college graduates who are just entering the workforce. Ford marketers point out that the Escort offers the standard features of economy cars in this price range but emphasize the extras, including a remote keyless entry system, safety cell construction, and a great sound system.

FIGURE 18.4 | **Ford Escort: Meeting Competition Objectives in Pricing**

Value Pricing

When discounts become normal elements of a competitive marketplace, other marketing-mix elements gain importance in purchase decisions. In such instances, overall product value, not just price, determines product choice. In recent years, a new strategy—**value pricing**—has emerged that emphasizes the benefits a product provides in comparison to the price and quality levels of competing offerings. This strategy typically works best for relatively low-priced goods and services.

Laundry detergents are a good example of value pricing. The label on Dash detergent proclaims *Value Price*, While Arm & Hammer's label assures customers that it *Cleans Great—Value Price, Too!* Yes detergent announces *Great Value!*, while Ultra Rinso claims *Super Value*, and the back label on Ultra Trend boasts that it offers *hard-working performance at a reasonable price*. The label on another detergent, All, simply advises customers to *Compare & Save*.

Value-priced products generally cost less than premium brands, but marketers point out that *value* does not necessarily mean *inexpensive*. The challenge for those who compete on value is to convince customers that low-priced brands offer quality comparable to that of a higher-priced product. An increasing number of alternative products and private-label brands has increased competition among marketers in recent years. In the dry cereal market, sales industry-wide have plummeted 15 percent. Kellogg, the number one cereal maker in the United States, watched market share drop drastically before it

MARKETING | **DICTIONARY**

value pricing Pricing strategy emphasizing benefits derived from a product in comparison to th price and quality levels of competing offerings.

The folic acid in

Because of childbearing age can help fight against certain brain and spinal cord birth defects in their babies by getting the recommended

Kellogg's Corn Flakes

amount of folic acid in their diets. Kellogg's Corn Flakes cereal has been an excellent source of folic acid for over six years.

can help reduce the risk

Call 1-800-468-9004 and learn more about how you can help yourself. With Kellogg's Healthier Life Is Within Your Reach.

of some birth defects.

Help yourself.

Kellogg's

This Kellogg ad focuses on the role folic acid in Kellogg's Corn Flakes can play in helping reduce the risk of some birth defects.

began implementing strategies based on price-value. Kellogg now focuses on promoting the quality ingredients and nutritional benefits of its cereals.[8]

Value pricing is perhaps best seen in the personal-computer industry. In the past few years, PC prices have collapsed, reducing the effectiveness of traditional pricing strategies intended to meet competition. In fact, PCs priced at under $600 are now the fastest growing segment of the market. In one year, this category has grown 657 percent and now accounts for almost 20 percent of PCs sold in stores. Industry leaders like Dell, Compaq, and Gateway cannot continue to cut prices, so they are adding features such as increased memory and 3-D graphic accelerator cards that increase speed.[9]

Prestige Objectives

The final category of pricing objectives, unrelated to either profitability or sales volume, is prestige objectives. Prestige pricing establishes a relatively high price to develop and maintain an image of quality and exclusiveness that appeals to status-conscious consumers. Such objectives reflect marketers' recognition of the role of price in creating an overall image of the firm and its goods and services.

Prestige objectives affect the price tags of such products as Waterford crystal, Alpha Romeo sports cars, Omega watches, and Tiffany jewelry. When a perfume marketer sets a price of $135 or more per ounce, this choice reflects an emphasis on image far more than the cost of ingredients. Analyses have shown that ingredients account for less than 5 percent of a perfume's cost. Thus, advertisements for Joy that promote the fragrance as the "costliest perfume in the world" use price to promote product prestige.

In contrast to low-price strategies used by marketers of economy cars, ads for the Bentley Azure target wealthy clientele interested in the vehicle's classic design that conveys their lifestyle. The Azure is flaunted as a sophisticated, turbocharged, 150-mile-per-hour sports car with a leather interior and a hand-polished walnut dashboard. Appearing in upscale magazines such as *Conde Nast Traveler*, the ads state: "Bentley. You don't park it, you position it."

While ads for luxury products, such as the one shown in Figure 18.5 for Royal Secret perfume, may hint at high prices, few openly mention price. Marketers tell perfume shoppers to "Do it for love." Cosmetics companies, in general, seldom talk price in their advertisements. More recently, however, marketers of prestigious products have experimented with their own version of value pricing. Cosmetics manufacturer Clinique, for example, now includes product samples and retail prices in its advertisements.

In the corporate world, private jet ownership imparts an image of prestige, power, and high price tags—too high for most business travelers to even consider. Recognizing that cost is the primary factor that makes jet ownership prohibitive for business travel, marketers at Flight Options have created an alternative in the marketplace. This new target market is willing to buy, and has authority to buy, but cannot afford a new Citation, Beechjet, Hawker, or Challenger aircraft. In efforts to satisfy this untapped market, Flight Options broke the price barrier by advertising pre-owned aircraft at 35 percent less than a new model. In addition to affordability and value, customers are granted a 30-day walk-away guarantee of satisfaction.

FIGURE 18.5 Royal Secret Marketers Emphasize Prestige

flightoptions.com

Pricing Objectives of Not-for-Profit Organizations

Pricing typically is a very important element of the marketing mix for not-for-profit organizations. Pricing strategy can help these groups to achieve a variety of organizational goals:

1. **Profit maximization.** While not-for-profit organizations by definition do not cite profitability as a primary goal, there are numerous instances in which they do try to maximize their returns on single events or a series of events. A $1,000-a-plate political fund-raiser is a classic example.

2. **Cost recovery.** Some not-for-profit organizations attempt to recover only the actual cost of operating the unit. Mass transit, publicly supported colleges, and bridges are common examples. The amount of recovered costs is often dictated by tradition, competition, and/or public opinion.

3. **Providing market incentives.** Other not-for-profit groups follow a lower than average pricing policy or offer a free service to encourage increased usage of the good or service. Seattle's bus system offers free service in the downtown area in an attempt to reduce traffic congestion, encourage retail sales, and minimize the effort required to access downtown public services.

4. **Market suppression.** Price can also discourage consumption. High prices help to accomplish social objectives independent of the costs of providing goods or services. Illustrations include tobacco and alcohol taxes, parking fines, tolls, and gasoline excise taxes.

METHODS FOR DETERMINING PRICES

Marketers determine prices in two basic ways—by applying the theoretical concepts of supply and demand and by completing cost-oriented analyses. During the first part of the 20th century, most discussions for price determination emphasized the classical concepts of supply and demand. During the last half of the century, however, the emphasis shifted to a cost-oriented approach. Hindsight reveals certain flaws in both concepts.

Treatments of this subject often overlook another concept of price determination—one based on the impact of custom and tradition. **Customary prices** are retail prices that consumers expect as a result of traditional and social habit. Candy makers have attempted to maintain traditional price levels by considerably reducing product size. Similar practices have prevailed in the marketing of soft drinks as bottlers attempt to balance consumer expectations of customary prices with the realities of rising costs.

Wm. Wrigley Jr. Co., manufacturer of such chewing gum standards as Juicy Fruit, Doublemint, and Big Red, took advantage of the weakness in the industry's customary pricing strategy by introducing a smaller-quantity pack at a lower price. While competitors continued to offer only seven-piece packs for 35 cents, Wrigley priced its five-piece packs at 25 cents. To spur impulse buying, the company prominently displayed the price on the package. The strategy was so successful that within two years of its inception, Wrigley discontinued selling seven-stick gum packs.

With over 800 convenient locations across the United States, Motel 6 has carved out a comfortable share of the lodging market by offering the best prices of any national chain. Its popular tag line, "We'll leave the light on for you," earned Motel 6 a position in the top 100 advertising campaigns of the century. In fact, it was the only motel chain to be included in the top 100 awards given by *Advertising Age*. Building market share based on the company's strong reputation and position as the nation's leader in the budget segment of the travel hospitality industry, Motel 6 marketers recently began offering a new program for extended-stay travelers. The new Studio 6 properties, shown in Figure 18.6, offer full kitchens, coffeemakers, voice mail, alarm clock, and other amenities for one low weekly rate.[10]

At some point, however, someone has to set initial prices for products. In addition, competitive moves and cost changes necessitate periodic reviews of price structures. The remaining sections delve into the issue of price determination. This section also considers how marketers can most effectively integrate the concepts to develop realistic pricing systems.

FIGURE 18.6   **Studio 6: Enhancing Value through Customary Prices**

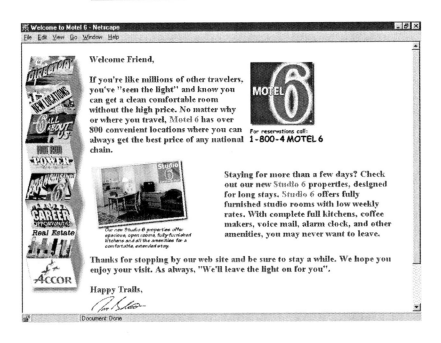

PRICE DETERMINATION IN ECONOMIC THEORY

Microeconomics suggests a way of determining prices that assumes a profit-maximization objective. This technique attempts to derive correct equilibrium prices in the marketplace by comparing supply and demand. It also requires more complete analysis than actual business firms typically conduct.

Demand refers to a schedule of the amounts of a firm's good or service that consumers will purchase at different prices during a specified period. **Supply** refers to a schedule of the amounts of a good or service that will be offered for sale at different prices during a specified time period. These schedules may vary for different types of market structures. Businesses operate and set prices in four types of market structures: pure competition, monopolistic competition, oligopoly, and monopoly.

Pure competition is a market structure with so many buyers and sellers that no single participant can significantly influence price. Pure competition presupposes other market conditions, as well: homogeneous products and ease of entry for sellers due to low start-up costs. While most of today's businesspeople encounter this market structure only in theory, the agricultural sector exhibits many characteristics of a purely competitive market, making it the closest actual example.

Monopolistic competition typifies most retailing and features large numbers of buyers and sellers. These diverse parties exchange heterogeneous, relatively well-differentiated products, giving marketers some control over prices.

Relatively few sellers compete in an **oligopoly**. Each seller may affect the market, but no single seller controls it. High start-up costs form significant barriers to entry for new competitors. Each firm's demand curve in an oligopolistic market displays a unique kink at the current market price. Because of the impact of a single competitor on total industry sales, competitors usually quickly match any attempt by one firm to generate additional sales by reducing prices. Price cutting throughout such an industry reduces total industry revenues. Oligopolies operate in the petroleum refining, automobile, and tobacco industries.

The availability of alternative air transportation in the form of such discount carriers as Southwest Airlines and Frontier Airlines forces established air carriers to maintain competitive airfares—or risk losing business to the upstarts. When these alternatives disappear, prices often rise. For example, before United Express began offering service to the Gulf Coast, the market had only one major airline—Delta. United Express was a welcome alternative for travelers who found prices two-thirds cheaper than the lowest competing fare.[11]

A **monopoly** is a market structure where only one seller of a product exists and for which there are no close substitutes. Antitrust legislation has nearly eliminated all but temporary monopolies, such as those created through patent protection and regulated monopolies, like utility companies. The government allows regulated monopolies in markets in which competition would lead to an uneconomical duplication of services. In return for such a license, government reserves the right to regulate the monopoly's rate of return.

Table 18.2 compares the four types of market structures on the following bases: number of competitors, ease of entry into the industry by new firms, similarity of competing products,

MARKETING | **DICTIONARY**

customary prices In pricing strategy, the traditional prices that customers expect to pay for certain goods and services.

demand Schedule of the amounts of a firm's product that consumers will purchase at different prices during a specified time period.

supply Schedule of the amounts of a good or service that firms will offer for sale at different prices during a specified time period.

pure competition Market structure characterized by homogeneous products in which there are so many buyers and sellers that none has a significant influence on price.

monopolistic competition Market structure involving a heterogeneous product and product differentiation among competing suppliers, allowing the marketer some degree of control over prices.

oligopoly Market structure involving relatively few sellers and barriers to new competitors due to high start-up costs.

monopoly Market structure involving only one seller of a good or service for which no close substitutes exist.

TABLE 18.2	Distinguishing Features of the Four Market Structures

	TYPE OF MARKET STRUCTURE			
CHARACTERISTICS	PURE COMPETITION	MONOPOLISTIC COMPETITION	OLIGOPOLY	MONOPOLY
Number of competitors	Many	Few to many	Few	No direct competitors
Ease of entry into industry by new firms	Easy	Somewhat difficult	Difficult	Regulated by government
Similarity of goods or services offered by competing firms	Similar	Different	Can be either similar or different	No directly competing goods or services
Control over prices by individual firms	None	Some	Some	Considerable
Demand curves facing individual firms	Totally elastic	Can be either elastic or inelastic	Kinked; inelastic below kink; more elastic above	Can be either elastic or inelastic
Examples	200-acre ranch	Gap stores	Texaco	Commonwealth Edison

degree of control over price by individual firms, and the elasticity or inelasticity of the demand curve facing the individual firm. Elasticity—the degree of consumer responsiveness to changes in price—is discussed in more detail in a later section.

Cost and Revenue Curves

Marketers must set a price for a product that generates sufficient revenue to cover the costs of producing and marketing it. A product's total cost is composed of total variable costs and total fixed costs. *Variable costs* change with the level of production (such as labor and raw materials costs), while *fixed costs* remain stable at any production level within a certain range (such as lease payments or insurance costs). *Average total costs* are calculated by dividing the sum of the variable and fixed costs by the number of units produced. Finally, *marginal cost* is the change in total cost that results from producing an additional unit of output.

The demand side of the pricing equation focuses on revenue curves. *Average revenue* is calculated by dividing total revenue by the quantity associated with these revenues. Average revenue is actually the demand curve facing the firm. *Marginal revenue* is the change in total revenue that results from selling an additional unit of output. Figure 18.7 shows the relationships of various cost and revenue measures; the firm maximizes its profits when marginal costs equal marginal revenues.

Table 18.3 illustrates why the intersection of the marginal cost and marginal revenue curves is the logical point at which to maximize revenue for the organization. Although the firm can earn a profit at several different prices, the price at which it earns maximum profits is $22. At a price of $24, $66 in profits are earned—$4 less than the $70 profit at the $22 price. If a price of $20 is set to attract additional sales, the marginal costs of the extra sales ($7) are greater than the marginal revenues received ($6), and total profits decline.

The Concept of Elasticity in Pricing Strategy

Although the intersection of the marginal cost and marginal revenue curves determines the level of output, the impact of changes in price on sales varies greatly. In order to understand why it fluctuates, it is necessary to understand the concept of elasticity.

Elasticity is the measure of responsiveness of purchasers and suppliers to price changes. The price elasticity of demand (or elasticity of demand) is the percentage change in the quantity of a good or service demanded divided by the percentage change in its price. A 10 percent increase

Explain price elasticity and its determinants.

FIGURE 18.7 | Determining Price by Relating Marginal Revenue to Marginal Cost

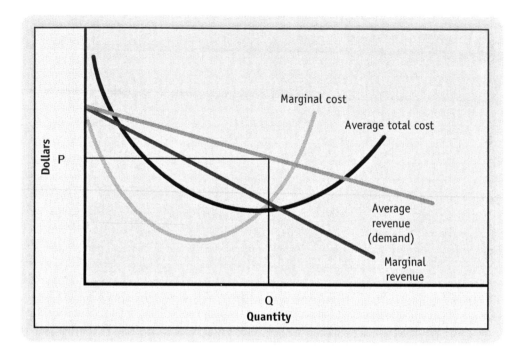

TABLE 18.3 | Price Determination Using Marginal Analysis

PRICE	NUMBER SOLD	TOTAL REVENUE	MARGINAL REVENUE	TOTAL COSTS	MARGINAL COSTS	PROFITS (TOTAL REVENUE MINUS TOTAL COSTS)
—	—	—	—	—	—	($50)
$34	1	$34	$34	57	$7	(23)
32	2	64	30	62	5	2
30	3	90	26	66	4	24
28	4	112	22	69	3	43
26	5	130	18	73	4	57
24	6	144	14	78	5	66
22	7	154	10	84	6	70
20	8	160	6	91	7	69
18	9	162	2	100	9	62
16	10	160	(2)	110	11	50

---

in the price of eggs that results in a 5 percent decrease in the quantity of eggs demanded yields a price elasticity of demand for eggs of 0.5. The price elasticity of supply of a product is the percentage change in the quantity of a good or service supplied divided by the percentage change in its price. A 10 percent increase in the price

MARKETING   DICTIONARY

elasticity Measure of responsiveness of purchasers and suppliers to a change in price.

continued on next page

of shampoo that results in a 25 percent increase in the quantity supplied yields a price elasticity of supply for shampoo of 2.5.

Consider a case in which a 1 percent change in price causes more than a 1 percent change in the quantity supplied or demanded. Numerically, that means an elasticity greater than 1.0. When the elasticity of demand or supply is greater than 1.0, that demand or supply is said to be *elastic*. If a 1 percent change in price results in less than a 1 percent change in quantity, a product's elasticity of demand or supply will be less than 1.0. In that case, the demand or supply is called *inelastic*. For example, the demand for cigarettes is relatively inelastic; research studies have shown that a 10 percent increase in cigarette prices results in only a 4 percent sales decline.

In countries such as Argentina and Brazil, where the annual inflation rate has been known to top 100 percent, prices on almost all products have risen accordingly. These higher prices have led to elastic demand for some items, such as houses and cars; many of the cars on Argentina's roads are over 10 years old, and the nation's housing market is severely depressed. For other products, demand has been inelastic; families continue to buy food because, after all, they need to eat. However, even if they do not affect demand, inflationary prices can alter consumers' buying patterns. Lower income Brazilians, for instance, buy all the food they can afford when they get each paycheck.

Determinants of Elasticity

Why is the elasticity of supply or demand high for some products and low for others? What determines demand elasticity? One major factor influencing the elasticity of demand is the availability of substitutes or complements. If consumers can easily find close substitutes for a good or service, the product's demand tends to be elastic. During the late 1990s, an increase in the number of businesses and individuals using e-mail cut into U.S. Postal Service (USPS) revenues. Fearing another price increase would only drive profits down further, marketers tried to boost revenues by adding value to current service offerings. None of these efforts generated enough revenues to cover rising costs, though, and finally marketers were forced to increase postage rates. In 1999, a penny was added to first-class postage and other rates were either increased or revised. Surprisingly, this smallest price change in USPS history allowed the USPS to reach its $200 million net income plan.[12] In another example, the relatively inelastic demand for motor oil reflects its role as a complement to a more important product, gasoline.

As increasing numbers of buyers and sellers complete their business transactions online, the elasticity of a product's demand is drastically affected. Take large discounters, for example. Small businesses and individual do-it-yourselfers shop Home Depot for tools, such as wheelbarrows; parents look for Furbies at Toys "Я" Us; and homeowners can go to Circuit City for new refrigerators or stoves. Today, however, the Internet lets consumers contact product manufacturers and service providers directly, often giving them better selections and prices for their efforts. (The power struggle between brick-and-mortar retailers and Internet suppliers is the topic of the Solving an Ethical Controversy in Chapter 19.) In the case of an item such as the wheelbarrow, which once was sold at almost identical prices at a relatively small number of retail outlets (inelastic demand), today's shoppers can find the item in dozens of different locations—traditional hardware stores, home-improvement centers, discount stores, and even some department stores. The one-wheelbarrow-fits-all approach has been replaced with different sizes, colors, and materials to match the specific needs of different users. The availability of different models and different prices for each combine to create a market characterized by demand elasticity.[13]

Elasticity of demand also depends on whether a product is a necessity or a luxury. For example, the Four Seasons chain of luxury hotels and resorts enjoys such a strong reputation for service, comfort, and exclusiveness that it has become a favorite among affluent individual travelers and business professionals. The combination of personal service and exclusiveness, depicted in Figure 18.8, attracts a select group of upscale travelers, who consider reservations at Four Seasons hotels essential components of their trips to Atlanta or Tokyo. Because such a customer views Four Seasons' accommodations as a necessity, not a luxury, sales remain strong despite the high room rates. Most people regard high-fashion clothes, such as a $2,000 Armani suit, as luxuries. If prices for designer outfits increase, people can respond by purchasing lower-priced substitutes instead. In

FIGURE 18.8	Four Seasons Hotels: Inelastic Demand for a Service Viewed as a Necessity by Upscale Travelers

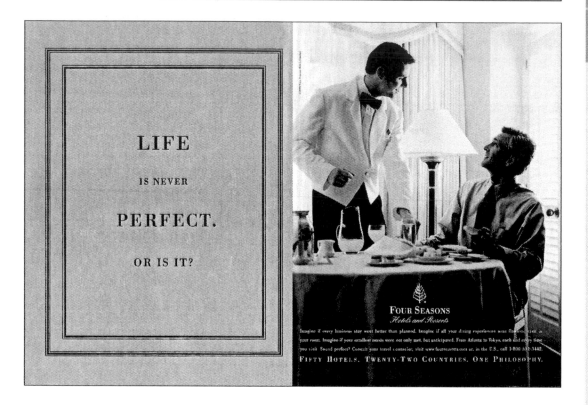

contrast, medical and dental care are considered necessities, so price changes have little effect on the frequency of medical or dental visits.

However, under the continuing influence of higher prices, some products once regarded as necessities may be dismissed as luxuries, leading to decreasing demand. For instance, German consumers have traditionally been eager buyers of brand-name consumer electronics goods. As prices and unemployment in Germany have risen, however, demand for these products has become highly elastic. As a result, retail outlets have encountered dramatically declining electronics sales.

Elasticity also depends on the portion of a person's budget that he or she spends on a good or service. People no longer really need matches, for example; they can easily find good substitutes. Nonetheless, the demand for matches remains very inelastic because people spend so little on them that they hardly notice a price change. In contrast, the demand for housing or transportation is not totally inelastic, even though these are necessities, because both consume large parts of a consumer's budget.

Elasticity of demand also responds to consumers' time perspectives. Demand often shows less elasticity in the short run than in the long run. Consider the demand for home air conditioning. In the short run, people pay rising energy prices because they find it difficult to cut back on the quantities they use. Accustomed to living with specific temperature settings, dressing in certain ways, and so forth, they prefer to pay more during a few months out of the year than to explore other possibilities. Over time, though, with global warming becoming a real and present danger, they may find ways to economize. They can better insulate their homes, plant shade trees, or even move to cooler climates.

Sometimes the usual patterns do not hold true, though. Alcohol and tobacco, which are not necessities but do occupy large shares of some personal budgets, are also subject to inelastic demand.

Elasticity and Revenue

bart.org

The elasticity of demand exerts an important influence on variations in total revenue as a result of changes in the price of a good or service. Assume, for example, that San Francisco's Bay Area Rapid Transit (BART) officials are considering alternative methods of raising more money for the city budget. One possible method for increasing revenues would be to change rail pass fares for BART commuters. But should the city raise or lower the price of a pass? The correct answer depends on the elasticity of demand for subway rides. A 10 percent decrease in fares should attract more riders, but unless it stimulates more than a 10 percent increase in riders, total revenue will fall. A 10 percent increase in fares will bring in more money per rider, but if more than 10 percent of the riders stop using the subway, total revenue will fall. A price cut will increase revenue only for a product with elastic demand, and a price increase will raise revenue only for a product with inelastic demand. BART officials seem to believe that the demand for rapid rail transit is inelastic; they raise fares when they need more money for the city budget.

Practical Problems of Price Theory

Marketers may thoroughly understand price theory concepts but still encounter difficulty applying them in practice. What practical limitations interfere with price setting?

First, many firms do not attempt to maximize profits. Economic analysis is subject to the same limitations as the assumptions on which it is based—for example, the proposition that all firms attempt to maximize profits. Second, it is difficult to estimate demand curves. Modern accounting procedures provide managers with a clear understanding of cost structures, so managers can readily comprehend the supply side of the pricing equation. But they find it difficult to estimate demand at various price levels. Demand curves must be based on marketing research estimates that often are less exact than cost figures. Although the demand element can be identified, it is often difficult to measure in real-world settings.

PRICE DETERMINATION IN PRACTICE

The practical limitations inherent in price theory have forced practitioners to turn to other techniques. **Cost-plus pricing**, the most popular method, uses a base-cost figure per unit and adds a markup to cover unassigned costs and to provide a profit. The only real difference among the multitude of cost-plus techniques is the relative sophistication of the costing procedures employed. For example, a local apparel shop may set prices by adding a 45 percent markup to the invoice price charged by the supplier. The markup is expected to cover all other expenses and permit the owner to earn a reasonable return on the sale of clothes.

In contrast to this rather simple pricing mechanism, a large manufacturer may employ a complex pricing formula requiring computer calculations. However, this method merely adds a more complicated procedure to the simpler, traditional method for calculating costs. In the end, someone still must make a decision about the markup. The apparel shop and the large manufacturer may figure costs differently, but they are remarkably similar in completing the markup side of the equation.

Cost-plus pricing often works well for a business that keeps its costs low, allowing it to set its prices lower than those of competitors and still make a profit. American discounter Wal-Mart keeps costs low by buying directly from manufacturers rather than going through wholesalers and other intermediaries. This strategy has helped the company in its rise to become the world's largest discount retailer.

Alternative Pricing Procedures

The two most common cost-oriented pricing procedures are the full-cost method and the incremental-cost method. *Full-cost pricing* uses all relevant variable costs in setting a product's price. In addition, it allocates those fixed costs that cannot be directly attributed to the produc-

SOLVING AN ETHICAL CONTROVERSY

Politics, Patents, and the Price of Loratadine

The debate seems to be never ending between a company's right to make money versus the public's right to low-cost medicine. Schering-Plough pharmaceutical company recently came face to face with this controversy, having enjoyed great success with Claritin, its prescription drug, containing loratadine, that combats allergies. Millions of allergy sufferers have purchased the medication, generating $2.3 billion in sales for the firm. In spite of the high demand, prices have not fallen because Schering-Plough holds the patent on the drug.

Patents are intended to protect companies as they enter the market with a new invention or innovation from competitors. In effect, patents create a monopoly situation to reward members by giving them time to re-coup their research-and-development costs. Schering-Plough and other drug companies not only obtain patents but frequently appeal for extensions. Recently, however, businesses have figured out how to use the po-litical process for monopoly-price protection that critics claim goes far beyond what is legitimate. With soaring drug prices, low-cost generic drug makers spend millions of dollars lobbying members of Congress not to ex-tend the patent on drugs. In one recent year, Schering-Plough had nine lobbying companies under contract and contributed more than $280,000 to the Democratic and Republican parties. Consumer advocate groups have joined the fight to stop patent extensions on drugs that typically cost 60 percent more than generic equivalents. Says one critic, "If they get away with it, it's a message to any company with a best-selling drug: 'You did it for Claritin, why not me?'"

 Should drug companies be allowed to extend patents?

Pro

1. Patents should be extended when companies need more time to recover their research and development costs associated with new medicines.

2. Drug prices do not always affect the consumer significantly since man HMOs and other group health programs cover many prescription drug Over half of Americans now receive discounted medicines through su managed-care programs.

3. Drug prices set by pharmaceutical companies are not aimed at hur ing the consumer but helping the company continue research an development.

Con

1. Patent extensions are anticonsumer and encourage monopolistic ma ket behavior.

2. Lobbying for patent extensions is an attempt to buy price protectic for large pharmaceutical companies. The giant drug companies are simp profiting from the illnesses of their consumers, rather than trying to he the sick.

3. Granting extensions undermines the primary purpose of a patent ar may result in high prices that force the consumer to forego neede medications.

Summary

Patents have long served to protect the creators of new goods and se vices. However, in any industry, the costs of production are reflected the prices charged. Since every product involves different cost levels, simple time limit on patents may be unrealistic for all products in industries.

Source: Bill Walsh, "Drugmaker Fights to Extend Patent on Best-Selling Claritin," *Mobile Reg ter*, July 1, 1999, pp. A1, A4.

---

tion of the specific item being priced. Under the full-cost method, if job order 515 in a printing plant amounts to .000127 percent of the plant's total output, then .000127 percent of the firm's overhead expenses are charged to that job. This approach allows the marketer to recover all costs plus the amount added as a profit margin.

The full-cost approach has two basic deficiencies. First, there is no consideration of competi-tion or demand for the item. Perhaps no one wants to pay the price the firm has calculated. Sec-ond, any method for allocating overhead (fixed expenses) is arbitrary and may be unrealistic. In manufacturing, overhead allocations often are tied to direct labor hours. In retailing, the square footage of each profit center is sometimes the factor used in computations. Regardless of the tech-nique employed, it is difficult to show a cause-effect relationship between the al-located cost and most products.

One way to overcome the arbitrary allocation of fixed expenses is with *incremental-cost pricing*, which attempts

MARKETING   DICTIONARY

cost-plus pricing Practice of adding a percentage of specified dollar amount (markup) to the bas cost of a product to cover unassigned costs and to provide a profit.

to use only those costs directly attributable to a specific output in setting prices. Consider a small-scale manufacturer with the following income statement:

Sales (10,000 units at $10)		$100,000
Expenses:		
Variable	$50,000	
Fixed	40,000	90,000
Net Profit		$10,000

Suppose the firm is offered a contract for an additional 5,000 units. Since the peak season is over, these items can be produced at the same average variable cost. Assume that the labor force would be idle otherwise. How low should the firm price its product in order to get the contract?

Under the full-cost approach, the lowest price would be $9 per unit. This figure is obtained by dividing the $90,000 in expenses by an output of 10,000 units. The incremental approach, on the other hand, could permit any price above $5, which would significantly increase the possibility of securing the additional contract. This price would be composed of the $5 variable cost associated with each unit of production plus a $.10-per-unit contribution to fixed expenses and overhead. With a $5.10 proposed price, the income statement now looks like this:

Sales (10,000 at $10; 5,000 at $5.10)		$125,500
Expenses:		
Variable	$75,000	
Fixed	40,000	115,000
Net Profit		$10,500

Profits thus are increased under the incremental approach.

Admittedly, the illustration is based on two assumptions: (1) the ability to isolate markets such that selling at the lower price will not affect the price received in other markets, and (2) the absence of legal restrictions on the firm. The example, however, does illustrate that profits can sometimes be enhanced by using the incremental approach.

st the major advantages and
ortcomings of using breakeven
alysis in pricing decisions.

Breakeven Analysis

Breakeven analysis is a means of determining the number of goods or services that must be sold at a given price in order to generate sufficient revenue to cover total costs. Figure 18.9 graphically depicts this process. The total cost curve includes both fixed and variable segments, and total fixed cost is represented by a horizontal line. Average variable cost is assumed to be constant per unit as it was in the example for incremental pricing.

The breakeven point is the point at which total revenue just equals total cost. In the example in Figure 18.9, a selling price of $10 and an average variable cost of $5 result in a per-unit contribution to fixed cost of $5. The breakeven point in terms of units is found by using the following formula, where the per-unit contribution equals the product's price less the variable cost per unit:

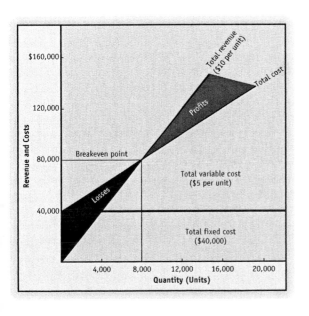

FIGURE 18.9 **Breakeven Chart**

$$\text{Breakeven Point (in Units)} = \frac{\text{Total Fixed Cost}}{\text{Per-Unit Contribution to Fixed Cost}}$$

$$\text{Breakeven Point (in Units)} = \frac{\$40,000}{\$5} = 8,000 \text{ units}$$

The breakeven point is found with the following formula:

$$\text{Breakeven Point (in Dollars)} = \frac{\text{Total Fixed Cost}}{1 - \text{Variable Cost per Unit Price}}$$

$$\text{Breakeven Point (in Dollars)} = \frac{\$40,000}{1 - \frac{\$5}{\$10}} = \frac{\$40,000}{0.5} = \$80,000$$

Once the breakeven point has been reached, sufficient revenues will have been obtained from sales to cover all fixed costs. Any additional sales will generate per-unit profits equal to the difference between the product's selling price and the variable cost of each unit. As Figure 18.9 reveals, sales of 8,001 units (1 unit above the breakeven point) will produce net profits of $5 ($10 sales price less per-unit variable cost of $5). Once all fixed costs have been covered, the per-unit contribution will become the per-unit profit.

Thomas Lipsky knew enough about breakeven analysis to convince himself that he could start a record label—and make money. With limited financing and even less clout in the music business, the Raleigh, North Carolina–based concert promoter knew he would not be signing hot groups like the teenybopper Backstreet Boys, who can sell 1.2 million copies of a new album in a single week. So he signed the only acts he could afford: 1980s rock groups like Slaughter and Warrant that featured gaudy guitar solos and oversized stage theatrics. Even though Slaughter had sold 3 million albums in 1990, they quickly fell off the charts—and Lipsky had much more modest expectations for the Las Vegas–based group.

The way to make money was contained within the breakeven formula. Slaughter already owned a recording studio, so the $100,000 advance Lipsky shelled out went into the band members' pockets. Another $150,000 was spent on promotion, much of which went to retailers to persuade them to stock his product. Lipsky's record company makes a gross profit of $5 per disc, so he starts making money once an album sells more than 50,000 copies. Even though the advances are meager, the band goes along with it because (1) nobody else is beating down their doors to record them, and (2) the new albums make it easier to convince concert promoters to book them for tours. Lipsky is happy; the band rocks; and breakeven analysis shows how profits can be gleaned from modest sales by shrewd marketers who can control overhead.[14]

Target Returns

Although breakeven analysis indicates the sales level at which the firm will incur neither profits nor losses, most firms' managers include some target profit in their analyses. In some instances, management sets a desired dollar return when considering a proposed new product or other marketing action. A retailer may set a desired profit of $250,000 in considering whether to expand to a second location. In other instances, the target return may be expressed in percentages, such as a 15 percent return on sales. These target returns can be modified as follows:

$$\text{Breakeven Point (including specified dollar target return)} = \frac{\text{Total Fixed Cost} + \text{Profit Objective}}{\text{Per-Unit Contribution}}$$

$$= \frac{\$40,000 + \$15,000}{\$5} = 11,000 \text{ units}$$

If the target return is expressed as a percentage of sales, it can be included in the breakeven formula as a variable cost. Suppose the marketing manager in the above example seeks a 10 percent return on sales. The desired return is $1 for each product sold (the $10 per-unit selling price multiplied by the 10 percent return on sales). In this case, the basic breakeven formula will remain unchanged, although the variable cost

MARKETING | **DICTIONARY**

breakeven analysis Pricing technique used to determine the number of products that must be sold at a specified price in order to generate enough revenue to cover total cost.

per unit will be increased to reflect the target return, and the per-unit contribution to fixed cost will be reduced to $4. As a result, the breakeven point will increase from 8,000 to 10,000 units:

$$\text{Breakeven Point} = \frac{\$40,000}{\$4} = 10,000 \text{ units.}$$

Evaluation of Breakeven Analysis

Breakeven analysis is an effective tool for marketers in assessing the sales required for covering costs and achieving specified profit levels. It is easily understood by both marketing and non-marketing executives and may help them decide whether required sales levels for a certain price are in fact realistic goals. However, it has its shortcomings.

First, the model assumes that costs can be divided into fixed and variable categories. Some costs, such as salaries and advertising outlays, may be either fixed or variable depending on the particular situation. In addition, the model assumes that per-unit variable costs do not change at different levels of operation. However, these may vary because of quantity discounts, more efficient utilization of the workforce, or other economies resulting from increased levels of production and sales. Finally, the basic breakeven model does not consider demand. It is a cost-based model and does not directly address the crucial question of whether consumers will actually purchase the product at the specified price and in the quantities required for breaking even or generating profits. The marketer's challenge is to modify the breakeven analysis and the other cost-oriented pricing approaches to incorporate demand analysis. Pricing must be examined from the buyer's perspective. Such decisions cannot be made in a management vacuum in which only cost factors are considered.

TOWARD REALISTIC PRICING

plain the superiority of odified breakeven analysis over e basic breakeven model and e role of yield management in icing decisions.

Traditional economic theory considers both costs and demand in determining an equilibrium price. The dual elements of supply and demand are balanced at the point of equilibrium. In actual practice, however, most pricing approaches are largely cost oriented. Since purely cost-oriented approaches to pricing violate the marketing concept, modifications that will add demand analysis to the pricing decision are required.

Consumer research on such issues as degree of price elasticity, consumer price expectations, existence and size of specific market segments, and buyer perceptions of strengths and weaknesses of substitute products is necessary for developing sales estimates at different prices. Because much of the resulting data involves perceptions, attitudes, and future expectations of present and potential customers, such estimates are likely to be less precise than cost estimates.

The Modified Breakeven Concept

The breakeven analysis method illustrated in Figure 18.10 assumes a constant $10 retail price regardless of quantity. But what happens at different retail prices? **Modified breakeven analysis** combines the traditional breakeven analysis model with an evaluation of consumer demand.

Table 18.4 summarizes both the cost and revenue aspects of a number of alternative retail prices. The $5 unit variable cost and the $40,000 total fixed cost are based on the costs utilized in the basic breakeven model. The expected unit sales for each specified retail price are obtained from marketing research. The table contains the information necessary for calculating the breakeven point for each of the five retail price alternatives. These points are shown in Part A of Figure 18.10.

The data shown in the first two columns of Table 18.4 represent a demand schedule that indicates the number of units consumers are expected to purchase at each of a series of retail prices. As Part B of Figure 18.10 shows, these data can be superimposed onto a breakeven chart to identify the range of feasible prices for the marketer to consider.

FIGURE 18.10   Modified Breakeven Chart: Parts A and B

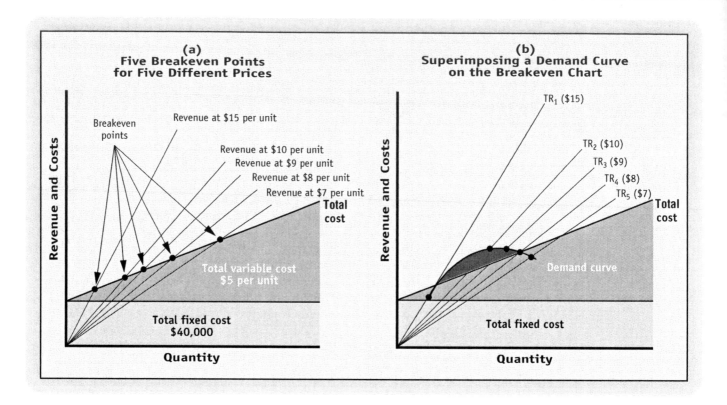

TABLE 18.4   Revenue and Cost Data for Modified Breakeven Analysis

	REVENUES			COSTS			
PRICE	QUANTITY DEMANDED	TOTAL REVENUE	TOTAL FIXED COST	TOTAL VARIABLE COST	TOTAL COST	BREAKEVEN POINT (NUMBER OF SALES REQUIRED TO BREAK EVEN)	TOTAL PROFIT (OR LOSS)
$15	2,500	$37,500	$40,000	$12,500	$52,500	4,000	$(15,000)
10	10,000	100,000	40,000	50,000	90,000	8,000	10,000
9	13,000	117,000	40,000	65,000	105,000	10,000	12,000
8	14,000	112,000	40,000	70,000	110,000	13,334	2,000
7	15,000	105,000	40,000	75,000	115,000	20,000	(10,000)

Figure 18.10 reveals that the range of profitable prices exists from a low of approximately $8 (TR$_4$) to a high of $10 (TR$_2$), with a price of $9 (TR$_3$) generating the greatest projected profits. Changing the retail price produces a new breakeven point. At a relatively

MARKETING   **DICTIONARY**

modified breakeven analysis Pricing technique used to evaluate consumer demand by comparing the number of products that must be sold at a variety of prices in order to cover total cost with estimates of expected sales at the various prices.

high $15 ($TR_1$) retail price, the breakeven point is 4,000 units; at a $10 retail price, it is 8,000 units; and at the lowest price considered, $7 ($TR_5$), it is 20,000 units.

The contribution of modified breakeven analysis is that it forces the marketer to consider whether the consumer is likely to purchase the number of units of a good or service required for achieving breakeven at a given price. It demonstrates that a large number of units sold does not necessarily produce added profits, since—other things equal—lower prices are necessary for stimulating additional sales. Consequently, it is important to consider both costs and consumer demand in determining the most appropriate price.

Yield Management

When most of a firm's costs are fixed over a wide range of outputs, the primary determinant of profitability will be the amount of revenue generated by sales. This situation is typical of such goods and services as the following:

- *theater tickets*—lower prices in the afternoons to offset low demand and higher prices in the evening when demand rises
- *lodging*—lower prices off season and higher prices during peak season periods; low-priced weekend rates
- *auto rental*—lower prices on weekends when business demand is low and higher prices during the week when business demand is higher
- *airfares*—low prices on nonrefundable tickets with travel restrictions such as advance-purchase and Saturday-night stay requirements and penalties for flight changes; high prices on refundable tickets that can be changed without penalty

The following example from the airline industry demonstrates how the strategy of **yield management** maximizes revenues in situations where costs are fixed.[15]

Airlines constantly monitor reservations on every flight. Beginning approximately 330 days before the flight, space is allocated between full-fare, discount-fare, and free tickets for frequent flyers who qualify for complimentary tickets. This allocation is monitored and adjusted at regular intervals until the actual departure.

Assume, for example, that Northwest Airlines has scheduled a 180-seat plane as Flight 1480 with an 8 A.M. departure from Memphis to Minneapolis on October 23. When Flight 1480 leaves its gate for departure, all costs associated with the flight (fuel, food, crew, and other operating expenses) are fixed. The pricing that maximizes revenues on this flight will also maximize profits. An examination of past sales indicates that Northwest could sell 40 to 60 round-trip, full-fare tickets at $600 per passenger and 100 to 150 round-trip restricted-fare tickets at $200 per passenger. Demand for frequent-flyer space should be at least 10 seats.

If Northwest reserves 60 seats for full-fare passengers and accepts reservations for 110 restricted-fare tickets but sells only 40 full-fare tickets (leaving 20 vacant seats), total revenues will be:

$$\text{Revenues} = (40 \times \$600) + (110 \times \$200)$$
$$= \$46,000$$

On the other hand, if Northwest's pricing decision makers want to reduce vacancies, they might decide to reduce the number of full-fare tickets to 20 and increase the restricted-fare tickets to 150. If the plane leaves the gate at full capacity, the flight will generate the following total revenues:

$$\text{Revenues} = (20 \times \$600) + (150 \times \$200)$$
$$= \$42,000$$

Instead of rigidly maintaining the allocations established nearly a year before the flight, Northwest will use yield management to maximize the revenue per flight. In this example, the airline initially holds 60 full-fare seats and accepts reservations for up to 110 restricted-fare seats. Thirty days before the October 23 departure, updated computer projections indicate that 40 full-fare seats are likely to be sold. The allocation is now revised to 40 full-fare and 130 restricted-fare tickets. A full flight leaves the gate and revenues are:

$$\text{Revenues} = (40 \times \$600) + (130 \times \$200)$$
$$= \$50,000$$

Applying yield management for the Memphis–Minneapolis flight increases revenues by at least $4,000 over the inflexible approach of making advance allocations and failing to adjust them based on passenger reservations and other data.

8

Identify the major pricing challenges facing online and international marketers.

GLOBAL ISSUES IN PRICE DETERMINATION

It is equally important for a firm engaging in global marketing to use a pricing strategy that reflects its overall marketing strategy. Prices must support the company's broader goals, including product development, advertising and sales, customer support, competitive plans, and financial objectives.

In general, there are five pricing objectives that firms can use to set prices in global marketing. Four of these are the same pricing objectives that we discussed earlier in the chapter: profitability, volume, meeting competition, and prestige. In addition, international marketers work to achieve a fifth objective: price stability.

In the global arena, marketers may choose profitability objectives if their company is a price leader that tends to establish international prices. Profitability objectives also make sense if a firm is a low-cost supplier that can make a good profit on sales.

Volume objectives become especially important in situations where nations lower their trade barriers to expose domestic markets to foreign competition. As the European Union lowered economic barriers between countries, for instance, competition for customers soared. A recent trend has been mergers of European firms to form larger companies that can achieve volume objectives. As one economist notes, "Merger activity [is] a way to get economies of scale." French grocery chain Carrefour, for example, recently acquired a former French competitor to become the world's second-largest retailer behind Wal-Mart.

Increased competition in Europe has also spurred firms to work toward the third pricing objective of meeting competitors' prices. Dutch corporation Philips Electronics offers U.S.-style coupons that give buyers 10 to 15 percent discounts off kitchen appliances. Aldi and Lidl, two German-owned food retailers, have opened discount outlets in France, forcing native French stores such as Carrefour to reduce prices. Automaker Fiat once boasted a 54 percent share of the Italian car market; its share has since dropped to 44 percent thanks to inroads from competitively-priced Ford of Europe, Inc. Fiat is fighting back by offering $1,600 rebates and zero-interest financing on certain models.

Prestige is a valid pricing objective in international marketing when products are associated with intangible benefits, such as high quality, exclusiveness, or attractive design. The greater a product's perceived benefits, the higher its price can be. Marketers must be aware, however, that cultural perceptions of quality can differ from one country to the next. Sometimes

One Cup.
Two Straws,
Please.

What's the best way to toast my sister's victory? With milk. It has 9 essential nutrients active bodies need. For best results, of course, serve in a silver cup.

got milk?

The endorsement fees that sports apparel and other consumer-goods marketers have paid to teenage tennis phenomenons Serena and Venus Williams are expected to be recouped through increased sales as the sisters take them to new heights—both in the United States and at major international events in London, Paris, and Melbourne. U.S. Open champion Serena Williams became the first African-American since Arthur Ashe in 1975 to win a Grand Slam singles title and the first African-American woman to do so since Althea Gibson in 1958.

MARKETING   DICTIONARY

yield management Pricing strategies designed to maximize revenues in situations such as airfares, lodging, auto rentals, and theater tickets where costs are fixed.

items that command prestige prices in the U.S. are considered run-of-the-mill in other nations; sometimes products that are anything but prestigious in America seem exotic to overseas consumers. American patrons, for instance, view McDonald's restaurants as affordable fast-food eateries, but in China they are seen as fashionable and relatively expensive.

The fifth pricing objective, price stability, is desirable in international markets although it is difficult to achieve. Wars, terrorism, economic downturns, changing governments and political parties, and shifting trade policies can alter prices. An example is the computer industry. A few years ago, U.S. computer manufacturers sold their products in Europe for 30 to 50 percent more than U.S. prices. Today, greater competition within the European Union has forced computer prices down until they average only 10 percent higher than the U.S. prices, barely enough to cover manufacturers' costs in retooling machines for the local market. Falling prices have slashed profits for both American and European manufacturers, including IBM, Compaq, and Olivetti.

Price stability can be especially important for producers of commodities—goods and services that have easily accessible substitutes that other nations can supply quickly. Countries that export international commodities, such as wood, chemicals, and agricultural crops, suffer economically when their prices fluctuate. A nation such as Nicaragua, which exports sugar cane, can find that its balance of payments changes drastically when the international price for sugar shifts. This makes it vulnerable to stiff price competition from other sugar cane producers.

In contrast, countries that export value-oriented products, rather than commodities, tend to enjoy more stable prices. Prices of electronic equipment and automobiles tend to fluctuate far less than prices of sugar cane or bananas.

STRATEGIC IMPLICATIONS OF PRICING IN THE 21ST CENTURY

This chapter has focused on traditional pricing concepts and methods—principles that are critical to all marketing strategies, especially in e-commerce. Consumers can now compare prices quickly, heightening the already intense competitive pricing environment. The Web allows for prices to be negotiated on the spot and anything can be auctioned. From airline tickets to automobiles, the Web allows consumers to name their price. The Coca-Cola Company marketers are currently testing variable pricing for vending machine soft drinks, based on time of day, temperature, and the historical demand curve. On a cold, wintry day, a 12-ounce can may cost only a quarter; on a dry, hot summer day, the price may be as high as $3![16]

Consumers will reap the greatest rewards of competition created by online price cutters. A recent study of prices on the Web found that books and music CDs were 9 percent to 16 percent lower online than at conventional stores. One research analyst explains how deep discount sites are empowering consumers in the pricing environment, "If you're a consumer and you're thinking about any kind of researched purchase, you're leaving thousands of dollars on the table if you don't at least look online. It's a great time to be a consumer. You have more power than you could possibly imagine."[17] In the near future, online shoppers will use electronic wallets that send intelligent agents out on the Net to find the lowest prices or even facilitate auctions in which merchants will bid to become the lowest-cost supplier for the products a consumer wants.

Electronic delivery of music, books, and a thousand other goods and services will only lead to further price reductions. E-commerce has smoothed out the friction of time, which kept pricing relatively static. Microsoft cofounder Bill Gates recently gave a futuristic view of what he sees as a "friction-free economy." The current obsession with time and the ability to measure it will change perceptions and pricing of tangible goods. Goods and services are no longer made before they are ordered and their prices will no longer be fixed; instead, prices will shift up and down.

While consumers rejoice, retailers worry as they watch their profit margins disappearing. Says Buy.com founder and CEO Scott Blum, "Every company is vulnerable, every company is under attack." The Internet discounter lures Web shoppers with low prices on brand-name products. That seems to be the blueprint for success: Spend generously to win new customers, offer the lowest prices possible, and then give them superior customer services to keep them loyal.[18]

ACHIEVEMENT CHECK SUMMARY

Read the learning objectives that follow, and consider the questions for each one. Answering these questions will reinforce your grasp of the most important concepts in the chapter and will allow you to check how well you have achieved these learning goals. Where a blank appears before a question, answer with *T* or *F* for true/false questions; for multiple-choice questions, choose the letter of the correct answer.

Objective 18.1: Outline the legal constraints on pricing.

1. _____ Unfair-trade laws require sellers to maintain minimum retail prices for comparable products.

2. _____ Price discrimination is prohibited under the Consumer Goods Pricing Act.

3. _____ Interstate usage of fair-trade laws was banned under the Robinson-Patman Act.

Objective 18.2: Identify the major categories of pricing objectives.

1. _____ Pricing objectives include all of the following except: (a) profit maximization objectives; (b) meeting competition; (c) market-share objectives; (d) quality performance objectives; (e) prestige objectives.

2. _____ Profits are (a) the most important objective for a firm; (b) the result of supply and demand; (c) a function of revenue and expenses; (d) determined primarily by the quantity of a product sold.

Objective 18.3: Explain price elasticity and its determinants.

1. _____ Elasticity is the measure of the responsiveness of manufacturers and distributors to inventory being held.

2. _____ If a good or service has close substitutes, demand tends to be elastic.

3. _____ When the measurement of elasticity in demand or supply is greater than 1.0, it is said to be elastic.

Objective 18.4: List the practical problems involved in applying price theory concepts to actual pricing decisions.

1. _____ All firms try to maximize profits.

2. _____ It can be difficult to estimate demand at various price levels.

3. _____ Using computer software, managers can accurately forecast demand for a product and thereby determine the price.

Objective 18.5: Explain the major cost-plus approaches to price setting.

1. _____ Cost-plus pricing approaches include incremental-cost pricing and full-cost pricing.

2. _____ Full-cost pricing takes competition and demand for the item into consideration.

3. _____ Incremental-cost pricing helps to overcome the arbitrary allocation of fixed expenses by only using costs directly attributable to a specific output in setting prices.

Objective 18.6: List the major advantages and shortcomings of using breakeven analysis in pricing decisions.

1. _____ Breakeven analysis (a) is a means of setting prices to determine rates of production; (b) is used in determining the quantity that must be sold to cover total costs; (c) assumes that per-unit variable costs will change at different levels of operation; (d) indicates how much profit will be made by producing a specified quantity of a good or service.

2. _____ Breakeven analysis (a) cannot reflect target return objectives; (b) considers how much of the product consumers will purchase; (c) is used to set profitability objectives; (d) is frequently used in price determination.

Objective 18.7: Explain the superiority of modified breakeven analysis over the basic breakeven model and the role of yield management in pricing decisions.

1. _____ Modified breakeven analysis helps marketers determine price regardless of demand.

2. _____ A large number of units sold does not necessarily produce added profits.

3. _____ Costs and consumer demand are equally important in determining the best price for a product.

Objective 18.8: Identify the major pricing challenges facing online and international marketers.

1. _____ A firm's global pricing strategy reflects its global marketing strategy.

2. _____ In addition to the four major categories of pricing objectives, marketers must consider price stability in their international pricing strategies.

3. _____ Internet marketers use the same pricing techniques as traditional marketers to reach global and domestic markets.

4. _____ Competitive pricing strategies are especially important to Web marketers because consumers can quickly search online for the best price.

Students: See the solutions section located on page S-3 to check your responses to the Achievement Check Summary.

Key Terms

price	supply
Robinson-Patman Act	pure competition
unfair-trade laws	monopolistic competition
fair-trade laws	oligopoly
profit maximization	monopoly
target-return objective	elasticity
Profit Impact of Market	cost-plus pricing
Strategies (PIMS) project	breakeven analysis
value pricing	modified breakeven analysis
customary prices	yield management
demand	

Review Questions

1. Distinguish between fair-trade laws and unfair-trade laws. As a consumer, do you support such laws? Would your answer change if you were the owner of a small retail store?

2. Identify the major categories of pricing objectives. Give an example of each.

3. What are the major price implications of the PIMS studies? Suggest possible explanations for the relationships they reveal.

4. Explain the concept of elasticity. Identify each factor influencing elasticity and give a specific example of how it affects the degree of elasticity in a good or service.

5. Explain the advantages of using incremental-cost pricing rather than full-cost pricing. What potential drawbacks exist?

6. Why do many firms choose to de-emphasize pricing as a marketing tool and instead concentrate on the other marketing mix variables in seeking to achieve a competitive advantage?

. How can locating the breakeven point assist in price determination? What are the primary dangers in relying solely on breakeven analysis in pricing decisions?

. What is the breakeven point for a product with a selling price of $40, average variable cost of $24, and related fixed cost of $37,500? What impact would a $4-per-unit profit requirement have on the breakeven point?

. Explain how yield management results in greater revenue than other strategies. Under what conditions is yield management a useful pricing strategy?

. Identify the factors that can affect prices in international and on-line marketing.

uestions for Critical Thinking

Categorize each of the following as a specific type of pricing objective. Suggest a company or product likely to utilize each pricing objective.

a. a 5 percent increase in profits over the previous year

b. prices no more than 6 percent higher than prices quoted by independent dealers

c. a 5 percent increase in market share

d. a 25 percent return on investment (before taxes)

e. following the price set by the most important competitor in each market segment

f. setting the highest prices in the product category to maintain favorable brand image

Describe the market situations that exist for the following products. Defend your answers.

a. local dry-cleaning service

b. DVD players

c. golf clubs

d. platinum

e. soybeans

f. remote control car alarms

g. razors

h. personal watercraft

How are the following prices determined and what do they have in common?

a. ticket to a museum exhibit

b. your college tuition fee

c. local sales tax rate

d. printing of business cards

4. WebTech Development of Nashville, Tennessee, is considering the possible introduction of a new product proposed by its research-and-development staff. The firm's marketing director estimates that the product can be marketed at a price of $70. Total fixed cost is $278,000, and average variable cost is calculated at $48.

a. What is the breakeven point in units for the proposed product?

b. The firm's president has suggested a target profit return of $214,000 for the proposed product. How many units must be sold in order to both break even and achieve this target return?

5. The marketing research staff at Cleveland-based Cyber Novelties has developed the following sales estimates for a proposed new item designed to be marketed through direct mail sales:

PROPOSED SELLING PRICE	SALES ESTIMATE (UNITS)
$8	55,000
10	22,000
15	14,000
20	5,000
24	2,800

The new product has a total fixed cost of $60,000 and a $7 variable cost per unit.

a. Which of the proposed selling prices would generate a profit for Cyber Novelties?

b. Cyber Novelties' director of marketing also estimates that an additional $.50 per-unit allocation for extra promotion will produce the following increases in sales estimates: 60,000 units at an $8 unit selling price, 28,000 units at $10, 17,000 units at $15, 6,000 units at $20, and 3,500 units at $24. Indicate the feasible range of prices if this proposal is implemented and results in the predicted sales increases.

c. Indicate the feasible price or prices if the $.50 per-unit additional promotion proposal is not implemented but management insists on a $25,000 target return.

1.   Unfair Trade Laws. Use a search engine to find recent news on predatory pricing practices for two different industries. In your summary identify the company or companies involved in each industry and the basis for the predatory pricing charges.

2.   Yield Management. The chapter discussion on yield management used theater tickets, lodging, auto rental, and airfares as examples to illustrate the concept of yield management. For this assignment, locate a specific pricing example of yield management in any area of interest to you. Bring your printout to class to use as an example during classroom discussion on the topic. A good site that you could use for this assignment comes from the Web site for the Phoenix Luxury Condominiums located on the Gulf of Mexico in Orange Beach, Alabama. At *www.brett-robinson.com,* you click on the photograph of the condominium for which you'd like rental rates. Included in the information that will appear is a breakdown of the seasons with dates, as well as the rates during each season.

3.   Strategic Implications of Pricing in the 21st Century. Go to www.quicken.com/shopping and complete the following: (a) Download and install the Quicken Shopper program. (b) Go through the steps of pricing a recent bestseller at a site such as *www.amazon.com* or *www.barnesandnoble.com* (without actually making a purchase) or of pricing a DVD or CD at a site such as *www.cduniverse.com, www.valueamerica.com,* or *www.dvdwave.com.* (c) Once you've selected an item, launch the Quicken Shopper and print out the results to bring to class.

brett-robinson.com

amazon.com

barnesandnoble.com

valueamerica.com

dvdwave.com

12

CHAPTER 21

Intellectual Property Rights

LEARNING OBJECTIVES
After studying this chapter, you should be able to:

1. *Explain how to obtain a copyright, a patent, and a trademark*
2. *Identify the rights obtained by owners of copyrights, patents, and trademarks*
3. *State the duration of the protection afforded owners of copyrights, trademarks, and patents*
4. *Set forth the remedies available to owners for infringement of intellectual property rights*
5. *List and explain the extent of protection provided by federal laws for owners of software and mask works*

383

Intellectual property comes in many forms: the writings of an author, the new product or process developed by an inventor, the company name "Microsoft," or the secret formula used to make Coca Cola. Federal law provides rights to owners of these works, products, company names, and processes called copyrights, patents, trademarks, and trade secrets. State laws provide protection for trade secrets. Federal laws and trade secrecy laws protect the special category of intellectual property rights relating to computer software development and use. This chapter discusses the federal and state laws governing these areas of intellectual property.

A. TRADEMARKS AND SERVICE MARKS

The Lanham Act, a federal law, grants a producer the exclusive right to register a trademark and prevent competitors form using that mark. This law helps assure a producer that it, and not an imitating competitor, will reap the financial, reputation-related rewards of a desirable product.

1. Introduction

A **mark** is any word, name, symbol, device, or a combination of these, used to identify a product or service.[1] If the mark identifies a product, such as an automobile or soap, it is called a **trademark**. If it identifies a service, such as a restaurant or dry cleaner, it is called a **service mark**.

The owner of a mark may obtain protection from others using it by registering the mark in accordance with federal law.[2] To be registered, a mark must distinguish the goods or service of the applicant from those of others. Under the federal statute, a register, called the *Principal Register,* is maintained for recording such marks. Inclusion on the Principal Register grants the registrant the exclusive right to use the mark. Challenges may be made to the registrant's right within five years of registration, but after five years the right of the registrant is incontestable.

An advance registration of a mark may be made not more than three years before its actual use by filing an application certifying a bona fide "intent-to-use." Fees must be paid at six-month intervals from the filing of the application until actual use begins.[3]

2. Registrable Marks

Marks that are coined, completely fanciful, or arbitrary are capable of registration on the Principal Register. The mark Exxon, for example, was coined by the owner. The name Kodak is also a creation of the owner of this trademark and has no other meaning in English, but it serves to distinguish the goods of its owner from all others.

A suggestive term may also be registered. Such a term suggests rather than describes some characteristics of the goods to which it applies and requires the consumer to exercise some imagination to reach a conclusion about the nature of the goods. For example, as a trademark for refrigerators, Penguin would be suggestive of the product's superior cooling and freezing features. As a trademark for paperback books, however, Penguin is arbitrary and fanciful.

Ordinarily, descriptive terms, surnames, and geographic terms are not registrable on the Principal Register.[4] A descriptive term identifies a characteristic or quality of an article or service, such as color, odor, function, or use. Thus, Arthriticare was held not to be registrable on the Principal Register because it was merely descriptive of a product used to treat symptoms of arthritis.[5] Boston Beer was denied trademark protection because it was a geographic term.[6]

An exception is made, however, when a descriptive or geographic term or a surname has acquired a secondary meaning; such a mark is registrable. A term or terms that have a primary meaning of their own acquire a *secondary meaning* when, through long use in

---

[1] 15 USC § 1127. *See also* Trademark Clarification Act of 1984, PL 98-620, 98 Stat 333.
[2] Lanham Act, 15 USC §§ 1050–1127.

[3] PL 100-667, 15 USC § 1051 (1988); effective November 16, 1989.
[4] A Supplemental Register exists for recording such marks. This recording does not give the registrant any protection, but it provides a source to which other persons designing a mark can go to make sure they are not duplicating an existing mark. *See Cushman v Mutton Hollow Land, Inc.,* 782 SW2d 150 (Mo Ct App 1990).
[5] *Bernard v Commerce Drug Co.,* 964 F2d 1338 (2d Cir 1992).
[6] *Boston Beer Co. v Slesar Bros. Brewing Co.,* 9 F3d 125 (1st Cir 1994).

connection with a particular product, they have come to be known by the public as identifying the particular product and its origin. **For example, the geographic Philadelphia has acquired a secondary meaning when applied to cream cheese. It is widely accepted by the public as denoting a particular brand rather than any cream cheese made in Philadelphia. Factors considered by a court in determining whether a trademark has acquired secondary meaning are the amount and manner of advertising, volume of sales, length and manner of use, direct consumer testimony, and consumer surveys.**

With a limited number of colors available for use by competitors along with possible shade confusion, courts had held for some 90 years that color alone could not function as a trademark. This legal rule was recently overturned by the U.S. Supreme Court in the *Qualitex* case. Now, if a color serves as a symbol that distinguishes a firm's goods and identifies their source without serving any other significant function, a color may, sometimes at least, meet the basic legal requirements for use as a trademark. **For example, Owens-Corning Fiberglass Corp. has been allowed to register the color pink as a trademark for its fiberglass insulation products.**

QUALITEX CO. v JACOBSON PRODUCTS CO., INC.
115 S Ct 1300 (1995)

Since the 1950s, Qualitex Co. has colored the dry-cleaning press pads it manufactures with a special shade of green-gold. In 1991 it registered its green-gold color on press pads as a trademark. Qualitex sued competitor Jacobson Products Co. for trademark infringement when Jacobson began to manufacture and sell press pads with a similar green-gold color. Qualitex won the lawsuit in U.S. district court, but the Ninth Circuit set the judgment aside because in its view the Lanham Act does not permit a manufacturer to register "color alone" as a trademark. The Federal Circuit had allowed Owens-Corning Fiberglass Corp. to register the color pink as a trademark for its insulation product. Because the Ninth Circuit and the Federal Circuit courts of appeals differed as to whether the law recognizes the use of color alone as a trademark, the U.S. Supreme Court granted certiorari.

BREYER, J.... I. The Lanham Act gives a seller or producer the exclusive right to "register" a trademark, 15 U.S.C. § 1052 (1988 ed. and Supp. V), and to prevent his or her competitors from using that trademark, § 1114(1). Both the language of the Act and the basic underlying principles of trademark law would seem to include color within the universe of things that can qualify as a trademark. The language of the Lanham Act describes that universe in the broadest of terms. It says that trademarks "includ[e] any word, name, symbol, or device, or any combination thereof." § 1127. Since human beings might use as a "symbol" or "device" almost anything at all that is capable of carrying meaning, this language, read literally, is not restrictive. The

courts and the Patent and Trademark Office have authorized for use as a mark a particular shape (of a Coca-Cola bottle), a particular sound (of NBC's three chimes), and even a particular scent (of plumeria blossoms on sewing thread)....

We cannot find in the basic objectives of trademark law any obvious theoretical objection to the use of color alone as a trademark, where that color has attained "secondary meaning" and therefore identifies and distinguishes a particular brand (and thus indicates its "source"). In principle, trademark law, by preventing others from copying a source-identifying mark, "reduce[s] the customer's costs of shopping and making purchasing decisions," 1 J McCarthy, McCarthy on Trademarks and Unfair Competition § 2.01[2], p. 2–3 (3d ed. 1994) (hereinafter McCarthy), for it quickly and easily assures a potential customer that *this* item—the item with this mark—is made by the same producer as other similarly marked items that he or she liked (or disliked) in the past. At the same time, the law helps assure a producer that it (and not an imitating competitor) will reap the financial, reputation-related rewards associated with a desirable product. The law thereby "encourage[s] the production of quality products," *ibid*, and simultaneously discourages those who hope to sell inferior products by capitalizing on a consumer's inability quickly to evaluate the quality of an item offered for sale....

...[We cannot] find a principled objection to the use of color as a mark in the important "functionality" doctrine of trademark law. The functionality doctrine prevents trademark law, which seeks to promote competition by protecting a firm's reputation, from instead inhibiting legitimate competition by allowing a producer to control a useful product feature. It is the province of patent law, not trademark law, to encourage invention by granting inventors a monopoly over new product designs or functions for a limited time, 35 U.S.C. §§ 154, 173, after which competitors are free to use the innovation. If a product's functional features could be used as trademarks, however, a monopoly over such features could be obtained without regard to whether they qualify as patents and could be extended forever (because trademarks may be renewed in perpetuity)....

See, *e.g., Kellogg Co.,* 305 U.S., at 119–120, (trademark law cannot be used to extend monopoly over "pillow" shape of shredded wheat biscuit after the patent for that shape has expired). This Court consequently has explained that. "[i]n general terms, a product feature is functional," and cannot serve as a trademark, "if it is essential to the use or purpose of the article or if it affects the cost or quality of the article," that is, if exclusive use of the feature would

put competitors at a significant non-reputation-related disadvantage. *Inwood Laboratories, Inc.* 456 U.S., at 850, n. 10,102 S.Ct., at 2186, n. 10. Although sometimes color plays an important role (unrelated to source identification) in making a product more desirable, sometimes it does not. And, this latter fact—the fact that sometimes color is not essential to a product's use or purpose and does not affect cost or quality—indicates that the doctrine of "functionality" does not create an absolute bar to the sue of color alone as a mark. See *Owens-Corning,* 774 F.2d, at 1123 (pink color of insulation in wall "performs no nontrademark function").

It would seem...that color alone, at least sometimes, can meet the basic legal requirements for use as a trademark. It can act as a symbol that distinguishes a firm's goods and identifies their source, without serving any other significant function. See U.S. Department of Commerce, Patent and Trademark Office, Trademark Manual of Examining Procedure § 1202.04(e), p. 1202–13 (2d ed. May, 1993) (hereinafter PTO Manual) (approving trademark registration of color alone where it "has become distinctive of the applicant goods in commerce," provided that "there is [no] competitive need for colors to remain available in the industry" and the color is not "functional"); see also 1 McCarthy §§ 3.01[1], 7.26 ("requirements for qualification of a word or symbol as a trademark" are that it be (1) a "symbol," (2) "use(d)...as a mark," (3) "to identify and distinguish the seller's goods from goods made or sold by others," but that it not be "functional"). Indeed, the District Court, in this case, entered findings (accepted by the Ninth Circuit) that show Qualitex's green-gold press pad color has met these requirements. The green-gold color acts as a symbol. Having developed secondary meaning (for customers identified the green-gold color as Qualitex's), it identifies the press pads' source. And, the green-gold color serves no other function. (Although it is important to use *some* color on press pads to avoid noticeable stains, the court found "no competitive need in the press pad industry for the green-gold color, since other colors are equally usable." Accordingly, unless there is some special reason that convincingly militates against the use of color alone as a trademark, trademark law would protect Qualitex's use of the green-gold color on its press pads.

II. Respondent Jacobson Products says that there are...special reasons why the law should forbid the use of color alone as a trademark. We shall explain, in turn, why we, ultimately, find them unpersuasive....

We...Courts traditionally decide quite difficult questions about whether two words or phrases or symbols are sufficiently similar, in context, to confuse buyers ....Legal standards exist to guide courts in making comparisons. See, *e.g.*, 2 McCarthy § 15.08; ("[S]trong" marks, with greater secondary meaning, receive broader protection than "weak" marks)....

Second, Jacobson argues, as have others, that colors are in limited supply. See, e.g., *NutraSweet Co.*, 917 F2d, at 1028; *Campbell Soup Co. v Armour & Co.*, 175 F.2d 795, 798 (CA3 1949). Jacobson claims that, if one of many competitors can appropriate a particular color for use as a trademark, and each competitor then tries to do the same, the supply of colors will soon be depleted. Put in its strongest form, this argument would concede that "[h]undreds of color pigments are manufactured and thousands of colors can be obtained by mixing." L. Cheskin, Colors: What They Can Do For You (1947). But, it would add that, in the context of a particular product, only some colors are usable. By the time one discards colors that, say, for reasons of customer appeal, are not usable, and adds the shades that competitors cannot use lest they risk infringing a similar, registered shade, then one is left with only a handful of possible colors. And, under these circumstances, to permit one, or a few, producers to use colors as trademarks will "deplete" the supply of usable colors to the point where a competitor's inability to find a suitable color will put that competitor at a significant disadvantage.

This argument is unpersuasive, however, largely because it relies on an occasional problem to justify a blanket prohibition. When a color serves as a mark, normally alternative colors will likely be available for similar use by others. See, e.g., *Owens-Corning*, 774 F.2d, at 1121 (pink insulation). Moreover, if that is not so—if a "color depletion" or "color scarcity" problem does arise—the trademark doctrine or "functionality" normally would seem available to prevent the anticompetitive consequences that Jacobson's argument posits, thereby minimizing that argument's practical force.

The functionality doctrine, as we have said, forbids the use of a product's features as a trademark where doing so will put a competitor at a significant disadvantage because the feature is "essential to the use or purpose of the article" or "affects [its] cost or quality." *Inwood Laboratories, Inc.*, 456 U.S., at 850, n. 10, 102 S. Ct., at 2186, n. 10. The functionality doctrine thus protects competitors against a disadvantage (unrelated to recognition or reputation) that trademark protection might otherwise impose, namely their inability reasonably to replicate important non-reputation-related product features....And, the federal courts have demonstrated that they can apply this doctrine in a careful and reasoned manner, with sensitivity....Although we need not comment on the merits of specific cases, we note that lower courts have permitted competitors to copy the green color of farm machinery (because customers wanted their farm equipment to match) and have barred the use of black as a trademark on outboard boat motors (because black has the special functional attributes of decreasing the apparent size of the motor and ensuring compatibility with many different boat colors). See *Brunswick Corp. v British Seagull Ltd.*, 36 F.3d 1527, 1532 (CA Fed.1994).

Jacobson points to many older cases— including Supreme Court cases—in support of its position....

These Supreme Court cases, however, interpreted trademark law as it existed *before* 1946, when Congress enacted the Lanham Act. The Lanham Act significantly changed and liberalized the common law to "dispense with mere technical prohibitions," S.Rep. No. 1333, 79th Cong., 2d Sess., 3 (1946), most notably by permitting trademark registration of descriptive words (say, "U-Build-It" model airplanes) where they had acquired "secondary meaning." See *Abercrombie & Fitch Co.*, 537 F.2d, at 9 (Friendly, J.). The Lanham Act extended protection to descriptive marks by making clear that (with certain explicit exceptions not relevant here), "nothing... shall prevent the registration of a mark used by the applicant which has become distinctive of the applicant's goods in commerce." 15 U.S.C. § 1052(f) (1988 ed., Supp. V).

This language permits an ordinary word, normally used for a nontrademark purpose (e.g., description), to act as a trademark where it has gained "secondary meaning." Its logic would appear to apply to color as well. Indeed, in 1985, the Federal Circuit considered the significance of the Lanham Act changes as they related to color and held that trademark protection for color was consistent with the "jurisprudence under the Lanham Act developed in accordance with the statutory principle that if a mark is capable of being or becoming distinctive of [the] applicant's goods in commerce, then it is capable of serving as a trademark." *Owens-Corning*, 774 F.2d, at 1120.

In 1988 Congress amended the Lanham Act, revising portions of the definitional language, but left unchanged the language here relevant. § 134, 102 Stat. 3946, 15 U.S.C. § 1127. It enacted these amendments against the following background: (1) the Federal Circuit had decided *Owens-Corning*; (2) the Patent and Trademark Office had adopted a clear policy (which it

still maintains) permitting registration of color as a trademark, see PTO Manual § 1202.04(e) (at p. 1200–12 of the January 1986 edition and p. 1202–13 of the May 1993 edition); and (3) the Trademark Commission had written a report, which recommended that "the terms 'symbol, or device'...not be deleted or narrowed to preclude registration of such things as a color, shape, smell, sound, or configuration which functions as a mark." The United States Trademark Association Trademark Review Commission Report and Recommendations to USTA President and Board of Directors, 77 T.M.Rep. 375, 421 (1987) (hereinafter Trademark Commission); see also 133 Cong.Rec. 32812 (1987) (statement of Sen. DeConcini) ("The bill I am introducing today is based on the Commission's report and recommendations"). This background strongly suggests that the language "any word, name symbol, or device," 15 U.S.C. § 1127, had come to include color.

Finally, when Congress re-enacted the terms "word, name, symbol, or device" in 1988, it did so against a legal background in which those terms had come to include color, and its statutory revision embraced that understanding.

Jacobson argues that there is no need to permit color alone to function as a trademark because a firm already may use color as part of a trademark, say, as a colored circle or colored letter or colored word, and may rely upon "trade dress" protection, under § 43(a) of the Lanham Act, if a competitor copies its color and thereby causes consumer confusion regarding the overall appearance of the competing products or their packaging, see 15 U.S.C. § 1125(a) (1988 ed. Supp. V).... Trademark law helps the holder of a mark in many ways that "trade dress" protection does not. See 15 U.S.C. § 1124 (ability to prevent importation of confusingly similar goods); § 1072 (constructive notice of ownership); § 1065 (incontestable status); § 1057(b) (prima facie evidence of validity and ownership).

Thus, one can easily find reasons why the law might provide trademark protection in addition to trade dress protection.

III. Having determined that a color may sometimes meet the basic legal requirements for use as a trademark and that respondent Jacobson's arguments do not justify a special legal rule preventing color alone from serving as a trademark (and, in light of the District Court's here undisputed findings that Qualitex's use of the green-gold color on its press pads meets the basic trademark requirements), we conclude that the Ninth Circuit erred in barring Qualitex's use of color as a trademark....

[Judgment reversed]

Questions

1. Does color alone meet the basic requirements for use as a trademark?
2. Assess the validity of the following statement: "Because of the limited number of basic colors, including red, orange, green, blue, yellow, violet, black and white, most new competitors would be placed at a disadvantage because of the depletion of the supply of usable colors."
3. Review the objectives of trademark law set forth in the decision and the ethical principles set forth in Chapter 2. Is it ethical for the owners of private label or store brand consumer products to design their private labels with closely similar trade dress or use colors similar to the national brand's trademarks?

Generic terms—that is, terms that designate a kind or class of goods, such as *cola* or *rosé wine*—are never registrable.

3. Trade Dress Protection

Firms invest significant resources to develop and promote the appearance of their products and the packages in which these products are sold so that they are clearly recognizable by consumers. **Trade dress** involves a product's total image, and in the case of consumer goods includes the overall packaging look in which each product is sold.

When a competitor adopts a confusingly similar trade dress, it dilutes the first user's investment and goodwill and deceives consumers, hindering their ability to distinguish between competing brands. The law of trade dress protection was settled in a recent U.S. Supreme Court decision,[7] and courts have subsequently become more receptive to claims of trade dress infringement under section 43(a) of the Lanham Act. In order to prevail, a plaintiff

must prove its trade dress is distinctive and nonfunctional and the defendant's trade dress is confusingly similar to the plaintiff's.[8] Thus, a competitor who copied the Marlboro cigarettes' package for its Gunsmoke brand cigarettes was found to have infringed the trade dress of the Marlboro brand.[9] Trade dress protection under the Lanham Act is the same as that provided a qualified unregistered trademark and does not provide all of the protection available to the holder of a registered trademark.

4. Injunction against Improper Use of Mark

A person who has the right to use a mark may obtain a court order prohibiting a competitor from imitating or duplicating the mark. The basic question in such litigation is whether the general public is likely to be confused by the mark of the defendant and to believe wrongly that it identifies the plaintiff. If there is this danger of confusion, the court will enjoin the defendant from using the particular mark.

---

7 *Two Pesos, Inc. v Taco Cabana, Inc.*, 112 S Ct 2753 (1992)

8 *Paddington v Attiki Importers and Distributors Inc.*, 996 F2d 577, 582 (2d Cir 1993).
9 *Philip Morris Inc. v Star Tobacco Corp.*, 879 F Supp 379 (SDNY 1995).

In some cases, the fact that the products of the plaintiff and the defendant did not compete in the same market was held to entitle the defendant to use a mark that would have been prohibited as confusingly similar if the defendant manufactured the same product as the plaintiff. **For example, it has been held that Cadillac as applied to boats is not confusingly similar to Cadillac as applied to automobiles; therefore, its use cannot be enjoined.**[10]

---

[10] *General Motors Corp. v Cadillac Marine and Boat Co.*, 140 USPQ (BNA) 447 (1964). See also *Amstar Corp. v Domino's Pizza Inc.*, 615 F2d 252 (5th Cir 1980), where the mark Domino as applied to pizza was held not to be confusingly similar to Domino as applied to sugar.

UNIVERSITY OF GEORGIA ATHLETIC ASS'N v LAITE
756 F2d 1535 (11th Cir 1985)

The University of Georgia Athletic Association (UGAA) brought suit against beer wholesaler Bill Laite for marketing Battlin' Bulldog Beer. The UGAA claimed that the cans infringed on its symbol for its athletic teams, which it had registered as a service mark and which depicted an English bulldog wearing a sweater with a *G* and the word *BULLDOGS* on it. Soon after the beer appeared on the market, the university received telephone calls from friends of the university. They were concerned that Battlin' Bulldog Beer was not the sort of product that should in any way be related to the University of Georgia. The university's suit was based on the theory of false designation of origin in violation of the Lanham Act. Laite contended that the University of Georgia Bulldog was not a valid service mark; that his bulldog was different from the university's; and that his cans bore the disclaimer "Not associated with the University of Georgia." The district court permanently enjoined Laite from marketing the beer under the challenged label design. Laite appealed.

KRAVITCH, C. J.... Laite's first argument on appeal is that the "University of Georgia Bulldog" is not a valid trade or service mark worthy of protection. Laite cites *Universal City Studios, Inc. v Nintendo Co.*, 578 F. Supp. 911 (S.D.N.Y. 1983), for the proposition that "[t]o make a successful claim of false designation of origin in violation of 43(a) of the Lanham Act, 15 U.S.C. § 1125(a), [plaintiff] must demonstrate that its trademark possesses 'secondary meaning'—'the power of a name or other configuration to symbolize a particular business, product or company....'" Laite contends that the record does not contain sufficient proof of secondary meaning, and that the vagueness of UGAA's mark, coupled with extensive third-party uses of the same or similar marks, demonstrates the absence of secondary meaning.... The general rule in this circuit is that proof of secondary meaning is required *only* when protection is sought for descriptive marks, as opposed to arbitrary or suggestive marks. We have long recognized that:

Service marks fall into four categories. A strong mark is usually fictitious, arbitrary or fanciful and is generally inherently distinctive. It is afforded the widest ambit of protection.... A descriptive mark tells something about the product; it is protected only when secondary meaning is shown.... In contrast to the above is the suggestive mark, which subtly connotes something about the service or product. Although less distinctive than a fictitious, arbitrary or fanciful mark...a suggestive mark will be protected without proof of secondary meaning.... Lastly, there are generic terms, which communicate 'information about the nature or class of an article or service,' and therefore can never become a service or trademark.

Thus, secondary meaning is best characterized not as a general prerequisite for trade or service mark protection, but as a means by which otherwise unprotectable descriptive marks may obtain protection. As one commentator has explained:

Secondary meaning converts a word originally incapable of serving as a mark into a full fledged trademark.... An arbitrary, fanciful, or otherwise distinctive word qualifies as a trademark immediately, because in the particular industry it has no primary meaning to overcome. Therefore it is initially registrable, and also protectable at common law. In the case of words with primary meaning, the reverse is true. Such words, be they descriptive or geographical, are initially nonregistrable and unprotectable unless and until they have attained secondary meaning as trademarks.

We therefore hold that...proof of secondary meaning is required in an action under section 43(a) only when protection is sought for a descriptive mark, as opposed to an arbitrary or suggestive mark. Turning to the mark at issue in the instant case, we are convinced beyond a shadow of a doubt that the "University of Georgia Bulldog" is not a descriptive mark. In our view, the portrayal of an English bulldog chosen by the university as a symbol for its athletic teams is, at best, "suggestive," if not downright "arbitrary." Thus, contrary to Laite's assertion, UGAA was not required to prove secondary meaning in order to prevail on its Lanham Act claim, and the district court did not err in granting injunctive relief to UGAA under section 43(a) despite the absence of proof of secondary meaning.

Laite's next argument is that the district court used the wrong factors in comparing the "Battlin' Bulldog" with the "University of Georgia Bulldog." Laite correctly points out that this circuit has recognized seven factors as relevant to the determination of a "likelihood of confusion" between two trade or service marks: (1) the type of mark at issue, (2) the similarity of design between the two marks, (3) the similarity

of product, (4) the identity of retail outlets and purchasers, (5) the identity of advertising media utilized, (6) the defendant's intent, and (7) actual confusion between the two marks....

As the district court pointed out, it is the combination of similar design elements, rather than any individual element, that compels the conclusion that the two bulldogs are similar. Had the cans of "Battlin' Bulldog Beer" been printed in different colors, or had the "Battlin' Bulldog" worn a different monogram on its sweater, we might have a different case. Instead, the cans are red and black, the colors of the University of Georgia, and the "Battlin' Bulldog" wears the letter "G." To be sure, the "Battlin' Bulldog" is not an exact reproduction of the "University of Georgia Bulldog." Nevertheless, we find the differences between the two so minor as to be legally, if not factually, nonexistent.

...Laite candidly admitted in the court below, and at oral argument in this court, that "Battlin' Bulldog Beer" was intended to capitalize on the popularity of the University of Georgia football program. In short, there can be no doubt that Laite hoped to sell "Battlin' Bulldog Beer" not because the beer tastes great, but because the cans would catch the attention of University of Georgia football fans.

Although we find the defendant's intent and the similarity of design between the two marks sufficient to support the district court's finding of a "likelihood of confusion," we also note that the remaining five factors either support the same conclusion or, at least, do not undermine it. For example, as we previously noted, the type of mark at issue in this case is at best "suggestive," if not downright "arbitrary." Such marks traditionally have been characterized as "strong." The fact that many other colleges, junior colleges, and high schools use an English bulldog as a symbol does not significantly diminish the strength of UGAA's mark, since almost all of the other schools (1) are geographically remote,

(2) use a different color scheme, or (3) have names that begin with a letter other than "G."...

The "Battlin' Bulldog's" football career thus comes to an abrupt end. Laite devised a clever entrepreneurial "game plan," but failed to take into account the strength of UGAA's mark and the tenacity with which UGAA was willing to defend that mark. Like the University of Georgia's famed "Junkyard Dog" defense, UGAA was able to hold its opponent to little or no gain.... [W]e find that the district court did not err, in fact or in law, when it granted permanent injunctive relief to UGAA....

[Judgment affirmed]

Questions

1. When is proof of secondary meaning required in a trademark or service mark infringement lawsuit?
2. In what category of service mark is the University of Georgia Bulldog?
3. What are the seven factors considered by this circuit court in determining whether "likelihood of confusion" exists between two marks?

5. Abandonment of Exclusive Right to Mark

An owner who has an exclusive right to use a mark may lose that right. If other persons are permitted to use the mark, it loses its exclusive character and is said to pass into the English language and become generic. **Examples of formerly enforceable marks that have made this transition into the general language are** *aspirin, thermos, cellophane,* **and** *shredded wheat.*

B. COPYRIGHTS

A **copyright** is the exclusive right given by federal statute to the creator of a literary or artistic work to use, reproduce, or display the work. Under the international treaty called the Berne Convention, copyright of the works of all U.S. authors are protected automatically in all Berne Convention nations, who have agreed under the treaty to treat nationals of other member countries like their own nationals.

A copyright does not prevent the copying of an idea but only the copying of the way the idea is expressed. That is, the copyright is violated when there is a duplicating of the words, pictures, or other form of expression of the creator but not when there is just use of the idea those words, pictures, or other formats express.

6. Duration of Copyright

Article 1, section 8 of the U.S. Constitution empowered Congress to "promote the Progress of Science and useful Arts, by securing for limited times to Authors and Inventors the exclusive Right to their respective Writings and Discoveries." The first U.S. copyright statute was enacted soon after in 1790 and provided protection for any "book, map or chart" for 14 years with a privilege to renew for an additional 14 years. In 1831 the initial 14-year term was extended to 28 years with a privilege for an additional 14 years. Under the 1909 Copyright Act, the protection period was for 28 years with a right of renewal for an additional 28 years.

Under the presently applicable copyright law, enacted in 1976, the duration of a copyright is the life of the creator of the work plus 50 years. The Copyright Act of 1976 brought the duration of U.S. copyright law into harmony with that of most comparable nations. Also under present law, if a work is a "work made for hire," the business employing the creator registers the copyright. This copyright runs for 100 years from creation or 75 years from publication of the work, whichever period is shorter. After a copyright has expired, the work is in the public domain and may be used by anyone without cost.

7. Copyright Notice

Prior to March 1, 1989, the author of an original work secured a copyright by placing a copyright notice on the work consisting of the word "copyright" or the symbol ©, the year of first publication, and the name or pseudonym of the author. The author also was required to register the copyright with the Copyright Office. Under the Berne Convention Implementation Act of 1988,[11] a law that adjusts U.S. copyright law to conform to the Berne Convention, it is no longer mandatory that works published after March 1, 1989, contain a notice of copyright. However, placing a notice of copyright on published works is strongly recommended. This notice prevents an infringer from claiming innocent infringement of the work, which would reduce the amount of damages owed. In order to bring a copyright infringement suit for a work of U.S. origin, the owner must have submitted two copies of the work to the Copyright Office in Washington, D.C., for registration.

8. What Is Copyrightable

Copyrights protect literary, musical, dramatic, and artistic work. Protected are books and periodicals; musical and dramatic compositions; choreographic works; maps; works of art such as paintings, sculptures, and photographs; motion pictures and other audiovisual works; sound recordings; and computer programs.

9. Rights of Copyright Holders

A copyright holder has the exclusive right to: (1) reproduce the work; (2) prepare derivative works, such as a script from the original works; (3) distribute copies of recordings of the work; (4) public performance of the work, including plays or motion pictures; and (5) public display, including display of paintings, sculptures, and photographs.

The copyright owner may assign or license some of the rights listed above and will receive royalty payments as part of the agreement. The copyright law also assures royalty payments. **To illustrate, Jessie Riviera is a songwriter whose songs are sung at public performances and are also recorded by performers on records, tapes, and CDs. Jessie is entitled to royalties from the public performance of her works. Such royalties, are collected by two performing right societies, the American Society of Composers, Authors and Publishers (ASCAP) and Broadcast Music Inc. (BMI), who act on behalf of the copyright holders. Jessie is also entitled to so-called mechanical royalties that refer to the royalty stream derived from "mechanically" reproduced records, tapes, and CDs.**[12] The principal payers of mechanical royalties are record companies and the rate is set by the Copyright Royalty Tribunal. The statutory rate is based on the greater of a flat fee or a per-minute, per-song, or per-record fee.[13]

In addition to rights under the copyright law and international treaties, federal and state laws prohibit record and tape piracy.[14]

10. Limitation on Exclusive Character of Copyright

A limitation on the exclusive rights of copyright owners exists under the principle of "fair use," which allows a limited use of copyrighted material in connection with criticism, parody, news reporting, teaching, and research. Four important factors to consider when judging whether the use made in a particular case is fair use include

(1) the purpose and character of the use, including whether such use is of a commercial nature or is for nonprofit educational purposes;
(2) the nature of the copyrighted work;
(3) the amount and substantiality of the portion used in relation to the copyrighted work as a whole; and
(4) the effect of the use upon the potential market for or value of the copyrighted work.[15]

In *American Geophysical Union v Texaco Inc.*, the court applied the four statutory standards to determine whether the defendant's photocopying of scientific journal articles was fair use.

---

[11] PL 100-568, 102 Stat 2854, 17 USC §§ 101 et seq.

[12] 17 USC § 115(a)(1).
[13] The rate as of January 1, 1996, is the greater of 6.6¢ per song or 1.25¢ per minute and is shared by the songwriter and a publishing company, if there is one.
[14] 17 USC §§ 1, 5, 20, 101; Wyo Stat Ann § 40-13-205.
[15] 17 USC § 107 (1993).

AMERICAN GEOPHYSICAL UNION v TEXACO INC.
60 F3d 913 (2d Cir 1995)

The American Geophysical Union and 82 other publishers of scientific and technical journals brought a class-action lawsuit against Texaco claiming that Texaco's unauthorized photocopying of articles from their journals constituted a copyright infringement. Texaco's defense was that the copying was fair use under section 107 of the Copyright Act of 1976. To avoid extensive discovery, the parties agreed to focus on one randomly selected Texaco scientist, Dr. Donald Chickering, who had photocopies of eight articles from the *Journal of Catalysis* in his files. The trial court judge held that the copying of the eight articles did not constitute fair use, and Texaco appealed.

NEWMAN, C.J.... Burdens of Proof and Standard of Review

Fair use serves as an affirmative defense to a claim of copyright infringement, and thus the party claiming that its secondary use of the original copyrighted work constitutes a fair use typically carries the burden of proof as to all issues in the dispute. Moreover, since fair use is a "mixed question of law and fact," *Harper & Row*, 471 U.S. at 560, 105 S.Ct. at 2230, we review the District Court's conclusions on this issue *de novo*, though we accept its subsidiary findings of fact unless clearly erroneous, see *Twin Peaks*, 996 F.2d at 1374....

First Factor: Purpose and Character of Use

The first factor listed in section 107 is "the purpose and character of the use, including whether such use is of a commercial nature or is for nonprofit educational purposes." Especially pertinent to an assessment of the first fair use factor are the precise circumstances under which copies of the eight *Catalysis* articles were made. After noticing six of these articles when the original copy of the journal issue containing each of them was circulated to him, Chickering had them photocopied, at least initially, for the same basic purpose that one would normally seek to obtain the original—to have it available on his shelf for ready reference if and when he needed to look at it. The library circulated one copy and invited all the researchers to make their own photocopies. It is a reason-able inference that the library staff wanted each journal issue moved around the building quickly and returned to the library so that it would be available for others to look at. Making copies enabled all researchers who might one day be interested in examining the contents of an article in the issue to have the article readily available in their own offices. In Chickering's own words, the copies of the articles were made for "my personal convenience," since it is "far more convenient to have access in my office to a photocopy of an article than to have to go to the library each time I wanted to refer to it." Affidavit of Donald Chickering at 11 (submitted as direct trial testimony) [hereinafter *Chickering testimony*]. Significantly, Chickering did not even have occasion to use five of the photocopied articles at all, further revealing that the photocopies of the eight *Catalysis* articles were primarily made just for "future retrieval and reference." *Id.*...

The photocopying of these eight *Catalysis* articles may be characterized as "archival"—*i.e.*, done for the primary purpose of providing numerous Texaco scientists (for whom Chickering served as an example) each with his or her own personal copy of each article without Texaco's having to purchase another original journal.... On balance, we agree with the District Court that the first factor favors the publishers, primarily because the dominant purpose of the use is a systematic institutional policy of multiplying the available number of copies of pertinent copyrighted articles by circulating the journals among employed scientists for them to make copies, thereby serving the same purpose for which additional subscriptions are normally sold, or, as will be discussed, for which photocopying licenses may be obtained.

Second Factor: Nature of Copyrighted Work

The second statutory fair use factor is "the nature of the copyrighted work." In assessing this factor, the District Court noted that the articles in *Catalysis* "are created for publication with the purpose and intention of benefiting from the protection of the copyright law," and that copyright protection "is vitally necessary to the dissemination of scientific articles of the sort that are at issue." 802 F.Supp. at 16. Nevertheless, the Court ultimately concluded that this factor favored Texaco because the photocopied articles were essentially factual in nature and the "'scope of fair use is greater with respect to factual than nonfactual works.'"...

Ultimately...the manifestly factual character of the eight articles precludes us from considering the articles as "within the core of the copyright's protective purposes," *Campbell*, 114 S.Ct. at 1175; see also *Harper & Row*, 471 U.S. at 563, 105 S.Ct. at 2232 ("The law generally recognizes a greater need to disseminate factual works than works of fiction or fantasy."). Thus, in agreement with the District Court, we conclude that the second factor favors Texaco.

Third Factor: Amount and Substantiability of Portion Used.

The third statutory fair use factor is "the amount and substantiality of the portion used in relation to the copyrighted work as a whole." The District Court concluded that this factor clearly favors the publishers because Texaco copied the eight articles from *Catalysis* in their entirety....

Despite Texaco's claims that we consider its amount of copying "minuscule" in rela-

tion to the entirety of *Catalysis*, we conclude, as did the District Court, that Texaco has copied entire works. Though this conclusion does not preclude a finding of fair use, it militates against such a finding, see *Sony*, 464 U.S. at 449–50, 104 S.Ct. at 792–93, and weights the third factor in favor of the publishers....

Fourth Factor: Effect Upon Potential Market or Value

The fourth statutory fair use factor is "the effect of the use upon the potential market for or value of the copyrighted work." Assessing this factor, the District Court detailed the range of procedures Texaco could use to obtain authorized copies of the articles that it photocopied and found that "whatever combination of procedure Texaco used, the publishers' revenues would grow significantly." The Court concluded that the publishers "powerfully demonstrated entitlement to prevail as to the fourth factor," since they had shown "a substantial harm to the value of their copyrights" as the consequence of Texaco's copying. See *id.* at 18–21.

Prior to *Campbell*, the Supreme Court had characterized the fourth factor as "the single most important element of fair use," *Harper & Row*, 471 U.S. at 566, 105 S.Ct. at 2233. However, *Campbell's* discussion of the fourth factor conspicuously omits this phrasing. Apparently abandoning the idea that any factor enjoys primacy, *Campbell* instructs that '[a]ll [four factors] are to be explored, and the results weighed together, in light of the purposes of copyright.' 114 S.Ct. at 1171....

Primarily because of lost licensing revenue, and to a minor extent because of lost subscription revenue, we agree with the District Court that "the publishers have demonstrated a substantial harm to the value of their copyrights through [Texaco's] copying," 802 F.Supp. at 21, and thus conclude that the fourth statutory factor favors the publishers.

Aggregate Assessment

We conclude that three of the four statutory factors, including the important first and the fourth factors, favor the publishers.... We therefore agree with the District Court's conclusion that Texaco's photocopying of eight particular articles from the *Journal of Catalysis* was not fair use.

Though we recognize the force of many observations made in Judge Jacob's dissenting opinion, we are not dissuaded by his dire predictions that our ruling in this case "has ended fair-use photocopying with respect to a large population of journals," 60 F.3d at 938–39, or, to the extent that the transactional licensing scheme is used, "would seem to require that an intellectual property lawyer be posted at each copy machine," *id.* at 937–38. Our ruling does not consider photocopying for personal use by an individual. Our ruling is confined to the institutional, systematic, archival multiplication of copies revealed by the record—the precise copying that the parties stipulated should be the basis for the District Court's decision now on appeal and for which licenses are in fact available. And the claim that lawyers need to be stationed at copy machines is belied by the ease with which music royalties have been collected and distributed for performances at thousands of cabarets, without the attendance of intellectual property lawyers in any capacity other than as customers....

[Affirmed]

Questions

1. Assess Texaco's position that the purpose and character of its use of the eight articles were for the legitimate reason of use in Dr. Chickering's research and they were not photocopied for resale.
2. Is the "market-effect" factor the single most important element of fair use?
3. Do you believe that the result of this decision will lead to the dire consequences of the posting of intellectual property lawyers at every copy machine, trying to enforce licensing schemes?

C. PATENTS

Under Article 1, section 8, of the U.S. Constitution, the founding fathers of our country empowered Congress to promote the progress of science by securing for limited times to inventors the exclusive rights to their discoveries. Federal patent laws established under Article 1, section 8, protect inventors just as authors are protected under copyright law authorized by the same section of the U.S. Constitution.

11. Types, Duration, and Notice

There are three types of patents, the rights to which may be obtained by proper filing with the Patent and Trademark Office (PTO) in Washington, D.C. The types and duration of patents are as follows:

(a) UTILITY PATENTS. *Utility* or *functional patents* grant inventors of any new and useful process, machine, manufacture, or composition of matter or any new and useful improvement of such devices the right to obtain a patent.[16] Prior to 1995 these utility patents had a life of 17 years from the date of grant. Under the Uruguay Round Table Agreement Act, effective June 8, 1995, the duration of U.S. utility patents was changed from 17 years from the date of grant to 20 years from the date of filing to be consistent with the patent law of General Agreement on Tariffs and Trade (GATT) member states.

(b) DESIGN PATENTS. A second kind of patent exists under U.S. patent law, which protects new and nonobvious ornamental features

---

[16]35 USC § 101.

that appear in connection with an article of manufacture.[17] These patents are called *design patents* and have a duration of 14 years. Design patents have limited applicability, for not only must they be new and have nonobvious ornamental features, but they must be nonfunctional as well. Thus, when the "pillow shape" design of Nabisco Shredded Wheat was found to be functional, the design patent was held invalid and not capable of design patent protection.[18]

(c) PLANT PATENTS. A third type of patent, called *plant patents*, protects the developers of asexual reproduction of new plants. The duration is 20 years from the date of filing, the same as applied to utility patents.

(d) NOTICE. The owner of a patent is required to mark the patented item or device using the word "patent" and must list the patent number on the device in order to recover damages from an infringer of the patent.

12. Patentability and Exclusive Rights

To be patentable an invention must be something that is new and not obvious to a person of ordinary skill and knowledge in the art or technology to which the invention is related. Whether an invention is new and not obvious in its field may lead to highly technical proceedings before a patent examiner, the PTO's Board of Patent Appeals, or the U.S. Court of Appeals for the Federal Circuit (CAFC). **For example, Thomas Devel's application for a patent on complementary DNA (cDNA) molecules encoding proteins that stimulated cell division was rejected by a patent examiner as "obvious" and affirmed by the PTO's Board of Patent Appeals. However, after a full hearing before the CAFC, which focused on the state of research in the field as applied to the patent application, Devel's patent claims were determined to be "not invalid because of obviousness."[19]**

The invention itself is what is patented. Thus, new and useful ideas and scientific principles by themselves cannot be patented. There must be an actual physical implementation of the idea or principle in the form of a process, machine, composition of matter, or device.

The patent owner has the exclusive right to make, use, or sell or import into the United States the product or process that uses the patented invention. It is a violation of U.S. patent law to make, use, sell, or offer to sell or import any patented invention within the United States without authority from the patent owner.[20]

D. SECRET BUSINESS INFORMATION

A business may have developed information that is not generally known but that cannot be protected under federal law. Or a business may want to avoid the disclosure required to obtain a patent or copyright protection of computer software. As long as such information is kept secret, it will be protected under state law relating to trade secrets.[21]

13. Trade Secrets

A **trade secret** may consist of any formula, device, or compilation of information that is used in one's business and is of such a nature that it provides an advantage over competitors who do not have the information. It may be a formula for a chemical compound; a process of manufacturing, treating, or preserving materials; and, to a limited extent, certain confidential customer lists.[22]

Courts will not protect customer lists if customer identities are readily ascertainable from industry or public sources or if products or services are sold to a wide group of purchasers based on their individual needs.[23]

---

17 *Id.* § 173.
18 *Kellogg Co. v National Biscuit Co.*, 305 U.S. 111 (1938).
19 *In re* Devel, 51 F3d 1552 (Fed Cir 1995).

20 35 USC § 27(a) (1995).
21 The Uniform Trade Secrets Act was officially amended in 1985. It is now in force in Alabama, Alaska, Arizona, Arkansas, California, Colorado, Connecticut, Delaware, Florida, Hawaii, Idaho, Illinois, Indiana, Iowa, Kansas, Kentucky, Louisiana, Maine, Minnesota, Mississippi, Montana, Nebraska, Nevada, New Hampshire, New Mexico, North Dakota, Oklahoma, Oregon, Rhode Island, South Carolina, South Dakota, Utah, Virginia, Washington, West Virginia, and Wisconsin. Trade secrets are protected in all states either under the Uniform Act or common law and under both criminal and civil statutes.
22 Restatement of Torts (second) § 757, Comment b. See also *Avnet, Inc. v Wyle Labs, Inc.*, 437 SE2d 302 (Ga 1993).
23 *Xpert Automation Systems Corp. v Vibromatic Co.*, 569 NE2d 351 (Ind Ct App 1990).

14. Loss of Protection

When secret business information is made public, it loses the protection it had while secret. This loss of protection occurs when the information is made known without any restrictions. In contrast, there is no loss of protection when secret information is shared or communicated for a special purpose and the person receiving the information knows that it is not to be made known to others.

When a product or process is unprotected by a patent or a copyright and is sold in significant numbers to the public, whose members are free to resell to whomever they choose, competitors are free to reverse engineer (start with the known product and work backwards to discover the process) or copy the article. **To illustrate, Crosby Yacht Co., a boatbuilder on Cape Cod, developed a hull design that is not patented. Maine Boatbuilders Inc. (MBI) purchased one of Crosby's boats and copied the hull by creating a mold from the boat it purchased. MBI is free to build and sell boats utilizing the copied hull.**

15. Defensive Measures

Employers seek to avoid the expense of trade secret litigation by limiting disclosure of trade secrets to employees with a "need to know." Employers also have employees sign nondisclosure agreements and they conduct exit interviews when employees with confidential information leave, reminding the employees of the employer's intent to enforce the nondisclosure agreement. In addition, employers have adopted industrial security plans to protect their unique knowledge from "outsiders," who may engage in theft, trespass, wiretapping, or other forms of commercial espionage.

E. PROTECTION OF COMPUTER SOFTWARE AND MASK WORKS

Computer programs, chip designs, and mask works are protected from infringement with varying degrees of success by federal statutes, restrictive licensing, and trade secrecy.

16. Copyright Protection of Computer Programs

Under the Computer Software Copyright Act of 1980,[24] a written program is given the same protection as any other copyrighted material regardless of whether the program is written in source code (ordinary language) or object code (machine language). **To illustrate, Franklin Computer Corp. copied certain operating-system computer programs that had been copyrighted by Apple Computer, Inc. When Apple sued Franklin for copyright infringement, Franklin argued that the object code on which its programs had relied were uncopyrightable "methods of operation." The Third Circuit held that computer programs, whether in source code or in object code embedded on ROM chips, are protected under the act.[25]**

In determining whether there is a copyright violation under the Computer Software Copyright Act, courts will examine the two programs in question to compare their structure, flow, sequence, and organization. Moreover, the courts in their infringement analysis look to see if the most *significant* steps of the program are similar rather than whether most of the program's steps are similar. To illustrate a copyright violation, substantial similarity in the structure of two computer programs for dental laboratory recordkeeping was found even though the programs were dissimilar in a number of respects but five particularly important subroutines within both programs performed almost identically.[26]

The protection afforded software by the copyright law is not entirely satisfactory to software developers because of the distinction made by the copyright law of protecting expressions but not ideas.[27] Also, section 102 (b) of the Computer Software Copyright Act does not provide protection for "methods of operation." A court has allowed a competitor to copy the identical menu tree of a copyrighted spreadsheet program because it was a non-

---

[24] Act of December 12, 1980, PL 96-517, 17 USC §§ 101, 117, 94 Stat 3015.
[25] 713 F2d 1240 (3d Cir 1983).
[26] *Whelan Associates v Jaslow Dental Laboratory*, 797 F2d 1222 (3d Cir 1986).
[27] *Autoskill Inc. v National Education Support Systems Inc.*, 994 F2d 1476 (10th Cir 1993).

copyrightable method of operation.[28] A move is now under way to enact broad new legislation that balances the need to protect the interests of software developers in their products while, after a reasonable time, providing accessibility to other developers so they may build on the technology for the public good. It has been suggested that the life of copyrighted software should be widely protected but drastically shortened from its present 75-year life.

17. Patent Protection of Programs

Patents have been granted for computer programs; for example, a method of using a computer to carry out translations from one language to another has been held patentable.

Patenting a program has the disadvantage that the program is placed in the public records and may thus be examined by anyone. This practice poses a potential danger that the program will be copied. To detect patent violators and bring legal action is difficult and costly.[29]

18. Trade Secrets

While primary protection for computer software is found in the Computer Software Copyright Act, industry also uses trade secret law to protect computer programs. When software containing trade secrets is unlawfully appropriated by a former employee, the employee is guilty of trade secret theft.[30]

19. Restrictive Licensing

To retain greater control over proprietary software, it is common for the creator of software to license its use to others rather than sell it to them. Such licensing agreements typically include restrictions on the use of the software by the licensee and give the licensor greater protection than that provided by copyright law. These restrictions commonly prohibit the licensee from providing, in any manner whatsoever, the software to third persons or subjecting the software to reverse engineering.

The *Data General* case illustrates the application of copyright law to the protection of computer software and the very significant damages available to the copyright holder for infringement. Notice that Data General alleged a count of trade secret misappropriation as well.

---

[28] *Lotus Development Corp. v Borland International, Inc.*, 49 F3d 807 (1st Cir 1995), *aff'd*, 116 S Ct 804 (1996).
[29] The Patent and Trademark Office has adopted guidelines for the examination of computer-related inventions. 61 CFR § 7478-02.

[30] As of the date of publication of this book, a new Article 2B of the Uniform Commercial Code is being prepared to regulate software transactions and licensing.

DATA GENERAL CORP. v GRUMMAN SYSTEMS SUPPORT CORP.
36 F3d 1147 (1st Cir 1994)

Data General (DG) developed a sophisticated computer program called ADEX to diagnose problems in its MV series of computers, DG's most advanced computer hardware. DG had 90 percent of the "aftermarket" for service to its computers. A group of third-party maintainers (TPMs) earned 7 percent of the available service revenue, and defendant Grumman was the leading TPM with 3 percent of the service business. In the mid-1980s DG altered its policy of liberally selling or licensing software diagnostics to TPMs, and it severely restricted the licensing of ADEX; it would not license ADEX to TPMs. Grumman found ways to skirt DG's ADEX restrictions, including using copies of ADEX that some former DG employees, in violation of their employment contracts, brought when they joined Grumman. DG brought suit alleging copyright infringement and misappropriation of trade secrets. Grumman counterclaimed alleging antitrust violations. The jury awarded DG $27,417,000 in damages and Grumman appealed.

STAHL, C.J.... In one count, DG alleged that Grumman's use and duplication of ADEX infringed DG's ADEX copyrights, and requested injunctive relief, 17 U.S.C. § 502 (1988), as well as actual damages and profits, 17 U.S.C. § 504(b) (1988). In another count, DG alleged that Grumman had violated Massachusetts trade secrets law by misappropriating copies of ADEX in violation of confidentiality agreements binding on former DG employees and DG service customers....

During the trial, it became evident that DG had made several errors in registering its ADEX copyrights. After Edward Gove, a DG official, testified that DG had deposited with the Copyright Office the correct excerpts of humanreadable "source code," Grumman introduced evidence that there were some errors in the deposits for the first three versions of ADEX. In rebuttal testimony, Gove confirmed that there were a number of minor, inadvertent errors in the deposits that would not affect the operation of the programs....

...Using a special verdict form, the jury found that DG had properly registered each of the ADEX copyrights.

Discussion

We first examine the two arguments that strike at the heart of DG's right to pursue its claims: DG's alleged failure to comply with the copyright registration requirements and the possible preemption of the state trade secrets claim by Section 301 of the Copyright Act....

Registration of a work with the Copyright Office provides several benefits to a plaintiff in an infringement action. First, although copyright protection attaches the day original expression is fixed in a tangible medium, see 17 U.S.C. § 102(a) and thus an infriger may be liable for infringement from that day forward, see 17 U.S.C. §

408(a) (providing that "registration is not a condition of copyright protection"), registration of the copyright is a prerequisite to suit under the Copyright Act, See 17 U.S.C. § 411(a). Second, upon accepting the registrant's application, fee, and deposit of a representative copy of the work, see 17 U.S.C. § 408, the Copyright Office issues a certificate of registration, which is admissible in an infringement action as "prima facie evidence of the validity of the copyright and of the facts stated in the certificate," 17 U.S.C. § 410(c) (1988). In the case of computer programs which, like ADEX, are either unpublished or published only in machine-readable form, the copyright owner must deposit "identifying portions of the program," generally the first and last 25 pages of the humanreadable source code 37 C.F.R. § 202.-20(c)(2)(vii) (1993). By questioning DG's compliance with the registration requirements, Grumman is effectively claiming that (1) DG may not claim infringement of those ADEX copyrights for which DG tendered a defective deposit; and (2) even if DG is free to bring such claims, it is not entitled to a presumption as to the validity of the copyrights at issue....

It is well established that immaterial, inadvertent errors in an application for copyright registration do not jeopardize the validity of the registration....

We conclude that there is no support in law or reason for a rule that penalizes immaterial, inadvertent errors in a copyright deposit. Accordingly, we find no flaw in the district court's instruction that such errors "do not impeach the validity and effect of the registration."

Refusal to Compel Production of Source Code

Grumman next argues that it was unfairly deprived of an opportunity to prove that the errors in the deposits were material. Specifically, Grumman claims that the district court abused its discretion when, during the trial, it refused to compel DG to produce roughly 40,000 pages of source code (on approximately 33,000 floppy disks) for each of the first three versions of ADEX (0.0 to 2.0)....

[We find no abuse of discretion to deny this request....]

Preemption of Trade Secrets Claim

Seeking to avoid the additional damages associated with the trade secrets remedies selected by DG, Grumman argues that the state claim is preempted by Section 301 of the Copyright Act, 17 U.S.C. § 301(a).

Section 301(a) precludes enforcement of any state cause of action which is equivalent in substance to a federal copyright infringement claim....

...To demonstrate misappropriation of trade secrets under Massachusetts law, DG must prove that "(1) MV/ADEX is a trade secret; (2) Data General took reasonable steps to preserve the secrecy of MV/ADEX; and (3) Grumman used improper means, in breach of a confidential relationship, to acquire and use the trade secret." *Grumman VI*, 825 F.Supp. at 357. The district court instructed the jury that "wrongful acquisition" is an element of a Massachusetts trade secrets claim, and that "[a]cquisition of a trade secret is wrongful...if it is by theft of property known to belong to another, or by *knowing participation in the breach of an express or implied confidentiality agreement* by, for instance, a former employee or customer of Data General." (Emphasis added.)... DG's theory was precisely that Grumman acquired ADEX by participating in the breach of confidentiality agreements binding on former employees and service customers of DG. Because the Copyright Act does not prevent the states from imposing liability for such conduct, the district court was correct to spare DG's trade secrets claim from preemption under Section 301(a)....

Grumman's Counterclaims

Grumman accused DG of willfully maintaining its monopoly in the aftermarket for service of DG computers in violation of Section 2 of the Sherman Act, 15 U.S.C. § 2, which prohibits the monopolization of "any part of the trade or commerce among the several States."... [O]n its willful maintenance claim, Grumman must demonstrate a genuine dispute about the existence of two elements; (1) DG's possession of monopoly power in the market for support services of DG computers; and (2) DG's maintenance of that power through "exclusionary conduct." *Town of Concord v Boston Edison Co.*, 915 F.2d 17, 21 (1st Cir.1990) (Breyer, C.J.)....

Grumman's primary contention is that DG's unilateral refusal to license ADEX to anyone other than qualified self-maintainers constitutes exclusionary conduct. Grumman also attacks as exclusionary DG's refusal to provide other service tools directly to TPMs. We first review the principles governing the analysis of a monopolist's unilateral refusal to deal, and then discuss whether a unilateral refusal to license a copyrighted work might ever deserve to be condemned as exclusionary. We hold below that the desire of an author to be the exclusive user of its original work is a presumptively legitimate business justification for the author's refusal to license competitors. We hold further that Grumman has not presented sufficient proof to rebut this presumption and thereby avert summary judgment. In particular, we find no merit in Grumman's contention that DG acted in an exclusionary fashion in discontinuing its liberal policies allowing TPM access to diagnostic software. Finally, we conclude that no reasonable jury could find that DG's restrictions on TPM access to other service tools amount to exclusionary conduct....

Copyright Law

Copyright law provides further guidance. The Copyright Act expressly grants to a copyright owner the exclusive right to distribute the protected work by "transfer of ownership, or by rental, lease, or lending." 17 U.S.C. § 106. Consequently, "[t]he owner of the copyright, if [it] pleases, may refrain from vending or licensing and content [itself] with simply exercising the right to exclude others from using [its] property."...We may also venture to infer that , in passing the Copyright Act, Congress itself made an empirical assumption that allowing copyright holders to collect license fees and exclude others from using their works creates a system of incentives that promotes consumer welfare in the long term by encouraging investment in the creation of desirable artistic and functional works of expression. See *Feist Publications, Inc. v Rural Tel. Serv. Co.,* 499 U.S. 340, 349, 111 S.Ct. 1282, 1290, 113 L.Ed.2d 358 (1991) ("The primary objective of a copyright is not to reward the labor of authors, but '[t]o promote the Progress of Science and useful Arts.'") (brackets in original) (quoting U.S. Const. art. I. § 8, cl. 8); *Sony Corp.,* 464 U.S. at 429, 104 S.Ct. at 782 (discussing goals and incentives of copyright protection); *Twentieth Century Music Corp. v Aiken,* 422 U.S. 151, 156, 95 S.Ct. 2040, 2044, 45 L.Ed.2d 84 (1975) ("The immediate effect of our copyright law is to secure a fair return for an 'author's' creative labor. But the ultimate aim is, by this incentive, to stimulate artistic creativity for the general public good.") We cannot require antitrust defendants to prove and reprove the merits of this legislative assumption in every case where a refusal to license a copyrighted work comes under attack. Nevertheless, although "nothing in the *copyright statutes* would prevent an author from hoarding all of his works during the term of the copyright," *Stewart,* 495 U.S. at 228–29, 110 S.Ct. at 1764 (emphasis added), the Copyright Act does not explicitly purport to limit the scope of the Sherman Act. And, if the Copyright Act is silent on the subject generally, the silence is particularly acute in cases where a monopolist harms consumers in the monopolized market by

refusing to license a copyrighted work to competitors.

We acknowledge that Congress has not been entirely silent on the relationship between antitrust and intellectual property laws. Congress amended the patent laws in 1988 to provide that "[n]o patent owner otherwise entitled to relief for infringement...of a patent shall be denied relief or deemed guilty of misuse or illegal extension of the patent right by reason of [the patent owner's] refus[al] to license or use any rights to the patent." 35 U.S.C. § 271(d) (1988). Section 271(d) clearly prevents an infringer from using a patent misuse defense when the patent owner has unilaterally refused a license, and may even herald the prohibition of all antitrust claims and counterclaims premised on a refusal to license a patent. *See* Richard Calkins, *Patent Law: The Impact of the 1988 Patent Misuse Reform Act and Noerr-Pennington Doctrine on Misuse Defenses and Antitrust Counterclaims,* 38 Drake L.Rev. 192–97 (1988–89). Nevertheless, while Section 271(d) is indicative of congressional "policy" on the need for antitrust law to accommodate intellectual property law, Congress did not similarly amend the Copyright Act.

Harmonizing the Sherman Act and the Copyright Act

Since neither the Sherman Act nor the Copyright Act works a partial repeal of the other, and since implied repeals are disfavored, we must harmonize the two as best we can, *id.,* mindful of the legislative and judicial approaches to similar conflicts created by the patent laws. We must not lose sight of the need to preserve the economic incentives fueled by the Copyright Act, but neither may we ignore the tension between the two very different policies embodied in the Copyright Act and the Sherman Act, both designed ultimately to improve the welfare of consumers in our free market system. Drawing on our discussion above, we hold that while exclusionary conduct can include a monopolist's unilateral refusal to license a copyright, an author's desire to exclude others from use of its copyrighted work is a presumptively valid business justification for any immediate harm to consumers.

Having arrived at the applicable legal standards, we may resolve Grumman's principal allegation of exclusionary conduct. Although there may be a genuine factual dispute about the effect on DG equipment owners of DG's refusal to license ADEX to TPMs, DG's desire to exercise its rights under the Copyright Act is a presumptively valid business justification....

For the foregoing reasons, we affirm the district court in every respect save for its failure to instruct the jury on its duty to consider Grumman's pleas for apportionment of Grumman's nonduplicative profits.

[Case remanded]

Questions

1. Did Grumman infringe DG's ADEX diagnostic computer software?
2. Consider Figure 2-1 in Chapter 2. What ethical principles were involved in this case? What problem was Grumman faced with? What should Grumman have done?
3. Under federal antitrust law, may a copyright owner refuse to license the copyrighted work to a competitor?

20. Semiconductor Chip Protection

The Semiconductor Chip Protection Act of 1984 (SCPA)[31] created a new form of industrial intellectual property by protecting "mask works" and the semiconductor chip products in which they are embodied against chip piracy. **Mask work** refers to the specific form of expression embodied in chip design, including the stencils used in manufacturing semiconductor chip products. A **semiconductor chip** product is a product placed on a piece of semiconductor material in accordance with a predetermined pattern that is intended to perform electronic circuitry functions. This definition includes such products as analog chips, logic function chips like microprocessors, and memory chips like RAMs and ROMs.

(a) DURATION AND QUALIFICATIONS FOR PROTECTION. The SCPA provides the owners of a mask work fixed in a semiconductor chip product the exclusive right for 10 years to reproduce and distribute their products in the United States and to import them into the United States. These rights fully apply to works first commercially exploited after November 8, 1984, the date of the law's enactment. However, the protection of the act only applies to those works that, when considered as a whole, are not commonplace, staple, or familiar in the semiconductor industry.

(b) APPLICATION PROCEDURE. The owner of a mask work subject to protection under the SCPA must file an application for a certificate of registration with the Register of Copyrights within two years of the date of the work's first commercial exploitation. Failure to do so within this period will result in forfeiture of all rights under the act. Questions concerning the validity of the works are to be resolved through litigation or arbitration.

(c) LIMITATION ON EXCLUSIVE RIGHTS. Under the SCPA's reverse engineering exemption, competitors may not only study mask works but may use the results of that study to design their own semiconductor chip products embodying their own original masks even if the masks are substantially similar (but not substantially identical) so long as their products are the result of substantial study and analysis and not merely the result of plagiarism.[32]

---

[31] PL 98-620, 98 Stat 3347, 17 USC § 901.

[32] *Id.* § 906.

Figure 21-1   Summary Comparison of Intellectual Property Rights

Type of Intellectual Property	Trademarks	Copyrights	Patents	Trade Secrets
Protection	Words, names, symbols, or devices used to identify a product or service	Original creative works of authorship such as writings, movies, records, and computer software	Utility, design, and plant patents	Advantageous formulas, devices, or compilation of information
Applicable Standard	Identifies and distinguishes a product or service	Original creative works in writing or in another format	New and nonobvious advances in the art	Not readily ascertainable, not disclosed to the public
Where to Apply	Patent and Trademark Office	Register of Copyrights	Patent and Trademark Office	No public registration necessary
Duration	Indefinite so long as it continues to be used	Life of author plus 50 years or 75 years from publication for "works for hire"	Utility and plant patents 20 years from date of application; design patents 14 years	Indefinite so long as secret is not disclosed to public

Innocent infringers are not liable for infringements occurring before notice of protection is given them and are liable for reasonable royalties on each unit distributed after notice has been given them. However, the continued purchasing of infringing semiconductors after notice has been given can result in penalties up to $250,000.

(d) REMEDIES. The SCPA provides that an infringer will be liable for actual damages and will forfeit its profits to the owner. As an alternative, the owner may elect to receive statutory damages of up to $250,000 as determined by a court. The court may also order destruction or other disposition of the products and equipment used to make the products.

ETHICS AND THE LAW

In the summer of 1996, the dance song "Macarena" hit the pop music scene and charts in the United States. The line-type dance inspired by the song is called the Macarena. At camps around the country, the song was played and children were taught the dance.

The American Society of Composers, Authors & Publishers (ASCAP) is the organization that serves as a clearinghouse for fee payments for use of copyrighted materials belonging to its members. ASCAP sent a letter to the directors of camps and non-profit organizations sponsoring camps (Girl Scouts, Boy Scouts, Camp Fire Girls,

American Cancer Association, and so forth) which warned them that licensed songs should not be used without paying ASCAP the licensing fees and that violators would be pursued. ASCAP's prices for the songs are, for example, $591 for the camp season for "Edelweiss" (from "The Sound of Music") or "This Land is Your Land."

Some of the nonprofit-sponsored camps charge only $44 per week per camper. The directors could not afford the fees and the camps eliminated their oldies dances and dance classes. ASCAP declined to offer dis-counted licensing fees for the camps.

Why did ASCAP work so diligently to protect its rights? What ethical and social responsibility issues do you see with respect to the nonprofit camps? Some of these camps are summer retreats for children who suffer from cancer, AIDS and other terminal illnesses. Does this information change your feelings about ASCAP's fees? What would you do if you were an ASCAP member and owned the rights to a song a camp wished to use?

SUMMARY

Property rights in trademarks, copyrights, and patents are acquired as provided primarily in federal statutes. A trademark or service mark is any word, symbol, or design, or a combination of these, used to identify a product (in the case of a trademark) or a service (in the case of a service mark). Terms will fall into one of four categories: (1) generic, (2) descriptive, (3) suggestive, or (4) arbitrary or fanciful. Generic terms are never registrable. However, if a descriptive term has acquired a secondary meaning, it is registrable. Suggestive and arbitrary marks are registrable as well. If there is likelihood of confusion, a court will enjoin the second user from using a particular registered mark.

A copyright is the exclusive right given by federal statute to the creator of a literary or artistic work to use, reproduce, or display the work for the life of the creator and 50 years after the creator's death.

A patent gives the inventor an exclusive right for 20 years from the date of application to make, use, and sell an invention that is new and useful but not obvious to those in the business to which the invention is related. Trade secrets that give an owner an advantage over competitors are protected under state law for an unlimited period so long as they are not made public.

Protection of computer programs and the design of computer chips and mask works is commonly obtained, subject to certain limitations, by complying with federal statutes, by using the law of trade secrets, and by restrictive licensing agreements. Many software developers pursue all of these means to protect their proprietary interests in their programs.

QUESTIONS AND CASE PROBLEMS

1. What qualities must an invention possess to be patentable?

2. Compare the protection afforded by a patent and the protection afforded by a trademark registration.

3. Banion manufacturers semiconductor chips. He wants to obtain protection for his mask works under federal law, particularly so that competitors will be prohibited from reverse engineering these works. Advise Banion of his legal options, if any, to accomplish his objective.

4. Jim and Eric work for Audio Visual Services (AVS) at Cramer University in Casper, Wyoming. For "expenses" of $5 and the provision of a blank tape, Jim and Eric used AVS facilities after hours to make tapes of Pearl Jam's CD "Vitology" for 25 friends or friends of friends from school. When Mrs. Mullen, who is in charge of AVS, discovered this and confronted them, Jim, a classics major, defended their actions, telling her, "It's de minimus...I mean, who cares?" Explain to Jim and Eric the legal and ethical ramifications of their actions.

5. Sullivan sold T-shirts with the name *Boston Marathon* and the year of the race imprinted on them. The Boston Athletic Association (BAA) sponsors and administers the Boston Marathon and has used the name *Boston Marathon* since 1917. The BAA registered the name *Boston Marathon* on the Principal Register. In 1986, the BAA entered into an exclusive license with Image, Inc., to use its service mark on shirts and other apparel. Thereafter, when Sullivan continued to sell shirts imprinted with the name *Boston Marathon*, the BAA sought an injunction. Sullivan's defense was that the general public was not being misled into thinking that his shirts were officially sponsored by the BAA. Without this confusion of source, he contended, no injunction should be issued. Decide. [*Boston Athletic Ass'n v Sullivan*, 867 F2d 22 (1st Cir)]

6. *Bambi*, written by Austrian citizen Felix Salten, was first published in Germany in the German language in 1923 without a copyright notice. A second edition was published in Germany in 1926 with a U.S. copyright notice and was timely registered in the United States in early 1927. In 1936 Salten assigned rights to the book to Sidney Franklin, who assigned his rights to Walt Disney Co. Disney released the *Bambi* motion picture in 1942, which had a derivative copyright from the *Bambi* book. Salten died in 1945, and the copyright in the *Bambi* book was renewed in 1954 by his daughter Anna Wyler. She executed agreements with Disney concerning derivative works from the *Bambi* book. Anna died in 1977 and her husband and two children assigned their rights to Twin Books Corp. in 1993. Twin Books sought profits from the rereleased Disney motion picture through the derivative copyrights emanating from the *Bambi* book. Disney contended that the book fell into the public domain in 1951 when Anna Wyler failed to timely renew the copyright at the end of its first 28-year period after first publication in 1923. Twin Books responded that it was renewed in 1954 within 28 years after the initial copyright was secured, which was 1926. Decide.

Even if the *Bambi* book copyright was timely renewed, how did Twin Books have standing to sue Disney for profits on the rereleased animated *Bambi* motion picture when the copyright on the *Bambi* book ended 56 years after 1926, in 1982? [*Twin Books Corp. v Walt Disney Co.*, 1996 Copyright Rep (CCH) 27,518 (9th Cir)]

7. Twentieth Century Fox (Fox) owned and distributed the successful motion picture *The Commitments*. The film tells the story of a group of young Irish men and women who form a soul music band. In the film the leader of the band, Jimmy, tries to teach the band members what it takes to be successful soul music performers. Toward that end, Jimmy shows the band members a videotape of James Brown's energetic performance of the song "Please, Please, Please." This performance came from Brown's appearance in 1965 on a TV program called the *TAMI Show*. Portions of the 1965 performance are shown in *The Commitments* in seven separate "cuts" for a total of 27 seconds. Sometimes the cuts are in the background of a scene and sometimes they occupy the entire screen. Brown's name is not mentioned at all during these relatively brief cuts. His name is mentioned only once later in the film, when Jimmy urges the band members to abandon their current musical interests and tune into the great soul performers, including James Brown: "Listen, from now on I don't want you listening to Guns & Roses and The Soup Dragons. I want you on a strict diet of soul. James Brown for the growls, Otis Redding for the moans, Smokey Robinson for the whines, and Aretha for the whole lot put together." Would it be fair use under U.S. copyright law for Fox to use just 27 seconds of James Brown cuts in the film without formally obtaining permission to use the cuts? Advise Fox as to what, if anything, would be necessary to protect it from a lawsuit. [See *Brown v Twentieth Century Fox Film Corp.*, 799 F Supp 166 (DDC)]

8. Sony Corp. manufactures video cassette recorders (VCRs) to tape television shows for later home viewing (time-shifting). Sony sold them under the trade name Betamax through retail establishments throughout the country. Universal City Studios and Walt Disney Productions owned the copyrights on some of the television programs that were broadcast on public airwaves. Universal and Disney brought an action against Sony and certain large retailers, contending that VCR consumers had recorded some of their copyrighted works that had been shown on commercially sponsored television and thereby infringed the copyrights. These plaintiffs sought damages and an injunction against the manufacture and marketing of VCRs. Sony contended that the noncommercial, home-use recording of material broadcast over public airwaves for later viewing was a fair use of copyrighted works. Decide. [*Sony Corp. v Universal Studios*, 464 US 417]

9. The menu commands on the Lotus 1-2-3 spreadsheet program enable users to perform accounting functions by using such commands as "Copy," "Print," or "Quit." Borland International, Inc. released its Quattro spreadsheet, a program superior to Lotus-1-2-3 that did, however, use an identical copy of the entire Lotus 1-2-3 menu tree but did not copy any of Lotus's computer code. Lotus believed that its copyright in Lotus 1-2-3 had been violated. Borland insisted that the Lotus menu command was not copyrightable because it is a method of operation

foreclosed from protection under section 102(b) of the Copyright Act of 1976. Decide. [*Lotus Development Corp. v Borland International, Inc.,* 49 F3d 807, 116 S Ct 904]

10. Diehr devised a computerized process for curing rubber that was based on a well-known mathematical formula related to the cure time, and he devised numerous other steps in his synthetic rubber-curing process. The patent examiner determined that because abstract ideas, the laws of nature, and mathematical formulas are not patentable subject matter, the process in this case based on a known mathematical formula was also not patentable. Diehr contended that all of the steps in his rubber-curing process were new and not obvious to the art of rubber curing. He contended also that he did not seek an exclusive patent on the mathematical formula except for its use in the rubber-curing process. Decide. [*Diamond v Diehr,* 450 US 175]

11. Aries Information Systems, Inc. (Aries), develops and markets computer software specifically designed to meet the financial accounting and reporting requirements of such public bodies as school districts and county governments. One of Aries' principal products is the POBAS III accounting program. Pacific Management Systems Corp. (Pacific) was organized by Scott Dahmer, John Laugan, and Roman Rowan for marketing a financial accounting and budgeting system known as FAMIS. Dahmer, Laugan, and Rowan were Aries employees before, during, and shortly after they organized Pacific. As employees, they each gained access to Aries' software materials (including the POBAS III system) and had information about Aries' existing and prospective clients. Proprietary notices appeared on every client contract, source code list, and magnetic tape. Dahmer, Laugan, and Rowan signed an Employee Confidential Information Agreement after beginning employment with Aries. While still employees of Aries, they submitted a bid on behalf of Pacific to Rock County and were awarded the contract. Pacific's FAMIS software system is substantially identical to Aries' proprietary POBAS III system. Aries sued Pacific to recover damages for misappropriation of its trade secrets. Pacific's defense was that no "secrets" were misappropriated because many employees knew the information in question. Decide. [*Aries Information Systems, Inc. v Pacific Management Systems Corp.,* 366 NW2d 366 (Minn Ct App)]

12. The plaintiff, Herbert Rosenthal Jewelry Corp., and the defendant, Kalpakian, manufactured jewelry. The plaintiff obtained a copyright registration of a jeweled pin in the shape of a bee. Kalpakian made a similar pin. Rosenthal sued Kalpakian for infringement of copyright registration. Kalpakian raised the defense that he was only copying the idea, not the way the idea was expressed. Was he liable for infringement of the plaintiff's copyright? [*Herbert Rosenthal Jewelry Corp. v Kalpakian,* 446 F2d 738 (9th Cir)]

13. Mineral Deposits Ltd. (MD Ltd.), an Australian company, manufactures the Reichert Spiral, a device used for recovering gold particles from sand and gravel. The spiral was patented in Australia, and MD Ltd. had applied for a patent in the United States. Theodore Zigan contacted MD Ltd., stating he was interested in purchasing up to 200 devices for use in his gravel pit. MD Ltd. agreed to lend Zigan a spiral for testing its efficiency. Zigan made molds of the spiral's components and proceeded to manufacture 170 copies of the device. When MD Ltd. found out that copies were being made, it demanded the return of the spiral. MD Ltd. also sought lost profits for the 170 spirals manufactured by Zigan. Recovery was sought on a theory of misappropriation of trade secrets. Zigan offered to pay for the spiral lent him by MD Ltd. He argued that trade secret protection was lost by the public sale of the spiral. What ethical values are involved? Was Zigan's conduct a violation of trade secret law? [*Mineral Deposits Ltd. v Zigan,* 773 P2d 609 (Colo Ct App)]

14. From October 1965 through July 1967, Union Carbide Corp. sold certain bulbs for high-intensity reading lamps under its Eveready trademark. Carbide's sales of electrical products under the Eveready mark exceeded $100 million for every year after 1963; from 1963 to 1967, Carbide spent $50 million in advertising these products. In 1969, the defendant, Ever-Ready, Inc., imported miniature lamp bulbs for high-intensity lamps with *Ever-Ready* stamped on their base. In two surveys conducted by Carbide, 50 percent of those interviewed associated Carbide products with the marks used by Ever-Ready, Inc. Carbide sought an injunction against Ever-Ready's use of the name Ever-Ready on or in connection with the sale of electrical products. No monetary damages were sought. Ever-Ready, Inc. contended that Carbide's trademark Eveready was descriptive and therefore the registration of the mark was improper and invalid. Carbide raised the defense that its mark had acquired secondary meaning. Decide. [*Union Carbide Corp. v Ever-Ready, Inc.,* 531 F2d 366 (7th Cir)]

15. Anheuser-Busch made an application for registration of the trademark LA and began marketing low-alcohol beer under the LA label. Following Anheuser-Busch's introduction of its product, the

Stroh Brewery Co. introduced Schaefer LA, also a low-alcohol beer. An action to enjoin Stroh's use of LA followed. Anheuser-Busch contended that the term LA was suggestive in that it required some imagination to connect it with the product and, accordingly, was a protectable trademark. Stroh argued that LA was generic or descriptive in nature, because the term is comprised of the initials of the phrase "low alcohol." Decide. [*Anheuser-Busch Inc. v Stroh Brewery Co.*, 750 F2d 631 (8th Cir)]

13

Competing in Global Markets

Learning Goals

1. Explain the importance of international business and the main reasons why nations trade.

2. Discuss the relationship of absolute and comparative advantage to international trade.

3. Describe how nations measure international trade and the significance of exchange rates.

4. Identify the major barriers that confront global businesses.

5. Explain how international trade organizations and economic communities reduce barriers to international trade.

6. Compare the different levels of involvement used by businesses when entering global markets.

7. Describe the types of international organizational structures available to businesses.

8. Distinguish between a global business strategy and a multidomestic business strategy.

MTV: At 20, It's the Coolest TV Channel around the World

A whole generation has grown up with MTV in the U.S. Now, a global generation of young people is growing up with their favorite MTV music and videos—in their own countries, in their own languages, with their own stars. From Russia to Australia to Brazil, people are tuning in. In the Philippines, MTV is the second most watched cable station. In Moscow's Red Square, 200,000 young people attend an MTV-sponsored concert. In a London suburb, 1,500 guests rock at an MTV-sponsored party.

MTV is international business—with a beat. There's a huge international market of young people out there who love music, and MTV is in the thick of it. Although now hugely successful, MTV's initial venture into foreign markets was hardly harmonious. First, the company tried piping in American programming—in English—throughout Europe. Viewers were interested in Michael Jackson but not much else that was American. Local competitors appeared, attracting both viewers and sponsors away from MTV. "We were going for the most shallow layer of what united viewers," admits CEO Tom Freston. "It didn't go over well." So MTV learned its lesson and began to pay more attention to the cultures and tastes of consumers in its foreign markets. A few years later, it launched five separate feeds to Europe, each designed to address the tastes of a particular region.

In providing custom-tailored programming, MTV increased the level of its involvement in different countries. Now local programming is routine in most MTV markets. "People root for the home team, culturally and musically," explains William Roedy, the London-based president of MTV's international networks. "Local repertoire is a worldwide trend. There are fewer global megastars." So, in India, where people love music from movie soundtracks, most of the MTV music comes from Hindi films. But any new MTV operation begins with a foundation of MTV values and procedures. The company begins by sending trusted employees—known as expatriates—to the new country. "We start with expatri-

ates to do a gene transfer of a company culture and operating principles," says Freston. Gradually, management and programming shift to the local culture. Describing the process in India, Freston notes, "We want them to be inside the Indian's head."

Government regulations have hindered MTV's global expansion. Some governments are so protective of their own business interests that they prohibit any foreign competition. Instead, they produce local look-alikes who imitate MTV's style. Such regulations have inhibited MTV's attempts to start channels in Canada and South Africa. Although MTV has a popular channel in Italy, the federal government is reducing the number of licensed broadcasters it will allow. And in Japan, MTV must have a local partner in order to expand. Political events have an impact on MTV broadcasts, as well.

After U.S. warplanes accidentally bombed the Chinese Embassy in Kosovo, the Chinese government refused to air an MTV awards program produced specifically for the Asian market. Eventually, the MTV Mandarin Music Honors program was aired for 300 million Chinese households, in partnership with the government-owned Chinese station. MTV has also had to learn from its own mistakes, much as it did with its programming errors in Europe. In India, MTV initially included the country's flag in its local logo, which many Indians found disrespectful.

Despite missing a few notes, MTV executives know that the company has a product with worldwide appeal—music—and a nearly unlimited potential market. The company's goal for this market is simple. "We want MTV in every household," says Roedy. That's every household, in every town, in every country.[1]

CHAPTER OVERVIEW

Consider for a moment how many products you used today that came from outside the U.S. Maybe you drank Brazilian coffee with your breakfast, wore clothes manufactured in Honduras or Malaysia, drove to class in a German or Japanese car fueled by gasoline refined from Venezuelan crude oil, and watched a movie on a television set assembled in Mexico for a Japanese company like Sony. A fellow student in France may be wearing Levi's jeans, using a Gateway or Compaq computer, and drinking Coca-Cola.

Like Volkswagen, Levi Strauss, Gateway, Sony, and The Coca-Cola Company, most U.S. and foreign companies recognize the importance of international trade to their future success. As Chapter 1 explains, economic interdependence is increasing throughout the world as companies seek additional markets for their goods and services and the most cost-effective locations for production facilities. No longer can businesses rely only on sales in domestic markets. Today, foreign sales are essential to U.S. manufacturing, agricultural, and service firms as sources of new markets and profit opportunities. Foreign companies also frequently look to America when they seek out new markets.

Thousands of products cross national borders every day. The computers that U.S. manufacturers sell in France are *exports*, domestically produced goods and services sold in markets in other countries. *Imports* are foreign-made products purchased by domestic consumers. Together, U.S. exports and imports make up about one-fourth the U.S. gross domestic product (GDP). U.S. exports exceed $950 billion each year, and annual imports total $1.2 trillion. That total amount is nearly double the nation's imports and exports just a decade ago.[2]

For dot.com powerhouses like eBay and Amazon.com, global markets mean global revenues. In Europe, eBay has been generating sales of $87 million, eight times the amount brought in by its largest competitor, a British company called QXL, which operates in 11 countries. In the first nine months after opening its European site, eBay was capturing a larger audience than QXL's in both Germany and Britain. Amazon.com has purchased online booksellers in Germany and Britain. Its European sales are five times greater than those of its key European competitor, BOL.[3]

Transactions that cross national boundaries may expose a company to an additional set of environmental factors—new social and cultural practices, economic and political environments, and legal restrictions. Before venturing into world markets, companies must adapt their domestic business strategies and plans to accommodate these differences.

This chapter travels through the world of international business to see how both large and small companies approach globalization. First, we consider the reasons nations trade, the importance and characteristics of the global marketplace, and the ways nations measure international trade. Then we examine barriers to international trade that arise from cultural and environmental differences. To reduce these barriers, countries turn to organizations that promote international trade and multinational agreements designed to encourage trade. Finally, we look at the strategies firms implement for entering global markets and how they develop international business strategies.

WHY NATIONS TRADE

As domestic markets mature and sales growth slows, companies in every industry recognize the increasing importance of efforts to develop business in other countries. McDonald's opens restaurants in Latin America, Nike sells shoes in the Philippines, and Amazon.com lures book buyers with fast delivery in Germany. These are only a few of the thousands of American companies taking advantage of foreign interest in their goods and services. Likewise, the U.S. market, with the world's largest purchasing power, attracts thousands of foreign companies to American shores. Large populations, substantial resources, and rising standards of living are boosting the attractiveness of many countries as targets for U.S. exports.

International trade is vital to a nation and its businesses because it boosts economic growth by providing a market for its products and access to needed resources. Companies in nations that promote global trade can expand their markets, seek out growth opportunities in other nations, and make their production and distribution systems more efficient. They also reduce their dependence on the economies of their home nations.

International Sources of Factors of Production

Business decisions to operate abroad depend on the availability, price, and quality of labor, natural resources, capital, and entrepreneurship—the basic factors of production—in the foreign country. The key factors for participating in the information economy are skilled human resources and entrepreneurship. The relative openness of the U.S. to immigration has permitted it to attract thousands of needed engineers and scientists from other countries. In contrast, in 2002, demand for skilled workers in Western Europe exceeded supply by 20 percent.[4] With talented workers so critical, companies tend to set up shop near the workforce they want to hire. The ability to locate near nine different universities lured Hewlett-Packard and Nokia to Barcelona, where both operate research and development facilities.[5]

Other key factors in choosing overseas markets include favorable regulatory conditions and healthy business climates. Companies that thrive on innovation and speedy decisions look for business environments where regulations will not slow them down. The freedom of this kind of environment positions organizations to attract the best talent worldwide. Amid the technology boom in the United States, the Dallas-based Baylor Institute for Immunology Research hired French biologist Nicolas Taquet. Not only could the U.S. facility offer him double what he was earning in France, but outside the government-dominated French bureaucracy, Taquet can more readily get the materials he needs for his cancer research. Although he misses his native country, Taquet says, "I'm so motivated here that I work weekends and nights. That wasn't the case back home."[6]

Many U.S. businesses have found international opportunities because many countries actively recruit them as sources of entrepreneurship and capital. As Russia's Internet population grows, the country's businesspeople want to get involved in Internet commerce. Russian start-ups are looking for U.S. investors who will bring not only money but also management talent. The United States, in contrast, has not only people who pioneered Internet commerce but also an enormous demand for investing in high-tech enterprises both at home and abroad.

One Russian company looking for management talent as well as capital is Kaspersky Lab, which develops and markets antivirus software. The company's revenues have grown steadily, but it needs help in becoming competitive internationally. Its CEO, Natalya Kaspersky, is looking for a foreign partner to assist with funding to expand and guidance in building a strong international image. So, she is seeking management expertise along with capital. Kaspersky points out that Russia's limited experience with capitalism requires her to find help outside her country: "We have only ten years of business history—where could people [in Russia] get business experience?"[7]

Trading with other countries also allows a company to spread risk, because different nations may be at different stages of the business cycle or in different phases of development. If demand falls off in one nation, the company may still enjoy strong demand in other nations. As discussed in Chapter 3, the U.S. has been enjoying the fruits of past investments in information technology. European countries are several years behind in making such investments. However, it is likely that Europe will soon begin enjoying similar gains in productivity and wealth as a result of expanded investment. Asia, which has recently been recovering from a recession, has increased its technology investments and may follow Europe, even as growth in the U.S. economy slows.[8] Later sections of the chapter discuss how these elements affect businesses.

Size of the International Marketplace

In addition to pursuing the production factors of human and natural resources, entrepreneurship, and capital, companies are attracted to international business by the sheer size of the global marketplace. Only 1 in every 5 people of the world's 6 billion-plus population live in relatively well-developed countries. The remaining 5 billion live in less-developed countries. The share of the world's population in the less-developed countries will continue to increase over the coming years because of differences in birth rates. Of the 78 million babies born each year, 19 of every 20 are born in the less-developed nations.[9]

As developing nations expand their involvement in global business, the potential for reaching new groups of customers dramatically increases. Firms looking for new sales are inevitably attracted to giant markets like China and India, with populations of 1.2 billion and 1 billion each. However, people alone are not enough to create a market. Economic demand also requires purchasing power. As Table 4.1 shows, population size is no guarantee of economic prosperity. Only two of the ten most populous countries, the U.S. and Japan, appear on the list of those with the highest per capita GDP.

Even though people in the developing nations have lower per capita incomes than those in the highly developed economies of North America and Western Europe, their huge populations do represent lucrative markets. Even when the high-income segments of those populations amount only to small percentages of all households, their sheer numbers may still represent significant and growing markets. Although overall India is very poor, it has somewhere between 150 million and 200 million well-educated middle-class consumers. In recent years, the Indian government has opened the country to more foreign trade, making this market even more attractive to business. Two companies that have recently responded to the lure of this giant marketplace by building factories in India are Kellogg Co. and Wm. Wrigley Jr. At present, few Indians chew gum or eat breakfast cereal, but these companies are betting young Indians will be willing to learn some new habits.[10]

Many developing countries have posted high rates of annual GDP growth. Compared with the 4 percent growth of the long U.S. economic expansion, South Korea recently enjoyed GDP growth of over 10 percent. China's growth moved at a 7 per-

Table 4.1   **The World's Top Ten Nations Based on Population and Wealth**

Country	Population (in millions)	Country	Per Capita GDP (in U.S. dollars)
China	1,247	Luxembourg	$33,700
India	1,001	United States	30,200
United States	282	Norway	27,400
Indonesia	216	Monaco	25,000
Brazil	172	Japan	24,500
Russia	146	United Arab Emirates	24,000
Pakistan	138	Switzerland	23,800
Bangladesh	127	Belgium	23,200
Japan	126	Denmark	23,200
Nigeria	104	Liechtenstein	23,000

In 20 years, Emerging Market GDP will grow from $8 trillion to $40 trillion (creating a new middle class).

These people can't wait to get started.

They're busy creating infrastructures, airlines, cars, buildings with elevators, offices and homes with air conditioners — and a growing appetite for comfort, security, travel — now. That's why we're in emerging markets.

Not as outsiders, but as integral partners. Making the best contacts, finding the best ventures, building the best work force, taking the best competitive positions and starting the best kind of growth curve — long and steady.

Sure, there may be bumps. But there's only one direction these markets can go in the next two decades. Forward. And only one way to capitalize on it.

Be there first.

Otis   Carrier   Pratt & Whitney   Sikorsky   Hamilton Standard   UT Automotive

United Technologies

FIGURE 4.1
The United Technologies Vision: Emerging Markets Are Growing

cent pace after two years of expanding in the range of 10 percent annually.[11] India's GDP growth has recently ranged from 5 to 6 percent annually.[12] These markets represent opportunities for global businesses, even though their per capita incomes lag behind those in more developed countries. Dozens of international firms are currently establishing operations in these and other developing countries to position themselves to benefit from local sales driven by rising standards of living. As Figure 4.1 explains, United Technologies is one of those companies: As the overall GDP of the emerging markets quintuples from $8 trillion to $40 trillion, its people will be buying everything from buildings with elevators to homes with air conditioning. United Technologies wants to ensure that some of those purchases include its Otis elevators and Carrier air conditioners.

In South America, the biggest Internet market is Brazil. The number of Internet subscribers tripled during the first three years of the 21st century to more than 6 million. Many are lured online by offers of free connections that banks are providing their customers. With the huge potential market in Argentina, Brazil, and other South American countries, not even competition as fierce as free services are discouraging companies that want to compete by selling paid subscriptions for Internet access. The leading contenders are a Brazilian service called Universo Online (UOL) and a Spanish company called Terra Networks. They are competing directly with the banks by offering free services, to be paid for through advertising sales. In addition, America Online has partnered with Venezuela's Cisneros Group to provide a paid-subscription service called AOL Latin America. Although UOL has the initial edge, not only in terms of the biggest subscriber base but also in the most content created in Portuguese, Brazil's official language, AOL believes its Brazilian joint venture will eventually enjoy the premium slice of this huge market.[13]

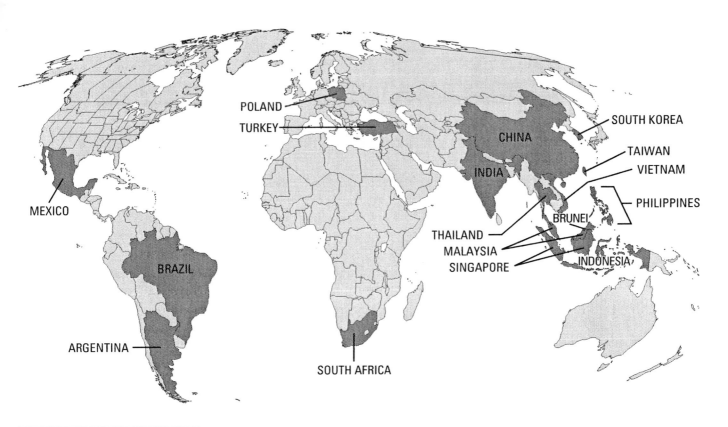

FIGURE 4.2
Major Emerging Markets for the 21st Century

Major World Markets

The major trading partners of U.S. firms include the country's northern and southern neighbors, Canada and Mexico. Other important global partners include Japan, China, Germany, and the United Kingdom. It is not a coincidence that these countries represent the world's major market regions: North America, Western Europe, the Pacific Rim, and Latin America. These regions encompass not only Germany, the United Kingdom, and Japan but also such emerging markets as India, Malaysia, and Vietnam. As Figure 4.2 shows, many of the world's most attractive emerging markets are located in Latin America and around the Pacific Rim.

North America   With a combined population of over 400 million and a total GDP of $9.2 trillion, North America represents one of the world's most attractive markets. The U.S.—the single largest market in the world and the most stable economy—dominates North America's business environment. Although less than 1 person in 20 lives in the U.S., the country's $8 trillion GDP represents more than one-fourth of total world output.[14] Major U.S.-based corporations like Citicorp, General Electric, and Motorola maintain sizable investments both around the world and in North America.

Canada, our neighbor to the north, is far less densely populated but has achieved a similar level of economic development. Two-thirds of Canada's GDP is generated in the services sector, and three of every four Canadian workers are engaged in service occupations. The country's per capita GDP places Canada near the top ten nations in terms of its people's spending power. Canada's economy is fueled by trade with the U.S. Exports to the U.S. are equivalent to about one-third of Canada's GDP. In addition, three-quarters of the nation's imports come from the United States. U.S. business is also attracted by Canada's human resources. Many of Canada's professionals have moved to the U.S., lured by the availability of jobs with higher pay and lower tax rates.[15]

South of the border, Mexico is moving quickly from developing-nation to industrial-nation status, thanks largely to the North American Free Trade Agreement, discussed later in this chapter. Stretching 2,100 miles from the Pacific Ocean to the Gulf of Mexico, the U.S.-Mexican border is home to 1,500 **maquiladoras,** foreign-owned businesses that manufacture products for export from this duty-free zone. About 450,000 Mexicans work in *maquiladoras* serving the clothing and automotive industries. Another 300,000 assemble electronics products, and 50,000 more are engaged in service *maquiladoras*—handling tasks ranging from laundering uniforms to answering phones and processing data.

These job creations are drawing Mexicans to towns near the U.S. border, and these towns are growing into cities. Higher incomes and greater urbanization are changing the Mexican culture and landscape. Greater buying power—and immigrant managers—are providing a market for car rental offices, fast-food restaurants, hotels, and other businesses.

Western Europe   Together, the nations of Western Europe, particularly Germany, the United Kingdom, France, and Italy, make up a sophisticated and powerful industrial region with a combined GDP three-fourths as large as that of the U.S. Solidifying the importance of this market is the European Union (EU), a 15-nation economic community discussed later in the chapter. International companies with headquarters in this region include Royal Dutch Shell, Nestlé, DaimlerChrysler, and Glaxo Wellcome. Significant investments from around the world are flowing into European nations, as foreign companies locate manufacturing and distribution facilities across the continent. Over half of U.S. investments in foreign companies flow to Europe.[16]

Ireland is Europe's fastest-growing economy. With a combination of tax cuts and investments in education, the country has made itself attractive to over 500 high-tech foreign firms, including Dell, Pfizer, and Microsoft. Intel's largest non-U.S. facility is a wafer fabrication plant west of Dublin that turns out Pentium III microchips. Ireland never prospered in the industrial age; it has moved straight from an agricultural to an information economy. Ireland is currently Europe's leading exporter of software, with an economy so strong that the nation is not just an exporter of high-tech products—it is an importer of human resources.[17]

The Pacific Rim   The major nations of the large and growing region known as the Pacific Rim are Australia, China (including Hong Kong), Indonesia, Japan, Malaysia, the Philippines, Singapore, South Korea, and Taiwan. The industries that fuel Asian economies—electronics, automobiles, and banking—are strong competitors to U.S. firms. In addition, Asia's technology-driven markets, rapid urbanization, and its growing middle class make this region a significant market for U.S. goods and services. See the "Clicks and Mortar" box for a description of how one Japanese entrepreneur is using the Internet to increase his company's competitiveness.

Leading the new cycle of growth are Korea, China, Malaysia, Taiwan, Singapore, and Hong Kong. China, whose 1.2 billion inhabitants have traditionally been known as a leading source of labor in manufacturing low-priced goods like toy dolls and clothing, is today challenging both the U.S. and Japan with its capabilities for low-cost production of high-tech products. Its leading exports to the U.S. are electrical machinery, toys and sports equipment, footwear, other machinery, and furniture and bedding.[18] Foreign companies also have operations in China. Intel has a production facility in Shanghai and is planning a research center for Beijing.[19]

China's biggest investor is a tiny seaport on the country's southern edge. Hong Kong was a British colony until 1997, when it rejoined the People's Republic of China. Under British rule, the government barely involved itself in business affairs, and as a result, Hong Kong developed a booming entrepreneurial economy. The Chinese government promised to grant Hong Kong a high degree of autonomy as a capitalist economy for 50 years. The Hong Kong government has kept taxes and

7-Eleven Gives Convenience Stores a New Meaning

Background. Imagine cruising into your local 7-Eleven store for your favorite flavor Slurpee and a bag of chips. While sipping your drink, you can browse through a few Web sites at the Internet terminal and maybe order a book and a CD. You decide you need some cash, so you click into the ATM and retrieve a few bucks. A week later, you come back to the 7-Eleven to pick up the book and CD you ordered. Where is this happening, you say?

What Happened? This scenario has been taking place for several years in Japan, a country that has suffered from an economic slowdown as well sluggish entry into e-commerce. Toshifumi Suzuki, CEO of 7-Eleven Japan, which owns 72 percent of all 7-Elevens in the U.S., thinks the idea makes perfect sense. More importantly, so do Japanese consumers.

The Response. Ninety-three percent of Japanese consumers who order books from the Web site Esbooks while in a 7-Eleven store opt to pick up their orders at the store instead of having them delivered at home. "The Japanese would rather pick up their goods and pay for them at a *konbini* [convenience store]," says Morihiko Ida, head of equities research at Century Securities. "So that could boost sales." Suzuki isn't stopping there. He plans to install ATMs at his 8,200 Japanese stores—among the first ATMs in Japan—which will allow 24-hour banking as well as payment for online purchases.

It's not surprising that Suzuki is bringing his own version of e-commerce to the United States. Starting with 250 stores in Texas, in-store computers will offer bill payment, payroll check cashing, money wiring, and ticket purchasing for entertainment events as well as travel. Next, Suzuki wants to convince online retailers to deliver products to the 7-Eleven distribution network so consumers can pick up their orders at the nearest store. Right now, the goods will have to be smaller items because 7-Eleven stores are small. And 7-Eleven employees will have to be trained to handle the systems. But they already restock empty shelves via handheld computer terminals. "Nobody else in the U.S. has that," notes James Keys, CEO of 7-Eleven U.S.

Today and Counting. So far, 7-Eleven Japan has managed to maintain steady growth in a sagging economy as well as attract once-reticent Japanese consumers to the Internet for their shopping. Who would have guessed that the maker of something as simple as a Slurpee might introduce e-commerce to a nation?

QUESTIONS FOR CRITICAL THINKING
1. Do you think Suzuki's ideas would be successful in the European Union? Why or why not?
2. As the Japanese economy recovers, how might 7-Eleven be affected?

Sources: Irene M. Kunii, "From Convenience Store to Online Behemoth?" *Business Week*, April 10, 2000, p. 64; Benjamin Fulford, "I Got It @ 7-Eleven," *Forbes*, April 3, 2000, pp. 53–54; Jim Rohwer, "Japan Goes Web Crazy," *Fortune*, February 7, 2000, pp. 115–118.

---

regulation at low levels compared with the rest of Asia, but it has increased government participation in the economy: Without soliciting bids, the government recently awarded land to a private developer to create facilities for high-tech businesses.[20]

Latin America During the 1990s, Latin American countries reduced government spending and encouraged investment. Privatization of port facilities, railways, telecommunications, mining, and energy attracted new industry. As a result, foreign investment in Latin America, particularly Brazil and Argentina, has grown, along with the goods and services available to consumers. Much of that investment came from the U.S. and Europe.[21]

However, cuts in government spending during the early years of this decade have taken their toll on people who relied on government services and jobs. Of the world's regions, Latin America has the largest gap between the incomes of the rich and poor.[22] Such trends have increased political instability, and investors have avoided such troubled countries as Colombia and Venezuela.

Despite such problems, Latin America is a big market for high-technology products. In particular, the Internet is providing new opportunities for Latin American businesses as Internet usage claims a growing share of the population.

With many Latin Americans living in poverty, governments and other agencies are trying to help their citizens gain access to Internet opportunities. In Peru, a nonprofit organization called the Peruvian Science Network (RCP) has helped to establish hundreds of public Internet centers and runs seminars to teach people about Internet businesses. @Altec Cyber Park, Latin America's first Internet host, stores hundreds of Web sites on its computer servers, so Latin Americans can link to local sites faster and at lower cost.

Besides providing the hardware and networks, businesses are finding opportunities in providing Internet-related services. Terra, shown in Figure 4.3, offers Web portals to Spanish-speaking customers in Spain and the U.S. as well as Latin America.

Absolute and Comparative Advantage

Few countries can produce all the goods and services their people need. For centuries, trading has been the way that countries can meet the demand. If a country can focus on producing what it does best, it can export surplus domestic output and buy foreign products that it lacks or cannot efficiently produce. The potential for foreign sales of a particular good or service depends largely on whether the country has an absolute advantage or comparative advantage.

A country has an *absolute advantage* in making a product for which it can maintain a monopoly or that it can produce at a lower cost than any competitor. For centuries, China enjoyed an absolute advantage in silk production. This luxurious fabric was woven from fibers recovered from silkworm cocoons, making it a prized raw material in high-quality clothing. Demand among Europeans for silk led to establishment of the famous *silk road*, a 5,000-mile link between Rome and the ancient Chinese capital city of Xian.

Absolute advantages are rare these days. But some countries manage to approximate absolute advantages in some products. Because many oil deposits are in the Middle East, these countries have a degree of control over oil supplies, which they sometimes manipulate to affect their income. Climate differences can give some nations or regions an advantage in growing certain plants. A rare, expensive herb called wasabi grows in valleys along Japan's mountain rivers. The Japanese use wasabi to make a hot green condiment for sushi. Because the absolute advantage of wasabi's rarity makes real wasabi so expensive, the version sold in most U.S. stores is a bland imitation concocted from horseradish and green food coloring. However, an American entrepreneur named Roy Carver III recently determined that his company, Pacific Farms, can grow the plant along Oregon's coast, where the microclimate resembles that of wasabi's natural habitat.[23]

A nation can develop a *comparative advantage* in a product if it can supply it more efficiently and at a lower price than it can supply other goods, compared with the outputs of other countries. China has long held a comparative advantage in producing toys and clothing due to very low labor costs. On the other hand, Japan has maintained a comparative advantage in producing electronics by preserving efficiency and technological expertise. By ensuring that its people are well educated, a nation can also develop a comparative advantage in providing skilled human resources.

Canon has recently adopted a strategy for research and development based on various nations' comparative advantage in engineering knowledge. Rather than basing all the company's research at its Tokyo headquarters, the company is planning to operate regional headquarters in Europe and the Americas, each focused on a different area of expertise. Engineers at Canon Research America in Palo Alto, California, concentrate on digital and networking technology. Engineers at Canon Research Center France focus on telecommunications. According to Canon's president, Fujio Mitarai, this is a departure from the past practice of making overseas research a

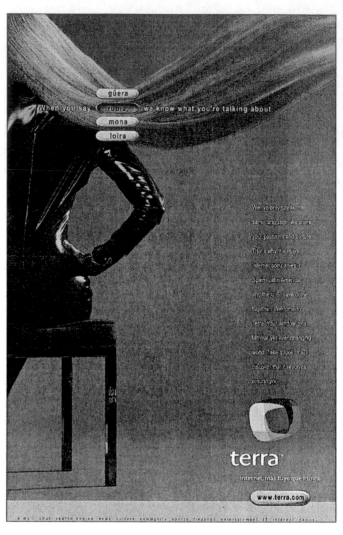

FIGURE 4.3
Terra: Web Portals for Latin America, Spain, and the United States

simple extension of Japanese activities: "From now on, we want to give birth to new value abroad. We want to make the best of the different kinds of expertise available in different countries."[24]

MEASURING TRADE BETWEEN NATIONS

Clearly, engaging in international trade provides tremendous competitive advantages to both the countries and individual companies involved. Any attempt to measure global business activity requires an understanding of the concepts of balance of trade and balance of payments. Another important factor is currency exchange rates for each country.

A nation's **balance of trade** is the difference between its exports and imports. If a country exports more than it imports, it achieves a positive balance of trade, called a *trade surplus*. If it imports more than it exports, it produces a negative balance of trade, called a *trade deficit*. The United States has run a trade deficit every year since 1976. Despite being the world's top exporter, the U.S. economy has an even greater appetite for foreign-made goods. At the beginning of the 21st century, the trade deficit set an all-time record high of $265 billion.[25]

As Figure 4.4 shows, U.S. exports have been growing, but imports have been growing faster. Because imports exceed exports, the trade balance shown in the shaded area is a deficit. This year, that deficit will surpass $1 trillion. Trade deficits with two countries—China and Japan—account for over half of this deficit.

A nation's balance of trade plays a central role in determining its **balance of payments**—the overall flow of money into or out of a country. Other factors also affect the balance of payments, including overseas loans and borrowing, international investments, profits from such investments, and foreign aid payments. Figure 4.5 illustrates the components of a country's balance of payments. To calculate a nation's balance of payments, subtract the monetary outflows from the monetary inflows. A

FIGURE 4.4
U.S. International Trade in Goods and Services

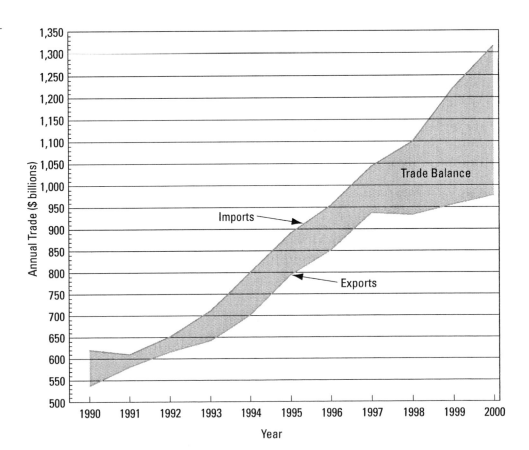

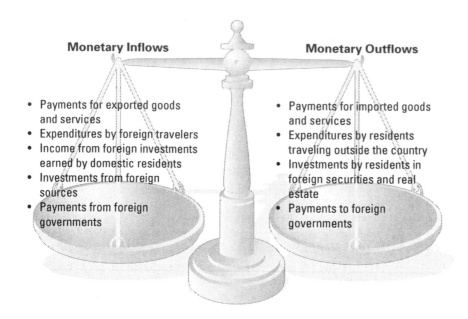

FIGURE 4.5
Components of the Balance of Payments

Monetary Inflows

- Payments for exported goods and services
- Expenditures by foreign travelers
- Income from foreign investments earned by domestic residents
- Investments from foreign sources
- Payments from foreign governments

Monetary Outflows

- Payments for imported goods and services
- Expenditures by residents traveling outside the country
- Investments by residents in foreign securities and real estate
- Payments to foreign governments

positive balance of payments, or a *balance of payments surplus*, means more money has moved into a country than out of it. A negative balance of payments, or *balance of payments deficit*, means more money has gone out of the country than enters it.

Major U.S. Exports and Imports

The United States, with combined exports and imports of over $2 trillion, leads the world in the international trade of goods and services. As listed in Table 4.2, the leading categories of goods exchanged by U.S. exporters and importers range from crops, including exports of wheat and soybeans and imports of coffee, to computers and electrical machinery. Strong U.S. demand for imported goods is partly a reflection of the nation's prosperity and diversity. In November 1999, for only the second time in the 20th century, the U.S. recorded a trade deficit in food and beverages. This deficit arose from the willingness of U.S. consumers to pay for imported fish, bananas, and coffee, as well as such treats as caviar and out-of-season fruits like strawberries in November or apples in May.[26]

Although the U.S. imports more goods than it exports, the opposite is true for services. U.S. exporters sell more than $270 billion in services annually. Much of that money comes from travel and tourism—money spent by foreign nationals visiting the United States. U.S. service exports also include business and technical services such as engineering, financial services, computing, legal services, and entertainment. Other services involve technologies developed by U.S. firms that earn royalties and licensing fees from users abroad. Many service exporters are well-known companies, including American Express, American Airlines, America Online, AT&T, Citibank, Walt Disney, Allstate Insurance, and Federal Express, as well as retailers such as Foot Locker, The Gap, Office Depot, Toys 'R' Us, and Costco.

As noted earlier in the chapter, businesses in many foreign countries want the expertise of U.S. financial and business professionals. In addition, entertainment is a major growth area for U.S. service exports. Disney, which already operates theme parks in France and Japan, is preparing to build a theme park on Hong Kong's Lantau Island. The company plans to invest $318 million to own a 43 percent share of the new Magic Kingdom plus three hotels. In addition, Disney will earn fees for managing the theme park, scheduled to open in 2005.[27]

To compete in a diverse global economy characterized by stiff competition for human talent, U.S. companies expanding abroad frequently require services in

BUSINESS DIRECTORY

➤ **balance of trade** *difference between a nation's exports and imports.*

➤ **balance of payments** *difference in money flows into or out of a country.*

Table 4.2 Top Ten U.S. Exports and Imports

Exports		Imports	
Electrical machinery	$66 billion	Vehicles	$119 billion
Vehicles	$54 billion	Computers and office equipment	$77 billion
Agricultural products	$51 billion	Electrical machinery	$54 billion
Computers and office equipment	$41 billion	Clothing	$54 billion
Airplanes	$35 billion	Televisions, VCRs, and other consumer electronics	$42 billion
General industrial machinery	$30 billion	Crude oil	$37 billion
Power-generating machinery	$29 billion	Agricultural products	$36 billion
Specialized industrial machinery	$27 billion	General industrial machinery	$29 billion
Scientific instruments	$24 billion	Power-generating machinery	$28 billion
Televisions, VCRs, and other consumer electronics	$23 billion	Specialized industrial machinery	$23 billion

these markets. When El Sitio USA set up a network of Spanish-language Web sites, it hired a Brazilian agency, Denison, Sao Paulo, to develop its advertising campaign. The bilingual campaign features baseball hero Sammy Sosa with the slogan, "To lugar en Internet," which means "your home on the Internet."[28]

With annual imports exceeding $1 trillion, the U.S. is by far the world's leading importer. American tastes for foreign-made goods, which show up as huge trade deficits with the consumer-goods exporting nations of China and Japan, also extend to European products. Last year, the 15 EU countries shipped more than $200 billion of merchandise, including Audi cars, Roquefort cheese, and high-tech machinery, to U.S. buyers, which is more than a 10 percent increase over the previous year.[29]

Exchange Rates

A nation's **exchange rate** is the rate at which its currency can be exchanged for the currencies of other nations. Each currency's exchange rate is usually quoted in terms of another currency, such as the number of Mexican pesos needed to purchase one U.S. dollar. Table 4.3 compares the values of several currencies against the U.S. dollar. Besides exchange rates for the currencies of various nations, the table shows the exchange rate for the euro, the currency of the EU. European consumers and businesses can use the euro to pay bills by check, credit card, or bank transfer. Euro coins and notes are also used in most EU-member countries.

Currency values fluctuate, or "float," depending on the supply and demand for each currency in the international market. In this system of *floating exchange rates*, currency traders create a market for the world's currencies based on each country's relative trade and investment prospects. In theory, this market permits exchange rates to vary freely according to supply and demand. In practice, exchange rates do not float in total freedom. National governments often intervene in the currency markets to adjust the exchange rates of their own currencies. In recent years, the euro has fluctuated greatly in value, from a high of $1.19 to a low of about $.80.[30]

Nations influence exchange rates in other ways as well. They may form currency blocs by linking their exchange rates to each other. Many governments practice protectionist policies that seek to guard their economies against trade imbalances. For instance, national governments sometimes take deliberate action to devalue their currencies as a way to increase exports and stimulate foreign investment. **Devaluation** describes a fall in a currency's value relative to other currencies or to a fixed

Table 4.3 Foreign Exchange Rates for Selected Currencies

	Country	Currency Unit	2001 Exchange Rate (per U.S. dollar)
	Canada	Dollar	1.5
	China	Renminbi	8.3
	European Union	Euro	1.1
	France	Franc	6.9
	Germany	Mark	2.1
	India	Rupee	45.9
	Italy	Lira	2,058.5
	Japan	Yen	118.1
	Mexico	Peso	9.8
	South Korea	Won	1,283.5
	Switzerland	Franc	1.6
	Thailand	Baht	42.6
	United Kingdom	Pound	0.7

standard. In Brazil, a recent currency devaluation made investing in that country relatively cheap, so the devaluation was followed by a flood of foreign investment. Pillsbury bought Brazil's Brisco, which makes a local staple, *pao de queijo*, a cheese bread formed into rolls and served with morning coffee. Other foreign companies invested in Brazil's construction, tourism, banking, communications, and other industries.[31] In Germany, few people complained about the falling value of the euro. Manufacturing fuels the nation's economy, with exports making up one-fourth of its GDP. At a devalued euro, manufacturing equipment priced in euros looks like a good deal to customers with dollars or yen to exchange.[32]

Exchange rate changes can quickly create—or wipe out—a competitive advantage, so they are important factors in decisions about whether to invest abroad. When the euro's value plunged relative to the U.S. dollar, American exports to Europe brought home fewer dollars at the new exchange rate. In Europe, the declining value of the euro meant that a price of 10 euros was not worth as much, so companies were pressured to raise prices, potentially fueling inflation. At the same time, the falling euro made European vacations more affordable for American tourists, because their dollars were worth more relative to the euro. In contrast, European travelers found that their euros bought less in America at the new exchange rate.

For an individual business, the impact of the euro's devaluation depends on where that business buys its materials and where it sells its products. Tellabs generates one-fifth of its sales in Europe, so the falling euro cut into its sales. However, the company also manufactures in Europe, so the falling euro also reduced the cost of manufacturing, measured in dollars. Tellabs predicted that the decline of the euro would have no effect on company profits. Other companies with significant

BUSINESS DIRECTORY

➤ **exchange rate** *value of one nation's currency relative to the currencies of other countries.*

sales in Europe, including McDonald's and Wm. Wrigley Jr., complained that the declining euro was reducing their revenues.[33]

Currencies that owners can easily convert into other currencies are called *hard* currencies. Examples include the euro, the U.S. dollar, and the Japanese yen. The Russian ruble and many central European currencies are considered *soft* currencies, because they cannot be readily converted. Exporters trading with these countries often prefer to barter, accepting payment in oil, timber, or other commodities that they can resell for hard-currency payments.

BARRIERS TO INTERNATIONAL TRADE

All businesses encounter barriers in their operations, whether they sell only to local customers or trade in international markets. Countries such as Australia, Germany, and New Zealand regulate the hours and days retailers may be open. Germany recently forced Wal-Mart to raise its prices to be more in line with local competitors. The differences and difficulties are multiplied many times over for businesses with international operations. Besides complying with a variety of laws and exchanging currencies, international companies may also have to reformulate their products to accommodate different tastes in new locations. Frito-Lay exports cheeseless Chee-tos to Asia, and Domino's Pizza offers pickled ginger pizzas at its Indian fast-food restaurants.

In addition to social and cultural differences, companies engaged in international business also face economic barriers as well as legal and political ones. Some of the hurdles shown in Figure 4.6 are easily breached, but others require major changes in a company's business strategy. To successfully compete in global markets, companies and their managers must understand not only how these barriers affect international trade but also how to overcome them.

Social and Cultural Differences

The social and cultural differences among nations range from language and customs to educational background and religious holidays. Understanding and respecting these differences are critical in the process leading to international business success. Businesspeople with knowledge of host countries' cultures, languages, social values, and religious attitudes and practices are well equipped for the marketplace and the negotiating table. Acute sensitivity to such elements as local attitudes, forms of address and expectations regarding dress, body language, and timeliness also help them to win customers and achieve their business objectives. Without this knowledge, companies may discover that their goods and services will not appeal to customers in foreign countries.

Language English may be considered the main language of business, but for much of the world, it is not the primary language. More people speak Mandarin Chinese and Spanish than English. English is the third most spoken language in the world, followed by Bengali, Hindi, Portuguese, Russian, Japanese, and German.[34] It is not

FIGURE 4.6
Barriers to International Trade

uncommon for students for whom English is not their first language to spend eight years of elementary and high school in English language classes. Understanding a business colleague's primary language may prove to be the difference between closing an international business transaction and losing the sale to someone else. Company representatives operating in foreign markets must not only choose correct and appropriate words but also translate words correctly to convey the intended meanings. Firms may also need to rename products or rewrite slogans for foreign markets.

Potential communication barriers include more than mistranslation. Companies may present messages through inappropriate media, overlook local customs and regulations, or ignore differences in taste. This sensitivity is especially critical in cyberspace. Web site developers must be aware that visitors to a site may come from anywhere in the world. Some icons that seem friendly to U.S. Internet users may shock people from other countries. A person making a high-five hand gesture would be insulting to people in Greece; ditto the index finger making a circle with the thumb in Brazil and a two-fingered peace sign with the back of the hand facing out in Great Britain. Even colors can pose problems. In the Middle East, people view green as a sacred color, so a green background on a Web page would be inappropriate there.[35]

Gift-giving traditions employ the language of symbolism. In China, for example, it is customary to give gifts at the lunar new year, but some types of gifts carry inappropriate meanings. For example, giving a clock is a bad idea, since the Chinese consider a clock to be a symbol of death.[36]

Values and Religious Attitudes   Even though today's world is shrinking in many ways, people in different countries do not necessarily share the same values or religious attitudes. Marked differences remain in workers' attitudes between traditionally capitalist countries and those adopting new capitalist systems and even among traditionally capitalist countries.

U.S. society places a higher value on business efficiency and low unemployment than European society, where employee benefits are more valued. The U.S. government does not regulate vacation time, and employees typically receive no paid vacation during their first year of employment, then two weeks' vacation, eventually working up to three or four weeks if they stay with the same employer for many years. In contrast, the EU mandates a minimum paid vacation of four weeks per year, and most Europeans get five or six weeks. Before Berlin bank employee Britta Niehoff left for a three-week bicycling trip, she told a newspaper reporter, "I am not like the Americans who believe the world would collapse if they were away from their workplace for more than two weeks. I work really hard, and for me real relaxation only starts after two weeks."[37] In these countries, a U.S. company that opens a manufacturing plant would not be able to hire any local employees without offering vacations in line with that nation's business practices.

U.S. culture values national unity with tolerance of regional differences. The U.S. is viewed as a national market with a single economy. European countries that are part of the 15-member EU are trying to create a similar marketplace. However, many resist the idea of being European citizens first and British, Danish, or Dutch citizens second. British consumers differ from Italians in important ways, and U.S. companies that fail to recognize this variation will run into problems with brand acceptance.

Religion plays an important role in every society, so businesspeople also must cultivate sensitivity to the dominant religions in countries where they operate. Understanding religious cycles and the timing of major holidays can help prevent embarrassing moments when scheduling meetings, trade shows, conferences, or events such as the dedication of a new manufacturing plant. People doing business in Saudi Arabia must take into account Islam's month-long observance of Ramadan, when work ends at noon. Friday is the Muslim Sabbath, so the Saudi workweek runs from Saturday through Thursday. Furthermore, Muslims abstain from alcohol and consider pork unclean, so gifts of pigskin or liquor would be offensive.

"Here, at our Multilingual Center, we put a strong accent on communications.

"As BellSouth service representatives, we answer billing and services questions from our non-English-speaking customers.

"We're from all over the world, but we all share the same goal—to go above and beyond to serve our customers' needs.

"And great things happen when we work together. We come up with new ideas...like our Spanish language telephone bill for our customers in Florida."

"We assist our customers in eight different languages."

Alexandra Angrand
Multilingual Center

BellSouth has many talented and dedicated people like Alexandra. We think they provide real service to our customers by helping them in new and creative ways.

BELLSOUTH
Nobody knows a neighbor like a neighbor.

http://www.bellsouth.com

BellSouth, a data, voice, and video communications company serving the southeastern states of the U.S., recognizes the increased diversity of its marketplace. This diversity has been increased by substantial immigration during the past 40 years. BellSouth has responded to the needs of its customers by offering assistance in eight different languages. The company even offers telephone bills in Spanish for the large number of Spanish-speaking households in Florida.

Economic Differences

Business opportunities are flourishing in densely populated countries such as China and India, as local consumers eagerly buy Western products. Although such prospects might tempt American firms, managers must first consider the economic factors involved in doing business in these markets. A country's size, per capita income, and stage of economic development are among the economic factors to consider when evaluating it as a candidate for an international business venture.

Infrastructure Along with other economic measures, businesses should consider a country's infrastructure. **Infrastructure** refers to basic systems of communication (television, radio, print media, telecommunications), transportation (roads and highways, railroads, airports), and energy facilities (power plants, gas and electric utilities). With widespread access to personal computers (PCs), the United States led the way in the use of Internet technology. However, many consumers in Western Europe, Japan, and Hong Kong own cellular phones. In Europe the rate of mobile-phone ownership exceeds that of the U.S. The availability of this technology makes these countries fertile soil for Internet businesses that adapt to wireless communication. Consumers in Hong Kong can use cell phones to place bids at the Cat-Street.com auction site. Mobile-phone subscribers in Finland can buy candy and soft drinks from vending machines or pay for car washes by pressing buttons on their phones.[38] Also, although North America has the greatest percentage of small businesses on the Internet, a larger share of German small businesses use the Internet to make purchases, and a larger share of British small businesses sell products online.[39]

Financial systems also provide a type of infrastructure for businesses. In the United States, buyers have widespread access to checks, credit cards, and debit cards, as well as electronic systems for processing these forms of payment. In many African countries, such as Ethiopia, no local business accepts credit cards, so travelers to the capital city Addis Ababa are warned to bring plenty of cash and traveler's checks. Lack of easy-to-use and affordable payment systems has slowed Internet commerce in Japan. Companies that issue credit cards discourage merchants with their terms—high fees for processing the cards, as well as burdensome paperwork and slow payment. When Echigo Meimon Shukai went online, the Japanese *sake* company arranged to accept payment by credit card. Credit card companies charged the firm 4 percent of each sale as a fee for processing payments, but they left plenty of work to Echigo. The company must add up its sales and fax the amounts to the credit-card companies. After that, Echigo must wait four weeks for payment. Not only that, but credit cards are expensive for Japanese consumers, so many of them don't even bother to get a card. They prefer to wire payments from a convenience store or post office. With these limits on the convenience of credit cards, it is no wonder that Japanese online consumers spend only 6 percent of the amount spent by U.S. online consumers.[40]

Currency Conversion and Shifts Despite growing similarities in infrastructure, businesses crossing national borders encounter basic economic differences: national currencies. Although many countries buy and sell in U.S. dollars, firms may trade in the local currency—the Mexican peso, Indonesian rupee, Swiss franc, Japanese yen, and English pound.

Foreign currency fluctuations may present added problems for global businesses. As explained earlier in the chapter, the values of the world's major currencies fluctuate in relation to each other. Rapid and unexpected currency shifts can make pricing in local currencies difficult. Shifts in exchange rates can also influence the attractiveness of various business decisions. A devalued currency may make a nation less desirable as an export destination, because of reduced demand in that market. However, devaluation can make the nation desirable as an investment opportunity, because investments there will be a bargain in terms of the investor's currency.

Political and Legal Differences

Similar to social, cultural, and economic differences, legal and political differences in host countries can pose barriers to international trade. China limits the use of encryption on Web sites and restricts Internet companies that want to raise money on international stock exchanges. Mexico's Federal Competition Commission has strengthened enforcement of that country's antitrust laws. Among other decisions, it prevented The Coca-Cola Company from acquiring Cadbury Schweppes brands in Mexico, on the grounds that the acquisition would give the company a 70 percent share of the Mexican soft-drink market.[41] To compete in today's world marketplace, managers involved in international business must be well versed in legislation that affects their industries.

Some countries impose general trade restrictions. Others have established detailed rules that regulate how foreign companies can operate. The one consistency among all countries is the striking lack of consistent laws and regulations governing the conduct of business.

Political Climate   An important factor in any international business investment is the stability of the political climate. The political structures of many nations promote stability similar to that in the U.S. Other nations, such as Indonesia, Congo, and Bosnia, feature quite different—and frequently changing—structures. Host nations often pass laws designed to protect their own interests, often at the expense of foreign businesses.

In recent years, the political structures of Russia, Turkey, the former Yugoslavia, Hong Kong, and several central European countries (including the Czech Republic and Poland) have seen dramatic changes. Such political changes almost always bring changes in the legal environment. Hong Kong's new status as part of China is an example of an economy where political developments produced changes in the legal and cultural environments. Since the collapse of the Soviet Union, Russia has struggled to develop a new market structure and political processes. The current president, Vladimir V. Putin, has strengthened law enforcement to help legitimate businesses by cracking down on the organized-crime figures who have built business empires on a pattern of bribery and extortion.[42]

Legal Environment   When conducting business internationally, managers must be familiar with three dimensions of the legal environment: U.S. law, international regulations, and the laws of the countries where they plan to trade. Some laws protect the rights of foreign companies to compete in the United States. Others dictate actions allowed for U.S. companies doing business in foreign countries.

The *Foreign Corrupt Practices Act* forbids U.S. companies from bribing foreign officials, political candidates, or government representatives. This act prescribes fines and jail time for U.S. managers who are aware of illegal payoffs. Until recently, many countries, including France and Germany, not only accepted the practice of bribing foreign officials in countries where such practices were customary, but they allowed tax deductions for these expenses. In 1999, representatives of the U.S., France, Germany, and 31 other countries signed the Organization for Economic

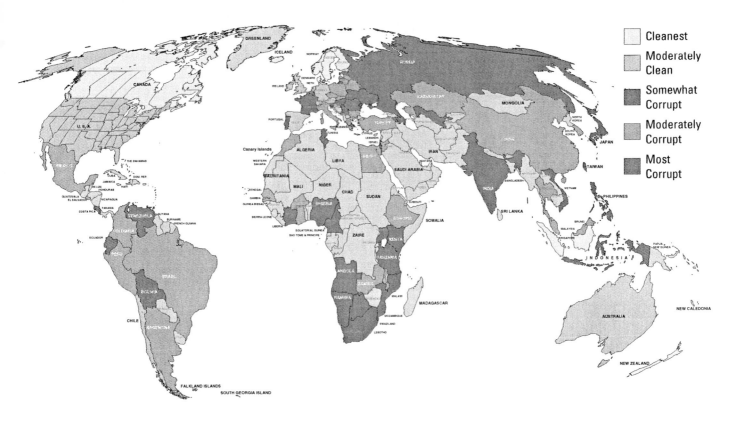

	Cleanest
	Moderately Clean
	Somewhat Corrupt
	Moderately Corrupt
	Most Corrupt

FIGURE 4.7
Corruption in Business and Government

Cooperation and Development Anti-Bribery Convention. This international agreement makes offering or paying bribes a criminal offense and ends the deductibility of bribes.[43]

Still, corruption continues to be an international problem. Its pervasiveness, combined with U.S. prohibitions, creates a difficult obstacle for Americans who want to do business in many foreign countries. Chinese pay *huilu,* and Russians rely on *vzyatka.* In the Middle East, palms are greased with *baksheesh.* Figure 4.7 compares 53 countries based on surveys of perceived corruption. This Corruption Perceptions Index is computed by Transparency International, a Berlin-based international organization that rates the degree of corruption in 90 countries observed by business-people and the general public.[44]

The growth of online business with the unfolding information age has introduced new elements to the legal climate of international business. Ideas, patents, brand names, trademarks, copyrights, and other intellectual property are difficult to police, given the availability of information on the Internet. However, some countries are adopting laws to protect information obtained by electronic contacts. Malaysia imposes stiff fines and long jail terms on those convicted of illegally accessing computers and using information that passes through them.

International Regulations   To regulate international commerce, the United States and many other countries have ratified treaties and signed agreements that dictate the conduct of international business and protect some of its activities. The U.S. has entered into many *friendship, commerce, and navigation* treaties with other nations. Such treaties address many aspects of international business relations, including the right to conduct business in the treaty partner's domestic market. Other international business agreements involve product standards, patents, trademarks, reciprocal tax policies, export controls, international air travel, and international communications.

In 2000, Congress granted China full trade relations with the U.S. China agreed to lower trade barriers, including subsidies that held down the prices of food exports, restrictions on where foreign law firms can open offices, and taxes charged on imported goods. China also promised to halve these taxes, called *tariffs*, over the course of five years. The United States, in exchange, granted China equal access to U.S. markets enjoyed by most other countries.[45]

Many types of regulations affect the actions of managers doing business in international markets. Not only must worldwide producers and marketers maintain required minimum quality levels for all the countries in which they operate, but they must also comply with numerous specific local regulations. European countries impose hundreds of regulations affecting marketers. Britain prevents advertisers from encouraging children to engage in such unhealthy behavior as eating frequently throughout the day or replacing regular meals with candy and snack foods. Sweden also places limits on television and radio ads directed to children 12 years and under.[46] Germany and France allow publishers to set prices that retailers charge for their books. Because companies like Amazon.com adhere to the fixed prices, German customers looking for English-language books can get better prices by buying at the U.K. Web site, even with the extra shipping costs. German law prohibits most price discounts, so cheap last-minute air fares are illegal on German Web sites. Without the ability to lure flyers by offering special deals, few European airlines sell tickets online.[47]

A lack of international regulations or enforcement can generate its own set of problems. Software piracy offers an example. China is especially notorious for piracy. Illegally copied U.S. software as well as music and movies cost American firms billions of dollars in lost revenues. Others copy consumer goods ranging from shampoo to cigarettes. Joseph M. Johnson, president of Bestfoods Asia's Chinese operations, estimates that one-fourth of the Skippy peanut butter sold in China is actually counterfeited.

U.S. companies are alarmed about the lost sales and possible damage to their brands' reputation if consumers become disappointed or even sick after using inferior fakes. Anheuser-Busch encountered Chinese retailers stocking Budweiser beer before they had ever seen a company sales representative. The labels on the bottles looked legitimate, but a sip of the contents immediately gave away the fact that the beer was pirated. Trying to keep ahead of the Chinese pirates, the company started using labels on which special images appear only when the bottles are cold.

Types of Trade Restrictions

Trade restrictions such as taxes on imports and complicated administrative procedures create additional barriers to international business. They may limit consumer choices while increasing the costs of foreign-made products. Trade restrictions are also imposed to protect citizens' security, health, and jobs. A government may limit exports of strategic and defense-related goods to unfriendly countries to protect its security, ban imports of insecticide-contaminated farm products to protect health, and restrict imports to protect domestic jobs in the importing country.

Trade restrictions grow out of a country's legal structure, often in response to the political environment. Some restrictions are intended to punish or protest countries' political actions. The *Helms-Burton* Act, a controversial law enacted in 1996, imposes trade sanctions against Cuba and permits U.S. companies and citizens to sue foreign companies and their executives if they use assets expropriated from U.S. owners to do business in Cuba. It also denies U.S. visas to executives of firms facing lawsuits for violating the act.

Other restrictions are imposed to promote trade with certain countries. Still others protect countries from unfair competition. Table 4.4 summarizes major arguments for and against trade restrictions.

Regardless of the political reasons for trade restrictions, most take the form of tariffs. In addition to tariffs, governments impose a number of nontariff—or administrative—barriers. These include quotas, embargoes, and exchange controls.

Table 4.4   Arguments for and against Trade Restrictions

For	Against
Protect national defense and citizens' health	Raise prices for consumers
Protect new or weak industries	Restrict consumer choices
Protect against a practice called *dumping*, in which products are sold for less abroad than in the home market, competing unfairly with domestic goods	Cause retaliation by other countries, which limits export opportunities for businesses
Protect domestic jobs in the face of foreign competition	Result in loss of jobs from international business
Retaliate for another country's trade restrictions	Cause inefficient allocations of international resources

Tariffs   Tariffs are taxes, surcharges, or duties on foreign products. Governments assess two types of tariffs—revenue and protective tariffs—both of which make imports more expensive for domestic buyers. Revenue tariffs generate income for the government. Upon returning home, U.S. leisure travelers who bring back goods are taxed 10 percent of the amount in excess of $400. This duty goes directly to the U.S. Treasury. The sole purpose of a protective tariff is to raise the retail price of imported products to match or exceed the prices of similar products manufactured in the home country. In other words, protective tariffs seek to level the playing field for local competitors.

Of course, tariffs create a disadvantage to companies that want to export to the countries imposing the tariffs. In addition, governments do not always see eye to eye on the reasons behind protective tariffs. The EU recently banned U.S. beef treated with growth hormones, on the grounds of health concerns. The U.S. government disputed these concerns and retaliated by imposing 100 percent tariffs on such European products as Roquefort cheese, Danish ham, Italian tomatoes, and German chocolate. These measures, which harmed both the European producers of these goods and the U.S. retailers that specialize in imported foods, were designed not so much to protect U.S. cheese, ham, tomato, and chocolate producers but to help beef producers by persuading Europe to change its policy. None of the U.S. tariffs applied to products produced in Britain, which did not support the EU ban on beef imports.[48]

Nontariff Barriers   Nontariff, or administrative, trade barriers restrict imports in more subtle ways than tariffs. These measures may take such forms as quotas on imports, unnecessarily restrictive standards for imports, and export subsidies. Because many countries have recently substantially reduced tariffs or eliminated them entirely, they increasingly use nontariff barriers to boost exports and control flows of imported products.

Quotas limit the amounts of particular products that countries can import during specified time periods. Limits may be set as quantities, such as number of cars or bushels of wheat, or as values, such as dollars' worth of cigarettes. Governments regularly set quotas for agricultural products and sometimes for imported automobiles. The U.S. government has imposed about 1,000 quotas related to clothing imports from various countries. All of these quotas are scheduled to be lifted by 2005.

Quotas help to prevent **dumping**, a practice that developed during the 1970s. In one form of dumping, a company sells products abroad at prices below its cost of production. In another, a company exports a large quantity of a product at a lower price than the same product in the home market and drives down the price of the domestic product. Dumping benefits domestic consumers in the importing market, but it hurts domestic producers. It also allows companies to gain quick entry to foreign markets.

Charges of dumping are difficult to prove, but most countries have the authority to set quotas if they suspect it. In addition to establishing quotas, companies can protect themselves against dumping by requesting that their government impose an antidumping duty, thus offsetting the cost advantage of the foreign good.

More severe than a quota, an **embargo** imposes a total ban on importing a specified product or even a total halt to trading with a particular country. In addition to their punitive effects, embargoes can protect citizens' health, as was the intent of the European ban on beef from animals treated with hormones. Embargo durations can vary to accommodate changes in foreign policy. The U.S. government recently began to restore diplomatic relations with Iran and lifted its embargo on carpets, dried fruits, pistachios, and caviar imported from that country. However, the United States maintained an embargo on Iran's biggest export, oil. Pistachios represent Iran's third-largest export, but the United States may not resume its place as a major buyer of the nuts. Since the first sack of pistachio seeds was sent from Iran to California, the state has developed its own pistachio crop. California growers say they still have an advantage because of high duties imposed on imported pistachios during the 1980s when Iranian companies were accused of dumping the nuts on the U.S. market. U.S. growers also insist they have developed a superior product in the meantime.[49]

Another form of administrative trade restriction involves **exchange controls**. Imposed through a central bank or government agency, exchange controls affect both exporters and importers. Firms that gain foreign currencies through exporting are required to sell them to the central bank or another agency. Importers must buy foreign currencies to pay for their purchases from the same agency. The exchange control authority can then allocate, expand, or restrict foreign exchange to satisfy national policy goals.

REDUCING BARRIERS TO INTERNATIONAL TRADE

Although tariffs and administrative barriers still restrict trade, overall the world is moving toward free trade. Several types of organizations ease barriers to international trade, including groups that monitor trade policies and practices and institutions that offer monetary assistance. Another type of federation designed to ease trade barriers is the multinational economic community, such as the EU. This section looks at the roles these organizations play.

Organizations Promoting International Trade

For the 50 years of its existence, the **General Agreement on Tariffs and Trade (GATT)**, an international trade accord, sponsored a series of negotiations, called *rounds*, that substantially reduced worldwide tariffs and other barriers. Major industrialized nations founded the multinational organization in 1947 to work toward reducing tariffs and relaxing import quotas. The last set of negotiations (the Uruguay Round) cut average tariffs by one-third, in excess of $700 billion, reduced farm subsidies, and improved protection for copyright and patent holders. In addition, international trading rules now apply to various service industries, with specific details yet to be resolved. Finally, the new agreement established the World Trade Organization (WTO) to succeed GATT. This new organization includes representatives from 135 countries, and others have applied to join. In 2000, the U.S. agreed to support China's membership in the WTO.

World Trade Organization Since 1995, the WTO has monitored GATT agreements among the member nations, mediated disputes, and continued the effort to reduce trade barriers throughout the world. Unlike provisions in GATT, the WTO's decisions are binding on parties involved in disputes.

The WTO has grown more controversial in recent years as it issues decisions that have implications for working conditions and the environment in member nations. The United States lost a dispute in which Brazil and Venezuela said the U.S. government had set a higher standard for emissions from foreign gasoline than from domestic supplies. The WTO ruled that the U.S. standard must be the same for imports and domestic products, so standards were reduced for U.S. gasoline. Environmentalists were dismayed that the government's decision would lead to increased air pollution. Concerns have also been expressed that the WTO's focus on lowering trade barriers encourages businesses to keep costs down through practices that may increase pollution and human rights abuses. Particularly worrisome is the fact that the organization's member countries must agree on policies, and the 77 developing countries tend not to be eager to lose their low-cost advantage by enacting stricter labor and environmental laws. As M.G. Quibria of Manila's Asianic Development Bank points out, "There's an Asian consensus that human rights should not be linked to trade." Other critics fret that if well-funded U.S. giants like fast-food chains, entertainment companies, and Internet retailers operate free of constraints on their entry into foreign markets, they will wipe out smaller foreign businesses serving the distinct tastes and practices of other countries' cultures.

Trade unions in developed nations complain that the WTO's support of free trade makes it easier to export jobs to low-wage countries. According to the U.S. Department of Commerce, about a million U.S. jobs are lost each year as a result of imports or movement of work to other countries. They are not always minimum-wage jobs either. General Electric's Aircraft Engines division runs a global engineering project employing 300 engineers in Brazil, India, Mexico, and Turkey. Hiring engineers in these developing nations helps General Electric lower costs. Although free trade can also contribute to economic growth, creating new jobs, all these concerns about WTO policy have led to protest demonstrations—sometimes violent—beginning with the WTO meeting in Seattle a few years ago.[50]

World Bank Shortly after the end of World War II, industrialized nations formed an organization to lend money to less-developed and developing countries. The **World Bank** primarily funds projects that build or expand nations' infrastructure such as transportation, education, and medical systems and facilities. The World Bank and other development banks provide the largest source of advice and assistance to developing nations. Often, in exchange for granting loans, the World Bank imposes requirements intended to build the economies of borrower nations.

The World Bank has come under fire for making loans with conditions that ultimately hurt the borrower nations. When developing nations are required to balance government budgets, they are sometimes forced to cut vital social programs. One World Bank official agrees that the critics are right in some situations: "Some of the conditions set were too harsh . . . and made tough economic conditions worse."[51] In addition, environmental and human rights activists maintain that the World Bank should consider the impact of its loans on the environment and the treatment of workers. Some observers believe that the organization is beginning to make progress in this regard.[52]

International Monetary Fund Established a year after the World Bank, the **International Monetary Fund (IMF)** was created to promote trade through financial cooperation, and in the process, eliminate barriers. The IMF makes short-term loans to member nations that are unable to meet their budgetary expenses. It operates as a lender of last resort for troubled nations. In exchange for these emergency loans, IMF lenders frequently extract significant commitments from the borrowing nations to address the problems that led to the crises. These steps may include curtailing imports or even devaluing currency. Throughout its existence, the IMF has worked to prevent financial crises by warning the international business community when countries encounter problems meeting their financial obligations. Often, the IMF lends to countries to keep them from defaulting on prior debts and to prevent economic crises in particular countries from spreading to other nations. However, like the WTO and World Bank, the IMF has come under criticism. One criticism is that economic problems sometimes arise because banks and other businesses become insolvent, not because of government policies. IMF restrictions on government spending then don't address the real economic problems plaguing some troubled economies.[53] The IMF has responded to criticism by establishing an independent group to review its policies and recommend reforms.[54]

Another concern is that IMF lending has placed many poor nations in an impossible position. Some countries owe far more money than they can ever hope to repay, and the debt payments make it impossible for their governments to deliver desperately needed services to their citizens. The nations of sub-Saharan Africa are hard-pressed to deal with the ravages of AIDS, yet their debt exceeds their GDP and is three times as high as their total annual exports. Critics maintain that situations like these can only be improved by forgiving the debt. Canceling $45 million of Uganda's debt payments permitted that nation to cut school tuition and almost double the number of children enrolled in primary school. The arguments in favor of debt forgiveness are primarily humanitarian, but the major argument against it is that it will merely encourage nations to borrow with no intent to repay their loans.[55]

International Economic Communities

International economic communities reduce trade barriers and promote regional economic integration. In the simplest approach, countries may establish a *free-trade area* in which they trade freely among themselves without tariffs or trade restrictions. Each maintains its own tariffs for trade outside this area. A *customs union* sets up a free-trade area and specifies a uniform tariff structure for members' trade with nonmember nations. In a *common market*, or economic union, members go beyond a customs union and try to bring all of their trade rules into agreement. The EU is an example.

One example of a free-trade area is the North American Free Trade Agreement (NAFTA) enacted by the U.S., Canada, and Mexico. Other examples of regional trading blocs include the MERCOSUR customs union (joining Brazil, Argentina, Paraguay, Uruguay, Chile, and Bolivia), and the ten-country Association of South East Asian Nations (ASEAN). To ensure continuing success in meeting its goal of creating peace, stability, and prosperity, ASEAN holds annual meetings at which members review developments and give directives for meeting economic and political challenges. Figure 4.8 shows the size of these economic communities.

NAFTA

NAFTA became effective in 1994, creating the world's largest free-trade zone with the U.S., Canada, and Mexico. By eliminating all trade barriers and investment restrictions among the three nations over a 15-year period, NAFTA opens more doors for free trade. The agreement also eases regulations governing trade in services, such as banking, and establishes uniform legal requirements for protection of intellectual property. The three signatory countries can trade with one another without tariffs or other trade barriers, simplifying shipments of goods across the partners' borders. Standardized customs and uniform labeling regulations create economic efficiencies and smooth import and export procedures.

By eliminating trade barriers, NAFTA expands choices of products and suppliers for consumers. Domestic producers in the U.S., Canada, and Mexico have gained access to a larger market. Many items are

BUSINESS DIRECTORY

➤ **North American Free Trade Agreement (NAFTA)** *1994 agreement among the U.S., Canada, and Mexico to break down tariffs and trade restrictions*

FIGURE 4.8
NAFTA, MERCOSUR, and ASEAN Free-Trade Areas

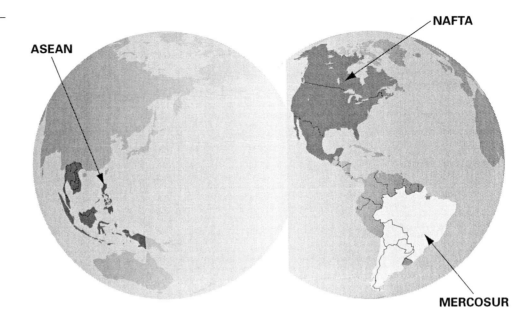

produced at lower per-unit costs than before NAFTA, because companies are able to plan for larger volumes of output.

Trade among the partners has increased steadily, with U.S. exports to Mexico growing at almost twice the rate of exports to other countries. Since NAFTA went into effect, Mexican exports grew from $52 billion to $137 billion, and foreign direct investment in Mexico doubled.[56] Critics blame NAFTA for causing more than 200,000 jobs to shift from the U.S. to Mexico. Especially hard hit were jobs in the apparel, electrical and electronic equipment, and transportation equipment industries. However, the Department of Commerce says trade with Canada and Mexico supports 2.6 million U.S. jobs and job loss is the result of changing technology, not international trade. Depending on their political agenda, observers are likewise split on whether NAFTA has helped or hurt the environment and labor conditions. Critics say producers have moved operations to Mexico to avoid stricter pollution controls and labor laws. Advocates of NAFTA argue that Mexico has improved conditions in order to trade with the U.S. and Canada.[57]

The growth of trade under NAFTA has encouraged the participants to pursue similar agreements with other countries. The Mexican government recently negotiated a NAFTA-style agreement with the EU.[58]

European Union

Perhaps the best-known example of a common market is the European Union (EU). The EU combines 15 countries, 350 million people, and a total GDP of $5 trillion to form a huge common market. Several central European countries and former Soviet republics have also applied for EU membership.

The EU's goals include promoting economic and social progress, introducing European citizenship as a complement to national citizenship, and giving the EU a significant role in international affairs. To achieve its goal of a borderless Europe, the EU is removing barriers to free trade among its members. This highly complex process involves standardizing business regulations and requirements, standardizing import duties and taxes, and eliminating customs checks, so that companies can transport goods from England to Italy as easily as from New York City to Boston.

Unifying standards and laws can contribute to economic growth. The EU established a common standard for mobile phones, called GSM. This standard enabled Nokia and Ericsson to develop a pan-European customer base for their cellular phones. Eventually, Nokia became the biggest seller of mobile communications devices worldwide.[59] But just as NAFTA sparked fears in the U.S. about free trade with Mexico, some people in Western Europe have worried that opening trade with countries like Poland, Hungary, and the Czech Republic will cause jobs to flow eastward to lower-wage economies.[60]

The EU also introduced the euro to replace currencies like the French franc and Italian lira. For the 11 member states that participated, potential benefits include eliminating the economic costs of exchanging one currency for another and simplifying price comparisons. Businesses and their customers have been able to make check and credit card transaction in euros since 1999, and euro notes and coins were introduced in 2002.

GOING GLOBAL

While expanding into overseas markets can increase profits and marketing opportunities, it also introduces new complexities to a firm's business operations. Before making the decision to go global, a company faces a number of key decisions, beginning with the following:

- Determining which foreign market(s) to enter
- Analyzing the expenditures required to enter a new market
- Deciding on the best way to organize the overseas operations

These issues vary in importance depending on the level of involvement a company chooses. Education and worker training in the host country would be much more important for a bank planning to open a foreign branch or an electronics manufacturer building an Asian factory than for a firm that is simply planning to export American-made products.

The choice of which markets to enter usually follows extensive research focusing on local demand for the firm's products, availability of needed resources, and ability of the local workforce to produce world-class quality. Other factors include existing and potential competition, tariff rates, currency stability, and investment barriers. A variety of government and other sources are available to facilitate this research process. A good starting place is the *CIA World Factbook,* which contains country-by-country information on geography, population, government, economy, and infrastructure.

U.S. Department of Commerce counselors at the agency's district offices offer a full range of international business advice, including computerized market data and names of business and government contacts in dozens of countries. As Table 4.5 shows, the Internet provides access to many resources for international trade information.

Levels of Involvement

After a firm has completed its research and decided to enter a foreign market, it can choose one or more of the entry strategies shown in Figure 4.9:

- Exporting or importing
- Entering into contractual agreements like franchising, licensing, and subcontracting deals
- Direct investment in the foreign market through acquisitions, joint ventures, or establishment of an overseas division

Although the company's risk increases with the level of its involvement, so does its overall control of all aspects of producing and selling its goods or services.

BUSINESS DIRECTORY

➤ **European Union (EU)** *15-nation European economic alliance.*

Table 4.5	International Trade Research Resources on the Internet	
Web Site and Address	**General Description**
Asia, Inc. www.asia-inc.com	Business news in Asia, featuring articles on Asian countries from India to Japan
Europages www.europages.com	Directory of and links to Europe's top 150,000 companies in 25 European countries
Emerging Markets Directory www.emdirectory.com	Links to sites with information about the emerging markets of Asia, Latin America, Europe, Africa, and the Middle East
World Trade Organization www.wto.int	Details on the trade policies of various governments
CIA World Factbook www.odci.gov/cia/publications	Basic facts about the world's nations, from geography to economic conditions
STAT-USA www.stat-usa.gov	Extensive trade and economic data, information about trends, daily intelligence reports, and background data (access requires paid subscription to the service)
U.S. Commercial Service www.usatrade.gov	Information about Commerce Department counseling services, trade events, and U.S. export regulations
U.S. Business Advisor www.business.gov	One-stop access to a range of federal government information, services, and transactions
U.S. State Department travel.state.gov/travel_warnings.html	Listing of the State Department's latest travel warnings about conditions that may affect safety abroad, supplemented by a list of consulate addresses and country information

Companies frequently combine more than one of these strategies. Web portal Yahoo! used joint ventures with local firms to gain a quick presence in Japan, Britain, France, Germany, and South Korea. Only after developing experience as an international company has Yahoo! begun to engage in direct investment by creating foreign subsidiaries. Waiting to develop expertise before moving overseas is risky for online businesses, though, because Web sites are so easy for competitors to copy. Alando, an auction Web site based in Germany, looks remarkably like eBay. Rather than fight the company, eBay entered Germany by acquiring Alando.[61]

Importers and Exporters   When a firm brings in goods produced abroad to sell domestically, it is an importer. Conversely, companies are exporters when they produce—or purchase—goods at home and sell them in overseas markets. An importing or exporting strategy provides the lowest level of international involvement, with the least risk and control.

Los Angeles Fiber Co., based in Vernon, California, sells fibers used to stuff cushions and pillows. Two of every five dollars of its annual sales are export sales. The company faces challenges when collecting payments from foreign customers, in part

FIGURE 4.9
Levels of Involvement in
International Business

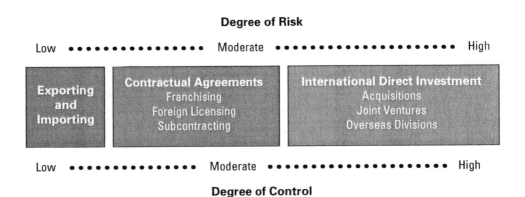

because foreign banks in many countries do not measure up to U.S. banking standards. The company has dealt with foreign banks that collect money from their customers, then take two to four weeks to move those funds into Los Angeles Fiber's bank account. Because of this delay, the firm's top managers have become experts in learning which banks they can rely on. Los Angeles Fiber encourages customers to open accounts with banks that meet its standards and has dropped customers that won't switch.[62]

Exports are frequently handled by special intermediaries called *export trading companies*. These firms search out competitively priced local merchandise and then resell it abroad at prices high enough to cover expenses and earn profits. When a retail chain like Dallas-based Pier One Imports wants to purchase West African products for its store shelves, it may contact an export trading company operating in a country such as Ghana. The local firm is responsible for monitoring quality, packaging the order for transatlantic shipment, arranging transportation, and handling the customs paperwork and other steps required to move the product from Ghana to the U.S.

Firms engage in exporting of two types: indirect and direct exporting. A company engages in *indirect exporting* when it manufactures a product, such as an electronic component, that becomes part of another product that is sold in foreign markets. The second method, *direct exporting,* occurs when a company seeks to sell its product in markets outside its own country. Often the first step for companies entering foreign markets, direct exporting is the most common form of international business. Firms that find success in exporting their products may then move on to other entry strategies.

In addition to reaching foreign markets by dealing with export trading companies, novice exporters may choose two other alternatives: export management companies and offset agreements. Rather than simply relying on an export trading company to assist in locating foreign products or foreign markets, an exporting firm may turn to an *export management company* for advice and expertise. These international specialists help the first-time exporter complete paperwork, make contacts with local buyers, and comply with local laws governing labeling, product safety, and performance testing. At the same time, the exporting firm retains much more control than would be possible with an export trading company.

An *offset agreement* matches a small business with a major international firm. It basically makes the small firm a subcontractor to the larger one. Such an entry strategy helps a new exporter by allowing it to share in the larger company's international expertise. The small firm also benefits in such important areas as international transaction documents and financing.

Countertrade   A sizable share of international trade involves payments made in the form of local products, not currency. This system of international bartering agreements is called **countertrade.**

A common reason for resorting to international barter is inadequate access to needed foreign currency. To complete an international sales agreement, the seller may agree to accept part of the purchase cost in currency and the remainder in other merchandise. Since the seller may decide to locate a buyer for the bartered goods before completing the transaction, a number of international buyers and sellers frequently join together in a single agreement.

Countertrade may often be a firm's only opportunity to enter a particular market. Many developing countries simply cannot obtain enough credit or financial assistance to afford the imports that their people want. Countries with heavy debt burdens also resort to countertrade. Russian buyers, with their country's soft currency, may resort to trading local products ranging from crude oil to diamonds to vodka as payments for purchases from foreign companies unwilling to accept Russian rubles. Still other countries, such as China, may restrict imports. Under such circumstances countertrade may be the only practical way to win government approval to import needed products.

Contractual Agreements   Once a company, large or small, gains some experience in international sales, it may decide to enter into contractual agreements with local parties. These arrangements can include franchising, foreign licensing, and subcontracting.

Franchising   Common among U.S. companies, franchising can work well for companies seeking to expand into international markets, too. A **franchise**, as described in detail in Chapter 5, is a contractual agreement in which a wholesaler or retailer (the franchisee) gains the right to sell the franchisor's products under that company's brand name if it agrees to the related operating requirements. The franchisee can also receive marketing, management, and business services from the franchisor. While these arrangements are common among leading fast-food brands such as Pizza Hut, McDonald's, and KFC, other kinds of service providers also often look to franchising as an international marketplace option.

The Howard Johnson hotel chain is using franchising to expand into Europe. Its franchise agreement with a U.K. business called Premier Hotels calls for Premier to develop 40 hotels in Austria, Belgium, Germany, Luxembourg, the Netherlands, Portugal, Spain, and Switzerland. Premier already operates Howard Johnson hotels in Great Britain. Calling on the experience of a European firm makes sense, because chain hotels are relatively uncommon in Europe. At the same time, the franchising arrangement enables the hotels to tap into the Howard Johnson's reservation system, which also includes specialized management software.[63]

Foreign Licensing   In a **foreign licensing agreement**, one firm allows another to produce or sell its product, or use its trademark, patent, or manufacturing processes in a specific geographic area. In return, the firm gets a royalty or other compensation.

Licensing can be advantageous for a small manufacturer anxious to launch a well-known product overseas. Not only does it get a market-tested product from another market, but little or no investment is required to begin operating. The arrangement can also allow entry into a market otherwise closed to imports due to government restrictions.

Licensing a brand is a $26 billion industry today. General Motors (GM) started engaging in licensing almost by accident. The company had been spending millions of dollars a year on lawsuits against companies that were placing GM brands on clothing. Then the company realized that caps and T-shirts bearing the Corvette logo could be a source of profits, not a drain on the legal department. GM has since negotiated over 1,200 licensing agreements to place its brands on goods from cologne to clothing, generating over $1 billion a year in revenues.

Most licensed brands are American, but Europeans have been jumping on the licensing bandwagon. Jaguar has licenses for its name on eyeglass frames, footwear, and fragrances. Aston Martin has a licensing program with makers of model cars and a video game.[64]

Subcontracting   The third type of contractual agreement, **subcontracting**, involves hiring local companies to produce, distribute, or sell goods or services. This move allows a foreign firm to take advantage of the subcontractor's expertise in local culture, contacts, and regulations. Subcontracting works equally well for mail-order companies, which can farm out order fulfillment and customer service functions to local businesses. Manufacturers practice subcontracting to save money on import duties and labor costs, and businesses go this route to market products best sold by locals in a given country.

Many high-tech firms rely on subcontractors known as contract electronics manufacturers (CEMs). The CEMs specialize in producing items from PC components to cell phones according to the specifications of the companies that design and market those products. Businesses currently using CEMs include Hewlett-Packard, Cisco, IBM, and Motorola. Companies with names like Solectron, Celectica, and

It's a standard business concept: If you want to enter a foreign market, buy a foreign company. That way, you don't have to worry about finding workers who speak the language or figuring out what types of goods and services consumers want. Going global this way would seem to be even easier for Internet companies, just by their boundaryless nature. That's what executives at Amazon, eBay, and Yahoo! thought. Amazon bought two small online booksellers—Bookpages in the United Kingdom and Telebuch in Germany. eBay acquired Alando.de, a German online auctioneer. Yahoo! followed a slightly different route by creating eight different country-specific Yahoo!s throughout Europe and is expanding into Asia.

Despite early and modest success, these three U.S. e-businesses are hardly dominating their European markets. Amazon was successful in circumventing German regulatory problems, and its two acquisitions now generate revenues of approximately $300 million a year. But there aren't really any more start-ups for it to buy in Europe; other European companies have already snapped them up. In the United Kingdom, British entrepreneur Timothy Jackson scooped eBay with his own online auction site, then quickly signed exclusive agreements in other European countries. eBay compounded its own problems by pricing items in U.S. dollars, which alienated many British customers. And although Yahoo! is Britain's number one portal, the French portal Wanadoo has many advantages, including being tied to the national telephone monopoly.

So far, these American Internet firms are not discouraged, and none has plans to pack its bags and head home. Fabiola Arredondo, managing director for Yahoo! Europe, believes that her company will duplicate its U.S. success in the long run. "Users who are comfortable with the Internet will be switching to Yahoo! more and more," she predicts. In fact, one reason Yahoo! has attained number-one status in Britain is because the national telephone company lost its monopoly. Should this occur in other countries, Yahoo! is ready to step in. But the American companies have a long way to go in foreign markets before their brand names carry the clout that they do at home. Acquiring local firms in foreign markets is the first step, not the last.

QUESTIONS FOR CRITICAL THINKING

1. In addition to acquiring local companies, what other steps can the American Internet companies take to increase their level of involvement in foreign markets?
2. In what ways can these companies create value for consumers in these markets?

Sources: Brian Bergstein, "Yahoo! Dumps Amazon," The Associated Press, September 19, 2000, abcnews.go.com; Chris Taylor, "All Boxed In," *Time*, September 4, 2000, www.time.com; "Yahoo! India Opens Today," Yahoo! press release, June 29, 2000, docs.yahoo.com; Katarzyna Moreno, "Global Pains," *Forbes*, March 20, 2000, pp. 286–288; John Schwartz, "EBay Greatly Expands Live Online Auction Bidding," *New York Times*, January 22, 2001, downloaded from www.nytimes.com, January 29, 2001.

Flextronics International not only assemble electronics but help with design, testing, and even product servicing. They are likely to operate more efficiently than the companies whose names are on the products because they invest in the latest software and manufacturing equipment and serve various customers. Flexible machinery and production tracking software enable companies like HMT Technology to track every detail of the manufacturing process, making immediate adjustments when problems arise or orders change. The company uses its technology to make disks for computers at a significantly lower cost than its Japanese competitors pay to make similar products.[65]

A key disadvantage of subcontracting is that companies cannot always control their subcontractors' business practices. As discussed in Chapter 2, several major U.S. companies have been embarrassed by reports that their subcontractors used child labor to manufacture clothing.

International Direct Investment Investing directly in production and marketing operations in a foreign country is the ultimate level of global involvement. Over time, a firm may become experienced and successful at conducting business in other countries through exporting and contractual agreements. Its managers may then decide to establish manufacturing facilities in those countries, open branch offices, or buy ownership interests in local companies.

In an *acquisition*, a company purchases another existing firm in the host country. An acquisition permits a company to gain an international presence very quickly, as discussed in the "Business Hits and Misses" box. Wal-Mart enjoyed an 86 percent increase in foreign sales after it acquired ASDA, a British supermarket chain with annual revenues of $14 billion.[66] Looking the other way across the Atlantic, the French company Infogames Entertainment is using acquisitions to help it break into the

Sikorsky Flies Around the World with Partners

Background. Gaining a foothold in a global marketplace can be tricky. Some companies fold under the increased competition; others turn to global suppliers for a competitive solution. Sikorsky Aircraft Corp. is one of the latter. Sikorsky makes helicopters for commercial and military use. The firm's copters are often seen on search and rescue missions, disaster relief flights, and U.S. Army or National Guard operations. One product, the Sikorsky Helibus, represents a current trend by companies attempting to gain a competitive edge in the global marketplace: forming a joint ventures.

What Happened? Sikorsky doesn't hire international participants in the Helibus project merely as subcontractors to produce or assemble parts according to the firm's blueprints. Instead, each of Sikorsky's partners has the authority to design the components they build. The cabin is designed and built by Mitsubishi Heavy Industries, and the cockpit module is designed by Aerospace Industrial Development Corp., both Japanese firms. The fuselage comes from Gamesa in Spain, and the vertical fin travels from China's Jingdezhen Helicopter Group. The landing gear and fuel sponsors are manufactured by Embraer in Brazil. All of these parts arrive at Sikorsky's Connecticut facility, where they are assembled—along with Sikorsky-built components such as the transmission and rotor system.

The Response. How does this design process work? Each partner has the responsibility to make its own technology infrastructure improvements. "We [try] not to dictate too much to them," says a Sikorsky manager. In other words, each of the partners assumes a certain amount of risk and responsibility in getting the Helibus to the launchpad. As fragmented as it sounds, the system works because of technology. Three-dimensional electronic modeling helps far-flung designers work together to spot and correct potentially costly—and dangerous—design conflicts. In fact, as various versions of the Helibus model were sent to partners, they spotted over 1,300 conflicts in design—before any of the components was actually manufactured, saving Sikorsky untold millions. Designers and engineers communicate via e-mail and the Internet. These communications take place in English, which is considered the universal language of the aerospace industry. The 3-D modeling and Internet communication make it possible for smaller teams to operate efficiently.

Today and Counting. In speaking of the relationship that Sikorsky shares with its foreign suppliers, "this is a leading edge concept," says David Burdick, vice president of engineering applications at Gartner Group. "The . . . partners are true design collaborators rather than design fulfillers. They have the authority to originate design intent rather than just process it." Is the collaboration working? The company recently signed an extremely competitive contract worth an estimated $186 million with the Austrian Ministry of Defense, and its revenues climbed to a lofty $1.4 billion in a recent year.

QUESTIONS FOR CRITICAL THINKING
1. In what ways might Sikorsky seek to increase its level of involvement in the global market?
2. What barriers to trade might Sikorsky face if it tries to increase its level of involvement in a country like China?

Sources: "Sikorsky Aircraft Corporation: About Us," company Web site, **www.sikorsky.com,** accessed January 29, 2001; "Sikorsky Wins Austrian Contract," Reuters Online News, October 9, 2000; Frank Colucci, "Hatching the Helibus," *Executive Edge,* June/July 1999, pp. 28–34.

---

huge American market for video games. The company's first major success, a haunted-house adventure called Alone in the Dark, helped the company establish a positive reputation among video game developers, but it needed a way to get shelf space in U.S. stores. So Infogames bought Accolade, a San Jose publisher of video games. With that deal, Infogames got not only Accolade's games but also a distribution channel through video game stores and major chains like Toys 'R' Us and Wal-Mart.[67]

Joint ventures allow companies to share risks, costs, profits, and management responsibilities with one or more host country nationals, as described in the "Clicks and Mortar" box. Like many auto companies in recent years, General Motors has increased its global role by entering into joint ventures with competitors in other countries. It recently exchanged stock shares with Fiat Auto, giving the U.S. and Italian carmakers a stake in each other's success. In addition, the two companies jointly run their European and Latin American engine and transmission factories. The shared operations are expected to save them billions of dollars through greater efficiency. GM has also formed alliances with Suzuki Motor Corp., Isuzu Motors, and Fuji Heavy Industries, a combination that accounts for one of every four cars produced in the world.[68]

By setting up an *overseas division,* a company can conduct a significant amount of its business overseas. This strategy differs from that of a multinational company

Table 4.6	The World's Top Ten Multinationals		
Rank and Company		**Corporate Headquarters**	**Revenues (in billions)**
1.	General Motors Corp.	United States	$177
2.	Wal-Mart Stores	United States	167
3.	ExxonMobil	United States	164
4.	Ford Motor Co.	United States	163
5.	DaimlerChrysler	Germany	160
6.	Mitsui	Japan	119
7.	Mitsubishi	Japan	118
8.	Toyota Motor	Japan	116
9.	General Electric	United States	112
10.	Itochu	Japan	109

in that a company with overseas divisions remains primarily a domestic organization with international operations. Gateway Computer, for instance, sells 10 percent of its products in Europe, the Middle East, and Africa. To serve these regions, the company operates a call center in Dublin, offering technical support and customer service. A call center in Ireland lets Gateway take advantage of low taxes, a skilled multilingual workforce, and Ireland's advanced telecommunications infrastructure. When Gateway set up the call center, it also got financial help from the Irish Development Authority. The call center also gives Gateway the advantage of being closer to its growing base of customers on the other side of the Atlantic.[69]

From Multinational Corporation to Global Business

A multinational corporation (MNC) is an organization with significant foreign operations. As Table 4.6 shows, firms headquartered in the U.S. and Japan dominate the list of the world's largest multinationals. Of the top 20 MNCs, the only exceptions to the U.S.-Japanese dominance are Germany's DaimlerChrysler, Royal Dutch/Shell (with headquarters divided between Britain and the Netherlands), France's AXA, Britain's BP Amoco, and Germany's Volkswagen.

Since the 1960s, when the first concerns surfaced about their influence on international business, MNCs have undergone a number of dramatic changes. For one, despite the continuing dominance of U.S. companies, America can no longer claim most of the top slots. Today's MNC is just as likely to be based in Japan (Sony, Nissan, and Matsushita, for example), with others based in Germany (DaimlerChrysler, Volkswagen) or Switzerland (Nestlé, Credit Suisse). Additionally, MNCs integrate capital, technologies, and even ideas from their various global operations. These operations no longer function as distant market outposts.

Many U.S. multinationals, including Nike and Wal-Mart, have expanded their overseas operations because they believe that domestic markets are peaking and foreign markets offer greater sales and profit potential. Other MNCs are making substantial investments in developing countries in part because these countries provide low-cost labor compared with the U.S. and Western Europe. In addition, many MNCs are locating high-tech facilities in countries with large numbers of technical-school graduates, such as India. But MNCs can experience difficulties in foreign markets, as the "Solving an Ethical Controversy" box discusses.

As MNCs contribute to a global economy, they reap the benefits of the global marketplace. Consumers in countries as geographically and culturally distant as Saudi Arabia and Canada shave with Gillette's razor blades, wash clothes with Procter & Gamble's Tide detergent, and use computers with Intel chips inside. Nike is crafting an international strategy aimed at both winning the marketing game

BUSINESS DIRECTORY

➤ **multinational corporation (MNC)** *firm with significant operations and marketing activities outside its home country.*

Goldman Sachs International provides financial infrastructure by financing developing businesses all over the world. In this ad from *The Economist* magazine, the company advertises its ability to provide support to make a big idea a success—wherever the company is located.

and enabling its international customers to win at the sports of their dreams. The company offers teens in Southeast Asia a line of footwear priced for households of limited means. Compared with the $50 to $150 shoes sold in the U.S., shoes in Nike's Play Series line are priced at the equivalent of about $25. The Play Series shoes are advertised to consumers in India, Indonesia, Malaysia, the Philippines, Singapore, and Thailand with the slogan "It's My Turn" beside images of national and international sports heroes. To help young people get their turn at sports, Nike has built Play Zone playgrounds with courts that can be used for games from basketball to badminton. The company has also donated equipment in rural areas. For Asian kids, some of whom play in bare feet, Nike is introducing the whole concept of wearing the right shoes for the game.[70]

Sources of Export Assistance

Regardless of the global business strategy that a company chooses, it may require export assistance. Companies can tap a variety of resources for this help. The U.S. Department of Commerce maintains a toll-free information hot line (1-800-USA-TRADE) that describes various federal export programs. The Web site of the Commerce Department's International Trade Administration (www.ita.doc.gov) also provides links to trade information, as well as Country Commercial Guides.

Companies can also seek advice from trade counselors at the Commerce Department's 68 district offices, who can offer information about exporting, computerized market data, and names of contacts in more than 60 countries. Some of these services are free; others are reasonably priced.

INTERNATIONAL ORGANIZATION STRUCTURES

The decision to go global must be followed by a series of additional decisions that specify the most appropriate organization structure for the expanded operation. The level of involvement in international business is a key factor in these decisions. Although a firm engaged in simple export activities may be best served by an export trading company, another company with extensive overseas sales may establish its own sales force for each country in which it operates. Figure 4.10 lists the alternative organization structures that are typical of global business firms.

Independent Agents

One method of entering international markets avoids the need to commit a major investment for developing and maintaining an overseas sales force: Using **independent agents**. These marketing intermediaries serve as independent sales forces in foreign markets, earning commissions on sales they book. They typically make sales calls on prospective customers, collect payments, and ensure customer satisfaction. Most cover limited geographic markets and hold down costs by representing multiple companies that produce related, noncompeting products.

Companies entering new foreign markets frequently rely on independent agents for several reasons:

- They understand their target markets, including customs and local environments.
- They represent minimal-risk entry alternatives for first-time exporters. If the firm is unhappy with an independent representative, it can terminate the relationship.
- Since most exporter–independent agent agreements specify compensation based on sales, they limit financial risks.

Exporters considering distributing through independent agents can secure names of local agents in various countries by contacting state export bureaus of the U.S. Department of Commerce. These agencies can also assist in developing sales agreements.

Licensing Agreements

As described earlier in the chapter, some firms try to increase revenues without making significant foreign investments by licensing their products, brand names, or production processes to other firms. Under this arrangement, the firm receiving the license has exclusive rights to use the production process or to manufacture and/or market the product in a specified market. In return, the firm granting the license typically receives an up-front fee plus an ongoing percentage of product sales.

Licensing agreements can be advantageous for companies seeking to enter foreign markets. License holders are usually large, well-known companies that depend on sales of the licensed products for their revenues. Because they invest more resources in the product than independent agents would, they often provide more effective representation in foreign markets. Also, licensing agreements are relatively inexpensive and easy to create. The license holder is familiar with the target market, and the exporting company can draw on its experience and expertise instead of spending money researching the market and culture.

Licensing agreements bring an important limitation, however: They usually specify long time periods. A company that wants to attract the best license holder in a market typically must grant exclusive rights to the product for five years or even longer. Firms may benefit from such time commitments if license holders provide effective support, but these contracts are difficult to terminate if the license holders prove to be ineffective partners.

Branch Offices

A branch office involves a different kind of commitment to foreign investment by a company. Instead of relying on a third party, the firm establishes its own overseas facility. In this way, it both improves its control and strengthens its presence in the host country. That was Trillium Digital Systems' objective when it opened a branch office in the United Kingdom. Trillium, which markets communications software, wanted to have people working in Europe to forge closer ties with its overseas customers and provide better support for its overseas sales representatives. A European office was a natural move for Los Angeles–based Trillium, because it has been selling globally from the start. The company's first customer was from France, and its second customer was from Japan. Trillium's hiring practices back up this level of commitment to multinational sales. Employees speak over two dozen different languages.[71]

FIGURE 4.10
Alternative Structures for International Organizations

Can Coke Go Local in Europe?

The Coca-Cola Company is living proof that being big doesn't necessarily mean being better when it comes to relationships in foreign markets. After several years of serious blunders, the dominant global soft-drink supplier is now trying to rebuild its relationships—and its reputation—in Europe. What went wrong? First, all decisions about advertising, products, and packaging were made at the company's Atlanta headquarters instead of carefully considering the values and tastes of each local market. Second, the company charged inappropriately high prices for Coke concentrate in foreign markets. Third, the firm alienated foreign government officials with its aggressive efforts to capture a bigger market share in their countries. Finally, the company reacted too slowly to a scare in Belgium in which cans of Coke were found to be contaminated with a sulfur compound. As a result, public trust crumbled, and Coca-Cola products were pulled from shelves in several European countries.

Does The Coca-Cola Company deserve a second chance to rebuild its relationship with European markets?

PRO

1. The Coca-Cola Company is making sincere efforts to right its previous wrongs in Europe. The company has hired local marketers, set up expanded communications offices, and is developing soft drinks—such as a pear-flavored drink in Turkey and a berry drink in Germany—geared toward local tastes.
2. The company has rehired Carl Ware, well-known for his previous work with local officials and community groups, as head of a global public affairs unit. In this move, "Coke will be able to sense the economic, political, and social sensitivities" in its European markets. Ware might insist on buying more raw materials locally and increasing the firm's involvement with local affairs.
3. Executives say they have learned their lesson from the way the contamination scare was handled. "The crisis had taught us the need to get closer to local consumers," says Marc Mathieu, president of the new Benelux and France division.

CON

1. The company should not be let off the hook for the contamination problem. "When you have a recall for any consumer-product company, you are floating in very dangerous water," says beverage analyst George Thompson.
2. The company had no contingency plan in place for such a consumer crisis. Such an oversight is inexcusable in such a large corporation.
3. The Coca-Cola Company has misread the European marketplace in other ways, especially in its aggressive attempts to acquire European companies and bully its way through government regulations.

SUMMARY

The Coca-Cola Company's future in Europe is anything but certain. Although attempts have been made to rebuild its reputation, sales have been slow to respond. Wary consumers have been sipping other soft drinks. Carl Ware admits, "We've got work to do."

Sources: William Echikson and Dean Foust, "For Coke, Local Is It," *Business Week*, July 3, 2000, p. 122; Dean Foust, "Will Coke Go Better with Carl Ware?" *Business Week*, January 24, 2000, p. 138; Nick Pachetti, "Tempest in a Coke Can," *Worth*, October 1999, pp. 51–56; James L. Graff, "A Big Fizzle for Coca-Cola," *Time*, June 28, 1999, **www.time.com**.

To maintain a branch office in another country, a firm must develop an understanding of both the local market and its culture. This requirement demands a more extensive investment in time and experience than working with an independent agent or licensee. Many firms choose to combine branch offices and licensing agreements. The two strategies can complement each other, since license holders provide access to the local market, and the branch office can oversee the activities of the license holder.

Strategic Alliances

Similar to a joint venture, a **strategic alliance** is an international business strategy in which a company finds a partner in the country where it wants to do business. These partnerships can create competitive advantages in new markets by allowing the parties to combine resources and capital into new, jointly owned business ventures. Both the risks and profits are shared, firms maintain control over their international activities, and they benefit from the local market expertise of their partners. A number of countries, including Mexico and China, have laws that require foreign firms doing business in their countries to work through such alliances.

With a growing number of travelers shopping for their plane tickets online, airlines have been forming alliances to sell tickets. One of these efforts is a seven-company venture of airlines based in the Asia-Pacific region. The airlines, including Australia's Qantas, Cathay Pacific Airways, and Singapore Airlines, post schedules and ticket prices at a Web site where customers can make purchases. When travelers buy directly from the airlines, the airlines don't have to pay commissions to travel agents. For this reason, airlines are trying to set up their own sites, rather than depending on independent sites like Expedia and Travelocity to sell tickets. Qantas hopes to save millions of dollars by selling online.[72]

Direct Investment

Unlike strategic alliances, a firm makes a **direct investment** in a foreign market when it buys an existing company or establishes a factory, retail outlets, or other facilities there. Direct investment entails the most complete involvement in foreign trade, but it also brings the most risk. Companies that invest directly in other countries must consider a number of issues discussed in this chapter, including the cultural environments, political stability, labor markets, and currency stability they will likely encounter.

As Figure 4.11 shows, U.S. companies—the most active in international direct investments—allocated over half of their $980 billion in total direct investment to Europe. The U.S. market is also a popular investment location for foreign investors, which recently invested over $800 billion in projects ranging from factories to dot.com enterprises.

When Matsushita Electrical Industrial Co. wanted to participate in Silicon Valley's innovation, the Japanese MNC planned to build its own laboratory. However, it quickly learned that U.S. engineers preferred to start their own businesses and capitalize on the Internet boom. So Matsushita adopted an investment strategy. It set up a venture capital fund to invest in U.S. start-ups working on technologies of interest to Matsushita. The company hopes to benefit from America's innovative, individualistic culture by helping to finance its entrepreneurs. At the same time, Matsushita's investment reflects a change from a manufacturing-oriented business philosophy to one that takes chances on future technology.[73]

DEVELOPING A STRATEGY FOR INTERNATIONAL BUSINESS

In developing a framework within which to conduct international business, managers must first evaluate their corporate objectives, organizational strengths and weaknesses, and strategies for product development and marketing. They can choose to combine these elements in either a global strategy or a multidomestic strategy.

Global Business Strategies

A global business (or *standardization*) strategy specifies a standardized, worldwide product and marketing strategy. The firm sells the same product in essentially the same manner throughout the world. Many companies simply modify their domestic business strategies by translating promotional

Two world-class heavy-equipment multinationals are Tokyo-headquartered Komatsu and U.S.-based Caterpillar. Komatsu's mining-equipment product line includes dump trucks, bulldozers, and loaders. Its Komatsu Mining Systems subsidiary provides software to use in controlling mining operations. In addition to its machinery and equipment, the company offers product service support "backed by Komatsu's on-site service, maintenance, and local support anywhere in the world."

FIGURE 4.11
Destinations and Sources of Direct Investment Dollars

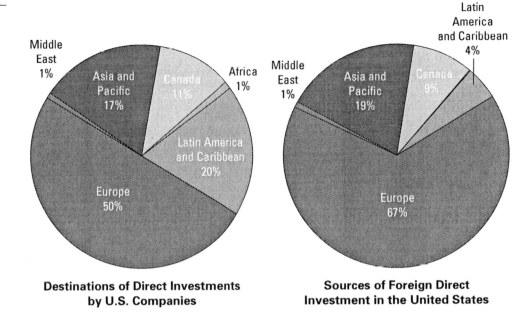

Destinations of Direct Investments by U.S. Companies

Sources of Foreign Direct Investment in the United States

brochures and product-use instructions into the languages of the host nations. Toyota adapts its marketing not only to international markets but to groups within nations. It is the biggest buyer of automobile advertising targeted to Hispanic Americans.[74]

Following its merger with Daimler Benz, Chrysler combined its international and U.S. sales and marketing divisions into a single global division. The objective of the change is to create and convey a single marketing message to its customers around the world, in support of global brands. DaimlerChrysler's first major test of the new global strategy was the launch of its PT Cruiser, a hybrid of a minivan and sport utility vehicle with 1930s-era styling. To prepare the advertising campaign, DaimlerChrysler's ad agency gathered ideas from offices in the different countries where the PT Cruiser would be sold. The only adaptations of the ads are translating the words into local languages and placing the steering wheel on the right in the United Kingdom, Australia, and Japan.[75]

A global marketing perspective can be appropriate for some goods and services and certain market segments that are common to many nations. The approach works for products with universal appeal, like Coca-Cola, and for luxury items like jewelry. Executives at Metabolife International are hoping that a global strategy will also work for its herbal remedies, as consumers change their views of health care. Americans are becoming more accustomed to the use of single herbs, but Chinese consumers have a vast and complex array of herbs, each combination designed for a specific symptom. Metabolife executives think the time may be right to introduce a product that will seem more sophisticated to Americans used to one-herb remedies, while simplifying the traditional complicated Chinese standards. Metabolife's line of remedies, under the brand Chinac, combines herbs targeted to particular ailments, such as colds, headache, or arthritis, but not to slight variations of symptoms in various forms of these ailments. Metabolife hopes that Americans and Chinese alike will appreciate the ease with which they can select the Chinac remedies.[76]

Multidomestic Business Strategies

Under a multidomestic business (or *adaptation*) strategy, the firm treats each national market in a different way. It develops products and marketing strategies that appeal to the customs, tastes, and buying habits of particular national markets. Companies that neglect the global nature of the Internet can unwittingly cause problems for potential customers by failing to adapt their strategy. Jo Van Samang, a marketing manager in Belgium, tried to order from a U.S.-based Internet company but failed when the site rejected his order because he did not fill in the "state" field on the order form. David Topping, marketing director for UpDate Marketing, a provider of marketing software, notes that European customers are less comfortable with online shopping than their U.S. counterparts. So Topping says a Web site that wants to attract European visitors should not simply assume they are ready to make a purchase. Topping recommends that Web sites be tailored to different comfort levels—perhaps offering lower-priced products on a site for Europeans so that they can build up comfort with online shopping or offering a list of places to buy products off line.[77]

Dell Computer tailors its Web sites to the needs of different regions. Of Dell's 80 Web sites, 34 have Internet business capabilities matched to the local country. Dell Japan offers an advanced form of its Premier Pages, customized for particular business customers. The Premier Pages for Dell Japan keep track of service needs and Dell's response, as well as providing news about Dell products. Sites are also customized to reflect differences in local languages and currencies. However, one thing is the same from region to region: Dell's commitment to service. This understanding of customers' needs—different languages but a common desire for good service—has helped Dell take the lead in selling computers online.[78]

When Maytag prepared to sell refrigerators and washing machines in China, it researched the ways it should adapt its marketing. The company thought it might bring its well-respected brand name to China, but consumer research indicated that the Chinese failed to recognize the Maytag name and also perceived American appliances as too big and bulky. In addition, Chinese consumers expected Japanese and European appliances to be more economical and innovative. Based on this information, Maytag decided to use the brand name Rongshida, after its Chinese partner, Hefei Rongshida. To offset the less favorable perceptions of American appliances, Rongshida's ads emphasize well-built appliances with valuable benefits of such features as hardworking washing machine parts and self-defrosting freezers.[79] As this example shows, learning about international customers is an important part of preparing for the global economy.

WHAT'S AHEAD

Examples in this chapter indicate that both large and small businesses are relying on world trade, not just major corporations. Chapter 5 examines the special advantages and challenges that small-business owners encounter. In addition, a critical decision facing any new business is the choice of the most appropriate form of business ownership. Chapter 5 also examines the major ownership structures—sole proprietorship, partnership, and corporation—and assesses the pros and cons of each. The chapter closes with a discussion of recent trends affecting business ownership, such as the growing impact of franchising and business consolidations through mergers and acquisitions.

BUSINESS DIRECTORY

➤ **multidomestic business strategy**   *developing and marketing products to serve different needs and tastes of separate national markets.*

➤ Summary of Learning Goals

1. **Explain the importance of international business and the main reasons why nations trade.**

The U.S. is both the world's largest importer and the largest exporter, although less than 5 percent of the world's population lives within its borders. With the increasing globalization of the world's economies, the international marketplace offers tremendous opportunities for U.S. and foreign businesses to expand into new markets for their goods and services. Doing busness globally provides new sources of materials and labor. Trading with other countries also reduces a company's dependence on economic conditions in its home market. Countries that encourage international trade enjoy higher levels of economic activity, employment, and wages than those that restrict it. The major world markets are North America, Western Europe, the Pacific Rim, and Latin America. Emerging markets such as China and Brazil will become increasingly important to U.S. businesses over the next decade.

2. **Discuss the relationship of absolute and comparative advantage to international trade.**

Nations usually benefit if they specialize in producing certain goods or services. A country has an absolute advantage if it holds a monopoly or produces a good or service at a lower cost than other nations. It has a comparative advantage if it can supply a particular product more efficiently or at a lower cost than it can produce other items.

3. **Describe how nations measure international trade and the significance of exchange rates.**

Countries measure the level of international trade by comparing exports and imports and then calculating whether a trade surplus or a deficit exists. This is the balance of trade, which represents the difference between exports and imports. The term *balance of payments* refers to the overall flow of money into or out of a country, including overseas loans and borrowing, international investments, profits from such investments, and foreign aid. An exchange rate is the value of a nation's currency relative to the currency of another nation. Currency values typically fluctuate, or "float," relative to the supply and demand for specific currencies in the world market. When the value of the dollar falls compared with other currencies, the cost paid by foreign businesses and households for U.S. products declines, and demand for exports may rise. An increase in the value of the dollar raises the prices of U.S. products sold abroad, but it reduces the prices of foreign products sold in the United States.

4. **Identify the major barriers that confront global businesses.**

Businesses face several obstacles in the global marketplace. Companies must be sensitive to social and cultural differences, such as languages, values, and religions, when operating in other countries. Economic differences include standard of living variations and levels of infrastructure development. Legal and political barriers are among the most difficult to judge. Each country sets its own laws regulating business practices. Trade restrictions like tariffs and administrative barriers also present obstacles to international business.

5. **Explain how international trade organizations and economic communities reduce barriers to international trade.**

Many international organizations seek to promote international trade by reducing barriers. The list includes the World Trade Organization, World Bank, and International Monetary Fund. Multinational economic communities create partnerships to remove barriers to flows of goods, capital, and people across the borders of member nations. Two major economic agreements are the North American Free Trade Agreement and the European Union.

6. **Compare the different levels of involvement used by businesses when entering global markets.**

Exporting and importing, the first level of involvement in international business, involves the lowest degree of both risk and control. Companies may rely on export trading or management companies to assist in distribution of their products. Contractual agreements such as franchising, foreign licensing, and subcontracting offer additional, flexible options. Franchising and licensing are especially appropriate for services. Companies may also choose local subcontractors to produce goods for local sales. International direct investment in production and marketing facilities provides the highest degree of control but also the greatest risk. Firms make direct investments by acquiring foreign companies or facilities, forming joint ventures with local firms, and setting up their own overseas divisions.

7. **Describe the types of international organizational structures available to businesses.**

Once a company's managers decide on the desired level of international involvement, they must choose the appropriate organizational structure for their overseas venture. An independent agent represents an exporter in a foreign market. A license holder typically makes a larger investment in the product than does an independent agent, and may be likely to provide better representation for the product. However, licensing arrangements require longer time commitments than working with independent agents. Branch offices are units of an international firm located in foreign countries. Strategic alliances are joint ventures with local companies that combine resources and capital to create competitive advantage.

8. **Distinguish between a global business strategy and a multidomestic business strategy.**

A company that adopts a global (or standardization) strategy develops a single, standardized product and marketing strategy for implementation throughout the world. The firm sells the same product in essentially the same manner in all countries in which it operates. Under a multidomestic (or adaptation) strategy, the firm develops a different treatment for each national market. It develops products and marketing strategies that appeal to the customs, tastes, and buying habits of particular national markets.

Business Terms You Need to Know

Other Important Business Terms

➤ Review Questions

1. How does a business go about deciding whether to trade with a foreign country? What are the key factors for participating in the information economy on a global basis?

2. According to Table 4.1, which country or countries represent attractive markets for foreign businesses? Why?

3. What is the difference between absolute advantage and comparative advantage? Give an example of each.

4. Can a nation have a favorable balance of trade and an unfavorable balance of payments? Why or why not?

5. Identify several potential barriers to communication when a company attempts to conduct business in another country. How might these be overcome?

6. Explain the concept of *infrastructure*. In what ways does the infrastructure of a foreign country affect a company's attempts to do business in that country?

7. Identify and describe briefly the three dimensions of the legal environment for global business.

8. What are the major nontariff restrictions affecting international business? Describe the difference between tariff and nontariff restrictions.

9. What is NAFTA? How does it work?

10. What are the key choices a company must make before making the final decision to go global?

➤ Questions for Critical Thinking

1. When Britain transferred Hong Kong to China in 1997, China agreed to grant Hong Kong a high degree of autonomy as a capitalist economy for 50 years. Do you think this agreement will hold up? Why or why not? Consider China's economy, population, infrastructure, and other factors in your answer.

2. The tremendous growth of online business has introduced new elements to the legal climate of international business. Ideas, patents, brand names, copyrights, and trademarks are difficult to monitor because of the boundaryless nature of the Internet. What steps could businesses take to protect their trademarks and brands in this environment? What steps might countries take? Do you think such steps should even be taken? Why or why not?

3. The WTO monitors GATT agreements, mediates disputes, and continues the effort to reduce trade barriers throughout the world. However, widespread concerns have been expressed that the WTO's focus on lowering trade barriers may encourage businesses to keep costs down through practices that may lead to pollution and human rights abuses. Others argue that human rights should not be linked to international business. Do you think that environmental and human rights issues should be linked to trade? Why or why not?

4. The IMF makes short-term loans to developing countries that may not be able to repay them. Do you agree that the IMF should forgive these debts in some cases? Why or why not?

5. Describe briefly the EU and its goals. What are the pros and cons of the EU? Do you predict that the EU alliance will hold up over the next 20 years? Why or why not?

➤ Experiential Exercise

Background: *Fortune* magazine has published "The *Fortune* Global 500," a statistical snapshot of the world's largest corporations, every year since 1990. This exercise is designed to (a) help you learn more about this important list, (b) see how much you already know about the biggest global businesses, and (c) learn some new things about global business.

Directions: Your instructor will direct you to either work alone or as a member of a group to answer these questions. Use the most recent edition of "The *Fortune* Global 500," which is published in *Fortune* magazine normally in late July or early August, or go to *Fortune*'s online version at **www.fortune.com/fortune/global500.**

1. On what is the Global 500 ranking based (for example, profits, number of employees, sales revenues)?
2. Among the world's ten largest corporations, list the countries represented with the number of companies from each country.
3. Identify the top-ranked company along with its Global 500 ranking and country for each industry classification listed in the following table:

Global 500 Rank	Industry Classification	Company	Country
	Food and Drug Stores		
	Industrial and Farm Equipment		
	Petroleum Refining		
	Utilities: Gas and Electric		
	Telecommunications		
	Pharmaceuticals		

4. _____ is the Global 500 company with the greatest assets.
5. _____ is the Global 500 company with the highest profits.
6. Each of the 500 corporations is identified by industry. In the following table, list the five top-ranked industries based on the number of companies in that industry that made the Global 500 list:

Rank	Industry Classification	Number of Companies
1		
2		
3		
4		
5		

7. In the following table, list the three industries with the fewest companies represented on the Global 500 list and list at least one company from each industry in column two:

Industry Classification	Company

8. In the following table, identify the top two employers in the world—the two companies employing more people than any other company:

Company	Industry	Employees	Country

9. Identify the two largest beverage companies in the world. Fill in their names and other information requested in the following table:

Global 500 Rank	Company	Sales Revenues

10. Which country has the greatest representation in the "Electronics, Electrical Equipment" industry classification? Which has the greatest representation in "Banks: Commercial and Savings"?

➤ Nothing but Net

1. **Going Global.** One of the most successful internationally focused companies is Finnish cell phone manufacturer Nokia. Visit the company's Web site and then list five interesting facts about Nokia.

www.nokia.com/main.html

2. **World Trade Organization (WTO).** Visit the WTO Web site. Prepare an oral report for your class on the WTO's organizational structure and the services it provides to member nations. Address the question of how WTO membership is determined.

www.wto.org

3. **European Monetary Union (EMU).** The EMU has recently experienced some growing pains. In 2000, Danish voters rejected a proposal to switch from their national currency, the krone, to the euro, and the British remain steadfast in retaining the pound sterling as the official currency of the United Kingdom. Use your search engine to find the latest information and news related to the EMU. Prepare a brief report outlining the current status and some of the major issues facing the EMU. The following Web site provides a good starting point.

http://fullcoverage.yahoo.com/fc/world/European Monetary Union

Note: Internet Web addresses change frequently. If you don't find the exact sites listed, you may need to access the organization's home page and search from there.

"We've known each other forever," say Gai Gherardi and Barbara McReynolds, co-owners and designers of an internationally acclaimed eyeglass company. They've been business partners forever, too—at least since 1979 when they founded L.A. Eyeworks as their own personal cure for, as they put it, "creative frustration." The pair had worked together in an optical store during the late 1960s and enjoyed the business, but they were bored with the eyeglass styles available. They had plenty of autonomy as employees—they held poetry readings and political discussions at the shop while they sold glasses—but they wanted to do something on their own. "We were pushing to do something new," recalls McReynolds.

When they opened their first shop on Melrose Avenue in Los Angeles, nothing much was going on in the neighborhood. They chose the location for that reason—the street was not going to dictate who the shoppers at the new store would be. To stock the store, they carefully selected uncirculated old stock from existing eyeglass manufacturers and transformed them by tinting the lenses and dyeing and changing the frame surfaces. They gave their store a clean, streamlined design so it would feature the glasses themselves. "We were successful from the first day," recalls Gherardi.

Pretty soon, the team was doing what they really wanted to—creating their own designs. They found a manufacturer in France who was willing to produce the frames and began showing their goods at optics-oriented trade shows. Orders poured in from retail department stores like Bendel's, fashion retailers, and optical buyers. Then in 1986 they decided to try a trade show in Paris. Ironically, although the show was a success, no one from France bought the glasses. Instead, customers came from Germany and Holland. The following year, Gherardi and McReynolds took their goods to trade shows in Milan and again in Paris. Customers from Belgium, Scandinavia, and Italy seemed to understand and love what they were doing, and the French were catching on. So they began to think about setting up a distribution warehouse in Europe.

"We looked at the best countries to do business in," says McReynolds. In other words, they identified the countries that supported the type of business in which L.A. Eyeworks engages. They reviewed tax structures, currency exchange rates, and ease of transportation. They settled on an industrial/office park run specifically to support international commerce. Located in France just one mile from the Swiss border and a stone's throw from the Geneva airport, the L.A. Eyeworks European operations headquarters handles business for Europe and the Middle East.

"We opened bank accounts in the countries where we were doing business and learned everything about shipping costs, currencies, and so forth," note the duo. At the same time, Gherardi and McReynolds were learning the complexities of conducting business on a global scale. For instance, invoicing practices vary from country to country, and customer service representatives need to speak several languages. "Customers want to speak in their own language," observes McReynolds. These language differences could be potential barriers to a company trying to establish a presence in another region of the world, but McReynolds and Gherardi simply view it as a challenge.

Cultural differences come into play as well, and both partners emphasize that their company strives to accommodate those differences. "But we needed to go forward as an American company representing the culture of our company and not let that go by the wayside. That's a really tricky thing," they pointed out. It has been important for L.A. Eyeworks to maintain its edgy image because that image is part of what customers are buying. Eyeglass shoppers like L.A. Eyeworks's new, risky designs because they represent leading design and fashion innovation. "Customers are interested in the energy that comes out of L.A.," says McReynolds. "They want in on it—the stories, the art, the culture." People everywhere want to sport frames with names like Chops, Zipper, Sprawl, or Nifty.

But there are some places in the world where L.A. Eyeworks—the product and the image—just doesn't work. For instance, in India, the economy simply can't support high-priced luxury goods (L.A. Eyeworks glasses sell for $275 a pair and up). And India has created a closed-door policy on manufacturing by charging extremely high duties on imports. The government prefers to have goods manufactured and sold within the country's borders. In addition, there is little protection of licensing or trademark rights. So L.A. Eyeworks does not feel that right now India would be a successful market. On the other hand, L.A. Eyeworks glasses can be found in Germany, Switzerland, Italy, France, England, Australia, Japan, Singapore, Hong Kong, New Zealand, Canada, and eastern Europe—to name just a few places.

The company's famous slogan, "A face is like a work of art—it deserves a great frame," seems to be as universal as the celebrity appeal that comes along with stars like Jodie Foster, Matthew Lillard, Jennifer Tilly, and Elton John, who wear the glasses, and some of whom model them in advertisements. Belinda Carlisle did one of the company's first ads. But not every ad works in every country. Recently, the company decided to photograph a Chinese Olympic basketball player—who happened to be the tallest woman in China—for one of its advertisements, thinking that Chinese customers would be attracted to it. Instead, it fell flat with the Chinese, but the American audience loved it.

McReynolds and Gherardi continue to push the boundaries of eyeglass design and fashion. And although their company's success has grown way beyond their first shop on Melrose Avenue, it has not outgrown the goal of the first sign that hung in that store: "changing the face of L.A." Perhaps the sign might be edited a bit to read, "changing the face of the world."

QUESTIONS

1. Latin America is identified as one of the world's most attractive emerging market regions, yet L.A. Eyeworks currently has only a minor presence there. Do you think this would be a good market for L.A. Eyeworks to pursue more actively? Why or why not?
2. In addition to those discussed in the case, what other trade barriers might L.A. Eyeworks face in different countries?
3. How do you think the European Union might affect L.A. Eyeworks?
4. What types of strategic alliances might L.A. Eyeworks form in order to grow into new areas?

Sources: Company Web site, **www.laeyeworks.com,** accessed April 14, 2001; Deborah Martin, "Benefit Big on Spectacle," *San Antonio Express-News,* November 23, 2000, p. 1E; Anne-Marie Otey, "FashionDish LA Dish," *FashionDish,* July 7, 2000, **www.fashiondish.com;** "Shades," *Los Angeles Magazine,* December 1997 [no page]. Permission for this material must be applied for directly to L.A. Eyeworks.

14

Electronic Commerce:
The Internet and
Online Business

Learning Goals

1. Discuss how the Internet provides new routes to business success.

2. Describe the increasing diversity of Internet users.

3. Summarize the Internet's four functions and give examples of each.

4. List the major forms of business-to-business e-commerce.

5. Name the major forms of business-to-consumer e-commerce.

6. Describe some of the challenges associated with Internet selling.

7. Describe how companies develop and manage successful Web sites.

8. Explain how global opportunities result from technological advances.

Razorfish Helps Customers Stay Afloat on the Internet

The Internet is an ocean of opportunity for businesses. It's also a place where many businesses can—and do—drown, simply because of its size and the number of predators lurking in its waters. Existing brick-and-mortar companies want to take advantage of the Internet to broaden their markets and streamline their operations, and some new companies are starting business solely on the Internet. They all have something in common: the need to establish their presence with a Web site. An effective Web site—one that is easy to find and easy to use—is essential for any company that wants to do business on the Internet. If the site is also attractive and offers useful information, it can build excitement and interest. But most companies don't know how to build the sites themselves. They don't have the technology or the expertise. And amateur-looking sites don't cut it anymore. In fact, numerous do-it-yourself sites have failed. That's where Razorfish glides into the picture.

Razorfish was founded in 1995 by Jeff Dachis and Craig Kanarick when they recognized that many fledgling Web sites failed because of poor design. Many sites drove consumers away because people couldn't figure out how to navigate through them, let alone conduct any kind of transaction. Dachis and Kanarick decided they would become the link between a business and its customers by designing and building better sites. "Everybody's slapping all this stuff together," says Dachis. "They aren't thinking about what the users want." Dachis and Kanarick named their company after a spiny-finned Mediterranean fish, just because its picture looked kind of cool in the dictionary. But the name has become synonymous with cutting-edge Web site design.

The Razorfish team's approach is to get to know their customers and understand the big picture before digging into the details of design. When working with the brokerage firm Charles Schwab Corp., Razorfish employees met with Schwab's executives to hammer out the broker's goals for its online division, Schwab.com. Since one of Schwab's main goals was to

attract new customers to the site and offer them an opportunity to open an account there, Razorfish designers eventually decided that the site's "Open an Account" link

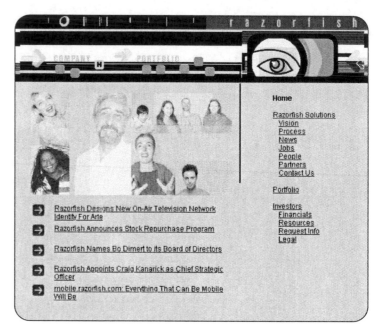

should be placed at the upper left-hand corner of the home page, where it would be simple to spot. Since many of Schwab's competitors downplay that link on their sites, Razorfish's approach was to highlight it, making it easy for new customers to use.

In addition to interviewing Schwab executives, Razorfish designers interviewed online traders, including some of its own employees. They asked questions such as "What's great about the online trading experience? What's terrible?" Then they put the answers to work. Razorfish also learned that many people were still using old-fashioned, small monitors, which meant that designers couldn't fill up the screen with unnecessary bells and whistles. And it's not good to allow important information to "fall off the screen," forcing the user to scroll up and down or back and forth. So the Schwab site had to be tightly designed. Then came the appearance of the site itself, which had to match the company's image. Schwab ultimately chose a pinstriped motif in soft blues. "It's a very business-oriented, strong, Wall Street-like color palette," notes Thomas Mueller, creative director for Razorfish.

With five offices in Europe and three in the United States, Razorfish has designed sites for brick-and-mortar companies such as CBS Corp. as well as Internet-based firms—called dot-coms—running the gamut from the Smithsonian Institution to underwear manufacturer Joe Boxer. In Britain, Razorfish has designed sites for the Spice Girls, NatWest, the Millennium Dome, the Paramount Comedy Channel, and British Aerospace. "The demand is still extremely high," remarks Mark Curtis, strategic solutions director for Razorfish. "The market for our kind of services is expanding at a rate of nearly 150 percent a year." One industry watcher says that concentrating on Europe is a good strategy for Razorfish. Because Europe is a few years behind the United States in business conducted on the Internet, Razorfish can learn from mistakes U.S. businesses make and can capture its share of the growing market in Europe.

The next time you log on to the Internet, pay attention to the sites you visit. Which do you like the most? Which do you hardly glance at? Razorfish wants to know what will make you and millions of other online shoppers return to its customers' sites and click that "buy now" key. They won't be the only fish in the Internet sea, but they are determined to be the strongest—and the sharpest.[1]

CHAPTER OVERVIEW

Like Razorfish and other businesses worldwide, more and more firms in every industry are operating in cyberspace. Increasingly, executives are asking themselves, "What does Internet technology mean to me and my business?" The Internet offers contemporary businesspeople a source of information, a means of communication, and a channel for buying and selling, all rolled into one. And the Internet offers tremendous opportunities for those who are willing to make the leap online.

In this chapter we describe the ways that the Internet is revolutionizing the face of business. We begin with an overview of the Internet, including its origins, scope, and components. Then we describe how individuals and businesses use the Internet. Later, we review electronic commerce and its implications for both businesses and consumers, including how companies use Web sites to further their objectives. The Internet also drives the globalization of business, so we investigate how e-commerce is helping companies take advantage of opportunities around the globe.

THE INTERNET: KEY TO BUSINESS SUCCESS

Want to find the cheapest price for a new car, computer, hotel room, or insurance? How about movie reviews and a schedule of what's playing in your neighborhood? Suppose you want to sell DVD players to affluent Mexican shoppers but don't know the size of the market or the applicable regulations. Just go online. With a few clicks of your computer's mouse, you can find the answer to just about any question. Besides looking up information, you can trade messages with friends and colleagues, join in an online discussion, play interactive games, listen to music, and make purchases. No wonder the average adult Internet user is expected to devote almost two years of his or her remaining life to online activities.

Although many people think of the Internet as a fairly recent development, it actually began in 1969 as a Department of Defense experiment that involved networking four computers to facilitate communications in the event of a nuclear war. Until about 1993, the Internet (or Net) remained an obscure computer network with few commercial applications. Today, however, this all-purpose, global network allows computer users anywhere to send and receive data, sound, and video content. Its growth has been phenomenal, with host computers doubling annually. By 2001, Internet users numbered 375 million people worldwide. By 2005, one person in ten will be a regular Internet user. In the United States, almost two-thirds of all Americans 12 years of age and older used the Internet in a recent year, and almost half of those logged on daily.[2]

A major factor in the Internet's growth was the introduction of technology that provided point-and-click access to the World Wide Web (or Web, for short). The Web is an interlinked collection of graphically rich information sources within the larger Internet. Web documents are organized into Web sites composed of electronic pages that integrate text, graphics, audio, and video elements. The pages include hypertext links, highlighted words or images that, when clicked on, whisk the user to other documents. Browsers are software programs that help users navigate the Web to locate, retrieve, and display information. By typing in search words or simply clicking on hypertext links, users can explore the Web. The most widely used Web browsers are Netscape Navigator and Microsoft Internet Explorer.

Today the Web is the most popular Internet resource. From just 100 Web sites in 1993, the scope of the Web has grown to more than 25 million registered domain names today.[3] A **domain name** is a Web site address. Although not every domain name has an operating Web site, the incredible increase in only a few years shows that the scope and potential of the Web are enormous.

Although the Internet has been considered an industry for only a few years, online transactions are already generating hundreds of billions of dollars in revenues.

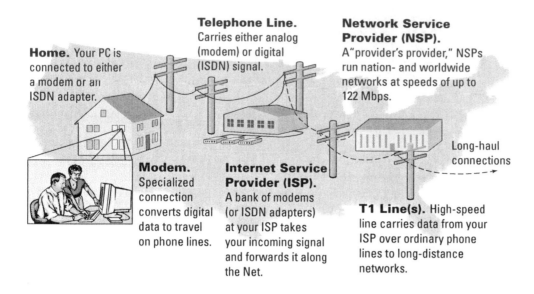

Home. Your PC is connected to either a modem or an ISDN adapter.

Telephone Line. Carries either analog (modem) or digital (ISDN) signal.

Network Service Provider (NSP). A "provider's provider," NSPs run nation- and worldwide networks at speeds of up to 122 Mbps.

Modem. Specialized connection converts digital data to travel on phone lines.

Internet Service Provider (ISP). A bank of modems (or ISDN adapters) at your ISP takes your incoming signal and forwards it along the Net.

T1 Line(s). High-speed line carries data from your ISP over ordinary phone lines to long-distance networks.

Long-haul connections

FIGURE 7.1
How Information Travels on the Internet

In addition, many types of companies are selling the hardware and software required for Internet use as well as providing support services. Telecommunications companies provide local and long-distance network transmission lines, and computer and electronics manufacturers supply resources that help to complete the Internet's infrastructure. Software developers create programs for a host of Internet applications such as multimedia transmissions and Web page design. Entertainment and media companies develop the content that Web surfers see, and service businesses offer Web site design and specialized software for electronic commerce. U.S. businesses spend an estimated $120 billion annually to develop or improve their presence on the Internet.[4] Also, many companies sell advertising on their Web pages to generate revenue.

How the Internet Works

The Internet is a remarkable system of cooperating networks. In seconds, you can send e-mail from Montana to Hong Kong, search the archives of European newspapers, plan your next vacation, gather product information, or buy a best-selling novel.

To understand how this complex system of networks operates, follow the journey of an e-mail message that you send to a friend in a different state. In the example shown in Figure 7.1, your message begins its Internet journey at your personal computer (PC), from which it travels through phone lines; modems convert digital data into analog form compatible with the phone lines. The data arrives at the modems of your Internet service provider (ISP), an organization that provides access to the Internet through its own series of local networks. Thousands of ISPs offer local Internet access to North American cybernauts.

This process is similar but faster if your friend has newer broadband technology, such as a **digital subscriber line (DSL)**, a cable modem, or a satellite link to the Internet. With DSL, data travel over standard telephone lines between computers and telephone switching stations, but a DSL router or modem makes the data move at higher frequencies and much faster speeds. This technology permits voice and DSL transmissions to be transmitted simultaneously over the same phone line, and the Internet connection is continuous, so the user does not have to dial up for

BUSINESS DIRECTORY

➤ **Internet (or Net)** *worldwide network of interconnected computers that lets anyone with access to a personal computer send and receive images and data anywhere.*

➤ **World Wide Web (Web)** *collection of resources on the Internet that offers easy access to text, graphics, sound, and other multimedia resources.*

➤ **Web site** *integrated document composed of electronic pages that integrate text, graphics, audio, and video elements, as well as hypertext links to other documents.*

➤ **Internet service provider (ISP)** *organization that provides access to the Internet, usually via the public telephone network.*

Using wireless technology, the OnStar vehicle communications system lets OnStar know if an air bag deploys or the vehicle is stolen. It can even send remote signals to unlock the car doors or diagnose an engine problem while the car is being driven.

Internet service. A cable connection uses the same line that supplies cable television programming. Satellite hookups have been relatively slow to catch on in the United States, where phone service is inexpensive and reliable. However, users in other countries have been faster to adopt satellite technology, which allows them to connect to the Internet from a cellular phone as well as a computer. In Finland, more than two-thirds of people use cell phones to connect to the Internet and look up information, send e-mail, and even make purchases.[5] But wireless technology is catching on in the U.S., as it offers faster downloading than a standard phone hookup can deliver. Wireless capabilities enable new applications of the Internet, such as General Motors' OnStar dashboard communications system, which lets drivers access the Internet from their cars. Drivers with OnStar can use the Internet to find a restaurant, make reservations, get driving directions, and even call for help if they have a flat tire along the way.[6]

What happens when the message reaches the recipient's ISP network? The answer to this question requires a basic understanding of client/server systems. The message you sent is stored with the ISP's **server,** a larger, special computer that holds information and then provides it to clients on request. A **client** is another computer or device that relies on the resources of one or more servers for help with its own processing. Traditionally, clients have been desktop PCs, but Internet users are increasingly connecting from various other devices, including laptop and palmtop computers, televisions, and cell phones. Servers efficiently distribute resources to a network of client computers as needed. When your friend wants to check his or her e-mail, the message travels back through phone, DSL, or cable lines or via wireless transmission to his or her modem.

The ISP functions as the intermediary for its customers. Monthly or hourly user fees cover the cost of equipment such as ISP modems, servers, related software, proprietary and leased networks, and in some cases original content. Some ISPs offer free services to consumers, but the trade-off for users is being forced to view large amounts of advertising posted on the site. Although many of them consider this barrage of ads more annoying than paying monthly subscription fees, the number of users of free ISP services continues to grow.

Who's on the Net?

Although the Internet was born in the United States, its users now live on every continent. At the beginning of the 21st century, 43 percent of Internet users were in the U.S., but the share of users from other countries is growing. By 2006, about three-quarters of the Internet user population will live outside the U.S.[7] As Figure 7.2 shows, of the world's 375 million Internet users, the four nations with the largest concentrations of Net users are located on three different continents: North America (United States), Asia (Japan), and Western Europe (Germany and the United Kingdom). South America, the fourth continent represented among the top ten, lists Brazil as the nation with the largest concentration located south of the equator.

Recent studies of U.S. Internet users reveal some major trends toward an increasingly diverse Net population:

- Although the Internet was once dominated by men, the gender gap has narrowed. Women now represent more than half of Internet users in the United States and a sizable share in other nations—more than a third in the United Kingdom and Germany and four in ten in Sweden.[8] Women were estimated to be 45 percent of the Internet's global population in 2001.[9]

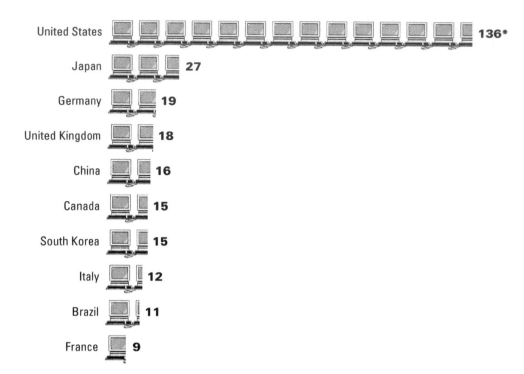

FIGURE 7.2
Top Ten Internet Users

United States 136*

Japan 27

Germany 19

United Kingdom 18

China 16

Canada 15

South Korea 15

Italy 12

Brazil 11

France .. 9

*Number of Internet users in millions.

- The earliest users of the Internet were disproportionately white and Asian American, but black and Hispanic Americans are now obtaining Internet access at a faster rate.[10]
- The average age of users is rising. The fastest-growing share of the Internet population is adults 45 years of age and older, and this age group spends more time on the Internet than 18- to 24-year-olds.[11]
- Net users tend to be more affluent and to attain higher levels of education than the general population.[12]
- Time spent online is rising, taking away from television and newspapers, as well as time spent in stores and with family and friends.[13]

Just as the population of individuals using the Internet is becoming more like the overall population, so is the mix of businesses on the Internet. A Web site once set a company apart as "high-tech," but most large businesses have by now established an Internet presence. Today, two of every five U.S. small businesses have Web sites, and more than two-thirds of them are connected to the Internet. Small businesses owned by women and minorities use the Net most often.[14]

Using the Net's Four Functions

What do these "Netizens" do online? As Figure 7.3 shows, one or more of four primary functions are performed on the Web: communication, information gathering and sharing, entertainment, and business transactions (e-commerce).

Communication   Most people go online to communicate. For both households and businesses, the most popular application of the Internet in the U.S. is e-mail. In fact, e-mails now outnumber regular mail by ten to one. Its popularity is easy to understand: e-mail is simple to use, travels quickly, and can be read at the receiver's convenience. Also, longer documents can be sent as attachments to e-mail messages.

FIGURE 7.3
Four Functions of the Internet

Communication
- E-mail
- Instant messaging
- Chat rooms
- Online communities
- Telephone and video conferencing

E-Commerce
- Electronic exchanges
- Extranets and private exchanges
- Electronic storefronts
- Online ticketing
- Auctions

Information
- Search engines
- Online publications
- Newsgroups
- Portals

Entertainment
- Games
- Radio and TV programming
- Music
- Electronic books
- Short movies

A more recent adaptation of e-mail is **instant messaging**. With this application, when someone sends a message, it is immediately displayed on the recipient's computer screen. As sender and recipient reply to one another, they can communicate in real time.

Another popular way to communicate online is through chat rooms. Chat rooms provide a forum in which a group of people can share messages. When someone sends a message, it is displayed for all to see. Users join chat sessions on topics that interest them. The resulting **online communities** are not only personally satisfying but an important force for businesses. Some companies participate in or even sponsor such communication. Playing Mantis has built a successful business manufacturing and selling car models and action figures from the 1960s. If you have older relatives who long for a model Corvette Stingray or The Phantom or Green Hornet action figures, you can send them to Playing Mantis to satisfy that need. In addition to manufacturing the toys, the company generates interest in them by participating in online chat rooms. Customer service manager Lisa Greco routinely participates in these discussions. In the mid-1990s, when online communication was still new, a Web site called Hobbytalk began sponsoring a bulletin board for collectors of Playing Mantis's line of Polar Lights models, later adding boards for other product lines. Greco routinely logs on to answer questions and announce new products. Over the years, regular visitors to the site have developed a sense of belonging to it—and a passion for Playing Mantis and its products. When Playing Mantis modernized its Web site, the launch was a mess, but high-tech members of this unofficial community patiently surfed the site and posted recommended fixes. Within days, the company got the site running properly. Greco and the other managers of Playing Mantis are convinced that this type of communication gives them an unbeatable edge—customers who feel like part of the company.[15]

Voice technology is now coming to the Web, and video-conferencing won't be far behind. Internet telephony allows users to use their computers to dial up and speak to friends and business associates alike. Voice messages are divided into segments called *packets*, which move over the transmission lines and are reassembled at the receiving end. Although the voice quality is currently not as good as regular telephone service and some packets can arrive out of sequence, the quality and reliability will improve in the future.

Businesses also use the Internet to communicate promotional messages. Marketers use the Web to build brand relationships and offer goods and services via e-mail, advertisements, sweepstakes, and more. Use of the Internet as a tool for marketing communications is discussed in Chapter 16.

Information In a recent consumer survey, 82 percent of Web users said getting information was one of the reasons they use the Internet.[16] Internet users meet their need for information at commercial sites such as AskJeeves and Northern Light, which search for information on topics entered by the user. Or they may visit online publications such as the *Chicago Tribune*'s and *The Wall Street Journal*'s online editions. Government sites provide a wealth of free data in the public domain. **Newsgroups** provide a forum for participants to share information on selected topics. Another fast-growing area of the Internet consists of sites providing online educational services. John Chambers, chief executive officer (CEO) of Cisco Systems, recently wrote in a *New York Times* editorial, "Education over the Internet is going to be so big, it's going to make E-mail usage look like a rounding error." One-third of U.S. colleges now offer some sort of accredited degree online, and private investment in education-related Internet companies more than doubled every year throughout most of the 1990s. These companies include publishers, schools, and corporate training services.[17]

With such an enormous variety of possibilities, some of the most popular Web sites are **portals**, sites designed to be a user's starting place when entering the World Wide Web. The most widely visited Web sites are Yahoo! (www.yahoo.com), America Online (www.aol.com), and Microsoft Network (www.msn.com).[18] All of these sites serve as portals, offering links to search engines, weather reports, news, yellow pages, maps, and other popular types of information, as well as e-mail, chat rooms, and the ability to bookmark favorite sites in order to click to them directly in the future.

Many sites specialize in particular types of information. For example, Travelocity, Expedia, Lowest Fare, and a number of other sites search for airline flights that meet the user's criteria for date, city, and price. Visitors to the UPS Web site (www.ups.com) can check the delivery status of their packages. Other sites offer product reviews, maps and driving directions, stock prices, sports coverage, and much, much more.

Businesses turn to the Web to gather information about their rivals and to assess industry trends. Executives can visit competitors' Web sites to learn about new-product announcements and check financial reports. They can read trade and business publications online and visit the Web sites of their professional organizations. Business-oriented Web portals offer links useful to businesspeople. The CEO Express Web site offers links to business publications, industry statistics, travel services, search engines, and other sites that can help with a manager's work. Other companies, including

Introducing Jeeves, the world's first Internet butler.
Just type a question in your own words and Jeeves promptly finds the answer.
How many calories am I burning? Where can I stay in Paris? How do I fix a flat tire?
Jeeves is asked millions of questions every day. What's yours?

Wanna know? Ask Jeeves Ask.com

The commercial Web site AskJeeves helps humanize online searches. Using the site is as simple as typing in a question you want answered. Want to know where to find the lyrics to your favorite song? Just type your question in at ASK.com and Mr. Jeeves will answer in a matter of seconds.

FIGURE 7.4
Web Page Sweepstakes Designed to Generate Customer Data

Yahoo!, Viador, and Microsoft, set up portals tailored to the individual needs of their business customers. These corporate portals combine a company's data with information from the Internet.

Companies can also use the interactive technology of the Internet to gather information about their customers. For example, some sites ask visitors for personal information through registration or sweepstakes entry forms. Figure 7.4 shows a sweepstakes site run by fastfreefun.com. To enter, visitors to this site provide their name, e-mail address, and other information. Sites that accept online orders gather the user-provided data, such as shipping addresses, along with purchase data. Even sites that do not ask for data can track the usage patterns of visitors to the site. With each type of data, marketers can adapt content, services, and advertising to their typical Web site users.

As an information source, the Internet is only as reliable as the individuals and companies who provide the information published there. Articles posted on Encyclopedia Britannica's Web site are likely to be more objective than Web sites put up by individuals to promote a particular viewpoint. Likewise, the ease of sending e-mail messages has markedly increased the speed with which people disseminate so-called urban legends, such as the story that the AIDS virus was on needles in gasoline pumps or flesh-eating viruses were found on banana peels. Because of the spread of misinformation, some practical cautions are essential for Web information gatherers:

- Know your source. Whenever you read information on the Web, make sure you have identified the provider of the information. Is it a reputable publication or news service, a known expert, or an organization or person with a position to promote? Recently, there has been a rash of attempts to manipulate stock prices by posting misinformation on investment sites. The rumor spreaders then try to cash in on the wild swings in stock prices—and they hurt other investors in the process.[19] The moral? Check the accuracy of information on the Web before acting on it.

- Investigate information by checking more than one source. The old saying "If it sounds too good to be true, it probably is" applies to the Internet just as it does in the rest of the world.

- Don't believe all the e-mail announcements forwarded to you, especially messages that urge you to "forward this to 20 friends." Check out the story at one of the Web sites that specialize in squelching false rumors and urban legends. These include the U.S. Department of Energy's Computer Incident Advisory Capability (CIAC), at ciac.llnl.gov, and About.com's Web pages titled "Virus Hoaxes" and "Urban Legends and Folklore." These sites are not only informative, but highly entertaining.

Entertainment Besides reading urban legends, Internet users are finding other entertainment online, including everything from concert Webcasts to online gaming. Some Internet users even participate in more than one form of entertainment at once. A study of children using the Internet found that 86 percent of teenage girls who go

With the Click of a Shutter, Camera World Becomes cameraworld.com

Background. Nearly 25 years ago, Korean-born businessman Jack Shin founded Camera World, a small retail shop for amateur photo buffs in downtown Portland, Oregon. When the business got going, he added a mail-order component that dovetailed easily with his retail operation. Shin assembled a simple order fulfillment and shipping infrastructure that was so efficient the company still uses it today, although the system was computerized in 1992.

From the beginning, Shin stuck to a few crucial principles. First, he refused to deal in "gray market" merchandise—goods not meant to be sold in the United States—which is so prevalent in the camera business. Instead, he developed solid relationships with executives from Fuji, Canon, Nikon, and others. Those relationships remain intact today. Second, he established the goal that mail-order customers would receive their merchandise within five days of ordering—no matter what. He also made returns simple and convenient. Third, he staffed the phones with a sales force made up of professional and qualified amateur photographers who could answer customer questions. As a result, Camera World developed a loyal following among camera manufacturers and consumers. "We make customers very happy, and they remember we give service, service, service. Repeat customers [are a] big part of our business," emphasizes Shin. Within a decade, Camera World was doing 70 percent of its business by mail order.

What Happened? Then markets and the world itself began to change, and Shin decided to sell out, with the help of Walt Mulvey, a retail-management expert who helped Shin ready the company for sale. Swedish-born businessman Alessandro Mina was looking for an opportunity and liked what he saw. "We saw this terrific sleeper and thought we could turn it into a full-fledged Net business," says Mina.

The Response. Mina and Mulvey took Camera World online. But they didn't take any shortcuts. "We made it a point to visit every supplier personally, take them out to dinner, and assure them that the business would continue," explains Mina. The suppliers went along. "At first we had some doubts about their ability to take over the business and move it to the Net, but they were able to build on the infrastructure to handle it," admits Eliott Peck, director and general manager for the camera division of Canon USA.

Today and Counting. In a 20,000-square-foot warehouse, workers scurry back and forth with order printouts and shipping boxes, filling orders in much the same way they always have. During the recent holiday shopping season, when many online companies failed to get their goods to customers, cameraworld.com fielded roughly 25,000 site visits a day, sold cameras at $600 apiece, and shipped 90 percent of its Internet orders within 24 hours. "We maintained heavy inventories to ship on time, and it all worked pretty well," says the company's new chief executive officer, Terry Strom. "But one thing's for sure: The Internet is raising the standard of performance for any retailer."

Recently updated, cameraworld.com's site is easy to use for both consumers and businesses. Cameraworld.com handles new and established commercial accounts as well as government accounts, in addition to all those shutterbugs who just want to take pictures of their vacations, family holidays, and pets. All customers get the same personalized treatment, which is why they keep coming back. Manufacturers remain loyal as well. On a scale of 1 to 10 among dealers, "I've always given them a 10," says Elliot Peck of Canon.

QUESTIONS FOR CRITICAL THINKING

1. Cameraworld.com has successfully used the Web to conduct transactions. What other ways might the company use the Internet to further strengthen its relationship with customers and suppliers?
2. Visit www.cameraworld.com and compare it with other sites you have visited. Is the site designed well? What are its strong points? If you detect any weak points, what improvements would you suggest?
3. Cameraworld.com is successful because of the strong infrastructure and relationship with suppliers and customers that it built before going online. Can you think of any other reasons why the company maintains success at e-commerce?

Sources: Company Web site, **www.cameraworld.com**, accessed February 6, 2001; Bronwyn Fryer, "When Something Clicks," *Inc. Technology* no 1, 2000, p. 62.; Robert Goldfield and Andy Giegerich, "Corillian, camerworld.com: Two Different Paths," *The Business Journal of Portland*, February 7, 2000, **www.bizjournals.com/portland**.

online listen to the radio at the same time. Other Web surfers manage to watch television while they are online. These mixed-media users, whom marketers call *telewebbers*, number an estimated 44 million in the U.S.[20]

Online providers of entertainment can offer competitive prices, speed, and boundless services. Games, radio programming, short movies, and music clips are available online, sometimes for free, with the costs borne by advertising on the Web site. And after decades of predictions that we will someday do most of our reading on computer screens, the technology finally seems to be in place. Products like the Rocket eBook allow users to download a book's contents from the Internet and read it on a handheld device that simulates a book. In 2000, Stephen King's novel *Riding the Bullet* became the first mass-market book published exclusively in electronic format. In the first day of the book's release, 400,000 copies were downloaded—or at least ordered, since the huge demand caused backups at booksellers' Web sites. That traffic may have indicated pent-up demand for high-tech publishing or perhaps the fact that the book was free on the first day it was offered.[21] Other titles have been published both in paper and electronically, including Mario Puzo's *Omerta* and Arthur Golden's *Memoirs of a Geisha*.

The availability of free content poses some ethical and business challenges, discussed later in the chapter. However, those issues are unlikely to chase entertainment off the Internet.

Business Transactions: E-Commerce   A newer application of Web technology, electronic business transactions, are growing at lightning speed. Customers can not only learn about companies and their products on the Internet but complete purchases. As discussed in Chapters 13 and 15, this gives the Web a key role in businesses' sales and distribution strategies. Organizations from multinational corporations to individual entrepreneurs have established a Web presence or have begun planning one. Today customers can go online to buy everything from toys and books to cars and business equipment. As growing numbers of companies sell their products on the Web, business success requires understanding the Web's advantages and its limitations and incorporating its use into a firm's overall business plans and strategies. The owners of Camera World built on its solid reputation when they took the business online, as the "Clicks and Mortar" box described.

A Web presence builds awareness of a company's products and brands, provides the means for one-on-one communication with customers, and can allow customers to place orders from anywhere in the world, at any time of day. At Ticketmaster's Web site, customers can purchase tickets to the upcoming Fiona Apple concert, printing them out on their own printer. They can also look up local entertainment listings and even sign up for an online dating service to find someone to invite to the concert.[22] These activities are the substance of *electronic commerce*, called *e-commerce* for short.

THE SCOPE OF ELECTRONIC COMMERCE

When a Silicon Valley giant like Oracle needs office furniture, its people naturally look online. They head for the Web site of a furniture company called CRI. By entering a password, they can view pages tailored to their purchase history, where they can see specifications, prices, and order forms. Not only does the site let customers place orders, but it allows them to plan office layouts by viewing, revising, and commenting on drawings. In addition, CRI plans to offer customers access to information about the status of their current orders and ways the company has resolved any past problems with their orders. So, the Web not only enables CRI and its customers to complete transactions, it also provides speedy, effective customer service.[23]

Like CRI and Oracle, companies around the world are discovering the advantages of electronic commerce (e-commerce), marketing goods and services over the Internet by exchanging information between buyers and sellers, while in the process minimizing paperwork and simplifying payment procedures. As with other types of buyer–seller interaction, e-commerce involves a chain of events for customer and seller. It starts with product information; moves through the order, invoicing, and payment processes; and ends with customer service.

The first wave of e-commerce brought techniques such as charge-card approval systems, point-of-sale terminals, scanners, and even early Internet selling—all activities focused mainly on lowering sellers' costs. As more firms discover the benefits of e-commerce, and as the Internet offers progressively more affordable services for almost any business, power begins to shift toward buyers, who gain access to a wider range of vendors.

A number of innovations promote both business-to-business and business-to-consumer e-commerce. One is encryption systems, which enable users to gather credit card numbers and other personal data required for completing transactions while protecting the security of purchasers. Another is the growing use of broadband technologies, which enable users to download more data at much faster speeds. Broadband makes technologies such as video and audio streaming more enjoyable and thus more attractive to users. With such developments, the number of businesses participating in e-commerce is growing fast. More than half of U.S. companies today have sold products online, twice the number making such sales just four years ago.[24]

The growth of e-commerce has attracted an army of specialized software firms and other service suppliers that provide expertise for firms taking their first steps into this competitive arena. As Figure 7.5 describes, global computer giant IBM offers its business customers both software and services designed to build virtual stores that go far beyond traditional Web sites. Although IBM originally was known as a producer of mainframe computers, it now generates one-fourth of its revenue from sales related to e-commerce—75 percent of that from software, services, and related technology. The company has a huge staff of consultants working on jobs ranging from designing Web sites to converting huge databases from "legacy" (old mainframe) systems to Internet systems. IBM will even run e-commerce systems for companies that want to outsource this activity. The company also sells its own personal computers online and offers answers to technical questions on its Web site. It even trains employees over the Internet as well as in classrooms. As a result, IBM's Internet presence is both generating sales and slashing costs.[25]

FIGURE 7.5
IBM's Key Role in Electronic Commerce

Profiting from E-Commerce

Much of the hype about e-commerce centers on sales of goods and services over the World Wide Web, but online product sales represent only one of several ways to generate revenue online. For example, two e-commerce businesses called Ezgov.com and GovWorks.com are partnering with governments to set up Web sites at which citizens can interact with government agencies to register cars, pay taxes, look for government jobs, and participate in government auctions, among other activities. The companies generate revenues by charging users a fee for each transaction and selling advertising space on their sites.[26]

So far, however, only a minority of companies report profits from their Web sites. Of sites catering to business customers, 27 percent were reported to be profitable in their first year. In contrast, among the sites that have survived at least three years, 42 percent claim to be profitable.[27] Profitability among online retailers—companies selling to consumers rather than business customers—is most common among those that already had off-line customers, including catalog retailers like Lands' End and Hanover Direct, whose catalogs include Gump's, the Company Store, and International Male. Such businesses have an advantage because consumers are more familiar with them and are reminded of the Web sites every time they look at the companies' catalogs.[28]

As Figure 7.6 shows, the business potential of e-commerce involves more than sales transactions.

BUSINESS DIRECTORY

➤ **electronic commerce (e-commerce)**   *process for online marketing of goods and services—including product information; ordering, invoicing, and payment processes; and customer service.*

FIGURE 7.6
Benefits of E-commerce

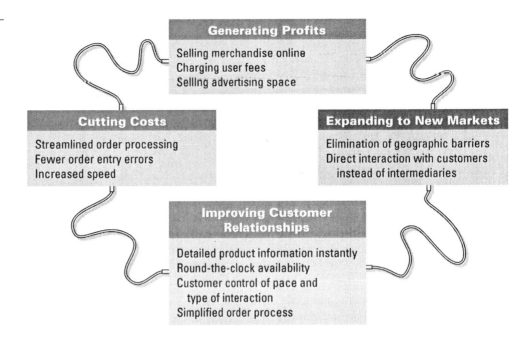

Generating Profits
Selling merchandise online
Charging user fees
Selling advertising space

Cutting Costs
Streamlined order processing
Fewer order entry errors
Increased speed

Expanding to New Markets
Elimination of geographic barriers
Direct interaction with customers
instead of intermediaries

Improving Customer Relationships
Detailed product information instantly
Round-the-clock availability
Customer control of pace and
type of interaction
Simplified order process

Companies also establish an Internet presence to expand beyond their geographic boundaries to reach new markets, cut costs, and improve customer relationships. Putting massive industrial catalogs on the Web, for example, saves publishing and postage costs. With a few keystrokes, customers can send orders and service requests directly from their computers to the seller's computer—cutting the need for inbound telemarketing personnel and other customer service representatives.

The two main types of e-commerce are transactions between businesses and transactions between businesses and customers. Both are offering new opportunities, but business-to-business e-commerce is taking the lead. Business-to-business transactions are fueling the growth of e-commerce and forging new relationships along the way.

Business-to-Business Transactions Lead the Way

One of the oldest applications of technology to business transactions is **electronic data interchange (EDI)**, computer-to-computer exchanges of invoices, purchase orders, price quotations, and other business documents between buyers and sellers. EDI requires compatible hardware and software systems to exchange data over a network. Use of EDI cuts paper flow, speeds the order cycle, and reduces errors. In addition, by receiving daily inventory status reports from vendors, companies can set production schedules to match demand.

Wal-Mart was one of the first major corporations to adopt EDI in the early 1990s. In fact, the retailer refused to do business with distributors and manufacturers that did not use compatible EDI standards. EDI is one of the major reasons Wal-Mart was able to operate with the efficiency that made it a market leader. It can buy just the products its customers want, just when it needs to restock its shelves, a system known as *quick response*.

From those early efforts to computerize business transactions, companies have taken the next technological leap—to the Internet—and are reaping rewards for doing so. **Business-to-business e-commerce, known as B2B,** is the use of the Internet for business transactions between organizations. One-fourth of all B2B transactions are expected to take place on the Internet in 2003, amounting to $2.8 trillion. This penetration of e-commerce is predicted to increase to more than 40 percent of B2B sales by 2005.[29] Those sales are spread out across many businesses. The number of U.S. businesses engaged in B2B e-commerce is expected to grow from 30 percent to more than 90 percent in one year.[30] Cisco Systems, Intel, and IBM are among the companies that generate billions of dollars in revenues online each year.

In addition to generating revenues from product sales, B2B e-commerce also provides detailed product descriptions whenever they are needed and slashes order-processing expenses. Business-to-business transactions, which typically involve more steps than consumer purchases, can be much more efficient on the Internet. Orders placed over the Internet typically contain fewer errors than handwritten ones, and when mistakes occur, the technology can quickly locate them. So, the Internet is an attractive option for business buying and selling. In some industries, relying on the Internet to make purchases can reduce costs by one-eighth.[31]

Initially, companies used their own Web sites to conduct isolated B2B transactions. Now the types of transactions and sites have become more varied. The principal forms of B2B e-commerce include electronic exchanges, extranets, and private exchanges.

Electronic Exchanges The earliest B2B e-commerce usually consisted of a company setting up a Web site and offering products to any buyer willing to make online purchases. More recently, businesses are buying and selling through **electronic exchanges,** Web-based marketplaces that cater to a specific industry's needs. General Motors, Ford, DaimlerChrysler, Renault, and Nissan are jointly investing in the start-up of an online parts exchange, called Covisint. Their plan, expanding on each company's earlier individual effort, is to create a global system through which each automaker can order all its parts and supplies. The contractors and subcontractors who participate can also buy from one another. The automakers hope that by posting planned design changes and actual production data on the system, they will encourage more efficient operations—for themselves and their suppliers. As Figure 7.7 shows, such savings can ultimately reduce the cost of a car by hundreds of dollars. The automakers also hope the system will bring auto manufacturers closer to building cars to meet individual orders, rather than trying to anticipate demand.[32] The "Clicks and Mortar" box explores another industry that has benefited from an electronic exchange, this time in the form of an auction.

The steel industry has also seen the advantages of electronic exchanges. At two Web sites, MetalSite.com and e-Steel.com, steel companies post data about product selection, availability, and prices. Steel buyers can visit the sites to look for the best deal and place orders. Steel makers benefit because they can find buyers for the excess inventory, and the buyers can find greater selection and better prices than they usually did when shopping by placing one phone call after another. LTV Corp., a U.S. steel-making giant, has used the Web site to unload tons of inventory, making the company more competitive with its foreign rivals. Francis P. Mangano, an LTV manager, says that without MetalSite, "we would have been selling roughly half of what we are selling now."[33]

Another example is the retail industry, which has set up the WorldWide Retail Exchange, in which nearly a dozen retailers, including Kmart, Safeway, and Britain's Marks & Spencer, conduct transactions with their suppliers. As with the automakers and steel industry, the retailers expect the exchange to help them reduce their overall cost of purchasing supplies and inventory and operate more efficiently. A notable holdout among exchange participants is Wal-Mart, the world's largest retailer. The firm's management believes that its participation in such a venture is more likely to benefit its competitors than to help Wal-Mart.[34]

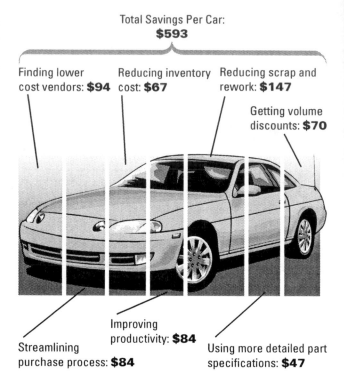

Total Savings Per Car: **$593**

Finding lower cost vendors: **$94**

Reducing inventory cost: **$67**

Reducing scrap and rework: **$147**

Getting volume discounts: **$70**

Streamlining purchase process: **$84**

Improving productivity: **$84**

Using more detailed part specifications: **$47**

FIGURE 7.7
How Online Parts Exchanges Save Money for Automakers

FreeMarkets Brings the Gavel Down on Prices

Background. Picture a bunch of ordinary purchasers scattered around the country, hunched over their computers, linked to each other and to a home base via the Internet. At home base, which looks like the control room of the Starship Enterprise, more computers hum and whir while a huge video screen displays rapidly changing prices. Look more closely, and you'll see that the prices are actually falling. You've already figured out that this is an Internet auction. But this isn't eBay, where the prices rise as buyers slap bids on everything from antique dolls to yard-sale mugs. This is FreeMarkets, where suppliers compete for the business of organizational buyers who might be purchasing anything from gears to printed circuit boards used in manufacturing their goods. FreeMarkets was founder Glen Meakem's idea.

What Happened? While working at General Electric, Meakem proposed that the company set up a system whereby suppliers would compete for General Electric's orders in live, open, electronic auctions. The Internet was still in its infancy, and servers were yet to appear. Yet Meakem was so enthusiastic that he exclaimed, "This idea will transform the global economy!" General Electric declined to become involved. Although GE is now considered one of the most-admired corporations, it was slow to adopt Internet technology; in 1994, when Meakem made his proposal, it was considered a nonissue.

The Response. Meakem decided to strike out on his own, founding FreeMarkets. Meakem understood that manufacturers spend roughly one-third of every dollar in sales on parts; about $5 trillion a year globally goes toward the purchase of industrial parts. In addition, the purchase process is usually inefficient, involving huge amounts of time and paperwork. Meakem decided to cut through the red tape. He developed a system whereby suppliers promise to deliver parts on a standardized schedule, with identical payment terms and inventory arrangements. The only variable is price. FreeMarkets consults with buyers and screens suppliers so that, by the time an auction takes place, each is familiar with the process and has the most information possible about issues such as quality ratings and manufacturing processes. The online auction itself takes less than half an hour. The price starts high and moves downward. On their own computer screens, sellers can see exactly how much their competitors have bid and how low they must drop to make the sale.

Today and Counting. So far, buyers and sellers love the system, and FreeMarkets claims a market cap of $7 billion. Giants like General Motors, United Technologies, Raytheon, Emerson Electric, and Quaker Oats, who thought they already knew how to play the parts-purchasing game, have found themselves saving another 15 percent on parts, materials, and services through FreeMarkets. "This FreeMarkets auction idea is revolutionizing procurement as we know it," says Kent Brittan, vice president of supply management of United Technologies. In fact, General Motors loves the system so much it has set up its own. Meakem isn't thrilled about the move, but it was bound to happen sooner or later. After all, imitation is the sincerest form of flattery.

QUESTIONS FOR CRITICAL THINKING

1. Think of an industry in which you think FreeMarkets might work well. Write a brief memo describing why you think your industry would benefit from online auctions.
2. As competition such as the General Motors program begins to appear, what steps can FreeMarkets take to stay ahead?

Sources: "What We Do," FreeMarkets Web site, **www.freemarkets.com**, accessed February 8, 2001; Larry Seben, "FreeMarkets Revenue Hits New Record," LocalBusiness.com—Pittsburgh, July 25, 2000, **www.localbusiness.com;** Shawn Tully, "The B2B Tool that Really Is Changing the World," *Fortune*, March 20, 2000, pp. 132-140; Geoffrey Colvin, "America's Most Admired Companies," *Fortune*, February 21, 2000, pp. 108-111.

Extranets and Private Exchanges   Internet commerce also offers an efficient way for businesses to collaborate with suppliers, partners, and customers through extranets, secure networks used for e-commerce and accessible through the firm's Web site by external customers, suppliers, or other authorized users. Extranets go beyond ordering and fulfillment processes by giving selected outsiders access to internal information. As with other forms of e-commerce, extranets provide additional benefits such as enhanced relationships with business partners. Intelsat, which operates global communications satellites, has an extranet called Intelsat Business Network (IBN). The more than 2,300 users of IBN log on from 400 organizations to check the availability of satellite capacity, view satellite maps, download corporate documents, and participate in discussion groups. Users can personalize their IBN account so that it shows information about only the services they use.[35]

Security and access authorization remain critical issues, and most companies create virtual private networks that protect communications traveling over public communications media. These networks control who uses a company's resources and what users can access. Also, they cost considerably less than leasing dedicated lines.

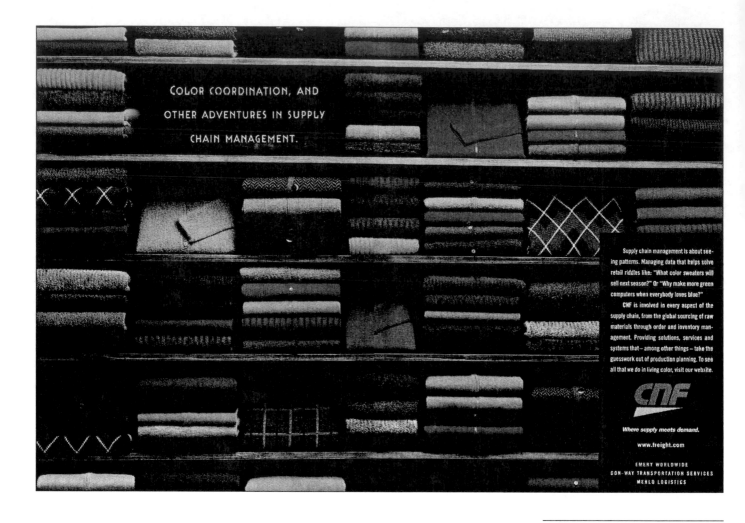

COLOR COORDINATION, AND
OTHER ADVENTURES IN SUPPLY
CHAIN MANAGEMENT.

Supply chain management is about seeing patterns. Managing data that helps solve retail riddles like: "What color sweaters will sell next season?" Or "Why make more green computers when everybody loves blue?"

CNF is involved in every aspect of the supply chain, from the global sourcing of raw materials through order and inventory management. Providing solutions, services and systems that – among other things – take the guesswork out of production planning. To see all that we do in living color, visit our website.

CNF

Where supply meets demand.

www.freight.com

EMERY WORLDWIDE
CON-WAY TRANSPORTATION SERVICES
MENLO LOGISTICS

FIGURE 7.8
Benefits from Allying with Distribution Partners

The next generation of extranets is the **private exchange,** a secure Web site at which a company and its suppliers share all types of data related to e-commerce, from product design through delivery of orders. A private exchange is more collaborative than a typical extranet, so this type of arrangement has sometimes been called "c-commerce."[36] The participants can use it to collaborate on product ideas, production scheduling, distribution, order tracking, and any other functions a business wants to include. Partners in a private exchange often form strategic alliances, similar to those described in Chapter 4. IBM has been creating a private exchange for its Personal Systems Group to use for product design, procurement, and logistics. The system permits IBM employees to identify qualified suppliers that can provide necessary components. The suppliers, in turn, can look up IBM's sales data and forecasts to manage their own inventory.[37] As Figure 7.8 shows, companies like CNF can participate in an exchange by providing services and data related to distributing goods.

Another variant of extranets is an *intranet,* which provides similar capabilities but limits users to an organization's employees. Intranets are discussed in Chapter 17.

Business-to-Consumer Transactions Gain Ground

One area of e-commerce that has consistently grabbed news headlines and attracted new fans is Internet shopping. Known as business-to-consumer e-commerce, or B2C, it involves selling directly to consumers over the Internet. Driven by convenience and improved

1. Books
2. CDs, DVDs, videos
3. Computer software
4. Travel-related services
5. Clothing/apparel

FIGURE 7.9
Top Five Products Purchased Online

Expedia.com is one of the successful new generations of B2C online travel services. In addition to offering discount rates, it supplies added value via simple-to-use and secure transactions and travel tips for each destination.

Introducing Expedia® Special Rates. Through direct negotiations with our hotel partners, we offer you exclusive prices on top quality hotels that beat standard rates by up to 70%. Plus you'll get all the other insights you need so you don't just book a trip, you book the right trip. Book the perfect flight. Reserve the right car. Easy and secure transactions, all at the right price. Backed by our 24-hour customer support.

Expedia.com
Don't just travel. Travel Right.

You can also find us under Travel on **msn**

security for transmitting credit-card numbers and other financial information, online retail sales, sometimes called *e-tailing*, have surpassed $30 billion and are climbing. Even with these increases, Internet retail sales are still a tiny fraction of the overall retail market. Only seven-tenths of one percent of all retail sales occur online.[38] In some product categories—computers, books, and audio and video recordings—online retailing has reached at least 10 percent of the market.[39] Figure 7.9 lists the top five products purchased online. Other popular online purchases include entertainment services, computer hardware, and specialty gift items.

A wide array of B2C e-commerce products are available. Industries such as investment and banking, online reservations and sales for travel and vacations, traditional retailing, and online auctions offer consumers a staggering array of products with just the click of a mouse. E-commerce has even invaded the staid world of legal services. At the Web site of eLawForum Corp., potential clients can describe their needs for legal work and invite bids from law firms. Assessing a lawyer's credentials and character online is difficult, so the approach might be too risky when the stakes are high. However, the cost-saving potential is attractive for someone looking to handle routine matters. For lawyers, eLawForum offers a way to attract new clients.[40]

Microsoft's Expedia online travel service represents another popular Internet business application. In addition to providing information and booking flights, hotel reservations, and auto rentals, the Web site supplies "insider" tips designed to resemble conversations with travelers who have recently visited the chosen destinations.

E-tailing and Electronic Storefronts   Major retailers are staking their claims in cyberspace. Many have set up **electronic storefronts,** Web sites where they offer items for sale to consumers. Wal-Mart received such a positive response to the launch of its electronic storefront that it expanded online product offerings from 2,500 to 40,000 items. Macy's and Bloomingdale's department stores have put their bridal registry, personal shopping, and interior-decorating services online. In a recent month, the top 20 Web retailers, measured in terms of the number of buyers, included such well-known names as Amazon.com, Ticketmaster, Barnes and Noble, Sears, Staples, and JCPenney.[41] Generally, retailers provide an online catalog at which visitors click on items they want to buy. These items are placed in a file called an **electronic shopping cart.** When the shopper indicates that he or she wants to complete the transaction, the items in the electronic shopping cart are listed on the screen, along with the total amount due, so that the customer can review the whole order and make any changes desired before making a payment.

Online retail selling works best for nontechnical products like flowers, books, compact discs, and travel and financial services. Even the sale of somewhat technical items, such as personal computers, has proven enormously successful through the combination of low prices, user-friendly Web sites, and 24-hour customer support offered by firms like Dell Computer and Gateway. In general though, cybershoppers like familiar goods that they can safely purchase without touching or trying out first. Marketing research firm Jupiter Communications predicts that the fastest-growing categories of online sales to consumers will be groceries, housewares, toys and specialty gifts like gourmet food, music, apparel, and videos.[42]

Developing Safe Online Payment Systems In response to consumer concerns about the safety of sending credit card numbers over the Internet, companies have developed secure payment systems for e-commerce. The most common forms of online payment are electronic cash, electronic wallets, and smart cards. Netscape Communications is one of several organizations that encrypt any sensitive information to protect consumers. **Encryption** is the process of encoding data for security purposes. When such a system is active, users see a special icon that indicates that they are at a protected Web site.

To increase consumer security, a group of companies, including Visa, Master-Card, and various technology suppliers, banded together to create Secure Electronic Transaction (SET), an industrywide standard for secure Internet payment transactions. Buyers using SET register with a bank and pay for purchases with **electronic cash** from their accounts using digital certificates that verify their identities. Adopting a standard technology provides consistency among merchants, card companies, software developers, and financial institutions. CyberCash is one company that specializes in providing secure online payment systems by incorporating SET into its encryption system.

An electronic wallet is another online payment method. An **electronic wallet** is a computer data file at an e-commerce site's checkout counter that contains not only electronic cash but credit card information, owner identification, and address. With electronic wallets, customers do not have to retype personal information each time they make a purchase at that site. Consumers simply click on the electronic wallet after selecting items, and their credit card payment information, name and address, and preferred mailing method is transmitted instantly.

Besides using electronic cash or wallets, online consumers have other choices for making payments. **Smart cards**—plastic cards that store encrypted information on embedded computer chips rather than magnetic strips—are convenient and better protected, so they are among the most popular methods of Internet payment. A smart card "reader" attaches to a shopper's computer, where the card is swiped for payment. In addition to storing e-cash, smart cards can also store data from several credit card companies, a driver's license number, and even health information. Other companies, including PayPal, Billpoint, and eMoneyMail, are offering online transfers of cash. When directed by the user, these programs send payments from a bank or credit card account to the recipient's account.[43]

E-Commerce Challenges

As noted earlier, e-commerce has its problems and challenges. Consumers are concerned about protecting their privacy and being victimized by Internet fraud, frustrated with unreliable and hard-to-use Web sites, and annoyed over the inconveniences of scheduling deliveries and returning merchandise. Businesses are concerned about fair use of their trademarks and copyrights, potential conflicts with business partners, and difficulty in measuring the effectiveness of Internet-based promotion. In addition to these issues, governments are looking to e-commerce for increased sales tax revenue. Internet retailers and government officials are now locked in a debate over the collection of sales tax for online purchases, as discussed in the "Solving an Ethical Controversy" box. Figure 7.10 summarizes the roadblocks to e-commerce.

Internet Security and Privacy Online security poses a major roadblock to the acceptance of consumer e-commerce, because consumers worry that information about them will become available to others without their permission. Marketing research indicates that privacy is the top concern of Internet users.[44] As the earlier discussion of Internet payments explained, concern about the privacy of credit card

FIGURE 7.10
Roadblocks to E-Commerce

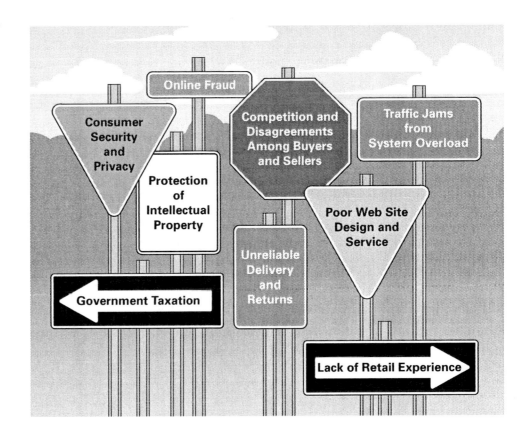

numbers has led to the use of secure payment systems. To add to those security systems, e-commerce sites require passwords as a form of authentication—that is, to determine that the person using the site is actually the one authorized to have access to the account. More recently, **electronic signatures** have become a way to enter into legal contracts such as home mortgages and insurance policies online. In 2001 a new federal law allows companies and individuals to use e-signatures.[45] With an e-signature, an individual obtains a kind of electronic identification and installs it in his or her Web browser. Signing the contract involves looking up and verifying the buyer's identity with this software.[46]

Thanks to cookies, the automatic data collection method introduced in Chapter 2, Web users leave electronic trails of personal information about their buying and viewing habits. The way that companies use cookies has the potential both to make visits to the Web site more convenient and to invade computer users' privacy. DoubleClick abandoned a plan to merge its data on Web use with a database of catalog orders, which would have given the company the ability to target online advertising to individual consumers based on their shopping habits.[47] Similarly, Amazon.com received such bad press over its plan to publicize customer shopping information by company or group, called Purchase Circles, that it now allows customers to request removal of their names. With a reported 23 million customers, Amazon's customer database is one of the largest online, and keeping its customers happy is critical to its success.[48]

Most consumers want assurances that any information they provide won't be sold to others without their permission. In response to these concerns, online merchants have been taking steps to protect consumer information. For example, many Internet companies have signed on with Internet privacy organizations like TRUSTe, shown in Figure 7.11. By displaying the TRUSTe logo on their Web sites, they indicate that they have promised to disclose how they collect personal data and what they do with the information. Prominently displaying a privacy policy is an effective way to build customers' trust.

E-Commerce and Taxes: Should They Meet?

If nothing is certain but death and taxes, then it was inevitable: lawmakers, traditional merchants, and Internet retailers are locked in a debate over whether Internet sales should be taxed. When Web-based retail sales began to take off, no one wanted to hamper its progress by slapping taxes on the activity. But now, state and local officials around the country—except in Alaska, Delaware, Montana, New Hampshire, and Oregon, which have no sales tax—are beginning to worry that their sales-tax base is slowly being eroded by increasing Internet retail transactions.

Should Internet sales be subject to tax?

PRO

1. Many states depend on sales taxes for revenues, and those revenues will decrease as shoppers increasingly turn to the Internet. States already lose some sales tax revenues to certain out-of-state mail-order and catalog sales. Failure to collect sales taxes will also ultimately hurt local brick-and-mortar businesses that are required to charge sales tax—and also pay property taxes—causing further erosion of the local tax base.

2. A tax break actually benefits consumers in upper income brackets, because they are the ones who can afford the computers as well as the goods and services offered on the Internet. Poorer consumers are thus stuck paying sales taxes when they shop at local businesses.

3. Several plans have been presented to calculate a simplified, streamlined sales tax so that it can be calculated and collected easily by both large and small Internet vendors.

CON

1. Collecting a sales tax will hamper the growth of e-commerce.
2. Introducing a sales tax will be extremely complicated, costing businesses more to implement than the actual taxes themselves.
3. Internet sales actually promote business activity elsewhere, for instance, increased shipping and other distribution functions, and so offset lost tax revenues.

SUMMARY

Internet retailers like the freedom that the current moratorium on taxes gives them. It provides them time to get sites up and running and, they hope, turn a profit. State and local officials, as well as brick-and-mortar businesses, fear that a continued ban on Internet sales tax will erode their own tax base and profitability. The issue has already gone before Congress more than once, and it will not go away anytime soon. The debates will continue over the need for breaks to allow new e-commerce sites to develop and the need for a level playing field for all businesses to compete.

Sources: Margret Johnston, "Legislators Debate Proposals for E-Commerce Taxes," *civic.com*, July 12, 2000, **www.cnn.com.technology**; David Hardesty, "Streamlined Sales Tax Project Moves Ahead," *E-Commerce Tax News*, July 9, 2000, **www.ecommercetax.com**; Mary Hillebrand, "U.S. Treasury Supports Internet Tax Ban," *E-Commerce Times*, June 6, 2000, **www.EcommerceTimes.com**; Howard Gleckman, "The Great Internet Tax Debate," *Business Week*, March 27, 2000, pp. 228–236; Howard Gleckman, "A First Step to Net Taxes," *Business Week*, September 20, 1999, p. 38; Ashlee Vance, "Trade Group Gives Technical Advice to Congress," CNN.com, downloaded from **www.cnn.com**, accessed February 6, 2001.

A policy is only as good as the company publishing it, though. Consumers have no assurances about what happens if a company is sold or goes out of business. Now-defunct Toysmart.com promised customers that it would never share their personal data with a third party. But when the company landed in bankruptcy court, it considered selling its database, one of its most valuable assets. And Amazon.com has told customers openly that if it or part of its business is purchased at some point, its database would be one of the transferred assets.[49] With these concerns, it is no wonder that some companies are profiting by selling software designed to protect privacy. For example, a program called Freedom enables the user to set up online identities, called "nyms." Online activity done under a nym uses encryption that makes the activity untraceable—even for law enforcement officials. Another package called PersonaValet allows users to determine which personal data to reveal when they visit Web sites that have installed software that works with PersonaValet.[50]

Such privacy features may become a necessary feature of Web sites if consumer concerns continue to grow. They also may become legally necessary. Already in the United States, the **Children's Online Privacy Protection Act (COPPA)** requires that Web sites targeting children younger than 13 years of age obtain "verifiable parental consent" before collecting any data that could be used to identify or contact individual users, including names and e-mail addresses.[51] Congress has also begun considering laws to protect the privacy of adult users.

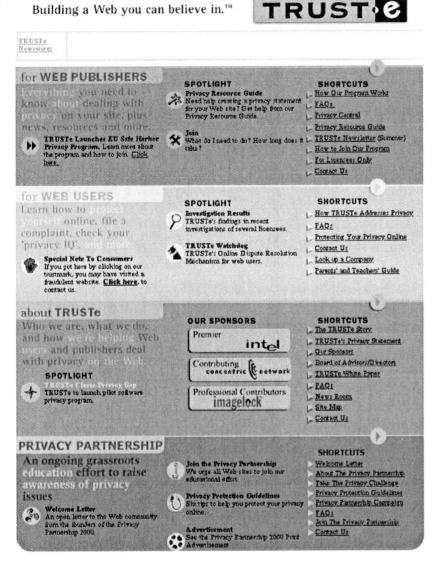

FIGURE 7.11
TRUSTe Organization Attempts to Build Customer Confidence Online

Security concerns are not limited to consumers. Employees are realizing that their employers can monitor their online behavior and e-mail messages at work. Some companies even specialize in helping employers use such information. Tacit Knowledge Systems builds a database from key terms in employees' e-mail. The primary objective is to help a company identify which employees have knowledge that they can contribute to the company—for example, knowledge about a particular competitor or type of product. Of course, many employees might be uncomfortable with their employer tracking what they write about. So, Tacit's software allows employees to decide which aspects of their personal profile they want to make public.[52]

Companies, too, are concerned about the privacy of their data, and with good reason. An employee of Legend Airlines recently discovered that an employee of American Airlines had logged into Legend's area of the Sabre scheduling and ticketing network. The American employee had correctly guessed the password of an acquaintance who worked at Sabre, using it to look up schedule information for Legend, and then failed to log off the system. The Legend employee discovered the intrusion a week later when the Sabre system wouldn't let the employee make scheduling changes because someone else— the American employee—was logged on. American insists that its employee was acting in good faith, and Sabre has since increased the security of its passwords.[53]

To prevent such intrusions, companies install combinations of hardware and software called firewalls to keep unauthorized Net users from tapping into private corporate data. A **firewall** is an electronic barrier between a company's internal network and the Internet that limits access into and out of the network. However, an impenetrable firewall is difficult to find. A determined and skilled hacker can often gain access. So, it is important for companies to test their Web sites and networks for vulnerabilities and provide backups of critical data in case an intruder breaches security measures.

Internet Fraud   Fraud is another barrier to e-commerce, and as more people go online, this crime is increasing. The Federal Bureau of Investigation and Department of Justice reported online auctions as the number-one source of fraud. They have logged more than 1,000 complaints a week and expect that rate to increase to 1,000 a day as the Internet Fraud Complaint Center becomes more widely used.[54] Auction fraud ranges from merchandise that does not match the description the bidder was given, such as fraudulent paintings, to products that were purchased but never delivered.

Investment scams are the second most common crime. Unreliable company information posted anonymously on the Web by disgruntled employees or predators who want to cash in on a stock's rise or fall are the most common "cybersmears." The misinformation can vary from untrue reports of problems with company products to character attacks on executives—anything to change the public's view of a company.[55] Law enforcement officials are gearing up to pursue online criminals, but untangling the layers of hidden online identities is proving difficult, though not impossible, to do. In the meantime, consumers and companies are being hurt by these fraudulent acts.

Traffic Jams Caused by System Overload   It sounded like a Web surfer's dream: the entire *Encyclopedia Britannica* available free online, for anyone with Internet access. Internet users anywhere could use that trusted source to look up articles on world history, art, or any other topic covered by that respected publication. But when the encyclopedia's content first became available, the reality was more like a nightmare. Users completely overloaded the Web site, and Encyclopedia Britannica's computers couldn't handle the traffic. The company went back to the drawing board and hired Akamai Technologies to handle content delivery through its own system of computers. A month later, the site relaunched successfully.[56] As Encyclopedia Britannica and Victoria's Secret—which suffered a similar traffic jam during the Webcast of a lingerie fashion show—have discovered, the Internet's increasing popularity has also increased the likelihood of delays and service outages, even as more users depend on their links. In addition, hackers can tie up a Web site with programs that flood it with inquiries. Whatever the cause of these traffic jams, they are costly in terms of lost business and frustrated customers.

Solutions to these problems are on the way. Internet service providers are adding capacity, and networking equipment manufacturers have recently introduced new technology capable of handling higher volumes of Internet traffic than older devices could manage. Many businesses also operate backup systems to ensure availability of Internet connections to customers. Companies like Akamai distribute content among thousands of computer servers, so that traffic to a Web site can be rerouted if it becomes too heavy.

Poor Web Site Design and Service   For e-commerce firms to attract customers—and keep them—companies must meet customer expectations. The biggest customer expectations are that they'll be able to find what they want without frustration and get questions answered. This obvious point has been a challenge on the digital frontier of cyberspace. Web sites are not always well designed and easy to use. In fact, two-thirds of Web shopping carts are abandoned before a customer places an order.[57] In other words, among the people who start selecting items to buy online, most of them change their minds before making a purchase. As Figure 7.12 suggests, some types of retailers have done much better than others in making online shopping a positive experience.

Surprisingly, many Web sites can receive e-mail but do not have a system for replying to the messages. Brightware, a provider of e-mail software, tested e-mail capabilities by sending a simple question—Who is your CEO and how do I contact him or her?—from a fictitious person to the biggest U.S. corporations at their e-mail addresses. The question was ignored by 62 percent of the companies, an increase from a similar test the year before. Among the companies that did reply, some took as long as two weeks. Commented Preston Dodd, an analyst with Jupiter Communications,

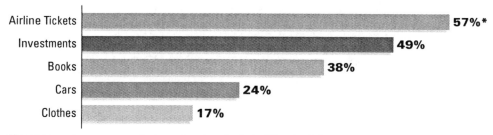

FIGURE 7.12
Five Products Consumers Would Prefer to Purchase Online

*Percentage of consumers preferring online shopping to traditional outlets.

"It's like giving somebody your phone number and they call for five days without getting an answer."[58]

Unreliable Delivery and Returns   Another challenge to successful e-commerce is merchandise delivery and returns. Retailers sometimes have trouble making deliveries to on-the-go consumers. And consumers don't want to wait for packages to be delivered. Also, if customers aren't satisfied with products, then they have to arrange for pickup or send packages back themselves. Several new companies are working to fill the need for reliable delivery and returns. PaxZone has established local businesses in the Chicago area that will receive shipments from retailers and arrange for returns from customers. The service is free to consumers, but the company charges a fee to the retailer, which benefits by not having to make repeated deliveries. An Arlington, Virginia, company called Brivo Systems has developed software that works with a "smart box" for home deliveries. Internet orders are given unique passwords, which the delivery person uses to gain access to the drop box.[59]

Lack of Retail Experience   "Pure-play" dot-coms—companies that started their lives online, without a history of traditional stores or catalogs—usually lack the expertise of running warehouses, customer service centers, and other aspects of selling to and satisfying customers. The 1999 Christmas season was the first big season of online retailing. Some 22 million consumers spent more than $5 billion on the Internet, but many of them were unimpressed with the experience. The ugly duckling of the season was the Toys 'R' Us Web site, which launched to great fanfare, then found it could not meet the demand. In mid-December, the company announced it could not guarantee delivery by Christmas Day, and dismayed parents around the country scrambled to find other sources of toys.[60] The "Business Hits and Misses" box describes some retailers' and shoppers' experiences with holiday e-tailing.

In contrast, Lands' End, which made its name as a service-oriented catalog retailer of classic clothing, has so far maintained its image online. As the company's Internet sales approach $100 million, its reliable distribution system has kept pace with the demand. Lands' End uses the same system for online sales as for its catalog orders.[61] Because of expertise in all parts of retailing, companies that combine their brick-and-mortar operations with e-commerce are gaining ground over those with little or no experience.

Competition and Disagreements Among Buyers and Sellers   Companies spend time and money to nurture relationships with their partners. But when a manufacturer uses the Internet to sell directly to customers, it can compete with its usual partners. Retailers often have their own Web sites, and they don't want their suppliers, the manufacturers, competing with them for sales. As e-commerce broadens its reach, producers must decide whether these relationships are more important than the potential of selling directly on the Web.

Mattel, well known for producing toys such as Barbie, Cabbage Patch dolls, and Matchbox cars, sells most of its products in toy stores and toy departments of other retailers, such as Wal-Mart. The company wants an Internet presence, but it would cut the retailers out of this important source of revenue if it sold toys online to consumers. Mattel cannot afford to lose the goodwill and purchasing power of giant retailers like Toys 'R' Us and Wal-Mart. So, the company sells only specialty products online, including pricey American Girl dolls, which were never sold in these stores, and software games.[62] In contrast, upscale toy retailers can sell Mattel products on the Internet competing with Mattel.

Pricing is another potential area of conflict. In their eagerness to establish themselves as Internet leaders, some companies have sold merchandise at unprofitable prices. This price slashing undercuts profits. American Leather sells custom leather furniture through upscale retailers, and each dealer serving a geographic area has an exclusive contract for the collections it offers in its area. But at least one dealer began

A holiday season was supposed to be the time that Internet retailers did everything except actually slide down chimneys to deliver toys. According to different sources, online sales for the year hovered between $8 billion and $10 billion, more than double the year before. Brick-and-mortar retailers like JCPenney and Toys 'R' Us hung out their Web shingles, and Internet startups like etoys, CDNow, and SmarterKids.com, got ready to rake in the money. As executives of these companies went to sleep at night, more than visions of sugar plums danced in their heads.

As it turned out, 22 million shoppers did spend more than $5 billion between Thanksgiving and Christmas. But it wasn't without a struggle. And if the major glitches hadn't occurred, that number might have been much higher. It seemed that the Grinch was determined to steal Christmas from the Web.

Web sites proved to be poorly designed and difficult to use. Customer frustrations mounted. When one customer logged on to JCPenney.com simply to order pajamas for his grandchildren, he clicked the pj's into his electronic shopping cart and then spent an hour trying to delete unwanted items that appeared there. When he finally found his way back to the main menu to process his final order, he discovered that some of the items he wanted were out of stock. Disgusted at the waste of his time, he canceled the whole order. Gap.com offered hundreds of products online but lacked a way for consumers to search through them. Wal-Mart.com didn't allow first-time shoppers to drop anything into their shopping carts without going through a lengthy check-in process.

Then there's the issue of supply and demand. So many shoppers decided to try making holiday purchases online that many companies—like JCPenney—simply ran out of stock. Perhaps the most publicized—and disastrous—story was of toysrus.com, which began the season with fanfare and a huge ad campaign designed to attract shoppers to the site. But by December, it was clear that the toy retailer couldn't fill all its orders, and large numbers of frustrated parents and grandparents were left empty-handed. Some e-customers were so put off by the experience that they vowed never to shop on the Internet again. "I doubt I will ever shop again online for Christmas," says one. "It is not worth the wait, lies, ill-informed customer service reps, and the hassle and stress."

All of this stress translates to real numbers. Only 2 percent of consumers who visit an online store actually buy anything, whereas in the "real" shopping world, more than 50 percent of consumers who visit a brick-and-mortar mall make a purchase, says one. What can online retailers learn from this experience?

"Reality caught up with the hype," remarks Lise Buyer, an e-tailing analyst at Credit Suisse First Boston. Even Buyer had a bad online experience. She tried to order a television as a gift for her dad from Amazon.com, until she learned that the shipping charges would be $100. But companies seem to be making sincere efforts to win back customers. One solution is to turn to the experts: software developers who can fix the glitches on Web sites. Barnes & Noble is considering a new tool from Inxight Software to help customers browse through its enormous databases. Interactive Pictures offers software to hotels, real estate brokers, and even auto manufacturers that allows customers to experience goods and services online with more realistic three-dimensional pictures. PeopleSupport is helping companies improve their customer service by providing online service representatives for their Web sites.

Retailers who work out the kinks in the way they deliver goods and services to their customers likely will survive; those who don't, won't. Either way, it's a pretty safe bet that in holiday seasons to come, they will be better prepared for the holiday spirit of giving.

QUESTIONS FOR CRITICAL THINKING

1. In addition to making Web sites easier to navigate, what steps might online retailers take to be prepared for busy holiday seasons?
2. In addition to difficult Web sites and lack of inventory, what other problems might online retailers face? What might be some potential solutions to these problems?
3. Although the primary function of the sites discussed here is e-commerce, how might these companies expand their functions to attract more customers and develop long-term relationships with them?

Sources: Quentin Hardy, "The Last Etail," *Forbes,* February 7, 2000, p. 71; Katrina Brooker, "The Nightmare Before Christmas," *Fortune,* January 24, 2000, pp. 24–26; Luisa Kroll, "Happy Together," *Forbes,* January 10, 2000, pp. 156–157; Silvia Sansoni, "Santa Claws," *Forbes,* December 27, 1999, pp. 282–284; "About Inxight," Inxight Web site, **www.inxight.com,** accessed February 6, 2001.

---

offering American Leather furniture at a discount to customers outside its market area. Other dealers complained, so American Leather established a policy that dealers were not to advertise the company's products on the Internet. Instead, American Leather offered links to local dealers on its own Web site and made plans to allow buyers to order online, with the sale to be directed to the dealer serving the consumer's geographic area.[63]

Protection of Intellectual Property   Along with privacy, intellectual property is difficult to protect on the Internet. Intellectual property is a trademark; invention; or literary, musical, artistic, photographic, or audiovisual work. The open sharing of information online can conflict with the desire of organizations to protect the use of their brand names, copyrights, logos, patents, and other intellectual property. Computer programmer David Simon recently tried to help his daughter watch her favorite cartoon series, *Pokémon*, by saving episodes on his family's home computer network. Her friends wanted to watch, too, so Simon posted them on a Web page for them to download. Eventually, he expanded the Web site to list television shows typed in from the newspaper TV listings, with instructions to click on Record and Play buttons to watch shows on demand. Thanks to a recommendation from a site called Netsurfer, Simon's site soon had tens of thousands of registered users, and would-be investors were contacting Simon. Then a dozen major entertainment companies, including AOL Time Warner and Walt Disney, sued Simon for illegally broadcasting their programming.[64] Their reaction is similar to that of recording companies when MP3 made downloading music files relatively easy and popular.

Even the choice of domain names can cause headaches for companies that have spent millions of dollars to develop a good reputation and widespread recognition. When the Internet was new and few companies understood the value of a Web presence, some individuals registered domain names that used companies' brand names, as well as the names of celebrities. When the companies got ready to go online, they were surprised to find that someone else had the right to use their name in cyberspace. At first, trade name owners had little recourse, but the legal environment has begun to change. The Anticybersquatting Consumer Protection Act imposes fines on people who in bad faith intend to profit from registering or using a domain name that is identical or similar to a company's trademark or an individual's name. The challenge for companies trying to protect their intellectual property is that the law requires them to show in court that the other party is using their name in bad faith in order to profit from it.[65]

Companies have used a variety of approaches to protect themselves in the free-wheeling world of the Internet. When a dissatisfied customer set up a Web site at www.dunkindonuts.org to post complaints about the food at Dunkin' Donuts, the doughnut chain initially threatened to sue him for misusing its trademarks. Instead, it arranged to buy the site and use it as a tool for obtaining consumer opinions, which brought a constructive end to a difficult situation. Ford Motor Co. at first thought it had something wonderful when Robert Lane, a diehard fan of the Ford Mustang, set up sites to share information about his favorite automobile. The company even gave him a press pass so he could write news for his fellow Mustang lovers. Anonymous sources sent Lane confidential company documents, and he regularly destroyed them until he became dissatisfied with the company. Ford began asking Lane to modify his site but rebuffed his requests that it sponsor his site. Lane began publishing the proprietary documents, and Ford sued him for publishing its trade secrets. Before Lane shut down the site, he posted about 100 more Ford documents there.

Not every company has had such an alliance backfire. Lucasfilm worked with fan sites for *Phantom Menace* to build excitement before the release of that Star Wars episode. Fan sites also drove much of the success of another movie, *The Blair Witch Project*.[66] The winners in cyberspace have to figure out how to participate in an environment where the flow of information is not always within their control. When information can zip around the globe within seconds, an after-the-fact lawsuit is not much protection.

MANAGING A WEB SITE: DOING BUSINESS ON THE INTERNET

Business Web sites serve many purposes. They broaden customer bases, provide immediate accessibility to current catalogs, accept and process orders, and offer personalized customer service. As technology becomes increasingly easy to use, anyone with a computer equipped with a modem can open an Internet account and place a simple Web site on the Internet. How people or organizations use their sites to achieve their goals determines whether their sites will succeed. Figure 7.13 lists some key questions to consider in developing a Web site.

Developing Successful Web Sites

Tod Johnson, CEO of the Media Metrix market-ing research firm, notes, "It's easy to build a bad Web site, harder to build a good one."[67] When judging Web sites, success means different things to different businesses. One firm might feel satis-fied by maintaining a popular site that conveys company information or reinforces name recogni-tion—just as a billboard or magazine ad does—without requiring any immediate sales activity. Web sites like those of *The New York Times* and *USA Today* draw many visitors who want the lat-est news, and Yahoo!, Netscape, C/Net, and ESPNSportsZone are successful because they attract millions of visitors. High-traffic sites like these add to their success by selling advertising space to other businesses.

- What is the purpose of the Web site?
- How can we attract repeat visitors?
- What external links should be established to draw visitors to the site?
- What internal links to databases and other corporate resources are needed?
- What should the domain name be?
- What should the site contain?
- How should it work?
- Who should put the site on the Net—company or Web host?
- How much money should be spent to set up and maintain the site?
- How current does information on the site need to be?

FIGURE 7.13
Questions to Consider in Developing a Web Site

Internet merchants need to attract customers who transact business on the spot. Some companies find success by hosting Web sites that offer some value-added ser-vice to create goodwill for potential customers. Organizations like the Mayo Clinic and accounting giant Ernst & Young provide useful information or links to related sites that people frequently visit. But to get people to stay at the site and complete a transaction, the site must also be secure, reliable, and easy to use.

Planning and Preparation What is the company's goal for its Web site? Answering this question is the first and most important step in the Web site development process. As we saw in the opening vignette, for Charles Schwab, the primary objec-tive was to sign up new customers. So, the discount broker's Web site designers put a link called "Open an Account" prominently in the upper left-hand corner of the home page. In addition, to reinforce Schwab's image as a respectable investment firm, the site uses a businesslike color scheme suggesting pinstripes.[68] Objectives for the Web site also determine the scope of the project. If the company's goal is to sell merchandise online, the site must incorporate a way for customers to place orders and ask questions about products, as well as links to the company's databases to track inventory and deliveries. As in this example, the plan includes not only the ap-pearance of the Web site but also the company's behind-the-scenes resources for making the Web site deliver on its promises.

Other key decisions include whether to create and maintain a site in-house or to contract with outside experts. Some companies prefer to retain control over content and design by producing their own sites. However, since acquiring the expertise to develop Web sites can be very time-consuming, hiring specialists may prove a more cost-effective option. Major companies have such complex needs that specialists are essential, so companies such as Macromedia are enlisted to provide both software and consulting services to clients for their Web sites, as illustrated in Figure 7.14.

Naming the Web site is another important early step in the planning process. A domain name should reflect the company and its products and be easy to remember. For companies in the United States, the last part of the domain name identifies an af-filiation category. Examples include .com for businesses, .org for organizations, .gov for government sites, and .edu for educational institutions. For companies outside the United States, the last part of the domain name identifies the country of origin, such as .ca for Canada and .jp for Japan. In addition to the existing dot-com, dot-gov, and dot-org addresses, seven new suffixes were approved and added to the Internet's naming system in late 2000. The new suffixes include .aero, .biz, .coop, .info, .museum, .name, and .pro. These suffixes were created to alleviate overcrowding in the .com domain and represent the first major addition of Internet addresses in more than a decade. With millions of dot-com names already registered, the search for a unique, memorable, and easily spelled name can be difficult.

FIGURE 7.14
Macromedia: E-Commerce Web Site Developer

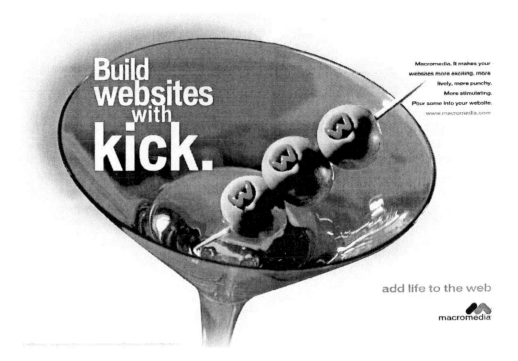

When Andrew Busey decided to create an e-commerce site for home furniture, he first thought of ForMyHome.com, which he was able to register, but it just wasn't catchy enough. So Busey and the design firm that was developing his site pondered the alternatives. Furniture.com was already taken, and its owner wanted $1 million for it. Eventually, they settled on Living.com. Not only is the name easy to spell, but the term is general enough to make sense if the site broadens its offerings beyond furniture. However, the California Association of Realtors had already registered the name. Busey negotiated the right to use the name in exchange for more than $100,000. The willingness of companies like Living.com to pay for the right to use a particular domain name reinforces the importance of this business asset. Living.com's competition appreciates the importance of domain names, too. Furniture.com has since registered three misspellings, Livng.com, Livign.com, and Lving.com, giving it the potential to capture customers with poor typing skills by setting up links to Furniture.com at those Web addresses.[69]

Content and Connections Content is one of the most important factors in determining whether visitors return to a site. People obviously are more inclined to visit a site that provides material that interests them. Many e-commerce Web sites try to distinguish themselves by offering information or online communities along with a chance to buy. For example, Tavolo is an electronic storefront for gourmet cooking supplies, and it lures traffic to the site with weekly menu planners, printer-ready recipes, and features that convert menus between metric and U.S. measurement systems, adjust measurements for different numbers of servings, and create shopping lists for weekly menus.[70] Many sites offer links to other sites that may interest visitors. Hyperlinks to related Web sites increase exposure and traffic, but they can also take visitors away before they buy anything.

Standards for good content vary for every site, but available resources should be relevant to viewers, easy to access and understand, updated regularly, and written or displayed in a compelling, entertaining way. When the World Wide Web was a novelty, a page with a picture and a couple of paragraphs of text seemed entertaining. But such "brochureware" falls far short of meeting today's standards for interactivity, including the ability to accept customer data and orders, keep up-to-the-minute inventory data, and respond quickly to customer questions and complaints. Also, today's Internet users are less patient about figuring out how to make a site do what it promises. They won't wait ten minutes for a video clip to download or click through five different pages to complete a purchase. So, a good Web site looks simple and intuitive to its users, a quality the developers can guarantee only by testing a site on its intended audience.

After making content decisions and designing the site, the next step is connecting to the Internet by placing the required computer files on a server. Companies can have their own dedicated Web servers or contract to place their Web sites on servers at ISPs or other host companies. Most small businesses lack the necessary expertise to set up and run their own servers; they are better off outsourcing to meet their hosting and maintenance needs. They also need to draw business to their site. This usually requires a listing with the major search engines, like Yahoo!, Lycos, and Excite.

Costs and Maintenance

As with any technological investment, Web site costs are an important consideration. The highly variable cost of a Web site includes not only development expenses but also the cost of placing the site on a Web server, maintaining and updating it, and promoting it. A reasonably tech-savvy employee with off-the-shelf software can create a simple piece of brochureware for a few hundred dollars. A Web site that can handle e-commerce will cost at least $10,000 and perhaps millions. Creating it requires understanding of how to link the Web site to the company's other information systems.[71]

Although developing a commercial Web site with interactive features can cost tens of thousands of dollars, putting it online can cost as little as $20 a month for a spot on a **Web host**'s server such as America Online.[72] And Web hosts deliver a huge audience. In a typical week, 30 million people visit the AOL site and another 25 million log on to Yahoo!. Like so much new technology, the cost of putting a site on a server is falling. ISPs like America Online, CompuServe, and NetCom host many commercial sites for basic monthly charges depending on the number of Web pages. A number of e-commerce service providers are offering services for a few hundred dollars or even for free. Treadmill Doctor, which repairs treadmills, set up a Web site to answer common questions about that type of exercise equipment. The company used a template from Bigstep.com to create the site and pays Bigstep $14.95 plus $.20 per transaction to host the site. Bigstep allows the company to update the site at no charge.[73] Similarly, Hodge Products sells combination locks on its www.combolock.com site, created using template software from a service called Sitematic. To operate the site, Hodge pays just under $40 a month to Sitematic, which processes all the transactions and lets Hodge offer up to 20 different products on its site.[74] Some e-commerce service providers also take care of listing the site with search engines, usually for an additional fee.

In addition to installation and connection fees, managers must ensure that their company's Web site stays current over time. Visitors don't return to a site if they know the information never changes or that claims about inventory or product selection are not current. Consequently, updating design and content is another major expense. In addition, site maintenance should include running occasional searches to test that links to the company's Web site are still active.

Measuring Web Site Effectiveness

How does a company gauge the return from investing in a Web site? Measuring the effectiveness of a Web site is a tricky process, and a site's answer depends on the purpose that it serves. Figure 7.15 lists some measures of effectiveness. Profitability is relatively easy to measure in companies that generate revenues directly from online product orders, advertising, or subscription sales. However, a telephone order resulting from an ad on a Web site still shows the sale as a phone sale, not a Web site sale, even though the order originated at the site.

FIGURE 7.15
Measures of Web Site Effectiveness

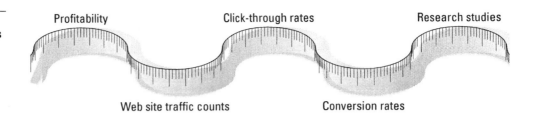

For many companies, revenue is not a major Web site objective. Only about 15 percent of large companies use their Web sites to generate revenue; the rest use them to showcase their products and to offer information about their organizations. For such companies, measures of success include increased brand awareness and brand loyalty, which presumably translate into greater profitability off-line.

Some standards guide efforts to collect and analyze traditional consumer purchase data, such as how many Ohio residents bought new Honda Accords the previous year, watched HBO's award-winning *The Sopranos,* or tried Burger King's new french fries. Still, the Internet presents several challenges for marketers. Although information sources are getting better, it is difficult to be sure how many people use the Internet, how often, and what they actually do online. Some Web pages display counters that measure the number of visits. However, the counters can't tell whether someone has spent time on the page or skipped over it on the way to another site, or whether that person is a first-time or repeat viewer.

Advertisers typically measure the success of their ads in terms of click-through rates, meaning the percentage of people presented with a banner ad who click on it, thereby linking to a Web site or a pop-up page of information related to the ad. Recently, the average click-through rate has been declining to about half of one percent of those viewing an ad. This rate is much lower than the 1.0 to 1.5 percent of responses to the average direct-mail advertisement. Low click-through rates have made Web advertising less attractive than it was when it was novel and people were clicking on just about anything online. Selling advertising has therefore become a less reliable source of e-commerce revenues.[75]

As e-commerce gains popularity, new models for measuring its effectiveness are being developed. A basic measurement is the conversion rate, the percentage of Web site visitors who make purchases. A conversion rate of 3 to 5 percent is average by today's standards.[76] A company can use its advertising cost, site traffic, and conversion rate data to find out the cost to win each customer. A company that spends $10,000 to attract 5,000 visitors to a Web site with a 4 percent conversion rate is obtaining 200 transactions, or .04 × 5,000. It spent $10,000 for those 200 transactions, so the advertising cost is $50 per transaction, meaning each of those customers cost $50 to acquire through the advertising campaign.

Among all categories of online advertisers, the average cost to get an online customer is $38. For Internet pure-plays, those only transacting business online, the cost is an astronomical $82, but the customer acquisition cost is just $11 per customer for retailers that also sell through stores or catalogs.[77] To be profitable, a site with an average conversion rate needs to generate a lot of revenue with each transaction—one reason many Internet start-ups have been having difficulty generating profits. So, e-commerce businesses are trying to boost their conversion rates by ensuring their sites download quickly, are easy to use, and deliver on their promises. At Net-Grocer, a low conversion rate meant that people were visiting the site but not buying anything. The Web site led off with a beautiful presentation of the company's mission statement, so visitors had to wait for it to download, then click through more pages before they could buy their groceries. The company shifted to an emphasis more characteristic of selling food—focus on the products coupled with coupons and fast links to make purchases. Soon the conversion rate had tripled, and the size of an average order grew as well.[78]

Besides measuring click-through and conversion rates, companies can study samples of consumers. Research firms such as PC-Meter and Relevant Knowledge recruit panels of computer users to track Internet site performance and evaluate Web activity; this service works in much the same way that ACNielsen monitors television audiences. The WebTrends service provides information on Web site visitors, including where they come from, what they see, and the number of "hits," or visits to the site, during different times of the day. Other surveys of Web users investigate their brand awareness and their attitudes toward Web sites and brands.

THE GLOBAL ENVIRONMENT OF E-COMMERCE

For many companies, future growth is directly linked to a global strategy that incorporates e-commerce. The United States leads the world in technology, communications infrastructure, and ownership of PCs and other consumer technology products, but Netizens live on every continent. Currently, 136 million Americans use the Internet, followed by 83 million in Europe, 69 million in the Asia-Pacific region, and millions more in South America, Africa, and the Middle East. Together, they spend well over $600 million online and are expected to spend ten times that amount in 2004.[79]

With so many users and so much buying power, the Internet creates an enormous pool of potential customers. Companies can market their goods and services internationally and locate distribution sources and trading partners. Customers can search for products at their convenience, browsing through online catalogs that always show current information. Brothers Sam and Shobit Gupta use the Internet as both a source of demand for their product and a way to work with customers. Their company, NetEcho, designs Web sites. Shobit Gupta supervises a team of designers in New Delhi, India, while Sam Gupta communicates with American clients from his home in Seattle. They start out with conference calls to learn about the culture of the company whose site they are designing. Then the programmers get to work. At the end of each workday, they post their work on the Internet for the client to review. Clients check the progress of the design and send feedback via e-mail, thus skirting the challenges of a 12-hour difference in time zones. Not only do clients get work comparable to that of U.S. design firms, they pay the much lower going rate for Indian programmers. NetEcho's satisfied clients include Technology Control Corp., which gave NetEcho the assignment to develop its Web site, then returned to the company when it was ready to expand the site.[80]

One practical implication of this global marketplace is the different languages that buyers and sellers speak. Reflecting the Internet's origins, more than half of users now communicate in English. However, the remainder use other languages, led by Japanese, German, Chinese, Spanish, and French.[81] As Figure 7.16 points out, Web site developers need to consider offering online information in more than one language. So far, however, three of every four Web pages are in English, slowing the adoption of the Internet in non-English-speaking countries.[82] Other international differences are important, too. Auction site eBay goofed in the United Kingdom by launching a site with prices given in U.S. dollars. After realizing that its British audience was offended, the company switched to local currency.[83]

E-commerce can heighten competition. In the virtual global marketplace, rivals can cross the oceans to enter your market. Many manufacturers use the Internet to search through online catalogs for the lowest-priced parts. No longer can local suppliers assume that they have locked up the business of neighboring firms. And U.S. firms cannot expect that their earlier experience with the Internet gives them an edge in foreign markets. Yahoo!, which has been in Europe longer than any other U.S.-based portal, operates eight country-specific versions. They represent 15 percent of Yahoo's total traffic, but

BUSINESS DIRECTORY

➤ **click-through rate**   *the percentage of people presented with a Web banner ad who click on it.*

➤ **conversion rate**   *the percentage of visitors to a Web site who make a purchase.*

Yahoo! enjoys the biggest slice of the market in the United Kingdom. In France, for example, the top portal is Wanadoo, which is the default portal of France's biggest Internet service provider, France Telecom.

Still, the Internet is a valuable way to expand a company's reach, especially for small businesses that would otherwise have difficulty finding customers overseas. Some customers are lured by the chance to save money compared with purchasing through other channels. David Butler, a retired sales manager in England, bought a Ford from a Belgian dealer and saved $5,000 off the price he would have paid at home. Inspired, he began shopping for a video camera from retailers based in the United States, where savings would far outweigh the costs of shipping and customs.[84]

WHAT'S AHEAD

The Internet is revolutionizing the way we communicate, obtain information, seek entertainment, and conduct business. It has created tremendous opportunities for B2B and B2C e-commerce. So far, B2B transactions are leading the way online. B2C e-commerce is undergoing a shakeout: Companies that combine expertise in traditional retailing with the new online technology have gained a firmer foothold in cyberspace.

In upcoming chapters, we look at other trends that are reshaping the business world of the 21st century: We explore the critical issues of how companies organize, lead, and manage their work processes; manage and motivate their employees; empower their employees through teamwork and enhanced communication; handle labor and workplace disputes; and create and produce world-class goods and services.

➤ Summary of Learning Goals

1. Discuss how the Internet provides new routes to business success.

The Internet, a worldwide network of interconnected computers, removes limitations of time and place so that transactions can occur 24 hours a day between people in different countries. It creates opportunities for companies that provide Internet infrastructure, access, and content, as well as for firms that use its resources in their business operations. The Internet offers a cost-effective way for managers to gather competitive intelligence; perform marketing research; showcase, sell, and in some cases distribute products; and offer customer service and technical support.

2. **Describe the increasing diversity of Internet users.**

From strictly a U.S. defense network, the Internet has grown to include users all over the world. The gender gap has also narrowed; women now represent roughly half of all Internet users. Ethnic and racial diversity is also increasing, with Asian Americans, African Americans, and Hispanic Americans going online in larger numbers. The average age of Internet users is also rising, reflecting the widespread acceptance of the Net.

3. **Summarize the Internet's four functions and provide examples of each.**

The Internet provides a means of communication through e-mail, instant messaging, and chat rooms. Internet telephony and videoconferencing are also being established online. The Net provides information services through search engines and portals, as well as online publications and newsgroups. Net entertainment is growing through online gaming, radio and television programming, electronic publishing, and music and movies. E-commerce, or online business transactions, make up the fourth function. E-commerce takes the form of electronic exchanges, extranets and private exchanges, electronic storefronts, online ticketing, and auctions.

4. **List the major forms of business-to-business e-commerce.**

Electronic data interchange was an early use of technology to conduct business transactions. E-commerce is the process of selling goods and services through Internet-based exchanges of data. It includes product information; ordering, invoicing, and payment processes; and customer service. In a B2B context, e-commerce uses Internet technology to conduct transactions between two organizations via electronic exchanges, extranets, and private exchanges.

5. **Name the major forms of business-to-consumer e-commerce.**

In a B2C context, e-commerce uses the Internet to connect companies directly with consumers. E-tailing and electronic storefronts are the major forms of online sales to consumers. Payment methods include electronic cash, electronic wallets, smart cards, and online transfers of cash.

6. **Describe some challenges associated with Internet selling.**

The growth of Internet retailing is currently limited by consumer security and privacy concerns, fraud, and system overload. In addition, poor Web site design and service, unreliability of delivery and returns, and lack of retail expertise can limit e-commerce success. The Internet can also generate conflict among buyers and sellers. Businesses also face challenges in protecting their intellectual property and proprietary data online.

7. **Describe how companies develop and manage successful Web sites.**

Businesses establish Web sites to expand their customer bases, increase consumer awareness of their products, improve customer communications, and provide customer service. Before designing a Web site, a company's decision makers must first determine what they want to achieve with the site. Other important decisions include who should create, host, and manage the site; how to promote it; and how much funding to allocate. Successful Web sites contain informative, up-to-date, and visually appealing content. Sites should also download quickly and be easy to use. Finally, management must develop ways of measuring how well a site accomplishes its objectives.

8. **Explain how global opportunities result from e-commerce.**

Technology allows companies to compete in the global market and workplace. Even the smallest firms can sell products and find new vendors in international markets. Through its own Web site, a company can immediately reach customers all over the world. Improved communications among employees in different locations create new ways of collaborating on projects.

Business Terms You Need to Know

Internet (Net) 248
World Wide Web (Web) 248
Web sites 248
Internet service provider (ISP) 249

electronic commerce
(e-commerce) 256
business-to-business e-commerce
(B2B) 258
extranets 260

business-to-consumer e-commerce
(B2C) 261
click-through rates 274
conversion rate 274

Other Important Business Terms

Review Questions

1. Describe the path your e-mail takes in traveling from your computer to your friend's. How would this path differ if your friend has a DSL connection?

2. Using the statistics cited in this chapter, construct a profile of the "typical" Internet user.

3. What are the four primary functions performed on the Web? Describe a practical business application of each.

4. Suppose your supervisor asked you to use the Internet to find the best supplier of office furniture for the new site your company is moving to. Explain several precautionary measures you might take as you gather information on furniture companies.

5. Discuss the benefits that a small company might enjoy by establishing a Web presence.

6. Name several ways that companies generate revenue online.

7. What are the differences between B2B and B2C e-commerce?

8. Describe several of the challenges that both businesses and consumers face as they engage in e-commerce. Cite some potential solutions to these problems.

9. If you were to advise the CEO of a company that wants to develop a Web site, what steps would you recommend that the company take to build a successful site?

10. In what ways do companies measure the effectiveness or success of a Web site?

Questions for Critical Thinking

1. Consider the following statement: "To remain competitive in the next decade, every business must have a Web site or at least be connected to the Internet." Do you agree or disagree? Why? If you disagree, name at least one type of business that you believe could succeed without the Internet.

2. More than 80 percent of Web users say that obtaining information is one of the reasons they use the Internet. How might an adventure travel company use this statistic to attract potential customers to its Web site?

3. Many businesses are banding together to form exchanges that serve large segments of an industry, such as the auto industry. However, Wal-Mart has decided not to follow this route. Do you think this is a wise decision for Wal-Mart? Why or why not?

4. Do you believe that companies should monitor employees' online behavior and e-mail messages at work? Why or why not? If so, discuss any boundaries you feel should be respected.

5. By setting up a Web site, companies can have instant access to a global marketplace. What are some advantages and disadvantages that a pure-play e-commerce company might encounter in setting up a Web site for global e-commerce? How would the advantages and disadvantages differ for a company with retail experience?

Experiential Exercise

Background: The Internet is a powerful resource for businesses. As the chapter explains, about 30 percent of U.S. businesses are currently engaged in B2B e-commerce, with nearly 90 percent online by 2002.

Directions: Assume you work for Paula Brewer, a small-business owner who is interested in developing a B2B e-commerce site on the Web. Research the Internet to find resources for Brewer to use in developing the company's new B2B Web site. You may wish to use **www.geobiz2biz.com,** an online directory with links to more than 100 Web sites for a wide variety of information resources, including the following:

- Web-based business solutions
- B2B auctions
- Procurement services
- Sales force management

- Supplier information
- Publicity/advertising
- Business tools

Print out the home page for either GeoBiz2Biz.com or a similar site you found. Submit a three-page report to Brewer that includes the home page printout of the Web site you recommend to get her started in B2B e-commerce. In the remainder of your report, summarize five links on the Web site you selected that you think are most important for her to visit. For each of the five sites listed in your report, include (1) the reason why you recommend the link as particularly important and (2) any necessary explanations about the link that would be helpful to Brewer.

≫ Nothing but Net

1. **B2B.** As noted in the chapter, IBM offers extensive consulting services, software, and hardware for firms engaged in e-commerce. Assume you're an entrepreneur and you'd like to expand your presence in the B2B market. Visit the IBM e-commerce Web site at

   www.ibm.com/e-commerce

   Read about the services offered by IBM to B2B entrepreneurs. Prepare a brief oral report to your class summarizing these services and some of the case studies where IBM has assisted firms in their B2B activities.

2. **Rating e-commerce Web sites.** Gomez.com is one of the leading authorities on e-commerce. As such, Gomez.com rates various e-commerce companies. Go to the Gomez.com Web site at

   www.gomez.com

   Prepare a brief report in which you identify the following:

   a. The highest-rated airline Web site

   b. The highest-rated e-toy Web site

   c. The methods Gomez.com uses to rate e-commerce sites

3. **Internet retailing experience.** Assume the role of a consumer who wishes to purchase the latest best-selling novel over the Internet. The two leading online booksellers are

   www.amazon.com

   www.bn.com (Barnes and Noble)

   Visit both sites and learn enough about each site so you can describe them both to a friend, including which you'd recommend and why.

   Note: Internet Web addresses change frequently. If you do not find the exact sites listed, you may need to access the organization's or company's home page and search from there.

In a few short years, the Internet has revolutionized the way companies do business. Of course, there have been huge successes as well as painful failures among the companies that have embraced the Internet—particularly those that have relied on the Internet for their very survival. But overall, the Internet offers global opportunities for a variety of individuals and organizations. One of those is Lycos Inc.

Founded in 1995, Lycos Network was initially an Internet portal—an entryway much like its larger competitors Yahoo! and America Online. Within a few years, experts predicted that the company would capsize in the Web, swamped by its giant competitors. "We were in danger of being an afterthought in early 1998," recalls Lycos chief financial officer Edward Philip. But a series of changes has turned Lycos around. Today, according to industry watcher Media Matrix, the company's collection of sites is the fourth-largest destination for people using the Web. "We had less funding and were late to market, yet we beat the odds and have flourished," boasts CEO Bob Davis. The company also has a new name: Terra Lycos. More on that later.

Lycos saved itself largely through a series of alliances and acquisitions, along with the introduction of new tools and services that benefit both consumers and business customers. One service, the "Lycos Daily 50 Report," helps marketers follow emerging consumer trends by tracking the topics that typical users search the Internet for. The report is simply a list of the fifty most popular search terms of the past seven days. It removes company names, porn sites, and Internet utility terms such as "chat room" and comes up with the fifty most useful words and phrases. "Our goal is to create an up-to-date list of the people, places, and things that Internet users are interested in," explains Jonathan Levine, director of content development. "It's a great way for people to stay current. For marketers, this tool can be used to get an idea about emerging consumer trends." This is just one way that the Lycos site helps create opportunities for other businesses.

During the past few years, Lycos has allied with or acquired companies such as Tripod Inc. and HotBot. Lycos and Bell Canada created a new company called Sympatico-Lycos, which would provide Canadians with expanded Internet resources for the business-to-business market. In the fall of 2000, Lycos became the "exclusive community provider for the Olympic Games," hosting and managing all Olympic athlete chats, message boards, and fan clubs for the Sydney Olympics. McDonald's joined the party as a sponsor of the Lycos Olympic site, in exchange for featured advertising. "This is a powerful combination linking two global leaders in support of the Sydney Olympic Games, and we look forward to continuing to work with McDonald's to further leverage the strengths of both companies," stated Jeff Bennett, senior vice president of corporate development at Lycos. Later, Lycos Asia received a license from the Chinese government to operate one of China's first foreign-owned Web sites. Previously, foreign-owned Web companies could function only through partnerships with Chinese institutions that would exert control over operations.

While all of these alliances are potential opportunities, they also increased the complexity of the company—and the complexity of its problems. So, Lycos hired its first chief information officer, Tim Wright. "They were looking for someone with experience in acquisitions, someone who knew how to handle multiple staffs of skilled people and knew how to blend disparate pieces together," Wright explains. In other words, Wright's job was to figure out how to weave technology and people together in a way that allowed workers and managers in the acquired companies to continue to do what they do best. He also showed them how their relationship with Lycos could actually increase their business. "We let [acquired companies] know right away that we can help them by redirecting our traffic to their site and recirculating traffic back their way," says Wright.

But the biggest deal for Lycos was still to come. The company agreed to be acquired by Spanish Internet service provider Terra Networks in a stock swap that valued Lycos at around $12.5 billion, with the idea that the merger would begin to create a megaportal to the Internet that would dominate Europe and Latin America. Pep Valles, the founder of Terra, views the deal as the global opportunity of a lifetime. "Who hits first hits twice," he remarks, repeating an old Spanish saying. "On the Internet, who hits first hits ten times." He sounds a bit like the first Lycos television commercial, which brought Lycos to the attention of many American consumers. The ad featured a black lab retriever named Lycos who streaked back and forth from the edge of the world to his owner, finding anything that his owner asked for. "Go get it!" the voice of Lycos's owner commanded. And Lycos did.

QUESTIONS

1. Using information in the chapter, outline three ways that you think Terra Lycos could help other businesses create opportunities for themselves using the Internet.
2. What methods might Terra Lycos use to measure the effectiveness of the various Web sites of its affiliates and subsidiaries?
3. Identify three challenges that managers of Terra Networks and Lycos will likely face as they merge the two organizations.
4. Visit the Terra Lycos Web site at **www.lycos.com**. As a user, what do you think its strengths and weaknesses are?

Sources: Lycos Web site, **www.lycos.com,** accessed January 19, 2001; "Lycos and McDonald's Form Global Marketing Relationship," *Business Wire,* September 20, 2000; "Lycos to Host All Athlete Chats for Sydney 2000 Olympic Games, *Business Wire,* September 13, 2000; Ross Kerber, "Lycos Asia Wins License in China," *The Boston Globe,* September 11, 2000, **www.boston.com;** Daniel Helft, "Terra's Terror," *The Standard,* July 3, 2000, **www.thestandard.com;** Stewart Deck, "Free To Be," *CIO Magazine,* June 1, 2000, **www2.cio.com;** Betsy Schiffman and Amy Doan, "Lycos and Terra Networks: A Marriage Made in Spain, *Forbes,* May 16, 2000, **www.forbes.com;** Jon Swartz, "Bob Davis, Lycos' Savior," *Forbes,* March 30, 2000, **www.forbes.com;** "Lycos Tool Highlights Emerging Consumer Trends," *Forbes,* September 15, 1999, **www.forbes.com.**

15

PROCUREMENT AND SUPPLY MANAGEMENT

LEARNING OBJECTIVES

After reading this chapter, you should be able to do the following:

- Understand the role and nature of procurement and supply management in a supply chain context.

- Explain the different types of inbound systems.

- Discuss the major materials-management activities.

- Understand the procurement process.

- Explain the risk/value technique for determining purchased item importance.

- Identify the four steps necessary for effective procurement.

- Explain the criteria for evaluating vendors.

- Examine the role of E-commerce in the procurement process.

LOGISTICS PROFILE

CBL Plastic Company

"Wow! That sure was a close call. We have to do everything possible to prevent such a situation from occurring in the future," said Bill Marley, president of CBL, to the operations team. Bill was referring to the critical shortage, two hours worth of material in the warehouse, of plastic pellets. Plastic pellets are the primary raw material used in the manufacture of CBL plastic injection molded parts.

Because of the near stockout of plastic pellets, CBL faced a potential operations stoppage. The plastic pellet supplier did not have a sufficient supply of recycled plastic, the base stock from which the pellets are made. After the pellet vendor located a new recycled plastic supplier and began production, a snowstorm hit the area and prevented the trucking companies from delivering the product to CBL.

When the inventory level dropped to a two-hour level, the truck arrived and saved CBL from shutting down the plant. If production had stopped, CBL would have incurred the overhead costs of the plant without any output as well as lost sales because it did not have sufficient inventories of finished product to meet customer orders. Bill did not have a good estimate of the cost of shutting down the plant and lost sales.

Now that the emergency was over, Bill convened his operations team to develop action plans to prevent a stockout of critical raw materials that could force a plant shutdown. To focus the operations team's efforts, Bill developed a number of strategic issues regarding the supply management process. The issues to be explored included:

1. The cost of a raw material stockout
2. The cause of the tier-one plastic pellet vendor's raw material supply problem
3. The availability of raw materials for the tier-two vendors
4. Potential of CBL switching to a backup plastic pellet vendor(s)
5. An analysis of the plastic pellet market, including suppliers, future supply capacity and demand, and raw material availability
6. Definition and identification of CBL's "critical" raw materials
7. The optimum number of vendors for critical raw materials
8. The optimum inventory level for critical and noncritical raw materials
9. Changes needed in policies and operating procedure to prevent supply disruptions

After presenting these issues to the operations team, Bill was certain the team would dig into the problem and come back next week with a list of additional issues and questions. After a few meetings, the team would be able to recommend strategies and tactics that would prevent the almost disastrous stockout condition from occurring again.

INTRODUCTION

Chapter 1 provided an overview of the logistics supply chain and indicated that today's environment requires management of the flow and storage of materials (raw materials, semifinished goods, and finished products) from vendor sources through to the ultimate customer. One convenient way to view the supply chain for a single company is to divide its logistics system into *inbound logistics* (materials management and procurement) and *outbound logistics* (customer service and channels of distribution).

common activities

The focus of this chapter is upon the inbound side of logistics systems, including procurement or purchasing and the related materials-management activities. It is important to note that the inbound and outbound logistics systems share common activities or processes, since both involve decisions related to transportation, warehousing, materials handling, inventory management and control, and packaging, as well as some other activities. Each of these common areas is covered in some detail in subsequent chapters of this book. The purpose of this chapter is to provide an overview of the materials-management and procurement activities of an inbound logistics system.

INBOUND LOGISTICS ALONG THE SUPPLY CHAIN

A dimension of the inbound system that deserves consideration at the outset is the differences that exist among the inbound systems of different companies. These differences have important implications for the design and management of logistics supply chains.

mining firm

As you move along a supply chain made up of a series of individual companies (see Figure 4–1), you will see important differences in the inbound systems of the companies. The start of a supply chain could very well be a mining operation involving the extraction of coal or some ore commodity. In this instance, the inbound logistics system is essentially a part of the extractive or production process. Therefore, inbound logistics would be very difficult to separate out for analysis from the mining operation except to the extent that the extractive company purchases supplies for use in the mining process that must be stored and transported prior to the extractive process. An important point here is that extractive companies would be most concerned about their outbound system, which

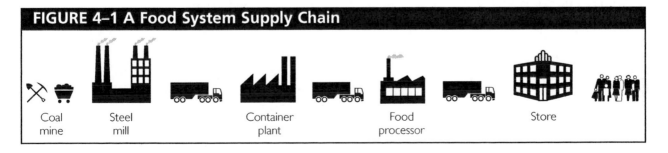

FIGURE 4–1 A Food System Supply Chain

Coal mine   Steel mill   Container plant   Food processor   Store would be involved in delivering appropriate quantities of their commodity at the right time and place to the next firm in the supply chain. The inbound system of the extractive company would probably not receive as much separate attention as would the inbound system at the next firm in the supply chain.

As we move along this hypothetical supply chain, the next company could be a steel manufacturer. The coal would be an important raw material for this firm, and it would probably transform the coal to coking coal in its coke plant. However, it could also buy coking coal from an intermediary company that buys coal and specializes in producing coking coal. (Obviously, if the latter were true, we would have another company in our supply chain.) **steel firm**

In addition to the coking coal, the steel company would utilize several raw materials from a variety of vendor sources to produce the steel. These materials would have to be procured in appropriate quantities, transported, stored, and their arrivals coordinated via the production planning process in advance of the manufacturing process for producing the steel. Therefore, the steel company would be very much aware of its inbound logistics system and the need to coordinate inbound logistics activities.

The steel company would have some interesting contrasts between its inbound and outbound systems. On the inbound side, the nature of the raw materials, coking coal, iron ore, and so on are such that they can be shipped in bulk in railcars and barges and stored outside in piles. On the other hand, the finished steel would need more sophisticated transportation, warehouses, inventory control, materials handling, and so on. Therefore, the inbound and outbound logistics systems could have some unique network design requirements.

Once the steel is produced, it would be ready to move along the supply chain to the next firm, which could be another manufacturer such as an auto or a container manufacturer. Assuming that the supply chain we are concerned about will ultimately result in food products in a store, the next point would be the container company that produces cans of various sizes for the food processors. It is important to note that the steel company would usually be a part of several supply chains. That is, the steel company may also be selling to auto manufacturers, office supply producers, and other types of manufacturers. **container firm**

After the can manufacturer, the next step in our supply chain would be the food manufacturing plant, where processed food would be added to the cans of various sizes. Food processing companies frequently add labels later, since the same can of peas, for example, could be sold under as many as eight to ten different company labels. By storing the cans as "brights" and adding the labels when orders are received, the level of inventory can be reduced because of the reduction of uncertainty. That is, it is much easier to forecast the total demand for a certain size of canned peas than it is to forecast the demand for each company's labeled cans of peas, since individual market shares change. **food firm**

Once an order for the peas has been received from a retailer, the labels can be added and the peas shipped to the retailer's warehouse or store. When the peas finally end up in the store for sale, we have reached the last point in our supply chain, although you could argue that the cycle is not complete until the can of peas ends up in a consumer's home. In fact, in today's environment, that can may be recycled after the peas are consumed and the materials may start back through part of the supply chain again—a reverse logistics system. **retail store**

TABLE 4–1 Industry Supply Chain Logistics Emphasis	
Industry	**Supply Chain Logistics Emphasis**
Extractive	One-way; outbound
Manufacturing	Two-way; inbound and outbound
Channel intermediary	Two-way; inbound and outbound
Retailer	Two-way; inbound and outbound
E-tailer	Two-way; inbound and outbound
End User	One-way; inbound

This rather lengthy discussion of the supply chain illustrates a number of interesting aspects of supply chain logistics. It shows that what is inbound for one company is frequently outbound for another company. Also, as we move along the supply chain, we are continually adding value, and the logistics costs will usually also increase because of the higher-value products. In addition, companies may be part of several supply chains.

The preceding discussion also indicates that the location in the supply chain channel determines the emphasis given to logistics. As shown in Table 4–1, an extractive industry has a one-way supply chain channel, outbound logistics. Conversely, an end user has a one-way supply channel that emphasizes inbound logistics. Manufacturers, channel intermediaries, retailers, and E-tailers have two-way supply chain channels, that is, these industries are concerned with both inbound and outbound logistics.

complexity Another important dimension of our discussion of inbound logistics systems is the difference in complexity that exists among companies. For example, an automobile manufacturer typically has about 13,000 individual parts in the inbound system in order to assemble or manufacture an automobile. The inbound system for the steel plant mentioned previously is relatively simple compared to that of the auto manufacturer. The steel company has a limited number of raw materials that are shipped in bulk and are stored outside. Some aspects of inbound logistics systems for steel production are challenging but not nearly as challenging as the inbound system for automobile production.

As was indicated previously, the focus of this chapter is the inbound systems for logistics. We examine each of the major activities that are a part of inbound systems. The discussion is limited on some of these activities, such as transportation and warehousing, since these topics receive extensive discussion in later chapters.

MATERIALS MANAGEMENT

integration Effective supply chain management requires careful coordination of the inbound system of logistics, which is frequently referred to as *materials management,* and the outbound system, which is usually called *physical distribution.* While the focus in this chapter is upon the inbound system, the integration of the inbound and outbound systems is extremely important to the efficient and effective management of the logistics supply chain. Information flow is often the key ingredient to the coordination of inbound and outbound logistics systems. Since information regarding product demand flows down the supply chain from the marketplace or customer and materials flow up the supply chain, the possibility exists that decisions related to the flow of materials will not be coordinated with the customer information flowing down. When there is a lack of integration, inefficiencies occur, especially with respect to inventory accumulation and/or lack of appropriate customer service levels. In today's complex environment, information needs to flow quickly in both directions for effective coordination.

Materials management can be described as the planning and control of the flow of materials that are a part of the inbound logistics system. Materials management usually includes the following activities: procurement, warehousing, production planning, inbound transportation, receiving, materials quality control, inventory management and control, and salvage and scrap disposal.

Procurement[1]

Effective procurement of goods and services contributes to the competitive advantage of an organization. The procurement process links members in the supply chain and assures the quality of suppliers in that chain. The quality of the materials and services that are input affects finished product quality and hence customer satisfaction and revenue. Input costs are a large part of total costs in many industries. With the importance of procurement as a determinant of revenues, costs, and supply chain relationships, it is easy to understand why it has recently been receiving more attention from both practitioners and academics.

importance

Procurement can be a complex process that is difficult at times to define, understand, and manage. However, to manage the process, it must be understood; to understand the process, it must be defined. Depending on the circumstances, procurement can be defined, in a narrow sense, as the act of buying goods and services for a firm or, in a broader perspective, as the process of obtaining goods and services for the firm. The procurement process is, however, more than just the culmination of an activity; it is the successful completion of a series of activities that often cut across organizational boundaries. To formalize the definition, then, procurement consists of all those activities necessary to acquire goods and services consistent with user requirements.

definition

Porter, in his value chain, identified the strategic importance of procurement, since it includes such activities as qualifying new suppliers, procuring different types of inputs, and monitoring supplier performance.[2] As such, procurement serves as a critical link between members of the supply chain.

The activities that follow for the procurement process apply to the purchase of both goods and services in industrial markets. (See Figure 4–2 for an overview of the procurement process.) These activities often cut across both functional boundaries (intrafirm) and organizational boundaries (interfirm) and cannot be effectively completed without input from all parties involved in the transaction. The successful completion of these activities maximizes value for both the buying and selling organizations, thereby maximizing value for the supply chain:

1. *Identify or reevaluate needs.* A procurement transaction is usually initiated in response to either a new or an existing need of a user (by an individual or

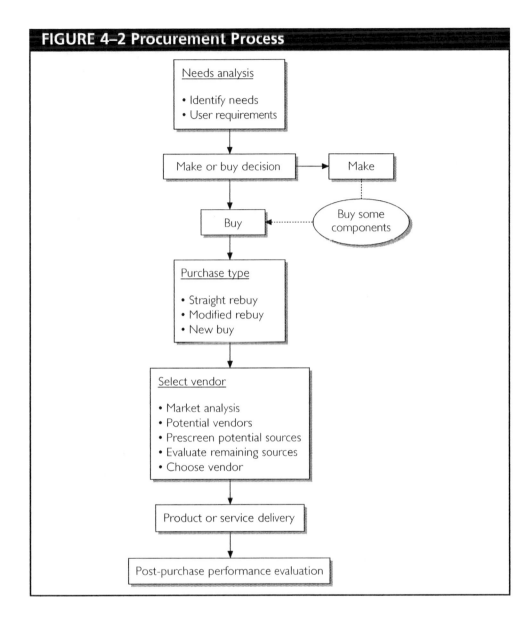

FIGURE 4–2 Procurement Process

Needs analysis

- Identify needs
- User requirements

Make or buy decision → Make

Buy ← Buy some components

Purchase type

- Straight rebuy
- Modified rebuy
- New buy

Select vendor

- Market analysis
- Potential vendors
- Prescreen potential sources
- Evaluate remaining sources
- Choose vendor

Product or service delivery

Post-purchase performance evaluation

department within the buyer's firm). In some instances, existing needs must be reevaluated because they change. In either case, once the need is identified, the procurement process can begin. The need can be identified by any of a variety of functional areas in the firm or even by someone outside the firm, for example, by customers.

2. *Define and evaluate user requirements.* Once the need has been determined, its requirement must be represented by some type of measurable criteria. The criteria may be relatively simple—for example, criteria for copy machine paper could be 8 ½ by 11-inch white paper of a certain bond weight—or they may be very complex if the company is buying a highly technical product. Using these criteria, the procurement professional can communicate the user's needs to potential suppliers.

3. *Decide whether to make or buy.* Before outside suppliers are solicited, the buying firm must decide whether it will make or buy the product or service to

satisfy the user's needs. Even with a "make" decision, however, the buying firm will usually have to purchase some types of inputs from outside suppliers. This step has become much more important today, when more companies are outsourcing in order to focus upon their "core" activities.

4. *Identify the type of purchase.* The type of purchase necessary to satisfy the user's needs will determine the amount of time needed for the procurement process and the complexity of the process. The three types of purchases, from least amount of time and complexity to most amount of time and complexity, are (1) a straight rebuy or routine purchase; (2) a modified rebuy, which requires a change to an existing supplier or input; and (3) a new buy, which results from a new user need. In a straight rebuy or modified rebuy, several of the activities discussed in the remainder of this section can be eliminated; for example, there is no need to identify all possible suppliers.

5. *Conduct a market analysis.* A source of supply can operate in a purely competitive market (many suppliers), an oligopolistic market (a few large suppliers), or a monopolistic market (one supplier). Knowing the type of market will help the procurement professional determine the number of suppliers in the market, where the power/dependence balance lies, and which method of buying might be most effective—negotiations, competitive bidding, and so on. The information about market type is not always apparent, and some research may be necessary using standard library sources such as *Moody's* or information from a trade association.

6. *Identify all possible suppliers.* This activity involves the identification of all possible suppliers that might be able to satisfy the user's needs. It is important at this stage to include possible suppliers that the buying firm has not used previously. Again, identifying all possible suppliers, especially with today's global environment, can be a challenge and may require some research. If the company is small, it may rely upon more common sources of such information, such as the telephone company's yellow pages directory.

7. *Prescreen all possible sources.* When defining and evaluating user requirements (as described in the second activity), it is important to differentiate between demands and desires. *Demands* for a product or service are those characteristics that are critical to the user; *desires* are those that are not as critical and are therefore negotiable. Prescreening reduces the pool of possible suppliers to those that can satisfy the user's demands. In some instances, prescreening can be a relatively simple task. For example, in the case of the copy paper, the supplier will have it on hand regularly or will not have it available dependably. With parts for a computer, the situation may require a series of tests by internal engineering staff.

8. *Evaluate the remaining supplier base.* With the possible pool of suppliers reduced to those that can meet the user's demands, it is now possible to determine which supplier or suppliers can best meet the user's negotiable requirements, or desires. This activity may be accomplished through the use of competitive bidding if the procurement item or items are fairly simple or standard and there is a sufficient number of potential vendors. If these conditions do not exist, more elaborate evaluation may be necessary, using engineering tests or simulated end-use situations, for example, to test seat belts for cars.

9. *Choose a supplier.* The choice of supplier also determines the relationship that will exist between the buying and supplying firms and how the "mechanics" of this relationship will be structured and implemented. This activity also

determines how the relationships with the nonselected suppliers will be maintained. The actual choice will be based upon criteria to be discussed subsequently, such as quality, reliability, total required price, and so on.

10. *Receive delivery of the product or service.* This activity occurs with the first attempt by the supplier or suppliers to satisfy the user's needs. The completion of this activity also begins the generation of performance data to be used for the next activity.

11. *Make a postpurchase performance evaluation.* Once the service has been performed or the product delivered, the supplier's performance must be evaluated to determine whether it has truly satisfied the user's needs. This also is the "control" activity. If supplier performance did not satisfy the user's needs, the causes for this variance must be determined and the proper corrective actions implemented.

external influences All of the activities identified in this section are subject to influences beyond the control of the procurement professional. These influences can determine how effectively each activity is performed. They include intraorganizational and interorganizational factors and external factors such as governmental influences. For example, a change in marketing needs or manufacturing process may require repeating all or some of the activities identified before the first iteration is completed. Financial failure of a potential vendor will also cause problems and necessitate repeated activities.

Importance of Item and Service Purchased[3]

The products and services purchased by a company are not all the same. Some products are more important and require greater procurement attention. Applying the same procurement strategies, tactics, and resources to supplying a computer manufacturer with paper clips and computer chips overlooks the differences in criticalness of each item to the firm's survival and profitability. That is, the computer company can survive without paper clips but not without computer chips.

The quadrant technique enables the supply chain manager to assess the importance of each product or service being purchased. The quadrant technique utilizes a two-by-two matrix to determine a procured item's relative importance on the basis of value and risk. The criteria used to delineate importance are *value* or profit potential and *risk* or uniqueness.

value The value criterion examines product or service features that enhance profits for the final product and the firm's ability to maintain a competitive advantage in the marketplace. For example, a computer chip that is faster or an operating system that is more user friendly will make the computer more desirable, thereby increasing demand for the product and, consequently, increasing profits. Alternatively, the addition of a gold-plated paper clip to the computer instruction manual probably will not increase computer sales or solidify a competitive advantage in the marketplace.

risk Risk reflects the chance of failure, nonacceptance in the marketplace, delivery failures, and source nonavailability. The risk of a paper clip failure is really not a significant risk for a computer manufacturer. That is, if a paper clip fails to hold a number of pieces of paper together, the operation of the company's computer should not be affected. However, if a computer chip fails, the computer will not operate and the marketplace will respond in a negative way. Thus, the computer chip poses a greater risk than the paper clip to a computer manufacturer.

FIGURE 4–3 Item Procurement Importance Matrix

R I S K	Distinctives High risk, low value Engineered items	Criticals High risk, high value Unique items Items critical to final product
	Generics Low risk, low value Office supplies MRO items	Commodities Low risk, high value Basic production items Basic packaging Logistics services

Value or Profit Potential

importance categories

Figure 4–3 depicts the value risk quadrant and categorizes item importance. Items of low risk, low value are identified as *generics;* and those of low risk, high value are *commodities.* Products or services that are high risk, low value are *distinctives;* while those of high risk, high value are *criticals.*

generics

Generics are low-risk, low-value items and services that typically do not enter the final product. Items such as office supplies and maintenance, repair, and operating items (MRO) are examples of generics. The administrative and acquisition processing costs are more significant than the purchase price of generics, and, for some generics, the administration and processing costs may exceed the price paid for the item or service. The strategic procurement thrust for generics is to streamline the procurement process to reduce the cost associated with purchasing generics. For example, the use of purchasing cards (corporate credit cards) reduces the number of checks written and the administrative costs associated with check payment, bank verification, and so on.

commodities

Commodities are items or services that are low in risk but high in value. Basic production materials (bolts), basic packaging (exterior box), and transportation services are examples of commodities that enhance the profitability of the company but pose a low risk. These items and services are fundamental to the company's finished product, thus making their value high. Risk is low because commodities are not unique items and there are many sources of supply. Because commodities are not unique, there is little brand distinction and price is a significant distinguishing factor. Freight and inventory are major procurement cost considerations for commodities. The procurement strategies used for commodities include volume purchasing to reduce price and just-in-time systems to lower inventory costs.

distinctives

Distinctives are high-risk, low-value items and services such as engineered items, parts that are available from only a limited number of suppliers, or items that have a long lead time. The company's customers are unaware of or do not care about the uniqueness of distinctives, but these products pose a threat to continued operation and/or high procurement cost. A stockout of distinctives results in stopping the production line or changing the production schedule to work around a stocked-out item, and both tactics increase production costs. Alternatively, using premium supply sources or premium transportation will eliminate the stockout but procurement costs will increase. The strategic focus for distinctives is developing a standardization program to eliminate or reduce the uniqueness of the distinctives, thereby changing these items to generics.

criticals Finally, *criticals* are high-risk, high-value items that give the final product a competitive advantage in the marketplace. As noted earlier, the computer chip used may give the computer a unique speed that differentiates it from all competitors. This unique computer chip increases the computer's value to the customer, and the risk of nonavailability is customer dissatisfaction and reduced sales. Criticals, in part, determine the customer's ultimate cost of using the finished product—in our example, the computer. The procurement strategy for criticals is to strengthen their value through use of new technologies, simplification, close supplier relations, and/or value-added alterations. The focus of critical procurement is on innovation to make the critical item provide greater market value to the finished product.

The preceding discussion of the quadrant technique emphasizes that not all items and services purchased are of equal importance. It also suggests that the supply chain manager must utilize varying procurement strategies based on the value and risk of the item. Greater resources and attention should be directed toward procuring criticals than toward generics. For example, one full-time procurement specialist may be assigned to purchasing one critical item—say, a computer chip—whereas one full-time person may be assigned to the purchase of hundreds of generics—office supplies.

In the next section, our attention is directed toward managing the procurement process.

Managing the Procurement Process. Managing the procurement process can be difficult for a multitude of reasons, ranging from inflexible organizational structures to inflexible organizational cultures. However, most firms should find the process relatively easy. What must be remembered when dealing with these activities is that all firms are different and will have different requirements for the procurement process. A four-step approach can be used and adapted to a firm's particular needs. Based on the previous discussion of the procurement process activities, the following steps can be used to maximize effectiveness:

1. *Determine the type of purchase.* In the procurement process, identifying the type of purchase (the fourth purchase activity) will many times dictate the complexity of the entire process. For example, a straight rebuy situation will mean that all of the procurement activities were completed previously (when the purchase was a new buy or modified rebuy), and the only activities necessary would probably be the fourth, ninth, tenth, and eleventh. A modified rebuy may also not require all of the activities, but a new buy would normally require performing all of the activities discussed earlier.

2. *Determine the necessary levels of investment.* The procurement process requires two major types of investments by the firm: time and information. Time is expended by the individuals involved in making the purchase; the more complex and important the purchase, the more time must be spent on it, especially if it is a new buy. Information can be both internal and external to the firm. Internal information is gathered concerning user requirements

ON THE LINE

HOW DELL DEFINES DIRECT

Before the first E-tailer ever set up shop, Dell Computer turned the personal computer industry on its ear by pioneering the idea of selling custom-built PCs directly to consumers. By developing and then staying focused on what he termed the *direct model*, Michael Dell built a $21 billion company that is both known for supply chain excellence and widely considered to have the right business model for the Internet age.

Michael Dell attributes his company's success to an unrelenting focus on the customer. "From the start, our entire business—from design to manufacturing to sales—was oriented around listening to the customer, and delivering what the customer wanted" has allowed Dell to eliminate all aspects of the business process that do not contribute directly to meeting customer needs.

Dell's success did not come without some growing pains. In the first few years, Dell learned tough but crucial lessons about the importance of parts inventory management and building to what the customers said they needed. And time and again it learned that continued success was tightly tethered to maintaining focus on the direct model.

Forming strong alliances with the suppliers who would make the direct model work was an important task. First Dell chose to source components from expert outside suppliers rather than build them itself. Dell found that this approach gave it the flexibility to rapidly scale operations as customer needs dictated and to gain access to the best components

in the world. Further, it believed in supplier partnerships where goals and strategies are shared freely—a dramatic departure from the traditional buy-bid cycle. When this approach to procurement worked so well, Dell was among the first companies to outsource significant portions of its logistics operations to third-party logistics providers.

To avoid the error, cost, confusion, and complexity that come from managing multiple suppliers, Dell partnered with only a few key suppliers and then brought these suppliers close to Dell's own business, both geographically and electronically. Dell required suppliers to site their facilities close to Dell's own manufacturing facilities to allow for better communication and service and faster time to market—all critical for a company that does not begin building a computer until it receives an order.

Today, Dell uses the Internet as a key part of its IT strategy: the company is now creating Web-based links for each of its suppliers to facilitate the rapid exchange of information such as component quality metrics, cost structures, and current and future demand forecasts. Providing suppliers with closer electronic links helps Dell continue to push for improved inventory velocity and better quality data and ultimately reduce the total cycle time from when Dell customers place an order to when they receive it.

Source: "How Dell Defines Direct," *Channels* 5, no. 1 (2000): 7. Reprinted with permission of *Channels*, a UPS Logistics Group publication.

and the implications that the purchase will have for the firm. External information concerning the input to be purchased may be gathered from supply chain members, from potential suppliers, and others. The more complex and important the purchase, the more information is needed for the procurement process to be effective. By determining the type of purchase (which is also a function of the user's needs), the procurement professional can determine the levels of investment necessary in the procurement process. Problems can occur when not enough or too much investment is made to satisfy a particular user's needs.

Determining the level of investment needed in time and information to adequately meet a user's requirements is a firm-specific process. Once the level of investment is decided, the procurement process can take place.

3. *Perform the procurement process.* This is a relatively easy step to describe but can be a complex step to perform, depending on the situation. It includes performing those activities necessary to effectively make a purchase and satisfy the user's requirements. This step also allows the procurement professional to collect data on the time and information actually used in making a specific purchase. The ability to measure the actual investment and how well a user's needs were satisfied is important to the final step in managing the procurement process.

4. *Evaluate the effectiveness of the procurement process.* This is a control step that asks two questions: (1) Were the user's needs satisfied? and (2) Was the investment necessary? Remember, the goal is to invest only enough time and information to exactly satisfy the user's needs. If the procurement process was not effective, the cause could be traced to not enough investment, not performing the proper activities, or mistakes made in performing one or more of the activities. In any case, when the procurement process is not effective, the manager must determine why and take corrective actions to make sure that future purchases will be effective. If the purchase satisfied the user's needs at the proper level of investment, the procurement process was effective and can serve as a reference for future purchases.

supplier relationship Thus, although the procurement process is complex, it can be managed effectively as long as the manager develops some systematic approach for implementing it. A key factor in achieving efficiency and effectiveness in this area is the development of successful supplier (vendor) relationships. In fact, many professional procurement/ materials managers agree that today's global marketplace requires developing strong supplier relationships in order to create and sustain a competitive advantage. Companies such as NCR and Motorola go so far as to refer to suppliers (vendors) as partners and/or stakeholders in their company. When vendors are "partners," companies tend to rely more upon them to provide input into product design, engineering assistance, quality control, and so on.

The buyer-supplier relationship is so important that it deserves special discussion. (Note that in our previous discussion of procurement activities, supplier relations were involved in at least five of the activities.) The next section provides additional discussion of supplier relationships.

vendor partners **Supplier/Vendor Evaluation and Relationships.** Many successful companies have recognized the key role that procurement plays in supply chain management and that supplier/vendor relationships are a vital part of successful procurement strategies "Good vendors do not grow on trees" is an adage that is often quoted by procurement professionals. This is especially true when companies reduce the total number of their suppliers, frequently in conjunction with total quality management (TQM) programs or just-in-time (JIT) production and inventory systems.

The strategy to utilize a smaller number of suppliers/vendors frequently means an alliance or partnership with suppliers/vendors because of the need to assure an adequate supply of quality materials over time at an optimum total acquired cost. The partnership/alliance concept encompasses more than just the procurement process, since partnerships are being developed today throughout the supply chain by companies. For example, partnerships are also evolving with transportation companies, contract logistics companies (third-party providers), and channel members.

At this stage, suffice it to say that procurement professionals today recognize that quality management necessitates quality materials and parts. That is, the final product is only as good as the parts that are used in the process. Also, we need to recognize that the customer satisfaction process begins with procurement.

Another dimension of the supplier relationship is that procurement contributes to the competitive advantage of the company, whether the advantage be one of low cost, differentiation, or a niche orientation (using Porter's generic strategies).[4] Therefore, the procurement management program has to be consistent with the overall competitive advantage that a company is seeking to attain in the marketplace. For example, we would expect that Honda or Toyota would approach procurement differently than would Mercedes Benz or Lexus.

Even with a partnership or strategic alliance with a vendor, certain key criteria need to be considered in any procurement situation. The typical but key vendor/supplier selection criteria are discussed in the section that follows.

Vendor Selection Criteria. Figure 4–4 provides an overview of the vendor selection criteria. The most important factor in vendor selection is usually quality. As was indicated earlier, quality often refers to the specifications that a user desires in an item (technical specifications, chemical or physical properties, or design, for example). The procurement professional compares the actual quality of a vendor's product with the specifications the user desires. In actuality, quality includes additional factors such as life of the product, ease of repair, maintenance requirements, ease of use, and

quality

FIGURE 4–4 Overview of Vendor Selection Criteria

Quality
- Technical specifications
- Chemical and physical properties
- Design
- Product life
- Ease of repair
- Maintenance
- Dependability

Reliability
- On-time delivery
- Performance history
- Warranty

Capability
- Production capability
- Technical capability
- Management
- Operating controls
- Labor relations

Financial
- Price
- Financial stability

Desirable Qualities
- Vendor attitude
- Training aids
- Packaging
- Vendor location
- Repair service

dependability. In today's TQM environment, not only are quality standards higher, but the supplier may also have to assume the major responsibility for quality.

reliability Reliability comprises delivery and performance history, the second- and third-ranked factors for most procurement professionals. To prevent production line shutdowns resulting from longer-than-expected lead times, the buyer requires consistent, on-time deliveries. Also, the performance life of the procured product directly affects the quality of the final product, the manufacturer's warranty claims, and repeat sales. Finally, in cases of material malfunction, the buying firm considers the vendor's warranty and claim procedure a reliability measure. Reliability is often considered a part of a total quality management program. It should also be noted that the growing reliance upon foreign vendors presents some special challenges to the achievement of reliability because of the distances involved.

capability The third major vendor selection criterion, capability, considers the potential vendor's production facilities and capacity, technical capability, management and organizational capabilities, and operating controls. These factors indicate the vendor's ability to provide a needed quality and quantity of material in a timely manner. The evaluation includes not only the vendor's physical capability to provide the material the user needs, but also the vendor's capability to do so consistently over an extended time period. The buying firm may answer this long-run supply concern by considering the vendor's labor relations record. A record of vendor-labor unrest resulting in strikes may indicate that the vendor is unable to provide the material quantity the user desires over a long time period. A firm that buys from this vendor will incur increased inventory costs for storing material in preparation for likely disruptions in the vendor's business due to labor strife. Again, sourcing from global suppliers makes this assessment more challenging.

financial Financial considerations constitute the fourth major vendor selection criterion. In addition to price, the buying firm considers the vendor's financial position. Financially unstable vendors pose possible disruptions in a long-run continued supply of material. By declaring bankruptcy, a vendor that supplies materials critical to a final product could stop a buyer's production. This criterion has become especially important in purchasing transportation service from truckload motor carriers. With the trend toward companies utilizing a smaller number of carriers, the financial failure of such a supplier is a major problem and source of disruption in a supply chain.

desirable qualities The remaining vendor selection factors may be grouped into a miscellaneous category of desirable, but not always necessary, criteria. Although the buyer might find the vendor's attitude difficult to quantify, attitude does affect the vendor selection decision. A negative attitude, for example, may eliminate a vendor for a buyer's consideration. The impression or image that the vendor projects has a similar effect on vendor selection. The importance of training aids and packaging will depend on the material the buyer is purchasing. For example, packaging is important to buyers of easily damaged material, such as glass, but not important to buyers purchasing a commodity that is not easily damaged, such as coal. Training aids would be significant to a firm selecting vendors to supply technical machinery such as computers and robots but not to a firm seeking office supplies. Likewise, a buyer would consider the availability of repair service more important when buying technical machinery.

vendor location Another vendor selection factor is geographical location. This factor addresses the issue of whether to buy from local or distant vendors. Transportation cost is one obvious aspect of this issue. Other factors, such as the ability to fill rush orders, meet delivery dates, provide shorter delivery times, and utilize greater vendor-buyer cooperation, favor the use of local suppliers. However, distant vendors may provide lower prices, greater technical ability, greater supply reliability, and higher quality. This is again a choice faced more frequently in today's global environment

The relative importance of the vendor selection factors will depend upon the material the buyer is purchasing. When a buyer purchases a computer, for example, technical capability and training aids may be more important than price, delivery, and warranties. Conversely, a buyer of office supplies would probably emphasize price and delivery more than the other factors. **factor importance**

All of the criteria just discussed are important or can be important in certain procurement situations. However, the one criterion that generates the most discussion and/or frustration for procurement specialists is price or cost. Therefore, some extended discussion of this criterion is necessary.

The Special Case of Procurement Price[5]

We begin by identifying the four generic sources of prices in procurement situations. This is somewhat basic but important to understand. The discussion of price becomes more complex when one adds an analysis of total acquired cost or value in the procurement process from a supply chain perspective. Total acquired cost and value are discussed after our description of price sources.

Sources of Price. Purchasing managers utilize four basic procedures to determine potential vendors' prices: commodity markets, price lists, price quotations, and negotiations. Commodity markets exist for basic raw materials such as grain, oil, sugar, and natural resources including coal and lumber. In these markets, the forces of supply and demand determine the price that all potential vendors will charge. Reductions in the supply of these materials or increases in demand usually result in increased prices; the converse is true for increases in supply or decreases in demand. **commodity markets**

Price lists are published prices that are generally used with standardized products such as gasoline or office supplies. The vendor's catalog, electronic or hard copy, describes the items available and lists their prices. Depending on the status, buyers may receive a purchaser discount from the list price. For example, a vendor may give a 10 percent discount to small-volume buyers (less than $1,000 per month) and a 35 percent discount to large-volume buyers (more than $10,000 per month). **price list**

Purchasers use the price quotation method for both standard and specialty items. It is particularly useful in promoting competition among suppliers. The process begins with the buyer sending potential vendors requests for quotes (RFQ). An RFQ contains all the necessary information regarding the specifications the purchaser requires and the manner in which potential suppliers are to present their offers. In turn, the vendors examine the cost they will incur in producing the material, considering the quantity the purchaser will order, the purchase's duration, and other factors that will affect the vendor's profitability. Finally, the purchaser compares the vendor's quoted price and offer specifications with those of other vendors. **price quotations**

The fourth procedure, negotiation, is useful when the other methods do not apply or have failed. Negotiation is particularly effective when the buyer is interested in a strategic alliance or long-term relationship. The negotiation process can be time-consuming, but the potential benefits can be significant in terms of price and quality. Negotiation is becoming more widely used by logistics managers buying goods and transport services. **negotiation**

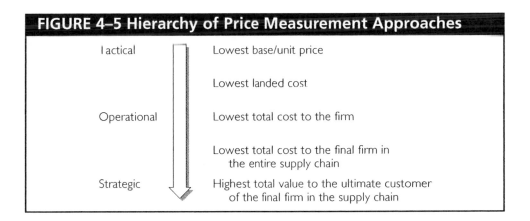

FIGURE 4–5 Hierarchy of Price Measurement Approaches

The objective of the procurement process is to purchase goods and services at the "best" price, which may not be the lowest price per unit at the vendor source. This is particularly true from a global supply chain perspective. In all four settings, the base price needs to be evaluated in a total acquired cost context.

A generalized spectrum of expanding procurement approaches to the supply chain concept is presented in Figure 4-5. At the first level, the firm evaluates procurement and logistics functions simply on the basis of lowest price or lowest cost, without strong regard to the total costs to the firm. In this context, it is difficult to attain a total cost savings unless a manager or group becomes directly responsible for the two or more interfacing functions that might offer a total cost savings. As a company attempts to move from the lowest base or unit price to taking a supply chain perspective to create highest value, the procurement function becomes more strategic in nature.

For customer satisfaction, all costs and factors that affect costs and create value should be captured in the total acquired cost. As Figure 4-5 indicates, a hierarchy of costs and other factors build upward from raw materials through manufacturing, to distribution, to final marketing and selection and use by the ultimate customer in order to determine total procurement cost and the highest total value.

For the buyer, the total procurement price is more than just the basic purchase price, as indicated in Figure 4-6. The following discussion starts with the base cost and delineates the additional direct and indirect costs that need to be considered:

Traditional basic input costs. This is the primary price of the product or materials as paid by the firm. It is the traditional price buyers seek through bidding, negotiating, or in requests for quotes. It is easily measured, and it has long been the hallmark against which buyer performance is measured; but, in a supply chain setting, it is only one factor for the firm to evaluate and consider in the acquisition process.

Direct transaction costs. These are the costs of detecting, transmitting the need for, and processing the material flow in order to acquire the goods. It includes the process of detecting inventory need, requisitioning, preparing and transmitting the order documentation to the supplier, receiving the acknowledgment, handling shipping documents, and receiving information about input to inventory. This area was made more efficient during the 1990s with the advent of internal electronic mail systems that automated the purchasing-requisition and order-transmission process.

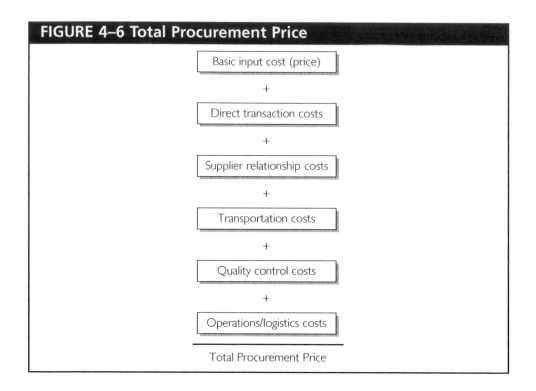

FIGURE 4–6 Total Procurement Price

Basic input cost (price)

+

Direct transaction costs

+

Supplier relationship costs

+

Transportation costs

+

Quality control costs

+

Operations/logistics costs

———————————

Total Procurement Price

Users inside the firm use electronic means to transmit their needs to purchasing. EDI and the Internet are extensions of this process outbound to the supplier.

The use of blanket or systems contracting can also reduce transaction costs. These include direct ordering by users to suppliers, single consolidated billing, and user inspection and checking. Direct transaction costs are overhead types of costs that are not easily visible, but they represent time and effort that are not available for more productive value-added activities. Suppliers and interfacing carriers that reduce the need for these activities represent value to the buying firm.

Supply relational costs. These are the costs of creating and maintaining a relationship with a supplier. They include travel, supplier education, and the establishment of planning and operational links between purchasing and the supplier's order-entry operation, as well as other links, including ones to traffic, engineering, research, and product development in both firms. In traditional purchasing settings, this includes the process of evaluating and certifying a supplier for quality and preferred supplier programs.

Landed costs. The inbound transportation flow includes two key cost elements: the actual transportation cost and the sales/FOB terms. There are four different transportation options with inbound movements—supplier-selected for-hire carrier or private carrier and buyer-selected for-hire carrier or private carrier.

The sales terms define which firm owns the goods during transportation as well as invoice payment requirements. Transportation terms pertain to the carrier in the move between the supplier and buyer firm. There are nearly a dozen possible transportation terms that include different carrier payment and loss and damage claim options. Each one presents different relative costs to each party in the linkage; and, for supply chain purposes, the one that can perform the task or own the goods at the lowest overall cost has an advantage that can contribute to the overall chain. Both sales and transportation terms must be considered, and there are different direct costs, responsibilities, and indirect implicit costs of cash flow that are affected by each one of them.

Quality costs/factors. Quality pertains to the conformance of goods to a desired specification. It includes the cost of conformance, nonconformance, appraisal, and ultimate use costs. The required quality specification is often balanced against what the supplier can easily provide nearly 100 percent of the time. Often a product specification that is extremely tight requires extra costs but results in higher quality, which may reduce total cost.

Operations/logistics costs. This group includes four key areas:

- Receiving and make-ready costs are the costs of those flow activities occurring between the inbound transportation delivery of a good and its availability for use by production or other processes. These include the cost of unpacking, inspect, counting, sorting, grading, removing and disposing of packaging materials (strapping, banding, stretch-shrink wrapping, pallets, etc.), and moving the good to the use point. A streamlined system such as direct forklift delivery to a production line is an example of an efficient receiving/make-ready process. Some leading edge carriers provide information links to the firm that include inspection checks, sequencing of the loads, and final count checks so that receiving processes can be reduced or eliminated.

- Lot-size costs directly affect space requirements, handling flow, unit price, and related cash flows. These are a major cost of inventories.

- Production costs can be affected by suppliers of even seemingly similar goods. Extruded plastic for high-quality towel rods is an example. The plastic is an extruded tube that must be inflated with air and slipped over a metal or wooden rod. Original raw material quality, differing production processes, and in-transit humidity can cause two suppliers' goods to affect the production line significantly. One might allow assembly of 200 units per hour, while another might split or not form properly, wasting 10 percent of the sleeves and requiring the production line to operate at a slower speed. Thus, each one has a different cost of production operation.

- Logistics costs are also important in both upstream and downstream settings. These are cost factors that are affected by product size, weight, cube, and shape and their resulting impact upon transportation, handling, storage, and damage costs. Purchased goods and packaging materials have a direct bearing upon these subsequent process costs.

All firms in the supply chain add cost and, hopefully, value to a product as it moves through the supply chain. Value is added by reducing total acquired cost or by enhancing the function of the product. Each firm in the supply chain can contribute to or detract from these factors. The key is to focus downstream in the supply chain, but it is also important to note the key role that the procurement process can play at each point along the supply chain by being aware of a product's total acquired cost. Ideally, the focus should be upon the total value at the end of the supply chain. Therefore, the analysis should also include indirect financial costs (payment terms), tactical input costs (vendor capabilities), and strategic business factors (factors that cause customers to buy the product).

Other Materials-Management Activities

As was indicated at the outset of this discussion, price can be a complex factor, since other aspects have to be considered as they relate to the base price. Thus far, the discussion of materials-management functions has focused solely upon procurement. We now turn to the additional materials-management activities.

Warehousing. The *warehousing* function concerns the physical holding of raw materials until a firm uses them. Chapter 8 discusses general warehousing functions and decision areas. Although storing the raw materials a manufacturer will use in the production process is basically the same as storing finished products, raw-materials storage and finished-goods storage differ notably in terms of the type of facility each requires, the value of the stored items, and product perishability.

Basic raw materials such as coal, sand, or limestone normally require an open-air warehouse facility; that is, a firm would merely dump the basic raw materials on the ground. Thus, the facility cost for storing basic raw materials is lower than the facility cost for storing other materials—finished goods, components, and other semifinished products, for example—that require an elaborate enclosed structure.

facilities required

The value of raw materials is usually lower than that of finished goods, since the manufacturer enhances the value of the finished material, or processed raw material, during the manufacturing process. Last, basic raw materials usually suffer less damage and loss than finished goods because raw materials have lower value and need no protection from the elements.

Chapter 8 discusses the warehousing function and the ways in which its activities and decisions affect logistics systems.

Production Planning and Control. In a manufacturing environment, *production planning and control* involve coordinating product supply with product demand. As Figure 4–7 shows, the starting point of the production planning and control process is the demand for the finished product the company produces and sells. This demand is the process's independent variable, since the seller cannot control customer demand.

The manufacturer must forecast, or estimate, customer demand. This sales forecast should indicate the sales amount the manufacturer expects for each item and the time period the sales projection covers. After establishing this independent customer demand, the manufacturer can provide the finished product supply either from available inventory or by producing the product. Thus, external demand establishes an internal demand for a finished product; and the manufacturer fills this demand from the existing stocks or from new production.

forecasting

When demand requires production, the production scheduling manager uses the sales forecast to develop a production schedule. A production planner's main concerns include the following:

- Number of units of a specified product to be produced
- Time intervals over which production will occur
- Availability of materials and machines to produce the number of units required within the specified time frame

Production control results as the production manager specifies time intervals and develops order schedules for raw materials to supply the production schedule. For

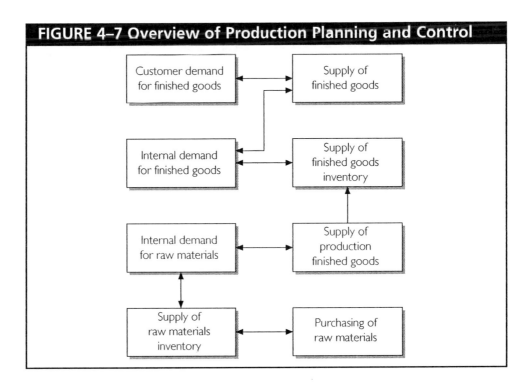

FIGURE 4–7 Overview of Production Planning and Control

example, suppose that sales forecasts estimate that a firm will sell 10,000 units of product A and 30,000 units of product B in March. The firm makes both products on the same machine, which produces 10,000 units per week. The production planner first determines how much, if any, production the firm requires to satisfy customer demand and to maintain target inventory levels. In this example, low inventory levels require the firm to produce all 40,000 units. Additionally, a special promotion has depleted product A's inventory quickly, giving product A scheduling priority. However, vendor labor strikes have made the material for product A unavailable until week 2. As a result, the production planner first schedules one week of product B, followed by one week of product A and then two weeks of product B. Obviously, this is a simple example.

Transportation. The *transportation* function manages the inbound transportation of materials. Transportation originates with the materials vendor, and the movement's destination is the buyer's plant. The inbound transportation activity supports the firm's supply effort in that the inbound transportation bridges the spatial and temporal gap existing between the buyer and the vendor, or seller.

The management of inbound transportation requires transportation knowledge and expertise similar to that necessary to handle the movement of finished goods outbound from the plant. The transportation manager must decide about the transportation mode, the routes, the rates, claims handling, carrier services, cost analysis, and regulations. Chapter 9 and Chapter 10 discuss these factors in detail.

vendor control   In some situations, the vendor controls inbound transportation. FOB-delivered terms of sale characterize such cases. When the buyer relinquishes the transportation function to the vendor, the buyer assumes that the vendor will ship the materials as cost-efficiently as possible. However, such an assumption is not always true. The buyer should periodically analyze the cost-effectiveness of the vendor's transportation decision.

For basic raw materials, the transportation activity may involve rail or water transportation, the modes companies most commonly utilize to ship large volumes of low-value, high-density products, such as coal or sand. With the advent of rail deregulation, many of these shipments are moving into plants under contract rates with the railroads. The contracts usually specify providing a specific rate and service in return for a guarantee that the shipper will tender the carrier a guaranteed amount of freight.

modal choice

Finally, inbound transportation is normally under less pressure to provide "rush" shipments than is outbound transportation. The demand for raw materials is much more stable and predictable than the demand for finished goods, since economies of production dictate long production runs, which give way to fixed production schedules. However, inbound transportation must occasionally handle a rush shipment—if a plant receives damaged raw materials, for example. Also, with increased use of JIT, inbound transportation requires much stricter schedules. Occasionally, when a problem develops, inbound transportation must expedite (rush) a shipment.

rush shipments

Receiving. The *receiving* process involves the actual physical receipt of the purchased material from the carrier. The receiving clerk, who must ensure that the goods a firm receives were those ordered and shipped, compares the materials indicated on the buyer's purchase order and the vendor's packing slip with the material the buyer has actually received. If discrepancies exist, the receiving department notifies the purchasing department, the material's users, and the accounts payable department.

inspection

Another critical inspection during the receiving process involves examining the received material for any physical damage. As is discussed in Chapter 10, claims against the carrier for damage are easier to make if the receiving clerk notes on the bill of lading that the buyer received the shipment in damaged condition. When such a notation appears on the bill of lading, the carrier is presumed guilty of damaging the material. Any legal action places the burden on the carrier to prove that the carrier was not guilty of damaging the freight. Not noting damage on the bill of lading does not preclude the payment of a damage claim, but it puts an additional burden on the receiver (or owner) of the material to prove that the shipment was damaged when the carrier delivered it. Inbound traffic departments and receiving departments usually coordinate freight claims handling activities.

damage claims

Quality Control. The *quality control* function, like the receiving function, attempts to ensure that the items a firm receives are those the firm ordered. However, the quality control function is directly concerned with defining the product's quality in terms of dimensions, design specifications, chemical or physical properties, reliability, ease of maintenance, ease of use, brand, market grade, and industry standard. The quality control area's specific concern is whether or not the product received meets the quality standards the buyer and seller set forth in the purchase agreement.

quality standards

The quality of the materials a manufacturer procures directly affects the quality of the finished product and, consequently, affects the sale of the finished product. If a firm sells a defective product, the product's buyer will become dissatisfied and may refuse to purchase the firm's product in the future. In addition, a manufacturer who uses inferior materials in production may be legally liable for a hazardous or unreliable product. Thus, quality control function responsibilities cover the spectrum from market to legal concerns.

quality implications

SUPPLY CHAIN TECHNOLOGY

BIBNET LINKS MICHELIN'S TIRE DEALERS

Michelin North America's dealers have a better spin on their tire needs than ever before, thanks to the creation of Michelin's on-line supply chain community. Just ask Belle Tire, Inc., Fallen Park, Michigan. The tire dealer, which has about fifty stores in the Detroit area, has been connected for the past three years to BibNet, Michelin's on-line community and, in that time, has reduced inventories, decreased the amount of handling required, and improved order accuracy.

Belle Tire is one of more than 300 Michelin dealers in North America connected to BibNet, which is named after the tire maker's mascot, Bib. These dealers use BibNet to order tires and determine inventory availability at Michelin's eight warehouses.

Michelin began putting BibNet together in 1966, using software from Entigo, a Pittsburgh-based electronic-commerce vendor. BibNet is technically an *Extranet,* which means the dealers dial into a private phone network to gain access to the tire manufacturer's systems and use a standard Web browser to view inventory status and place orders for tires and parts electronically. "It allows for the sales channels to completely automate all of their ordering processes via the Web," says James Graham, Entigo's president.

But, the community offers more to its dealers than just Web-based procurement. Leo Zannetti, Belle Tire's director of purchasing, says that his company also can obtain access to Michelin's tire inventory system (TIMS). TIMS keeps track of the dealer's sales, the stock of tires on hand, and its orders. The system then consolidates the dealer's orders and suggests a shipment replenishment order twice a week.

From all accounts, participation in BibNet has had a positive effect on Belle Tire's operations. Zannetti reports that the software optimization of the procurement process has reduced inventory, resulting in the need for less warehouse space. On top of that, Belle Tire has initiated direct store replenishment for fifteen of its larger stores, which can accommodate tractor-trailer deliveries from Michelin. The other stores are resupplied daily from Belle Tire's main warehouse. "The product that's directly shipped cuts down on handling," says Zannetti. He has identified one other benefit as well: "Because the purchase orders are sent electronically, there are fewer mistakes."

Michelin believes that its on-line community will ultimately eliminate unneeded inventory for both the manufacturer and its dealers. "Because of the visibility of orders from the time the dealer places them to the time they leave the warehouse," says Tom Hall, Michelin's manager of electronic commerce, "there will be fewer mistakes in the order-fulfillment process."

Source: "BibNet Links Michelin's Tire Dealers," *Logistics* (February 2000): 47. Copyright Cahners Business Information. Reprinted by permission.

---

sample Normally, inspecting each item that a buyer purchases is neither possible nor desirable. Quality inspectors usually examine a limited sample of the items purchased. For example, a quality inspector wanting to determine whether the life of a given vendor's light bulbs met longevity specifications would test a sample of the vendor's light bulbs. The quality control department would statistically examine the results and, on the basis of the tested sample, would decide to accept or reject the order received. The increased emphasis on quality in recent years has required vendors to develop their own statistical quality control programs. Today, many buyers insist upon total or 100 percent quality.

value of scrap **Salvage and Scrap Disposal.** The final activity in the materials-management function involves *disposing of salvage, scrap,* excess, and obsolete materials. Although primarily concerned with buying, the materials management department has assumed this selling responsibility, since most marketing or sales departments must concentrate on selling the firm's finished products.

Scrap and salvage material that is useful to others has a certain value, and the disposal of these items provides income for the firm. The recent recycling trend has provided a ready market for many scrap and salvage items. For example, companies are using used oils and other scrap items such as olive pits and corncobs as fuel sources; and, as recent years of double-digit inflation have sent new equipment prices beyond the ability of many potential buyers to pay, more companies are buying or salvaging used equipment.

Certain scrap materials cannot be sold but must be disposed of in a safe and prescribed manner. One such commodity group is hazardous wastes—materials that are ignitable, corrosive, reactive (volatile), or toxic. Disposing of these hazardous materials is quite costly, and the generator of such materials is under specific legal liability to dispose of them properly.

disposal

The materials-management function, as we indicated, occurs on the inbound side of the logistics pipeline. Customer service and distribution activity channels are on the pipeline's outbound side; but a firm must tightly coordinate both inbound and outbound logistics in today's highly competitive marketplace.

ELECTRONIC PROCUREMENT

The computer and the World Wide Web have created some dramatic changes in the business world. It is becoming quite common for consumers to research products and services; locate retail outlets; and, with the click of a mouse, purchase goods and services—all in the convenience of one's home. There is much attention to business-to-consumer (B2C) E-commerce, but the majority of the E-commerce transactions are business to business (B2B). B2B purchases are estimated to be $1.3 to $2.0 trillion by 2003.[6]

Procurement was the business process that made early application of E-commerce. Initially, companies utilized electronic data interchange (EDI) technology to connect with their major customers to process purchase orders, send notifications of shipment, and transfer funds. However, EDI technology is costly and requires special technology to implement. The advent of the publicly available Internet has eliminated the investment and technology problems associated with EDI and opened the door to increased application of E-commerce techniques to procurement.

The most common use of E-commerce today is to research vendor and product information. This is a primary reason that some vendors have only a Web site on the Internet to merely advertise their products. However, other companies have advanced on-line procurement systems that permit a buyer to electronically check available stock, negotiate price, issue an order, check on the status of the order, issue an invoice, and receive payment. The ultimate E-commerce procurement system is still in the development stage and will evolve over time.

Advantages

The advantages of E-commerce procurement are shown in Figure 4–8. An obvious advantage is the lowering of procurement operating costs. The reduction of paperwork and the associated cost of paper processing, filing, and storing is a major cost-saving area of E-commerce. Many companies have a goal of being paperless, but few have obtained that goal at this time.

Another paper reduction possible with E-commerce is electronic funds transfer. Paying vendor invoices electronically eliminates the cost of preparing, mailing, filing, and storage of the checks. Estimates of the cost of writing a check vary from a low of $10 to a high of $85, the majority of this cost being the cost of accounts payable personnel.

Reduced sourcing time means increased productivity because a procurement specialist spends less time per order and can place more orders in a given time period. Likewise, the seller utilizing E-commerce can increase the productivity of customer service representatives. Many of the questions asked by the buyer can be answered on-line, thereby saving time for both the buyer and seller personnel.

Given the real-time nature of E-Commerce information, sellers have up-to-date information on demand and can adjust production/purchases to meet the current demand level. This same real-time information enables the buyer to establish controls that will coordinate purchase quantities with requirement quantities and monitor spending levels. That is, the buyer is now in the position of monitoring the quantity of an item ordered, received, and on-hand and comparing it to the amount needed, and doing this in a real-time mode. The same is true for monitoring spending activities against budgeted amounts.

Electronic procurement affords efficiency in the process by utilizing fewer resources to produce a given level of purchases. With a click of the mouse, a purchasing manager can search the world for alternative supply sources of a product or service. With another click of the mouse, the manager can then ascertain information about the sources identified through the electronic search. All of this research is done in the office without phone calls, additional personnel, or outside sources.

FIGURE 4–8 Advantages of Electronic Procurement

Lower operating costs
- Reduce paperwork
- Reduce sourcing time
- Improve control over inventory and spending

Improve procurement efficiency
- Find new supply sources
- Improve communications
- Improve personnel use
- Lower cycle times

Reduce procurement prices
- Improve comparison shopping
- Reduce overall prices paid

A significant efficiency factor of E-commerce is improved communication. The buyer can secure information from the vendor's company—product line, prices, and product availability. The seller can obtain information regarding requests for proposals, blueprints, technical specifications, and purchase requirements from the buyer. Also, the seller can improve customer service by communicating the status of the order, giving the buyer advance notice of any delays in the order fulfillment due to stockout conditions or transportation. As noted earlier, E-commerce permits the seller to gain real-time information to more accurately predict demand.

This improved communication via E-commerce aids in reducing order cycle time. All the time elements incorporated in order cycle time are reduced. The time to place the order is reduced to seconds. The buyer knows prior to placing an order whether the vendor has product available. The seller monitors demand instantaneously and is in a better position to adjust supply with current demand and to reduce or eliminate a stockout condition.

Better use of procurement personnel is made possible by relieving them of the clerical tasks associated with processing the order, such as typing purchase orders, mailing them to the vendor, and checking the status of the order via phone. The procurement manager is now free to focus attention on the long-term strategic procurement issues such as long-term item availability, opportunities for supply chain efficiencies, innovative products, and so on.

Reduced procurement prices have resulted from the ability of a buyer to gain access to pricing information from more potential vendors. With more vendors bidding for the business, the buyers are finding lower prices forthcoming. In addition, the procurement manager has the ability to view on-line the qualities of different vendor products and services, making comparison much easier. The overall effect of increased comparison shopping and increased number of potential vendors is lower prices.

Disadvantages

Like most things in life, E-commerce does have some drawbacks. The most frequently voiced concern about using the Internet for procurement is security. Recent examples of attacks on B2C E-commerce companies such as Amazon.com and eBay where the computers were overloaded with orders and operations were stopped give many executives much concern about E-commerce security. Also, there is concern regarding the vulnerability of credit card numbers transmitted over the Internet or stored on a vendor's system to theft by a computer hacker.

Another problem is the lack of face-to-face contact between the buyer and seller. Buying and selling via E-commerce reduces the ability to build close supplier relationships. This can be overcome by making a concerted effort to develop and enhance personal communications with the vendor.

Other concerns deal with technology. More specifically, there are concerns with the lack of standard protocols, system reliability, and technology problems. Lastly, there is reluctance on the part of some to invest the time and money to learn the new technology. For the most part, these concerns are diminishing daily as new and improved technology is developed and the business community demands the use of E-commerce.

Common Applications

E-commerce is most often used to purchase high-volume, low-value, low-risk items, or generics. The most frequently E-purchased items include office supplies, office equipment, computer hardware/software, and travel. Items within these categories are quite standard, and there are many sellers available. Also, the sellers of these products have been leaders in the development of B2B systems.

This does not mean that other products are not electronically purchased. There is a growing trend toward B2B transactions in such basic products as chemicals, plastics, and metals. Virtually any item purchased by today's businesses will eventually be available through E-commerce within the next few years.

Types of E-commerce Models[7]

There are four basic types of E-commerce business models used in procurement: sell-side system, electronic marketplace, buy-side system, and on-line trading community.

The *sell-side system* is a Web site administered by a seller. The site is usually free to the buyer and offers B2B service with the seller who establishes the site. Examples include OfficeMax (http://www.officemax.com), Staples (http://www.staples.com), McMaster-Carr (http://www.mcmaster.com), Global Computer Supplies (http://www.globalcomputer.com), and Newark Electronics (http://www.newark.com). A buyer can log on to the sell-side Web site and review products, prices, and services and place an order. The buyer cannot track or control spending with the sell-side system, and the Web sites are somewhat difficult to locate.

Another seller-operated B2B service is the *electronic marketplace*. The electronic marketplace is an amalgam of electronic catalogs from vendors within a market. The marketplace is administered by a third party, not one of the vendors. The electronic marketplace provides a one-stop sourcing site for buyers who can examine the offerings of many different vendors at one Web location. Like the sell-side system, the electronic marketplace does not permit the buyer to track or control spending. Examples of electronic marketplaces include the Plastics Network (http://www.plasticsnet.com), E-Chemicals (http://www.e-chemicals.com) and MetalSite (http://www.metalsite.com).

The buyer-controlled B2B service is known as the *buy-side system*. This B2B system is housed on the buyer's system and administered by the buyer. The buyer preapproves the vendors that have access to the system, and the prices of the vendors' products and services have been prenegotiated. These systems permit tracking and controlling procurement spending and reduce unauthorized purchases. However, the cost of the buy-side system is very high due to the cost of developing and administering the system with a large list of vendors. The buy-side system is usually the domain of large companies.

Recently, Ford announced the establishment of buy-side procurement systems. The companies expect to save millions of dollars as a result of processing purchase orders electronically. The Ford system is known as Auto Exchange and will permit its thousands of suppliers to receive and process purchase orders electronically. After focusing on procurement, the system will be used for supply chain planning;

consolidating demand; and, finally, collaborative design and shortening of the product release cycle. Although Ford will benefit from the procurement aspects of its buy-side system, there will be many value-added services, efficiencies, and economies realized from its application to the total supply chain.

The final basic electronic business model is the *on-line trading community.* The on-line trading community is maintained by a third-party technology vendor where multiple buyers and multiple sellers in a given market can conduct business. The difference between the on-line trading community and the electronic marketplace is that the electronic marketplace is focused on providing information about sellers, whereas the on-line community permits the buyers and sellers to conduct business transactions.

The on-line trading company may be viewed as an electronic auction. The buyer indicates the type of product, quantity, and so on desired; and the sellers respond. In a downward auction, the buyer states a maximum time period to receive the best bid from potential vendors. At the end of the time period, the buyer selects the vendor(s) with the lowest price and will conduct negotiations, if necessary, to finalize the transaction. Examples of on-line trading companies include Travelocity (http://www.travelocity.com), eBay (http://www.ebay.com), and the National Transportation Exchange (http://www.nte.net).

Electronic procurement is here and will continue to grow. It will not replace all procurement activities, but it could reach 80 percent or more of a company's total purchase order activity. Electronic procurement focuses on the processing of orders and maintaining a source of real-time information for better decision making. Procurement specialists focus on selecting vendors, negotiating prices, monitoring quality, and developing supplier relations.

SUMMARY

- The supply chain can be viewed as inbound logistics and outbound logistics; the focus of this chapter is on the inbound system. Effective supply chain management requires the careful coordination of inbound and outbound systems.

- Inbound logistics systems can vary in terms of importance, scope, cost, and complexity, depending on where the company is located in the supply chain, the nature of the product, and the market situation in which the product is sold.

- The procurement area plays a major role in materials management, and procurement is an important link in the supply chain.

- The procurement process can be broken down into a set of activities that include identifying a need, defining and evaluating user requirements, deciding whether to make or buy, identifying the type of purchase, performing a market analysis, identifying potential suppliers, prescreening possible vendors, evaluating remaining suppliers, choosing a vendor, receiving delivery of the product or service, and making a postpurchase evaluation.

- Not all purchased items are of equal importance. Using the criteria of risk and value, the quadrant technique classifies items into four importance categories: generics, commodities, distinctives, and criticals. Generics have low risk, low value; commodities have low risk, high value; distinctives have high risk, low value; and criticals have high risk, high value.

- The procurement process activities can be more effectively managed by following a four-step process: (1) determine type of purchase; (2) determine necessary level of investment; (3) perform the procurement process; (4) evaluate the effectiveness of the procurement process.

- In selecting vendors, a number of criteria should be utilized, including quality, reliability, capability, financial viability, and other factors, such as location.

- There are four basic sources of price: commodity markets, price lists, price quotation, and price negotiation.

- The purchase price is a matter of great importance, but it is much more complex than just the base unit price, since it requires the analysis of added value along the supply chain to deliver the highest total value to the ultimate customer.

- In addition to procurement costs, materials management includes warehousing, production planning and control, traffic, receiving, quality control, and salvage and scrap disposal.

- Electronic procurement has become widely used in business because of the publicly available Internet. The advantages include lower operating costs, improved efficiency, and reduced prices, with the primary disadvantage being security. There are four basic types of electronic procurement models: sell-side, electronic marketplace, buy-side, and on-line trading community systems.

STUDY QUESTIONS

1. Inbound logistics systems can vary in scope and complexity among different companies. Explain the differences that can exist between inbound logistics systems. What is the source of the differences?

2. The procurement process can be described in terms of a set of activities that should be used in the purchase of goods and services. Briefly discuss these activities.

3. Maximizing the effectiveness of the procurement process is a major goal of an organization. What steps can be taken to help ensure that the process is maximized?

4. A key part of the procurement process is the selection of vendors. What criteria are commonly used in this selection process? Which criteria should be given the highest priority? Why?

5. What are the major sources of prices in the purchase of goods? Under what circumstances would these sources be utilized?

6. What are the components of total acquired cost? Is it realistic to expect companies to consider all of these components?

7. Using the risk/value technique, categorize the importance of the following items for an automobile manufacturer: engine, tires, gasoline, paper for the employee newsletter, a uniquely designed and engineered muffler, and rail car service to dealers. Describe the rationale you used to ascertain each categorization.

8. What role does warehousing play in materials-management systems? Can the importance of warehousing vary among companies? Explain.

9. Discuss the advantages and disadvantages of using E-commerce in the procurement process.

10. Describe the different types of E-commerce business models available for procurement, and point out their respective benefits and disadvantages.

NOTES

1. This section is adapted from R. A. Novack and Stephen W. Simco, "The Industrial Procurement Process," *Journal of Business Logistics* 12, no. 1 (1991): 145–65.

2. Michael E. Porter, *Competitive Advantage* (New York: The Free Press, 1985), 11–16.

3. This section is adapted from Joseph L. Cavinato, "Quadrant Technique: Key to Effective Acquisition and Access," *ARDC Spectrum, Report #11,* Acquisition Research & Development Center, State College, Pa.

4. Porter, 33–34.

5. This section is adapted from J. L. Cavinato, "A Total Cost/Value Model for Supply Chain Competitiveness," *Journal of Business Logistics* 13, no.2 (1992): 285–99.

6. Cherish Karoway Whyte, "E-Procurement the New Competitive Weapon," *Purchasing Today* (April 2000): 25.

7. The material in this section is adapted from Mark Vigoroso, "Buyers Prepare for Brave New World of E-Commerce," *Purchasing* (22 April 1999).

CASE 4–1 ■ Durable Vinyl Siding Corp.

The Durable Vinyl Siding Corporation (DVS) is a leading U.S. manufacturer of vinyl siding products for home and commercial buildings. In 2000, the company had record sales of $250 million—a 15 percent increase over 1999 and the tenth year of double-digit growth. Mr. Mark Talbott, president, was very pleased with the positive sales figures for 2000 but was growing increasingly concerned about the trend of the bottom-line numbers. During the past five years, the net profit margin had slipped from 7.2 percent in 1996 to 4.5 percent in 2000.

At the monthly executive team meeting, Mark pointed out the downward trend of net profits and challenged the team to increase the bottom line by 1.0 to 2.0 percentage points for the next year. Mark pointed out to the team members that price pressure from competing siding companies and increasing costs were the primary reasons for the declining profit margins. He asked each team member to develop a strategic plan to accomplish the profit goals.

Margaret Klisure, director of purchasing, was reviewing the purchasing data the procurement team had gathered in preparation for developing a purchasing strategic plan. First, procurement costs had increased from 57 percent of sales in 1996 to 65 percent of sales in 2000. The procurement staff increased by five people during this same time period. DVS now manufactures 1,500 SKUs and purchases over 5,000 SKUs of materials to support the manufacture, sale, and delivery of its finished goods line.

The items purchased include vinyl base products, paints, office supplies, packaging, lumber for pallets, warehouse equipment, maintenance and operating items, and transportation services. In total, DVM spent $162.5 million in 2000 for these items and the operation of the procurement department. For each 1.0 percent reduction in procurement expenditures, Margaret calculated an increase of 0.65 percent in net profits (assuming $250 million in sales).

The purchasing department operation was basically the same as it was in 1996. Margaret was recently appointed director of purchasing following the retirement of the previous director who was the head of purchasing since the founding of the company over twenty years before. Most of the purchasing tasks are completed manually. A computer is used for internal control of inventory levels and for printing invoices. There is no procurement computer system in place, and there is no use of E-commerce for purchasing. The purchasing staff consists primarily of buyers who are assigned to particular product groups; for example, a person is responsible for purchasing all the vinyl raw materials, one person purchases transportation, and so on.

Over the years, the buyers have become very adept at gaining price concessions from vendors. However, this has created some very serious warehousing problems for DVM. For example, last week Mark Talbott called an emergency meeting with the directors of manufacturing, warehousing, sales, and purchasing to seek a solution to the overcrowding in the warehouse. The warehouse was completely full, forcing DVS to go off-site to store finished goods. A review of the items stored in the warehouse indicated that there was a six-month supply of corrugated packaging material, a ten-month supply of paints, and a four-month supply of lumber. Also, the inventory levels of over 50 percent of the finished good SKUs exceeded a two-year supply at current sales levels.

With only one warehouse in the system, DVM had to optimize the utilization of this facility. If DVM had to use an outside warehouse for short-term storage, it incurred a 15 percent penalty in the form of higher storage, order picking, and transportation costs. In addition, the cost of capital rose last year because of the actions of the Federal Reserve; and the total purchasing expenditure included the cost of money tied up in inventory.

Margaret also knew that the buyers' productivity was declining because the annual number of orders was declining in light of the addition of staff last year. The buyers noted the need for more time to research potential vendors and to maintain good vendor relations as the prime reason for the lower productivity.

Margaret's primary objective was to reduce procurement costs while maintaining the product quality and efficiency of procurement. Price concessions from vendors did not appear to be a major source of cost savings, particularly for the basic vinyl raw materials. She concluded that the primary areas for efficiency enhancements were in computerization and E-commerce.

Case Questions

1. What organizational changes would you suggest for DVM procurement?

2. What types of computerization changes would you recommend?

3. How would E-commerce benefit DVS procurement?

4. Would you recommend the same computer and E-commerce strategies for all 5,000 SKUs purchased? If not, how would these strategies differ?

5. What strategies do you suggest for maintaining procurement service levels?

16

TRANSPORTATION MANAGEMENT

LEARNING OBJECTIVES

After reading this chapter, you should be able to do the following:

- Define proactive transportation management.

- Discuss the five transportation management strategies: reducing the number of carriers, negotiating with carriers, contracting with carriers, consolidating shipments, and monitoring service quality.

- Explain the current economic regulation (deregulation) of transportation.

- Distinguish among the transportation documents: bill of lading, freight bill, and freight claims.

- Compare the domestic terms of sale with international Incoterms.

- Explain cost of service and value of service ratemaking and the effect of shipment weight and distance on freight rates.

- Discuss terminal and line-haul services offered by carriers.

LOGISTICS PROFILE

Mastering the Art of Advance Planning

Intensive advance planning, painstaking attention to detail, and constant communication—these are without doubt the most important factors in the success of NBC Olympics' effort to ship television broadcasting equipment and supplies to Sydney, Australia, for the 2000 Summer Olympics.

Both NBC and Fritz Cos., which handles the broadcaster's freight forwarding and customs brokerage, have staff members dedicated full time to the Olympics effort. In addition to daily, ad hoc telephone communications, there are weekly conference calls between NBC Technical Logistics, staff members in the United States and Sydney, Fritz's managers in the United States, and the Olympics project team at Fritz's Sydney office. During those calls, the four groups update each other on the past week's activities and plan for upcoming shipments. Staff members also enter updated information into Fritz's customer-service "Response Tracking" software, Microsoft Excel spreadsheet files, or Microsoft Access database files; these are quickly and easily shared with all parties in both countries when sent as E-mail attachments.

Advance planning occupied much of the groups' time. Every one of the thousands of items that NBC brought into Australia over a ten-month period must leave the country within a few weeks after the Games end. And items in each departing shipment must be matched with their original import documentation. The shipments, moreover, must be consolidated with others that are headed for the same destination. And they have to leave by certain dates to ensure that they arrive at their destinations before they are needed at other events.

To make all that happen, NBC and Fritz planned the exact order in which every item and piece of equipment must be shipped back from Sydney. The logistics service provider booked space with air and ocean carriers long in advance. And Fritz's customs brokers made sure when the original shipments were exported that all of the import documentation needed for re-entry into the United States was ready to go.

Nothing in this enormous program was left to chance. When NBC and Fritz began their collaboration, says Fritz Client Relations Manager Dave Smith, the shipper and forwarder wrote a 150-page operations manual to ensure that there would be no "holes." "A lot of thought went into this," he says. "Very talented people at both NBC and Fritz recognized the magnitude of this project and made sure there was a process in place for each item that needed to be there. . . . When we turned on the TV to watch the Olympics, we felt proud to say, 'I was a part of that.' "

Source: "Mastering the Art of Advance Planning," *Logistics Management* (September 2000): 55. Copyright Cahners Business Information. Reprinted with permission.

INTRODUCTION

Transportation costs, which represent approximately 40 to 50 percent of total logistics costs and 4 to 10 percent of the product selling price for many companies, may represent logistics management's major concern. Transportation decisions directly affect the total logistics costs, costs in other functional areas of the firm, and costs within other logistics channel members. This chapter focuses on the daily transportation management activities in today's deregulated transportation environment, concentrating specifically on carrier pricing, services, and documentation. We first direct our attention toward transportation management strategy.

MANAGEMENT STRATEGY

seeking parity

The passage of the transportation deregulation acts in 1977 and 1980 drastically changed the business climate within which the transportation manager operates. Before those acts, the climate emphasized the ability to operate effectively within regulation confines. Good transportation managers were those who worked within the system to ensure that competitors were not getting better rates or services, that is, who sought to achieve regulatory parity among transportation users.

The bureaucratic red tape of transportation regulation placed a stranglehold on management initiative. Innovative transportation management was difficult to develop because of regulatory constraints. By necessity, transportation managers armed themselves with a list of "thou shalt nots" that would squelch any and all suggestions company managers put forth.

Today, the transportation environment has changed and the regulations shackling management decisions are gone. A transportation manager can no longer utilize the regulatory constraints to prevent a competitor from gaining a competitive advantage when a carrier offers the competitor better rates and services. In fact, contracting, the elimination of tariff-filing requirements, and the publication of individual carrier tariffs prevent the transportation manager from knowing what rates and services a carrier is providing to competitors.

Proactive Management Approach

With the regulatory safety net gone, today's transportation manager must rely on traditional management techniques, using a proactive approach to identify and solve transportation problems and to provide the company with a competitive advantage in the marketplace. (See the Logistics Profile for an example of transport planning.)

A proactive management approach seeks to identify transportation problems and to postulate solutions that benefit the whole company. Without a regulatory rule book, transportation management is free to concentrate on innovative solutions to today's logistics and transportation challenges. Only managers' abilities and creativity and normal business law constraints limit the benefits of this proactive business strategy.

For example, suppose that a firm's sales decline in a particular market results from longer and less-dependable lead times than those provided by the competition in that market. If the firm makes a modal switch from rail to truck, the increased cost of truck service would force the firm to increase prices or to incur a loss, neither of which is acceptable. Negotiating with carriers, establishing carrier contracts with prescribed service levels, and modifying loading procedures are alternatives that the transportation manager may explore to improve services and sales while maintaining acceptable costs.

negative versus positive approach

Today, the transportation manager actively participates in solving company problems. Companies no longer look upon transportation as a necessary evil; rather, transportation contains fundamental solutions to problems that plague a company's functional areas. Thus, today's transportation manager must understand other functional areas, as well as the entire company, so as to seek logistics strategies that support other departmental and corporate strategies.

Reducing the Number of Carriers

market power

By reducing the number of carriers it uses, a shipping firm increases the freight volume and freight revenue that it gives to a carrier, thereby increasing its ability to have the carrier provide the rates and services the shipper needs. As the shipper concentrates its freight business in a limited number of carriers, the shipper becomes more important to each carrier; and each carrier, in becoming more dependent on the shipper's business, is more willing to negotiate with the shipper.

Being one of the carrier's largest customers gives the shipper significant negotiating power: the fear of losing the shipper's business motivates the carrier to comply with the shipper's demands for better rates and service levels. In essence, the shipper who is one of the carrier's A customers (part of the 20 percent of the carrier's customers who provide 80 percent of the carrier's sales revenue) possesses market power with the carrier.

strategic alliance

This concentration of freight in a limited number of carriers not only increases market power but also permits a company to develop a strategic alliance with the carriers it uses. In a strategic alliance, the shipper and the carrier, recognizing their mutual dependency, strive to be efficient so that both can survive and prosper. In addition to reducing transportation costs, the improved working relations within the strategic alliance reduce other logistics costs such as information processing, inventory, and warehousing.

Reducing the number of carriers a firm uses may also increase the possibility of providing a carrier with balanced loads of raw materials inbound and finished goods outbound. By reducing excess capacity, a balanced-load pattern enables the carrier to reduce its costs and to offer lower rates. In addition, providing the carrier with balanced loads may increase the carrier's service level.

risks

A negative risk associated with concentrating business in a limited number of carriers is the firm's increased dependency on the carrier it uses. A shipper who uses only ten carriers is much more vulnerable to shipment disruptions and resulting customer service declines than is a shipper who uses 100 carriers. With the 100-carrier strategy, losing one carrier requires the shipper to reallocate only 1 percent of its freight volume among the remaining ninety-nine carriers, which should pose no problem to carrier capacity and customer service levels. In the ten-carrier scenario, however, losing one carrier requires the shipper to secure shipping capacity equivalent to 10 percent of the shipper's volume, which the remaining nine carriers may not have the capacity to handle. This will force the shipper to use carriers unfamiliar with the shipper's freight, shipping procedures, and customer service requirements; will normally disrupt operating systems and customer service levels; and, possibly, will lead to higher transportation costs, since crisis stage allows the shipper little market power to negotiate favorable rates.

Single sourcing is the ultimate concentration of market power. By using one carrier, the shipper realizes the maximum market power for the freight dollars spent. Corporate-wide single sourcing poses a substantial risk of complete disruption of transportation operations if the carrier fails. However, single sourcing occurs at one facility or for one product (inbound or outbound).

Negotiating with Carriers

Today, carrier negotiation is the norm, and, in some situations, a daily function. The transportation manager must possess negotiating skills sufficient to secure the desired service level at the least cost. Successful carrier negotiation has enabled many companies either to remain competitive in the market or to increase competitive advantage through improved carrier service levels.

negotiating constraints

Market forces and regulatory constraints determine the negotiable factors between the carrier and the shipper. Generally, the negotiated factors revolve around the rates and services the carriers provide. The remaining economic regulations, the STB (see the following section), and antitrust scrutiny imposed upon the truck and rail common carriers govern the negotiated rates and services; air carrier negotiations are subject to antitrust scrutiny only.

The marketplace determines the negotiable factors, assuming that these factors violate no regulatory constraints. The shippers' operational needs, customer demands, and company objectives determine the areas where negotiations will begin. The shipper brings these needs to the carrier, who decides (negotiates) whether these needs are realistic. More than likely the carrier will respond with a counterproposal that offers something less than what the shipper requested.

At other times the carrier will initiate negotiations. The carrier, who may have a specific need to eliminate an empty backhaul, specify pickup times, or increase tonnage, entices a shipper to respond, usually by offering a concession, such as a reduced rate. The shipper will analyze the carrier proposal and either accept or reject the offer or request a greater concession.

market power

Throughout this negotiation, the market power each party enjoys influences the outcome. The shipper possesses market power in terms of the transportation business available in a given time period and can increase this market power by limiting the number of carriers it uses. The carrier possesses market power in terms of the carrier's importance to the shipper—that is, the availability of equal or better-quality service substitutes.

Contracting with Carriers

The Motor Carrier Act of 1980, the Staggers Act of 1980, and the ICC Termination Act of 1995 increased shippers' ability to enter into contracts with carriers. Contracting enables the shipper to eliminate the uncertainties in rates and services that common carriers provide. Through the contract terms, the shipper can specify the rate and level of service that the carrier will provide and can dictate noncompliance penalties, thereby fixing service levels during the contract period.

tailored service

Contracting permits shippers that desire specialized services to purchase a unique or tailored service level that may not be available from the regulated or common carrier. The common carrier must provide service to all shippers without discrimination or preferential treatment, whereas the regulated carrier, which does not have the same regulatory requirement, provides a generic level of service to the shipping public. The regulated carrier service is a unilateral agreement in which the carrier, through its rate and rules tariffs, specifies the level of service that will be provided. The shipper has no input into the service decision, and the carrier can make changes without the shipper's approval or knowledge in some cases.

In contrast to the unilateral agreement of the regulated carrier, the contract is a bilateral agreement whereby the shipper and the carrier define the level of service and rates. When the two parties agree, a contract containing the mutually agreed-upon terms is implemented. Changes to the contract can be made only with the consent of both parties, in contrast to the unilateral carrier actions with regulated carrier service.

Shippers using motor transportation have adopted contracting to cover all types of shipments including TL, LTL, small package, and local delivery. As noted earlier, a current shipper strategy is to reduce the number of carriers used, with many shippers using a core carrier approach. The core carrier tactic utilizes a limited number of carriers—eight or ten carriers—to provide the bulk of the transportation service to the shipper. The core carriers are under contract to the shipper, and the contract specifies special services required, the rates associated with these special services, and a penalty clause for nonperformance.

examples

Rail transportation has widely adopted contracting. A railroad negotiation normally establishes a contract rather than the rate discount common to motor carrier negotiations. Rail contracts normally specify a rate, the type of equipment the carrier will provide, and the service level the shippers expect (a fifteen-day maximum transit time on shipments from Chicago to Seattle, for example). The contract also dictates a minimum or guaranteed quantity that the shipper will tender to the carrier during the contract life.

Companies implementing the just-in-time (JIT) system use contracting to ensure safe, consistent, and fast service. The JIT system emphasizes low inventory levels and a reliance upon transportation to deliver goods as customers and logistics nodes need them. Transportation delays decrease production, increase inventory costs, and disrupt operations, which defeats JIT's objectives. Contracting with all transportation modes ensures the required transportation service level.

JIT

Consolidating Shipments

The freight volume a shipper tenders to a carrier directly relates to the freight rate the carrier charges. By consolidating shipments, the transportation manager can reap the benefits of the lower rates carriers charge for larger shipment volumes. That is, the manager may increase the weight of the shipment the shipper tenders to the carrier to the level that will enable the carrier to use TL (truckload) or CL (carload) rates. In addition, the motor carrier tariffs provide rate discounts at multiple weight levels such as 1,000 pounds, 2,000 pounds, and 5,000 pounds, thus encouraging shippers to consolidate small shipments into larger ones.

As a general rule, carriers charge lower rates for shipping larger quantities. Carrier cost per weight unit transported (pound, hundredweight, or ton) decreases as the shipment weight increases. For example, the carrier pickup cost does not vary with shipment size. The per-pound carrier pickup cost for a 2,000-pound shipment is 50 percent of that for a 1,000-pound shipment. (If the pickup cost is $50, the pickup cost per pound is $0.05 for the 1,000-pound shipment and $0.025 for the 2,000-pound shipment.) TL rates requiring 25,000-to 30,000-pound shipments may be 30 to 60 percent lower than LTL rates.

shipment size and rates

A shipper may utilize freight consolidation to support a competitive price marketing strategy. By consolidating shipments, the transportation manager realizes a

quantity discounts

lower carrier rate; and the shipper can translate this lower transportation cost per unit into a lower price for buyers purchasing the larger quantity. Thus, shippers can coordinate the quantity discounts they offer buyers with the rate reductions possible with consolidated shipment sizes.

Freight consolidation is also being used to control the shipping cost of B2C E-commerce. The typical B2C shipment is small, moves to residential destinations, and is delivered by the U.S. Postal Service (USPS), a major carrier providing the residential delivery service. USPS rates are based on weight and distance (zones); the greater the distance (zones traversed), the higher the rate. By consolidating B2C shipments, the shipper can move the consolidated load at lower TL rates to a postal station near the customer's residence, thereby minimizing the distance (zones) the shipment is moved and the USPS rate. The new USPS plus the TL rate and consolidation costs must be lower than the all USPS rate to make the freight consolidation of B2C shipments economical. However, customer service may dictate the use of a higher freight cost freight consolidation program because the transit time may be lower than an all USPS system.

Monitoring Service Quality

product differentiation

Transportation service quality can differentiate a company's product, thereby providing the company with a competitive market advantage. An ability to get the product to the customer on a consistent, timely, and undamaged basis reduces the buyer's inventory and stockout costs. Thus, product differentiation through the transportation service a company provides is a significant nonprice marketing strategy.

service/cost trade-off

However, a trade-off exists between transportation service quality and cost. The transportation manager must compare the quality of service required by buyers of the finished product against the level the shipper currently provides. If the buyers require three-day transit time and the shipper provides two-day transit time, the transportation manager is providing a better and more costly service level than the buyers demand. The transportation manager might correct the service level by negotiating a lower rate with the carrier in return for a longer transit time (three-day delivery instead of two-day delivery) or utilizing a slower but lower-cost mode of transportation.

A fundamental element for implementing service quality monitoring is information. The transportation manager must have information regarding the customer service demands and the service level that current carriers provide. Without this information, the transportation manager cannot make a rational transportation service/cost decision that meets the shipper's established logistics and corporate goals.

Normal transportation documentation—the bill of lading, freight bill, customer shipping document, and so on—does not contain transportation service data. These source documents do not indicate the number of days the shipment is in transit, the transit time consistency, or the frequency and extent of shipment damage. The transportation manager must obtain these data directly from the shipment's receiver.

transit time

The bill of lading, freight bill, and customer shipping document indicate the date the shipper dispatched the shipment to the carrier, but not the date the consignee received it. Many carriers offer electronic notification of delivery and can provide transit time data by shipment.

Figure 10–1 is an example of a carrier evaluation report that bases its evaluation criteria upon the carrier selection factors discussed in Chapter 9. The figure assigns

FIGURE 10–1 Carrier Evaluation Report

Carrier: _____   Time period: _____

Maximum Rating	Evaluation Criteria	Carrier Rating	Comments
	Meets pick-up schedules		
	Meets delivery		
	Transit time		
	Overall		
	Consistency		
	Claims		
	Frequency		
	Timely settlement		
	Equipment		
	Availability		
	Condition		
	Driver		
	Customer acceptance		
	Courtesy		
	Attitude		
	Scope of operations		
	Operating authority		
	Computer		
	Electronic billing		
	Billing		
	Errors		
	Timeliness		
	Tracing capabilities		
	Problem solving		
	Innovativeness		
	Management		
	Attitude		
	Trustworthiness		
	Financial		
	Operating ratio		
	Cash flow		
	Profitability		
	Rates		
	Accessorial charges		
	Handles rush shipments		
100	Total weighted rating		

Evaluator: _____   Date: _____

each criterion a maximum rating totaling 100 and gives the carrier's performance in each service and financial area a numerical rating. The sum of the weighted ratings provides an evaluation score for each carrier.

Using a carrier evaluation system like the one Figure 10–1 depicts provides the transportation manager with information that is vital to the achievement of the transportation, logistics, and corporate customer service strategies and goals.

Federal Regulation[1]

Federal regulation of transportation has been with us since the Act to Regulate Commerce passed in 1887. The years immediately preceding the enactment of this law were full of turmoil, for both shippers and carriers. Inland transportation was basically by railroad, and the carriers charged high rates when possible and discriminated against small shippers. Control over the transportation industry was important to U.S. economic growth and to assure a stable transportation service supply compatible with the needs of an expanding society.

public interest   We find the basis for federal economic regulation of transportation in transportation's significance to the overall economy of the United States. Transportation enables business to accomplish the very foundation of economic activity—the exchange of commodities from areas of oversupply to areas of undersupply. The transportation activity benefits all citizens; thus, we could argue that the government should provide transportation, just as it provides public interest functions such as the court system and national defense.

Traditionally, however, private enterprise has provided freight transportation. Through the dollars shippers spend, the marketplace identifies the resources that transportation companies commit to various transportation services and considers this resource allocation to be more efficient than that a governmental, political allocation could produce. Since the free enterprise marketplace has imperfections that may allow monopolies to develop, government control of transportation attempts to allocate resources in the public's interest by maintaining and enforcing the competitive market structure.

marketplace controls   Current federal economic regulation of transportation is very minimal, and the forces of the marketplace are the major controls used to enforce a competitive market structure. The lessening of federal regulatory controls over transportation began in 1977 with the deregulation of air transportation and followed in 1980 with reduced regulation over trucking and rail transportation. Virtual deregulation occurred with the enactment of the ICC Termination Act of 1995, which eliminated the Interstate Commerce Commission, reduced or eliminated most economic regulation over motor and water carriers, and established the Surface Transportation Board (STB) to administer the remaining railroad regulations. The current status of federal regulation of the modes follows:

- *Motor and Water Carriers.* All rate and tariff-filing regulations are eliminated except for household goods and noncontiguous trade (continental United States and Alaska, for example). The common carrier concept is eliminated, but the carriers are held liable for damage. All carriers may contract with shippers. Antitrust immunity is granted carriers for collective ratemaking (for

ON THE LINE

TRANSPORTATION: THE FORGOTTEN FACTOR

The talk at supply chain management events and in supply chain management articles covers a wide spectrum—how to design a supply chain; how to synchronize supply with demand; how to form alliances with your suppliers; how to select the right technology; and, of course, the hottest topic of all, how to understand—and then leverage—the power of the Internet.

Now, all of these issues are important and rightly deserve a prominent position on conference agendas and in books and periodicals. The problem, however, is that in most of the discussions about effective supply chain management, one element is conspicuously missing, or at least underrepresented. And that is transportation.

The move to the E-economy has brought about many changes in the way we move goods and information through the supply chain. But one reality has not changed. The customer's most direct—and often most lasting—impression of you is based on how your product is physically delivered to its place of business.

The quality of the product's packaging and its condition upon arrival are crucial, though often overlooked, factors in the overall business transaction. The timeliness of delivery is absolutely essential, too, because more and more companies are operating on strict delivery schedules. How fast claims are processed or shipment problems are resolved are central parts of the total supply chain experience. So are the attitude, appearance, and professionalism of the driver who delivers the freight. (And no, it is not too much of a stretch to assert that the driver helps create the customer's overall impression of you and

your product—whether we are talking about your private fleet or a for-hire carrier.)

Logistics managers need to keep these considerations in mind as they investigate the various electronic exchanges and dot-com marketplaces that are proliferating today. Certainly, these technologies have a place in the new economy—and anyone who would foreclose on using them probably does a disservice to his or her company.

Yet, transportation remains the final and most direct link to the customer. For this reason, transportation management and carrier selection cannot be an afterthought or a secondary responsibility assigned to someone with no real experience. And the idea of going out blindly into the electronic market and making transportation decisions based on price alone is an invitation to disaster.

Companies expend tremendous amounts of time and resources determining the right configuration for their distribution network or evaluating the right supply chain technology. The same type of rigorous analysis should be applied to the evaluation and selection of transportation options for actually moving the freight to the customer. This is the last link in a supply chain that stretches all the way back to the sourcing of the raw material. If there is a problem at this critical juncture, then all of the excellent planning and executing that went before could go for naught.

Source: Francis J. Quinn, "Transportation: The Forgotten Factor," *Logistics Management* (September 2000): 45. Copyright Cahners Business Information. Reprinted by permission.

example, joint publishing of a freight classification), and the carriers must provide tariffs (containing rates and rules) to shippers upon request. In essence, there is little federal economic control exercised over these modes.

- *Railroads.* In theory, rail economic regulation still exists. The STB has jurisdiction over rail rates and rules, as well as routes, services, facilities, and mergers. The railroads are subject to the common carrier obligations to provide service to all shippers; to not discriminate against persons, places, or commodities; to charge reasonable rates; and to be liable for damage to the goods. The filing of rail tariffs and contracts is not required. The railroad industry remains the most highly regulated transportation mode, but complete rate deregulation exists over certain types of rail traffic—piggyback and fresh fruits, for example.

- *Air Transportation.* In 1977, economic regulation of air transportation was eliminated; the marketplace determines rates and services. Safety regulation, however, remains a major thrust of federal controls over air carriers. Such safety regulations as the controls over the number of landings and takeoffs permitted at an airport indirectly determine the level of service provided by an air carrier and whether an air carrier can provide service to a particular airport (availability of landing slots).

- *Freight Forwarders and Brokers.* Both forms of transportation are required to register with the STB, and the broker must post a $10,000 surety bond to ensure the carrier used will receive payment from the broker. However, there are no federal economic controls over the rates or services provided by these two intermediaries. A freight forwarder is considered a carrier and is held liable for freight damage, whereas the broker is not considered a carrier and is not liable for freight damage.

DOCUMENTATION—DOMESTIC

Domestic transportation utilizes a number of different documents to govern, direct, control, and provide information about a shipment. This section focuses on the bill of lading, freight bill, claims, and F.O.B. terms of sale—the documentation that is most prevalent in interstate transportation.

Bill of Lading

contract receipt

The *bill of lading* is probably the single most important transportation document. It originates the shipment, provides all the information the carrier needs to accomplish the move, stipulates the transportation contract terms, acts as a receipt for the goods the shipper tenders to the carrier, and, in some cases, shows certificate of title to the goods. Figure 10–2 shows a typical bill of lading.

All interstate shipments by common carriers begin with the issuance of a properly completed bill of lading. The information on the bill specifies the name and address of the consignor and consignee, as well as routing instructions for the carrier. The bill also describes the commodities in the shipment, the number of items in each commodity description, and the commodity's class or rate. Many shippers provide their own bills of lading (short form), which show the shipper's preprinted name and describe the commodities the company most commonly ships. This reduces the time required to fill out the bill, thereby eliminating delays at the shipper's loading facilities. Electronic bills of lading are being used in situations where the carrier and shipper have a strategic alliance established.

nonnegotiable

Straight Bill of Lading. The *straight bill of lading* is a nonnegotiable instrument, which means that endorsement of the straight bill cannot transfer title to the goods the straight bill names. For firms using the straight bill of lading, the terms of sale

FIGURE 10–2 Bill of Lading

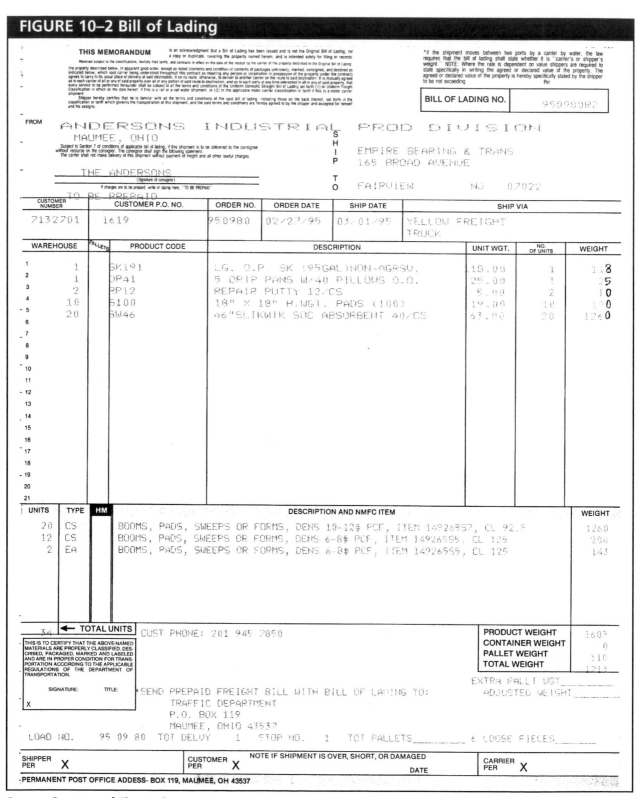

Source: Courtesy of The Andersons Management Corporation. Used with permission.

upon which the buyer and seller agreed, the buyer and seller generally dictate where title to the goods passes. The carrier does not require presentation of the straight bill's original copy to effect delivery; the carrier must simply deliver the goods to the person or firm the straight bill of lading names as consignee.

negotiable

Order Bill of Lading. The *order bill of lading* is a negotiable instrument showing certificate of title to the goods it names. Using the order bill of lading enables the consignor to retain security interest in the goods.[2] That is, the consignee must pay the goods' invoice value to obtain the original copy of the order bill of lading that must be presented to the carrier for delivery.

Contract Terms. The bill of lading contains the *terms of contract* for movement by common carrier. The contract is between the shipper and the common carrier for the movement of the freight that the bill of lading identifies to the consignee that the bill identifies. The bill of lading contract contains nine sections. Section 1, delineating the extent of the carrier's liability, is a primary contract term.

exceptions to liability

The major terms of the common carrier's contract of carriage as found in the bill of lading sections are as follows:

1. *Common carrier liability.* The carrier is held liable for all loss, damage, or delay to the goods except for the following:

   Act of God—loss resulting from any unavoidable natural catastrophe. If the carrier had sufficient opportunity to avoid the catastrophe, the carrier is liable and cannot use this exception.

   Act of public enemy—loss resulting from armed aggression against the United States.

   Act of shipper—loss resulting from shipper's improper loading, packaging, or concealment of goods being shipped.

   Act of public authority—loss resulting from public agencies taking or destroying goods by due process of law.

   Inherent nature of the goods—the normal or expected loss of the products (e.g., evaporation).

2. *Reasonable dispatch.* The shipper holds the carrier liable for the actual loss or damage that results from an unreasonable delay in transit. No specific rule exists for determining reasonable time. The shipper examines the shipment's specifics to see if the delay was unreasonable under given circumstances.

3. *Cooperage and baling.* The owner pays such costs. The carrier may compress cotton or cotton linters and may commingle bulk grain shipments destined to a public elevator with other grain.

4. *Freight not accepted.* The carrier may store at the owner's cost any property the consignee does not remove within the free time. After notifying the consignor, the carrier may sell at public auction property the consignee refuses.

5. *Articles of extraordinary value.* The carrier is not obligated to carry documents or articles of extraordinary value unless the classification or tariff specifically rates such items. This is one area where a common carrier can refuse to provide service.

6. *Explosives.* The shipper shall give the carrier full written disclosure when shipping dangerous articles. If there is no disclosure, the shipper is held liable for any damage such goods cause.

7. *No recourse.* The carrier has no legal recourse back to the shipper for additional charges after making delivery. If the shipper signs the no recourse clause and the carrier delivers the shipment, the carrier has recourse only to the consignee for additional freight charges for the shipment.

8. *Substitute bill of lading.* When a bill of lading is an exchange or substitute for another, the subsequent bill of lading shall encompass the prior bill's statements regarding shipment value, election of common law liability, and consignor's signature.

9. *Water carriage.* If water transportation is involved, the water carrier is liable for negligence in loading, and is responsible for making the vessel seaworthy and for outfitting and manning the vessel.

10. *Alterations.* The carrier's agent must note any changes, additions, or erasures to make such alterations enforceable.

The discussion of the bill of lading contract terms describes the contract of carriage with a common carrier, railroad. Many contracts signed with motor carriers hold the carrier to these liability terms. Current regulations hold regulated motor carriers liable for cargo damage, but the regulations permit the motor carrier to limit its liability through released value rates (to be discussed subsequently) and maximum liability rules found in the carrier's rules tariff. Examples of the motor carrier liability limits include a maximum liability of $50,000 if the entire shipment is damaged or a maximum liability limit of $2.50 per pound. Freight claims are discussed in a subsequent section. **liability limits**

Freight Bill

The *freight bill* is the carrier's invoice for the charges the carrier incurs in moving a given shipment. The freight bill lists the shipment, the origin and destination, the consignee, the items, total weight, and total charges. In addition, the freight bill specifies the credit time period for payment. Note that the carrier is not obligated to extend credit to the shipper and the carrier may require prepayment of the charges if, in the opinion of the carrier, the commodity's value is less than the freight charge. **definition**

A brief description of the carrier's credit payment terms is typically found on the freight bill, but the carrier's rules tariff contain the credit payment terms in detail. The transportation manager should have a working knowledge of the carrier's credit payment terms because some carriers have excessive penalties for not paying within the allowed credit period and/or discounts for paying early. **credit terms**

For example, some carriers provide a credit payment period of thirty days. Shippers who pay promptly (within ten days) are afforded a discount (2 percent, for example). However, if payment is not received within thirty days, the carrier's penalty may be loss of all discounts (average of 55 percent for LTL shipments) plus a 10 percent late charge fee.

Freight bills may be either prepaid or collect. The prepaid or collect basis determines when the carrier will present the freight bill, not necessarily whether the shipper will pay the charges in advance or after the movement's completion. On a *prepaid* shipment, the carrier presents the freight bill on the effective day of shipment. On a *collect* shipment, the carrier presents the freight bill on the effective day **prepaid or collect** of delivery. In both cases, the shipper must pay the bills within the maximum days of credit from presentation; but, on the collect basis, the carrier extends the payment due date by the length of the transit time.

freight bill auditing
Freight bill auditing can be performed either internally or externally. The trend today is for shippers to outsource the freight bill auditing function because most shippers lack the expertise and resources for economical and efficient freight bill auditing. With the advent of computerized tariffs and the use of simpler rate structures, especially in conjunction with contracting, freight bill auditing involves matching the computer-generated charge with the carrier's freight bill. If the two do not match, the freight bill is given to a transportation manager to resolve. Often times, the audit occurs prior to payment of the freight bill.

Claims

time limits
The *freight claim* is a document (with no prescribed format) that the shipper files with the carrier to recoup monetary losses resulting from loss, damage, or delay to the shipment or to recover overcharge payments. The shipper must file in writing freight claims with the carrier (originating, delivering, or on whose line damage occurred) within nine months of delivery or, in the case of loss, within nine months of reasonable delivery. If a contract of carriage governs, the contract may stipulate a different filing time period. Air carrier claim filing times are generally less than nine months and vary by carrier.

Damage may be either visible or concealed. *Visible damage,* usually discovered at delivery, is damage that the consignee detects before opening the package. *Concealed damage* is not detected until the consignee opens the package. A problem arises with determining whether concealed damage occurred while the goods were in the carrier's possession or in the consignee's possession. Many carriers stipulate that the shipper must file concealed damage claims within fifteen days of delivery. This does not overrule the nine-month limitation, but the carrier will look more favorably upon the claim if the shipper files it within the stated policy period.

claim value
The following principle establishes the damage claim's value: The claim shall restore the claimant to a condition as good as that in which the claimant would have been had the carrier safely delivered the goods. To determine this value, the claimant utilizes the original invoice, price catalog, and other factors to show the commodity's market value at destination. For commodities that do not have a ready market value, such as one-of-a-kind items, the claimant may use cost accounting records to determine value.

A *released value* is an exception to the full value liability obligation. At the time of shipment, the shipper may elect to release the value of the shipment to something less than its full value. This election reduces the carrier's liability in case of damage to the amount stipulated by the shipper. In return, the shipper usually receives a lower freight rate.

Another exception to the full value liability is the automatic released-value rules that some carriers place in their rules tariffs. The automatic released value states that the value of the product is automatically reduced (released) to that stipulated in the tariff unless the shipper states otherwise on the bill of lading at the time of shipment. Finally, some carriers have limits on the maximum liability for a shipment.

F.O.B. Terms of Sale

The *F.O.B. terms of sale* determine the logistics responsibility that the buyer and seller will incur. Originally, F.O.B. referred to the seller's making the product free of transportation charges to the ship, or "free on board." More specifically, the F.O.B. terms of sale delineate (1) who is to incur transportation charges, (2) who is to control movement of the shipment, and (3) where the title passes to the buyer.

transportation responsibility

The F.O.B. term specifies the point to which the seller incurs transportation charges and responsibility and relinquishes title to the buyer. For example, *F.O.B. delivered* indicates that the seller incurs all transportation charges and responsibility to the buyer's destination and that title passes to the buyer at delivery. *F.O.B. origin* means the opposite: the buyer incurs all transportation charges and responsibility, and title passes to the buyer at the shipment's origin.

The terms a firm utilizes to sell its products or to purchase its raw material directly affect the magnitude of the transportation function. A firm that purchases raw materials F.O.B. origin and sells its finished product F.O.B. delivered would require extensive transportation management. In such a situation, the firm controls carrier selection and warehousing and also incurs transportation charges for all commodity movements. The firm can pass this responsibility on to the buyer or supplier by altering the terms of sale, thereby lessening its transportation management requirements.

The F.O.B. term also defines the party responsible for filing a damage claim. The party that possesses title to the goods must file the claim. If damage occurs after the shipment reaches the named point, the buyer would be responsible for filing the claim. Conversely, if damage occurs before the shipment reaches the named point, the seller would file the claim.

DOCUMENTATION—INTERNATIONAL

Export documentation is far more complicated than the documentation that domestic shipments require. Since the transaction involves different nations, political as well as economic considerations affect the documentation required. Specific documentation requirements vary widely from country to country. It is necessary to complete each document accurately, for a mistake may delay the shipment's delivery.

For discussion purposes, we group the various documents into two categories: sales and transportation. Much of the information the documents require is similar, but each document serves a different purpose.

Sales Documents

The *sales contract* is the initial document in any international business transaction, and export sales contracts exhibit little uniformity. To reduce time and cost, the export sales contract should completely and clearly describe the commodities, price, payment terms, transportation arrangements, insurance requirements, the carriers, and any special arrangements the agreement may require.

sales contract

letter of credit   After negotiating the sales contract, the parties involved must determine the method of payment. The *letter of credit,* the most common payment method, provides a high degree of protection. Other forms of payment include cash, consignment, and open account. The letter of credit is a bank's assurance that the buyer will make payment as long as the seller meets the sales terms (export sales contract terms) to which the parties have agreed. When the seller complies with the sales conditions that the letter of credit states and presents a draft drawn in compliance with the letter of credit, the buyer makes payment to the exporter.

A letter of credit is drawn up and used in the following manner:

1. The buyer and seller make a contract for the sale of goods.
2. The buyer arranges for its bank to issue the seller a letter of credit in the sale amount.
3. The buyer's bank places the amount in the seller's bank.
4. The seller prepares a draft against the deposit and attaches the draft to the following documents:
   —Clean, negotiable bill of lading
   —Certificate of insurance
   —Seller's invoice
   —Letter of credit
5. The seller endorses the order bill of lading to the bank and receives the money.
6. The seller's bank endorses the bill of lading to the buyer's bank.
7. The buyer's bank endorses the bill of lading to the buyer.
8. The buyer takes the bill of lading to the carrier and picks up the shipment.

Terms of Sale

The international terms of sale are known as *Incoterms.* Unlike domestic terms of sale, where the buyers and sellers primarily use F.O.B. origin and F.O.B. destination terms, there are thirteen different Incoterms. Developed by the Paris-based International Chamber of Commerce in 1936, these Incoterms are internationally accepted rules defining trade terms.

The Incoterms define responsibilities of both the buyer and the seller in any international contract of sale. For exporting, the terms delineate buyer or seller responsibility for:

- Export packing cost
- Inland transportation (to the port of export and from port of import)
- Export clearance
- Vessel or plane loading
- Main transportation cost
- Cargo insurance
- Customs duties
- Risk of loss or damage in transit

departure contract   **E terms.**   The *E terms* consist of one Incoterm, *Ex Works* (EXW). This is a departure contract that means the buyer has total responsibility for the shipment. The seller's responsibility is to make the shipment available at its facility. The buyer agrees to take possession of the shipment at the point of origin and to bear all of the cost and risk of transporting the goods to the destination. (See Table 10–1 for additional responsibilities of the E terms.)

TABLE 10–1 Summary of Incoterms Cost Obligations

Cost or Activity	EXW	FCA	FAS	FOB	CFR	CIF	CPT	CIP	DAF	DES	DEQ	DDU	DDP
Export packing	B	S	S	S	S	S	S	S	S	S	S	S	S
Export clearance	B	S	S	S	S	S	S	S	S	S	S	S	S
Inland transport (domestic)	B	S	S	S	S	S	S	S	S	S	S	S	S
Vessel/plane loading	B	B	B	S	S	S	S	S	S	S	S	S	S
Main transport	B	B	B	B	S	S	S	S	S	S	S	S	S
Cargo insurance	B	B	B	B	B	S	B	S	S	S	S	S	S
Customs duties	B	B	B	B	B	B	B	B	B	B	S	B	S
Inland transport (foreign)	B	B	B	B	B	B	B	B	B	B	B	B	S
Mode applicability	X	X	W	W	W	W	X	X	X	W	W	X	X

B = buyer; S = seller; W = water carrier; X = air, motor, rail, intermodal.

F Terms. The three *F terms* obligate the seller to incur the cost of delivering the shipment cleared for export to the carrier designated by the buyer. The buyer selects and incurs the cost of main transportation, insurance, and customs clearance. *FCA,* Free Carrier, can be used with any mode of transportation. Risk of damage is transferred to the buyer when the seller delivers the goods to the carrier named by the buyer.

FAS, Free Alongside Ship, is used for water transportation shipments only. Risk of damage is transferred to the buyer when the goods are delivered alongside the ship. The buyer must pay the cost of "lifting" the cargo or container on board the vessel. *F.O.B.,* Free on Board, is used only for water transportation shipments. The risk of damage is transferred to the buyer when the shipment crosses the ship's rail (when the goods are actually loaded on the vessel). The seller pays the lifting charge. (See Table 10–1 for additional responsibilities of the F terms.)

shipment contract

C Terms. The four *C terms* are shipment contracts that obligate the seller to obtain and pay for the main carriage and/or cargo insurance. *CFR,* Cost and Freight, and *CPT,* Carriage Paid To, are similar in that both obligate the seller to select and pay for the main carriage (ocean or air to the foreign country). *CFR* is used only for shipments by water transportation, while *CPT* is used for any mode. In both terms, the seller incurs all costs to the port of destination. Risk of damage passes to the buyer when the goods pass the ship's rail (CFR) or when delivered to the main carrier (CPT).

CIF, or Cost, Insurance, Freight, and *CIP,* Carriage and Insurance Paid To, require the seller to pay for both main carriage and cargo insurance. The risk of damage is the same as that for CFR and CPT. (See Table 10–1 for additional responsibilities of the C terms.)

D Terms. The *D terms* obligate the seller to incur all costs related to delivery of the shipment to the foreign destination. There are five D terms; two apply to water transportation only, and three apply to any mode used. All five D terms require the seller to incur all costs and the risk of damage up to the destination port.

arrival contract

DAF, Delivered at Frontier, means that the seller is responsible for transportation and incurs risk of damage to the named point at the place of delivery at the frontier of the destination country. For example, DAF Laredo, Texas, indicates that the seller is responsible for making the goods available at Laredo, Texas. The buyer is responsible for customs duties and clearance into Mexico. DAF can be used with all modes.

DES, Delivered Ex Ship, and *DEQ,* Delivered Ex Quay (wharf), are used with shipments by water transportation. Both terms require the seller to select and pay for the main carriage. Under DES, the risk of damage is transferred when the goods are made available to the buyer on board the ship, uncleared for import at the port of destination. The buyer is responsible for customs clearance. With DEQ, risk of damage is transferred to the buyer when the goods, not cleared for import, are unloaded onto the quay (wharf) at the named port of destination.

DDU, Delivered Duty Unpaid, and *DDP,* Delivered Duty Paid, are available for all modes. DDU requires the seller to incur all costs, except import duties, to the named place in the country of importation. Risk of damage passes to the buyer when the goods are made available, duties unpaid, at the named place. (DDU is similar to DES.) DDP imposes the same obligations on the seller as DDU plus the additional responsibility of clearing the goods for import and paying the customs duties. (DDP is similar to DEQ.) (See Table 10–1 for additional responsibilities of the D terms.)

Transportation Documents

export declaration

After the buyer and seller reach an agreement as to sales and credit terms, the exporter files with exit port customs an *export declaration* (see Figure 10–3), which provides the Department of Commerce with information concerning the export shipment's nature and value. The required information usually includes a description of the commodity, the shipping weight, a list of the marks and numbers on the containers, the number and dates of any required export license, the place and country of destination, and the parties to the transaction.

export license

A company requires an *export license* to export goods from the United States. These licenses fall into one of two categories. The *general license* allows the export of most goods without any special requirements. The commodities this license covers are general in nature and have no strategic value to the United States. On the other hand, certain items whose export the government wishes to control require a *validated export license.* Commodities requiring this type of license include military hardware, certain high-tech items such as microprocessors and supercomputers, and other goods for which control is in the national interest.

invoices

The *commercial invoice,* which the seller uses to determine the commodity's value less freight and other charges is basically the seller's invoice for the commodities sold. The letter of credit and companies or agencies often require this invoice to determine the correct value for insurance purposes and for assessing import duties. Some countries have special requirements (language, information requested, etc.) for the commercial invoice. Many countries also require a special form called a *consular invoice* for any incoming shipments. The consular invoice, which allows the country to collect import statistics, is usually written in the importing nation's language.

FIGURE 10–3 Shipper's Export Declaration

U.S. DEPARTMENT OF COMMERCE - BUREAU OF THE CENSUS - INTERNATIONAL TRADE ADMINISTRATION

FORM **7525-V** (1-1-88)   **SHIPPER'S EXPORT DECLARATION**   OMB No. 0607-0018

1a. EXPORTER *(Name and address including ZIP code)*

ZIP CODE

2. DATE OF EXPORTATION

3. BILL OF LADING/AIR WAYBILL NO.

b. EXPORTER'S EIN (IRS) NO.

c. PARTIES TO TRANSACTION
☐ Related   ☐ Non-related

4a. ULTIMATE CONSIGNEE

b. INTERMEDIATE CONSIGNEE

5. FORWARDING AGENT

6. POINT (STATE) OF ORIGIN OR FTZ NO.

7. COUNTRY OF ULTIMATE DESTINATION

8. LOADING PIER *(Vessel only)*

9. MODE OF TRANSPORT *(Specify)*

10. EXPORTING CARRIER

11. PORT OF EXPORT

12. PORT OF UNLOADING *(Vessel and air only)*

13. CONTAINERIZED *(Vessel only)*
☐ Yes   ☐ No

14. SCHEDULE B DESCRIPTION OF COMMODITIES,
15. MARKS NOS., AND KINDS OF PACKAGES.   *(Use columns 17—19)*

D/F (16)	SCHEDULE B NUMBER (17)	CHECK DIGIT	QUANTITY — SCHEDULE B UNIT(S) (18)	SHIPPING WEIGHT *(Kilos)* (19)	VALUE (U.S. dollars, omit cents) *(Selling price or cost if not sold)* (20)

21. VALIDATED LICENSE NO./GENERAL LICENSE SYMBOL

22. ECCN *(When required)*

23. Duly authorized officer or employee   The exporter authorizes the forwarder named above to act as forwarding agent for export control and customs purposes.

24. I certify that all statements made and all information contained herein are true and correct and that I have read and understand the instructions for preparation of this document, set forth in the **"Correct Way to Fill Out the Shipper's Export Declaration."** I understand that civil and criminal penalties, including forfeiture and sale, may be imposed for making false or fraudulent statements herein, failing to provide the requested information or for violation of U.S. laws on exportation (13 U.S.C. Sec. 305; 22 U.S.C. Sec. 401; 18 U.S.C. Sec. 1001; 50 U.S.C. App. 2410).

Signature

Confidential - For use solely for official purposes authorized by the Secretary of Commerce (13 U.S.C. 301 (g).

Title

Export shipments are subject to inspection by U.S. Customs Service and/or Office of Export Enforcement.

Date

25. AUTHENTICATION *(When required)*

The "Correct Way to Fill Out the Shipper's Export Declaration" is available from the Bureau of the Census, Washington, D.C. 20233.

carnet When a seller makes a shipment in a sealed container, a *carnet* is often issued. A carnet indicates that the shipment has been sealed at its origin and will not be opened until it reaches its final destination. The container may then pass in transit through intermediate customs points without inspection. Carnets are very useful for intermodal shipments and for containers crossing several national boundaries between origin and destination. Much of the overland shipping in Europe travels under carnet.

A destination country that has made a treaty agreement to give favorable import duty treatment to certain U.S. goods often requires a *certificate of origin,* which certifies that the goods' origin is the United States. This prevents a shipper from applying the favorable import duty to foreign goods that the shipper merely reshipped from the United States.

bill of lading The initiating document for any international shipment is the bill of lading (B/L). One bill of lading, the *export bill of lading,* could govern the domestic portion of the move (from plant to port of exit), the intercountry portion (by ocean or air), and the foreign portion (from port of entry to final destination in a foreign country). In practice, most shipments move under a combination of domestic and ocean (or air) bills of lading.

The *ocean bill of lading* is similar to the domestic bill of lading discussed earlier. The ocean bill of lading serves as the contract of carriage between the carrier and the shipper. It sets down the terms of shipment and designates the origin and destination ports. It also supplies shipment information, such as the quantity and weight, the freight charges, and any special handling requirements. The ocean bill of lading is hardly uniform. The carrier is able to add conditions to the bill of lading as long as the additions are not contrary to law.

As discussed earlier, *order bills of lading* also provide evidence of ownership. Sellers can use these negotiable documents to transfer title of the goods.

The carrier issues a *clean bill of lading* when the cargo arrives aboard ship in good condition. If the goods show evidence of damage, the carrier will note this on the bill of lading and will not issue a clean B/L. After processing all the bills of lading, the carrier prepares a *ship's manifest,* which summarizes the cargo aboard the ship, listed by port of loading and destination.

liability The primary bill of lading contract terms concern the ocean carrier's liability. The Carriage of Goods by Sea Act of 1936 states that the ocean carrier is required to use due diligence to make its vessel seaworthy and is held liable for losses resulting from negligence. The shipper is liable for loss resulting from perils of the sea, acts of God, acts of public enemies, inherent defects of the cargo, or shipper negligence. Thus, the liability of the ocean carrier is less than that imposed upon a domestic carrier.

The terms of sale may also require a *certificate of insurance.* This certificate will state that the buyer or seller has obtained insurance adequate to cover any losses resulting during transit.

dock receipt After the carrier has delivered the goods at the dock, the steamship agent issues a *dock receipt* indicating that the domestic carrier has delivered the shipment to the steamship company. This document can be used to show compliance with a letter of credit's payment requirements and to support damage claims.

airway bill Another increasingly important document is the *universal airway bill,* a standardized document that air carriers use on all international air shipments. By reducing required paperwork to one document, the carrier reduces processing costs. Having a standardized document also helps to speed shipments through customs.

Improving Documentation

It has been said that international trade moves on paper and without the proper paperwork, documentation, the shipment will stop. To say the least, international documentation is very cumbersome, costly, and time consuming. Efforts are being made to reduce the reliance on paper documents and to move toward the use of electronic documents. This is true of the industrialized nations, but many of the developing nations of the world are not technically advanced and the paper document will remain the mainstay in these countries.

Electronic data interchange (EDI) and the Internet hold much promise in achieving the goal of less international documentation. Importers and exporters, as well as carriers and intermediaries, are beginning to exchange international documentation data via the Internet and EDI. The U.S. government has developed the Automated Brokerage System (ABS) to automate the import documentation process for customs house brokers. For exports, the Bureau of the Census has developed the Automated Export System, an EDI-based system for electronic filing of the Shipper's Export Declaration (SED), and it expects by 2002 to have paperless reporting of SED export information.

electronic filing

Computer software programs are available to produce the international document required for a shipment to/from a specific country. These programs can produce the document in the specified language and make as many copies as necessary. The completed documents can then be sent electronically to the importing country, carriers, intermediaries, and financial institutions. For companies that are long-standing trading partners, such software provides substantial savings in paper cost, personnel time, errors, and shipping delays.

Finally, an international classification system, the *Harmonized Commodity Description and Coding System,* has been developed to identify specific products with an internationally accepted identification number. The Harmonized Code permits consistent classification for transportation elements such as documentation and duties.

Harmonized Code

BASES FOR RATES

This section directs attention toward the bases carriers use or the factors they consider in determining rates. The following factors usually affect the rate: (1) the cost and value of service, which affect the different rates the carrier establishes for different commodities; (2) distance; and (3) the volume or weight of the shipment.

Cost of Service

Basing rates upon the *cost of service* considers the supply side of pricing. The cost of supplying the service establishes the floor for a rate; that is, the supply cost permits the carrier's viability by providing the rate's lower limit (see Figure 10–4).

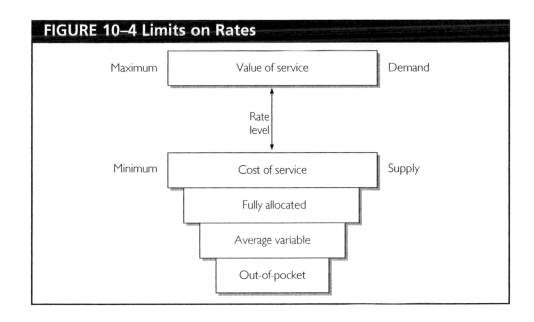

FIGURE 10–4 Limits on Rates

Maximum	Value of service	Demand
	Rate level	
Minimum	Cost of service	Supply
	Fully allocated	
	Average variable	
	Out-of-pocket	

cost concepts   A continual problem of what cost basis to use has plagued this area. Carriers have used fully allocated (average total) costs, as well as average variable costs and out-of-pocket (marginal) costs. In essence, this problem sets up subfloors to the lower rate limit: the carrier will base the higher limit upon fully allocated costs and will base the lower limit upon out-of-pocket costs.

common costs
joint costs   Common and joint costs also increase the problem of using service cost as a basis for rates. The carrier incurs common and joint costs when producing multiple units of output; the carrier cannot directly allocate such costs to a particular production unit. (*Joint cost* is a particular type of common cost in which the costs a carrier incurs in producing one unit unavoidably produce another product. For example, moving a commodity from A to B unavoidably produces the movement capacity and cost from B to A—the backhaul.) The procedure the carrier uses to assign these costs determines the cost basis, permitting latitude for cost variations and, consequently, for rate variations.

Value of Service

Value of service pricing considers the demand side of pricing. We may define value of service pricing as "charging what the traffic will bear." This basis considers the transported product's ability to withstand transportation costs. For example, in Figure 10–5, the highest rate a carrier can charge to move producer A's product to point B is fifty cents per unit. If the carrier assesses a higher rate, producer A's product will not be competitive in the B market area. Thus, value of service pricing places the upper limit upon the rate.

rationale   Generally, rates vary by transported product. The cost difference associated with various commodity movements may explain this, but this difference also contains the value of service pricing concept. For higher-value commodities, transportation charges are a small portion of the total selling price. From Table 10–2, we can see that the transportation rate for diamonds, for a given distance and weight, is 100 times

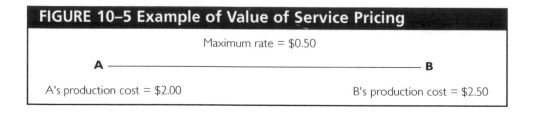

FIGURE 10–5 Example of Value of Service Pricing

Maximum rate = $0.50

A ———————————————————————————— B

A's production cost = $2.00   B's production cost = $2.50

TABLE 10–2 Transportation Rates and Commodity Value

	Coal	Diamonds
Production value per ton*	$30.00	$10,000,000.00
Transportation charge per ton*	10.00	1,000.00
Total selling price	$40.00	$10,001,000.00
Transportation cost as a percentage of selling price	25%	0.01%

*Assumed.

greater than that for coal; but transportation charges amount to only 0.01 percent of the selling price for diamonds, as opposed to 25 percent for coal. Thus, high-value commodities can sustain higher transportation charges; and carriers price the transport services accordingly—a specific application of demand pricing.[3]

Distance

Rates usually vary with respect to *distance;* that is, the greater the distance the commodity moves, the greater the cost to the carrier and the greater the transportation rate. However, certain rates do not relate to distance. One example of these is a *blanket rate.*

blanket rate

A blanket rate does not increase as distance increases; the rate remains the same for all points in the blanket area the carrier designates. The postage stamp rate is one example of a blanket rate. No matter what distance you ship a letter, your cost as shipper (sender) is the same. In transportation, carriers have employed blanket rates for a city's commercial zone,[4] a given state, region, or a number of states, for example. In each case, the rate into (out of) the blanket area will be the same no matter where the destination (origin) is located in the blanket area.

tapering rate

Most transportation rates do increase as distance increases, but the increase is not directly proportional to distance. This relationship of rates to distance is known as the *tapering rate principle.* As Figure 10–6 shows, the rate increases as distance increases, but not linearly. The rate structure tapers because carriers spread terminal costs (cargo handling, clerical, and billing) over a greater mileage base. These terminal costs do not vary with distance; as the shipment's movement distance increases, the terminal cost per mile decreases. The intercept point in Figure 10–6 corresponds to the terminal costs.

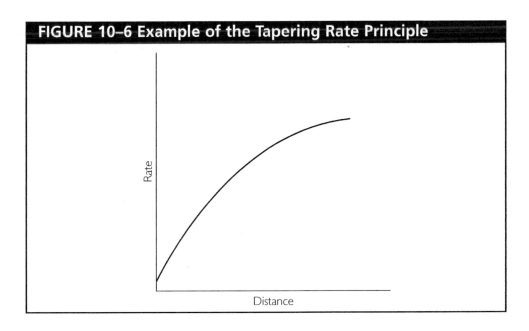

FIGURE 10–6 Example of the Tapering Rate Principle

Weight of Shipment

Carriers quote freight rates in cents per hundredweight (actual weight in pounds divided by 100 = hundredweight, or cwt) and determine the total transportation charge by the total weight of the shipment in cwt, and the appropriate rate per cwt. The rate per cwt relates to the shipped volume: carriers charge a lower rate for volume shipments and a higher rate for less-than-volume quantities. In essence, carriers offer a quantity discount for shipping large volumes (buying service in a large quantity).

quantity discount   Railroads term these quantity discounts carload (CL) and less-than-carload (LCL); motor carriers call them truckload (TL) and less-than-truckload (LTL). The CL and TL rates represent the lower, volume rates; and the LCL and LTL rates denote the higher, less-than-volume rates.

One noteworthy exception to the rate-volume relationship is the any-quantity (AQ) rate, which bears no relationship to volume shipped. The rate per cwt remains constant regardless of the volume a firm tenders to the carrier for shipment; that is, no quantity discount is available.

The pragmatics of carrier pricing are presented in Appendix 10A, following this chapter.

TRANSPORTATION SERVICES

The preceding material does not entirely delineate the nature of the transportation service. Carriers may seem merely to provide commodity movement service between two facilities; in reality, the carrier provides terminal and line-haul services as well as basic transport service. For some services, but not all, the carrier charges no additional fee. The transportation manager must recognize and take advantage of these "extra" services.

Terminal Services

Although carrier terminal operations fall outside the logistics manager's direct control, exploring the nature of this operation provides the logistics manager with some knowledge of the constraints that carrier terminals impose upon the provision of transportation service.

Terminal Functions. Essentially, the carrier's terminal performs five basic functions: consolidation, breakbulk, shipment service, vehicle service, and interchange. Performing these functions requires time and, therefore, affects the total transit time a carrier provides.

Consolidation is the combining of many less-than-volume shipments into one large **consolidation** shipment that the carrier can transport economically. Thus, if a shipper tenders a 2,000-pound shipment, the carrier will combine this shipment with other small shipments before dispatching it on toward destination. *Breakbulk* is just the oppo- **breakbulk** site; when a consolidated shipment arrives at the destination terminal, the carrier must break down the many shipments in the vehicle for dispatch to the individual consignees.

Through *shipment service,* the carrier provides freight-handling services for consolidation and dispersion and performs the clerical, billing, routing, and other functions for the shipment. *Vehicle service* essentially maintains a sufficient vehicle supply. The carrier must constantly review vehicle distribution among terminals to ensure a supply sufficient to provide the transport service the shipping public and regulatory requirements demand. Finally, *interchange* provides freight-exchange facilities for carriers coordinating to provide through service.

In addition to the preceding functions, the carrier's terminal provides pickup and delivery service. Pickup and delivery involve picking up movement-ready freight at the shipper's plant or making ultimate shipment delivery at the consignee's plant. Carriers may or may not charge for this service; the shipper must consult the carrier's rules and accessorial tariffs.

Loading and Unloading. The consolidation function embraces the carrier's obligation to load and unload small shipments. For TL- and CL-size shipments, the shipper is required to load the vehicle and the consignee is required to unload it; but, if a firm wishes, the carrier will perform these services at an added cost. The shipper must consult the carrier's rules to determine loading (or unloading) requirements.

The carrier grants the shipper or consignee a specified amount of free time to load **demurrage** or unload a vehicle and assesses charges for holding the vehicle beyond the free **and detention** time; these are known as *demurrage* (rail) and *detention* (motor) charges. For railroads, the free time for loading or unloading a boxcar is twenty-four to forty-eight hours, Saturdays, Sundays, and holidays excluded. The demurrage charge per railcar per day held varies by carrier.

The motor carrier industry has no standard detention rules and charges. Consequently, a shipper must consult each carrier's rules tariff to determine free time and detention charges. As a general rule, detention charges for holding the power unit and driver beyond the free time are higher than for holding the trailer only.

Shipment Monitoring. As noted earlier, carriers quote transportation rates in terms **weighing** of cents per cwt. Thus, the carrier needs the shipment's exact weight determined so that the carrier realizes the appropriate revenue and the shipper pays the correct charges. The carriers maintain weighing devices that the regulatory commissions control. A shipper may request a carrier to reweigh a vehicle and its contents if the shipper feels the original weight is in error. For some commodities, the carrier and shipper use an agreed weight per package, case, carton, or other container. If an agreed weight is in effect, the number of shipped packages times the agreed weight determines the total shipment weight.

tracing

In many situations, the transportation manager must know where a shipment is or when it will arrive at its destination. Such information eliminates customer ill will and stockouts and improves the utilization of materials-handling equipment and labor. Carriers provide this monitoring function, known as tracing and expediting. *Tracing* is tracking a shipment's movement to determine its location in the trans-

expediting

portation pipeline. *Expediting*, which utilizes the same procedure as tracing, has the objective of getting the shipment to its destination quicker than normal. Some motor carriers use satellites to monitor a vehicle's exact location.

electronic tracing

Technology has drastically improved the tracing and expediting functions. Many carriers have Internet-based information systems that enable the shipper to trace the location of the shipment by using the shipment's bill of lading or airway bill number. Depending on the system configuration, the shipper can trace the progress of the shipment in the carrier's system. As the shipment traverses a system checkpoint (terminal), the carrier's information system updates the status of the shipment. Motor carriers and ground expedited and air express carriers have made great strides in the use of Internet-based tracing systems.

global positioning system

The motor carriers have been adopting the use of the Global Positioning System (GPS) that can pinpoint the location of a vehicle within a matter of feet. The GPS utilizes a system of satellites that triangulates the position of the vehicle to give the shipper and carrier an exact location of the shipment in real time. And, with the addition of a computer terminal in the vehicle, the carrier can communicate to the driver any delivery or routing changes required.

Line-Haul Services

Carriers also provide line-haul services that permit the logistics manager to effect changes in the original shipping order and to realize savings in transportation costs. The line-haul services are reconsignment and diversion, pool car (or truck) service, stopping in transit, and transit privilege.

Reconsignment and Diversion. Carriers use *reconsignment and diversion* interchangeably to mean a change in the shipment's destination and/or consignee with the shipper paying the through rate from origin to final destination. There is, however, a technical difference between the two. Reconsignment permits the shipper to change the destination and/or consignee after the shipment has reached its original destination but before the carrier has delivered it to the original consignee. Diversion enables the shipper to effect the same changes while the shipment is en route and before it reaches the original destination.

benefit

Shippers use reconsignment and diversion extensively in the movement of perishable products (fruits, etc.) and movements in which the original consignee refuses the shipment or cancels the order. Shippers may start perishable products in movement before they have a buyer, using the time in transit to obtain a buyer. Having found a buyer, the shipper issues a reconsignment or diversion order with the buyer named as consignee. Or, when an original buyer decides not to accept an

SUPPLY CHAIN TECHNOLOGY

THE HOME DELIVERY PORTAL

Obviously, the home delivery of goods and services is a tremendous E-commerce target market, but receipt of those goods and services also presents one of the biggest challenges. While many of the dot-com companies schedule home deliveries around the needs of the customer, other clients may require goods to be left when they are not home. However, the millions of Americans who use the latest technology to buy and receive over the Internet typically do not have a technologically advanced "mailbox" capable of receiving those purchases. With this market in mind, companies like Deliverybox.com and mentalPhysics.com (formerly Smart Box) have moved beyond the concept stage and have experimented with "receptacle" designs and some are seeking design patents.

To meet the diverse containerization needs of home-delivered goods, the designs vary in size and may be temperature controlled. For security purposes, some designs have access codes that only the owner and approved delivery company know. Streamline.com provides its customers with free

refrigerators and fits their garages with keypad entry systems for delivery when the customers are not home. An independent receptacle, however, may be required if carriers are unwilling to commingle their delivered goods with another carrier's.

There are several physical challenges with these new mailboxes, including the size, which is about the size of a small hotel honor-bar refrigerator, and placement. Placement of the receptacle will be relatively easy if you live in a house with a two-car garage; however, it becomes a problem if you are an apartment dweller. Regardless of the physical challenges associated with these receptacles, this new age of Internet home shopping presents the case for an apparent need for the "home delivery portal." Consumers have computer access to place orders day or night, and package carriers like FedEx and UPS, as well as the new dot-com delivery companies, could drive efficiencies further if they have the opportunity to leverage their networks and infrastructures to operate twenty-four/seven, utilizing current unused capacity.

Source: "The Home Delivery Portal," *Parcel Shipping & Distribution* (March 2000): 28. Reprinted by permission.

---

order, the shipper can utilize a reconsignment or diversion order to change the shipment's destination to a new buyer location or to have the shipment stopped and returned to the seller's location. These services permit the shipper to amend the original contract (bill of lading) with the carrier and to realize the benefits of the lower through rate (the tapering rate principle) from origin to new destination.

Pooling. *Pool car or pool truck service* permits the shipper to combine many LCL or LTL shipments into one CL or TL shipment and to send it to one destination and one consignee. The lower CL or TL rate applies to the combined shipments and thus effects savings for the shipper. Since the service requires one destination and one consignee, the shipper usually sends the shipment to a warehouse or drayage firm,[5] which breaks down or disperses the consolidated shipment into individual shipments and delivers them to the appropriate consignees. The warehouse manager or drayage firm assesses a fee for this service. For inbound movements, the opposite is possible: the warehouse manager can combine small shipments from a firm's suppliers and present them to a carrier, who delivers them to the firm's plant under a lower high-volume rate.

Stopping in Transit. Another service, *stopping in transit* (also known as *drop shipping*), allows the shipper to complete loading or to partially unload freight, and to pay on the highest weight in the vehicle at any time the lower TL or CL rate

FIGURE 10–7 Example of Stopping-in-Transit Service

Toledo ———————————— Chattanooga ———————————— Atlanta

45,000 lb.   25,000 lb.   20,000 lb.
(Total shipment)

Rates per cwt

	LTL	TL	Minimum Weight
Toledo to Chattanooga	$7.50	$5.00	45,000 lb.
Toledo to Atlanta	$8.00	$5.50	45,000 lb.

Stop-off charge = $55.00 per stop-off

between the most distant destination and the origin. The shipper assesses a stop-off charge for each intermediate stop, but not for the final destination.

Figure 10-7 shows an example of stopping-in-transit service. The shipper at Toledo has two customers, located at Chattanooga and Atlanta, that have purchased 25,000 and 20,000 pounds respectively. The shipper has two shipping options for these two shipments: (1) as two LTL shipments and (2) as one stopping-in-transit shipment. The cost of each is as follows:

1. Two LTL shipments:
   Toledo to Chattanooga = 250 cwt @ $7.50 = $1,875.00
   Toledo to Atlanta = 200 cwt @ $8.00 = <u>1,600.00</u>
   Total cost = $3,475.00

2. Stopping-in-transit shipment:
   450 cwt @ $5.50 = $2,475.00
   Stop-off charge = <u>55.00</u>
   Total cost = $2,530.00

Use of the stopping-in-transit service saves $945.00.

Transit Privilege. The final line-haul service is the *transit privilege*, which permits the shipper to stop the shipment in transit and to perform some function that physically changes the product's characteristics. With this privilege, carriers charge the lower through rate (from origin to final destination) rather than the higher combination of rates from origin to transit point and from transit point to final destination. Carriers have established the transit privilege for grain milling, steel fabrication, lumber processing, and storage of various commodities for aging.

SUMMARY

Transportation management encompasses the day-to-day functions of the transportation process. Considerable knowledge is required of transportation pricing, services, and regulation, both domestic and international, to manage the transportation process and to operate the logistics system efficiently.

- Transportation management embraces a proactive philosophy to identify and solve transportation problems.

- To increase negotiating power and facilitate partnerships, shippers are using a limited number of carriers.

- Carrier negotiating and contracting are a natural outgrowth of carrier deregulation. Both activities result in lower freight costs and improved services.

- Shipment consolidation is a strategy that combines smaller shipments into a larger shipment to realize lower freight rates inherent in carrier pricing.

- Economic regulation of transportation placed controls over carrier entry, prices, and services. Today, economic deregulation of transportation emphasizes the marketplace, not government, as the mechanism for control.

- Carrier performance quality is measured with a carrier evaluation technique that uses a rating scale to rate carrier performance.

- Domestic documentation includes the bill of lading, freight bill, and freight claim. The bill of lading is the contract of carriage and a receipt for the goods tendered to the carrier. The freight bill is the carrier's invoice, and the freight claim is a shipper request for reimbursement for freight loss and damage.

- Common carriers are liable for all loss and damage, with limited exceptions.

- International documentation consists of financial, customs, and transportation documents.

- For domestic trade there are basically two terms of sale, whereas for international trade there are thirteen.

- Transportation rates are based on either cost of service or value of service. Cost of service reflects the carrier's cost, while value of service considers how much the shipper is willing to pay.

- Freight rates vary with distance and weight. Rates increase with distance and weight shipped.

- In addition to basic movement service, carriers offer terminal and line-haul services. Terminal services include the terminal functions, loading and unloading, and shipment monitoring. Reconsignment and diversion, pooling, stopping in transit, and transit privilege are line-haul services.

STUDY QUESTIONS

1. Describe the transportation management philosophy existing today, pointing out the major strategies firms use.

2. Discuss the concept of market power and show how it relates to carrier negotiation and carrier contracting.

3. How would a transportation manager monitor the quality of service provided by the carriers used?

4. What is the basis of economic regulation of transportation? Explain the rationale for economic deregulation of transportation.

5. How has economic deregulation of transportation impacted shippers?

6. Describe the function of the following documents: bill of lading, freight bill, freight claim, certificate of origin, letter of credit, carnet, dock receipt, and airway bill.

7. Discuss the cost implications to the buyer of the thirteen Incoterms.

8. What is the economic implication of cost of service, value of service, shipment weight, and shipment distance in carrier pricing?

9. Discuss the economic and operation impact of a carrier's terminal services upon the shipper and carrier rates.

10. Describe the circumstances under which a company would utilize the line-haul services of reconsignment and diversion, pooling, stopping in transit, and transit privilege.

NOTES

1. For a thorough discussion of transportation regulation, see John J. Coyle, Edward J. Bardi, and Robert A. Novack, *Transportation*, 5th ed. (Cincinnati, Ohio: South-Western College Publishing, 2000), Chapter 2.

2. When using a straight bill of lading, the shipper can retain security interest in the goods by using the C.O.D. (cash on delivery) service carriers offer. With a C.O.D. shipment, the carrier collects the invoice price of the shipment before delivering the shipment to the consignee.

3. We could argue that for high-valued goods the carrier bears a higher cost because of the increased liability risk in case of damage.

4. We define the commercial zone as the city proper plus surrounding points, determined by population, and the rates to the city apply to the surrounding points within this limit.

5. A *drayage firm* is a motor carrier specializing in providing pickup and delivery service.

CASE 10–1 ■ Specialty Metals Company

During the past two months, Thomas Train, vice president of transportation for Specialty Metals Company, a metals servicing company with operations in ten midwestern states, has been soliciting bids for the movement of tool steel, a specialty steel used for manufacturing tools and related products. Tom's goal is to reduce the shipping cost of this high-value steel. The supplier is located in Weirton, West Virginia, 350 miles from Specialty's Toledo, Ohio, service center. Steel Haulers, Inc., a regional contract motor carrier, currently moves the tool steel under contract. Steel Haulers' current rates are incremental: $2.80/cwt for shipments weighing less than 150 cwt, $2.60/cwt for shipments between 150 and 250 cwt, $2.40/cwt for shipments between 250 and 400 cwt, and $2.25/cwt for shipment weights in excess of 400 cwt up to a maximum of 450 cwt. The carrier submitted a rate of $2.25/cwt for weights in excess of 400 cwt two hours before the submission deadline for the carrier proposals.

For various equipment, financial, and/or management reasons, Tom has eliminated all but two carrier proposals. One of the two remaining carrier proposals is from Flatbed, Inc., a contract motor carrier that has an excellent reputation for providing specialized steel hauling service. Flatbed submitted a rate of $2.60/cwt with a minimum weight of 100 cwt; the carrier gives no discounts for larger shipments. The second carrier under consideration is the Middlewest Railroad, which submitted a piggyback rate of $2.45/cwt with a minimum of 200 cwt; the rate is for Plan 2, door-to-door piggyback service with a maximum shipment weight of 400 cwt per load. Both motor carriers will provide one-day transit time, while the piggyback transit time is three days.

The final proposal Tom is considering is a private trucking proposal submitted by the transportation department. The estimated total operating cost for the private fleet (including overhead and depreciation) is $50,000 per year; the investment the vehicles require is $85,000. This annual operating cost equates to $2.50/cwt with a minimum of 400 cwt per shipment and fifty shipments per year. The private truck proposal recognizes Specialty's inability to provide a load for the backhaul from Toledo to Weirton. But, given today's deregulated environment, the proposal assumes the private fleet will be able to solicit return loads from other Toledo shippers 30 percent of the time and generate $15,000 in annual backhaul revenue.

Specialty has a contract with the steel mill to purchase two million pounds of tool steel per year. Last year, tool steel shipments averaged 250 cwt per order. Tool steel has a purchase value of $250/cwt. Unloading costs would be the same under each proposal. The chief financial officer estimates Specialty's annual inventory carrying cost per dollar of average inventory stored to be 20 percent (15 percent for the cost of money and 5 percent for the cost of insurance, taxes, and handling); he estimates the cost to place an order to be $75. The inventory-in-transit cost is 15 percent per year.

Case Question

Tom indicated that he would decide on the bid proposals today. Given the facts of the different proposals, what would you advise Tom to do?

APPENDIX 10A

THE PRAGMATICS OF CARRIER PRICING

One of the most difficult and confusing responsibilities of a logistics manager is determining the prices of various transportation services available for a logistics system's use. Determining how much it will cost to move a barrel of pickles from Toledo, Ohio, to New York City is not always easy.

To appreciate the problem, consider the nature of a transportation service. It would be simple if carriers sold all transportation service on the basis of ton-miles; that is, if we had to pay X dollars to move one ton of a product one mile. But carriers do not sell transportation services in ton-miles; rather, carriers sell transportation services for moving a specific commodity (pickles) between two specific points (Toledo and New York City). This fact gives us a glimpse of the enormous magnitude of the transportation pricing problem. There are more than 33,000 important shipping and receiving points in the United States. Theoretically, the number of different possible routes would be all the permutations of the 33,000 points. The result is in the trillions of trillions. In addition, we must consider the thousands and thousands of different commodities and products that firms might ship over any of these routes. On top of that, we must consider the different modes and different companies within each mode. We may also need to consider each commodity's specific supply-and-demand situation over each route.

Class Rates

Since quoting trillions and trillions of rates is impossible, the transportation industry has taken two major steps toward simplification.

shipping points The first step was to consolidate the 33,000 shipping points into groups by dividing the nation into geographic squares. The most important shipping point (based on tonnage) in each square serves as the *rate base point* for all other shipping points in the square, reducing the potential number of distance variations for ratemaking purposes. The carriers determined the distances from each base point to every other base point and published them in the National Rate Basis Tariff. The distance between any two base points is called the *rate basis number*. This first simplifying step reduced the number of possible origins and destinations for pricing purposes.

rate basis number The second step deals with the thousands and thousands of different items that firms might ship between any two base points. The railroads have established a national scale of rates, which gives a rate in dollars per hundredweight (cwt) for each rate basis number. (Motor carriers have individual rate scales.) These rate scales are the basis for a simplified product classification system.

classification procedure *Classification* simply means grouping together products with similar transportation characteristics so that one rating can be applied to the whole group. The four primary classification characteristics are density, stowability, ease or difficulty of handling goods, and liability. High-demand and high-value items might be placed in class 100, which means that carriers will charge them 100 percent of the *first class rate*. Low-value items, such as coal, might be placed in class 50, which means carriers will charge them 50 percent of the first class rate. This percentage number is a *class rating*, the group into which carriers place a commodity for ratemaking purposes.

Now the number of possible pricing situations is small enough to allow the formation of a transportation pricing system. We determine the price of moving a particular item between two particular points as follows: First, look up the rate basis point for the origin and for the destination. Then determine the rate basis number between the two base points. Next, determine the classification rating (class rating) for the particular product to be shipped. Then find the rate in the class rate tariff that corresponds to the appropriate rate basis number and class rating. Finally, multiply this rate, which is in cents per cwt, by the total shipment weight in cwt to determine the cost to move that specific product between those two points.

tariff

The word *tariff* commonly means almost any publication that a carrier or a tariff publishing agency produces that concerns itself with the pricing or service the carrier performs. All the information a shipper needs to determine the cost of a move is in one or more tariffs.

example

Now look at an example of the mechanics involved in determining the class rate charges for a motor carrier shipment. A firm wishes to ship 4,000 pounds of putty in steel-lined drums with metal covers from Reading, Pennsylvania, to Washington, D.C.:

1. The rate basis number in Table 10A–1 is 98 (at the intersection of Reading, Pennsylvania, and Washington, D.C., in the vertical and horizontal portions of the tariff, respectively).

2. The class ratings and minimum weight, found in the classification for putty in steel-lined drums with metal covers (see Table 10A–2), are LTL = 55, TL = 35, and minimum weight = 36,000 lb. For interstate shipments we use the LTL rating of 55.

TABLE 10A–1 Table of Rate Basic Numbers

| To Rate Groups | From Rate Groups (All Cities in Pennsylvania) | | | | | | | |
| | Allentown | Altoona | Bellefonte | Reading | Scranton | State College | Williamsport | York |
	Apply Rate Basis Numbers							
Baltimore . . . . MD	84	73	86	62	64	92	76	98
Barnesville . . . MD	103	94	122	96	95	132	102	117
Newark . . . . . . NJ	98	90	96	101	92	113	84	76
Newark . . . . . . NY	61	76	60	76	76	76	60	77
New York . . . . NY	96	92	92	101	96	111	87	73
Washington. . . DC	109	96	111	98	90	118	103	122
Wilmington . . . DE	98	66	98	84	66	107	83	101

Source: MAC Tariff 2-M.

TABLE 10A–2 National Motor Freight Classification

Item	Articles	Classes		
		LTL	TL	MW
149500	PAINT GROUP, Articles consist of Paints, Paint Material, or Putty, as described in items subject to this grouping, see Note, item 149502.			
149502	NOTE—Commodities listed under this generic heading when tendered for shipment in Package 2452 are to be classified under the same provisions that apply when tendered to the carrier in boxes.			
149520	Aluminum, or Bronze Powders, or Filters, in barrels, boxes, or Package 2258	60	40	30
149580	Blue, ultramarine, forms or shapes, in barrels or boxes or in double bags	70	40	30
149590	Blue, ultramarine, lumps or powdered, see item 600000 for classes dependent upon agreed or released value:			
Sub 1	In containers in barrels or boxes	70	40	30
Sub 2	In bulk in double bags, double-wall paper bags, barrels, or boxes	55	35	36
150110	Putty in containers in barrels, boxes, or crates or in bulk in barrels, steel putty drums, kits, pails, or tubs, or steel-lined drums or tubs with metal or wooden covers	55	35	36

Source: National Motor Freight Classification 100-P.

3. The table of class rates gives the applicable rate (see Table 10A–3); the intersection of the horizontal line of rate basis number 98 (the 92 to 99 group) and the vertical line of class 55 determine this rate. Since the 4,000-pound shipment falls between weight groups 2,000 and 5,000, we must compute the charges under both weight groups to determine the lowest cost. The appropriate rates are $2.33/cwt for 2,000 pounds and $1.77/cwt for 5,000 pounds.

4. We find the transportation charge by multiplying the rate per cwt by the number of cwt in the shipment, or

$$4,000 \text{ lb} = \frac{4,000}{100} = 40 \text{ cwt}$$

The firm could ship the 40 cwt under the 2,000-pound rate of $2.33 or under the 5,000-pound rate of $1.77 as follows:

40 cwt @ $2.33 = $93.20
50 cwt @ $1.77 = $88.50

In this case, the shipper would elect the 4,000-pound shipment as a 5,000-pound shipment—in essence, shipping 1,000 pounds of phantom weight—and pay $88.50 rather than $93.20.

weight break We can compare the cost of shipping at a volume higher than actual weight to realize a lower rate and lower shipping cost with the cost of shipping at the actual weight by determining the *weight break*. The weight break is the shipment size that equates the transportation charges for different rates and weight groups. That is,

TABLE 10A–3 Class Tariff

Rate Basis No.	Weight Group	Classes 100	85	70	60	55	50	45	40	35
		Rates in Cents per 100 Pounds								
60 to 67	500 LTL	408	358	312	273	256	239			
	1,000 LTL	361	314	268	236	223	207			
	2,000 LTL	297	255	216	189	175	161			
	5,000 LTL	216	184	151	130	119	108			
	Truckload	169	144	120	103	95	89	82	73	64
76 to 83	500 LTL	470	410	355	311	291	270			
	1,000 LTL	421	365	310	273	256	238			
	2,000 LTL	356	304	256	223	208	191			
	5,000 LTL	271	230	190	163	149	136			
	Truckload	223	191	158	135	125	116	107	97	84
	TL 30,000	221	189	156	133	123	114	101	90	80
84 to 91	500 LTL	496	432	374	325	304	282			
	1,000 LTL	449	388	330	288	271	251			
	2,000 LTL	385	329	278	241	223	205			
	5,000 LTL	304	258	213	182	167	152			
	Truckload	263	223	187	159	147	136	125	113	98
	TL 30,000	261	221	185	157	145	134	118	105	93
92 to 99	500 LTL	514	448	386	336	314	291			
	1,000 LTL	467	404	342	299	281	260			
	2,000 LTL	403	345	290	252	233	214			
	5,000 LTL	322	274	225	193	177	161			
	Truckload	285	242	201	171	158	147	136	122	106
	TL 30,000	283	240	199	169	156	145	129	114	101
100 to 109	500 LTL	566	492	423	367	343	317			
	1,000 LTL	519	448	379	330	310	286			
	2,000 LTL	455	389	327	283	262	240			
	5,000 LTL	374	318	262	224	206	187			
	Truckload	342	290	240	206	188	170	165	149	130
	TL 30,000	342	290	240	206	188	170	156	139	121
110 to 125	500 LTL	598	519	444	387	361	334			
	1,000 LTL	549	474	399	349	326	302			
	2,000 LTL	484	413	345	299	278	255			
	5,000 LTL	399	339	279	239	219	200			
	Truckload	365	310	254	219	200	185	177	159	138
	TL 30,000	365	310	254	219	200	185	168	152	131

Application of weight groups: 500 LTL: Applies on LTL or AQ shipments weighing 500 pounds or more but less than 1,000 pounds. 1,000 LTL: Applies on LTL or AQ shipments weighing 1,000 pounds or more but less than 2,000 pounds. 2,000 LTL: Applies on LTL or AQ shipments weighing 2,000 pounds or more but less than 5,000 pounds. 5,000 LTL: Applies on LTL or AQ shipments weighing 5,000 pounds or more. Truckload: Subject to minimum weights in NMFC (Note A). 30,000: Applies on truckload shipments where actual or billed weight is 30,000 pounds or more (Note A).

Note A: Where the charge under the rates for TL 30,000 pounds is lower than the charge under the rates for TL shipments subject to minimum weights of less than 30,000 pounds.

$$\text{LV rate} \times \text{WB} = \text{HV rate} \times \text{MW}$$

where

$$\begin{aligned} \text{LV rate} &= \text{lesser-volume rate} \\ \text{WB} &= \text{weight break} \\ \text{HV rate} &= \text{higher-volume rate} \\ \text{MW} &= \text{minimum weight for higher-volume rate} \end{aligned}$$

Plugging in the numbers from the example used here, we find the weight break to be

$$\begin{aligned} \$2.33 \times \text{WB} &= \$1.77 \times 50 \text{ cwt} \\ \text{WB} &= 37.98 \text{ cwt} \end{aligned}$$

Next, we can establish a simple decision rule for shipping clerks to use to determine when it is economical to ship a shipment at a volume higher than the volume a firm is actually shipping. In this example, the decision rules are:

shipping decision rules

1. If the shipment weighs between 2,000 and 3,798 pounds, ship the actual weight at the 2,000-pound rate of $2.33/cwt.

2. If the shipment weighs between 3,798 and 5,000 pounds, ship at 5,000 pounds (minimum weight) at the 5,000-pound rate of $1.77/cwt.

3. If the shipment weighs more than 5,000 pounds but less than the truckload minimum weight, ship the actual weight at the 5,000-pound rate of $1.77/cwt. (*Note:* a weight break exists between the 5,000-pound rate and the truckload rate.)

Exception Ratings (Rates)

Carriers publish exception ratings when the transportation characteristics of an item in a particular area differ from those of the same article in other areas. For example, large-volume movements or intensive competition in one area may require the publication of an exception rating; the exception rating supersedes the classification. The same procedures described earlier apply to determining the exception rate, except now we use the exception rating (class) instead of the classification rating. Table 10A–4 gives an example of an exception tariff.

Continuing with the earlier example, an exception rating is available under item number 150110 of the exception tariff for the putty moving from Reading, Pennsylvania, to

TABLE 10A–4 Exception Tariff

	Exceptions to National Motor Freight Classification			
	Classes (Ratings)			
Item	**Articles**	**LTL**	**TL**	**MW**
150110	Putty, in containers in steel-lined drum or tubs with metal or wooden covers	50	35	36

Washington, D.C. It lists a class rating for LTL quantities of 50. The exception rating of class 50 takes precedence and results in a rate of $2.14 for 2,000 to 5,000 pounds and $1.61 for 5,000 pounds to a truckload (see Table 10A–3).*

Using the exception rating, we find that the cost to ship 4,000 pounds of putty is 50 cwt @ $1.61 = $80.50. The exception rate produces a savings of $8.00, or 9.0 percent of the class rate.

Commodity Rates

Carriers can construct a commodity rate on a variety of bases. The most common is a specific rate concerning a specific commodity or related commodity group between specific points and generally by specific routes. Commodity rates are complete in themselves and are not part of the classification system. If the rate does not specifically state the commodity you are shipping, or if the origin-destination (O-D) is not one that the commodity rate specifically spells out, then the commodity rate does not apply for your particular movement. A published commodity rate takes precedence over the class rate or exception rate on the same article between the specific points.

commodity specific

direction specific

O-D (origin-destination) specific

Carriers offer this type of rate for commodities that firms move regularly and in large quantities. But such a pricing system, which completely undermines the attempts to simplify transportation pricing through the class rate structure, has caused transportation pricing to revert to the publishing of a multiplicity of rates and adds greatly to the pricing system complexity.

Table 10A–5 gives an example of a commodity tariff. Using the putty shipping example, we find that a commodity rate exists in item 493 in Table 10A–5. Item 493, which applies to classification items 149500 to 150230, includes putty, as shown in Table 10A–2. Note that the commodity rate specifies a route from Reading, Pennsylvania, to Washington, D.C., the example problem's origin and destination. However, Table 10A–5 lists only a TL rate with a minimum weight of 30,000 pounds.

*We find the exception rates for class 50 in Table 10A–3 at the intersection of class 50 and rate basis 92 to 99 for 2,000 LTL and 5,000 LTL.

TABLE 10A–5 Commodity Tariff

Commodity Rates in Cents per 100 Pounds

Item	Commodity	From	To	TL Rate	Min. Wt.
493	PAINTS GROUP, as described in NMFC Items 149500 to 150230, rated Class 35	Reading . . . PA	Baltimore . . . . . MD	79	23M
			Beltsville . . . . . . MD	82	30M
			Washington . . . DC	82	30M

We can compare the class, exception, and commodity rates for the movement of putty from Reading, Pennsylvania, to Washington, D.C., in truckload quantities (36,000 pounds or more) as follows:

$$\text{Class rate} = \$1.01/\text{cwt}$$
$$\text{Exception rate} = \$1.01/\text{cwt}$$
$$\text{Commodity rate} = \$0.82/\text{cwt}$$

zip code

As we can see from this comparison, the commodity rate is the lowest, 18.8 percent less than the class rate and the exception rate.

Many LTL and express carriers use U.S. Postal Service zip codes to identify origins and destinations. The *zip code commodity rates* specify rates for named commodities from a specific origin to multiple destinations identified by a zip code.

Other Rates

In addition to class rates, exception rates, and commodity rates, many special rates have developed over the years to meet very specific situations. The most prevalent and most important of these special rates are all-commodity, released-value, actual-value, deferred, multiple-vehicle, incentive, and innovative rates.

All-Commodity Rates. All-commodity rates, also known as freight-all-kinds (FAK) rates, are a recent development in which the carrier specifies the rate per shipment either in dollars per hundredweight or in total dollars per shipment with a specified minimum weight. The shipped commodity or commodities are not important. These rates tend to price transportation services by cost rather than by the value of service and are used mostly by shippers who send mixed-commodity shipments to a single destination.

released value

actual value

Value Rates. Of a whole host of value rates, released-value rates and actual-value rates are the most important. The degree of liability (commodity value) the carrier assumes determines these rates. Generally, a common carrier is liable for the actual value of any goods lost or damaged while in the carrier's custody. Carriers base a released-value rate on the assumption of a certain fixed liability, usually stated in cents per pound. Usually this fixed liability is considerably less than the actual value of the goods. As a result of this limited liability, the shipper receives a lower rate.

Carriers use released-value rates extensively in the shipment of household goods and use actual-value rates when goods considered to be the same commodity—jewelry, for example—vary greatly in value. In these cases, a single rate is not desirable because some shipments have a high-liability potential whereas other shipments have a low liability potential. The actual-value rates make allowances for this potential difference, and the rate the carriers charge reflects the liability difference. The 1980 deregulation acts reduced the ICC constraints on motor carrier and railroad use of value rates. Today, motor carriers may offer value rates without STB approval.

Deferred Rates. Deferred rates are most common in air transportation. In general, they allow the carrier to charge a lower rate for the privilege of deferring a shipment's arrival time. For example, Federal Express offers a two-day two-pound package delivery rate that is 42 percent lower than the rate for priority, 10:00 A.M. next-day delivery. A deferred rate allows the carrier to move shipments at the carrier's convenience as long as the shipment arrives within a reasonable time or by the scheduled deferred delivery date. This allows the carrier to use the deferred-rate shipments as "filler freight" to more fully load its vehicles.

Multiple-Vehicle Rates. Carriers offer multiple-vehicle rates as a special incentive rate to firms shipping multiple-vehicle loads of a particular commodity at one time to a single destination. Motor carriers first used these rates to overcome the fact that a railcar holds more than a truck. By publishing lower multiple-vehicle rates, the motor carriers competed more effectively with the railroads. Multiple-vehicle rates also reduce commodities' transportation costs, thus allowing those commodities to move to more distant markets. The savings that carriers achieve by economies of scale justify lower rates. The railroads can often demonstrate savings in multiple-vehicle pickups. Multiple-vehicle rates have progressed to the unit train rates that rail carriers give for whole trainloads of commodities such as coal, ore, and grain.

Incentive Rates. A carrier publishes incentive rates, or in-excess rates, to encourage heavier loading of individual vehicles so that the carrier can improve its equipment utilization. One rate covers all cargo up to a certain minimum weight, and a lower rate covers all cargo in excess of the minimum weight.

in-excess rates

Innovative Rates. Shippers commonly negotiate rates with carriers. The negotiated rate could take the form of (1) a discount from the prevailing rate, a situation common to shippers that ship small shipments under class rates; (2) a commodity rate for TL shipments that move in large volumes on a regular basis—for example, 40,000 pounds per day, seven days per week; and (3) a contract rate (rail) for very large freight volumes—for example, 800 carloads (80,000 tons) per year.

The following are examples of the rates that shippers and carriers have negotiated in recent years:

- *Density-based rating.* A lower rating (classification or exception) is possible when the shipper increases product density; the increased product density permits heavier loading of the carrier's vehicle, thus spreading the cost over a larger number of weight (pricing) units.

- *Specific description.* Shippers seek a specific commodity description for a commodity that does not fit an existing classification description; for example, defective goods being returned to the plant have a lower value, liability, and so forth than if perfect, and thus should receive a lower rating.

- *Loading and unloading allowance.* The carrier is responsible for loading and unloading LTL-size shipments. If the shipper and consignee perform this function, the carrier realizes a lower cost and passes it on to the shipper and consignee.

- *Aggregate tender rate.* The carrier gives a lower rate to the shipper who presents multiple shipments at one time. The carrier realizes a lower pickup cost per shipment, while the shipper delays delivery by aggregating shipments before dispatch.

- *Mileage rate.* This rate is quite common for truckload-type freight; carriers base it upon the number of miles the shipment moves, regardless of the commodity or the shipment's weight.

- *Contract rate.* Railroads may negotiate a specific rate with a shipper for moving a given commodity volume between specified points. These rates, which require large volumes, 600 cars or more per year, are appropriate for the movement of bulk commodities or manufactured products that move regularly between specific points in large volumes. The shipper may specify service constraints and penalties for noncompliance.

Ocean Freight Rates. Carriers set ocean freight rates at a level that will cover all the expenses of operating the ship, the ship's capital cost, and any charges specific to the voyage. The rates cover items such as fixed costs for crew, maintenance, repair, and insurance, and variable costs such as fuel, port fees, dockage, and cargo handling. The carrier and the shipper balance these factors against the cargo type, as well as the voyage's length and special requirements, to arrive at an agreeable price.

Ocean freight rates are typically quoted on a weight-ton or measurement-ton basis. There are three weight tons: short = 2,000 pounds; long = 2,240 pounds; and metric = 2,205 pounds. The measurement ton is 40 cubic feet. The carrier will use whichever ton generates the greatest revenue. For example, a 100-cubic-foot shipment weighing 3,500 pounds will be charged for 2.5 measurement tons (100 cubic feet divided by 40 cubic feet per measurement ton) rather than 1.563 metric tons (3,500 pounds divided by 2,205 pounds).

Container rates are quite common for shipping manufactured products. The container rate does not vary by the weight shipped in the container. Generally, container rates are quoted from port to port, not shipment origin to shipment destination. Land transportation costs are added to the container rate to get the through rate.

Finally, ocean carriers add numerous surcharges to the basic rate. Example surcharges include fuel, currency, port congestion, out-of-port differential, trans-shipment, and terminal handling.

As the following example indicates, the container rate for moving a container from Charleston, South Carolina, to Antwerp, Belgium, is only 54.8 percent of the total ocean freight charge.

Rate per 40-foot container	$1,201
Currency adjustment factor	408
Terminal handling charge	500
Fuel adjustment factor	80
Total container rate	$2,189

Study Questions

1. Determine the cost of shipping 8,500 pounds of blue, ultramarine, powdered paint in bulk in double bags to Newark, New York, from State College, Pennsylvania.

2. What is the freight cost to move 22,000 pounds of putty from Reading, Pennsylvania, to Baltimore, Maryland? The putty is in a container in a steel-lined tub with a wooden cover.

3. Calculate the shipping cost to move 1,500 pounds of aluminum powders in Package 2452 to Baltimore, Maryland, from Reading, Pennsylvania.

4. You are shipping a ten-pound box ($12'' \times 12'' \times 12''$) of dry roasted peanuts in the shell from Atlanta, Georgia, 30001, to Chicago, Illinois, 60601. Comparing the charges for this shipment by FedEx (http://www.fedex.com), UPS (http://www.ups.com), and the U.S. Postal Service (http://www.usps.gov), which carrier would you use for: (1) next-day delivery, (2) second-day delivery, and (3) third- or fourth-day delivery?

SUGGESTED READING

Cattani, K. D., "Supply Chain Planning for Demand Uncertainties," *Supply Chain Management Review* (Winter 2000): 25–28.

Cooke, J. A., "Logistics Ropes in Inventory," *Logistics Management and Distribution Report* (July 2000): 49–62.

Cunningham, R., "Balancing Inventory and Service Levels," *APICS Journal* (August 1998): 42–47.

Hoffman, K. C., "Clarity Brought to Window Maker's Supply Chain," *Global Logistics and Supply Chain Management* (May 2001): 40–44.

LaLande, B., "Why So Much Inventory," *Supply Chain Management Review* (Summer 1999): 7–8.

Lindhart, J. A., "The Peaks and Valleys of Inventory Record Accuracy," *APICS Journal* (July 1998): 34–38.

Murphy, J. V., "Customer Driven Supply Chains," *Global Logistics and Supply Chain Strategies* (April 2001): 40–49.

Sankar, R., "Inventory Management Across the Retail Supply Chain," *Supply Chain Management Review* (Winter 2000): 56–63.

Waller, M., M. E. Johnson, and T. Davis, "Vendor-Managed Inventory in Retail Supply Chains," *Journal of Business Logistics* 20, no. 1 (1999): 183–204.

Chapter 6
Managing Inventory Flows in the Supply Chain

Ballou, R. M., "Evaluating Inventory Management Performance Using a Turnover Curve," *International Journal of Physical Distribution and Logistics Management* 30, no. 1 (2000): 72–85.

Claycomb, C., C. Dröge, and R. Germain, "The Effect of Just-in-Time with Customers on Organizational Design and Performance," *International Journal of Logistics Management* 10, no. 2 (1999): 37–58.

Das, C., and R. Tyagi, "Effect of Correlated Demands on Safety Stock Centralization," *Journal of Business Logistics* 20, no. 1 (1999): 205–214.

Dröge, C., and R. Germain, "The Just-in-Time Inventory Effect," *Journal of Business Logistics* 20, no. 1 (1999): 53–72.

Pfol, H. C., O. Cullmann, and W. Stolzle, "Inventory Management with Statistical Process Control," *Journal of Business Logistics* 20, no. 1 (1999): 101–120.

Schuster, Edmund W., Stuart J. Allen, and Michael P. D'Itri, "Capacitated Materials Requirements Planning and Its Application in Process Industries," *Journal of Business Logistics* 21, no. 1 (2001): 169–186.

Schwarz, L. B., and Z. K. Wong, "The Design of a JIT Supply Chain," *Journal of Business Logistics* 20, no. 1 (1999): 141–164.

Tracey, M., "The Importance of Logistics Efficiency to Customer Service and Firm Performance," *International Journal of Logistics Management* 9, no. 2 (1998): 65–82.

Tyagi, R., and C. Das, "Extension of the Square Root Law for Safety Stocks to Demands with Unequal Variances," *Journal of Business Logistics* 19, no. 2 (1998): 197–203.

Vokurka, R. J., and R. R. Lummas, "The Role of Just-in-Time in Supply Chain Management," *International Journal of Logistics Management* 11, no. 1 (2000): 38–98.

Chapter 7
Inventory Decision Making

Ackerman, Kenneth B., *Practical Handbook of Warehousing*, 4th ed. (New York: Chapman & Hall, International Thomson Publishing, 1999).

Ackerman, Kenneth B., *Warehousing Profitability: A Manager's Guide* (K.B. Ackerman Co., 1999).

Foger, Gary, "Productivity Climbs with Real-Time Warehouse Control," *Modern Materials Handling* 49, no. 3 (April 1994): 38–40.

"Hot New Trends in Packaging," *Modern Materials Handling* (October 2001).

James, Aaron, "Re-Inventing the Public Warehouse," *Logistics Management Distribution Report* (May 1, 2000).

Jedd, Marcia, "Trends in Selecting Distribution Centers Are All Over the Map," *Global Logistics & Supply Chain Strategies* (March 2001).

Kulwiec, Ray, "Materials Handling and the Supply Chain," *Modern Materials Handling* (March 21, 1999).

Murphy, Paul R., and Richard F. Poist, "In Search of Warehousing Excellence: A Multivariate Analysis of HRM Practices," *Journal of Business Logistics* 14, no. 2 (1993): 145–164.

Thompkins, James A., Yavuz A. Bozer, Edward Frazelle, Joe Tanchoco, and John White, *Facilities Planning* (New York: John Wiley & Sons, 1996).

Towle, William H., *Warehousing Law* (Cawley Press, LTD, 1988).

Chapter 8
Warehousing Decisions

Chapter 9
The Transportation System

Bowman, Robert J., "Are Bigger Ocean Carriers Better? Shippers and Lines Don't See Eye to Eye," *Global Logistics & Supply Chain Strategies* (March 2000).

Clott, Christopher B., "Ocean Freight Intermediaries: An Analysis of Non-Vessel Operating Common Carriers (NVOCC's) and Maritime Reform," *Transportation Journal* 40, no. 2 (Spring 2001): 17–26.

Contrill, Ken, "Air Express Carriers Stress Time-Definite Service in U.S.-Europe Trade," *Global Sites and Logistics* (October 1998): 28–35.

Cooke, James A., "Logistics Exchanges and ASPs: On the Evolutionary Path," *Logistics Management Distribution Report* (December 2000).

Coyle, John J., Edward J. Bardi, and Robert A. Novack, *Transportation*, 5th ed. (Cincinnati, Ohio: South-Western College Publishing, 2000).

Crum, M.R., D. A. Johnson, and B. J. Allen, "A Longitudinal Assessment of EDI Use in the Motor Carrier Industry," *Transportation Journal* 38, no. 1 (Fall 1998): 15–28.

Evers, Philip T., and Carol J. Johnson, "Performance Perceptions, Satisfaction, and Intention: The Intermodal Shipper's Perspective," *Transportation Journal* 40, no. 2 (Spring 2001): 27–39.

Hoffman, Kurt C., "Tight Supply Chains Respond to Guaranteed Truck Service," *Global Logistics & Supply Chain Strategies* (February 2000).

Milligan, Brian, "Transportation Can Provide a Competitive Edge—Or Take It Away," *Purchasing* (January 13, 2000).

"Will Tomorrow's Transportation System Be Viable?" *Logistics Management Distribution Report* (April 2001).

Chapter 10
Transportation Management

Bardi, Edward J., Prabir K. Bagchi, and T. S. Raghunathan, "Motor Carrier Selection in a Deregulated Environment," *Transportation Journal* 29, no. 1 (Fall 1989): 4–11.

Bardi, Edward J., and Michael Tracey, "Transportation Outsourcing: A Survey of U.S. Practices," *International Journal of Physical Distribution & Logistics Management* 15, no. 1 (1985): 15–21.

Bradley, Peter A., Mary Collins Holcomb, Karl B. Manrodt, and Richard H. Thompson, "Trends and Issues in Logistics: Ninth Annual Survey of the Giants of Shipping," *Council of Logistics Management Annual Conference Proceedings* (2000): 99–110.

Con, Larry A., "Establishing Effective Transportation Controls in a Decentralized Company," *Council of Logistics Management Annual Conference Proceedings* (1995): 391–398.

Cooke, James A., "Logistics Exchanges and ASPs: On the Evolutionary Path," *Logistics Management Distribution Report* (December 2000).

"Driving Shipper and Transport Provider Networks to Optimal Performance, While Improving the Bottom Line for Both," *Logistics Management Distribution Report* (March 2001).

LaLonde, Bernard J., James M. Masters, Arnold B. Maltz, and Lisa R. Williams, *Evolution Status and Future of the Corporate Transportation Function* (American Society of Transportation and Logistics, 1991).

Liberatore, Matthew J., and Tan Miller, "A Decision Support Approach for Transport Carrier and Mode Selection," *Journal of Business Logistics* 16, no. 2 (1995): 85–116.

Manrodt, Karl, "Trading Exchanges in Transportation," *Logistics Management Distribution Report* (December 2000).

Murphy, Paul R., and Patricia K. Hall, "The Relative Importance of Cost and Service in Freight Transportation Choice Before and After Deregulation: An Update," *Transportation Journal* 35, no. 1 (Fall 1995): 30–38.

Quality in Customer-Supplier Relationships

CHAPTER OUTLINE

The needs of customers too often are overshadowed by short-term business objectives. Peter Senge of MIT tells a story about a company that embraced total quality management but found its stock price steadily declining. One of the main objectives of their quality initiative was to reduce new product introduction time. In the effort to meet this objective (on which the managers were measured and rewarded), the new products became increasingly simple and mundane.

143

In Japanese the same word—*okyakusama*—means both "customer" and "honorable guest." World-class organizations are obsessed with meeting and exceeding customer expectations. Many companies such as Disney and Nissan Motor Co.'s Infiniti division were built on the notion of satisfying the customer. The service philosophy of Home Depot, cited by Wal-Mart's CEO as *the* best retail organization in the United States, is "Every customer has to be treated like your mother, your father, your sister, or your brother."

Many businesses traditionally have kept suppliers at arm's length, but the quality of output can be no better than the quality of the input. In 1982 IBM purchased some parts from a Japanese manufacturer. According to the specifications, IBM would accept 300 defective parts per million of the product. The response from Japan raised a lot of questions and gave IBM the opportunity to change its perspective on quality and relationships with suppliers. The Japanese commented, "We have a hard time understanding North American business practices. But the 3 defective parts per 10,000 have been included and are wrapped separately. Hope this pleases."[1]

Developing strong and positive relationships with customers and suppliers is a basic principle of total quality. This chapter will

- demonstrate the importance of customer-supplier relationships to achieving total quality;
- identify the principles and practices of quality customer-supplier relationships;
- give examples of effective partnerships between customers and suppliers; and
- compare the TQ approach to customers and suppliers to conventional organizational theories.

CUSTOMER-SUPPLIER RELATIONSHIPS AND TOTAL QUALITY

From the TQ perspective, every company is part of a long chain (actually many long chains) of customers and suppliers.[2] Each company is a customer to its suppliers and a supplier to its customers, so it does not make sense to think of a company as only one or the other (Figure 4.1). One implication of this concept is that your customer's customers are, in a sense, your customers as well. Sometimes a company must focus on both their immediate customers and those next in the chain. Procter & Gamble, for example, works hard to satisfy the needs of both the people who use their products and the retail establishments that sell them, labeling the former "consumers" and the latter "customers."

Companies should try to establish the same kinds of productive relationships with their suppliers that they have with their customers. By developing partnerships, customers and suppliers can build relationships that will help them satisfy their shared customers further along the customer-supplier chain.

FIGURE 4.1 THE CUSTOMER-SUPPLIER CHAIN

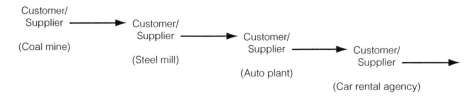

This is why we have written one chapter on customer-supplier relationships, rather than separate chapters on customers and suppliers.

The idea of creating mutually beneficial relationships with both customers and suppliers is a major departure from the traditional approach to customer and supplier relationships (CSRs). As one book on quality recently put it, "The historical picture of customer-supplier relationships has been one of self-interested adversaries negotiating against each other to maximize their slice of the pie at the expense of the other."[3] The authors go on to say that the focus of CSRs under TQ is on expanding the pie rather than on arguing over its division.

The Importance of Customers

The importance of customers has evolved over the years, from viewing the customer as a buyer to increase profitability, to viewing the customer as an active partner and the focus of all quality activities. Customer satisfaction translates directly into increased profits. Loyal customers spend more, refer new clients, and are less costly to do business with. Studies have shown that it costs about five times more to attract new customers than to keep old ones and that satisfied customers purchase more and are willing to pay higher prices. At IBM, for instance, each percentage point in improved customer satisfaction translates into $500 million more revenue over five years.[4] Although Home Depot customers spend only about $38 each visit, they shop 30 times annually and spend more than $25,000 throughout a lifetime.[5] Poor quality products and services, on the other hand, lead to customer dissatisfaction in the form of complaints, returns, and unfavorable word-of-mouth publicity. Dissatisfied customers purchase from competitors. One study found that customers are five times more likely to switch because of perceived service problems than for price concerns or product quality issues.[6] Studies have also shown that dissatisfied customers tell at least twice as many friends about bad experiences than they tell about good ones.

For many companies, "The Customer Comes First" is a guiding principle (see the box about Southwest Airlines). It is impossible to overstate the importance of customers to TQ. Customers are at the very center of every TQ activity, and devotion to satisfying them is the first principle of TQ. Customers are recognized as the guarantee of the organization's continued existence. Therefore, a focus on customers, rather than internal issues, is the foundation of the TQ approach to management. Customer-driven quality is recognized as a core value of the Malcolm Baldrige National Quality Award. The award guidelines state:[7]

> Quality is judged by customers. Thus, quality must take into account all product and service features and characteristics that contribute value to customers and lead to customer satisfaction, preference, and retention. Value and satisfaction may be influenced by many factors throughout the customer's overall purchase, ownership, and service

---

Flying the Customer-Friendly Skies[8]

Southwest Airlines began on June 18, 1971, with flights to Houston, Dallas, and San Antonio. It has grown to become the fifth largest U.S. airline in terms of domestic customers carried. The airline operates more than 2,150 flights daily with more than 23,000 employees. Known for its legendary service, the Southwest culture ensures that it serves the needs of its Customers (with a capital *C*) in a friendly, caring, and enthusiastic manner. Kevin and Jackie Freiberg, authors of *NUTS! Southwest Airlines' Crazy Recipe for Business and Personal Success*, note that legendary service is a key component of Southwest's culture.

> Southwest wants its customers to experience service that makes a lasting impression, service that is kind and loving, service that is fun and makes them laugh. . . . Thus, Southwest will go a long way to defend and support an employee who may violate a company policy to bend toward the customer. The company instills in every employee the idea that happy, satisfied customers who return again and again create job security.

Every one of the approximately 1,000 customers who write to the airline gets a personal response (not a form letter) within four weeks, and frequent fliers even get birthday cards. The airline even moved a flight up a quarter hour when five medical students who commuted weekly to an out-of-state medical school complained that the flight got them to class 15 minutes late.

Customer focus applies to internal customers also; each operating division identifies an internal customer. Mechanics who service planes target the pilots who fly them, and marketers treat reservation agents as customers. It is not unusual to find pilots helping ground crews unload baggage. As Executive VP Colleen Barrett stated: "We are not an airline with great customer service. We are a great customer service organization that happens to be in the airline business."

Southwest has been one of the most profitable airlines in the United States. In many years, the airline has been recognized for best baggage handling, fewest customer complaints, and best on-time performance. It has been recognized with numerous honors, including one of America's Most Admired Corporations by *Fortune* magazine in 1995.

experiences. These factors include the company's relationship with customers that helps build trust, confidence, and loyalty.

The Importance of Suppliers

Suppliers—those companies that provide the organization with goods and services that help them to satisfy the needs of their own customers—are also crucial to successful TQ. A manufacturing company assembling parts made by suppliers illustrates this point: The final product cannot be any better than the parts that go into it. If a supplier's performance is of consistently high quality, its customer can decrease or eliminate costly incoming inspections that add no value to the product. For these reasons, organizations such as Ford Motor Company and Motorola have increasingly demanded tangible progress in quality from all their suppliers. Companies that do not accept this requirement are dropped from supplier lists. The importance of suppliers is at least as great when they provide training, software, or other goods or services that do not physically become part of the final product; they will influence its quality, nevertheless, by shaping the quality of the processes used to produce it.

However, as Terry A. Carlson, corporate vice president of purchasing for Maytag stated, "Superior quality, consistent service, and competitive pricing are just the price of entry to get into the game." What sets world-class suppliers apart from the rest are a formal company-wide effort to continually improve their products and services, the ability and willingness to align products, processes, and business strategies with customers for mutual success, and a proven ability to be an industry leader in developing new technologies and products.[9]

In business today, operations are often highly decentralized and dispersed around the world. Consequently, managing a complex network of suppliers becomes a critical interorganizational issue. Suppliers play a vital role throughout the product development process, from design through distribution. Suppliers can provide technology or production processes not internally available, early design advice, and increased capacity, which can result in lower costs, faster time-to-market, and improved quality for their customers. In turn, they are assured of stable and long-term business. At Chrysler, for example, suppliers are involved early in the design process.[10] As a result, Chrysler often finds out about new materials, parts, and technologies before other automakers.

Increasingly, suppliers are viewed as *partners* with customers, because there usually is a co-dependent relationship. A powerful example of supplier partnerships is the response that occurred when a fire destroyed the main source of a crucial $5 brake valve for Toyota.[11] Without it, Toyota had to shut down its 20 plants in Japan. Within hours of the disaster, other suppliers began taking blueprints, improvising tooling systems, and setting up makeshift production lines. Within days, the 36 suppliers, aided by more than 150 other subcontractors, had almost 50 production lines making small batches of the valve. Even a sewing-machine company that had never made car parts spent 500 person-hours refitting a milling machine to make just 40 valves a day. Toyota promised the suppliers a bonus of about $100 million "as a token of our appreciation."

PRINCIPLES FOR CUSTOMER-SUPPLIER RELATIONSHIPS

Three governing principles describe CSRs under total quality:

- recognition of the strategic importance of customers and suppliers,
- development of win-win relationships between customers and suppliers, and
- establishing relationships based on trust.

First, an organization must recognize that its customers and suppliers are absolutely crucial to its success. Although this may sound obvious, many organizations seem to be driven by the need to observe standard operating procedures. Those companies maintain rigid boundaries between jobs, rather than trying to meet customer expectations. Consider the following letter from a hotel desk clerk to the popular newspaper columnist Abigail Van Buren:

> Dear Abby:
> I am a desk clerk at a resort hotel. I would like the public to know that we are not maintenance men. We cannot repair television sets or break into their automobiles when they have locked their keys inside the car. We do not unplug toilets or change lightbulbs, and we can't repair the telephone.
> Also, we are not in "housekeeping," so we can't bring them extra wash cloths, towels, pillows, blankets, or toilet paper. We are not bellmen either, so please don't ask us to carry luggage or run errands.
> Now I will tell you what front desk clerks *are* paid to do: greet and register incoming guests, and make sure that outgoing guests see the cashier about paying their bill and turning in their key before departing. Thank you.
>
> Desk Clerks[12]

Although some division of labor is to be expected in any organization, the writer seems ignorant of his or her responsibility for guaranteeing customer satisfaction, preferring to focus on what he or she can't do. As the first and last contact a guest makes with the hotel, front desk personnel probably have the largest impact on guest satisfaction of anyone. It is frightening to imagine how much damage this individual's attitude has done to his or her organization. Of course, the responsibility for this attitude may ultimately rest with the hotel organization that apparently has created a system in which people are more interested in maintaining boundaries than in serving customers.[13]

Fortunately, Abby seems to have grasped the central principle of TQ much better than her correspondent:

I doubt that you can speak for all hotel and motel desk clerks through-out the world. In the name of good customer relations, you should be prepared to handle all questions and complaints to the satisfaction of the guests so they will want to return to your establishment.[14]

Customers must be at the center of the organizational universe. Satisfying their needs leads to repeat business and positive referrals, as opposed to one-shot business and negative referrals. Suppliers must also be considered crucial to organizational success, because they make it possible to create customer satisfaction. Neither the quality nor the cost of the organization's product can be brought to competitive levels and continuously improved without the contributions of suppliers.

The second principle of customer-supplier relationships is the need to develop mutually beneficial (often called win-win) relationships between customers and suppliers. This was discussed previously as working together to increase the size of the pie, rather than competing over how to divide it. The goal of building partnerships with customers and suppliers can be seen as an extension of the teamwork principle that applies to all TQ activities and as a recognition that the needs of both partners must be satisfied if productive long-term relationships are to be created. W. Edwards Deming has advocated these principles for decades, as is evident in his 14 points (chapter 2). Joseph Juran suggests some key differences between adversarial and teamwork relationships with suppliers.[15] Traditionally, customers have used many different suppliers for the same purchased item, and they typically have been awarded short-term (annual) contracts. This practice fosters a competitive situation in which suppliers strive to outbid each other, and may sacrifice quality for cost. A teamwork relationship results in the need for fewer suppliers, with many items being single-sourced. With few suppliers, companies do not have to rely on annual bidding, and can award longer-term contracts. This enhances the motivation to work together for mutual benefits. For instance, quality planning is performed jointly, rather than independently. This helps both the customer and supplier focus on "fitness for use" to meet customer needs rather than simply trying to conform to specifications. It also fosters a spirit of continuous improvement, in which larger customers often help smaller suppliers develop their quality management systems and process capabilities. Similar ideas were also advocated by Deming in his 14 points.

The third principle of effective CSRs is that they must be based on trust rather than suspicion. The point noted by Juran observes that a critical distinction between adversarial and teamwork relationshps is a "pattern of collaboration." Adversarial relationships are characterized by secrecy and a tendency to look over suppliers' shoulders. Teamwork relationships, on the other hand, are characterized by openness and full disclosure of both capabilities and problems.

The costs of mistrust are staggering: Witness the tremendous number, detail, and rigidity of rules that characterize the U.S. Department of Defense's contracts with suppliers. The suppliers often incur substantial costs in terms of

---

Partnering with Internal Customers[16]

GTE Supply negotiates contracts, purchases products, and distributes a vast array of goods needed for telephone operations, from office supplies to telecommunications equipment. Its major customers are internal network, business, and telephone operations customer groups at each GTE local telephone company. The company created a systematic, highly effective process of obtaining and using information from internal customers, making partners of previously adversarial groups, reducing costs, and improving customer satisfaction. This was based on systematically surveying internal customers and using the results as a basis for quality improvement. Respondents rate GTE Supply on how well it

- Provides complete information,
- Understands customers' needs,
- Does the job right the first time,
- Provides timely responses to questions and requests,
- Makes it easy to do business with,
- Follows up on services, and
- Provides clear communication.

Other questions seek information about overall satisfaction, quality, and value, and open-ended questions ask about improvement opportunities. Detailed reports and analyses are provided to managers, who use the information to set objectives and to develop and implement action plans.

The survey and quality improvement process has transformed the organization from one of the worst-regarded to one of the best-regarded organizations in the company. They learned that extensive, focused communication with internal customers can produce spectacular increases in satisfaction levels and decrease costs and cycle times.

---

both money and time due to multiple levels of review and inspection. Although a certain level of rigidity is to be expected in the acquisition of weapons, it is harder to understand when applied to more ordinary items.

Aside from the obvious teamwork implications for relationships based on trust versus suspicion, monitoring supplier or customer behavior does not add any value to the product. If a trusting relationship between customers and suppliers can be developed so that neither must check up on the behavior of the other, the costs of monitoring, such as inspection and auditing, can be avoided. Many Japanese firms do not inspect items purchased from other companies in Japan; they do, however, often inspect those purchased from America. Trust is not a blind leap into the unknown; it is developed over time "through a pattern of success by all parties to fully and faithfully deliver that which was promised."[17] In other words, trust depends upon trustworthy behavior by both parties in a CSR.

Practices for Dealing with Customers

How can these principles be translated into specific practices? The most basic practices for dealing with customers are (1) to collect information constantly on customer expectations, (2) to disseminate this information widely within the organization, (3) to use this information to design, produce, and deliver the organization's products and services, and (4) to effectively manage relationships with customers.

Collect Customer Information

As seen in the GTE Supply example, acquiring customer information is critical to understanding customer needs and identifying opportunities for improvement. The Japanese auto industry is known for trying to understand customer needs so thoroughly that they can incorporate design features that customers would never have asked for but love once they experience them. Teams of automobile designers visit people at home and observe how they live in order to anticipate their automotive needs. Hideo Sugiura, executive vice president of Honda, comments on his company's efforts to anticipate customer needs: "We should not try to sell things just because the market is there, but rather we should seek to create a new market by accurately understanding the potential needs of customers and society."[18] Lexus, Toyota's luxury car line, has succeeded dramatically in this manner and is consistently at the top of owner satisfaction surveys.

Perhaps one of the best examples of understanding customer needs and using this information to improve competitiveness is Frank Perdue's chicken business.[19] Perdue learned what customers' key purchase criteria were. These included a yellow bird, high meat-to-bone ratio, no pinfeathers, freshness, availability, and brand image. He also determined the relative importance of each criterion and how well the company and its competitors were meeting each one. By systematically improving his ability to exceed customers' expectations relative to the competition, Perdue gained market share even though his chickens were premium priced. Among Perdue's innovations was a used jet engine that dried the chickens, allowing the pinfeathers to be singed off. As discussed in chapter 1, Perdue not only addressed his customer's satisfiers, but also their exciters/delighters as well.

Some of the most popular ways to collect information about customers are surveys, service evaluation cards, focus groups, and listening to what customers say during business transactions, especially when they complain. Some companies, such as Marriott Hotels, have developed elaborate methods for keeping abreast of customer needs. This is not a low-profile activity at Marriott: Chairman Bill Marriott, Jr., himself reads approximately 800 letters from customers and 15,000 guest questionnaires every month![20] The rewards of taking customer information seriously are also apparent at Marriott, where occupancy rates are consistently 10 percent above the industry average. (For an example from manufacturing, see box, "Promoting Customer Delight at U.S. Precision Lens," on page 153.)

Sending employees into customer facilities, another popular practice, provides not only feedback from customers, but also valuable information to employees about the importance of what they do. A manager in a foundry that follows this practice commented:

> We take shop floor people and take them out to the customer's plant. We want them to see the final product in place. It gets our employees out in the world to meet the customers. They get to know the customers better and really by doing that, the employees get to have a better, more caring attitude. Because they know more about what's going on.

Having top managers of the company act as customers of their own organizations—renting a room in their own hotel or buying a suit from a retail outlet—is another way to better understand customer needs. This not only gives them a sense of the quality of service, but also makes them more sensitive to how the organizational policies they have created actually affect customers.[21]

A newer approach to collecting customer information is to monitor the Internet.[22] In recent years, the growth of the Internet is offering companies a fertile arena for finding out what consumers think of their products. Internet users frequently seek advice from other users on strengths and weaknesses of products, share experiences on service quality, or pose specific problems they need to resolve. By monitoring the conversations on Usenet discussion groups, managers can obtain valuable insights on customer perceptions and product or service quality problems. In open forums, customer comments can often be translated into creative product improvements. In addition, the Internet can be a good source of information about competitors' products. The cost of monitoring Internet conversations is minimal compared to the costs of other types of survey approaches, and customers are not biased by any questions that may be asked. However, the conversations may be considerably less structured and unfocused and thus may contain less usable information. Also, unlike a focus group or telephone interview, inaccurate perceptions or factual errors cannot be corrected.

Beyond getting a thorough understanding of customer needs, companies also need to assess how well their products and services are meeting customer needs. Some companies have developed unconventional and innovative ways of understanding customers. British Airways has installed video kiosks at Heathrow Airport outside London and at Kennedy Airport in New York. Upset customers can enter the booth and create a video message for BA's management. The videos have proven so informative that, although they were initially viewed only by executives, frontline employees demanded and were given access to them. One important aspect of this method is that it gives people a sense of the emotion associated with customer response to the quality of service ("You lost my *&%$# baggage!"), which cannot easily be conveyed by checking a number from one through five on a customer satisfaction survey, especially when done weeks later. Texas Instruments created a simulated

---

Promoting Customer Delight at U.S. Precision Lens[23]

U.S. Precision Lens (USPL) is the world's largest manufacturer of lens systems for projection televisions. Since 1986 USPL has been a wholly-owned subsidiary of Corning, Inc. The major requirements for success in selling to projection television manufacturers such as Philips and Sony are product quality, delivery, product innovation, and customer service. USPL's goal in each area is "customer delight" through exceeding customer expectations.

USPL understands customer needs through a system it describes as "simple, reliable, and effective"—they ask them what their needs are. Company executives travel frequently to Europe and the Far East to meet with senior members of customer organizations, and customers visit USPL with similar frequency. During these visits, competitors' products are also discussed, so USPL can set a direction for continuous (they say "relentless") improvement. Planning sessions prior to visits allow input to the data-gathering process from across the organization. Trips are not the exclusive preserve of senior managers; hourly "associates" (employees) also visit customers and share their impressions on their return.

Interestingly, the primary medium of day-to-day communication between USPL and its customers is the fax. This is partly due to the time zone differences between USPL and its customers. The CEO sees every fax message from customers, and USPL's policy is to respond to all faxes within 24 hours. Also, the home telephone numbers of USPL's senior executives are provided to customers, and they use them.

USPL uses a survey to procure ratings of its own service quality, as well as that of its competitors, on the dimensions of assurance, responsiveness, reliability, empathy, and "tangibles." In response to feedback through this and other means, USPL has bar-coded container labels, vacuum sealed parts, and placed a native speaker in Japan to represent the company.

These and other TQ-oriented practices at USPL have paid tremendous dividends to the company. USPL received the SONY President Award in 1991 as the highest-rated supplier for quality and delivery. Philips presented USPL the Supplier Total Quality Award that same year. Electrohome made USPL its supplier of the year for 1990. The ultimate reward for quality, however, is in attracting and maintaining demand for the organization's products. In this category as well USPL is outstanding: The company's market share is approaching 70 percent.

---

classroom to understand how mathematics teachers use calculators, and a manager at Levi Strauss used to talk with teens who were lined up to buy rock concert tickets.

Disseminate Customer Information

After people in the organization have gathered information about customer needs, the next step is to broadcast this information within the organization. After all, if the people in the firm are going to work as a team to meet customer expectations, they must all be "singing from the same hymnbook," as the saying goes. Information does little good if it stays with the person or department that brought it into the organization. Wainwright Industries has a unique approach. A room at the headquarters building, named Mission Control by one of the managers who is a Star Trek fan, serves as the company's key information center. Not only are customer report cards displayed on a wall (along with other key quality and business information), but green and red flags are used to designate customers for whom everything is going well or a problem has arisen. Red flags signal the convening of a customer team to address the problem.

Richard Whiteley, vice chairman of The Forum Corporation, a customer satisfaction–oriented consulting firm, has a vivid way to describe this need: "Saturate your company with the voice of the customer."[24] Saturation is an attractive way of describing what organizations need to do: If the organization is awash in information about customer needs, it is much harder to downplay customer expectations in favor of administrative convenience or the need to follow procedures.

AT&T, which won two Baldrige Awards in 1992 and another in 1994, is one organization trying to maintain a constant customer focus. Jerre Stead, president of Global Business Communications Systems, tells people in his unit: "I say if you're in a meeting, any meeting, for 15 minutes and we're not talking about customers or competitors, raise your hand and ask why. If it goes on for half an hour, leave! Leave the meeting!"[25]

Customer information must be translated into the features of the organization's products and services. This is the bottom line of quality customer-supplier relations from the supplier's point of view: giving the customers what they want. Translating customer needs into product features can be done in a structured manner using Quality Function Deployment (QFD), a technique discussed in chapter 3. QFD allows people to see how aspects of their products and services relate to customer satisfaction and to make informed decisions about how their products should be improved. The overall process of using information from customers to provide quality products is summarized in Figure 4.2.

Use Customer Information

Customer information is worthless unless it is used. Customer feedback should be integrated into continuous improvement activities. For example, by listening to customers, Bank One opened nearly 60 percent of its 1,377 branches in Ohio and Texas on Saturdays and 20 percent on Sundays. A 24-hour customer hotline is also available. Since the early 1980s, Xerox has surveyed tens of thousands of customers annually and tracked the results through its Customer Satisfaction Measurement System (CSMS).[26] The data guide continuous improvements within the corporation. For instance, the CSMS uncovered the fact that customers wanted one-call, one-person problem resolution. As a result, Xerox created six Customer Care Centers, staffed by specially trained customer care representatives who handle some 1.2 million telephone calls and about one

FIGURE 4.2 THE CUSTOMER-DRIVEN QUALITY CYCLE

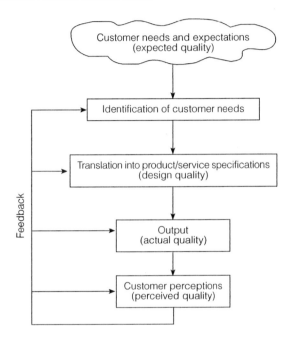

million written inquiries each year. Employees are cross-trained and empowered to adjust bills, correct forms, or take other steps to solve problems single-handedly. Any problems that cannot be resolved instantly are given a 10-day resolution deadline. The files remain open until customers confirm that they are totally satisfied with Xerox actions. CSMS data also showed that customer satisfaction is linked to cycle time—the elapsed time between the reporting phone call and the solution of the problem. The data also showed that simply knowing when a technician will arrive has a positive effect on customer satisfaction. Xerox modified the system to call customers shortly after problems are reported and give them an estimated time of arrival.

Binney & Smith, the company that produces Crayola crayons and markers, makes it a point to improve its products by taking advantage of customer feedback. Many of the letters the company receives from parents laud the role that crayons play in the artistic development of their children. Some letters complained that the markers created permanent stains in children's clothes. After two years of research, Binney & Smith responded by developing a new line of washable markers. Marker sales doubled, demonstrating the company's ability to learn and provide what customers are looking for.[27] More recently Binney & Smith sponsored a contest in which customers could name one of 16 new crayon colors the company created for its Big Box. "Part of our reason for introducing new colors came from consumer suggestions. More than 50 percent said they wanted us to expand and add new colors," according to Brad Dexler, a company spokesman.

Manage Customer Relationships

A company builds customer loyalty by developing trust and effectively managing the interactions and relationships with customers through customer-contact employees. Truly excellent companies foster close and total relationships with customers. These companies also provide easy access to their employees. AT&T Universal Card Services, for instance, has an 800 number, fax, and access for the hearing impaired 24 hours every day throughout the year, translation services for 140 languages, and bilingual Spanish/English operators. Customers are also informed if they will have to wait more than a minute. Customers of Ames Rubber Corporation have immediate access to top division management, manufacturing personnel, quality engineers, sales and service representatives, and technical support staff.

In services, customer satisfaction or dissatisfaction takes place during *moments of truth*—every instance in which a customer comes in contact with an employee of the company. Moments of truth may be direct contacts with customer representatives or service personnel, or when customers read letters, invoices, or other company correspondence. One study concluded that 70 percent of customers leave a supplier because of poor quality service, not problems with products per se, and many companies are struggling to bring their service up to the level of their products.[28] One of the main areas on which companies have focused is telephone service, especially how long it takes to get someone on the phone and to get one's question answered or order taken. Many companies have worked to make sure that phone calls are answered on the third ring, but to AMP, Inc., the world's largest manufacturer of electronic interconnection systems, three rings is an eternity. Customer calls to AMP are answered within six seconds—that is, on the first ring. Why such an ambitious goal? AMP found that 8 percent of their customers were hanging up before their calls were answered under the three-ring standard. They don't lose many calls now.[29]

Customer-contact employees are particularly important. They are the people whose main responsibilities bring them into regular contact with customers—in person, by telephone, or through other means. Companies must carefully select these employees, then extensively train and empower them to meet and exceed customer expectations. Job applicants often go through rigorous screening processes. At Universal Card Services, for instance, every applicant completes a two-part general aptitude test. The company then invites successful candidates to participate in additional testing, which includes a customer service role-playing exercise. Each applicant is asked to handle simulated incoming and outgoing calls. After completing the initial screening test, each candidate must pass a background check, credit check, and a medical evaluation, including drug testing, before being hired.

Service standards are measurable performance levels or expectations that define the quality of customer contact. Service standards might include technical standards, such as response time (answering the telephone within two rings), or behavioral standards (using a customer's name whenever possible). Companies need to communicate and continually reinforce their service standards. Finally, a company should implement a process for tracking adherence to the standards and providing feedback to the employees to improve their performance. Information technology supplies the data for effectively tracking conformance to customer service standards.

Despite all efforts to satisfy customers, every business experiences unhappy customers. Complaints can adversely affect business if not dealt with effectively. Many customers do not complain because they feel it wouldn't do any good or they are uncomfortable with the process. World-class organizations make it easy for customers to complain. Besides providing easy access to the company using toll-free telephone numbers (which should be adequately staffed and supported), many firms actively solicit complaints. Nissan, for instance, telephones each person who buys a new car or brings one in for significant warranty work. Its objective is to resolve all dissatisfaction within 24 hours.[30] Effective resolution of complaints increases customer loyalty and retention. At the Ritz-Carlton Hotel Company, for example, employees can spend up to $2,000 to resolve complaints with no questions asked.

Customers in the Fine Arts[31]

Car dealers have customers, bookstores have customers, but how about symphony orchestras and art museums? Traditionally, such organizations have acted as if they were your customer. But fine arts organizations in Cincinnati, spurred both by economic necessity and the proximity and influence of several quality-conscious corporations, have begun to think hard about satisfying customers. Some of the results:

- The Cincinnati Symphony Orchestra has initiated a series of concerts on Thursday nights. Dress is more casual for these concerts, and tickets can be easily exchanged.
- The Taft Museum has doubled the number of events it holds—from 20 to 40 per season.
- The Cincinnati Opera has begun scheduling series of operas linked by a popular theme. For example, "Pretty Women" included *Carmen* and *The Barber of Seville*.

The increased focus on satisfying customers, which has begun to pay off economically, is reflected by statements from leaders in these organizations. Paul A. Stuhireyer III, managing director of the opera, believes that "the goal should not be an international reputation while losing sight of what [local customers] want. . . . I want to make sure we're still putting 3,000 people into Music Hall for each performance. Then I know we're taking care of the citizens of Cincinnati." Gretchen Mehring, Cincinnati Art Museum director of public service, puts it: "Our primary focus is the family, especially the children. We're not operating a museum or creating exhibitions to appeal to art experts."

Practices for Dealing with Suppliers[32]

Although the principles of CSRs are the same in dealing with suppliers as they are with customers, the practices are somewhat different. In many companies, suppliers are treated as if they were actually a part of the organization. For example, functions such as cafeteria service, mailroom operations, and information processing are being performed by suppliers at their customers' facilities. As more and more of this type of outsourcing is done, the lines between customer and supplier become increasingly blurred.

To ensure that suppliers can provide high quality and reduce costs associated with incoming inspection or testing, many companies provide many types of assistance to their suppliers in developing quality assurance programs or solving quality problems. Joint conferences, training, incentives, recognition, and long-term agreements help to improve suppliers' abilities to meet key quality requirements. The Delco Moraine Division, a manufacturer of automotive brake controls, uses an awareness program that includes a videotape presentation emphasizing quality shown at supplier plants. After viewing the tape, supplier employees were better able to relate their work to Delco. Similarly, Chrysler instituted a program with its suppliers to identify cost reduction ideas; both parties benefit from the lower costs.

Many companies segment suppliers into categories based on their importance to the business and manage them accordingly. For example, at Corning, Level 1 suppliers, who provide raw materials, cases, and hardware, are deemed critical to business success and are managed by teams that include representatives from engineering, materials control, purchasing, and the supplier company. Level 2 suppliers provide specialty materials, equipment, and services and are managed by internal customers. Level 3 suppliers provide commodity items and are centrally managed by purchasing.[33]

In general, the fundamental practices for dealing with suppliers are (1) to base purchasing decisions on quality as well as cost, (2) to reduce the number of suppliers, (3) to establish long-term contracts, (4) to measure and certify suppliers' performance, and (5) to develop cooperative relationships and strategic alliances."

Base Purchasing Decisions on Quality and Cost

The first and most obvious practice is that purchasing decisions should be based on the quality of the product and not just its cost.[34] This, however, goes against the grain in most organizations. Generally speaking, the technical people will determine the specifications for a product to be purchased, and then the purchasing department will solicit bids or check prices with several suppliers and negotiate the contract with the one that fills the order. Purchasing personnel have traditionally been rewarded primarily for negotiating low prices, and thus this has been their focus. Supplier firms have often responded to this situation in the obvious way: by doing whatever they need to do (including sacrificing quality) to maintain low prices.

Beyond the compromises this creates for the quality of the final product, there are two other problems with this approach. First, low purchase cost often does not equal low overall cost. If a cheap (in both senses of the word) part causes a large amount of scrap or leads to high warranty costs, it may end up with a higher overall cost, often referred to as life-cycle cost. Second, pressing suppliers for ever-lower prices will minimize their profits. Although this benefits the customer in the short run, in the long run it keeps suppliers operating so close to the bone that they forgo capital investments, maintenance, and other expenses necessary to improve or even maintain their quality.[35]

Reduce the Number of Suppliers

Firms pursuing TQ also reduce the number of suppliers they work with to the point of having only one supplier for some components. Xerox has reduced its suppliers by about 90 percent—from more than 4,000 to about 450 in 1990.[36] In the automotive industry, General Motors had cut domestic suppliers by 45 percent, from 10,000 down to 5,500, by 1991. Ford Motor Company had likewise reduced their number of suppliers from 1,800 down to 1,000.[37] This also goes against the grain of conventional purchasing practices, as it increases the dependence of the organization on the supplier, thus weakening its bargaining position and exposing it to the possibility of an interruption in supply in the case of a labor stoppage or similar problem with the supplier.

Several advantages offset these disadvantages. For one thing, administrative costs are greatly reduced.[38] (Imagine the time to be saved by eliminating the paperwork associated with 90 percent of suppliers!) Also, cutting the number of suppliers reduces the variability in the incoming products, making it much easier to control the quality of outgoing products. This is because there are fewer "special causes" of variation, to use Deming's term.

The type of intensive CSRs that characterize TQ simply cannot be maintained with a large number of suppliers. The significance of partners (like friends or vice presidents) is lost if you have too many of them. For these reasons, many organizations continue to reduce the number of suppliers with which they do business.

Establish Long-Term Contracts

Related to the idea of fewer suppliers is the practice of establishing long-term contracts with suppliers (see box, "Changing Ford's Supplier Relationships: Easier Said Than Done," on page 161). Establishing long-term contracts allows suppliers to make greater commitments to improving the quality of products and provides greater opportunity for joint improvement efforts and the development of teamwork across organizational boundaries.

Measure and Certify Supplier Performance

Texas Instruments measures suppliers' quality performance by parts per million defective, percentage of on-time deliveries, and cost of ownership.[39] An electronic requisitioning system allows a paperless procurement process. More than 800 suppliers are linked to Texas Instruments through an information exchange system. Integrated data systems track the incoming quality and timeliness of deliveries as materials are received. Analytical reports and on-line data are used to identify material defect trends. Performance reports are sent each month to key suppliers. Joint customer-supplier teams are formed to communicate and improve performance. A supplier management task force of top managers directs current and strategic approaches to improving supplier management practices.

Supplier certification is used by many companies as the focal point of their supplier management system. Formal programs typically are established to rate and certify suppliers who provide quality materials in a cost-effective and timely manner. At the Gillette Company, the supplier certification program begins with Gillette identifying those suppliers with a proven ability to meet its specifications.[40] Once a supplier is selected to participate, Gillette expects them to establish a preproduction planning system to assess the capability of their process to meet Gillette's specifications. Feedback is offered in the form of recommended changes that will improve quality, reduce cost, or facilitate ease of manufacture.

Some companies, such as Motorola, have suppliers rate them as customers. Motorola uses a 15-member council of suppliers that rates Motorola's practices and offers suggestions for improving, for example, the accuracy of production schedules or design layouts that Motorola provides.[41]

Develop Cooperative Relationships and Strategic Alliances

The cornerstone of TQ-style customer-supplier relationships is cooperation. In a sense, practices such as long-term contracts and fewer suppliers create an environment in which cooperation can flourish. Similar to the operation of teamwork within an organization (see chapter 7), quality customer-supplier relations help both parties to achieve their goals.

One common form that cooperation takes is the early involvement of suppliers in the design of new products.[42] Early involvement allows suppliers to make cost-cutting and quality-improving suggestions about the design while changes are relatively easy and inexpensive to make. When the product design is not revealed to suppliers until late in the process, often out of concern that it will be leaked to competitors, such opportunities are lost. Security concerns can be dealt with through nondisclosure agreements.[43]

Another indication of cooperation is the effort of customers to help suppliers improve quality, which can take many forms. Many TQ-oriented corporations present quality-improvement seminars for their suppliers.[44] Juran recommends joint quality planning between customers and suppliers, featuring the exchange of quality-related information.[45] Although customers traditionally have hammered suppliers to lower their prices, in a cooperative relationship the focus is on helping suppliers to lower their costs, which will ultimately benefit both parties.[46]

Today, suppliers are being asked to take on greater responsibilities to help their customers. As companies focus more on their core competencies—the things they do best—they are looking outside their organizations for assistance with noncritical support processes. Customer-supplier partnerships represent an important strategic alliance in achieving excellence and business success. Benefits of such partnerships include access to technology or distribution channels not available internally, shared risks in new investments and product development, improved products through early design recommendations

> ## Changing Ford's Supplier Relationships: Easier Said Than Done[47]
>
> Ford Motor Company was among the first companies to try to change its relationships with suppliers to be consistent with total quality. In 1983 Ford's purchasing vice president, L.M. Chicoine, sent a statement throughout Ford's purchasing organization to the effect that he would like to see more supplier contracts written for periods of more than one year. After six months he learned that there was virtually no increase in the number of long-term contracts.
>
> Mr. Chicoine found that the reason for this lack of change was a procedure requiring buyers to get authorization from two levels of supervision for any contract greater than one year. Most buyers, not seeing any great rewards to them from negotiating long-term contracts, and seeing very clearly the extra hassle involved in getting two additional levels of approval, simply did not attempt to negotiate long-term contracts. A one-word change was all that was needed. The new policy stated that any contract for less than one year would require two additional levels of authorization, leading to historic changes in the nature of Ford's supplier relationships.

based on supplier capabilities, and reduced operations costs through better communications. For example, FedEx and Jostens formed a strategic partnership that enabled both to benefit from new sales of scholastic jewelry and yearbooks.[48] They took advantage of each others' strengths: Josten provided a high-quality product with superior service, and FedEx provided reliable high-volume, short-interval delivery for these time-critical products.

QUALITY CUSTOMER-SUPPLIER RELATIONSHIPS IN ACTION

Many of the aspects of quality CSRs we have been discussing are illustrated by the relationship between GE Appliance and DJ Inc., both of Louisville, Kentucky.[49] In nine years, DJ went from being one of 100 GE suppliers of plastic parts to being its sole source. DJ improved its quality by taking advantage of GE's supplier seminars in statistical process control (SPC). The company must have studied hard, as it has not had a single lot of parts rejected by GE since 1978. Early involvement in product design is commonplace for these two companies. In one typical case, DJ recommended a minor change in product design that reduced the cost of a part by more than 5 percent and increased its expected life by 16 percent. This example typifies the advantages enjoyed by companies with quality customer-supplier relationships.

Granite Rock Company of Watsonville, California, a 1992 Malcolm Baldrige Award winner, has also devoted itself to absorbing and making use of information from customers.[50] Bruce Woolpert, who shares with his brother Steve the CEO title at Granite Rock, believes that the role of manager is "to make sure there's a flood of information coming into the company." Where does the flood come from? Granite Rock has its customers rate its performance against its competitors in "report cards," longer surveys, quick-response cards, and focus groups. Information on what customers need and what is being done to satisfy them is distributed throughout the company via team meetings, an annual recognition day, and the appropriately titled company newsletter, *Rock Talk.*

Granite Rock learned that quarry customers wanted to pick up rock very quickly at any time of the day or night. To satisfy this need, the company invested a great deal of money in Granite Xpress, a system that allows customers to pull up to the quarry, check the computer for their order, and insert a magnetic card to load their own orders. Not only does this system operate 24 hours a day, but it has reduced the time at the quarry for truckers from 30 minutes to 10.

Granite Rock personnel also frequently make trips to benchmark other companies, both in their industry (aggregate and concrete producers) and out of their industry (a gold mine). Perhaps the furthest afield they have roamed is to Domino's Pizza, another company that is concerned about on-time delivery. Domino's told Granite Rock where to get better maps and suggested that they adopt Domino's practice of writing house numbers on maps.

CUSTOMER-SUPPLIER RELATIONS IN ORGANIZATION THEORY

Much of the organization literature has argued that firms should consider customers as partners for success.[51] As far back as 1973, Gersuny and Rosengren argued that diverse customer roles require new bonds of interdependence and an increasingly complex social network that crosses traditional organizational boundaries.[52] They identified four distinct roles for customers:

1. resource,
2. worker (or co-worker),
3. buyer, and
4. beneficiary (or user).

A fifth role has emerged from work in the human service area: Customers can be a key outcome, or product, of value-creating transformation activities, such as education and health delivery. In the first two roles, customers act as inputs to the transformation process, while in the last three, they act as outputs. Each of these roles is instrumental in creating competitive quality within a firm.

In reviewing the organizational literature for these roles, Lengnick-Hall[53] suggests that the following organizational practices are positively related to the competitive quality of production processes and outcomes:

• practices that deliberately select and carefully manage customer resources, foster an effective alliance between the firm and its customer resources, and improve the quality of its customer resources;

- practices that provide clear opportunities for coproduction, enhance customer abilities as coproducers, and increase customer motivation toward coproduction;
- activities that foster trust, develop interdependence, share information, and initiate friendly, mutually beneficial customer-organization bonds;
- activities that foster unambiguous communication with users, focus on meeting customer needs, offer realistic previews, achieve dimensions of quality that customers truly care about, and ensure that actual use is consistent with intended use; and
- activities that create opportunities for direct communication and interaction between users and production/core service personnel.

Thus, firms should design systems that involve and empower customers throughout the input-transformation-output system, rather than merely rely on customers to define their preferences and evaluate the products and services provided to them. This conclusion is certainly the foundation of modern TQ approaches and is reflected in the Baldrige Award criteria.

One example of this in practice is ADAC Laboratories, a manufacturer of high-technology health care equipment and a 1996 Baldrige winner. Not only does ADAC survey customers and potential customers and measure satisfaction, they invite customers to participate in strategic planning meetings, have lunch with customers attending new equipment training sessions, and host formal user group meetings to help prioritize product enhancements, share tips on new uses, and provide other information.

Total quality can also be related to a number of traditional organizational theories. The following sections discuss TQ's relationship with the resource dependence perspective and the theory of integrative bargaining.

The Resource Dependence Perspective

The organizational theory most directly comparable to the TQ view of customer-supplier relations is the resource dependence perspective (RDP) developed by Jeffrey Pfeffer and Gerald Salancik.[54] This perspective—which deals with how organizations manage to get the resources they need from their environment—resembles TQ in some ways, yet differs in others.

The most important similarity between the two perspectives is their mutual emphasis on the idea that the sources of an organization's success lie outside its boundaries. Although the idea that customers ultimately grant the organization its continued existence has become familiar as a fundamental principle of TQ, Pfeffer and Salancik point out that much organization theory focuses on the internal operations of organizations, giving less emphasis to the organization's environment:

Most current writers give only token consideration to the environmental context of organizations. The environment is there, somewhere outside the organization, and the idea is mentioned that environments constrain or affect organizations. . . . After this, the task of management is considered. Somehow, the things to be managed are usually within the organization, assumed to be under its control, and often have to do with the direction of low-level hired personnel. When authors get down to the task of describing the running of the organization, the relevance of the environment fades.[55]

According to the RDP, the effectiveness of an organization should be understood in terms of how well it meets the demands of external groups and organizations that are concerned with its actions and products. This is similar to the TQ conception of quality as meeting or exceeding customer expectations. There is an interesting difference, however, between the RDP concept of effectiveness and the TQ concept of quality.

TQ has traditionally focused almost exclusively on the organization's customers—that is, those who purchase the organization's products and provide the wherewithal for the organization's continued survival. The RDP perspective, however, recognizes that organizations must satisfy the demands of not only customers, but also other entities in the environment, including various government agencies, interest groups, shareholders, and—to some extent—society as a whole.

A government regulatory agency can make life miserable for an organization it does not believe is following government regulations—for example, a coal mine with inadequate safety procedures or a restaurant with unsanitary practices. In the extreme case, the government can even shut down an operation. Interest groups can influence customers to boycott a product for reasons unrelated to the quality of the product itself. Certain brands of California wine were boycotted for years because of alleged mistreatment of the migrant farmworkers who picked their grapes.

In recent years, shareholders of public corporations have become a constituency to be reckoned with. They are making increasing demands on how corporations operate, including not only economic but also social and environmental aspects of performance, such as minority hiring and use of recyclable materials.

From this perspective it is clear that although customers are important, groups and organizations other than customers can play a major role in determining an organization's success. TQ advocates can take two avenues in dealing with this issue. The first is to enlarge the concept of customers to include all those who have a stake in the organization. Following this logic, an organization would not be seen as practicing TQ unless it met the expectations of all of its constituencies, not just its customers in the traditional sense. However, different groups are apt to have very different expectations for the behavior of an organization, thus making it quite difficult to satisfy all parties.

The other avenue is for TQ advocates to recognize that although providing quality to customers is the overriding focus of an organization's activities, satisfying customers alone will not necessarily guarantee continued success, due to the potential influence of other constituencies. Interestingly, this perspective has recently been incorporated into the Baldrige Award criteria:

A company's leadership needs to stress its responsibilities to the public and needs to practice good citizenship. This responsibility refers to basic expectations of the company—business ethics and protection of public health, safety, and the environment. . . . Company planning should seek to prevent problems, to provide forthright company response if problems occur, and to make available information needed to maintain public awareness, safety, and confidence. Companies should not only meet all local, state, and federal laws and regulatory requirements. They should treat these and related requirements as areas for continuous improvement "beyond mere compliance."

Another similarity between TQ and RDP is in their recognition of interdependence between organizations as a fact of organizational life that must be managed effectively.

In the current dense environment . . . interdependencies are the problem. The dominant problems of the organization have become managing its exchanges and its relationships with the diverse interests affected by its actions. . . . The increasing density of relationships among diverse interests has led to less willingness to rely on unconstrained market forces. Negotiation, political strategies, the management of the organization's institutional relationships—these have all become more important.[56]

Thus the RDP shares with TQ the idea that managing interdependencies with other organizations is a key to success. The two perspectives diverge again, however, when it comes to how such interdependencies should be managed. Quality customer-supplier relationships are seen from the TQ perspective as consisting of mutually beneficial partnerships. Such an option, however, is not anticipated in the RDP. From this perspective, interdependence should be managed by some combination of gaining as much control as possible over the other organization, minimizing the other party's control over one's own organization, making it difficult for the other organization to monitor and influence one's behavior, and so on.

When compared to the protection of self-interest inherent in the recommendations of the RDP, the TQ win-win doctrine sounds somewhat naive. Yet most organizations practicing TQ and building partnerships with their customers and suppliers have traditionally managed customer-supplier relationships in the manner suggested by the RDP and have been dissatisfied with the results. The partnership efforts are mostly in their early stages, and there is no guarantee that they will ultimately succeed. As of now, however, they are the preferred method of many firms for managing interdependence.

Integrative Bargaining

The idea of building cooperative relationships that benefit both parties to a negotiation is not something that was created by writers or practitioners of TQ.

The idea of mutually beneficial relationships and win-win bargaining comes from a long tradition of research and writing on conflict management and negotiation.[57]

The idea behind this research tradition is that both parties will benefit more in the long run if they work together to help each other, rather than each one striving to win each round of negotiation. This tradition has been appropriated by writers on TQ, perhaps because it is consistent with the idea of customer orientation and teamwork. This is another area where TQ doctrine derives in a straightforward manner from existing organizational theory.

SUMMARY

Customers are the focus of companies practicing TQ, and those companies recognize that they cannot satisfy their customers without strong partnerships with their suppliers. The principles for developing quality customer-supplier relationships are

- recognizing the centrality of customers and the importance of suppliers,
- developing win-win relationships, and
- building up and acting on trust.

The practices for implementing these principles in dealing with customers are

- collecting information relentlessly about what customers want,
- distributing this information broadly within the organization,
- designing one's products and services in accord with customer demands, and
- managing customer relationships.

Practices for creating effective relationships with suppliers include developing long-term relationships with a limited number of suppliers chosen on the basis of quality, developing cooperative relations characterized by early supplier involvement in product design, and working together to improve quality and reduce costs. TQ principles and practices for customer-supplier relations are related to organizational theories of resource dependence and negotiation.

REVIEW AND DISCUSSION QUESTIONS

1. What can be learned about customer-supplier relationships from the story about IBM and its Japanese supplier?
2. Draw a diagram of a customer-supplier chain that includes at least four organizations. What attributes of quality are required at each link in the chain? How does quality at the beginning of the chain influence quality at the end?
3. Why are suppliers important to a company's quality efforts?
4. Identify three practices through which companies can better understand their customers' needs.

5. Think of a type of customer that you know reasonably well. Try to identify some unmet needs of this type of customer and to think of some new features of the products and/or services they purchase that would excite them. Why do you think these features are not being offered?

6. Identify a customer-supplier relationship in which you are involved. How does it compare to the principles and practices of TQ relationships? In what specific ways could adopting some of the principles and practices discussed in this chapter improve this relationship?

7. How do the terms used for customers in different industries and occupations (for example, patients, clients, passengers, students) influence how people in these industries think about their customers?

8. How would TQ and the resource dependence perspective differ in describing the quality and effectiveness of a state university?

9. Can you think of a situation in which customers are not important to the success of an organization?

10. How should an organization go about deciding who its customers are? Identify the customers of a university, a government agency, and a movie producer.

CASES

The Case of the Missing Reservation

Mark, Donna, and their children, along with another family, traditionally attended Easter brunch at a large downtown hotel. This year, as in the past, Donna called and made a reservation about three weeks prior to Easter. Because half the party consisted of small children, they arrived 20 minutes prior to the 11:30 reservation to assure being seated early. When they arrived, however, the hostess said that they did not have a reservation. The hostess explained that guests sometimes failed to show and that she would probably have a table available for them before long. Mark and Donna were quite upset and insisted that they had made a reservation and expected to be seated promptly. The hostess told them, "I believe that you made a reservation, but I can't seat you until all the people on the reservation list are seated. You are welcome to go to the lounge for complimentary coffee and punch while you wait." When Mark asked to see the manager, the hostess replied, "I am the manager," and turned to other duties. The party was eventually seated at 11:45, but was not at all happy with the experience.

The next day, Mark wrote a letter to the hotel manager explaining the entire incident. Mark was in the MBA program at the local university and taking a course on total quality management. In the class, they had just studied issues of customer focus and some of the approaches used at the Ritz-Carlton Hotel, a 1992 Baldrige Award winner. Mark concluded his letter with the statement, "I doubt that we would have experienced this situation at a hotel that truly believes in quality." About a week later, he received the following letter:

We enjoy hearing from our valued guests, but wish you had experienced the level of service and accommodations that we strive to achieve here at our hotel. Our restaurant manager received your letter and asked me to respond as Total Quality Lead.

Looking back at our records we did not show a reservation on the books for your family. I have addressed your comments with the appropriate department head so that others will not have to experience the same inconveniences that you did.

Thank you once again for sharing your thoughts with us. We believe in a philosophy of "continuous improvement," and it is through feedback such as yours that we can continue to improve the service to our guests.

Discussion Questions

1. Were the hostess's actions consistent with a customer-focused quality philosophy? What might she have done differently?
2. How would you have reacted to the letter that Mark received? Could the Total Quality Lead have responded differently? What does the fact that the hotel manager did not personally respond to the customer tell you?

Pro Fasteners, Incorporated

Pro Fasteners of San Jose, California, has been particularly innovative in building quality customer-supplier relationships.[58] Inspired by such books as Crosby's *Quality Without Tears* and quality-oriented companies such as Nordstrom, President Steve Braccini conceived of a radical new role for his company, which provides industrial hardware and components to the electronics industry.

In the late 1980s, many of Pro's customers were making the kinds of changes we have discussed, such as buying from fewer suppliers and using long-term contracts. They were asking more of their suppliers, including a commitment to keep them stocked with their product, quality guaranteed. Braccini realized that his customers were really saying they didn't want to have to worry about their parts inventory and that Pro Fasteners could do a better job of managing it than they could—and at a lower cost to boot. As Braccini put it, "Suddenly, the customer could cut his in-house staff. He'd have no purchasing costs, no receiving costs, no quality-assurance costs."

With this vision of being excruciatingly close to the customer came some significant management and organizational challenges for Pro Fastener. They would need to learn to anticipate customer needs. They would have to be on the cutting edge of quality. They would need the computer power to keep track of hundreds of thousands of parts. Most important, they would need committed and adaptive people in the organization to pull this off.

Using teams, among other methods, Pro Fastener has made a great deal of progress in turning the quality vision into reality. One team found a way to ship

100 percent correct parts with 100 percent on-time delivery to Applied Materials, a major customer. Another team responded to customer complaints about setting up credit with a $100 "courtesy account" that can be opened immediately, with no credit check. Hundreds of similar changes have transformed the company, particularly its relationships with customers.

The changes did not come easily. Employees often wondered whether Braccini knew what he was doing. His wife and partner was especially concerned about the amount of responsibility that was given to associates. Braccini created an employee quality group called the Continuous Improvement Council (CIC), which eventually decided to kick all of the managers off the quality teams. If a new style of organization was being born, the labor pains were awful.

However, the quality CSRs Pro Fasteners has developed have paid off in a big way. Despite a recession, the company's sales rose 20 percent between 1989 and 1992, and the company won more than 50 quality awards during this period. Overall, as one purchasing agent puts it, "They're the best." What else could you ask for in a supplier?

Discussion Questions

1. How does Pro Fasteners illustrate the principles of customer-supplier relationships discussed in this chapter?
2. If the company had failed in this attempt to change the nature of its business, what would have been the likely causes?
3. What role can information systems play in managing customer-supplier relationships?

Lands' End: The Secrets of Success

Lands' End, a popular and very successful catalog company, recently shared with customers the secrets of its success. The following are some of the things they had to say:[59]

Here at Lands' End, in the heartland of America, we still believe the customer comes first. . . . There are four basic ways we put the customer first. We hope you'll take a few minutes to read about them. Then decide if you'd like to be treated that way yourself.

1. **Make your merchandise as good as you can.** Our goal has always been to make our clothing and accessories as good as they could possibly be. By adding back features others have taken out over the years. By using the finest fabrics available. By inspecting the finished goods by eye to make sure they measure up.

2. **Always, always price it fairly.** It's our policy to mark up products modestly, just enough to give us a fair profit and to give you a terrific value. Admittedly, we have a few advantages. We're direct merchants with no middlemen taking a bite out of the profits. We don't spring for glitzy,

budget-busting advertising. . . . Our main headquarters is in Dodgeville, Wisconsin, surrounded by cornfields (no kidding).

3. **Make it a snap to shop for, 24 hours a day.** Our store never closes. We're open around the clock every day of the week to accommodate the varied schedules and different time zones of our customers. . . . Should you have detailed questions, we'll hook you up with one of our Specialty Shopper operators. They're our elite corps—the best of the best—able to answer any questions you might have about styling, fit, color matching, and more.

4. **Guarantee it. Period.** We strive for perfection, but sometimes a flawed product slips through. The color may be a shade too dark. A button may break. A seam may unravel. In those cases, we beg your tolerance and offer you one final protection. If at any time you are not completely satisfied, return the item for a full refund or exchange. And please, never feel bad about sending something back. We'd rather a truckload of returns than one dissatisfied customer.

Discussion Questions

1. How is Lands' End practicing total quality in its products and services?
2. How would the experience of purchasing a shirt through a catalog company differ from purchasing the same shirt from a department store? Could they both represent high quality?

ENDNOTES

1. Reported in "Total Quality Management and Competitiveness" by G. Pouskouleli, *Engineering Digest*, December 1991, pp. 14–17. The Japanese response is based on a story in the *Toronto Sun* by S. Ford, April 25, 1983, p. 6.

2. This idea has been promoted by Richard J. Schonberger in his book, *Building a Chain of Customers*. New York: The Free Press, 1990.

3. Arthur R. Tenner and Irving J. DeToro, *Total Quality Management: Three Steps to Continuous Improvement*. Reading, Mass.: Addison-Wesley, 1992, p. 197.

4. David Kirkpatrick, "Breaking Up IBM," *Fortune*, July 27, 1992, pp. 44–58.

5. Patricia Sellers, "Companies That Serve You Best," *Fortune*, May 31, 1993, pp. 74–88.

6. The Forum Corporation, *Customer Focus Research*, Executive Briefing, Boston, 1988.

7. Sources: Southwest Airlines home page, http://iflyswa.com; Richard S. Teitelbaum, "Where Service Flies Right," *Fortune*, August 24, 1992, pp. 117–118; and Kevin Freiberg and Jackie Freiberg, *NUTS! Southwest Airlines' Crazy Recipe for Business and Personal Success*, Austin, TX: Bard Press, 1996.

8. 1998 Criteria For Performance Excellence, Malcolm Baldrige National Quality Award. Gaithersburg, Md.: National Institute of Standards and Technology, United States Department of Commerce.

9. Tim Minahan, "What Makes a Supplier World-Class," *Purchasing*, Vol. 125, No. 2, August 13, 1998, pp. 50–61.

10. Justin Martin, "Are You as Good as You Think You Are?" *Fortune*, September 30, 1996, pp. 142–152.

11. Valerie Reitman, "Toyota's Fast Rebound after Fire at Supplier Shows Why It's Tough," *Wall Street Journal*, May 8, 1997, p. 1.

12. As seen in Dear Abby column by Abigail Van Buren. Dist. by Universal Press Syndicate. Reprinted with permission. All rights reserved.

13. We are indebted to David Waldman for this insight.

14. As seen in Dear Abby column by Abigail Van Buren. Dist. by Universal Press Syndicate. Reprinted with permission. All rights reserved.

15. J.M Juran, *Juran on Leadership for Quality: An Executive Handbook.* New York: The Free Press, 1989.

16. James H. Drew and Tye R. Fussell, "Becoming Partners with Internal Customers," *Quality Progress*, Vol. 29, No. 10, October 1996, pp. 51–54.

17. John Carlisle, quoted in Tenner and DeToro, *Total Quality Management.*

18. Richard C. Whitely, *The Customer-Driven Company, Moving from Talk to Action.* Reading, Mass.: Addison-Wesley, 1991. p. 7.

19. Robert D. Buzzell and Bradley T. Gale, *The PIMS Principles: Linking Strategy to Performance*, New York: The Free Press, 1987.

20. Marriott's approach to gathering information from customers is discussed in detail in Whiteley, *The Customer-Driven Company.*

21. See Benson P. Shapiro, V. Kasturi Rangan, and John J. Sviokla, "Staple Yourself to an Order," *Harvard Business Review*, July–August 1992, pp. 113–122.

22. Byron J. Finch, "A New Way to Listen to the Customer," *Quality Progress*, Vol. 30, No. 5, May 1997, pp. 73–76.

23. Based on Houghton Award Application 1992, U.S Precision Lens, Inc.

24. Whiteley, *The Customer-Driven Company.*

25. Quoted in "Could AT&T Rule the World?" by David Kirkpatrick. *Fortune*, May 17, 1993.

26. "Quality '93: Empowering People With Technology," advertisement, *Fortune*, September 1993.

27. Whiteley, *The Customer-Driven Company.*

28. Whiteley, *The Customer-Driven Company.*

29. Dick Schaaf,"Complex Quality: AMP Rings Up Service Success," *Quality Imperative*, September 1992, pp. 16–26.

30. "Focusing on the Customer," *Fortune*, June 5, 1989, p. 226.

31. Based on "Arts Groups Try to Keep the Customer Satisfied" by Owen Findsen and Cliff Radel, *Cincinnati Enquirer*, February 7, 1993.

32. These practices are based on *The Deming Route to Quality and Productivity* by William W. Scherkenbach (Rockville, Md.: Mercury Press, 1988) and on *Juran on Leadership for Quality* by Joseph M. Juran (New York: The Free Press, 1989).

33. Larry Kishpaugh, "Process Management and Business Results," presentation at the 1996 Regional Malcolm Baldrige Award Conference, Boston, Massachusetts.

34. This idea has long been championed by Deming. See the discussion of his 14 points in chapter 2.

35. For a discussion of these two points, see David N. Burt, "Managing Suppliers Up to Speed," *Harvard Business Review*, July–August 1989, pp. 127–135.

36. Tenner and DeToro, *Total Quality Management.*

37. John R. Emshwiller, "Suppliers Struggle to Improve Quality as Big Firms Slash Their Vendor Rolls." *Wall Street Journal*, August 16, 1991, B2.

38. Patrick J. McMahon, "Supplier Involvement," chapter 9 in *The Improvement Process* by H. James Harrington (New York: McGraw-Hill, 1987).

39. Texas Instruments Defense Systems & Electronics Group, Malcolm Baldrige Application Summary (1992).

40. Mike Lovitt, "Responsive Suppliers Are Smart Suppliers," *Quality Progress*, June 1989, pp. 50–53.

41. McMahon, op. cit.

42. This point is discussed by Randall S. Schuler and Drew L. Harris in *Managing Quality: The Primer for Middle Managers*, Reading, Mass.: Addison-Wesley, 1992.

43. McMahon, op. cit.

44. McMahon, op. cit.

45. Juran, *Juran on Leadership for Quality.*

46. Schuler and Harris, *Managing Quality.*

47. W.W. Scherkenbach, *The Deming Route to Quality and Productivity.* Washington, D.C: CEEP Press, 1986, p. 131.

48. AT&T Corporate Quality Office, *Supplier Quality Management: Foundations*, 1994, p. 52.

49. This example is discussed by David N. Burt in "Managing Suppliers Up to Speed," *Harvard Business Review*, July–August 1989, pp. 127–135.

50. The section on Granite Rock is based on "The Changemasters" by John Case, *INC.*, March 1992, pp. 58–70.

51. Cynthia A. Lengnick-Hall, "Customer Contributions to Quality: A Different View of the Customer-Oriented Firm," *Academy of Management Review*, Vol. 21, No. 3, 1996, pp. 971–824.

52. C. Gersuny and W.R. Rosengren, *The Service Society*, Cambridge, Mass.: Schenkman Press, 1973.

53. Lengnick-Hall, "Customer Contributions to Quality: A Different View of the Customer-Oriented Firm."

54. Jeffrey Pfeffer and Gerald R. Salancik, *The External Control of Organizations: A Resource Dependence Perspective*, New York: Harper & Row, 1978.

55. Ibid, pp. 257–258.

56. Pfeffer and Salancik, *The External Control of Organizations*, p. 94.

57. See, for example, David W. Johnson and Frank P. Johnson, *Joining Together: Group Theory and Group Skills*, Englewood Cliffs, N.J.: Prentice-Hall, 1975; Max H. Bazerman and Roy J. Lewicki (eds.), *Negotiating in Organizations*. Beverly Hills: Sage Publications, 1983; M. Afzalur Rahim, "A Strategy for Managing Conflict in Complex Organizations," *Human Relations*, Vol. 38, No. 1, 1985, pp. 81–89.

58. The material on Pro Fasteners is based on "Quality with Tears" by John Case, *INC.*, June 1992, pp. 82–93.

59. Lands' End Direct Merchants. Reprinted with permission.

INDEX